OCÉANO ATLÁNTICO

La Habana

CUBA

Santiago

PENÍNSULA DE YUCATÁN

JAMAICA

HAITÍ

REPÚBLICA
DOMINICANA

Santo Domingo

San Juan

Ponce

PUERTO RICO

MAR CARIBE

Belmopan

BELICE

HONDURAS

Tegucigalpa

León

NICARAGUA

Managua

Lago de
Nicaragua

Canal de Panamá

Panamá

COSTA RICA

San José

PANAMÁ

Caracas

VENEZUELA

Río Orinoco

Río Magdalena

Bogotá

COLOMBIA

BRASIL

Motivos de conversación

THIRD EDITION

Motivos de conversación
Essentials of Spanish

TEACHER'S EDITION

Robert L. Nicholas
University of Wisconsin, Madison

María Canteli Dominicis
St. John's University, New York

Eduardo Neale-Silva
Late of the University of Wisconsin, Madison

McGraw-Hill, Inc.
New York St. Louis San Francisco Auckland Bogotá Caracas Hamburg
Lisbon London Madrid Mexico Milan Montreal New Delhi Paris
San Juan São Paulo Singapore Sydney Tokyo Toronto

This is an  book.

Motivos de conversación
Essentials of Spanish

Copyright © 1992, 1988, 1984 by McGraw-Hill, Inc. All rights reserved. Printed in the United
States of America. Except as permitted under the United States Copyright Act of 1976, no part
of this publication may be reproduced or distributed in any form or by any means, or stored in a
database or retrieval system, without the prior written permission of the publisher.

1 2 3 4 5 6 7 8 9 0   VNH VNH   9 0 9 8 7 6 5 4 3 2

ISBN   0-07-046708-0 (Student Edition)
ISBN   0-07-046713-7 (Instructor's Edition)

This book was set in 10/12 Galliard by Black Dot Graphics.
The editors were Leslie Berriman, Heidi Clausen, Stacey Sawyer, and Peggy Hines;
the production supervisor was Tanya Nigh;
the text designer was Adriane Bosworth;
the illustrator was Axelle Fortier;
the photo researcher was Judy Mason;
the cover designer was Francis Owens.
Von Hoffman Press was printer and binder.

Cover photograph: Stuart Cohen/Comstock

Library of Congress Cataloging-in-Publication Data

Nicholas, Robert L.
    Motivos de conversación : essentials of Spanish / Robert L.
  Nicholas, María Canteli Dominicis, Eduardo Neale-Silva. —3rd ed.
      p. cm.
  Includes index.
  "This is an EBI book"—T.p. verso.
  ISBN 0-07-046708-0
  1. Spanish language—Grammar—1950— 2. Spanish language—Textbooks for foreign
speakers—English.   I. Dominicis, María Canteli.   II. Neale-Silva, Eduardo.   III. Title.
PC4112.N53   1992
468.2'421—dc20
                                                                    91-27906
                                                                       CIP

C O N T E N T S

LECCIÓN 14

De viaje por España   283

LECCIÓN 15

De viaje por Hispanoamérica   300

To the Instructor

Motivos de conversación, third edition, is a brief Spanish textbook for beginners. It presents the essentials of Spanish grammar as well as practice of vocabulary, communication, and reading skills in eighteen lessons, a preliminary lesson, and six reading/review sections. The title reflects the book's primary goal, which is to convey meaning within situational and cultural contexts, thereby motivating the student to use Spanish actively.

Each chapter of *Motivos de conversación* features thematic core vocabularies, real-life situations in the form of dialogues or narrative passages, and brief grammatical explanations. These features are accompanied by exercises for learning basic forms and constructions, models for controlled expression, and a wide variety of communicative activities that encourage student creativity. Frequent **Memoprácticas** offer students suggestions on how to study, memorize, and create their own learning aids. The presentation of grammar *per se* and the manipulation of words as grammatical components are minimized in the text, while a personal, creative use of Spanish by students is encouraged.

To facilitate lesson planning and the assigning of homework, each of the eighteen lessons in *Motivos de conversación* is divided into three main parts:

1. **Gráficos** This section promotes initial self-expression through visuals and brief dialogues or narrative passages followed by personalized questions. It also serves as an informal introduction to the essential vocabulary and grammatical points that are developed in detail in other parts of the lesson. A feature called **Estudio de palabras** presents cognate study and word-building patterns to help students make associations among words. Each **Gráficos** section concludes with a **Vista cultural,** a brief photographic insight into Hispanic culture.

2. **Gramática esencial** Each lesson presents three to six grammar points in a condensed format, with exercises corresponding to each point immediately following the explanation. Only essential, first-year material is included. Instructors should, of course, supplement grammar explanations whenever they feel it is necessary. **Para resumir y repasar,** which concludes each **Gramática esencial** section, synthesizes the vocabulary and grammar of the current lesson in an initial exercise called **En persona** and

then, in the remaining exercises, reinforces key grammatical points from earlier lessons. Answers to the exercises in **Para resumir y repasar** are found in Appendix 3.

3. **Comunicación**   This section begins with a **Texto,** a dialogue or a narrative, and/or **De la vida real,** various pieces of authentic material from Hispanic publications. Both the **Texto** and the realia illustrate in context the grammatical points and vocabulary presented in the lesson. These segments are followed by **Para conversar más** activities, which also provide an opportunity for synthesis; that is, students can demonstrate their mastery of the information presented in the lesson by completing activities that encourage working with others. Each lesson concludes with a **Motivo cultural** (*Cultural Note*) that includes a photograph and explains in detail certain aspects of Hispanic culture.

In addition, after every three lessons, *Motivos de conversación* includes an **Ampliaciones** section that allows students to assess their progress on a regular basis. **Ampliaciones** contain readings, **Repasos visuales** (visually cued reviews), and **Exámenes de repaso** (self-tests). Each reading includes a prereading section (**Antes de leer**) that presents reading hints and strategies incorporated into an exercise format. Postreading exercises (**Después de leer**) are also provided at the end of each reading to check students' comprehension.

The answers to the **Exámenes de repaso** are given in Appendix 4. Other appendices include verb charts (Appendix 1) as well as information on punctuation, capitalization, and syllabication (Appendix 2). Complete Spanish-English and English-Spanish vocabularies, based on the text's active vocabulary, are also provided.

Motivos de conversación can be adapted easily to beginning programs that meet either three, four, or five times weekly. Because the **Vocabulario activo** lists at the end of each lesson include terms introduced only in the **Gráficos** and **Gramática esencial** sections, courses meeting three days a week can omit **Comunicación** and concentrate on the **Gráficos** and **Gramática esencial** of each lesson. Courses meeting four or five days a week can add the **Comunicación** section for synthesis and enrichment. In this case, instructors may wish to assign the new vocabulary presented in the **Comunicación** section as active vocabulary, in addition to the **Vocabulario activo** at the end of the lesson.

Major Changes in the Third Edition

Motivos de conversación has been rewritten to update and expand the cultural information, to further contextualize the exercises, and to refine the grammar explanations. Many of the changes in the third edition are based on valuable suggestions from instructors across the country who have used the second edition.

- The number of preliminary chapters has been reduced from two to one.
- The grammar sections have been slightly resequenced. For example, the preterite and imperfect tenses are now presented, respectively, in Lessons 5 and 8, both one lesson earlier than in the second edition.
- Many of the dialogues and cultural notes have been revised or rewritten.
- The exercises and activities are virtually all contextualized in the third edition, and there are more pair/group activities.
- **Vista cultural,** a brief photographic insight into Hispanic culture, appears at the end of the **Gráficos** section. This feature is in Spanish in all eighteen chapters of the text.
- Each **Comunicación** section of the new edition contains a **Motivo cultural** box that presents in-depth Hispanic cultural information accompanied by a photograph. Brief **Motivo cultural** boxes that do not include photographs also appear in other sections of the text. The **Motivos culturales** are in English throughout the text.
- **Para resumir y repasar** incorporates a communicative activity called **En persona,** which synthesizes the grammar and vocabulary of the current lesson, in addition to one or two exercises that review material from previous lessons.
- Realia has been added to each lesson in the new **De la vida real** segment of the **Comunicación** section. This material comes from many different Spanish-speaking countries and presents students with a glimpse into everyday life in the Hispanic world. The realia is accompanied by activities that encourage students to read the material for general understanding and for particular information, as well as to interact with one another using the material as a point of departure.
- The final three readings in the **Ampliaciones** sections have been replaced with authentic Spanish-language articles.
- The **Antes de leer** portion of the **Ampliaciones** sections has been expanded to guide students through various reading hints and strategies by giving them specific tasks to complete before reading each selection.
- The new full-color format of *Motivos de conversación* vividly depicts the people, places, and heritage of the Spanish-speaking world.
- The annotated *Instructor's Edition* has been substantially expanded.

Supplementary Materials

- The *Instructor's Edition* provides extensive marginal notes on vocabulary and grammar presentation, together with suggestions for many additional exercises, including listening comprehension and oral practice.
- The *Instructor's Manual* contains lesson plans, a short sample test for every lesson, supplementary class aids, and methodological suggestions.

These recommendations offer the instructor various approaches to difficult points of grammar, more detailed explanations (when appropriate), rationales for the organization of class materials, hints on how to vary the presentation of each lesson, and aids in presenting students with strategies for avoiding common pitfalls and clarifying areas of confusion.

◆ The *Workbook/Laboratory Manual* provides additional exercises on grammar and vocabulary and a complete listening program. With one preliminary and eighteen regular lessons that correspond to the text and tapes, the *Workbook/Laboratory Manual* is designed for independent study. Students may check their answers against those given in the back of the *Workbook* to assess their progress.

◆ The *Tape Program* contains abundant exercises to assist students in aural/oral practice, either on first exposure to the material or as a review. It includes new listening materials as well as many of the text's exercises and dialogues. The variety of voices used on the tapes gives students a wide range of practice in listening to and imitating native speakers. The *Tape Program* is available free of charge from the publisher; the same program can also be made available for purchase by students.

◆ The *Tapescript* consists of a complete transcription of the *Tape Program*. One copy of the *Tapescript* is included with each *Tape Program*. Additional copies are also available free of charge.

◆ The *Instructor's Resource Kit* contains supplementary materials coordinated with the chapters of the student text. It includes communicative games and activities, transparency masters from the student text, and additional realia.

◆ The *McGraw-Hill Electronic Language Tutor* (*MHELT 2.0*) includes most of the more controlled activities from the student text. This CAI (computer-assisted instruction) program has been dramatically altered and improved for the third edition. It is available free to adopting institutions in Apple, IBM, and Macintosh formats.

◆ A set of *color slides* provides students with visual images from various parts of the Spanish-speaking world. Each set of slides is accompanied by descriptive commentary and activities for classroom use. One set of slides is available to each adopting institution.

◆ *Juegos comunicativos* consists of a set of computerized games in Spanish. It is available free to adopting institutions in Apple format.

◆ The *McGraw-Hill Video Library of Authentic Spanish Materials* consists of various volumes of video materials. Also available is the *McGraw-Hill Video for Beginning Spanish*. This twenty-three-part video program provides students with real-world experiences from the Spanish-speaking world and is easily coordinated with the themes and situations of **Motivos de conversación.** It includes the complete scripts as well as suggested pre- and postviewing activities. For further information on videos to accompany **Motivos de conversación,** consult your local McGraw-Hill representative.

Acknowledgments

The authors and publisher would like to express their gratitude to the following instructors whose criticism and advice contributed to the preparation of this revised edition (the mention of their names here does not constitute an endorsement of this text or of its methodology):

Marc Accornero	Mission College
Jim M. Baker	Lubbock Christian University
Pilar Bellver	West Virginia University
Virgil H. Blanco	Middlesex County College
Jeff Bruner	Trenton State College
José H. Córdova	Bennington College
Clara Estow	University of Massachusetts, Harbor Campus
Frank M. Figuerroa	Eckerd College
Anne Fountain	Peace College
Phyllis Golding	Queens College
Josiane Guilleux	Montgomery County Community College
Mary A. Harris	Howard University
Ray E. Horst	Houghton College
Ann N. Hughes	Mercer University
Judith D. Luckett	Rollins College
Nicholas Mason-Browne	Coe College
Ricardo Naves-Ruiz	University of Massachusetts, Boston
Howard N. Peters	Valparaiso University
Alex R. Quiroga	Salem State College
Elliot Ramer	Middlesex County College
Ramiro Ramírez	Anna Maria College
D. Doris Reppen	Christopher Newport College
Andrea Rice-Mikkelsen	Mary Washington College
Stephen Richman	Mercer County College
Linda Sites	Piedmont Virginia Community College
Darío Valdes	Mt. Wachusett Community College
José A. Velázquez	Houghton College
Joseph Zdenek	Winthrop College

Finally, the authors would like to thank the following members of the editorial and production staff who assisted in various aspects of the preparation of the third edition: Heidi Clausen, Leslie Berriman, Thalia Dorwick, Laura Chastain, Stacey Sawyer, Tanya Nigh, Francis Owens, Karen Judd, and Phyllis Snyder. A special thank-you is due Axelle Fortier, whose illustrations grace the third edition.

To the Student

Motivos de conversación is designed to give you the opportunity to start speaking Spanish from the very beginning of your study; even in the first few lessons you will be encouraged to express yourself in Spanish. We feel this is the most important goal of language learning, and we hope that your experience never becomes a mere rote memorization of rules. Becoming really fluent in Spanish means using Spanish words and constructions automatically. Although you will not become fluent immediately, your ability to say a considerable number of things in Spanish right away may surprise you! Here are some simple suggestions to help you become a good language learner.

1. Memorization is a necessary part of language learning—it is one of the key factors in achieving fluency. Effective memorization consists of three steps. First, associate words and phrases you are trying to memorize with something else: for example, **árbol** (*tree*) with English *arbor,* or **¡No se preocupe Ud.!** (*Don't worry!*) with the noun *preoccupation.* Second, repeat what you have learned as many times as possible until the use of the word or sentence becomes automatic. Third, learn to concentrate only on Spanish when you are studying Spanish: ten minutes of concentrated study are far better than an hour of unfocused attention. The sections called **Memopráctica** will offer more hints and suggestions on how to study and memorize new vocabulary and constructions. Incorporate these hints and suggestions into your study routines whenever possible.

2. Many of the drawings, photos, and written exercises in this text will depict situations for you. Try to imagine yourself in those situations and then speak the Spanish required by that situation. Imagine, for example, that you have to buy a ticket in a hurry because your train is leaving in three minutes. How can you say, quickly and clearly, "One return ticket to Barcelona, please"? Someday catching that train may depend on your ability to express yourself quickly and clearly.

3. Check your progress often by taking the **Exámenes de repaso** that appear after every third lesson in the **Ampliaciones** sections (the answers are given in Appendix 4) and by using the *Workbook* regularly—again, checking your answers. The tape program is another useful learning tool: with

two or three short lab periods per week you will make rapid progress toward proficiency in Spanish.

4. Remember that learning isolated words is of limited value. Language is connected speech: brief exchanges, short dialogues, and so on. Practicing vocabulary and constructions in conversational contexts will help you learn more efficiently and make your language usage more natural.

5. Learn to pronounce Spanish accurately from the very beginning by paying close attention to the pronunciation of fluent speakers of the language. If your pronunciation is sloppy, listeners may not understand you, and you will not achieve your goal of communicating what you want to say.

6. Pay close attention to details of form, such as spelling. A change of a single letter, or one wrong accent, may make all the difference in the meaning conveyed by a word. **Converso** (*I converse*) is not the same as **conversó** (*he or she conversed*), and **puerto** (*port*) is very different from **puerta** (*door*).

7. Study with one or more friends. The practice will be very helpful and, more importantly, when you begin to teach Spanish to another person, you will really begin to learn it yourself.

One of the most important prerequisites for learning a foreign language is the sincere desire to learn it. The potential rewards for learning Spanish are enormous. Not only will you acquire a useful tool of communication, but you will learn about other people and how they think and live, about how other countries and cultures have solved common human problems. Good luck in achieving these goals!

LECCIÓN PRELIMINAR

Un grupo de estudiantes comentan un libro favorito.

Nombres y personas

Me llamo...	*My name is . . .*
¿Cómo te llamas tú?	*What is your name? (familiar)*
¿Cómo se llama usted?	*What is your name? (polite)*
¿Cómo se llama él/ella?	*What is his/her name?*

Presentation: Introduce yourself in Spanish and have students repeat phrases after you. Use choral and individual repetition.

Virginia Isabel
María
Carmen Gloria
Paulina Alicia Sara
Dolores Juana
Bárbara

Eduardo Tomás
Diego Carlos
Jorge
Alberto Enrique
Roberto Miguel
José (Pepe)

Ask several individuals their names and tell them yours. This is a good time to assign Spanish names or have students select their own.

Tú and usted

In Spanish it is important to distinguish between **tú** and **usted,** both of which mean *you.* The familiar form, **tú,** is generally used among close friends, family members, and classmates, and with small children and pets. The polite form, **usted** (abbreviated **Ud.** or **Vd.**), is usually used when speaking with older persons, casual acquaintances, and anyone whose social or professional status requires formality and respect.

Presentation: Summarize or read section to students, since they may not have prepared any of this preliminary chapter before class.

Note: Tell students that the text will address them as *Ud.,* although they will be expected to use the *tú* form when working with each other. Also, tell them that the abbreviation *Ud.* will be used throughout the text.

◆ MOTIVO CULTURAL*

A Hispanic person has two last names: the first is the father's family name and the second the mother's. If María **Gómez** Contreras married Ricardo **Plaja** Pelegrín, their son José would be called José **Plaja Gómez,** because the grandfather's name on each side is passed on.

Expansion: Ask students to give the full names of the children of the following couples: *Antonio Rodríguez Puértolas* and *Anita Buero García (Luis); Francisco Ruiz Ramírez* and *Adela Garza Sánchez (Victoria); Alberto Silva Castro* and *Tina Serrano Negrún (Carmen).* Try different combinations of names. These names could also be reviewed later for additional pronunciation practice.

*Cultural information will be given in this section throughout the text.

Actividad

With several classmates, take turns asking one another's names.

MEMOPRÁCTICA *

Here are four general principles you should follow while studying Spanish. (1) Begin using expressions in Spanish right away; don't just learn rules or talk *about* Spanish. (2) When studying Spanish, concentrate totally. Allow nothing to divert your attention. (3) Study in short but frequent sessions rather than for extended periods of time. (4) Above all, remember that a positive attitude is the first step toward learning a language.

Another suggestion is to familiarize yourself with the components of the *Motivos de conversación* program. First, examine the format of the text. (Don't forget the self-tests called **Exámenes de repaso,** appendices, and glossaries!) As the course progresses, use the Workbook and Laboratory Manual regularly, checking your answers with those given in the back. In addition, regular attendance at the language laboratory will help you develop facility in listening and responding in Spanish. If possible, take advantage of the computer software supplied with the program. A broad-based approach to the study of Spanish will bring you the best results.

---

*Suggestions for learning how to use this text and how to study Spanish will be given in this section.

The Spanish Vowels

There are five basic vowel sounds in Spanish. Unlike their English counterparts, Spanish vowel sounds are crisp and do not "glide." For example, the **o** in English *hello* sounds like the **ow** in *crow;* Spanish would cut the **o** shorter and would add no second vowel sound. Try to say the Spanish **aló** crisply, with no **u** sound at the end.

Repeat the following sounds after your instructor.

a: approximately like **a** in *father.*

a	da	la
ama	sala	casa

e: approximately like **e** in *they*

e	de	me
Elena	elemento	Venezuela

i: approximately like **i** in *marine*

i (y)*	mi	ti
Silvia	Lima	Misisipí

o: approximately like **o** in *Coca* but without the glide of *Cola*

o	lo	yo
oro	todo	modo

u: approximately like **u** in *Julie*

u	tu	su
un	luna	mucho

The Spanish Alphabet

a	a	Álava	j	jota	Jerez	rr	erre	Sierra Madre
b	be	Bogotá	k†	ka	kilómetro	s	ese	San Salvador
c	ce	Celaya, Cuba	l	ele	Lima	t	te	Tegucigalpa
ch	che	Chile	ll	elle	Callao	u	u	Uruguay
d	de	Durango	m	eme	Maracaibo	v	ve	Venezuela
e	e	Ecuador	n	ene	Nicaragua	w†	doble ve,	whisky
f	efe	Florida	ñ	eñe	España		ve doble	
g	ge	Guatemala,	o	o	Orinoco	x	equis	examen
		Génova	p	pe	Paraguay	y	i griega	Yauco
h	hache	Honduras	q	cu	Quito	z	zeta	Zaragoza
i	i	Iguazú	r	ere	Guadalajara			

*When it stands alone in a sentence, the letter **i** is written **y** and means *and*.
†The **k** and the **w** are not Spanish letters. They are found only in words of foreign origin.

Presentation: Model all words; have entire class, groups, and individuals repeat quickly. Point out for a crisp pronunciation of Spanish vowels, students should maintain muscle tension in lips for duration of the sound.

Suggestion: To facilitate choral repetition of alphabet, say three letters at a time: *a, be, ce* (pause for imitation); and so on. Emphasize pronunciation of words and phrases rather than individual sounds.

Suggestion: Write these series on board and have students repeat them: *ca, co, cu—ce, ci; ga, go, gu —ge, gi.*

Suggestion: Tips for trilling *r* and *rr:* (1) Barely touch the ridge behind the upper front teeth with the tip of the tongue while puffing air over the top of the tongue. (2) Simulate the *rd* and *rt* combinations by saying quickly "potter though" (*pardo*) or "potter toe" (*parto*). (3) Repeat "pot o' tea" several times in rapid-fire succession.

Optional: Have students spell out their names or some of the better-known Spanish place names: *Los Ángeles, Guadalajara, Valencia, Cuba, Sacramento, Buenos Aires, San Luis Obispo, Alamogordo, Sierra Nevada, Guatemala.*

Cognados

Cognates

Words that are identical or similar in two languages are known as *cognates*. Because of the numerous cognates shared by Spanish and English, you can begin your study of Spanish with a large "passive" vocabulary. However, be careful with the pronunciation of these cognates. While they look alike, they don't sound alike!

Here is a list of several common nouns and adjectives. You will see that all Spanish nouns have gender; that is, they are either masculine or feminine. Words modifying or qualifying nouns must also reflect this gender. In Spanish there are four forms of the word *the:* **el, la, los,** and **las. El** is used before singular masculine nouns and **la** is used before singular feminine nouns. **Los** and **las** are the plural forms for **el** and **la.** You will learn more about these forms in **Lección uno;** for now, just learn to recognize them and practice the forms given below.

Most adjectives end in **-o** when they refer to masculine nouns and in **-a** when they refer to feminine nouns. Other adjectives keep the same ending for both masculine and feminine forms.

Pronounce the following lists and ask your instructor about words you don't recognize.

SUSTANTIVOS (*NOUNS*)	ADJETIVOS (*ADJECTIVES*)	
	o/a	**No Change**
la institución	americano/a	admirable
el capitalismo	estupendo/a	ideal
el comunismo	famoso/a	idealista
la democracia	magnífico/a	importante
el socialismo	mexicano/a	imposible
la educación	necesario/a	improbable
la clase	práctico/a	inevitable
la gramática	religioso/a	inteligente
la persona	romántico/a	interesante
el actor/la actriz	sincero/a	popular
el estudiante/la estudiante		posible
el presidente/la presidente (la presidenta)*		probable
el profesor/la profesora		realista
el senador/la senadora		responsable

Presentation: For additional pronunciation practice, have students repeat cognates and articles after you. Students need *not* memorize all words here, but point out that they will be able to recognize cognates because of similarity to English. Remind students that although words may look alike in Spanish and English, they do not sound alike.

Optional: Try these words for additional pronunciation or listening practice: *la monarquía, el anarquismo, la república, la dictadura, el líder, liberal, conservador, superior, inferior, animal, general, capitán, policía, guardia, conductor, atención, cruel, estúpido, generoso.*

Suggestion: Point out to students that when they look up an English adjective in an English-Spanish dictionary, it will usually give only the masculine form of the Spanish adjective. They can find out whether it has a feminine form by looking it up in the Spanish-English portion of the dictionary.

Emphasis: Stress footnote and give other examples: cliente/clienta, dependiente/dependienta, médico/médica.

*Current usage fluctuates between **la presidente** and **la presidenta.**

Asking Questions

One way to form a question in Spanish is to invert the word order of the sentence, placing the verb before the subject.

STATEMENT: Ella se llama Carmen.   QUESTION: ¿Cómo se llama ella?

Note that an inverted question mark is placed at the beginning of the question.

When asking a question that anticipates a yes-or-no answer, Spanish speakers often keep the normal word order and simply raise their voice at the end of the sentence.

STATEMENT: María es inteligente.   QUESTION: ¿María es inteligente?

Presentation: Present section orally and model examples. Explain two intonation patterns included. Model patterns using names of students in your class: ¿ _____ es inteligente (famoso/a, idealista, realista, americano/a)? —Sí (No), _____ es _____.

Actividades

Suggestion A: For maximum practice, students ask and answer questions in pairs. For additional group and pair activities, consult the Instructor's Resource Kit.

A. Responda. *Answer the questions based on the drawings.*

MODELO:

¿Es popular Elena? →
Sí, Elena es popular.

1. ¿Es idealista Juan?

2. ¿Es religiosa Isabel?

3. ¿Es importante el señor Rivera?

4. ¿Es inteligente la profesora Franco?

5. ¿Es romántico Alberto?

B. Responda según los modelos. (*Answer according to the models.*)

MODELO: ¿Es famosa la senadora? → Sí, señor, la senadora es famosa.

¿Es Ud. famoso/a? → No, señora, no soy* famoso/a.

1. ¿Es impaciente el profesor?
2. ¿Es estupenda la actriz?
3. ¿Es importante el presidente?
4. ¿Es necesaria la educación?
5. ¿Es excelente el café colombiano?
6. ¿Es Ud. generoso/a?
7. ¿Es Ud. sincero/a?
8. ¿Es Ud. mexicano/a?
9. ¿Es Ud. famoso/a?
10. ¿Es Ud. realista?

Saludos y conversaciones

1. —Hola, me llamo Juan Ortiz Mejía. ¿Y Ud.?†
—Me llamo María Pelayo Díaz.
—¿De dónde es Ud., señora?
—Soy de Madrid. ¿Y Ud.?
—Soy de la Argentina.

2. —Buenos días, señorita.
—Buenos días, don Antonio.
—¿Cómo está Ud.?
—Bien, gracias, ¿y Ud.?
—Muy bien, gracias.

3. —Buenas tardes. Me llamo Arturo, y mi amigo se llama Pedro. ¿Cómo te llamas tú?
—Me llamo Alicia.
—¿De dónde eres tú, Alicia?
—Soy de la Ciudad de México, ¿y tú?
—Soy de Los Ángeles, y Pedro es de Los Ángeles también.

*To make a sentence negative, place **no** immediately before the verb.

Es estudiante. → **No** es estudiante.
¿Es Ud. doctor? → No, **no** soy doctor.

†Direct dialogue in Spanish is indicated by dashes, not by quotation marks as in English.

1. *Hello, my name is Juan Ortiz Mejía. And yours? —My name is María Pelayo Díaz. —Where are you from, madam? —I'm from Madrid, and you? —I'm from Argentina.* **2.** *Good morning, miss. —Good morning, don Antonio. —How are you? —Well, thank you, and you? —Very well, thank you.* **3.** *Good afternoon. My name is Arturo and my friend's name is Pedro. What is your name? —My name is Alicia. —Where are you from, Alicia? —I'm from Mexico City, and you? —I'm from Los Angeles and Pedro is from Los Angeles too.*

En la Universidad de Barcelona. —¿Un examen? ¡Ay, no!

Actividades

DIÁLOGO 1

1. ¿Cómo se llama el señor?
2. ¿Cómo se llama la señora?
3. ¿De dónde es la señora? ¿y el señor?

DIÁLOGO 3

1. ¿Cómo se llama el amigo de Arturo?*
2. ¿De dónde es Alicia?
3. ¿De dónde es Arturo?

DIÁLOGO 2

1. ¿Cómo se llama el señor?
2. ¿Cómo está la señorita?
3. ¿Cómo está el señor?

Expansion: Additional oral questions: **1.** ¿De dónde es el presidente... ? **2.** ¿De dónde es (*name of famous actor/actress*)? **3.** ¿De dónde eres tú? **4.** ¿Cómo se llama el presidente (*un actor favorito*)? **5.** ¿Cómo se llama un violinista (*pianista*) famoso?

Emphasis: Point out footnote and give additional examples of expressing possession: *la profesora de Juan; el nombre de la profesora; la amiga de Alberto; la familia de Antonio.*

Optional: In groups, students ask each other their names and where they are from.

Me gusta/te gusta/le gusta

Note: Introduce these as lexical items to be memorized; do not try to explain constructions now. Just point out that they mean "I (you, he, she) like(s)." Forms are presented here only to encourage students to communicate complete thoughts in Spanish.

These phrases can be used to talk about likes and dislikes.

Profesor, ¿le gusta la música moderna? —Sí, me gusta mucho.
Pepe, ¿te gusta el coche? —No, no me gusta nada.

Professor, do you like modern music? —Yes, I like it a lot.
Pepe, do you like the car? —No, I don't like it at all.

To talk about more than one item, use **gustan.**

Me gustan los actores italianos.
¿Te gustan las novelas de Agatha Christie?

I like Italian actors.
Do you like Agatha Christie's novels?

Note in several of the preceding examples that Spanish sometimes uses the definite article (**el, la, los, las**) when English omits it.

Suggestion: For rapid oral practice, give singular and oral cues and ask students to reply with *me gusta mucho* or *me gustan mucho*: *la música, las novelas, el profesor (la profesora), los coches americanos, los estudiantes, (names of two students), La Ciudad de México, el presidente.*

Actividades

Suggestion A: Divide class into small groups to give students maximum opportunity for oral practice and to help them become relaxed using Spanish with each other.

A. ¿Qué (*What*) te gusta? Responda en español. *Ask a classmate what he or she likes.*

MODELO: ¿Te gusta el océano? →
Sí, me gusta mucho el océano. (No, no me gusta mucho.)

1. ¿Te gusta la universidad?
2. ¿Te gusta la televisión? ¿el teatro?
3. ¿Te gusta la música popular? ¿la música clásica?

---

*Spanish does not use an apostrophe to show possession: **el amigo de Carlos** = *Carlos's friend* (*the friend of Carlos*).

4. ¿Te gusta el tenis? ¿el golf?
5. ¿Te gustan los deportes (*sports*)?
6. ¿Te gustan las discotecas?
7. __¿?__ **Posibilidades:** las matemáticas, la biología, la filosofía, la arquitectura clásica (moderna), el comunismo, el capitalismo, el vólibol, las comedias (tragedias)

B. ¿Qué le gusta? *Ask your instructor about his or her likes and dislikes.*

1. ¿Le gusta el fútbol? ¿el béisbol?
2. ¿Le gusta la literatura?
3. ¿Le gusta la Coca-Cola?
4. ¿Le gusta el chile con carne?
5. ¿Le gustan los restaurantes McDonald's?
6. ¿Le gustan los tacos?
7. __¿?__

Suggestion B: Try to answer creatively using cognates to expand value of exercise as listening practice. Examples: **1.** *¡Me gusta mucho el béisbol! ¡(Name of player) es fantástico!* **2.** *Mi novela favorita es _____.*

El calendario

Los días de la semana (*Days of the Week*) y los números 1–31

OCTUBRE						
lunes	martes	miércoles	jueves	viernes	sábado	domingo
1 primero* (uno)	2 dos	3 tres	4 cuatro	5 cinco	6 seis	7 siete
8 ocho	9 nueve	10 diez	11 once	12 doce	13 trece	14 catorce
15 quince	16 diez y seis	17 diez y siete	18 diez y ocho	19 diez y nueve	20 veinte	21 veinte y uno
22 veinte y dos	23 veinte y tres	24 veinte y cuatro	25 veinte y cinco	26 veinte y seis	27 veinte y siete	28 veinte y ocho
29 veinte y nueve	30 treinta	31 treinta y uno				

Note: See the Instructor's Manual for Student Worksheets. These worksheets provide additional practice for pairs of students and are useful for mechanical drills since they expand student practice and minimize the instructor's role.

Note: This section presents additional vocabulary so students can carry on limited conversation on variety of topics. For now, concentrate on pronunciation and memorization; no need to explain grammatical constructions.

Compound numerals from sixteen through nineteen and twenty-one through twenty-nine can be written as one word: **dieciséis, diecisiete, veintiuno, veintiocho,** and so on. Those ending with a monosyllabic number (**dos, tres, seis**) carry a written accent when written as one word: **veintidós, veintitrés, veintiséis.** Note also the z → c change before i in **dieciséis, diecisiete.**

Emphasis: Point out footnote and be sure students realize they should use *uno* when counting but *primero* when referring to the calendar.

---

*As shown in this calendar, cardinal numbers are used for all dates except the first of the month, which is expressed with the ordinal number **primero** instead of **uno.**

VOCABULARIO IMPORTANTE

Si hoy es lunes, mañana es   *If today is Monday, tomorrow is*
martes y ayer fue domingo.   *Tuesday and yesterday was Sunday.*

Motivo cultural

Hispanic calendars generally show Monday (**lunes**) as the first day of the week.

Estaciones y meses (*Seasons and Months*)

LA PRIMAVERA   EL VERANO   EL OTOÑO   EL INVIERNO

marzo, abril, mayo   junio, julio, agosto   septiembre, octubre, noviembre   diciembre, enero, febrero

Suggestion: Most of these exercises can be reviewed in pairs or small groups. When working in pairs, A tests B (whose text is closed) and then they reverse roles. Encourage students to work quickly. When small-group activity has ended, test students on a few items from each exercise.

Expansion B:
1. 13 − 6 **2.** 22 + 4
3. 14 + 13 **4.** 30 − 19
Also encourage students to invent a few mathematical problems of their own.

Optional B: Give students answers and ask them to supply original problem: 17 (11 + 6 or 24 − 7).

Actividades

A. *Practice counting with a classmate; continue the sequences logically.*

1. 1, 2, 3...
2. 31, 30, 29...
3. 2, 4, 6...
4. 1, 3, 5...
5. 3, 6, 9...
6. 4, 8, 12...
7. 5, 10, 15...

B. Matemáticas. *Do these problems and create others. Pronounce all numbers.*

MODELOS: 2 + 4 = 6 dos más cuatro son* seis (dos y cuatro son seis)
8 − 3 = 5 ocho menos tres son cinco

1. 2 + 3 son _____.
2. 4 + 5 son _____.
3. 7 + 1 son _____.
4. 6 + 1 son _____.
5. 30 − 13 son _____.
6. 18 + 12 son _____.
7. 15 − 4 son _____.
8. 10 + 11 son _____.
9. 17 − 4 son _____.
10. 31 − 3 son _____.
11. 29 − 6 son _____.
12. 14 + 16 son _____.

*Son (*Are*) is the plural of es (*is*).

C.   Días y números. *Practice days and numbers with a classmate, using the calendar shown earlier.*

1. Choose a date from the calendar and your classmate will state which day of the week it is.
2. Your classmate will call out the name of a day and you will give all the dates that fall on it.

D.   Conteste. *Practice the following questions with a classmate. Refer to the calendar for other days of the week and dates.*

DÍAS DE LA SEMANA

1. Si hoy es el 12, ¿qué día es?
2. Si mañana es el 5, ¿qué día es?
3. Si ayer fue (*yesterday was*) el 19, ¿qué día es hoy?

FECHAS (*DATES*)

4. Si mañana es sábado 13, ¿qué fecha es hoy?
5. Si ayer fue el 29, ¿qué fecha es hoy?
6. Si ayer fue el 9, ¿qué fecha es hoy?

E.   Estaciones y meses. Complete.

1. Los meses de la primavera son _____, _____ y _____.
2. Mi (*My*) estación favorita es _____.
3. Mis (*My*) meses favoritos son _____, _____ y _____.
4. Hay* _____ días en noviembre/agosto/febrero.
5. Hay tres _____ en una estación.

E S T U D I O   D E   P A L A B R A S†

Here are several commands and interrogative words that you will hear in the classroom and see in the exercises of this text. Pronounce them after your instructor.

MANDATOS (*COMMANDS*)

cambie	*change*	haga	*do, make*
complete	*complete*	invente	*invent*
conteste/responda	*answer*	prepare	*prepare*
dé	*give*	pronuncie	*pronounce*
diga	*tell*	repita	*repeat*

Caution: Model pronunciation of words. Remind students to avoid Anglicizing pronunciation of cognates.

*****Hay** means *there is, there are* and **¿hay?** means *is there?, are there?*: **hay un estudiante en la clase** (*there is one student in the class*); **hay dos estudiantes...** (*there are two students . . .*).
†A variety of useful expressions and ways to help you recognize and learn new groups of words will be presented in this section.

INTERROGACIONES (*QUESTIONS*)

¿cómo?	*how? what?*	¿qué?	*what?, which?*
¿dónde?	*where?*	¿quién(es)?	*who?, whom?*

Note that all of these interrogative words have an accent mark.

Encuesta (*Opinion poll*). *Try to find out as much as you can from your classmate. Use as many of the question-and-answer cues as possible.*

MODELO: ¿Quién es sentimental?
yo, mi (*my*) actor favorito →
Yo soy sentimental.
Mi actor favorito, Tom Cruise, es sentimental.

1. ¿Quién es generoso/a (estupendo/a, importante, sincero/a, mexicano/a)?
el presidente, yo, el estudiante, Ud., el profesor (la profesora)
2. ¿Qué es necesario/a?
la educación, la universidad, el café colombiano, la televisión
3. ¿Cómo es el profesor (la profesora) (el presidente, Ud., su [*your*] actor favorito, su amigo/a)?
inteligente, liberal, religioso/a, excelente, popular, sentimental
4. ¿De dónde es Ud. (su actriz favorita, el profesor [la profesora], el presidente)?
Hispanoamérica, los Estados Unidos, California, España, el Canadá, la capital

---

¿Qué hora es?

What Time Is It?

A. To express time in the present, use **es** with one o'clock and **son** with all other hours.

Es la una.

Son las nueve.

NOTE: **La** is used with the first hour (one o'clock) and **las** with all others because it is understood that they correspond to **hora** (*hour*) and **horas.**

B. To express *quarter* and *half hour,* Spanish uses **cuarto** and **media,** respectively. Use **y** to refer to fractions of time up to the half hour; after the half hour use **menos** with the next hour.

Es la una **y cuarto.**   Es la una **y media.**   Son las diez **menos diez y ocho.**

C. References to hours may be clarified by adding the phrases **de la mañana** (*a.m.*), **de la tarde/noche** (*p.m.*), and **en punto** (*on the dot*).

Son las nueve de la mañana (noche).
Son las cinco de la tarde.
Son las doce en punto.

It is nine o'clock in the morning (at night).
It is five o'clock in the afternoon.
It is twelve o'clock on the dot.

D. When no specific time is mentioned, use the expressions **por la mañana (tarde, noche).**

La clase de español es por la mañana.

The Spanish class is in the morning.

E. Use **a la...** or **a las...** to indicate at what time something happens.

¿A qué hora es la fiesta? —Es a la una.
¿A qué hora es la clase de español? —A las doce.

When is the party? —At one o'clock.
When is the Spanish class? —At twelve o'clock.

Actividades

A. ¿Qué hora es? Use Ud. **de la mañana, de la tarde** y **de la noche.**

1. p.m.   2. p.m.   3. p.m.   4. a.m.

Son las _____.   Es la _____.   Son las _____.   Es la _____.

5. a.m.   6. p.m.   7. a.m.   8. p.m.

_____.   _____.   _____.

B. ¿A qué hora? *No one in the López family comes home at the same time. What time do the following family members come home?*

MODELO: Estela, 3:15 → A las tres y cuarto.

1. Inés, 1:45
2. el señor López, 5:15 p.m.
3. Raúl y Hernán, 6:30 p.m.
4. La señora López, 8:00 p.m. en punto

C. Un día típico. *Tell when you usually do the following activities, first using **por la mañana, por la tarde,** or **por la noche,** and then giving a specific time.*

1.

2.

3.

4.

Note: Each lesson in text ends with variety of communication exercises. Encourage students to learn short dialogues thoroughly so they can use them comfortably and even change them slightly in speaking with classmates.

Note: Refer to the Instructor's Manual for the chapter quiz covering the Preliminary Lesson. (Quizzes for all lessons are included in the IM.)

Conversación

Pronuncie y aprenda de memoria. (*Pronounce and memorize.*)

1. —Buenas noches, señora Gómez Contreras. ¿Cómo está Ud.?*
   —Bien, gracias. ¿Y Ud.?
   —Muy bien.

2. —Buenas tardes, Julia.
   —Hola, ¿qué hay?
   —Pues... nada de nuevo. ¿Y cómo estás tú?
   —Así así. Ahora, a la clase de español.
   —Adiós. Hasta mañana.
   —Hasta luego. Buenas tardes.

*1. *Good evening, Mrs. Gómez Contreras. How are you? —Fine (Well), thanks. And you? —Very well (Great).* **2.** *Good afternoon, Julia. —Hello, how are you (what's up)? —Well . . . nothing new. And how are you? —So-so. Now (I'm off) to Spanish class. —Good-bye. Until (See you) tomorrow. —Until (See you) later. Good afternoon.*

Actividad

With a classmate, take turns greeting each other, asking how you are, and saying good-bye.

Vocabulario activo

Before going on to **Lección 1,** you should know all of the following words from the **Lección preliminar** as well as all the cognates and classroom commands studied in those sections.

Sustantivos (*Nouns*)

el amigo/la amiga	(male/female) friend
el estudiante/la estudiante	(male/female) student
el profesor/la profesora	(male/female) professor, instructor
el señor	man, gentleman; sir
la señora	woman, lady; madam
la señorita	young lady; miss
el día	day
la estación	season
la fecha	date
el mes	month
la semana	week

Adverbios

¿cómo?	how?, what?
¿dónde?	where?
¿qué?	what?, which?
¿quién(es)?	who?, whom?
ayer	yesterday
hoy	today
mañana	tomorrow
mucho	a lot; much
muy	very
pues	well
sí	yes
no	no

Saludos y conversaciones (*Greetings and Conversations*)

buenos días	good morning
buenas tardes	good afternoon
buenas noches	good evening; good night
hola	hello
adiós	good-bye
hasta luego	until (I see you) later
hasta mañana	until (I see you) tomorrow
¿Cómo está Ud.?	How are you? (*pol.*)
¿Cómo estás (tú)?	How are you? (*fam.*)
¿Qué hay?	What's up? What's new?
(muy) bien, gracias	(very) well (fine), thanks
así así	so-so
nada de nuevo	nothing new
¿De dónde es Ud.?	Where are you from? (*pol.*)
¿De dónde eres tú?	Where are you from? (*fam.*)
Soy de...	I'm from . . .
Me llamo...	My name is (I call myself) . . .
¿Cómo se llama Ud.?	What's your name? (*pol.*)
¿Cómo te llamas (tú)?	What's your name? (*fam.*)
¿Cómo se llama él/ella?	What's his/her name?
¿Quién es él/ella?	Who is he/she?

La hora (*Time, Hour*)

¿A qué hora es (la clase)?	At what time is (the class)?
A la una en punto.	At one o'clock on the dot.
A las dos y media.	At two thirty.
Por la mañana/tarde/ noche.	In the morning./In the afternoon./At night.
¿Qué hora es?	What time is it?
Es la una y cuarto.	It's quarter after one.
Son las dos menos diez.	It's ten of two.
Son las seis de la mañana.	It's six in the morning.
Son las cinco de la tarde.	It's five in the afternoon.
Son las once de la noche.	It's eleven at night.

Otras palabras

a	to
de	of; from
más	plus
menos	minus
si	if
y	and

Verbos

(yo) soy	I am
(tú) eres	you (*fam.*) are
(Ud./él/ella) es	you (*pol.*) are; he/she is
me gusta(n)	I like
te gusta(n)	you (*fam.*) like
le gusta(n)	you (*pol.*) like; he/she likes
hay	there is, there are

Números

uno, dos, tres, cuatro, cinco, seis, siete, ocho, nueve, diez, once, doce, trece, catorce, quince, diez y seis (dieciséis), diez y siete (diecisiete), diez y ocho (dieciocho), diez y nueve (diecinueve), veinte, veinte y uno (veintiuno), veinte y dos (veintidós), veinte y tres (veintitrés), veinte y cuatro (veinticuatro), veinte y cinco (veinticinco), veinte y seis (veintiséis), veinte y siete (veintisiete), veinte y ocho (veintiocho), veinte y nueve (veintinueve), treinta, treinta y uno

Días de la semana

lunes, martes, miércoles, jueves, viernes, sábado, domingo

Meses y fechas

enero, febrero, marzo, abril, mayo, junio, julio, agosto, septiembre, octubre, noviembre, diciembre

el primero de...	the first of . . .

Estaciones

la primavera, el verano, el otoño, el invierno

Mis compañeros de clase

Estudiantes chilenos en una clase en la Universidad de Santiago

METAS

Comunicación: The **metas** (*objectives*) of this lesson are to learn basic vocabulary and expressions needed in the classroom. The material presented will enable you to talk about different classroom situations and to begin working in Spanish with other students.

Estructuras: 1. Singular Articles 2. Gender of Nouns 3. Plurals of Articles and Nouns 4. Agreement and Position of Adjectives 5. Subject Pronouns 6. Present Tense of **-ar** Verbs

GRÁFICOS

La sala de clase

The Classroom

1. la mesa	7. el profesor
2. la silla	8. la profesora
3. la puerta	9. el reloj
4. la ventana	10. el borrador
5. la tiza	11. la mochila
6. la pizarra	

1. el libro	7. el alumno
2. el lápiz	8. la alumna
3. el bolígrafo	9. el mapa
4. el papel	10. la pared
5. el dibujo	11. la calculadora
6. el cuaderno	12. el diccionario

MEMOPRÁCTICA

The purpose of the drawings in the **Gráficos** sections is to provide a context that will make learning new vocabulary easier. Try to "see" the new vocabulary in related groups of images rather than as abstract, individual words. Associate the numbered words with the numbered drawings and then pronounce them. Next, cover the words with your hand or a piece of paper and identify the objects in each drawing. As you study the dialogues, review the drawings frequently and try to vary your descriptions of them. You will notice that the characters in many drawings have been given names; this should also help you to remember the context of the vocabulary presentation. The more images you can associate with new words as you study them, the easier it will be for you to remember them.

Actividades

A. Relaciones. *In each group, indicate the word that is not related to the others.*

1. la ventana, el dibujo, el lápiz
2. el libro, el papel, la alumna
3. el mapa, la pared, la profesora
4. el bolígrafo, el cuaderno, la silla
5. la puerta, el alumno, el profesor
6. la mesa, la pizarra, la tiza
7. la mochila, los libros, la puerta
8. la sala, la mesa, la silla
9. el diccionario, el reloj, el libro
10. la calculadora, el borrador, la pizarra

B. Identificaciones. *With a classmate, point out objects or persons in the classroom. Your partner will name the items or individuals in Spanish. Then reverse roles.*

Expansion B: Questions relating to your classroom: **1.** *¿Qué libro de gramática usa Ud.?* **2.** *En la clase, ¿quién pregunta y quién contesta?* **3.** *¿Quién pronuncia las palabras nuevas?* **4.** *¿Es Motivos un libro difícil?*

La clase de español

Note: The dialogues in *Motivos de conversación* are not intended to be memorized; rather, students should learn key terms to be able to repeat the information in the dialogues in their own words. However, to illustrate how easy memorization can be, write a dialogue on the board and have students dramatize it several times, as you erase key words. Challenge students to repeat the entire dialogue once it is completely erased.

◆ PRESENT TENSE **-ar** VERBS ◆	
converso	*I converse*
conversa	*you* [Ud.] (*he/she*) *converse(s)*
pregunto	*I ask*
pregunta	*you* [Ud.] (*he/she*) *ask(s)*
contesto	*I answer*
contesta	*you* [Ud.] (*he/she*) *answer(s)*
enseño	*I teach*
enseña	*you* [Ud.] (*he/she*) *teach(es)*
uso	*I use*
usas	*you* [tú] *use*
estudio	*I study*
estudias	*you* [tú] *study*
pronuncio	*I pronounce*
pronuncias	*you* [tú] *pronounce*

Julia conversa *con* Carla, su amiga mexicana. Carla pregunta *sobre varias cosas* y Julia contesta las *preguntas.*

⟶ *with / about / various things questions*

CARLA: ¿Te gusta la clase de español?

JULIA: Sí, me gusta mucho. Es una clase muy interesante.

CARLA: ¿Quién enseña la clase?

JULIA: La profesora Jiménez enseña *todas* las clases de español básico. Es una profesora estupenda. ⟶ *all*

CARLA: ¿Usas un libro *difícil*? ⟶ *difficult*

JULIA: No, uso *Motivos de conversación.* Es muy *fácil.* ⟶ *easy*

CARLA: ¿Qué estudias *ahora*? ⟶ *now*

JULIA: Estudio los *nombres* de las cosas *en* la sala de clase: la puerta, el lápiz, la ventana, el dibujo y la calculadora. ⟶ *names / in*

CARLA: ¡Fantástico! Tú pronuncias muy bien todas las *palabras nuevas.* ⟶ *words / new*

Actividades

A. Asociaciones. *What do the following people do?*

1. Julia _____ con Carla, _____ las preguntas de Carla, _____ un libro fácil y _____ los nombres de las cosas en la sala de clase.
2. Carla _____ con Julia y _____ sobre varias cosas.
3. La profesora Jiménez _____ todas las clases de español básico.
4. ¿Y Ud.?

Now tell where you use these objects.

5. Uso el bolígrafo en (*on*) _____.
6. Uso la tiza en _____.
7. Uso el mapa en _____.

B. La clase de español. *Alternate asking and answering the following questions with a classmate.*

1. ¿Qué estudias ahora?
2. ¿Usas un libro difícil?
3. ¿Qué palabras nuevas estudias?
4. ¿Qué pronuncias muy bien?
5. ¿Cómo se llama la profesora (el profesor)?
6. ¿Qué enseña? ¿Qué usa en la pizarra?

Suggestion C: Have students present monologues in small groups and then select a few for presentation in front of class.

C. Un monólogo. *Prepare a brief monologue using the following verbs in a logical sequence:* **estudio, converso, pregunto, pronuncio, uso, contesto, __¿?__** . *Begin with* **En la clase... .**

En *la biblioteca*

Library

◆	MORE PRESENT TENSE VERBS	◆
entro	*I enter*	
entra	*you* [Ud.] (*he/she*) *enter(s)*	
trabajo	*I work*	
trabaja	*you* [Ud.] (*he/she*) *work(s)*	
preparo	*I prepare*	
prepara	*you* [Ud.] (*he/she*) *prepare(s)*	
practico	*I practice*	
practica	*you* [Ud.] (*he/she*) *practice(s)*	
hablo	*I speak*	
habla	*you* [Ud.] (*he/she*) *speak(s)*	

Cultural expansion: Point out to students that Spanish surnames (*Jiménez, Pérez*) used in first two dialogues are among most common in Hispanic world (also mention *García, Martínez, González*), roughly equivalent to Smith or Jones. Telephone directories of large Hispanic cities have pages of these names. Have students check the phone book in your city for Hispanic names. How many listings for *García, Martínez, Pérez*, etc. can they find?

Suggestion: Model the verbs in the verb chart. Be especially careful with accentuation patterns.

La profesora Jiménez entra en la biblioteca, donde trabaja el *joven* Mario.   *young man*

PROFESORA: Mario, ¿trabaja Ud. *aquí?*   *here*
MARIO: Sí, *pero sólo* trabajo por la tarde.   *but / only*
PROFESORA: Y ¿*cuándo* prepara las *lecciones* de español?   *when / lessons*
MARIO: Por la mañana y por la noche, pero *también* practico el español   *also*
aquí.
PROFESORA: ¿*Verdad?* ¿Habla Ud. español en la biblioteca?   *Really?*
MARIO: Sí, *a veces* converso con el director, *que* es de Bogotá, Colombia.   *at times / who*
PROFESORA: ¡*Ah, sí!* Es el profesor Pérez. Soy *amiga de él.* Yo soy de Colombia   *Right! / a friend of his*
también.

Actividades

A. Preguntas informativas. Conteste.

1. ¿En dónde entra la profesora Jiménez?
2. ¿Quién trabaja en la biblioteca? ¿Cuándo?
3. ¿También estudia Mario el español? ¿Cuándo?
4. ¿Con quién conversa Mario a veces?
5. ¿De dónde es el profesor Pérez?
6. ¿Es amiga de él la profesora Jiménez?

Now pretend you're Mario and answer these questions as he would.

7. ¿Dónde trabaja Ud., joven? ¿Trabaja sólo por la mañana?
8. ¿Cuándo prepara Ud. las lecciones de español?
9. ¿Con quién practica Ud. el español a veces?

B. En la clase. *Ask a classmate the following questions, using both of the words or phrases in parentheses.*

1. ¿Quién (enseña, habla) en la clase?
2. ¿Dónde trabaja hoy (la profesora, Mario)?
3. ¿Qué estudias (aquí, en la biblioteca)?
4. ¿Con quién (conversas, practicas) en la clase?
5. ¿Quién (pronuncia bien el español, conversa en la biblioteca)?
6. ¿Cuándo (preparas, estudias) la lección de español?
7. ¿Cuándo (entras, hablas) en la clase de español?

ESTUDIO DE PALABRAS

Once you learn the Spanish equivalents of certain frequently occurring suffixes, you can predict the forms of many Spanish cognates. Here are several common suffixes.

INGLÉS (*ENGLISH*)		ESPAÑOL	
-sion *(-tion)*	{ *session* *indication*	**-sión** **(-ción)**	{ sesión indicación
-ly	{ *really* *sincerely*	**-mente**	{ realmente sinceramente
-ty	{ *liberty* *identity*	**-tad (-dad)**	{ libertad identidad
-ure	{ *architecture* *literature*	**-ura**	{ arquitectura literatura
-y	{ *history* *sociology*	**-ia (-ía)***	{ historia sociología

The names of many school subjects follow these patterns. Others are very close cognates of English words. You should easily recognize the meaning of the following words.

la música
las matemáticas
el álgebra
las ciencias (naturales, físicas, sociales)

las lenguas
la medicina
la química (orgánica, inorgánica)

Exprese en inglés.

1. fraternidad
2. especialmente
3. clarificación
4. antropología

5. generalmente
6. cultura
7. educación
8. pasión

9. claridad
10. economía
11. identificación
12. generosamente

Expansion: Additional words for students to express in English: *probablemente, realidad, ilusión, intensidad, inteligentemente, contribución.* Remind them to try to avoid pitfall of pronouncing Spanish cognates like English counterparts.

VISTA CULTURAL†

Cultural expansion: Mention some differences between North American and Hispanic universities. For example, Hispanic universities generally do not have competitive sports teams, university housing, or extracurricular activities.

La Universidad Nacional Autónoma de México está en la Ciudad de México. Es una universidad muy famosa. Tiene (*It has*) aproximadamente 300.000 estudiantes. Muchos de los líderes de la nación se graduaron en este importante centro de educación.

---

*You will have to memorize when an accent mark is needed.

†Brief photographic insights into different aspects of Hispanic culture will be presented in this section.

GRAMÁTICA ESENCIAL

1. Singular Articles

Note: Most numbered grammar topics in text are introduced with excerpts of drawings and accompanying dialogues from *Gráficos*. Students can be asked to dramatize lines and to add other new words.

—¿Te gusta la clase de español?
—Sí, me gusta mucho. Es una clase muy interesante.

	DEFINITE ARTICLE		INDEFINITE ARTICLE	
Masculine	el	*the*	un	*a*
Feminine	la	*the*	una	*a*

2. Gender of Nouns

—¿Usas un libro difícil?
—No, uso *Motivos de conversación.* Es muy fácil.
—¿Qué estudias ahora?
—Estudio los nombres de las cosas en la sala de clase como la puerta, el lápiz, la ventana, el dibujo y la calculadora.

Most Spanish nouns ending in **-o** and those referring to males are masculine. Most nouns ending in **-a** and those referring to females are feminine. Definite and indefinite articles *must agree* with the nouns they accompany.

MASCULINE		FEMININE	
el amigo	un amigo	la amiga	una amiga
el profesor	un profesor	la profesora	una profesora

A few nouns ending in **-a,** however, are masculine: **el día, el mapa.** Most nouns ending in **-d** or **-ción (-sión)** are feminine.

la ciu**dad** (*city*)   una lec**ción**   una universi**dad**   la conversa**ción**

Since the gender of nouns is not always predictable, learn nouns along with their definite article, **el** or **la: el lápiz, la clase, el papel, el inglés, el agua** (*water*).*

Actividades

A.   Un repaso (*review*). *Return to the drawings on page 18. Covering the printed words and following the numbers, identify the objects in Spanish and give their correct definite articles.*

B.   ¿**Un** o **una?**

1. universidad
2. clase
3. conversación
4. día
5. ciudad
6. español
7. señor
8. ocasión
9. lección

C.   Identificaciones. Complete según (*according to*) los modelos. *Identify these people.*

> MODELO: Carmen es <u>una</u> alumna inteligente.

1. Tomás es _____ alumno extraordinario.
2. Elena es _____ joven española.
3. La señora Díaz es _____ profesora famosa.
4. Martín es _____ joven italiano.
5. Carmen es _____ amiga generosa.

Now describe these people.

> MODELO: <u>El</u> joven es <u>un</u> alumno argentino.

6. _____ señorita es _____ persona sincera.
7. _____ señora es _____ profesora mexicana.
8. _____ joven es de _____ ciudad colombiana.
9. _____ profesor es _____ señor español.
10. _____ alumna es _____ señorita de Toronto.

3. Plurals of Articles and Nouns

¡Fantástico! Tú pronuncias muy bien todas las palabras nuevas.

*****El** is required with feminine nouns beginning with a stressed **a** or **ha.**

	DEFINITE ARTICLE		INDEFINITE ARTICLE	
Masculine	los	*the*	unos	*some*
Feminine	las	*the*	unas	*some*

Suggestion: All examples given in the grammar presentations, as well as the grammar section exercises, provide excellent pronunciation practice.

Always use a plural article with a plural noun. Remember these rules when making nouns plural:

1. Add **-s** to nouns ending in a vowel.

    el alumn**o** → **los** alumn**os**   la mes**a** → **las** mes**as**

2. Add **-es** to nouns ending in a consonant.

    la ciuda**d** → **las** ciuda**des**   el profeso**r** → **los** profeso**res**

3. A noun that ends in **-z** changes the **z** to **c** before adding **-es.**

    el lápi**z** → **los** lápi**ces**   la vo**z** (*voice*) → **las** vo**ces**

4. A noun that ends in **-n** or **-s** with an accent mark on the last syllable drops the accent mark in the plural.

    la lec**ción** → **las** lec**ciones**   el in**glés** → **los** in**gleses**

Actividades

A.   Cambie al singular.

1. los españoles
2. los profesores
3. unos días
4. las clases
5. unos señores
6. los lápices
7. unas lecciones
8. las puertas
9. los meses

B.   Cambie al plural. *Change each numbered noun to the plural, giving the correct definite or indefinite article. Then relate each noun to one or more of the lettered categories.*

1. papel
2. mapa
3. silla
4. libro
5. lápiz
6. dibujo
7. novela
8. nación

a. la educación
b. la biblioteca
c. la geografía
d. el arte
e. la literatura

C.   Una descripción. *Working with a classmate, name as many objects as possible on this student's desk. Use indefinite articles.*

MODELO: Hay un/una/ unos/unas _____ en la mesa.

4. Agreement and Position of Adjectives

La profesora Jiménez enseña todas las clases de español básico. Es una profesora estupenda.

mesa
silla
cuaderno

A. All adjectives in Spanish agree in gender with the nouns they modify. Adjectives ending in **-o** change the **-o** to **-a** when they modify a feminine noun.

un amigo famos**o**   **una** ciudad famos**a**

Most adjectives not ending in **-o** remain the same when modifying a singular noun, whether masculine or feminine.

un libro **especial**   **una** clase **especial**
un bar **interesante**   **una** lección **interesante**

Adjectives of nationality are an exception. If they end in a consonant, an **-a** is added for the feminine form. Note that the extra syllable often results in an accent being dropped.

el amigo **español** → **la** amiga **española**
un señor **francés** (*French*) → **una** señora **francesa**
un compañero **alemán** (*a German classmate*) → **una** compañera **alemana**
un joven **inglés** → **una** joven **inglesa**

B. All adjectives must also agree in number with the nouns they modify. To make an adjective plural, add **-s** if the adjective ends in a vowel and **-es** if it ends in a consonant:

el alumno **inteligente** → **los** alumnos **inteligentes**
una lección **especial** → **unas** lecciones **especiales**

Adjectives of nationality ending in a consonant add **-es** to form the masculine plural and **-as** to form the feminine plural.

muchos amigos aleman**es**   varias universidades español**as**

C. Note that all articles precede the nouns they modify. Similarly, adjectives indicating quantity and number (**muchos, varias**) also precede the noun. Most descriptive adjectives (**interesante, francés, inteligente**) follow the noun.

Actividades

A.   Descripciones. *The international center at your university is having a party for some of the new students. Describe the following people at the party.*

> MODELO: Claudine es _____ señorita _____ (francés). →
> Claudine es una señorita francesa.

1.   Pablo es _____ estudiante _____ (español).
2.   Akbar y Sabim son _____ estudiantes _____ (inteligente).
3.   La joven es _____ compañera _____ (alemán).
4.   Pierre es _____ estudiante _____ (francés).
5.   El señor Valle es _____ profesor _____ (estupendo).
6.   Diana es _____ joven _____ (inglés).
7.   María y Alicia son _____ estudiantes _____ (mexicano).
8.   Juan es _____ joven _____ (idealista).
9.   Wolf y Hans son _____ compañeros _____ (alemán).
10.   La profesora Jiménez es _____ profesora _____ (interesante).

B.   Descripciones. *Tell the nationality of the following people.*

Now describe the people in each drawing. **Possible adjectives:** romántico, generoso, artístico, inteligente, interesante, famoso, tímido, sentimental, popular, cruel

5. Subject Pronouns

—Mario, ¿trabaja Ud. aquí?
—Sí, pero sólo trabajo por
   la tarde.

Presentation: Present
subject pronouns using
people in class. Point at
yourself (*yo*), then to student, saying *tú*, then to
un compañero de clase
(*él*), and so on. Explain
that Spanish uses subject
pronouns less than Eng-
lish, often for clarification
or emphasis. Tell class
that *vosotros* form is presented but not empha-
sized in book, and men-
tion your preference
concerning its use.

SINGULAR		PLURAL	
yo	*I*	nosotros/as	*we*
tú	*you (fam.)*	vosotros/as	*you (fam.)*
usted	*you (pol.)*	ustedes	*you (pol.)*
él	*he*	ellos	*they*
ella	*she*	ellas	*they*

In Spanish there is no word for *it* as a subject.

Es importante.   *It is important.*

Except for **ustedes,** the plural pronouns are either masculine or feminine
according to the gender of the group they refer to. If the group includes
males and females, the masculine form is used.

¿Estudian Isabel y Tomás con Juana? —No, **ellos** estudian con
   Carmen.

Vosotros, the plural of **tú,** is used extensively in Spain but rarely in
Hispanic America. There, **ustedes** serves as the plural of both **tú** and **usted.**
As mentioned in the **Lección preliminar, usted** is usually abbreviated to
Ud. or **Vd.; ustedes** is abbreviated to **Uds.** or **Vds.**

Actividades

A.   ¿De quién habla Ud.? *What subject pronouns would you use to refer to these
people?*

1.   una amiga
2.   un cliente
3.   las profesoras
4.   tú mismo/a (*yourself*)
5.   un amigo y tú mismo/a

6. los señores García (*the Garcías*)
7. dos amigos
8. el presidente
9. un doctor

B. ¿Con quién habla Ud.? *Would you use **Ud., Uds., tú,** or **vosotros** when speaking to these people?*

1. la profesora Jiménez
2. un compañero de clase
3. tres amigas íntimas (en España)
4. el director de la biblioteca
5. papá y mamá (en Hispanoamérica)
6. el profesor Pérez y la profesora Franco

6. Present Tense of *-ar* Verbs

—¿Habla Ud. español en la biblioteca?
—Sí, a veces converso con el director, que es de Bogotá, Colombia.

Suggestion: Write an English regular verb conjugation on the board to show the English equivalents of the six verb forms.

I sing	we sing
you sing	you sing
he/she sings	they sing

Warm-up: Write chart on board for present tense of *hablar* and list other first-conjugation verbs used in lesson: *contestar, conversar, enseñar, entrar, estudiar, practicar, preguntar, preparar, pronunciar, trabajar, usar.* Then say the following short sentences and ask students to repeat them, conjugating verbs to agree with new subjects given: **1.** *Contestamos las preguntas. (Ud., tú)* **2.** *Converso en español. (vosotras, Uds.)* **3.** *La profesora enseña francés. (yo, nosotros)* **4.** *El alumno entra en la sala de clase. (ellas, tú)* **5.** *¿Estudias las palabras nuevas? (Ud., Uds.)* **6.** *Practico las palabras. (nosotras, vosotros)* **7.** *Preguntan sobre los verbos. (Ud., él)* **8.** *Preparáis la lección. (yo, ella)* **9.** *Pronunciamos los nombres. (Uds., tú)* **10.** *Trabajas por la tarde. (ellas, nosotros)* **11.** *Mario usa un lápiz. (tú, Uds.)*

Spanish verbs are divided into three conjugations, according to the ending of the infinitive.* Verbs ending in **-ar** belong to the first conjugation, those ending in **-er** and **-ir** to the second and third conjugations, respectively. Examples of verbs in each of these conjugations are **estudi*ar*** (*to study*), **comprend*er*** (*to understand*), and **viv*ir*** (*to live*).

The present tense of first-conjugation verbs is formed by dropping the **-ar** ending of the infinitive and adding the following endings.

Emphasis: Point out the footnote and ask students under what main entry in the Spanish dictionary the following verbs would be found:
1. *converso* **2.** *usas* **3.** *entro* **4.** *preparan* **5.** *estudiamos* **6.** *practica* **7.** *trabajáis* **8.** *hablo* **9.** *enseñan* **10.** *contestamos*

SINGULAR	PLURAL
-o	-amos
-as	-áis
-a	-an

*The infinitive is the form of the verb listed in the dictionaries as the main entry. Its equivalent in English is the form preceded by *to*: *to* speak, *to* study, *to* work.

The majority of **-ar** verbs are regular; that is, they follow this general pattern.

hablar (*to speak*)

Singular	(yo)	habl**o**	*I speak*
	(tú)	habl**as**	*you speak*
	(usted, él/ella)	habl**a**	*you speak, he/she speaks*
Plural	(nosotros/as)	habl**amos**	*we speak*
	(vosotros/as)	habl**áis**	*you speak*
	(ustedes, ellos/ellas)	habl**an**	*you speak; they speak*

NOTE 1: The Spanish present tense has three possible English translations.

hablo = *I speak, I am speaking, I do speak*

NOTE 2: Subject pronouns are usually omitted in Spanish, since the verb endings indicate the subject.

Estudi**o** español hoy. *I study Spanish today.*
Habl**as** inglés. *You speak English.*

NOTE 3: To make a sentence negative in Spanish, place **no** before the verb.

Ellas **no** trabajan mañana. *They do not work (are not working) tomorrow.*

Actividades

Expansion A: Ask students to change sentences from singular to plural and vice versa:
1. *¿Hablas alemán?*
2. *Pronuncio los verbos.*
3. *Estudia la lección uno.*
4. *Usáis el cuaderno.*
5. *Contestamos las preguntas.* **6.** *Enseñan español y alemán.* **7.** *Entro en la clase.* **8.** *Practicas los verbos.* **9.** *Preparan las preguntas.* **10.** *Conversamos en inglés.*

A. ¿De quién habla? *Eduardo keeps telling you about different people's activities without mentioning anyone by name. Give all the pronouns to show which people he could be talking about.*

MODELO: Estudian español. →
Ellos (Ellas, Uds.) estudian español.

1. Habla con Carmen.
2. Pronuncian el español.
3. Estudias en la clase.
4. Practica las dos lenguas (*languages*).
5. Contestan las preguntas.
6. Entramos en la biblioteca.
7. Conversáis en francés.
8. Enseña el español básico.
9. Preparo la lección.
10. Usas el bolígrafo.

B. Actividades en la clase de español. *Everyone seems to be doing the same thing today. Tell who else is doing the activity of the first person mentioned.*

MODELO: Mario prepara la lección de español... (yo) →
(Yo) Preparo la lección de español...

1. La profesora Jiménez enseña la clase de español básico. Ahora ella entra en la sala de clase. Ella pregunta a los alumnos sobre varias cosas, usa la pizarra y practica con ellos las palabras nuevas.
(yo, tú, los profesores, nosotras)

2. Yo examino el mapa de España que hay en la pared y estudio los nombres de las ciudades y regiones. Pronuncio los nombres de las ciudades y también converso con los compañeros de clase (*classmates*) sobre España y los españoles.
(los alumnos, Julia y Ud., tú, Ud.)

C. Conversaciones entre (*between*) estudiantes. *With a classmate, present these dialogues in class, giving the correct form for the infinitive in each case.*

1. —Soy una persona muy ocupada (*busy*). Por la mañana (trabajar), por la tarde (estudiar) historia y biología y por la noche (practicar) el español.
—Yo también soy una persona ocupada. Por la tarde (preparar) las lecciones para (*for*) mis clases y por la noche (enseñar) inglés a un compañero argentino.

2. —Julia, ¿por qué no (contestar) Ud. cuando la profesora (preguntar) las palabras nuevas?
—Porque soy tímida y a veces no (estudiar) mucho. Los compañeros de clase (pronunciar) el español correctamente, pero yo no.

D. Confesiones. *In five or six short sentences, tell a classmate about yourself.* **¿Qué estudia Ud.? ¿Dónde? ¿Cuándo?** (*When?*) **¿Con quién?** (*With whom?*) **¿Cuál** (*Which*) **es su clase favorita?**

*Para resumir y repasar**

To Summarize and Review

A. En persona: Mi amiga argentina. *Imagine that a student is visiting you from Argentina and wants to know about your Spanish class. From memory, tell him or her about the classroom (mention both objects and activities), your classmates (describe some of them, including their study habits), and the instructor. When finished, compare your comments with those of your classmates to see who was able to say the most.*

Expansion C: Write following cues on board and have students develop short speeches based on them: **1.** *En la clase: el profesor (la profesora) preguntar... ; yo contestar... y pronunciar... ; otro estudiante no estudiar... , no practicar... .* **2.** *En la biblioteca: nosotros entrar... , conversar... y trabajar... ; yo hablar... , preparar... y... .*
Review: Ask following questions: **1.** *¿Dónde prepara Ud. la lección?* **2.** *¿Dónde practica el español?* **3.** *¿Con quién conversa Ud. en español?* **4.** *¿Qué usa en la clase?* **5.** *¿Cómo se llama el profesor (la profesora) de la clase de español?* **6.** *¿Qué lengua(s) habla el profesor (la profesora)?*

Suggestion D: Have pairs of students tell each other their "confessions"; if there is time, assign students a new partner and have them repeat the activity.

Although *En persona* exercises will probably be done in class, the rest of this section is designed for home study. When possible, answers are provided in Appendix 3.

---

*The **Para resumir y repasar** section summarizes the grammar points of the present lesson in the **En persona** exercises, then reviews those of previous lessons in the following exercises. The majority of the exercises in this section are designed for home study. Whenever possible, answers are provided in Appendix 3.

B.   Mandatos. Complete con un mandato.

Cambie	Conteste	Dé
Invente	Prepare	Repita
Complete	Responda	Haga
Diga	Pronuncie	

1.   _____ según (*according to*) los modelos.
2.   _____ las palabras nuevas después de (*after*) la profesora.
3.   _____ una descripción original para (*for*) mañana.
4.   _____ todas las preguntas.
5.   _____ las preguntas con un verbo de la lista.
6.   _____ una descripción del dibujo.
7.   _____ a las preguntas afirmativamente.
8.   _____ todos los cognados con la acentuación correcta en español.
9.   _____ la hora exacta.
10.   _____ una situación nueva.
11.   _____ cómo se llama la señora.

C.   Complete los diálogos lógicamente.

1.   —Buenos días, señor (señorita).
    —__¿?__
    —¿Cómo está Ud.?
    —__¿?__
    —Muy bien, gracias.
2.   —Buenas tardes. Me llamo Arturo, y mi amigo _____.
    —¿Cómo _____ tú?
    —Me llamo Alicia.
    —¿De dónde _____ tú, Alicia?
    —Soy _____, ¿y tú?
    —Soy _____ también.

D.   Problemas de matemáticas. *Fill in each blank with the correct answer to the problem. Choose from the numbers below.*

1.   veintisiete menos catorce   _____
2.   once más diez   _____
3.   treinta y uno menos trece   _____
4.   quince más once   _____
5.   dieciocho menos siete   _____

E.   Diga qué hora es.

1.   2.   3.

Comunicación

De la vida real

Note: If students want to fill out the table of personal information in the ad, remind them of the meaning of *apellido* and explain that *localidad* = the city or town of one's residence, *C.P.* = *código postal, D.N.I.* = *Documento nacional de identidad.*

LA UNIVERSIDAD DE DESCANSO[a]

En un futuro próximo, los miembros de las diferentes comunidades universitarias españolas, podrán disfrutar[b] de la nueva Ciudad Universitaria Internacional de Villajoyosa. Se trata de un complejo[c] residencial y cultural destinado al deporte,[d] al ocio[e], y, cómo no, a congresos, reuniones, simposios o conferencias. La ventaja[f] de este centro frente a otros similares es que permanecerá[g] en funcionamiento todo el año y no sólo en determinadas temporadas.

[a]*rest*
[b]*podrán... will be able to enjoy*
[c]*Se... It is a complex*
[d]*sports*
[e]*leisure*
[f]*advantage*
[g]*will remain*

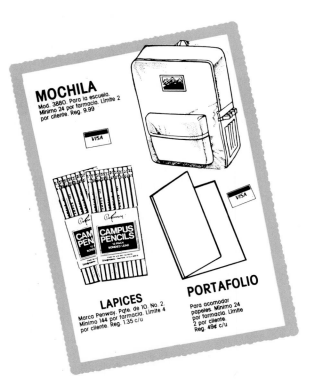

MOCHILA
Mod. 3880. Para la escuela.
Mínimo 24 por farmacia. Límite 2
por cliente. Reg. 9.99

VISA

LAPICES
Marca Penway. Pqte. de 10. No. 2,
Mínimo 144 por farmacia. Límite 4
por cliente. Reg. 1.35 c/u

PORTAFOLIO
Para acomodar
papeles. Mínimo 24
por farmacia. Límite
2 por cliente.
Reg. 49¢ c/u

VISA

Suggestion: The *Comunicación* section presents authentic materials in Spanish. They have been carefully selected to correspond to the lexical and grammatical level of each lesson, although students will encounter terms they do not know. Students should be told that even though they may not understand everything they read, they should be able to get the gist of a reading and gather all the information requested. In the early lessons, you may find it helpful to use some English when working with the realia. This will not lessen the cultural value of these items.

It has been necessary to offer translations in the exercises of this section more often than in other sections due to the nature of the material. Encourage students to integrate these items into their active vocabulary, if possible. In any case, tell them not to be intimidated by this practice. It is an aid to help them with the authentic Spanish materials.

Note: Abbreviations in the Mochila ad: *Mod.* = *Modelo, Reg.* = *Regular, Pqte.* = *Paquete, c/u* = *cada uno.*

A. Reserva de libros de texto. *Take turns asking and answering the following questions with a classmate.*

1. ¿Qué libros te parecen (*seem*) interesantes? ¿fáciles? ¿difíciles? (Me parecen...)
2. ¿Qué libros son para estudiar una lengua? ¿una ciencia?
3. ¿Estudias una de estas materias (*one of these subjects*) ahora? ¿Qué materias te gustaría (*would you like*) estudiar? (Me gustaría estudiar...)

Suggestion B: Since this reading is rather advanced, remind students that they are reading to get the gist of the article and to gather the short list of information requested in the exercise. You might first ask them to read through the article and list the cognates they find; being able to understand the numerous cognates here will boost their reading confidence. Also, ask them to examine the drawing and explain how it relates to the text of the article.

B. La universidad de descanso. *First read the article all the way through once. Then, while reading through it a second time, make a list of all of the cognates you find, and gather the information below.*

1. el nombre de la nueva universidad
2. el nombre de la ciudad
3. las funciones del nuevo complejo

Now, with a classmate, give a brief summary of what you learned in this article.

C. Material para las clases. Lea (*Read*) el anuncio (*advertisement*) de la mochila. *After reading through the advertisement, take turns answering the following questions with a classmate.*

1. ¿Para quién es la mochila?
2. ¿Qué lleva (*carry*) generalmente un(a) estudiante en la mochila?
3. ¿Cuántas (*How many*) mochilas por cliente es el límite?
4. ¿Cuántos portafolios por cliente es el límite?
5. ¿Qué llevas en tu (*your*) mochila? ¿Cuántos libros? ¿lápices? ¿portafolios?

Note: First have students answer these questions from their own experience. Then have them alternate asking and answering them with a classmate (using *tú*). Both could then report their findings to the class.

Para conversar más

Entrevistas (*Interviews*). *Interview several of your classmates, using the following questions.*

1. ¿Qué lenguas hablas?
2. ¿Enseñas el español?
3. ¿Te gusta el español?
4. ¿Dónde y con quién practicas el español?
5. ¿Cuándo te gusta estudiar? ¿por la mañana? ¿por la tarde? ¿por la noche?
6. ¿Contestas preguntas en la clase de español?
7. ¿Trabajas? ¿Dónde? ¿Cuándo?

MOTIVO **CULTURAL**

The educational system in the Hispanic world is quite different from that of the United States and can also vary from one country to another. Generally, students attend elementary school (**escuela primaria** or **colegio**) for six to eight years and then go on to high school (**escuela secundaria, liceo,** or **colegio**) for another four to six years. Secondary studies are more extensive in Spanish-speaking countries than in the United States, and students graduate with a degree called **el bachillerato,** which is roughly equivalent to our junior college degree. In some countries, students attend an additional year or two of **preparatoria** before entering the university.

Every student must choose a course of study on entering the university, since all students working for a particular degree (**título**) take the same prescribed courses. Students are required to take as many as eight different subjects in a single academic term and are rarely offered the option of taking an elective. The lecture system is even more prevalent than it is in the United States, and university students often take oral as well as written exams.

Vocabulario activo

Adjetivos

alemán, alemana	German
difícil	difficult
español(a)	Spanish
fácil	easy
francés, francesa	French
inglés, inglesa	English
nuevo/a	new
todo/a	all
varios/as	several; various

Sustantivos

LENGUAS	LANGUAGES
el alemán	German
el español	Spanish
el francés	French
el inglés	English

LA SALA DE CLASE

el/la alumno/a	student
el bolígrafo	ballpoint pen
el borrador	eraser
la calculadora	calculator
la clase	class
el/la compañero/a (de clase)	classmate
el cuaderno	notebook
el dibujo	drawing
el diccionario	dictionary
el lápiz	pencil
la lección	lesson
el libro	book
el mapa	map
la mesa	table
la mochila	backpack
el papel	paper
la pared	wall
la pizarra	chalkboard
la puerta	door
el reloj	clock

la sala de clase	classroom
la silla	chair
la tiza	chalk
la ventana	window

OTROS SUSTANTIVOS

la biblioteca	library
la ciudad	city
la cosa	thing
el/la joven	young man/woman
el nombre	name
la palabra	word
la pregunta	question
la universidad	university

Verbos

contestar	to answer
conversar	to converse, talk
enseñar	to teach
entrar (en)	to enter
estudiar	to study
hablar	to speak
practicar	to practice
preguntar	to ask (*a question*)
preparar	to prepare
pronunciar	to pronounce
trabajar	to work
usar	to use

Otras palabras y expresiones

ahora	now
aquí	here
a veces	sometimes; at times
con	with
¿cuándo?	when?
en	in, on
pero	but
que	that; who
sólo	only
también	also, too
¿verdad?	really?

Mi ciudad

Un parque en el centro de la Ciudad de México,
la capital más poblada del mundo.

METAS

Comunicación: In this lesson you will learn vocabulary and expressions related to your city and neighborhood. You will learn how to talk about where you live and activities you do downtown, including going to a café and conversing with friends.

Estructuras: 7. More on the Definite Article 8. Possessive Adjectives 9. Present Tense of **-er** and **-ir** Verbs 10. Irregular Present Tense Verbs: **hacer, decir, tener, venir** 11. Numbers: 20–1,000,000

GRAFICOS

Los edificios del centro

Downtown Buildings

1. la calle
2. el autobús
3. el banco
4. la tienda
5. el edificio de oficinas
6. el almacén/los almacenes*
7. el cine
8. el hotel
9. el bar
10. el edificio de apartamentos
11. el taxi
12. el automóvil/ el coche/el carro/ el auto
13. el metro
14. el café/la cafetería
15. el restaurante

Suggestion: Model pronunciation of new vocabulary words. Review plural forms of words, especially inclusion or absence of the accent mark in *autobús, automóvil,* and *almacén.* Include *camión* from following *Motivo cultural.*

Expansion: Mexican *peseros* are taxis that carry groups of individuals along fairly established routes for varying numbers of *pesos,* according to the distance the passenger travels. *Peseros* offer the commuter more comfort and flexibility than an *autobús* as only a modest increase in price. It is considerably more expensive for one person to hire a taxi.

MOTIVO CULTURAL

Spanish names for everyday objects often vary from country to country. *Motivos de conversación* will present some of the most common variants. For example, while **automóvil** is common everywhere, the word **auto** is used predominantly in South America; **carro** is used in Mexico and most of the Caribbean; **coche** is used in Spain. The word for *bus* is **autobús** in most countries, but **camión** is used in Mexico, and other words for *bus* are preferred in other countries.

*In Spain, the word **almacén** is used in the plural.

Suggestion A and B:
Spot-check orally students' preparation of A and B. Have them look at drawing as you go over B; vary order of sentences.

Expansion: Read following statements based on *Gráficos* drawing. Students answer true or false orally or in writing; ask them to correct false statements. **1.** *El cine se llama Cine Colón.* **2.** *Un autobús entra en el cine.* **3.** *Muchos señores trabajan en la calle.* **4.** *El hotel se llama Hotel Velázquez.* **5.** *Una profesora enseña en el almacén.* **6.** *Un taxi entra en el restaurante.* **7.** *Muchas personas entran en el metro.* (All statements are false.)

Actividades

A. Identificaciones.

1. Transportes: a. _____ b. _____ c. _____ d. _____

2. Edificios: a. _____ b. _____ c. _____ d. _____

3. Dónde comer (*to eat*) o beber (*to drink*):

   a. _____ b. _____ c. _____ d. _____

B. Asociaciones. *Bernardo is only six and he wants to know what the following things are. Match the descriptions to the items to help explain what they are.*

1. la tienda
2. la calle
3. el banco
4. el almacén
5. el cine
6. el edificio de oficinas

a. La gente (*People*) deposita los pesos aquí.
b. Es una tienda grande (*big*).
c. Muchas personas trabajan aquí.
d. La gente ve (*see*) películas (*movies*) aquí.
e. Es un almacén pequeño (*small*).
f. Es para (*for*) los coches y los autobuses.

En el café del* centro

At the Downtown Café

Note: Point out that plural of *joven* is *jóvenes* and briefly explain contraction *del.* (See footnote.)

	PRESENT TENSE VERBS	
bebo	*I drink*	
bebe	*you (he/she) drink(s)*	
tomo	*I take, drink*	
toma	*you (he/she) take(s), drink(s)*	
vendo	*I sell*	
vende	*you (he/she) sell(s)*	
compro	*I buy*	
compra	*you (he/she) buy(s)*	
como	*I eat*	
come	*you (he/she) eat(s)*	
abro	*I open*	
abre	*you (he/she) open(s)*	
discuto	*I argue, discuss*	
discute	*you (he/she) argue(s), discuss(es)*	

1. el hombre
2. la mujer, la joven
3. la cerveza
4. el jugo de naranja
5. la señora vieja, la vieja
6. los billetes de lotería
7. el joven
8. el sándwich
9. la leche
10. el señor viejo, el viejo
11. el periódico
12. el vino

*Del is a contraction of **de** + **el**. It means *of the* or *from the*. (See **Gramática esencial** 7.)

En una mesa, un hombre bebe cerveza y su amiga toma *jugo de naranja.* Una   *orange juice*
señora vieja vende *billetes de lotería* y el hombre compra el *número trescientos*   *lottery tickets*
cincuenta y cinco. Es un *regalo para su* amiga.   *number 355 / present / for / his*

En *otra* mesa, un joven come un sándwich de *jamón* y *queso* y toma *leche,* y un   *another / ham / cheese / milk*
5 señor viejo abre el periódico. El señor bebe vino *mientras* discute las *noticias* del   *while / news*
día con el joven. —¿Mi opinión personal? Pues, yo *digo* que... no me gusta *la*   *I say*
política. No me gusta el presidente. No me gusta...   *politics*

Note: Stress that *otro* by itself means "another" and that *un otro* is incorrect. (See also the last paragraph of *En mi barrio Gráfico.*)

Note: It's good practice for students to read aloud in class occasionally. A narrative segment like this lends itself especially well to such oral practice.

◆ MOTIVO CULTURAL

In Hispanic countries it has long been traditional for individuals to sell lottery tickets on the street. A portion of the funds collected is often used to support schools, hospitals, organizations for the blind, and so on.

Actividades

Suggestion A: Warm up class with pantomimed actions to illustrate verbs given in *Gráficos: beber jugo de naranja/cerveza, comprar/vender billetes de lotería, comer un sándwich, abrir el periódico.* Ask students to create original sentences to describe your actions.

Suggestion B: Say the following words and ask students to complete the expressions: *jugo de... , billetes de... , noticias del... , sándwich de... , opinión... .*

A.   En el café del centro. *Using the following questions as a guide, tell what the characters in the drawing are doing.*

1. el hombre: ¿qué toma? ¿qué compra? ¿para quién es?
2. la señora vieja: ¿qué vende?
3. el joven: ¿qué come? ¿qué bebe?
4. el señor viejo: ¿qué abre? ¿qué bebe?
5. el señor y el joven: ¿qué discuten?

B.   ¿Qué hace Ud.? *(What do you do?) You don't do any of the things la señora López asks you about. Using the indicated words, tell her what you do.*

> MODELO: ¿Vende Ud. libros? (periódicos)
> —No, vendo periódicos.

1. ¿Bebe Ud. cerveza en los bares? (vino)
2. ¿Compra Ud. libros en la calle? (billetes de lotería)
3. ¿Discute Ud. la política con sus amigos? (noticias)
4. ¿Toma Ud. jugo de naranja por la mañana? (leche)
5. ¿Come Ud. un sándwich de queso? (jamón)

Expansion C: Have students give short monologues about their activities (cue them with questions given if necessary): **1.** *un café* (¿Qué comes en un café? ¿Qué bebes? ¿A qué hora?) **2.** *una calle* (¿Cómo se llama la calle? ¿Qué compras allí?) **3.** *los amigos* (¿Cómo se llaman? ¿Conversas con ellos todos los días? ¿Dónde? ¿Qué discutes con ellos?)

C.   Conversación. *With a classmate, take turns asking these questions. Only the questioner's book should be open.*

1. ¿Te gusta comprar regalos? ¿Para quién(es)?
2. ¿Qué tomas en un café?
3. ¿Qué comes en un restaurante?
4. ¿Qué compras en la calle?
5. ¿Qué no te gusta comer?
6. ¿Qué sándwiches te gustan?
7. ¿Qué discutes con los amigos?
8. ¿Qué abres en la clase?

En mi barrio

In My Neighborhood

◆ MORE PRESENT TENSE VERBS ◆

vivo	*I live*
vive	*you (he/she) live(s)*
necesito	*I need*
necesita	*you (he/she) need(s)*
deseo	*I desire*
desea	*you (he/she) desire(s)*
miro	*I look at*
mira	*you (he/she) look(s) at*
leo	*I read*
lee	*you (he/she) read(s)*
escribo	*I write*
escribe	*you (he/she) write(s)*

Suggestion: Ask students to describe scene, cueing them with questions if necessary: **1.** *¿Son grandes o pequeñas las casas de la calle?* **2.** *¿Son grandes o pequeños los edificios?* **3.** *¿Es bonita o fea la calle?* **4.** *¿Dónde hay un reloj?* **5.** *¿Qué hay en el parque?* **6.** *¿Quién toma fotos?* **7.** *¿Qué lee el hombre?* **8.** *¿Qué escribe la mujer?*

Suggestion: Have students cover the list of words and look at the *Gráfico.* Then read the numbers and ask them to give the word corresponding to each one.

Note: Point out that two meanings of *banco,* "bench" and "bank," are given in this lesson.

1. el parque	6. las flores	bueno/a *good*	malo/a *bad*
2. la casa	7. el banco	bonito/a *pretty*	feo/a *ugly*
3. el árbol	8. la iglesia	barato/a *cheap*	caro/a *expensive*
4. la fuente	9. la cámara	antiguo/a *old, ancient**	nuevo/a *new*
5. el agua	10. la carta	pequeño/a *small*	grande *large*

¿*Por qué* no vivo en el centro? *Porque* los apartamentos *allí* son muy caros y muy feos. En mi barrio los apartamentos son buenos y relativamente baratos. *No tengo* coche, pero hay metro y también autobuses.

    Mi calle es bonita. *Tiene* casas pequeñas, edificios de apartamentos grandes,
5 un cine, un café y una iglesia antigua. No necesito *reloj*; si deseo *saber* la hora, miro el reloj de la iglesia. En el parque hay flores, árboles y una fuente *de mármol.*†

    Ahora no hay *mucha gente*‡ en el parque. Una *muchacha toma fotos* con *su* cámara. En un banco, un hombre lee el periódico. En otro banco, una mujer escribe una carta.

Why / Because / there
I don't have

It has

watch / to know
of marble
many / people / girl / takes pictures / her

Emphasis: Point out first note and ask students whether they would use *antiguo/a* or *viejo/a* with the following: **1.** *don Antonio* **2.** *la música* **3.** *la amiga* **4.** *el estudiante* **5.** *el libro*

---

*Although both **antiguo/a** and **viejo/a** may be used to describe objects, only **viejo/a** can be used to describe people.

†**De** is used here to indicate what the fountain is made of. You will learn more about this usage in **Gramática esencial 13.**

‡**La gente** is a singular noun and takes a singular verb.

MOTIVO CULTURAL

The various neighborhoods of a large Hispanic city are called **barrios.** The word refers to the cluster of houses, apartments, parks, shops, cafés, and other small businesses that together form a neighborhood.

Cultural expansion: Elaborate on concept of *barrio*. Students from small towns and rural areas may know little about vitality of typical Hispanic *barrio*: e.g., that people shop daily in small neighborhood shops (with separate stores for dairy products, bread, fruit, meat, etc.). Such outings are important socially, allowing neighbors to chat and keep up on local gossip.

Actividades

Antonyms: Students give the opposite of each adjective you say: **1.** *grande (pequeño)* **2.** *bueno (malo)* **3.** *bonito (feo)* **4.** *barato (caro)* **5.** *antiguo (nuevo)*

A. Descripciones. *Describe each item below logically.*

MODELO: el edificio... → El edificio es grande.

1. la muchacha
2. las casas del barrio
3. los apartamentos del centro
4. los apartamentos del barrio
5. la fuente
6. la iglesia

Expansion B: **1.** *¿Qué necesito si deseo tomar fotos?* **2.** *¿Dónde leo las noticias?* **3.** *¿Qué transporte uso si no tengo coche?* **4.** *¿Qué miro si deseo saber la hora?* **5.** *¿Qué necesito si deseo escribir una carta?*

B. Conversación. *Imagine you live in the neighborhood described on page 41. With a classmate, take turns asking and answering the following questions about your* **barrio.**

1. ¿Por qué no vives en el centro? ¿Cómo son los apartamentos allí?
2. ¿Cómo son los apartamentos de tu barrio?
3. ¿Cómo es tu calle?
4. ¿Qué hay en tu calle?
5. ¿Qué hay en el parque?
6. ¿Dónde hay agua?
7. ¿Qué miras si deseas saber la hora?
8. ¿Escribes cartas o lees el periódico en el parque?
9. ¿Necesitas un coche en tu barrio? ¿Por qué (no)?
10. ¿Vive mucha gente en tu barrio?

ESTUDIO DE PALABRAS

Here are some expressions of agreement and disagreement.

Claro (que sí).	*Of course.*	No estoy de	*I disagree.*
De acuerdo.	*Agreed.*	acuerdo.	
Es verdad.	*It's true.*	No es verdad.	*It isn't true.*

React to these statements with an expression of agreement or disagreement. Don't use the same expression twice.

1. En todos los parques hay árboles.
2. Los apartamentos del centro son baratos.

Expansion: Ask students to use expressions of agreement or disagreement to react to your statements: **1.** *Escribo una carta con un bolígrafo.* **2.** *Compro libros en un café.* **3.** *Necesito una cámara para tomar fotos.* **4.** *Vivo en el metro.* **5.** *Leo las noticias en un libro.* **6.** *Hay árboles y flores en el parque.* **7.** *Bebo cerveza en la clase.* **8.** *Compro billetes de lotería en la iglesia.*

3. Leo las noticias en el periódico.
4. Las fuentes tienen agua.
5. Escribo una carta con tiza.

VISTA CULTURAL

En esta plaza del centro de Santiago, la capital de Chile, hay tiendas, árboles, flores y una fuente con mucha agua. Santiago es una ciudad muy grande: más de cuatro millones de personas viven allí. Tiene una zona antigua con iglesias y edificios coloniales y otra zona moderna. También tiene barrios residenciales elegantes y tres universidades importantes.

Show location of Chile and Santiago on map. Give students additional information: Chile has about 4,300 km. of coastline since it is over 10 times as long as it is wide. Its name comes from the Araucan Indian word *chilli,* which means "place where the land ends." Chile has important copper and nitrate mines; in fact, more minerals are mined there than in any other Hispanic country. Another well-known city in Chile is Viña del Mar, a fashionable seaside resort where one of the most famous Pan-American festivals of music takes place every year.

GRAMÁTICA ESENCIAL

7. More on the Definite Article

El señor bebe vino mientras discute las noticias del día con el joven.

A. There are only two contractions in Spanish: **a + el = al; de + el = del.**

BUT: a la   a los   a las   de la   de los   de las

Suggestion A: Write two model sentences on board to emphasize different forms: **1.** *Discuten las noticias del día* (*de los periódicos, de la clase, de las profesoras*). **2.** *Habla al cliente* (*a los clientes, a la clienta, a las clientas*). Then have students substitute cues you give orally: *hombres, periódico, carta, jóvenes* (note: can be either *de los* or *de las*), *barrio, almacén, mujer, señoras.*

Note: *De + él* never contract.

El alumno necesita **al*** profesor.	*The student needs the professor.*
Vivo en un edificio **del** centro.	*I live in a downtown building.*
BUT: El alumno necesita **a la** profesora.	*The student needs the professor.*
¿Por qué estudias el mapa **de las** Américas?	*Why are you studying the map of the Americas?*

B. Nouns used in a general sense are preceded by the definite article except when the idea of "some" or "any" (a certain amount or quantity) is conveyed.

El jugo de naranja tiene vitamina C.	*Orange juice has vitamin C.*
Me gustan mucho **los** árboles.	*I like trees very much.*
BUT: Deseo jugo de naranja.	*I want (some) orange juice.*
No hay árboles en mi calle.	*There aren't any trees on my street.*

Suggestion B: Explain that some verbs convey the idea of amount or quantity and can serve as markers for omission of definite article: *hay, tener, necesitar, comprar, vender.* Examples: *Las flores son bonitas.* but *Hay flores en el parque. El dinero es necesario.* but *No tengo dinero hoy. La leche tiene vitaminas.* but *Necesitamos leche. Me gusta el queso.* but *Compro queso. Los billetes de lotería son baratos.* but *¿Vende Ud. billetes de lotería?*

C. There is no standard practice for using the definite article with the names of countries. As a general rule, *Motivos de conversación* uses the article with these countries:

la Argentina	el Paraguay
el Brasil	el Perú
el Canadá	la República
el Ecuador	Dominicana
los Estados Unidos	el Uruguay
el Japón	

BUT: **España, Francia, Italia,** and so on. Note that the definite article is part of the name of **El Salvador.**

D. The definite article is used with titles except in direct address.

El profesor Sánchez es de México.	*Professor Sánchez is from Mexico.*
El capitán García es un amigo muy bueno.	*Captain García is a very good friend.*
BUT: Señorita López, ¿de dónde es Ud.?	*Miss López, where are you from?*

---

*The preposition **a** must be used in Spanish before direct objects that refer to specific persons. You will learn more about this usage in **Gramática esencial** 18.

Actividades

A. *Professor Sánchez is an avid people watcher. Tell who he's looking at now.*

> MODELO: El profesor mira a los alumnos. (viejo) →
> El profesor mira al viejo.

1. amigos
2. clase
3. hombre
4. mujer
5. señoritas
6. joven

Professor Sánchez is also an avid talker. What is he talking about now?

> MODELO: El profesor habla de los problemas. (noticias) →
> El profesor habla de las noticias.

7. edificios grandes
8. regalo para su amigo
9. tienda del barrio
10. árbol del parque
11. iglesias antiguas
12. cine de la plaza

B. En un café del centro. ¿Con o sin (*without*) el artículo definido?

_____[1] doctor Fernández vive en Buenos Aires, _____[2] capital de _____[3] Argentina. Todos _____[4] días visita un café de _____[5] centro de _____[6] ciudad. Le gusta _____[7] café y también _____[8] cerveza. _____[9] camarero (*waiter*) pregunta: «¿Desea tomar _____[10] cerveza también hoy, _____[11] doctor Fernández?»

C. Preguntas y respuestas. *With a classmate, take turns asking and answering the following questions according to the indications.*

> MODELO: El coche, ¿es de la mujer? (hombre) →
> No, el coche es del hombre.

1. El reloj, ¿es del banco? (iglesia)
2. Lima, ¿es la capital de Venezuela? (Perú)
3. El vino que bebes, ¿es de Chile? (Estados Unidos)
4. El periódico, ¿es de España? (Japón)
5. La casa, ¿es de Carlos Jiménez? (señora Ruiz)

Expansion C: Pick up items (*un libro, un cuaderno,* etc.) belonging to students and ask to whom they belong: **1.** ¿Es el/la _____ del estudiante (de la estudiante, del hombre, de la mujer, etc.)? **2.** ¿De quién es? (*Es del profesor [de la profesora].*) Include practice with plural forms.

Optional: Write model on board: *Quito es la capital del Ecuador.* Have students create new sentences, using correct contractions, with oral cues: **1.** *Lima / Perú* **2.** *Buenos Aires / Argentina* **3.** *La Ciudad de México / México* **4.** *Tokio / Japón* **5.** *San Salvador / El Salvador*

8. Possessive Adjectives

¿Mi opinión personal? Pues, yo digo que...

mi, mis	*my*	nuestro/a/os/as	*our*
tu,* tus	*your (fam. s.)*	vuestro/a/os/as	*your*
su, sus	*your, his/her/its*	su, sus	*your (pl.), their*

Possessive adjectives precede the noun they modify and agree with the thing possessed, not with the possessor. **Mi, tu,** and **su** agree only in number with the noun possessed, while **nuestro** and **vuestro** agree in both number and gender.

Mi casa tiene muchas ventanas.	*My house has many windows.*
Tus cartas son interesantes.	*Your letters are interesting.*
Nuestro hotel es muy caro.	*Our hotel is very expensive.*
Su amigo vende coches.	*Your (His/Her, Their) friend sells cars.*

Emphasis: Stress that possessive adjectives agree in gender and number with nouns they modify and that plurals end in -*s: mi → mis; tu → tus; su → sus. Nuestro* and *vuestro* have four forms; other possessive adjectives have only two.

Oral practice: Change to plural: **1.** *mi periódico* **2.** *tu regalo* **3.** *su reloj* **4.** *mi cámara* **5.** *tu coche* **6.** *su billete*

Since **su** and **sus** have more than one meaning, the following constructions are used quite often to clarify who the possessor is.

su amigo = el amigo de él (de ella, de Ud., de ellos, de ellas, de Uds.)
sus amigas = las amigas de él (de ella, de Ud., de ellos, de ellas, de Uds.)

Actividades

Optional: Students change *nuestro* and *vuestro*, as appropriate, to combine with following words you state or write on board: **1.** *almacenes* **2.** *banco* **3.** *restaurantes* **4.** *autobús* **5.** *automóviles* **6.** *tienda* **7.** *apartamentos*

Optional: Ask questions pointing at different objects in the class and have students answer using the opposite possessives. **1.** (point at your pen) *¿Es mi bolígrafo? (Sí, es su bolígrafo.)* **2.** (point at the books of several students) *¿Son vuestros libros? (Sí, son nuestros libros.)* **3.** (point at a student's backpack) *¿Es tu mochila? (Sí, es mi mochila.)* and so on.

A. Nuestros gustos (*tastes*). *Find out whether your classmate likes some things of yours by asking him or her a question like the models below.*

MODELO: —¿No te gusta mi reloj? (¿No te gustan mis relojes?)
　　　　　—Sí, me gusta tu reloj. (Sí, me gustan tus relojes.)

1. amigos	4. regalo	7. automóvil
2. fotos	5. bolígrafo	8. calle
3. cámaras	6. flores	9. casa

B. En el café del centro. *Tell what these people are doing. Use logical verbs and possessive adjectives that correspond to the subjects.*

1. Laura y yo _____ _____ sándwiches.
2. La mujer _____ _____ billetes de lotería.
3. Nosotros _____ _____ opiniones.
4. Ellas _____ _____ ventana.
5. Tú _____ _____ leche.
6. Ud. _____ _____ jugo de naranja.

---

*The subject pronoun **tú** (*you*) is distinguished from the possessive adjective **tu** (*your*) by its accent.

Note: With regard to the footnote, remind students of *el/él.*

C. ¡Qué mala memoria! (*What a bad memory!*) *Don Guillermo's memory isn't what it used to be. Answer his questions with the correct information. Change the possessive adjectives if necessary.*

> MODELO: *Tu* amigo se llama Julio, ¿no? (Ricardo) →
> No, *mi* amigo se llama Ricardo.

1. *Nuestra* amiga Laura es estudiante, ¿no? (profesora)
2. El café *del señor García* se llama «Las Delicias», ¿verdad? («La Rosa»)
3. El carro *de ustedes* es alemán, ¿no? (mexicano)
4. *Tu* profesora es francesa, ¿verdad? (española)
5. *Sus* cámaras son caras, ¿no? (baratas)

9. Present Tense of *-er* and *-ir* Verbs

En un banco, un hombre lee
el periódico. En otro banco,
una mujer escribe una carta.

The present indicative of second- and third-conjugation verbs (**-er** and **-ir** verbs, respectively) is formed by dropping the **-er** and **-ir** endings of the infinitive and adding the following endings:

comer (*to eat*)		**vivir** (*to live*)	
como	*I eat*	vivo	*I live*
comes	*you eat*	vives	*you live*
come	*you eat, he/she/it eats*	vive	*you live, he/she/it lives*
com**emos**	*we eat*	viv**imos**	*we live*
com**éis**	*you eat*	viv**ís**	*you live*
com**en**	*you, they eat*	viv**en**	*you, they live*

Presentation: Model pronunciation of *comer* and *vivir*. Ask students to identify similarities and differences between these endings and those of *-ar* verbs.

Note that the only difference between the two sets of endings is in the first and second persons plural.

Here are the second- and third-conjugation verbs presented so far in this lesson:

-er		-ir	
beber	*to drink*	abrir	*to open*
comer	*to eat*	discutir	*to discuss; to argue*
leer	*to read*	escribir	*to write*
vender	*to sell*	vivir	*to live*

Actividades

Warm-up A: Students answer these cued questions: **1.** *Yo leo el (name of local newspaper). ¿Qué periódico lee Ud. (leen Uds.)?* **2.** *En la clase abro mi libro. ¿Qué abre Ud. (abren Uds.)?* **3.** *Yo bebo Coca-Cola. ¿Qué bebe Ud. (beben Uds.)?* **4.** *Ella y yo vivimos en (name of your city). ¿Dónde vivimos (viven ellos)?* **5.** *Yo como enchiladas. ¿Qué comen Uds. (coméis vosotros)?*

Rapid oral translations: **1.** we live **2.** they write **3.** I argue **4.** you (*Ud.*) buy **5.** she reads **6.** he sells **7.** you (*vosotros*) drink **8.** you (*tú*) open

Expansion B: Act out pantomimes and have students describe in oral or written form what you are doing: **1.** *Enter* establishment, *buy* something, and *drink* it. **2.** *Open* package, *look* inquisitively at contents, then *eat* it. **3.** *Read* newspaper, *write* down reaction, then *discuss* it with friend.

Suggestion C: Have students tell class what they learned from interviews.

A. Mis amigos y yo en la ciudad. Diga qué hacen estas personas.

MODELO: ellas, Ud.   leer el periódico → Ellas leen el periódico.
Ud. lee el periódico.

Ud., nosotras
1. abrir un periódico
2. leer el editorial
3. discutir las noticias del día

tú, ellos
4. comer un sándwich de jamón y queso
5. beber jugo de naranja
6. escribir una carta en el café

yo, vosotros
7. no vivir en el centro de la ciudad
8. visitar la plaza central
9. vender regalos en un almacén

B. Una tarde en la ciudad. *Use the* **yo** *form of the following infinitives to describe what you do at a café and when you go downtown. Then use the* **él/ella** *form to describe what a friend does. Can you also use the* **ellos** *and* **nosotros** *forms quickly?*

EN EL CENTRO

1. no vivir
2. mirar
3. entrar
4. hablar
5. comprar

EN EL CAFÉ

6. abrir
7. leer
8. discutir
9. comer
10. beber

C. ¿Qué te gusta? *Take turns asking and answering these questions with a classmate.*

1. ¿Hay un restaurante muy bueno donde te gusta comer? ¿Cómo se llama? ¿Comes allí todos los días? ¿Qué te gusta comer allí?
2. Cuando comes en un restaurante, ¿bebes agua, vino o cerveza?
3. ¿En qué tiendas entras generalmente cuando necesitas comprar cosas? ¿En qué tiendas entras sólo para mirar y no para comprar?
4. ¿Qué periódico lees? ¿Lees noticias de otros países?

10. Irregular Present Tense Verbs:
hacer, decir, tener, venir

Pues, yo digo que... no me gusta la política.

The verbs below do not follow the patterns of regular **-er** and **-ir** verbs, so it is necessary to memorize their different forms. Note that all four have a common feature, the **g** in the first person singular.

-er: hacer (*to make; to do*)	**-ir: decir** (*to tell, say*)	**-er: tener** (*to have*)	**-ir: venir** (*to come*)
hago	digo	tengo	vengo
haces	dices	tienes	vienes
hace	dice	tiene	viene
hacemos	decimos	tenemos	venimos
hacéis	decís	tenéis	venís
hacen	dicen	tienen	vienen

Actividades

Warm-up exercises:
Change singular to plural or plural to singular: **1.** *Hablan mucho.* **2.** *Decimos «buenos días».* **3.** *Tengo dos libros.* **4.** *¿Cuándo vienen Uds.?* **5.** *¿Qué hago yo?* **6.** *¿Qué dices?* **7.** *¿Qué hacéis?*

Rapid oral translations: **1.** I have **2.** I do **3.** they come **4.** we say **5.** he has **6.** I come **7.** she says **8.** they have

A. ¿Qué hacemos para la fiesta (*party*)? Complete con una forma de **hacer.**

1. Ellas _____ las invitaciones.
2. Yo _____ el café.
3. Nosotros _____ sándwiches de queso.
4. Vosotros _____ jugo de naranja.
5. Ella _____ el té (*tea*).
6. ¿Qué _____ tú?

Optional A: Oral questions with *hacer:* **1.** ¿Qué hacemos en la clase? **2.** ¿Qué hacen Uds. en una tienda? **3.** ¿Qué hace Ud. en el centro? **4.** ¿Qué hace Ud. todos los días? **5.** ¿Qué hacen los estudiantes en la biblioteca?

B. Cosas que hago todas las mañanas. Complete la narración con una forma del verbo indicado.

Todas las mañanas yo (hacer) las mismas (*same*) cosas. Si (tener) tiempo, (tomar) café. A las ocho, (decir) adiós a la familia y (venir) a trabajar al centro.

C. *Now change exercise B to tell what the following people do each morning:* **tú, ella, nosotros, vosotras,** *and* **ellos.**

D. En mi bar favorito. Invente oraciones (*sentences*).

1. Yo / tener / un bar favorito
2. Nosotros / hacer / muchas cosas / allí todos los días
3. Yo / conversar / amigos
4. Tomás y yo / beber / vino y cerveza
5. Hoy / no venir / Juan y Alberto
6. Nosotros / discutir / noticias del día
7. Tomás / decir / que / el presidente _____

11. Numbers: 20–1,000,000

Una señora vende billetes de lotería y el hombre compra el número trescientos cincuenta y cinco.

20	veinte	200	doscientos/as
30	treinta	300	trescientos/as
40	cuarenta	400	cuatrocientos/as
50	cincuenta	500	quinientos/as
60	sesenta	600	seiscientos/as
70	setenta	700	setecientos/as
80	ochenta	800	ochocientos/as
90	noventa	900	novecientos/as
100	cien(to)		

1.000	mil	1.000.000	un millón
2.000	dos mil	2.000.000	dos millones

Beginning with **treinta,** the multiples of ten end in **-a** and are not combined in a single word: **treinta y uno, cuarenta y siete.**

Ciento is shortened to **cien** when it is directly followed by a noun, whether masculine or feminine.

Multiples of one hundred may be either masculine or feminine.

Hay ciento cincuenta y cinco muchachos en la escuela.	*There are 155 children in the school.*
Hay cien hombres y doscientas mujeres aquí.	*There are 100 men and 200 women here.*

In Spain and in many Spanish American countries a period is used in place of a comma to indicate thousands: **1.000; 17.361.210.** Conversely, a comma is often used where English uses a decimal point: **$3.036,41; 2,5%.**

Numerals above 1000, including years, are never read in Spanish by hundreds.

Hay 1.700 (mil setecientos) autobuses en la ciudad de San Juan.	*There are one thousand seven hundred (**not** seventeen hundred) buses in the city of San Juan.*
Nací en 1970 (mil novecientos setenta).	*I was born in (the year) one thousand nine hundred seventy (**not** nineteen seventy).*

Millón is always followed by **de** in Spanish if used in conjunction with a noun: **dos millones de discos. Mil,** however, does not require **de,** and it is always singular: **dos mil discos.**

Optional A: Ask these math problems orally: **1.** ¿Cuántos son 184 − 23? (161) **2.** ¿Cuántos son 355 + 437? (792) **3.** ¿Cuántos son 49.522 − 1.022? (48.500) **4.** ¿Cuántos son 15 + 69? (84) **5.** ¿Cuántos son 3.000.000 + 17.000.000? (20.000.000)

Actividades

Optional: Have a student write on the board the numerals corresponding to the amounts you dictate. The others will check for mistakes. *diez mil quinientos quince, veintitrés mil cuatrocientos dos, seiscientos sesenta y siete, cuatrocientos veinticinco, ochenta y ocho, siete mil ciento dos, treinta y un mil treinta y uno, nueve mil cuatrocientos trece, un millón setecientos mil doscientos veinticinco, noventa y tres mil quinientos cuarenta y tres.* Then ask students to read the figures on the board.

A.   Exprese en español según (*according to*) los modelos.

MODELOS: 22 + 14 = _____. → Veinte y dos más catorce son treinta y seis.
88 − 23 = _____. → Ochenta y ocho menos veintitrés son sesenta y cinco.

1.   16 + 23 = _____.
2.   15 + 17 = _____.
3.   19 − 14 = _____.
4.   59 + 41 = _____.

5.   80 − 13 = _____.
6.   90 − 19 = _____.
7.   800 − 600 = _____.
8.   42 − 22 = _____.

B.   De compras (*Shopping*). *How much do you expect to pay for these items? Give your answers in dollars (**dólares**).*

1.   un coche japonés
2.   un reloj
3.   un sándwich de jamón

4.   una casa pequeña
5.   una cámara alemana
6.   *Motivos de conversación*

Suggestion A: In doing this activity, you may have to encourage students by giving them some cues. How will you get downtown?: *Tomar un taxi / el metro / el autobús / su carro.* Things you may want to do there: **1.** comprar... en... **2.** comer... en... **3.** conversar en... con... **4.** mirar... en... **5.** tomar fotos de... con... .

Para resumir y repasar

A.   En persona: Una visita al centro. *A friend wants to go downtown with you. Tell him/her how you will get there and at least five things you want to do. Name at least five locations you want to visit and use five different verbs. Then ask your friend what he/she wants to do downtown.*

B.   Pregúntele* a otro alumno (otra alumna) si... (*Ask another student if . . .*)

****Le** is an indirect object pronoun. In this case it refers to **otro alumno (otra alumna).** Learn to recognize this command + pronoun construction, because it will appear in directions to other exercises. Indirect object pronouns are explained in **Gramática esencial** 40.

1. estudia español todos los días
2. trabaja en la biblioteca
3. desea hablar dos lenguas
4. prepara bien las lecciones
5. conversa con los compañeros de clase

C. Sustantivos y adjetivos. Cambie según (*according to*) los modelos.

MODELO: Son bueno / amigas → Son buenas amigas.

1. Compro mucho / libros, lápices, cuadernos, tiza
2. Visitamos varios / ciudades, países, barrios, plazas

MODELO: Escriben de las profesoras nuevas. (barrio) →
Escriben del barrio nuevo.

3. Uso el bolígrafo nuevo. (palabras, dibujos, mapa, lápices)
4. Converso con la joven famosa. (profesoras, inglés, francesa, españoles)

COMUNICACIÓN

Texto: Laura escribe a su amiga

Cultural expansion: While introducing *Texto,* underscore following cultural points: Some Hispanic cities are immense: Buenos Aires (over 11 million people), Mexico City (over 20 million), Madrid (5 million). Streets are almost always crowded with people; Hispanics are gregarious and are on streets (in cafés, stores, etc.) several times every day. Until recent years living in suburbs and commuting to work in central city was not common. Most people still prefer to live in city, even in downtown areas.

Suggestion: Ways to proceed with this *Texto:* (1) Model pronunciation of first couple of sentences in each paragraph; (2) assign each student in groups of four or five one paragraph to summarize; (3) then select one student to present general summary to class.

Querida Rosita: *Dear*

¿Cómo estás? Hoy no tengo clases y *paso el rato* en el centro. La   *I am killing time*
ciudad es grande y en la Plaza Colón hay muchos autobuses, coches y
taxis. En las ciudades hispánicas, *como* en las ciudades de los Estados   *as*
Unidos, el tráfico es un problema muy serio.

Son las diez y media de la mañana y hay en la calle muchos
hombres y mujeres, jóvenes y viejos. *Algunos* trabajan en el centro;   *Some*
otros viven aquí, en edificios de apartamentos modernos.

Hay muchos clientes en las tiendas y en el banco *todo el día.*   *all day long*
Muchos de ellos compran en Gómez, un almacén elegante de la Plaza
Colón.

Escribo en una mesa del café Las Delicias. Aquí los amigos toman
café o vino, comen y también conversan y comentan las noticias. Es una
buena *manera* de pasar el rato.   *way, manner*

Me gusta mucho vivir en esta ciudad, pero *echo de menos* a los   *I miss*
amigos como tú.

Cariños,   *Love*
Laura

Hablando del texto. Summarize Laura's letter by individual paragraphs. Use the questions as a guide.

1. ¿Tiene clases hoy? ¿Dónde pasa el rato? ¿Qué hay en la Plaza Colón? Qué problema es muy serio en las ciudades hispánicas?
2. ¿Qué hora es? ¿Dónde hay muchos jóvenes y viejos? ¿Qué hacen?
3. ¿Dónde hay muchos clientes? ¿Qué almacén hay en el centro? ¿Es pequeño o grande, probablemente?
4. ¿En qué café escribe Laura? ¿Quiénes toman café o vino allí? ¿Qué comentan? ¿Es una mala manera de pasar el rato?

De la vida real

¡COMPRE YA SU BOLETO![a]

100
millones de sucres
POR[b] UN SOLO BOLETO DE S/.500

PLAN DE PREMIOS[c]

PRIMER PREMIO
$100'000.000,oo

2ª PREMIO:	20'000.000,oo
3ª PREMIO:	15'000.000,oo
4ª PREMIO:	10'000.000,oo
5ª PREMIO:	6'000.000,oo
6ª PREMIO:	1'000.000,oo
7ª PREMIO:	1'000.000,oo
8ª PREMIO:	1'000.000,oo
9ª PREMIO:	1'000.000,oo
10ª PREMIO:	1'000.000,oo
11ª PREMIO:	1'000.000,oo
12ª PREMIO:	1'000.000,oo
13ª PREMIO:	1'000.000,oo
14ª PREMIO:	1'000.000,oo
15ª PREMIO:	1'000.000,oo

9 PREMIOS POR APROXIMACIONES DE 5 CIFRAS S/.1'000.000,oo c/u	9'000.000,oo
9 PREMIOS POR TERMINALES DE 5 CIFRAS S/.1'000.000,oo c/u	9'000.000,oo
90 APROXIMACIONES AL PREMIO MAYOR	9'000.000,oo
99990 TERMINALES AL PREMIO MAYOR	72'000.000,oo

100.113 BOLETOS PREMIADOS CON **260'000.000,oo**

Adquiéralo también en todos los puntos de venta identificados con:

JUNTA DE BENEFICENCIA
LOTTO
1888 — 1989
DE GUAYAQUIL

S/. 100'000.000

Las utilidades[d] de LOTTO se destinarán a la construcción, equipamiento y mantenimiento[e] del nuevo Hospital para Niños[f] Alejandro Mann que la Junta de Beneficencia[g] de Guayaquil construirá en La Garzota.

[a]*billete*
[b]*for*
[c]*prizes*
[d]*profits*
[e]*maintenance*
[f]*Children*
[g]Junta... *Public Welfare Board*

A.   ¡Compre ya su boleto! Este anuncio (*advertisement*) es de Guayaquil, Ecuador. La unidad monetaria (*monetary unit*) del Ecuador es el sucre (S/.). Lea el anuncio y conteste las preguntas.

1. ¿Cuántos (*How many*) sucres gana (*win*) Ud. con el primer premio? ¿y con el 2° (segundo) (*second*) premio? ¿y con el 6° (sexto) (*sixth*)?
2. ¿Cuánto cuesta (*How much is*) un boleto?
3. ¿Para (*For*) qué usa las utilidades del Lotto la Junta de Beneficencia de Guayaquil? (Para...)
4. ¿Desea Ud. comprar un boleto? ¿Por qué (no)?

B.   La lotería de Puerto Rico. *You are trying to sell the lottery tickets above to a classmate. Alternate asking and answering the following questions about the tickets.*

1. ¿Qué números tiene Ud.?
2. ¿Cuánto cuesta un billete?
3. ¿De cuánto es el primer premio?
4. ¿De qué fecha son los billetes?
5. ¿Por qué vende Ud. billetes viejos?

Motivo cultural

There is often little difference between a **café,** a **cafetería,** and a **bar** since all three sell alcoholic beverages and you can get a cup of coffee and a snack as easily in a **bar** as in a **café** or **cafetería.** Generally, all three are well-lit, popular gathering spots where friends can spend time together. In the warmer months, **cafés al aire libre,** sidewalk cafés, are especially popular.

The word **cafetería** refers to a coffee shop, not to a self-service cafeteria like the ones in the United States. Self-service

cafeterias, called **auto-servicios,** are becoming more common in the Hispanic world.

Expansion A: Return to drawings in *Gráficos* and have students make as many statements as they can (and as fast as they can!) about each one. Students' fluency should be much improved at this point in lesson.

Para conversar más

A. En la ciudad. Describa qué pasa (*what is happening*) en los dibujos.

1. comprar y vender / la tienda
2. comer / beber / el restaurante
3. vivir / la ciudad
4. discutir / los amigos

B. Entrevista (*Interview*). Pregúntele a otro alumno (otra alumna)...

1. si vive en un apartamento o en una casa; si es grande o pequeño/a su apartamento o casa
2. si tiene coche
3. si viene a la universidad todos los días
4. qué clases tiene
5. qué días viene a la clase de español
6. qué le gusta hacer en la clase de español
7. cómo pasa el rato en una cafetería / en una tienda en el centro

Tell the class what you learned about your classmate from this interview.

Vocabulario activo

Adjetivos

antiguo/a	old
barato/a	inexpensive, cheap
bonito/a	pretty, beautiful
bueno/a	good
caro/a	expensive
feo/a	ugly
grande	large
malo/a	bad
otro/a	other, another
pequeño/a	small, little
viejo/a	old

Sustantivos

PERSONAS

la gente	people
el hombre	man
el/la muchacho/a	boy/girl
la mujer	woman
el/la viejo/a	old man/woman

EDIFICIOS (*BUILDINGS*)

el almacén (los almacenes)	department store(s)
el apartamento	apartment

el banco	bank
el bar	bar
el café	café; restaurant
la cafetería	coffee shop
la casa	house; home
el cine	movie theater
el edificio de apartamentos	apartment building
el edificio de oficinas	office building
el hotel	hotel
la iglesia	church
el restaurante	restaurant
la tienda	store

EN LA CALLE

el autobús	bus
el automóvil	automobile, car
el barrio	neighborhood
la calle	street
el carro	car
el centro	downtown
el coche	car
el metro	subway
el parque	park
la plaza	central plaza, mall
el taxi	taxi

PARA BEBER Y COMER

el café	coffee
la cerveza	beer
el jamón	ham
el jugo de naranja	orange juice
la leche	milk
el queso	cheese
el sándwich	sandwich
el vino	wine

EN EL PARQUE

el agua	water
el árbol	tree
el banco	bench
la flor	flower
la fuente	fountain

OTROS SUSTANTIVOS

el billete de lotería	lottery ticket
la cámara	camera
la carta	letter
la foto(grafía)	photo(graph)
las noticias	news
el periódico	newspaper
la política	politics
el regalo	gift
el reloj	watch, clock

Verbos

abrir	to open
beber	to drink
comer	to eat
comprar	to buy
decir	to say, tell
desear	to desire, want
discutir	to argue; to discuss
escribir	to write
hacer	to do; to make
leer	to read
mirar	to watch; to look at
necesitar	to need
tener	to have
tomar	to drink
vender	to sell
venir	to come
vivir	to live

Otras palabras y expresiones

allí	there
Claro (que sí).	Of course.
De acuerdo.	Agreed.
Es verdad.	It's true.
muchos/as	many
No es verdad.	It isn't true.
No estoy de acuerdo.	I disagree.
para	(intended) for
¿por qué?	why?
porque	because
todos los días	every day
tomar fotos	to take pictures

Números

veinte, treinta, cuarenta, cincuenta, sesenta, setenta, ochenta, noventa, cien(to), doscientos/as, trescientos/as, cuatrocientos/as, quinientos/as, seiscientos/as, setecientos/as, ochocientos/as, novecientos/as, mil, un millón

Posesivos

mi(s), tu(s), su(s), nuestra/a/os/as, vuestro/a/os/as, su(s)

La ropa que llevo

En una boutique de Madrid. —¡Me encanta! ¿Cuánto cuesta?

METAS

Comunicación: In this lesson you will learn vocabulary and expressions related to clothes and accessories. You will talk about the way you dress and shop for clothes. In addition, you will learn to describe the conditions and characteristics of people and objects.

Estructuras: 12. More Irregular Present Tense Verbs: **estar, ser, dar, ir** 13. **Ser** Used to Express Identification, Origin, Material, and Possession 14. **Estar** Used to Express Location 15. **Ser** and **estar** with Adjectives 16. Present Participles and Progressive Forms

GRÁFICOS

La ropa

Verbs

llevar, usar *to wear*

Adjectives

cómodo/a *comfortable*
incómodo/a *uncomfortable*

1. el traje
2. la camisa
3. la corbata
4. los pantalones
5. el zapato
6. el vestido
7. el abrigo

8. el bolso/la bolsa/la cartera*
9. el sombrero
10. la bota
11. los pantalones cortos
12. la camiseta
13. la sandalia
14. la blusa

15. la falda
16. el calcetín
17. el tenis
18. la chaqueta
19. el suéter
20. los (pantalones) vaqueros/los jeans

Gráficos expansion: Students state (or write down) whether item of clothing is generally used by woman (*mujer*), man (*hombre*), or both (*hombre y mujer*):
1. *falda* **2.** *blusa* **3.** *zapatos* **4.** *pantalones* **5.** *corbata* **6.** *calcetín* **7.** *bolso* **8.** *vestido* **9.** *botas* **10.** *camisa*

Footnote: You may also want to add that *el jersey* is the preferred word for "sweater" in Spain. Another version of "blue jeans" is *los bluyines*.

Note: Students should also learn to use the verb *usar* to mean "to use", as this usage appears frequently in *Motivos*.

Actividades

A. La ropa que me gusta. *Tell your classmates what you are wearing now* (**Ahora llevo...**). *Then explain what you like to wear* (**Me gusta llevar/usar...**) *in the following situations.*

1. por la tarde en agosto
2. por la mañana en febrero
3. en un concierto de música rock
4. en la iglesia en octubre
5. en una entrevista de trabajo (*job interview*)
6. en la clase de español
7. un sábado por la mañana

*La bolsa** is used in Mexico; **la cartera** is common in the rest of Spanish America.

B. Mil dólares. *You are on a shopping spree with the $1000 you have just been given as a gift. Explain what you are buying and how much each item costs. Stop when you have spent all your money.*

MODELO: Compro un traje nuevo; gasto (*I spend*) $150.

C. Preguntas personales. Pregúntele a un compañero (una compañera).

1. ¿Hay muchas tiendas de ropa en la ciudad donde vives? ¿Venden ropa cara o barata, bonita o fea? ¿Te gusta ir de compras (*go shopping*) allí? ¿Qué compras, generalmente?
2. ¿Qué ropa nueva necesitas ahora?
3. ¿Qué usas más frecuentemente: botas, sandalias, tenis o zapatos? ¿Cuántos pares (*pairs*) de zapatos, tenis y botas tienes?
4. ¿Son cómodas las sandalias?

Miguel *lava* su chaqueta

Washes

Adjectives
alto/a *tall*
bajo/a *short*

delgado/a *thin*
gordo/a *fat*

listo/a *smart*
tonto/a *dumb*

◆ PRESENT TENSE ◆	
estoy	*I am*
está	*you (pol.) are; he/she/it is*
soy	*I am*
eres	*you (fam.) are*
es	*you are; he/she/it is*
voy	*I go*
va	*you go; he/she/it goes*
doy	*I give*
da	*you (he/she/it) give(s)*

MIGUEL: ¡Mi chaqueta está *manchada!*   *stained*

LUIS: Claro, si lavas una chaqueta *blanca* con unos pantalones *negros*...   *white / black*

MIGUEL: Es verdad. ¡Qué listo soy! Pero, voy a la *fiesta* de Silvia *esta noche.*   *party / tonight*
¿Ahora qué llevo? ¿mi chaqueta vieja?

LUIS: Hay una solución muy fácil: *te presto* mi chaqueta *de piel o* mi camisa   *I'll lend you / leather / or*
azul de lana.   *blue / wool*

MIGUEL: Pero tú eres delgado y bajo y yo soy alto y *un poco* gordo.   *a little*

LUIS: *Entonces te doy* mi suéter *rojo,* que es de una *talla* grande.   *Then / I'll give you / red / size*

MIGUEL: De acuerdo. Me gusta tu suéter rojo. ¡Gracias, Luis! Eres un amigo muy bueno.

Actividades

A. Los problemas de Miguel.

1. ¿Qué problema tiene Miguel con su chaqueta?
2. ¿De qué color son los pantalones de Miguel?
3. ¿Por qué no desea llevar la camisa de lana de Luis a la fiesta?
4. ¿Qué suéter va a llevar Miguel a la fiesta? ¿Por qué?

B. Antónimos. *As your classmate reads each word aloud, give its opposite.*

1. alto
2. delgado
3. fácil
4. tonto
5. pequeño
6. cómodo
7. feo
8. barato

C. ¿Es Ud. un buen actor (una buena actriz)?

1. Act out the dialogue in groups of two, changing the appearance of the characters and the garments and colors.
2. Create a dialogue with two or three exchanges in which you lend a piece of clothing to a friend. Why does he/she need it? What color is it? What is it made of? What size is it?

D. Preguntas personales. Conteste las preguntas.

1. ¿Cómo es Ud.? (*What are you like?*) ¿Bajo/a? ¿Delgado/a? ¿Tonto/a?
2. ¿Adónde (*Where*) va Ud. después de (*after*) la clase de español?
3. ¿Cuál es su color favorito?
4. ¿Presta Ud. su ropa a sus amigos?
5. ¿Da Ud. su ropa vieja o manchada a Goodwill?
6. ¿Qué talla usa Ud.?

Comprando una blusa

Adjectives
contento/a *happy*
triste *sad*

rico/a *rich*
pobre *poor*

joven *young*

Verbs
aceptar *to accept*
buscar *to look for*
ganar *to earn*
gastar *to spend*
pagar *to pay*

Present Participles
estoy comprando *I am buying*
está comprando *you (he/she) are (is) buying*

estoy hablando *I am speaking*
está hablando *you (he/she) are (is) speaking*

Alina es una *chica* joven y *simpática*. Es de México, pero vive en Los Ángeles. Ahora está hablando con la *dependienta* en el Almacén Neptuno. Busca una blusa elegante, pero tiene poco *dinero,* porque no gana mucho.

girl / nice, pleasant

salesclerk

money

Note: Additional colors, if you wish to give them to the class: *anaranjado* (orange), *pardo* (brown), *violeta, morado* (purple).

ALINA: *¿Cuánto cuesta* la blusa *rosada?*

How much does . . . cost / pink

DEPENDIENTA: Sólo treinta y dos dólares, señorita.

ALINA: ¡Es muy cara, señora! Yo no soy rica.

DEPENDIENTA: *Es de seda,* señorita, y *está rebajada* de treinta y nueve dólares. Aceptamos *tarjetas de crédito.*

It's silk / it's reduced

credit cards

ALINA: Es verdad que es *preciosa,* pero *no quiero* gastar mucho. *¿Cuál** es el *precio* de la blusa *amarilla?*

darling, very pretty / I don't want

What is / price / yellow

DEPENDIENTA: Es *más barata.* Sólo veinticinco dólares. La blusa *verde* también cuesta veinte y cinco dólares.

cheaper ("more cheap") / green

ALINA: Compro *la amarilla.* Combina bien con mi falda *color café.* (Alina, muy contenta, paga los veinticinco dólares.)

the yellow one / brown

DEPENDIENTA: Gracias, señorita. Adiós.

Suggestion: Encourage students to make educated guesses about cognates. Although *aceptamos* and *dólares* should offer no difficulty, *Combina* cannot be translated literally. It should be read as "It matches . . ."

Note: You could mention that Los Angeles is the city with the second largest Mexican population in the world.

Note: Explain following points in dialogue: (1) comparative *más barata* (more cheap, cheaper); (2) elliptical construction *la amarilla* (the yellow one).

Expansion C: Bring additional pictures to class or refer to photos in text for more practice with colors.

Optional: Try this directed conversation with your class: **1.** *Pregúntele Ud. a (name of student) cuántas blusas (camisas) tiene.* **2.** *Pregúntele a (another student) qué va a hacer mañana.* **3.** *¿Qué lleva Ud. (él, ella) ahora? ¿Le gusta su blusa (falda, camisa)?* **4.** *Pregúntele a (another student) qué mira cuando está en la calle.*

Actividades

A. Comprando una blusa. Conteste las preguntas sobre el diálogo.

1. ¿De dónde es Alina? ¿Dónde vive? ¿Cómo es ella?
2. ¿Qué está haciendo? ¿Qué busca?
3. ¿Por qué no quiere gastar mucho dinero?
4. ¿Cuál de las blusas que Alina está mirando es más cara? ¿Cuánto cuesta? ¿Por qué es tan (*so*) cara?
5. ¿Aceptan tarjetas de crédito en el Almacén Neptuno?
6. ¿Qué blusa compra Alina? ¿Cuánto paga?

B. Justificaciones. *Playing the role of the clerk (**el dependiente, la dependienta**), give several reasons why a classmate (**el cliente, la clienta**) should buy a shirt or a blouse. Your partner responds with reasons why he/she should not buy it.*

C. Colores. *How many colors can you name?*

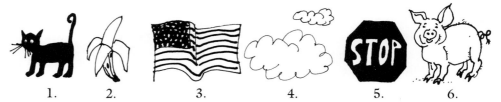

1.   2.   3.   4.   5.   6.

---

*You have seen both **¿qué?** and **¿cuál(es)?** used to express *what?* and *which?* in Spanish. In general, **¿qué?** expresses *what?* and can be followed by a noun or a verb. **¿Cuál(es)?** usually expresses *which?* and can only be followed by a verb. **¿Qué?** is not followed by the verb *to be* unless one asks for a definition.

¿Qué es «rosado»? —«Rosado» es un color.   ¿Cuál es tu color favorito? —El rosado.

Review: Since several adjectives are used in dialogues of this lesson, this is a good time to review agreement of nouns and adjectives. Write on board *antiguo, malo, pequeño, bueno, caro, feo, barato, bonito, grande.* Then say each item while pointing at corresponding adjective and ask students to give the correct form of the adjective: **1.** *la iglesia* **2.** *el cine* **3.** *las plazas* **4.** *la gente* **5.** *los vinos* **6.** *el edificio de apartamentos* **7.** *las casas* **8.** *el almacén* **9.** *los restaurantes*

Suggestion: You can use drawings on board and props you bring to class to illustrate adjectives in exercise. If possible, bring one photo or page from catalogue for each pair of students so they can drill each other.

Now give the colors of the following garments.

1. la camisa de lana de Luis
2. los pantalones de Luis
3. el suéter grande de Luis
4. la ropa que Ud. lleva hoy
5. la blusa que cuesta $32
6. las blusas que cuestan $25
7. la falda de Alina
8. la ropa del profesor (de la profesora)

D. Opiniones. Exprese su reacción con un adjetivo apropiado.

cómodo/incómodo	elegante/ridículo	pobre/rico
contento/triste	fácil/difícil	tonto/listo

1. Si gano mucho dinero en la lotería, estoy...
2. Si llevo pantalones cortos y corbata, estoy...
3. Si llevo zapatos muy pequeños, estoy...
4. Si quiero ir de compras y no tengo dinero, estoy...
5. Si llevo una blusa de seda, estoy...
6. Si Luis aprende (*learns*) una lección en diez minutos, la lección es muy... o Luis es muy...
7. Si Luis estudia todo el día (*the whole day*) pero no aprende una lección, la lección es muy... o Luis es muy...
8. Si mi amigo Fernando gana mucho dinero, él es...

ESTUDIO DE PALABRAS

Here are some useful expressions you can use when you go shopping.

¿Cuánto cuesta... ?	*How much does . . . cost?*
Cuesta...	*It costs . . .*
¿Tiene la talla... ?	*Do you have size . . . ?*
Sí, tengo tallas desde la... hasta la...	*Yes, I have sizes from . . . to . . .*
¿Cuál es su número de zapato?	*What is your shoe size?*
Mi número de zapato es...	*My shoe size is . . .*
¿Qué le parece?	*What do you think (of it)?*
(No) Me gusta.	*I (don't) like it.*
Me queda grande (pequeño, bien).	*It's too large (too small, just right).*
Voy a comprar el vestido (los pantalones, etcétera).	*I'm going to buy the dress (the pants, etc.).*

Actividad

Con un compañero (una compañera), prepare un breve diálogo sobre su visita a una tienda.

MEMOPRÁCTICA

In memorizing new material, you are more likely to be successful if you develop systematic study habits. For example, jot down on a flash card or a slip of paper some new words from tomorrow's lesson and begin going over them as you leave class today. Go over them— English to Spanish and then Spanish to English—as you walk to your next destination. Before your next class, take advantage of the two or three minutes you have to wait for the instructor to review the list. Try to look at the new words for a few moments every hour or so; frequent reviews throughout the day will fix the words more firmly in your mind than will a single, lengthy study period.

Emphasis: Mention effectiveness of learning new vocabulary little by little every day rather than trying to memorize hundreds of words a few hours before test.

VISTA CULTURAL

Muchos países de Hispanoamérica tienen sus propios (*own*) bailes (*dances*) típicos. Generalmente, estos bailes muestran (*show*) influencia de las antiguas culturas indias o de las tradiciones del pueblo rural, combinadas con las tradiciones de los españoles. Aquí vemos a un grupo de bailarines (*dancers*) en una pequeña plaza de San José, Costa Rica. Llevan el traje

(*costume*) típico de este baile folclórico: las mujeres llevan vestidos de muchos colores y los hombres llevan pantalones y camisas blancas.

GRAMÁTICA ESENCIAL

12. More Irregular Present Tense Verbs: *estar, ser, dar, ir*

—¡Mi chaqueta está man-
chada! Pero, voy a la fiesta
de Silvia esta noche.
¿Ahora qué llevo?
—Te doy mi suéter rojo.
—¡Eres un amigo muy bueno!

In the **Gráficos** section of this lesson, you learned the **yo** and **usted** forms of these irregular verbs. Here are the remaining forms of the present tense. Note that all four verbs share one irregularity, the **-y** ending of the first person singular.

estar *(to be)*	ser *(to be)*	dar *(to give)*	ir *(to go)*
estoy	soy	doy	voy
estás	eres	das	vas
está	es	da	va
estamos	somos	damos	vamos
estáis	sois	dais	vais
están	son	dan	van

Expansion: Divide class into *ser* group and *estar* group. Call on each alternately to supply as quickly as possible forms of either verb that correspond to following subjects: **1.** *Uds.* **2.** *la señora Díaz* **3.** *los alumnos* **4.** *vosotros* **5.** *Carlos y yo* **6.** *tú* **7.** *él y María* **8.** *Juan y yo* **9.** *Juan y Jacinto* **10.** *yo*

Actividades

A. Sonia es muy optimista. Haga oraciones (*sentences*) nuevas según las indicaciones para expresar lo que (*what*) ella dice sobre las personas indicadas.

1. Las alumnas son simpáticas. (nosotras, Uds., tú, Luis y Alina, yo)
2. La dependienta está contenta. (yo, vosotras, tú, Amalia y Alfredo, nosotras)

B. Hoy hay liquidación en el Almacén Neptuno. Diga quiénes van al almacén y quiénes compran algo.

1. Miguel va al Almacén Neptuno. (ellas, Alina y yo, Uds., tú, vosotros)
2. Mamá da el dinero a la dependienta. (los clientes, Uds., tú y Rodrigo, nosotros)

C. Una conversación telefónica. Complete la conversación con la forma apropiada de los verbos entre paréntesis.

MIGUEL: ¡Hola! Habla Miguel. ¿(Estar[1]) Juanita en casa?
JUANITA: Sí, Miguel. (Ser[2]) (*I am*) Juanita.
MIGUEL: Juanita, ¿qué tal? ¿(Dar[3]) tú una fiesta el sábado?
JUANITA: No, yo no (dar[4]) una fiesta, pero Jaime sí (dar[5]) una. ¿(Ir[6]) tú a la fiesta de Jaime?
MIGUEL: Sí, Luis y yo (ir[7]) en mi coche.
JUANITA: ¡Ah! ¿Tú (ser[8]) amigo de Luis?
MIGUEL: Sí, Luis y yo (ser[9]) muy buenos amigos. ¿Quién más (ir[10]) a la fiesta?
JUANITA: A ver... Alina y Laura (ir[11]) y también el nuevo estudiante español.
MIGUEL: ¡Estupendo! Entonces, nos vemos (*we'll see each other*) el sábado.
JUANITA: De acuerdo.

13. *Ser* Used to Express Identification, Origin, Material, and Possession

Alina es de México...
La blusa es de seda...

A. The verb **ser** is used to indicate that one noun or pronoun is equal to another noun or pronoun.

José es cliente de esa tienda.   *Joe is a client of that store.*
Yo soy dependiente.   *I am a salesclerk.*

Note in these examples that the noun or pronoun before the verb and after it refer to the same person (**José = cliente, yo = dependiente**).

Suggestion A: To illustrate identification with *ser*, have students list their own identities (*soy hombre, soy mujer, soy alumno, soy norteamericano*, etc.). Stress that unlike *ser*, *estar* never links subject with noun or pronoun.

B. When **ser** is used to tell where a person or thing is from, it is followed by the preposition **de.**

Somos **del** Canadá.   *We're from Canada.*

C. **Ser** plus **de** expresses what material a thing is made of.

Mi abrigo es **de** alpaca y es del Perú.   *My coat is (made of) alpaca, and it's from Peru.*

D. **Ser** with the preposition **de** also expresses possession.

El vestido es **de** María.   *The dress is María's.*
¿Las botas? Son **de** la señora Andújar.   *The boots? They are Mrs. Andújar's. (They belong to Mrs. Andújar.)*

14. *Estar* Used to Express Location

Ahora Alina está en el Almacén Neptuno.

The verb **estar** (often followed by the preposition **en**) is used to express location.

Tu camiseta está en la silla.   *Your T-shirt is on the chair.*
¿Dónde está el Almacén Neptuno?   *Where is (the department store) Neptuno?*

BAJOS
HOTEL ROMANO
PALACE

OK CLOTHING COMPANY

LOCAL 6
ACAPULCO, GRO.
TEL. 44688

SUPER OFERTAS

ETIQUETA ROJA
$10,000 ($4 US)
RED LABEL

ETIQUETA AZUL
$15,000 ($6 US)
BLUE LABEL

BIG SALE

PRECIOS POR COLORES

ETIQUETA VERDE
$20,000 ($8 US)
GREEN LABEL

ETIQUETA AMARILLA
$27,000 ($10 US)
YELLOW LABEL

PRICE BY COLORS

Actividades

A. ¿De dónde son? ¿Qué son? *Using the lists given, state where these people are from and describe what they do. If you don't know, guess!*

PERSONA	PAÍS	PROFESIÓN
1. Carlos Salinas de Gortari	Puerto Rico	atleta
	Cuba	líder político/a
2. Juan Carlos I (Primero)	España	presidente
	México	escritor (*writer*)
3. Rita Moreno	Colombia	actriz
4. José Canseco		rey (*king*)
5. Gabriel García Márquez		
6. Fidel Castro		

B. ¿Dónde están? Conteste.

1. ¿En qué países están estas (*these*) ciudades? Toronto, Barcelona, Acapulco, Bogotá, Buenos Aires
2. Generalmente, ¿dónde está Ud. por la mañana (por la tarde, los sábados, los veranos)?
3. ¿Dónde están ahora el Presidente Salinas, Fidel Castro y el rey Juan Carlos I?

C. En los Almacenes Gómez. Ud. es dependiente/a; describa los siguientes (*following*) artículos a un cliente.

> MODELO: la corbata → La corbata es de seda.

1. la blusa	lana
2. la falda	seda
3. la chaqueta	mármol
4. el suéter	piel
5. la mesa	alpaca

D. ¡Adivine Ud.! (*Guess!*) *One student will think of an article of clothing that someone in the class is wearing; the others will try to guess the garment and its owner by asking questions. The person who guesses correctly then gets to pick the next article of clothing.*

> MODELO: ¿Es bonito/a o feo/a? ¿Es nuevo/a o viejo/a? ¿Es grande o pequeño/a? ¿De qué color es? Etcétera.

E. Un monólogo. *With your classmates, take turns telling a few things about yourself based on the following questions and suggestions.*

1. ¿Quién eres? (nombre)
2. ¿De dónde eres? (el Canadá, California,...)
3. ¿Qué eres? (americano/a, estudiante,...)
4. ¿Cómo eres? (alto/a, bajo/a, simpático/a, inteligente...)

15. *Ser* and *estar* with Adjectives

—¡Es muy cara, señora! Yo
no soy rica.
—Está rebajada de treinta y
nueve dólares.

When used with an adjective, **ser** expresses a characteristic considered to be inherent. For example, **rico/a, pobre, joven,** and **viejo/a** are used with **ser** to classify a person according to social class or age group. **Estar** used with an adjective describes a current state and may indicate that some change has taken place. For example, **Ellos están gordos** suggests that they weren't fat previously. **Estar** used with an adjective also implies a quality or sensation that is unexpected, in which case it can convey the meaning of *to feel, to taste,* or *to look.* For example, **estar** used with **joven** or **viejo/a** suggests that the person *looks* young or old even if it isn't so. Compare the following examples.

ser: INHERENT TRAITS	**estar:** STATES OR UNEXPECTED TRAITS
El hielo es frío. *Ice is cold.*	La sopa está caliente. *The soup is hot.*
Ella es (una persona) enferma. *She is (a) sickly (person).*	Ella está enferma ahora. *She is sick now.*
Juan es alto. *John is tall.*	La hierba está alta. *The grass is tall.*
Él es joven. *He is young.*	Él está joven para su edad. *He is (looks) young for his age.*
El café es siempre bueno aquí. *The coffee is always good here.*	El café está bueno. *The coffee (This particular coffee) tastes good.*

When an adjective expresses a state, whether it is permanent or not, **estar** must be used.

Ud. siempre está cansada. *You are always tired.*
El general está ocupado. *The general is busy.*
Lucía y Guillermo están enamo- *Lucía and Guillermo are in love.*
rados.

This rule also applies to adjectives that describe a mood.

Yo siempre estoy contento. *I am always happy (in a happy mood).*

¿Cómo es... ? requests a description of the essential nature of someone or something.

¿Cómo es el dependiente?   *What is the clerk like?*

¿Cómo está... ?, on the other hand, inquires about the health or condition of someone or something.

¿Cómo está la muchacha?   *How is the girl (feeling)?*

Actividades

Optional: To review other adjectives, say these sentences and ask students to complete with adjective. Possible answers suggested in parentheses: **1.** *El español es* _____ *(fácil).* **2.** *El profesor (La profesora) de español es* _____ *(inteligente).* **3.** *El libro de*

A.   Descripciones. *Use **ser** or **estar** as appropriate to describe these scenes. Choose from these adjectives:*

bueno/a	enamorado/a	pobre
cansado/a	enfermo/a	rico/a
delgado/a	gordo/a	triste
elegante	nuevo/a	

1. Eva   2. Don Andrés   3. María, 1989   4. María, 1992   5. Paquito   6. Mis amigos

español es _____ (bueno). **4.** La clase de español no es _____ (difícil). **5.** Kareem Abdul Jabbar es _____ (alto). **6.** George Burns es _____ (viejo). **7.** Rosanne Barr es _____ (gorda).

B.   Sus compañeros de clase. *Take turns describing different classmates.*

1. ¿Quién es?	4. ¿Cómo está hoy?
2. ¿De dónde es?	5. ¿Qué ropa lleva?
3. ¿Cómo es?	6. ¿Cuáles son sus colores favoritos, probablemente?

C.   Excusas. *Give several reasons why you must refuse.*

¿Quieres ir a la fiesta de Jaime?   ¿Por qué no llevas mis pantalones?

1. estar cansado/a	4. Tú eres... y yo...
2. estar enfermo/a	5. Son...
3. mis pantalones nuevos, manchados	6. El color...

Optional listening comprehension: Present brief monologue to class in which you describe yourself and your tastes. Elaborate on following cues and add other information if you wish: **1.** ¿Cómo es? (alto/a, etc.) **2.** ¿Cómo está hoy? **3.** ¿Qué ropa lleva a clase (al cine, al trabajo, a una fiesta)? **4.** ¿Cuáles son sus colores favoritos? ¿Cuáles no le gustan? **5.** ¿En qué tienda(s) compra su ropa? ¿Dónde está(n)? **6.** ¿Qué accesorios usa con frecuencia? You can write questions on board or distribute them for students to prepare own monologues.

D.   **¿Ser o estar?**

Yo siempre voy de compras a El Gigante que _____[1] en el centro, porque _____[2] un almacén muy grande. Casi (*Almost*) todos los dependientes _____[3] simpáticos. Me gusta charlar con una dependienta en particular porque _____[4] muy lista. _____[5] de Mazatlán. Hablamos de la plaza donde _____[6] los hoteles. En la tienda hay un dependiente que no me gusta. _____[7] de la capital y ¡no _____[8] muy simpático!

16. Present Participles and Progressive Forms

Alina está hablando con la dependienta.

Present participle is the name given in English to the verb form ending in *-ing*. Its Spanish counterpart is formed by adding **-ando** to the stems of **-ar** verbs and **-iendo** to the stem of **-er** and **-ir** verbs.*

trabajar	trabajando	*working*
comer	comiendo	*eating*
discutir	discutiendo	*discussing*

The present participle can be used with **estar** to express an action in progress at the present time. Although the present tense in Spanish can also convey this idea (**Escribo una carta** = *I am writing a letter*), **estar** followed by the present participle (**Estoy escribiendo una carta**) emphasizes the progressive meaning.

Emphasis: Stress that in Spanish present progressive never expresses future actions. Example: "I am going to Spain in June." *Voy a España en junio.* Also, it would not be used to tell what someone is doing over a period of time. Example: "She's studying Spanish this semester." *Ella estudia español este semestre.*

Actividad

Un día agitado (*busy*). *Read these paragraphs aloud to your classmate, substituting appropriate present progressive forms for the italicized present tense forms. Your classmate will then retell the information, changing the present progressive forms accordingly (**A las doce estás comiendo...**).*

1. Por la tarde. A las 12:00 *como* un sándwich de jamón y queso. A las 2:00 *busco* mi bolígrafo y *escribo* una carta a mi amiga. A las 3:00 *trabajo* en un almacén de ropa. A las 4:00, un dependiente y yo *bebemos* Coca-Cola.
2. Por la noche. A las 8:00, Enrique y yo *preparamos* la lección de español para mañana y *discutimos* varios problemas de gramática. Yo *leo* un ejercicio y Enrique *lee* las preguntas. A las 9:00 *hablo* por teléfono con un compañero. A las 10:00, mi familia y yo *miramos* las noticias del día en la televisión.

---

*The present participles of **-er** and **-ir** verbs whose stems end in a vowel use the ending **-yendo:** **leer** → **leyendo.**

Para resumir y repasar

A. En persona: ¡De compras! (*Shopping!*) *Your grandmother will pay for your shopping spree, but there's a catch. Although she won't set a spending limit, neither will she pay for any unwise purchases. Carefully select five items to buy and justify each to your grandmother (a classmate) so you don't get stuck with the bill.*

Posibilidades:

Es caro/barato...   Es de seda (lana, piel)...
Es elegante/práctico/a...,   Está rebajada de...
Es para el verano/invierno...

B. Mire el dibujo y conteste las preguntas.

1. ¿Qué hace la mujer?
2. ¿Qué hace el hombre?
3. ¿Qué come el joven?
4. ¿Qué toma el joven?
5. ¿Qué bebe el señor viejo?

Now use the following suggestions to elaborate on your answers. Give imaginary answers when necessary.

1. ¿Qué compra el hombre?
2. ¿Cómo es el hombre?
3. ¿Cómo es la señora vieja?
4. ¿Qué discuten el joven y el señor viejo?
5. ¿Cómo es el señor viejo?

COMUNICACIÓN

De la vida real

Cosmos
La comodidad
de lo informal

Diseño. Estilo. Calidad.
Una afortunada coincidencia.

Un armario[a] sin vaque-
ros es como un jardín[b]
sin flores. ¡Le falta algo[c]!

[a]closet
[b]garden
[c]Le... Something's missing!

Calidad antes que[a]cantidad: el armario del perfecto
caballero debe estar compuesto por[b]unas piezas
básicas que den el juego necesario para adaptarse a
todas las situaciones. Estas son tres prendas que no
fallan:[c]una chaqueta de lana, unos vaqueros y un
jersey de cuello[d]alto.

PIEZAS DE DOBLE VALOR[e]

[a]antes... *before*
[b]debe... *should be composed of*
[c]*fail*
[d]*collar*
[e]*value*

MODA[a]

Estilo Latino

Sensualidad y rigor.
Una composición
estudiada.[b]Para hacer
teatro. Para definir la
identidad. La silueta
triunfa: toma formas
que no esconden[c]el
cuerpo.[d]La fantasía se
encuentra[e]en mil y un
detalles.[f] Voluntad de
un estilo que no es
desmemoriado.
Lo de hoy y de aquí
siempre tiene reso-
nancia a lo de ayer
y de allá.

[a]*fashion*
[b]*studied*
[c]*hide*
[d]*body*
[e]se... *is found*
[f]*details*

Note: Point out the style of the *Estilo latino* ad: At the beginning there are no verbs; then there are only verbal phrases; finally, subject and predicate come together in two complete sentences, as if form and content were at last united (i.e., the model). Have students examine other ads in this collage, to identify the stylistic intent of the ad agency. A brief discus-sion in English at this level might enhance interest.

Suggestion: Have different students read the brief ads aloud as if they were radio or television announcers. These ads provide excellent pronunciation practice.

A. Estilo latino. Con frecuencia los anuncios comerciales (*advertisements*) presentan estereotipos. Lea el anuncio y diga qué significan (*mean*) estos cognados: estilo, sensualidad, composición, teatro, identidad, silueta, triunfa, formas, fantasía. ¿Qué estereotipos presenta este anuncio?

B. Piezas de doble valor. *Although you may not know all of the vocabulary in this advertisement about the ideal wardrobe, you should be able to get the general meaning of it. First, read the advertisement through once. On the second reading, look for the following words or the answers to the following questions.*

1. two different words that mean article (of clothing)
2. a synonym for **suéter**
3. If **calidad** means quality, what do you think **cantidad** means?
4. If **dama** means *lady,* and **caballero** is its opposite, what does **caballero** mean?

Which of these sentences best expresses the main idea of the advertisement?

1. A real gentleman never has three pieces of clothing in his wardrobe.
2. There are three pieces of clothing that every well-dressed man needs to have.

¿Y usted? *Now answer the following questions about your own wardrobe.*

1. ¿Qué es más importante para Ud., la calidad de la ropa, o la cantidad?
2. ¿Cuáles son las piezas básicas que tiene Ud. en su armario?
3. ¿Le gustan los vaqueros? ¿Cuántos tiene en su armario?

C. Moda para los que tienen clase. Estudie la foto y conteste las preguntas con un compañero (una compañera).

1. ¿Cuántos muchachos hay en la foto?
2. ¿Quién es más alto?
3. ¿Están tristes?
4. ¿Qué ropa llevan?
5. ¿Qué objetos llevan para las clases?

Para conversar más

A. En el Almacén Neptuno. ¿Qué hacen y dicen las tres personas del dibujo? Con un compañero (una compañera) invente un diálogo con estos verbos: **ser, pagar, mirar, necesitar, tener, buscar.**

B.   Preguntas personales. Conteste.

1.   ¿Gasta Ud. mucho o poco en ropa? ¿Paga Ud. a veces con tarjeta de crédito? ¿Cuándo?
2.   ¿Cuánto cuesta ahora una camisa/blusa buena? ¿Cuál es el precio de un suéter/abrigo bueno?
3.   ¿Cuándo lleva Ud. pantalones vaqueros?
4.   ¿Usa Ud. más frecuentemente zapatos o botas?
5.   ¿Cuándo lleva traje un joven? ¿Usan sombrero más frecuentemente los jóvenes o los viejos?

Mᴏᴛɪᴠᴏ ᴄᴜʟᴛᴜʀᴀʟ

While Hispanic young people value comfort and informality in dress, they are generally very style-conscious. For this reason small, fashionable boutiques abound in the larger cities, along with the large department stores. **El Corte Inglés** (*The English "Cut"*) and **Galerías Preciados** are two of Spain's most well-known department store chains. Colombia has **Éxito** and Buenos Aires has Harrod's, originally a branch of the famous London store.

Hispanic students used to dress very formally. Years ago, for example, young men were expected to wear a suit and tie to class, but in recent years dress codes have been relaxed considerably. Today many college students attend classes in jeans and sandals, much like their North American counterparts. And many imitate dress styles popularized by American and English rock stars.

Vocabulario activo

Adjetivos

alto/a	tall	**de lana**	(made of) wool
bajo/a	short (*person*)	**de piel**	(made of) leather
cansado/a	tired	**de seda**	(made of) silk
cómodo/a	comfortable	**enamorado/a**	in love
contento/a	happy	**enfermo/a**	ill
delgado/a	thin	**gordo/a**	fat
		incómodo/a	uncomfortable
		joven	young

listo/a	smart
manchado/a	stained
ocupado/a	busy
pobre	poor
poco/a	(a) little
rebajado/a	reduced
rico/a	rich
simpático/a	nice, pleasant (*person*)
tonto/a	dumb
triste	sad

Sustantivos

LA ROPA (*CLOTHING*)

el abrigo	coat
la blusa	blouse
el bolso (la bolsa)	purse
la bota	boot
el calcetín	sock
la camisa	shirt
la camiseta	T-shirt
la cartera	purse
la corbata	necktie
la chaqueta	jacket
la falda	skirt
los jeans	jeans
los pantalones	pants
los pantalones cortos	shorts
la sandalia	sandal
el sombrero	hat
el suéter	sweater
la talla	size
el tenis	sneaker
el traje	suit
los (pantalones) vaqueros	jeans
el vestido	dress
el zapato	shoe

LOS COLORES

amarillo/a	yellow
azul	blue
blanco/a	white
color café	brown
negro/a	black
rojo/a	red
rosado/a	pink
verde	green

OTROS SUSTANTIVOS

el/la chico/a	boy/girl
el/la dependiente/a	salesclerk
el dinero	money
la fiesta	party
el precio	price
la tarjeta de crédito	credit card

Verbos

aceptar	to accept
buscar	to look for
dar	to give
estar	to be
ganar	to earn
gastar	to spend
ir	to go
ir de compras	to go shopping
llevar	to wear
pagar	to pay
prestar	to lend
ser	to be
usar	to wear; to use

Otras palabras y expresiones

¿Cómo es/son _____?	What is/are _____ like?
¿Cuál(es)?	What?; Which?
¿Cuánto cuesta?	How much does it cost?
entonces	then
más	more
o	or
que	that, which
quiero	I want

Instrucciones

la oración	sentence
según	according to
siguiente	following, next

Lectura (*Reading*)

The **Lectura** section, appearing after every three lessons in **Motivos de conversación,** develops your ability to work with longer, more difficult readings. The selections are accompanied by prereading strategies, notes, and post-reading activities to facilitate your recognition of the new words, to help you understand the reading, and to make logical associations between related forms.

The numbered items in the Spanish text are new words for which translations are given at the end of the reading. Try to guess their meanings from context before you consult the translations.

Antes de leer (**Before Reading**)

One way to boost your comprehension of a reading in Spanish is to try to develop an expectation of what it is about before you start reading. Approaching a passage with even a general notion of its focus will facilitate your understanding of it. Among the elements of the reading that you can glance at for this purpose are the title, any accompanying drawings, photos, or notes, the basic structure of the selection (is it an advertisement, an essay, a dialogue?, etc.), and any introductory material.

Examine the map on page 78 and the title of the reading. After reading the brief introduction, the first marginal note on cognates, and the **Nota** at the end, try to answer the following basic questions.

> *Who* is speaking?
> *What* precise topic is he/she talking about?
> *Where* is the country located?
> *Which* city is its capital?

Were you able to answer these questions without referring back to the text? If so, your cursory reading of the beginning and the end of the selection was helpful. Now read the entire dialogue carefully. It develops as a series of questions and answers between the instructor and some of her students. Try to put yourself in the place of a student. Be creative in associating Spanish cognates with their English counterparts and try to guess the parts of speech of new words by examining their contexts carefully.

Note: Emphasize importance of learning how to read efficiently; encourage students to go over suggestions and hints in *Antes de leer* sections carefully. Suggest students create memory aids of their own.

76

Una lección de geografía

La profesora Jiménez enseña una lección sobre la *geografía* hispanoamericana. Ahora habla de los transportes en uno de los países[1] del hemisferio occidental.

PROFESORA: ¿Cuál es la línea aérea más antigua del continente americano?

MARIO: Ummm. ¿Una línea aérea de los Estados Unidos?

PROFESORA: No. La primera línea aérea es creación de otro país.

JOSÉ: El Ecuador, posiblemente.

PROFESORA: No. Es un país que exporta esmeraldas a *todo* el *mundo*.

MARIO: ¿El Perú?

PROFESORA: No, no, no. Es un país que produce un café excelente.

RAÚL: ¡El Brasil!

PROFESORA: No. No es el Brasil.

JOSÉ: Entonces, ¿qué país es?

PROFESORA: Tiene dos costas, una en el Océano Pacífico y otra en el Mar Caribe.

¿De qué país habla la profesora Jiménez?

Nota: La profesora habla de Colombia, un país que tiene tres enormes *cordilleras* y un territorio muy extenso en la región amazónica. Su capital es Bogotá.

geografía: Some cognates are easy to recognize: **geografía, hemisferio, occidental, creación, exporta, esmeraldas, produce,** and so on. Others may be less obvious: **transportes, línea aérea, antigua, costa, extenso.**

todo: Knowing a word's part of speech can help you guess its meaning; is **todo** a noun, adjective, or verb?

mundo: Again, be creative. Think of English *mundane.*

cordilleras: Examine the context: Colombia has three of these, and they are part of the larger **Cordillera de los Andes.** Can the map provide some clues?

MOTIVO CULTURAL

Because of its mountainous terrain, Colombia was the first country to realize fully the advantages and convenience of commercial air travel. The elevation of Bogotá is 2,660 meters (8,660 feet).

---

[1]*countries*

Después de leer (After Reading)

A. Invente oraciones. *Invent a brief sentence in Spanish based on the following phrases.*

1. línea aérea
2. esmeraldas
3. café
4. dos costas
5. la capital

B. Identifique. *Identify the following features of Colombia by studying the accompanying map.*

1. tres cordilleras
2. un río (*river*)
3. la capital
4. un océano
5. una región tropical

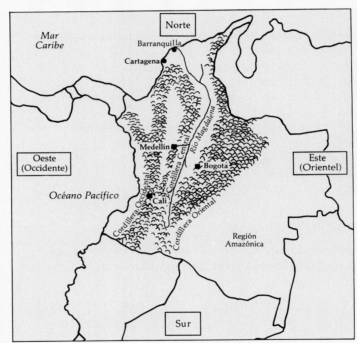

Suggestion: Bring a map of South America and/or Colombia to class in order to provide additional details of Colombian topography to your students. You may also want to point out the cities, mountains, rivers, etc. of nearby countries (Venezuela, Panama, Peru, etc.). Did they know Panama used to be part of Colombia, but broke away (at the suggestion of the United States) to facilitate construction of the Panama Canal?

Challenge: Close your book and give the preceding information about Colombia from memory.

C. Responda en español.

1. ¿Cuáles son las ciudades principales de Colombia?
2. ¿Qué exporta Colombia?
3. ¿Cómo se llama la capital de Colombia?
4. ¿Cuántas cordilleras hay en Colombia?
5. Colombia tiene costas en un océano y un mar. ¿Cómo se llaman?
6. ¿Qué otros países hay en el mapa?

Repaso visual*

Without looking back, describe the actions in each drawing in as many sentences as you can. You may want to keep in mind questions like the following.

¿Qué hay en el dibujo?   ¿Dónde están las personas?   ¿Con quién conversan?
¿De qué hablan?   ¿Cómo son las personas?

---

*This section repeats drawings featured in the **Gráficos** section of the previous three lessons.

Examen de repaso 1*

A. ¿El o la?

En la clase: _____¹ lápiz _____² mapa _____³ pared _____⁴ papel
En el centro: _____⁵ calle _____⁶ almacén _____⁷ cine _____⁸ autobús
La ropa: _____⁹ traje _____¹⁰ zapato _____¹¹ suéter _____¹² camiseta

B. Cambie según (*according to*) el modelo.

MODELOS: Los *alumnos* son inteligentes. (alumnas) →
Las alumnas son inteligentes.

Los *alumnos* son inteligentes. (alumna) →
La alumna es inteligente.

1. Los *lápices* son nuevos.
_____ sillas _____.
_____ mapa _____.
_____ dibujos _____.
_____ cámara _____.

2. Los *clientes* son argentinos.
_____ amiga _____.
_____ señor _____.
_____ señoras _____.
_____ profesores _____.

C. Aquí hay varios pares (*pairs*) de verbos. *Do you know them all?*
_____ yes _____ no

1. a. desear   b. necesitar
2. a. dar   b. prestar
3. a. leer   b. escribir
4. a. beber   b. comer
5. a. comprar   b. vender
6. a. ir   b. venir
7. a. decir   b. hacer
8. a. estudiar   b. enseñar

Invente oraciones con los verbos usando los pronombres indicados.

1. a. yo (desear)
   b. nosotros (necesitar)
2. a. Juan y María (leer)
   b. tú (escribir)
3. a. Uds. (ir)
   b. ella (venir)
4. a. El (decir)
   b. vosotros (hacer)

Ahora exprese b en inglés.

D. ¿Qué hora es?

1.

2.

3.

---

*The answers to the **Exámenes de repaso** may be found in Appendix 4.

80

E. Dé los colores apropiados.

1.

2.

3.

F. Exprese en español.

1. 4.658 cars
2. 1.000.000 women
3. my shoes
4. our skirts

G. Complete la conversación con la forma correcta de **ser** o **estar**.

ALICIA: ¿Quién _____[1] la alumna nueva de la clase?

ELVIRA: _____[2] Marisa Sánchez.

ALICIA: ¿De dónde _____[3] ella?

ELVIRA: Ella y sus padres (*parents*) _____[4] de México. Los padres _____[5] muy contentos aquí, pero Marisa _____[6] triste.

ALICIA: ¿Por qué? Nuestro país _____[7] muy bueno.

ELVIRA: Sí, pero todos sus amigos _____[8] en México.

ALICIA: No. Eso no es verdad. Ahora tú y yo vamos a _____[9] sus amigas. Vamos a hablar con ella.

H. Conteste.

1. ¿Tiene Ud. clases todos los días?
2. ¿Dónde lee Ud. las noticias?
3. ¿Qué hace Ud. en la clase?
4. ¿Qué le gusta hacer con los amigos?
5. ¿Va al cine mucho? ¿Con quién va usualmente?

I. Vocabulario. Complete.

1. Siempre tienen _____. (*good prices*)
2. ¿ _____ vive Ud.? (*Where*)
3. Las preguntas no son _____. (*difficult*)
4. Compramos dos bolsos _____. (*cheap but good*)
5. Señoritas, ¿ _____? (*do you teach several classes*)
6. No compramos bolsos porque _____ caros. (*they are*)
7. La profesora es _____. (*young and smart*)
8. Hay _____ alumnos en esta clase. (*53*)

Mi familia

Una familia feliz: mamá, papá y dos hermanitas.

METAS

Comunicación: In this lesson you will learn vocabulary and expressions related to the family. You will talk about your own family, describe your favorite relatives, make a family tree, and discuss family visits and outings.

Estructuras: 17. Irregular Present Tense of **conocer, saber, oír, poner, salir, traer, ver** 18. Uses of the Preposition **a** 19. Idioms with **hacer** and **tener** 20. Affirmative Familiar Commands

GRÁFICOS

Parientes* de tres generaciones

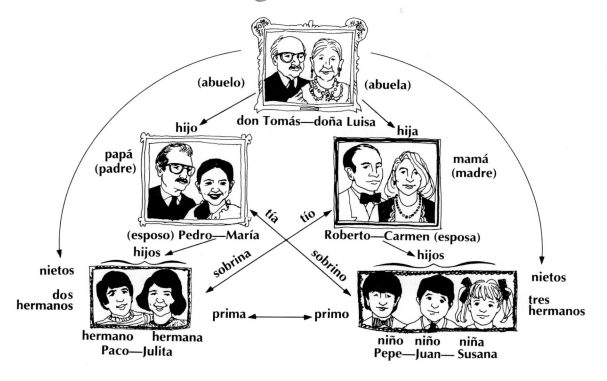

*Parientes is a false cognate. It means *relatives,* not *parents. Parents* is expressed in Spanish as **padres.**

los hijos	*sons; son(s) and daughter(s)**
los nietos	*grandchildren; granddaughter(s) and grandson(s)*
los niños	*boys; boy(s) and girl(s); children**
los novios	*sweethearts; bridegrooms; bride(s) and bridegroom(s)*
los padres	*fathers; father(s) and mother(s); parents*
los primos	*cousins; male and female cousins*
los señores	*men; Mr. and Mrs.*
los sobrinos	*nephews; niece(s) and nephew(s)*
los tíos	*uncles; aunt(s) and uncle(s)*

Exprese en español.

Hoy vienen a casa todos nuestros parientes. Mis (*parents*[1]) tienen muchos (*brothers and sisters*[2]). Por eso (*Therefore*), yo tengo numerosos (*uncles and aunts*[3]). Todos ellos tienen muchos (*children*[4]). Por eso, yo también tengo muchos (*cousins*[5]). Mis (*grandparents*[6]) no vienen porque mi (*grandmother*[7]) está enferma.

Suggestion A: Spot-check some of the questions for listening comprehension by changing key words: **1.** ¿Cómo se llama la abuela de Paco y Julita? **2.** ¿Quién es el hijo de don Tomás? **3.** ¿Cuántos hijos tienen Pedro y María? **4.** ¿Cómo se llama la tía de Paco y Julita? **5.** ¿Cuántos primos tiene Susana? **6.** ¿Quiénes son los padres de Paco y Julita? **7.** ¿Cuántos adultos y cuántos niños hay en la familia? **8.** ¿Qué esposos tienen más sobrinos?

Suggestion B: If students need cues, write these questions on board: **1.** ¿Quién es? **2.** ¿Qué hace? ¿Estudia o trabaja? ¿Dónde? **3.** ¿Dónde vive? **4.** ¿Qué lengua(s) habla? **5.** ¿Es rico o pobre?

Expansion B: Create a living family tree in class. Students assume roles of *abuelos, hijos, nietos, tíos,* and *primos.* Do in front of class or in the middle of class (if chairs are arranged in semicircle). Give students names and let them explain their relationships to others in "tree."

Actividades

A. La familia de don Tomás y doña Luisa. Estudie el dibujo en la página anterior y conteste las preguntas.

1.   ¿Cómo se llama el abuelo de Paco y Julita?
2.   ¿Quién es la esposa de don Tomás?
3.   ¿Cuántos sobrinos tienen Pedro y María?
4.   ¿Cómo se llama la prima de Paco y Julita?
5.   ¿Cuántos hermanos tiene Susana?
6.   ¿Quiénes son los tíos de Paco y Julita?
7.   ¿Cuántos nietos hay en la familia?
8.   ¿Qué esposos tienen más hijos?
9.   ¿Cuántas generaciones hay en el dibujo?
10.   ¿Hay más mujeres o más hombres en la familia?

B. Su familia. Ud. es una de las personas en el dibujo. Explique (*Explain*) la relación entre (*between*) Ud. y los otros miembros de la familia. Entonces, describa a su pariente favorito.

C. Una entrevista (*An interview*). Pregúntele a un compañero (una compañera)...

1.   ¿Cuántos hermanos tienes?
2.   Si tienes hermanas, ¿cómo se llaman? (Mis hermanas...)

*****Hijos** refers to a couple's children of any age; **niños** is generally used only with children under twelve.

—¿Tienen Uds. hijos?
—Sí, tenemos tres niños pequeños.
—Pues yo tengo sólo un hijo, y ya está casado.

3. ¿Cuántos primos tienes?
4. ¿Tienes parientes famosos?
5. ¿Cómo es tu abuela (abuelo)? (Mi abuela...)
6. ¿Dónde vive ella (él)?
7. ¿Hay muchos nietos en tu familia? (En mi familia...)
8. ¿Son niños o niñas?
9. ¿Cómo es tu padre (madre)? (Mi padre...)

D. El árbol familiar. Prepare un árbol familiar para una telenovela (*television soap opera*). Describa al menos (*at least*) tres de las relaciones entre (*between*) los miembros de la familia. **Adjetivos posibles:** cruel, ambicioso/a, generoso/a, romántico/a, hermoso/a, famoso/a, rico/a, interesante, bueno/a, malo/a, listo/a, simpático/a.

La visita de los parientes

◆ IRREGULAR PRESENT TENSE VERBS ◆	
veo	*I see*
ve	*you (he/she/it) see(s)*
traigo	*I bring (take along)*
trae	*you (he/she/it) bring(s) (take[s] along)*
pongo	*I put*
pone	*you (he/she/it) put(s)*
oigo	*I hear*
oye	*you (he/she/it) hear(s)*
salgo	*I leave, go out*
sale	*you (he/she/it) leave(s), go(es) out*

1. el mantel
2. el plato*
3. el vaso
4. el pan
5. los cubiertos
6. la copa
7. la taza
8. la cuchara
9. la cucharita
10. el tenedor
11. el cuchillo
12. la servilleta
13. la jarra

LUIS: Los domingos *casi siempre* veo a mis parientes porque comen en mi casa.

OLGA: Es *duro* para tu mamá. Mucho *trabajo,* ¿verdad?

LUIS: No, porque mi abuela trae parte de la *comida. Además, cada* uno de nosotros *ayuda. Por ejemplo,* mi hermana *mayor* pone el mantel, las

almost / always

hard / work

food / Besides / each

helps / For example / older

***Plato** can also mean a dish or culinary specialty, as well as a course or part of a meal.

servilletas y los platos; mi hermano Perico pone las copas, las tazas, los vasos y la jarra con el agua, y mi hermana *menor lleva* el pan y los cubiertos a la mesa.

younger / carries

OLGA: Y tú, ¿qué haces?

LUIS: Oigo música o *llamo por teléfono* a mi *novia*, y *después, si hace buen tiempo*, salgo a *caminar un rato* con mis tíos *por* el barrio.

call on the telephone / girlfriend / afterward if the weather is good / to walk / for a while / through

OLGA: ¡Huy! ¡*Qué vida!*, ¿no? ¡Tú no haces *nada*!

What a life! / anything (nothing)

Note: Explain that since a double negative is not correct in English, *nada* is often translated as "anything."

◆ M OTIVO CULTURAL

Comida means *food* in Spanish, but it can also mean *meal*. As such, it is employed in a general sense but also refers to the large midday meal in Spain and to dinner (supper) in many places in Spanish America.

Actividades

A. Comprensión. Conteste las preguntas sobre el diálogo.

1. ¿Qué día ve Luis a sus parientes? ¿Por qué?
2. ¿Cuántos hermanos tiene Luis? ¿Cuántas hermanas?
3. ¿Quién trae parte de la comida?
4. ¿A quién llama Luis por teléfono?
5. ¿Qué hace Luis si hace buen tiempo?
6. ¿Por dónde camina Luis con sus tíos?

B. Imagine que Ud. es miembro de la familia de Luis. Diga qué hace Ud. para (*in order to*) ayudar.

MODELO: Mi abuela trae la comida. (vino) →
Yo traigo el vino.

1. Nuestros tíos traen el queso. (leche)
2. Mi prima mayor pone el mantel. (los platos)
3. Perico pone los vasos. (la jarra con el agua)
4. Mi hermana menor lleva el pan a la mesa. (las copas)
5. Luis pone las cucharas y las cucharitas. (los tenedores)
6. Mi sobrino lleva las servilletas a la mesa. (los cuchillos)

C. Preguntas personales. Pregúntele a un compañero (una compañera).

1. ¿Cuándo (no) sales con tus amigos?
2. ¿Ves a tus parientes frecuentemente? ¿Dónde viven?
3. ¿Siempre ayudas tú con los trabajos domésticos? Por ejemplo, ¿pones los cubiertos y las tazas en la mesa? ¿Qué otras cosas haces?
4. En tu opinión, ¿qué trabajos domésticos son duros?

Suggestion B: Assign the roles of Luis's family to different students and cue them with pantomimed actions to tell the class what they do when their relatives come on Sundays: **1.** *La hermana mayor de Luis (poner el mantel / las servilletas / los platos).* **2.** *Perico (poner las copas / las tazas / los vasos / la jarra con el agua).* **3.** *La hermana menor de Luis (llevar a la mesa el pan / los cubiertos). Luis (oír música / llamar por teléfono / caminar por el barrio).*

Optional C: Ask students to prepare short speech explaining activities they do with their friends and relatives. Suggestions: *salir en el auto, mirar la televisión, comer en casa (en un restaurante), ayudar a mamá, poner la mesa, limpiar la casa, discutir las noticias, oír música, conversar.*

Un perrito para Carmina

1. la frutería
2. los plátanos/
   las bananas
3. las manzanas
4. la tienda de animales
5. el perro
6. el perrito*
7. el gato
8. el gatito/el gatico*
9. la niña

◆ IRREGULAR PRESENT TENSE VERBS ◆

conozco	*I know (am acquainted with)*
conoces	*you know (are acquainted with)*
sé	*I know (a fact)*
sabes	*you know (a fact)*

◆ FAMILIAR COMMANDS ◆

di	*tell; say*
haz	*do; make*

ELENA: *¡Mira* los perritos y los gatitos! Son preciosos. Quiero comprar un perrito para Carmina, la hija de mi primo Ramón. ¿Conoces a Ramón? — *Look (at)*

CLAUDIA: Conozco a Ramón, pero... ¿no es *soltero?* — *single*

ELENA: No, es *casado* y tiene dos hijos. — *married*

CLAUDIA: *Dime,* ¿por qué no compras un gatito? ¡Son *tan monos!* — *Tell me / so cute*

ELENA: Porque sé que le gustan más los perros. Es un *premio,* ¿sabes?, porque la niña *aprende* a leer y *saca muy buenas notas* en la *escuela.* ¿*Me ayudas a escoger* el perrito? — *prize / is learning / gets very good grades / school / Will you help me choose*

CLAUDIA: *No puedo; tengo prisa. Tengo que* ir a la frutería a comprar manzanas y plátanos. — *I can't / I'm in a hurry / I have to*

ELENA: *Comprendo.* Pero, *hazme* un favor, el perrito es una *sorpresa* y... — *I understand / do me / surprise*

CLAUDIA: De acuerdo; *no voy a* decir nada. — *I'm not going to*

Listening Comprehension A: Write cues on board: (1) *frutería,* (2) *tienda de animales.* Read aloud the following sentences and ask students to associate them with one of two cues: **1.** *Me gustan mucho los plátanos.* **2.** *Busco un perrito para Carmina.* **3.** *Voy a comprar manzanas.* **4.** *Necesito un gato.*

Actividades

A. ¿Cierto o falso? *Correct the false statements.*

1. Elena va a comprar un gato.
2. Carmina es la sobrina de Ramón.

Cultural expansion: Explain how dialogue exemplifies prevalence of small stores and specialty shops in Hispanic world. Every *barrio* has a *farmacia, frutería, lechería, panadería, carnicería, zapatería, ferretería, papelería,* etc.

Optional: (See note on next page). Explain...

*The endings **-ito, -ita,** and occasionally other endings, such as **-ico, -ica,** indicate smallness in Spanish.

Optional: Explain that there are other suffixes that indicate smallness like -*ín*, -*ina* (*pequeñín*) and -*illo*, -*illa* (*chiquillo*). Also, note that regional usage often favors a given suffix. For instance, in Mexico and Puerto Rico -*ito*, -*ita* are the preferred endings in all cases while in Cuba, Dominican Republic, Costa Rica, Colombia, Venezuela and other countries -*ico*, -*ica* are preferred when there is a *t* in the preceding syllable (*perrito* but: *gatico*).

3. Claudia no conoce a Ramón.
4. Un hombre que tiene esposa es soltero.
5. Elena sabe que a Carmina le gustan más los gatos.
6. Carmina aprende a escribir en la escuela.
7. Claudia tiene prisa y no puede entrar en la tienda de animales con Elena.
8. Claudia ayuda a escoger el perrito.
9. La gente compra manzanas y plátanos en las fruterías.
10. Claudia no comprende que el perrito es una sorpresa.

B. Preguntas personales. Pregúntele a un compañero (una compañera).

1. ¿Cuántos primos tienes?
2. ¿Conoces a todos tus primos?
3. ¿Son solteros o casados tus primos?
4. ¿Sabes dónde viven todos tus primos?
5. ¿Son más monos los perritos que los gatitos? ¿Por qué?
6. ¿Qué animales hay en tu casa? Si hay un perro, ¿quién sale a caminar con el perro?
7. ¿Sacas buenas o malas notas en la escuela? ¿Recibes (*Do you receive*) un premio cuando sacas buenas notas?

◆ VISTA CULTURAL

Suggestion: Find photos of and information about Spanish royal family in Spanish magazines and bring them to class.

Ésta es la familia real (*royal*) española. Juan Carlos I (Primero) es rey (*king*) de España desde (*since*) la muerte (*death*) de Francisco Franco en 1975. Su esposa, la reina (*queen*) Sofía, es de Grecia. Juan Carlos y Sofía tienen tres hijos: las princesas* Elena y Cristina, y el príncipe Felipe.

Aunque (*Although*) Felipe es el hijo menor, probablemente va a ser rey un día porque en España las mujeres no heredan (*inherit*) el trono. Felipe habla varias lenguas, practica deportes (*sports*) y es un joven muy simpático.

---

*Spanish princesses are also called **infantas**.

GRAMÁTICA ESENCIAL

17. Irregular Present Tense of
conocer, saber, oír, poner, salir, traer, ver

—Y tú, ¿qué haces?
—Yo oigo música o llamo
por teléfono a mi novia, y
después, si hace buen
tiempo, salgo a caminar
un rato...

In the **Gráficos** section of this lesson, you learned two forms of irregular verbs. All except **oír** are irregular only in the first person singular. Here are the complete conjugations:

> **conocer: conozco,** conoces, conoce, conocemos, conocéis, conocen
> **saber:** **sé,** sabes, sabe, sabemos, sabéis, saben

Conocer means *to know* in the sense of being acquainted or familiar with a person, a city, and so on. **Saber** means *to know* a fact, *to know* how to do something (**sé leer** = *I know how to read*).

> **oír:** **oigo, oyes, oye,** oímos, oís, **oyen**
> **poner:** **pongo,** pones, pone, ponemos, ponéis, ponen
> **salir:** **salgo,** sales, sale, salimos, salís, salen
> **traer:** **traigo,** traes, trae, traemos, traéis, traen
> **ver:** **veo,** ves, ve, vemos, veis, ven

In addition to the **g** in its **yo** form, **oír** has another change: the **i** of the present tense endings changes to **y** in three of the six persons of the conjugation. This change always occurs when **i** comes between two vowels. For this reason, the present participles of **oír** and **traer** are **oyendo** and **trayendo,** respectively, like **creer** (**creyendo**) and **leer** (**leyendo**).

Actividades

A. Ana está enferma. *Retell the story, substituting the subjects indicated (on the following page) for* **la madre** *and changing the corresponding verbs.*

La madre trae leche para Ana, pero *ve* que Ana no bebe la leche. Después, *la madre oye* que la niña está llorando (*crying*), y *sabe* inmediatamente que está enferma. *Pone* a Ana en el coche y *sale* con ella para (*in the direction of*) la casa del doctor que *conoce*, el Dr. Jiménez.

1. yo   2. tú   3. los padres   4. vosotros   5. nosotras

Now answer these questions as if you were Ana's mother. Try to give an original twist to some of your answers.

1. ¿Qué traes?
2. ¿Qué ves?
3. ¿Qué oyes?
4. ¿Qué sabes inmediatamente?
5. ¿A quién conoces?
6. ¿Dónde pones a la persona enferma?

B. Preguntas personales. Conteste.

1. ¿Conoce Ud. un barrio interesante en esta (*this*) ciudad? ¿Qué ve Ud. allí generalmente?
2. ¿Sabe Ud. hablar español? ¿Sabe Ud. leer o escribir otra lengua?
3. ¿Oye Ud. mucho tráfico desde (*from*) su casa o apartamento? ¿Es un problema para Ud.?
4. ¿Siempre trae Ud. un sándwich a la universidad, o sale a comer con los amigos? ¿Sale Ud. a comer frecuentemente? ¿A qué restaurante?
5. Cuando sus parientes comen en su casa, ¿pone un mantel elegante? ¿Qué pone Ud. en la mesa?

Optional: Drill use of *saber* and *conocer*. **1.** No _____ al primo de Elena, pero _____ que vive en México. **2.** Nosotros _____ conjugar los verbos irregulares. **3.** Yo _____ que tú _____ bien la ciudad de Chicago. **4.** ¿_____ Ud. cuánto cuestan los plátanos? **5.** Mi hermanita menor no _____ leer. **6.** Todos mis amigos _____ mi número de teléfono. **7.** Vosotros _____ dónde vive el profesor. **8.** Tú _____ poner la mesa muy bien.

18. Uses of the Preposition *a*

—Conozco a Ramón, pero... ¿no es soltero?
—No, es casado y tiene dos hijos.

Suggestion: Explain that the clue to the use of *a* is often a specific versus an unspecific direct object. *Deseo comprar un gato* and *Necesito una secretaria* don't refer to a specific cat or secretary while *Cuido a mi gato* and *Aprecio a mi secretaria* do. You may also want to mention that *a* can be used with personified things: *Temo a la muerte* and *Quiero a los Estados Unidos*.

The preposition **a** is used in the following ways.

1. Before direct objects that refer to specific persons and often to intelligent animals

Conocen a la hija de don Tomás.	*They know don Tomas's daughter.*
No traigo a mi perro a la escuela.	*I don't bring my dog to school.*
BUT: No conozco la ciudad.	*I don't know the city.*

The personal **a** is not generally used with **tener.**

Tengo tres hijos.	*I have three sons.*

2. Certain verbs always take **a** when followed by an infinitive: **aprender, enseñar, invitar,** and verbs of motion like **ir, venir,** and **salir.**

Ella aprende a hablar bien el español.	*She is learning to speak Spanish well.*
Él no enseña a la clase a cantar porque no sabe cantar.	*He doesn't teach the class to sing, because he doesn't know how to sing.*
Mi tía viene a ayudar a mi madre.	*My aunt comes to help my mother.*

3. The phrase **ir a** + *infinitive,* meaning *to be going to* (*do something*), is one way to express the future in Spanish.

Voy a ver a mis parientes mañana.	*I am going to see my relatives tomorrow.*
Mi madre no va a comprar el mantel rosado.	*My mother is not going to buy the pink tablecloth.*

Vamos a + *infinitive* has two possible meanings: *Let's* (*do something*) or *We are going to* (*do something*).

Vamos a comer ahora.	$\begin{cases} \textit{Let's eat now.} \\ \textit{We are going to eat now.} \end{cases}$

The context will reveal which meaning is intended.

Actividad

*Supply the preposition **a** if necessary.*

¿Qué veo y a quién veo?

En la sala de clase veo ____[1] la profesora y ____[2] mis compañeros. Miro por la ventana y veo ____[3] la calle y ____[4] los automóviles. También veo ____[5] el café Las Delicias. Un joven en la calle está invitando ____[6] su amiga ____[7] tomar algo en el café.

¿Qué oigo y a quién oigo?

Oigo ____[8] la profesora que habla y enseña ____[9] los alumnos que aprenden ____[10] conjugar los verbos. Oigo ____[11] la música de un radio. Oigo ____[12] el ruido (*noise*) del tráfico en la plaza. También oigo ____[13] una mujer que llama ____[14] su perro: «Cuchicuchi, ven ____[15] comer».

¿Qué conozco y a quién conozco?

Conozco ____[16] Pedro y conozco ____[17] el barrio donde él vive con su familia. Sé que Pedro tiene ____[18] tres hermanas, pero yo sólo conozco ____[19] la hermana que aprende ____[20] hablar francés en la universidad. Sé que ella va ____[21] la cafetería ____[22] tomar café con su amiga Carla todos los días y que sale ____[23] bailar con su grupo todos los viernes.

Suggestion: Give verbs followed by the preposition *a,* asking students to complete sentences with logical infinitives: **1.** *Aprendemos a...* (*escribir bien, pronunciar las palabras*) **2.** *Enseño a...* (*hablar español, leer correctamente, conjugar los verbos*) **3.** *Invito a mis compañeros a...* (*estudiar, ir a mi casa, oír música, caminar por el barrio*) Do the same with verbs of motion, having students complete with likely places: **4.** *Vamos a...* (*la biblioteca, la cafetería, el almacén*) **5.** *Todos los días vengo a* (*la clase, la universidad*) **6.** *Sales a...* (*la calle, la plaza, el parque*)

Suggestion: Give sentences in the present tense and have students change them using the construction *ir a* + infinitive. **1.** *Yo no compro un perrito.* **2.** *Elena y Claudia no compran un gatito.* **3.** *Carmina aprende a leer rápido.* **4.** *Carmina también saca buenas notas.* **5.** *Nosotros escogemos las manzanas.* **6.** *Uds. compran plátanos.* **7.** *Claudia no dice nada.* **8.** *Yo no traigo a mi perro a la escuela.*

Oral practice: Write a list of words on the board: *mis amigos, sus hijos, las servilletas, la tienda de animales, la ciudad, doña Luisa.* Then give the following sentences orally, asking students to substitute direct objects as you point to words on the board. They will need to decide whether an *a* is needed with the new object. **1.** *Oigo música.* **2.** *José lleva frutas en su coche.* **3.** *Lavo a los niños.* **4.** *Visito a mis abuelos.* **5.** *No conozco a tu primo.* **6.** *Veo muchos platos en la mesa.*

19. Idioms with *hacer* and *tener*

Tengo prisa. Tengo que ir a la frutería a comprar manzanas y plátanos.

A. The following **hacer** idioms describe the weather.*

¿Qué tiempo hace?	*How is the weather?*
Hace mucho calor (fresco, frío, sol, viento).	*It is very hot (cool, cold, sunny, windy).*
Hace mal tiempo.	*The weather is bad.*

B. Several idioms with **tener** refer to bodily sensations.

¿Qué tienes (tiene, tienen...)?	*What's wrong with you (him, them . . .)?*
Tengo (tiene, tienen...) calor (frío, hambre, sed, sueño).	*I am (he is, they are . . .) hot (cold, hungry, thirsty, sleepy).*

C. There are many other important **tener** idioms.

tener _____ años = *to be _____ years old*

¿Cuántos años tiene Ud.?	*How old are you?*
Tengo veinte y tres.	*I am twenty-three.*

tener que = *to have to*

Yo tengo que hacer eso.	*I have to do that.*

tener razón, no tener razón = *to be right, to be wrong*

Uds. tienen razón.	*You are right.*
Pues, no tenemos razón.	*Well, we're wrong.*

tener ganas de (+ *infinitive*) = *to feel like* (*doing something*)

Hoy no tengo ganas de trabajar.	*I don't feel like working today.*

tener prisa = *to be in a hurry*

Note: You may wish to mention use of *hay* with weather phenomena: *Hay nubes (viento, sol).* "It is cloudy (windy, sunny)."

Suggestion: Ask students how weather is in following places: *¿Qué tiempo hace en Alaska* (*la Florida, California, Montana, Nueva York*) *en verano* (*en invierno, en primavera, en otoño*)?

---

*All idioms with **hacer** and **tener** contain nouns. Spanish speakers literally say, for example, *I have thirst*. Therefore, if they wish to intensify the idiom, they must use the adjective **mucho/a.**

¿Por qué corres? —Porque tengo mucha prisa.

Why are you running? —Because I am in a big hurry.

tener miedo = *to be afraid*

Tengo miedo cuando oigo ruidos por la noche.

I'm afraid when I hear noises at night.

tener cuidado = *to be careful*

Debes tener cuidado con las copas; son muy caras.

You should be careful with the wine glasses; they are very expensive.

Actividades

Optional oral questions:
1. ¿Qué toma Ud. cuando tiene sed? **2.** ¿Qué come Ud. cuando tiene hambre? **3.** ¿Cuántos años tiene Ud.? **4.** ¿Tiene Ud. frío (calor) ahora? **5.** ¿Qué hace Ud. cuando tiene frío (calor)? **6.** ¿Cuándo tiene Ud. ganas de trabajar (estudiar)? **7.** ¿Qué tiene ganas de hacer en este momento? **8.** ¿Cuándo tiene Ud. prisa? **9.** ¿Tiene Ud. prisa ahora? ¿Por qué? **10.** ¿Quién siempre tiene razón en su familia?

A. ¿Qué tienen mis parientes? *Make a logical comment using idioms with tener.*

1. Mi abuela busca su abrigo.
2. Mi tío Armando decide llevar hoy camiseta y pantalones cortos.
3. Mi hermana Alicia bebe varios vasos de Coca-Cola.
4. Mi sobrino ve *La hija de Drácula* en el cine.
5. Mi primo Ernesto va a comer dos sándwiches y después una manzana y un plátano.
6. Mi hermano Perico dice la verdad.
7. Mi sobrina Carmina es muy joven.
8. Mi padre va caminando muy rápido por la calle.
9. Mi hija siempre mira bien cuando cruza (*crosses*) la calle.
10. Me voy a la cama (*I go to bed*) inmediatamente después de comer.

B. ¿Qué tiempo hace...

1. en el mes de marzo en Los Ángeles?
2. en las playas (*beaches*) de Acapulco?
3. el 22 de diciembre en Maine?
4. en agosto en el Sáhara?
5. en febrero en Chicago?
6. en su ciudad en octubre?

C. Confesiones. Complete lo que dicen estas (*these*) personas.

Irma, una chica que tiene diecisiete años

1. Tengo ganas de salir con mis amigos, pero mi padre dice que tengo que...
2. Deseo mirar la televisión ahora, pero tengo que...

Doña Clara, una señora que tiene cuarenta años

3. Tengo cuarenta años, pero digo a mis amigos que...
4. Siempre tengo que lavar los platos, pero tengo ganas de...

20. Affirmative Familiar Commands*

Dime, ¿por qué no compras un gatito? ¡Son tan monos!

A. Affirmative commands with regular verbs. The **tú** affirmative command is spelled the same as the third person singular of the present indicative tense. Compare (**él**) **escucha** (*he listens*) with **¡escucha tú!** (*listen!*).

-ar: mirar	¡mira (tú)!	*look!*
-er: beber	¡bebe (tú)!	*drink!*
-ir: escribir	¡escribe (tú)!	*write!*

B. Affirmative commands with irregular verbs. The irregular familiar commands must be memorized. Here are the most common.

decir	¡di (tú)!	*say, tell!*		salir	¡sal (tú)!	*leave!*
hacer	¡haz (tú)!	*do, make!*		tener	¡ten (tú)!	*have!*
ir	¡ve (tú)!	*go!*		venir	¡ven (tú)!	*come!*
poner	¡pon (tú)!	*put, place!*				

Suggestion: Mimic the following actions and ask students to give familiar commands for them. **1.** *Mira a tu compañero/a.* **2.** *Bebe.* **3.** *Escribe en tu cuaderno.* **4.** *Ve a la ventana.* **5.** *Pon el libro en la mesa.* **6.** *Sal de la clase.* **7.** *Ven aquí.*

Actividades

A. Instrucciones a un amigo. *You have just moved into a new apartment and are having a housewarming party. Using familiar commands, ask a classmate to do the following to get to your new place and to help you prepare the party.*

> MODELO: escribir estas instrucciones en un papel →
> Escribe estas instrucciones en un papel.

1. decir a todos los compañeros que tenemos una fiesta
2. salir de tu casa temprano
3. venir antes de las cinco
4. tomar el autobús número 22
5. ir hasta la Plaza de Colón
6. bajar en Colón y caminar tres calles
7. tener cuidado con mi perro al entrar

---

*The negative familiar command forms will be presented in **Gramática esencial** 26.

8. lavar las ventanas
9. poner el mantel y los platos en la mesa
10. ir a la frutería a comprar manzanas
11. comprar pan, jamón y queso
12. hacer los sándwiches

B.   Carmina educa a su perrito. *Use the familiar commands corresponding to the infinitives given, to express the orders Carmina gives her new puppy.*

1. escuchar con atención
2. comer toda la comida que pongo en tu plato
3. beber la leche
4. venir cuando te llamo
5. ir a la sala
6. poner la pata (*paw*) en la silla
7. salir al patio
8. tener cuidado con los coches en la calle

Para resumir y repasar

A.   En persona: Una cena (*dinner*) para sus parientes. *Together with your older sister or brother (a classmate), plan a large dinner party for your relatives. First, make a list of the relatives you would like to invite. Since neither of you has enough chairs, glasses, plates, silverware, etc., for everyone, you should also decide which relatives to ask to bring these items and which to ask to bring food items. Finally, decide what needs to be done for the party, and using commands, tell each other which tasks to do.*

B.   ¿Ser o estar?

Los amigos

1. Anselmo _____ un buen amigo; _____ muy simpático.
2. Rosita _____ una persona alegre, pero hoy _____ triste.
3. Carmen _____ de Colombia, pero _____ en México ahora.
4. La señora Ramírez tiene buen humor; siempre _____ contenta.
5. Héctor siempre contesta bien en clase; _____ muy listo.

En casa

6. Juan y yo tenemos poco dinero; _____ pobres.
7. Por eso, nuestro nuevo apartamento no _____ muy grande.
8. Trabajamos mucho porque deseamos _____ ricos.
9. Trabajamos mucho todos los días y _____ muy cansados.
10. Pero no me gusta trabajar en casa; por eso, los platos de ayer todavía _____ en la mesa.

COMUNICACIÓN

De la vida real

ESPERAª, VOY A PREGUNTARLE SI QUIERE IR A JUGAR CONTIGOᵇ

SI...

TEO DICE QUE NO PUEDE, TIENE QUE ESTUDIAR.

ªWait
ᵇjugar... *play with you*

Note: Point out the prevalence in conversational Spanish of constructions learned in this lesson: *voy a preguntarle*, *ir a jugar*, *tiene que*. In the second joke an infinitive (*errar*) is used as the subject, as is often the case in English as well as Spanish.

A. Teo tiene que estudiar. Lea el chiste (*joke*) y conteste las preguntas.

1. ¿Quién llama por teléfono?
2. ¿Qué quiere la persona que llama?
3. ¿Qué contesta Teo?
4. ¿Qué dice la señora?
5. ¿Quién es la señora?

B. Errar es humano. Mire el chiste y decida si es verdad o no que...

1. el niño tiene miedo.
2. el padre lleva una corbata blanca.
3. el padre va a dar un premio al niño.
4. el padre está furioso.
5. errar es humano.

ERRAR ES HUMANO

Para conversar más

Optional questions: 1. *¿Cuántos hermanos tiene Ud.? ¿Cuántos hay en su familia en total, entonces?* 2. *¿Conoce Ud. a los padres de sus amigos? ¿Cómo son?* 3. *¿A qué miembro de su familia le gusta contar (tell) chistes? ¿Cómo son sus chistes?* 4. *Para Ud., ¿es muy importante su familia? Explique.*

A.   Su familia. Escriba o diga a la clase varias oraciones sobre un miembro particularmente interesante de su familia. Ideas:

1.   ¿Qué pariente es?
2.   ¿Cómo se llama?
3.   ¿Dónde vive?
4.   ¿Cuántos años tiene?
5.   ¿Qué hace?
6.   ¿Dónde trabaja/estudia?

7.   ¿Es casado/a?
8.   ¿Tiene hijos? ¿Cuántos?
9.   ¿Cómo es? (alto, bajo, listo, simpático, alegre, etcétera)?
10.   ¿Es mayor/menor que (*than*) Ud.?

B.   Teatro. *With a classmate, prepare a skit to present to the class on one of the following topics.*

1.   Su tía y Ud. *You are studying hard for an exam, but your aunt is lonely and wants to talk. She tells you about . . . You interrupt and explain that . . . Finally, she tells you a joke.*
2.   Su novio/a y Ud. *Your boyfriend/girlfriend wants to go to . . . and invites you to come along. You want to go, but your family is having a big celebration at home. Your friend insists, you insist, and finally . . .*
3.   Un amigo (una amiga) y Ud. *You and a friend are talking about your cousin. Your friend reminds you that he/she doesn't know your cousin and asks whether the cousin is married. You explain that your cousin is single. The friend asks . . . and you answer . . .*

C.   Una familia grande y feliz (*happy*). Comente sobre los siguientes aspectos de la escena.

1.   número de adultos
2.   número de nietos
3.   cuántos años aproximadamente tiene cada persona

4.   los padres
5.   relaciones de familia entre los niños
6.   el perro y el gato

D. Una persona famosa. Describa Ud. a la clase una persona famosa. Sus compañeros tienen que adivinar (*guess*) la identidad de la persona.

1. ¿Cómo es?
2. ¿Dónde vive?
3. ¿Dónde trabaja?
4. ¿Gana mucho dinero?
5. ¿Es listo?
6. ¿Qué dicen los periódicos de él/ella?

MOTIVO CULTURAL

In the Hispanic culture, the concept of family includes not only parents and children but other relatives as well. It is not uncommon for grandparents and single aunts and uncles to share a household with a couple and their children. Family members feel a strong bond with each other and a sense of loyalty toward the group that proves very valuable in times of difficulty.

Today, however, many young people in small towns and rural areas are leaving home and moving to large cities in search of better job opportunities. Because of this, the nuclear family is becoming more and more common.

Traditionally, the Hispanic father has been the provider and the head of the household, while the wife's role has been to keep house and care for the children. These roles are also changing; very often, especially in large cities, both husband and wife work outside the home.

Vocabulario activo

Adjetivos

cada	each, every
casado/a	married
duro/a	hard
mayor	older
menor	younger
mono/a	cute
soltero/a	single

Sustantivos

LOS PARIENTES (*RELATIVES*)

el/la abuelo/a	grandfather/grandmother
el/la esposo/a	husband/wife
el/la hermano/a	brother/sister
el/la hijo/a	son/daughter
la madre	mother

el/la nieto/a	grandson/granddaughter
el/la niño/a	child; boy/girl
el padre	father
los padres	fathers; parents
el/la primo/a	cousin
el/la sobrino/a	nephew/niece
el/la tío/a	uncle/aunt

PARA COMER Y BEBER

la banana	banana
la comida	food; meal
la copa	wine glass
los cubiertos	silverware
la cuchara	spoon
la cucharita	teaspoon
el cuchillo	knife
la frutería	fruit stand, store
la jarra	pitcher
el mantel	tablecloth
la manzana	apple
el pan	bread
el plátano	banana
el plato	plate
la servilleta	napkin
la taza	cup
el tenedor	fork
el vaso	glass

LA TIENDA DE ANIMALES

el gatito	kitten
el gato	cat
el perrito	puppy
el perro	dog

OTROS SUSTANTIVOS

la escuela	school
el/la novio/a	boyfriend/girlfriend
el premio	prize
el rato	short time, little while
la sorpresa	surprise
el trabajo	work
la vida	life

Verbos

aprender	to learn
ayudar	to help

caminar	to walk
comprender	to understand
conocer	to know (be acquainted with)
llevar	to take; to carry
oír	to hear
poner	to put
saber	to know (*a fact, how to do something*)
salir	to leave, go out
traer	to bring
ver	to see

Otras palabras y expresiones

además	besides
casi	almost
después	afterward
hace buen/mal tiempo	the weather is good/bad
hace calor/fresco/frío/ sol/viento	it is hot/cool/cold/ sunny/windy
hazme un favor	do me a favor
llamar por teléfono	to call on the telephone
nada	nothing (anything)
para	for, in the direction of
por	through, in
por ejemplo	for example
¿Qué tienes?	What's wrong with you?
sacar buenas notas	to get good grades
siempre	always
tener _____ años	to be _____ years old
tener calor/frío/ hambre/sed/sueño	to be hot/cold/hungry/ thirsty/sleepy
tener cuidado	to be careful
tener ganas de + *infinitive*	to feel like (*doing something*)
tener miedo	to be afraid
tener prisa	to be in a hurry
tener que + *infinitive*	to have to (*do something*)
tener razón/no tener razón	to be right/to be wrong

La comida que me gusta

Las naranas están muy baratas en este mercado de frutas.

METAS

Comunicación: In this lesson you will learn vocabulary and expressions involving food and meals. You will use them to talk about food-related activities, including shopping for, preparing, and eating meals.

Estructuras: 21. The Preterite Tense 22. Irregular Preterites: **hacer, venir, dar, ir, ser** 23. Shortened Adjectives 24. **Por** and **para** Contrasted

GRÁFICOS

Frutas, legumbres, carnes y mariscos

Fruits, Vegetables, Meats, and Seafood

Las frutas

1. la piña
2. la sandía
3. las uvas
4. la pera
5. la naranja
6. el melocotón
7. la fresa

Las legumbres (hortalizas, verduras)*

8. la lechuga
9. el maíz
10. la papa, la patata
11. la cebolla

Expansion: Explain that fruits and vegetables are often referred to by different terms in different countries. For instance, *el melocotón* is called *el duranzo* in some countries, while string beans are called both *las judías verdes* and *las habichuelas.* Additional vocabulary: *la cereza, la toronja, el mango, la papaya; la calabacita, la remolacha, los pimientos; la sartén, la olla, la espátula, la licuadora.*

Otras legumbres

los frijoles *beans*
los guisantes *peas*
el pepino *cucumber*
el tomate *tomato*
la zanahoria *carrot*

Las carnes y los mariscos

el atún *tuna*
el bistec *steak*
los camarones *shrimp*
la carne de cerdo *pork*
la carne de cordero *lamb*

la carne (de res) *beef*
la chuleta *chop*
el pavo *turkey*
el pescado *fish*
el pollo *chicken*
el salmón *salmon*

Expansion A: ¿Qué ingredientes necesita Ud. para hacer... *tortillas?, sopa?*

Emphasis: Point out footnote, asking students to list the items that would fit into the stricter definitions of these categories.

Actividades

A. Recetas (*Recipes*) básicas. Complete.

1. Para hacer una buena ensalada (*salad*) es necesario comprar _____.
2. Para hacer una ensalada de frutas es necesario tener _____.
3. Los _____ son mariscos que usamos para hacer un coctel delicioso.
4. Cuando invito a mis amigos a comer en el verano, siempre preparo dos legumbres: _____ y _____.
5. La _____ es una fruta tropical.

*While **legumbres** may refer only to legumes (beans and so on) and **verduras** to greens, both, along with **hortalizas,** are often used generically to mean *vegetables*.

B. Preferencias. Conteste.

1. ¿Cuál le gusta más, la carne de cerdo o la carne de res? ¿el pescado o el pollo? ¿el atún? ¿el pavo? ¿el salmón?
2. ¿Cuántas veces come Ud. carne (pescado, pollo) cada semana?
3. ¿Cuáles son sus legumbres (frutas) favoritas?
4. ¿Cuál es el precio de una buena chuleta de cerdo (de cordero) ahora? ¿y de un buen bistec?
5. ¿Qué sándwiches prefiere: de atún, de pavo, de ensalada de pollo o un sándwich vegetariano?
6. ¿Qué ensaladas prefiere: de pollo, de camarones, de patatas, de atún o de legumbres?

C. Un juego (*game*). Describa una fruta o legumbre y un compañero (una compañera) adivina (*guesses*) qué fruta o legumbre es.

MODELO: Es muy larga y delgada y es de color naranja. →
¡Es una zanahoria!

Las compras de doña Rosa

◆ THE PRETERITE ◆

-ar: gastar	
gasté	*I spent*
gastaste	*you spent*
gastó	*you (he/she) spent*
comprar	
compré	*I bought*
compraste	*you bought*
compró	*you (he/she) bought*
tomar	
tomé	*I drank, took*
tomaste	*you drank, took*
tomó	*you (he/she) drank, took*
-er: comer	
comí	*I ate*
comiste	*you ate*
comió	*you (he/she) ate*
-ir: subir	
subí	*I went up*
subiste	*you went up*
subió	*you (he/she) went up*

1. la botella de aceite
2. el paquete de azúcar
3. la bolsa
4. la caja de cereal
5. el helado
6. la lata de sopa
7. el carrito (de las compras)
8. el paquete de harina

LOLI: ¡Hola, mamá! *¡Cuántas* bolsas traes!   *How many*

DOÑA ROSA: Sí, y gasté una *barbaridad* en el supermercado y en la tienda de   *a lot*
don Ramiro. *¡Ni me preguntes cuánto!* El precio de los *comestibles*   *Don't even ask how much! / food items*
subió mucho.

LOLI: Ah, ¡jugo de naranja! *¡Qué bueno!* Pepito tomó todo el jugo ayer.   *How nice!*

DOÑA ROSA: También compré una caja de cereal Pitufo, que te gusta, y helado
porque Pepito comió todo el helado de fresa *anoche.*   *last night*

LOLI: ¿Y qué más compraste? ¿Qué *cenamos* hoy?   *eat (for) dinner*

DOÑA ROSA: Compré varias latas de sopa, unas chuletas de cerdo, guisantes y
aceite. Voy a *cocinar* las chuletas *como* te gusta. ¡Ah! También   *cook / as*
traigo harina y azúcar para hacer un *postre* especial.   *dessert*

LOLI: ¿Por qué no haces plátanos *fritos**? Son el plato favorito de papá y   *fried*
son muy *ricos.*   *delicious*

Cultural expansion: In recent years, large supermarkets have become more and more popular in Hispanic world. In Mexico, *Gigante* is chain of immense supermarkets. *Aurerá* was one of first chains in Spain; now there are several others. As with clothing, Hispanics tend to spend high percentage of income on food.

Actividades

A. Las compras de doña Rosa. Usando la información del diálogo, haga el papel (*play the role*) de doña Rosa y describa sus compras. Su compañero/a de clase contesta como Loli.

DOÑA ROSA

1. jugo de naranja
2. una caja de cereal Pitufo
3. helado de fresa, porque...
4. chuletas de cerdo
5. como gustarte / también harina y azúcar, para...

LOLI

Pepito / ayer
gustarme
¿qué? / cenar
¿cómo? / cocinar
plátanos fritos / el plato...

Ahora, comente sobre los cuatro miembros de la familia de doña Rosa: Loli, Pepito, doña Rosa y el padre.

Suggestion A: Have students practice in pairs; later, several pairs present dialogue to class. Be sure to assign last part of activity; possible cues to write on board: *Loli → chuletas y Pitufo; Pepito → jugo de naranja y helado; el padre → plátanos fritos; doña Rosa → una barbaridad.*

Reminder: See the Instructor's Resource Kit for worksheets designed for pair work.

B. En el supermercado. ¿Qué recipiente (*container*) corresponde a las siguientes cosas? **Las posibilidades:** botella, lata, caja, paquete, bolsa

1. _____ de cereal
2. _____ de vino
3. _____ de sopa
4. _____ de aceite
5. _____ de azúcar
6. _____ de plástico
7. _____ de harina
8. _____ de helado

Variation B: State sentences including the wrong container. Students to correct. **1.** *una bolsa de vino* **2.** *una botella de cereal* **3.** *una lata de azúcar* **4.** *una caja de sopa* One student could create such sentences and another correct them.

C. Otro juego. *In groups of three, take turns asking each other questions and answering. Keep the round-robin conversation going as long as possible.*

MODELO: —¿Qué comiste ayer en el almuerzo (*lunch*)?
—Comí un sándwich de atún. ¿Y tú?

***Plátanos fritos** is a favorite dish in the Caribbean countries. It is made with a kind of large banana called a *plantain,* which, when ripe, is cut vertically into thick slices and deep fried.

¿Desayuno, almuerzo o cena?

Breakfast, Lunch, or Dinner?

◆ MORE REGULAR PRETERITES ◆

desayunar	
desayuné	*I ate breakfast*
desayunaste	*you ate breakfast*
desayunó	*you (he/she) ate breakfast*

salir	
salí	*I went out*
saliste	*you went out*
salió	*you (he/she) went out*

◆ IRREGULAR PRETERITES ◆

hacer	
hice	*I did, made*
hiciste	*you did, made*
hizo	*you (he/she) did, made*

ser; ir	
fui	*I was; I went*
fuiste	*you were; you went*
fue	*you were, (he/she/it) was; you (he/she/it) went*

1. el café con leche
2. los huevos
3. la mantequilla
4. los panecillos
5. la sal
6. la pimienta
7. las tostadas
8. la mermelada

Cultural expansion: It is common in large cities in Spain for people to snack in bars and cafés during day. They frequently prefer to eat breakfast at nearby café rather than at home and also have snack at 11:00 or 12:00 (coffee and roll or glass of wine and hors d'oeuvre) before midday meal and another in evening before dinner.

As pointed out in the footnote, the kind of breakfast Nicanor ate in this dialogue is not the norm in most Spanish-speaking countries.

RENATO: Sólo son las once, pero tengo mucha hambre.

NICANOR: ¿No desayunaste?

RENATO: Sí, desayuné. *Bueno, solamente* tomé café con leche. Casi siempre como un panecillo con mermelada por la mañana, pero mi madre *no hizo las compras* ayer y no *había* nada de comer en casa.

Well / only

didn't go shopping / there wasn't

NICANOR: Pues, *con razón* tienes hambre. Yo, esta mañana, salí de casa *temprano*, fui a la Cafetería Sanborns y comí huevos rancheros* con frijoles, tostadas con mantequilla, jamón, queso...†

no wonder

early

RENATO: ¡Hombre! Eso no fue un desayuno; ¡fue un gran almuerzo... o *más bien* una cena!

rather

Suggestion: Model pronunciation of preterite forms in *Gráficos*. Use brief game if you wish: Designate three sections of class as *yo*, *tú*, and *él*; ask following questions and point quickly to student who answers with person corresponding to his/her section. Model: *¿Quién desayunó temprano hoy?* (*tú/él/yo*)

Actividades

A. ¿Desayunó Ud.? En grupos de dos, contesten la pregunta de dos maneras.

1. Sí, tomé... y comí...

2. No, porque...

---

*Eggs with chili peppers and tomatoes
†Although Nicanor ate a heavy breakfast, this is not customary in most Hispanic countries. See the **Motivo cultural** on page 119.

Optional:
1. ¿Cuándo salió de casa Nicanor? 2. ¿Qué comió Renato? 3. ¿Adónde fue Nicanor? ¿Qué hizo allí? 4. ¿A qué hora desayunó Ud. esta mañana? 5. ¿A qué hora salió Ud. para la universidad?

B. Su desayuno favorito. Prepare oraciones para describir un desayuno especial que Ud. comió en un restaurante. ¿En qué restaurante? ¿A qué hora de la mañana? ¿Con quién(es) fue Ud. al restaurante? ¿Qué comió? ¿Qué tomó? ¿Cuánto costó? ¿Quién pagó?

C. ¿Qué ocurrió (*happened*) ayer en su casa? Conteste.

1. ¿Quiénes desayunaron en su casa? ¿A qué hora de la mañana?
2. ¿Tomaron café con leche o café solo?
3. ¿Comieron tostadas o panecillos? ¿con mantequilla o mermelada?
4. ¿Prepararon huevos rancheros? ¿frijoles y jamón?
5. ¿Quién hizo las compras? ¿Cuándo salió de casa? ¿Qué compró?

VISTA CULTURAL

La palabra **tortilla** tiene diferentes significados en distintos países del mundo hispano. En España, por ejemplo, la tortilla típica es de huevos y patatas. Generalmente los españoles comen la tortilla como (*as*) parte del almuerzo o de la cena, o sola, como merienda (*snack*). En México, la tortilla es un tipo de *pancake* hecho de (*made from*) harina de maíz. A

veces se come* con las comidas, como el pan, pero también se dobla* y se ponen* varios ingredientes en el centro.

---

*Note that the word **se** before the verb changes the verb's meaning slightly.

> **come** (*he/she/it*) *eats* → **se come** (*one thing*) *is eaten*
> **ponen** (*you/they*) *put* → **se ponen** (*two or more things*) *are put*

You will see this construction throughout *Motivos de conversación.* Learn to recognize it, for it is used frequently in Spanish.

Emphasis: Point out the footnote, adding any additional explanation necessary. This usage appears throughout *Motivos* and students need to be able to recognize it; they will not, however, be asked to produce this construction until it is formally presented.

ESTUDIO DE PALABRAS

Knowing all the words related to one basic form will greatly increase your vocabulary. Look at the following word families and try to guess what all the words mean. Can you conjugate all of them? Hint: Think of the English suffixes *-pose* and *-tain*.

poner

componer	proponer
deponer	disponer
oponer	suponer

tener

contener	obtener
detener	retener
mantener	sostener

Presentation: Explain that all these verbs are conjugated like *tener* and *poner*. Ask students at random to give forms for different persons in present tense. This will serve as review of *tener* and at same time facilitate use of new verbs in future.

GRAMÁTICA ESENCIAL

21. The Preterite Tense

Sí, y gasté una barbaridad en el supermercado y en la tienda de don Ramiro. ¡Ni me preguntes cuánto! El precio de los comestibles subió mucho.

There are two simple past tenses in Spanish: the preterite and the imperfect (presented in **Lección 8**). The preterite expresses a past action that had a definite beginning and end. The duration of the action is unimportant; the essential thing is that the action is viewed by the speaker as being over and done with. Compare the preterite and the present tense as shown below.

PRESENT		PRETERITE	
(yo) compro	*I buy,* *do buy,* *am buying*	(yo) compré	*I bought,* *did buy*
(él) escribe	*he writes,* *does write,* *is writing*	(él) escribió	*he wrote,* *did write*

Suggestion: Model pronunciation of all regular preterite forms; emphasize stress on the *yo* and *Ud.* forms.

In the **Gráficos** section of this lesson, you used the **yo, tú,** and **Ud.** (él/ella) preterite forms of some verbs. Here are the complete conjugations of **-ar, -er,** and **-ir** verbs in the preterite. Note that the preterite endings are added to the stem of the infinitive.

gastar (*to spend*)	correr (*to run*)	subir (*to go up*)
gasté	corrí	subí
gastaste	corriste	subiste
gastó	corrió	subió
gastamos	corrimos	subimos
gastasteis	corristeis	subisteis
gastaron	corrieron	subieron

As you can see, the preterite endings of **-er** and **-ir** verbs are the same. Note that the first person plural of **-ar** and **-ir** verbs (**gastamos, subimos**) has the same ending in both the preterite and the present; context generally reveals which tense is intended.

To preserve the original sound of the stem consonant, the first person singular (**yo**) preterite ending of certain verbs contains spelling changes.

practicar	c → qu	practico → practiqué
pagar	g → gu	pago → pagué
cruzar (*to cross*)	z → c	cruzo → crucé

Yet another kind of spelling change occurs in the preterite: When it appears between two vowels, the **i** of the third-person (**Ud., él/ella** and **Uds., ellos/as**) preterite ending changes to **y.**

corrió *and* corrieron   BUT   leyó *and* leyeron

Actividades

A. Un cuento (*story*). Complete en el pretérito según el modelo.

MODELO: yo / comer / en el hotel →
Yo comí en el hotel.

1. yo / decidir / salir / ayer por la tarde
2. yo / entrar / un restaurante nuevo para comer algo
3. yo / comer / bistec, patatas y muchas otras cosas
4. yo / beber / una copa de vino
5. yo / no salir / hasta (*until*) muy tarde

Now retell the "story" using these subjects: **mi madre y yo, ellas, Ud., tú.**

Expansion: Practice three verbs given in box with short questions and answers. Write basic sentence in each case on board: **1.** *Yo gasté 26 dólares ayer.* **a.** *¿Cuánto gasté?* **b.** *¿Cuándo gasté yo 26 dólares?* **c.** *¿Gastó esa cantidad (name of student)?* **2.** *Elvira corrió por la calle.* **a.** *¿Quién corrió?* **b.** *¿Por dónde corrió ella?* **c.** *¿Corrieron Uds. por la calle?* **3.** *Alberto, Juan y Ud. subieron en el ascensor.* **a.** *¿Cómo subió Alberto?* **b.** *¿Y cómo subieron Ud. y Juan?* **c.** *¿Cómo subimos nosotros?*

Listening practice: Read following sentences; students indicate whether verb is in present or preterite: **1.** *Llego temprano.* **2.** *Practico mucho.* **3.** *Comencé a comer a las dos.* **4.** *Llegué el lunes pasado.* **5.** *Leen todas las cartas.* **6.** *Yo pagué el café.* **7.** *No gastamos mucho.* **8.** *¿Por dónde corrió ella?* **9.** *Comemos a las tres hoy.*

B. Contradicciones. Ud. y un amigo (una amiga) hablan de los preparativos (*plans*) para el almuerzo. Ud. hace preguntas con las palabras de la columna izquierda; él o ella contesta en negativo con las palabras de la columna derecha.

MODELO: ver, jugo → ¿Viste jugo en el supermercado?
sólo vino y cerveza → No, sólo vi* vino y cerveza.

1. buscar, pollo	pescado
2. ver, tortillas	sólo huevos
3. comprar, arroz (*rice*) y frijoles	guisantes y lechuga
4. preparar, pan	pasteles
5. cocinar, chuletas	filetes

C. ¿Qué hicieron ayer? **Verbos posibles:** abrir, escribir, comprar, estudiar, comer, beber, entrar, pagar, llevar, mirar, leer, gastar, vender

1.  2.  3.  4.

22. Irregular Preterites: *hacer, venir, dar, ir, ser*

Casi siempre como un panecillo con mermelada por la mañana, pero mi madre no hizo las compras ayer y no había nada de comer en casa.

Suggestion: Model pronunciation of irregular preterite forms. Point out that *yo* and *Ud.* forms of irregular preterites are not stressed on last syllable, as are regulars.

---

*The first- and third-person singular forms of **ver** (**vi, vio**) do not have a written accent mark in the preterite.

Several common verbs do not follow the regular pattern for forming the preterite tense. However, these irregular preterites have certain features in common: none bears an accent on the final syllable, and all of them form the preterite on an irregular stem.

hacer: hice, hiciste, hizo, hicimos, hicisteis, hicieron
venir: vine, viniste, vino, vinimos, vinisteis, vinieron
dar: di, diste, dio, dimos, disteis, dieron
ir/ser: fui, fuiste, fue, fuimos, fuisteis, fueron

NOTE 1: The verb **dar,** a first-conjugation (**-ar**) verb, takes the preterite endings of **-er/-ir** verbs.

NOTE 2: The preterite of **ir** is exactly like the preterite of **ser.** In Spanish, *I went* and *I was* are both (**yo**) **fui.** The context will clarify which meaning is intended.

Review: Review regular preterite by handing a prop (pencil, dollar bill, etc.) to various students and posing series of questions: **1.** *¿Qué tomó él?* **2.** *¿Qué tomó Ud.?* **3.** *¿Y qué tomaste tú?* **4.** *¿Qué tomaron ellos?* **5.** *¿Qué tomaron Uds.?* **6.** *¿Qué tomasteis vosotros?* Continue with other verbs and props.

Optional: Rapid questions and answers: **1.** *¿Viniste ayer? (Vine ayer.)* **2.** *¿Fuiste esta mañana?* **3.** *¿Hizo Ud. el trabajo?* **4.** *¿Dieron Uds. una fiesta?* **5.** *¿Vinisteis temprano?* **6.** *¿Hicieron ellos mucho?* **7.** *¿Fuisteis todos?* **8.** *¿Fueron los profesores?*

Actividades

A. ¿Qué pasó en la fiesta? Conteste con el verbo en el pretérito según las indicaciones.

1. Alicia *dio* una fiesta el viernes pasado (*last*). (yo, tú, ellos)
2. Ana y Marcos *vinieron* a las 9:00. (Esteban, tú, nosotros)
3. Lucho *vino* más tarde. (yo, tú, Juana y María)
4. La abuela de Alicia *hizo* unas galletitas (*cookies*) deliciosas para la fiesta. (ellos, nosotras, yo)
5. Laura *hizo* una torta (*cake*) de limón. (Miguel y Pablo, Ud., tú)
6. Los otros *compraron* bombones de chocolate y helado. (el novio de Alicia, yo, mis abuelos)
7. Después de la fiesta, Miguel y yo *fuimos* a una discoteca. (la abuela de Alicia, mis amigos, Ud.)

B. Anoche en casa. Usando el pretérito, hágale las preguntas de la columna izquierda a su compañero/a. Él o ella contesta según las palabras de la columna derecha.

1. ¿qué / hacer / tú / anoche?
2. ¿qué / leer?
3. ¿qué / preparar / tú?
4. ¿quién / venir / a la cena?
5. ¿a qué hora / venir?
6. ¿quién / comer / todo el pollo?
7. ¿quién / preparar / el café?
8. ¿adónde / ir / Uds. / después de cenar?
9. ¿qué / hacer / Uds. / después?

yo / leer
un libro de cocina
yo / preparar / arroz con pollo
yo / invitar / a _____
venir / a las _____
_____ / comer / todo el pollo
_____ / preparar / el café
_____ ¿?
_____ ¿?

Suggestion A: For extra verb practice, cue students with these questions to reconstruct story in exercise A: **1.** *¿Qué hizo Ud. ayer?* **2.** *¿En dónde entró Ud. después?* **3.** *¿Qué comió y qué bebió?* **4.** *¿Cuándo salió Ud.?*

Oral transformation drill: Students rapidly change verbs to preterite: **1.** *Hago el café.* → *Hice...* **2.** *Vengo por la mañana.* → *Vine...* **3.** *Vamos al mercado.* → *Fuimos...* **4.** *Dan dinero a todos.* → *Dieron...* **5.** *Doy muchos regalos.* → *Di...* **6.** *Hacemos las preguntas.* → *Hicimos...* **7.** *¿Vienes con ellos?* → *¿Viniste... ?*

Optional: *Preguntas para hacerles a los otros.* Tell students to select five verbs from earlier lessons to form questions asking a classmate and you about your activities yesterday or last week.

Optional review: Read verbs quickly as students indicate on paper if form is present or preterite: **1.** *habló* **2.** *vio* **3.** *dan* **4.** *fue* **5.** *dieron* **6.** *pagué* **7.** *bebo* **8.** *saliste* **9.** *hace* **10.** *decimos* **11.** *tomó* **12.** *doy* **13.** *di* **14.** *veo* **15.** *tengo* **16.** *coméis* **17.** *termino* **18.** *hizo* **19.** *salió* **20.** *caminaron*

Suggestion B: Have students present brief speeches to class in which they explain what they did last night at home.

Follow-up: Dictation: 1. *Los niños cruzaron la calle solos.* **2.** *¿Por qué no fuiste tú con ellos?* **3.** *No llegué a casa hasta las tres.* **4.** *Pero ellos no salieron hasta las tres y media.*

23. Shortened Adjectives

¡Hombre! Eso no fue un desayuno; ¡fue un gran almuerzo... o más bien una cena!

The adjectives **bueno** and **malo** may precede or follow the noun. If they precede a masculine singular noun, they drop the final **-o.** This shortening does not take place with the feminine form.

un hombre malo (bueno)	*an evil (good) man*
una(s) amiga(s) buena(s)	*a (several) good friend(s)*
un mal (buen) hombre	*a bad (fine) man*
una(s) buena(s) amiga(s)	*a (several) close friend(s)*

Grande, which means *large* when it follows a noun, is shortened to **gran** when it precedes a noun; it then means *great* or *famous.*

Vivo en una casa grande.	*I live in a big house.*
Es una gran profesora.	*She is a great (famous) teacher.*

Ordinal numbers generally precede the nouns they modify and agree with them in gender and number. The first three ordinal numbers are **primero/a** (*first*), **segundo/a** (*second*), and **tercero/a** (*third*). **Primero** and **tercero** are shortened before a masculine singular noun: **el primer autobús, el tercer día.** Otherwise, these adjectives are not shortened: **la primera casa de la calle, los primeros números.**

Emphasis: Stress difference between *gran* and *grande*. Example: *un gran señor, un señor grande.*

Note: Because ordinal numbers are not presented until later in text, these three common ordinals are given here.

Actividades

Variation A: After students have gone over Exercise A, you can use it as a "Mad-lib." Call for different adjectives at random, then reread the passage with the new adjectives. It may make no sense but should garner some laughs.

A. Una cena inolvidable (*unforgettable*). Complete con una forma apropiada de **bueno, malo, grande, primero, segundo** o **tercero.**

La semana pasada (*last*) invité a unos ____[1] amigos a cenar en mi casa. Sólo vinieron tres, porque los otros saben que soy un cocinero (*cook*) muy ____.[2] Pero la verdad es que preparé una ____[3] cena. El ____[4] plato fue una sopa de albóndigas (*meatballs*), el ____[5] fue patatas fritas y pescado; y el ____[6] plato fue bistec. También compré un ____[7] vino blanco para el pescado y un vino tinto muy ____[8] para la carne.

B. Mi restaurante favorito. En grupos pequeños, describa una gran cena en su restaurante favorito. **Comentarios posibles:** ¿Adónde fue Ud. a cenar? ¿Con quién(es) fue? ¿Cuándo fue? ¿Cuál fue el primer plato que comió? ¿y el segundo? ¿Cuánto costó la cena? ¿Quién pagó?

MEMOPRÁCTICA

Study with a classmate whenever you can. Systematic teamwork has a variety of benefits. It keeps you on a regular study schedule and makes study a social event. It also helps with oral comprehension, one of the most difficult skills to master, since you and your partner can take turns reading sentences, paragraphs, and questions aloud. One of the most important benefits is that both of you have the opportunity to act as the instructor. When you begin to teach someone else, you really begin to teach yourself!

---

24. *Por* and *para* Contrasted

También traigo harina y azúcar para hacer un postre especial.

Por and **para** are both equivalents of English *for*, but they are not interchangeable. They also express several other English prepositions.

A.   Movement (**por**) versus destination (**para**)

por	*type of movement*
along, *down,* *by,* *around,* *through*	Camino **por** la calle. *I walk along (down) the street.*
	Siempre paseamos **por** el parque. *We always stroll around (in) the park.*
	Amalia entró **por** la puerta principal. *Amalia entered through the main door.*
para	*goal of movement*
for	Él sale **para** Lima mañana. *He leaves for Lima tomorrow.*

The following diagram illustrates the difference between **por** and **para** in the paragraph below.

Cuando iba para la casa de mi amigo, pasé por el supermercado y decidí entrar. Fui por los pasillos buscando diferentes cosas. Compré algunas y salí a la calle por la puerta principal. Iba de nuevo para la casa de mi amigo.

When I was going to my friend's house, I passed by the supermarket and decided to go in. I went along the aisles looking for different things. I bought some and went back outside through the main door. I was on the way to my friend's house again.

B. Duration of time (**por**) versus specific moment (**para**)

por *for, during*	*period of time* Va a estar en la ciudad **por** varios días. *He is going to be in the city for several days.*
para *for, by*	*point in time, deadline* Tengo que hacer el trabajo **para** el lunes. *I have to do the work by Monday.*

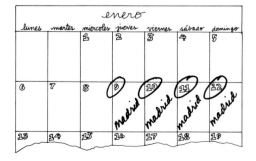

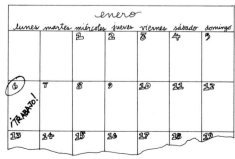

Va a estar en la ciudad por varios días.   Tengo que hacer el trabajo para el lunes.

C. Other uses of **para**

1. *For* (meant for someone; to be used for)

> Los uvas son **para** Silvia.   *The grapes are for Silvia.*
> Necesitamos copas **para** vino.   *We need wine glasses for the wine.*

2. *In order to* + infinitive*

> Es necesario cocinar mucho **para** ser un buen cocinero.   *It is necessary to cook a lot (in order) to be a good cook.*
> **Para** ir al restaurante Los Porches tengo que subir por la Calle Seis.   *(In order)† To go to the restaurant Los Porches I have to go up Sixth Street.*

3. *For* (considering / contrary to expectations)

> Este café está demasiado frío **para** mi gusto.   *This coffee is too cold for my taste.*
> Tú eres muy alto **para** un niño de diez años.   *You are very tall for a ten-year-old boy. (He's six feet tall.)*

D. Other uses of **por**

1. *For* (to indicate price or exchange)

> Pagué veinte mil pesos **por** esa cena.   *I paid 20,000 pesos for that dinner.*
> Compramos tres plátanos **por** un dólar.   *We bought three plantains for one dollar.*

2. *For* (to imply replacement)

> Hoy trabajo **por** mi padre.   *Today I'm working for (instead of, in place of) my father.*

3. *Because of, out of, for the sake of, on account of, on behalf of* (to explain the motivation behind an action)

> No dije nada **por** respeto a mi abuelo.   *I said nothing out of respect for my grandfather.*
> A veces los padres hacen sacrificios **por** sus hijos.   *Sometimes parents make sacrifices for their children.*
> Ellos están muy contentos **por** la invitación a comer.   *They are very happy on account of the invitation to dine.*

4. In expressions such as

> ¡Por Dios!   *For Heaven's sake!*
> por ejemplo   *for example*

---

*As with any preposition, the infinitive is the only verb form that can follow **para**.
†Note that although *in order* is sometimes omitted in English, **para** is never omitted in Spanish.

por eso	*for that reason*
por favor	*please*
por fin	*finally*
por la mañana (la tarde, la noche)	*in the morning (the afternoon, the evening)*
por supuesto	*of course*
por teléfono	*by (on the) telephone*

Actividades

A.   **¿Por o para?** *Tell whether the italicized word(s) would be **por, para,** or an expression with **por**. Do not translate the sentences.*

1. *At night* she always enters the restaurant *by* the back door.
2. She is working *for* the cook since he's sick.
3. She came early *in order to* consult him.
4. *Please* buy these fresh vegetables *for* our lunch.
5. She was walking *along* the long road.
6. He's a very good cook *for* a beginner.
7. The telegram *for* him *finally* arrived at three.
8. *For heaven's sake!* He ran out *through* the main door.
9. I wouldn't give him ten cents *for* his luck today.
10. When I spoke to him *on the phone,* I told him that rest is good *for* his illness.

B.   Lo que (*What*) mis padres hacen por mí. **¿Por o para?**

Mis padres siempre hacen mucho _____¹ mí. _____² ejemplo, mañana ellos salen _____³ la Ciudad de México donde van a estar _____⁴ dos semanas, y hoy _____⁵ la tarde mi madre va a ir al supermercado _____⁶ comprarme (*buy me*) comida. Ellos saben que cuando yo estoy solo (*alone*), no como muy bien, y _____⁷ eso, mi madre va a comprarme muchas legumbres. Ella cree (*believes*) que las legumbres son esenciales _____⁸ comer bien. _____⁹ supuesto, yo prefiero comer hamburguesas y papas fritas, pero voy a comer legumbres _____¹⁰ ella.

C.   Asociaciones lógicas. Complete con un sustantivo (*noun*) o infinitivo.

El tiempo

1. Hace demasiado frío para...
2. Hace demasiado calor para...
3. Hace mucho viento para...

En la sala de clase

4. Es necesario ser inteligente para...
5. Repita, por...
6. Ella es demasiado lista para...

De compras

7. ¿Cuánto pagaste por... ?
8. Ella compró un regalo para...
9. Rosita volvió a su casa por...

Sentimientos (*Feelings*)

10. Estoy contento/a por...
11. A veces digo esas cosas por...
12. Ramírez hizo algo heroico. Dio su vida por...

Pan de fibras. Tipo pistola, elaborado con harina, agua, levadura, masa madre y harina de fibras.

Pan de aceite. Redondo, pan dulce para meriendas o desayunos, elaborado con harina, agua, levadura, sal, azúcar, anises, aceite de oliva, pasas, huevos y ajonjolí.

Pan chapata. Plano, rectangular, elaborado con harina, agua, sal, levadura y masa madre.

Pan de leña. Pistola, elaborado con harina, sal, agua, levadura, y masa madre.

Pan payés. Redondo, elaborado con harina, agua, sal, levadura y masa madre.

Pan de rosca candeal. Redondo, elaborado con harina, agua, sal, levadura, masa madre (esta masa se refina mucho).

Pan estrella. Redondo, elaborado con harina, agua, sal, levadura, masa madre (masa candeal)

Pan rústico. Redondo, elaborado con harina, agua, sal, levadura y masa madre.

Pan inglés. Molde, elaborado con harina, agua, levadura y harina de fibras.

Pan integral de trigo. Molde, elaborado con harina integral, trigo prensado, harina de salvado, sal, levadura, agua y masa madre.

Para resumir y repasar

A. En persona: Al supermercado. Ayer Ud. decidió ir de compras porque sus compañeros de apartamento no fueron la semana pasada. Por supuesto, a la hora de salir para el supermercado, sus compañeros de apartamento decidieron que ellos también necesitaban (*needed*) varias cosas para la cena que preparan para unos amigos hoy. Primero haga una lista de todas las cosas que Ud. compró. Después, explíquele la situación a un compañero (una compañera) y dígale:

1. qué compró
2. qué tipo de comida es cada cosa (fruta, legumbre, carne o marisco)
3. para quién compró el/la...
4. en qué plato va a usar el/la...
5. cuánto costó

B. Modismos. Invente oraciones originales con las palabras siguientes.

hacer

1. enero / Alaska
2. mayo / Acapulco
3. octubre / Chicago
4. agosto / Los Ángeles
5. diciembre / San Antonio

tener

6. Llevo un suéter y una chaqueta porque...
7. Voy a comer un sándwich porque...
8. ¡No soy viejo/a! Sólo...
9. Tengo un examen muy importante mañana. Por eso,...
10. Necesito agua ahora porque...

Optional: You may want to assign this outside work to some students. *Informes meteorológicos. Oscar Clavín es de Buenos Aires, Argentina; Mercedes Marcet es de Madrid, España, y Guillermo Narváez es de Managua, Nicaragua. Busque la sección meteorológica internacional de su periódico y diga qué tiempo hace en cada lugar y qué ropa deben llevar los tres.*

C. Una cena para su madre. Hoy viene su madre a comer y Ud. necesita la ayuda de su esposo/a. Use mandatos familiares afirmativos. *Can you add suggestions of your own at the end?*

1. salir de casa a las cinco de la tarde
2. ir a la tienda de don Ramiro
3. comprar azúcar y plátanos
4. decirle a don Ramiro que necesitas plátanos y no bananas
5. traer todas las compras a casa rápidamente
6. abrir una lata de leche condensada
7. leer las instrucciones de la receta (*recipe*)
8. hacer...
9. ...
10. ...

COMUNICACIÓN

La comida en familia es una ocasión importante en todo el mundo hispánico. —¿No quieres más?

Texto: Una típica comida española

Mi amigo Ramón vive con su familia en la Moncloa,* y *yo paso* a veces por su casa. Ayer por la tarde, cuando pasé, vi a su madre en el balcón. Conversamos y *me invitó* a comer con ellos. Acepté muy contento, porque la señora es una *cocinera* excelente.

5   El primer plato fue una sopa de pescado y *luego* vino una tortilla española. Un *arroz* con pollo suculento fue el plato principal. *Sirvieron* la ensalada de lechuga y tomate después del plato principal y no *al principio*, como en los Estados Unidos. Comimos mucho pan, pero no vi mantequilla en la mesa. Por supuesto, no bebimos agua: los padres de Ramón tomaron vino blanco y los

10   jóvenes tomamos una *sangría* que preparó mi amigo. Y de postre, la madre hizo un *flan* delicioso. *Al final*, bebimos café.

Me gustó mucho esta cena con la familia de Ramón. Voy a pasar por su casa todos los días—¡y espero ver siempre a su madre en el balcón!

I pass

she invited me
cook
afterward
rice / They served
at the beginning

wine and fruit punch
custard / At the end

---

*The Moncloa district is located in northwestern Madrid and encompasses the university campus. This section of the city is known for its boulevards, parks, and promenades.

Hablando del texto. Describa el menú en casa de Ramón.

1. El primer plato...
2. Luego,...
3. El plato principal...
4. Después del plato principal,...
5. Los padres bebieron...
6. Los jóvenes bebieron...
7. De postre...
8. Al final...

De la vida real

¡Buenos días, desayuno!

Tus hábitos cambian,[a] mejoran.[b] Nuevas y saludables[c] costumbres como hacer deporte[d] o vigilar el peso[e] forman ya parte de tu vida diaria. Pero... ¿y el desayuno?

Un buen desayuno es el primer ejercicio que debes[f] practicar cada día. Y es, precisamente, lo que no hacemos la mayoría de los españoles. Desayunamos poco y mal. Olvidamos[g] que el desayuno es una comida tan importante como las demás[h] y que de los primeros alimentos que tomemos depende la energía de todo el día.

Por ello, Nestlé ha editado[i] el libro «¡Buenos días, desayuno!» con informaciones, consejos y sugerencias para que el desayuno ocupe el lugar que le corresponde[j] en la alimentación.

Verás[k] qué fácil es poner en práctica la sana[l] costumbre de desayunar bien.

[a] *change*
[b] *improve*
[c] *healthy*
[d] hacer... *to play sports*
[e] vigilar... *to watch one's weight*
[f] *you should*
[g] *We forget*
[h] tan... *as important as the others (meals)*
[i] ha... *has published*
[j] para... *so that breakfast occupies its proper place*
[k] *You will see*
[l] *healthy*

¡Buenos días, desayuno!

A. ¡Buenos días, desayuno! Primero lea rápidamente el anuncio y haga una lista de todos los cognados.

¿Encontró los siguientes cognados: hábitos, costumbres, forman, parte, diaria, ejercicio, practicar, precisamente, mayoría, energía, informaciones, ocupe?

Ahora lea el anuncio, buscando la información necesaria para contestar las preguntas.

1. ¿A quién(es) se dirige el anuncio? (*Whom does the ad address?*) ¿Qué formas de verbo usa el anuncio? ¿Por qué?
2. Según el anuncio, ¿cómo cambian los hábitos de la gente que lee el anuncio?
3. ¿Cuáles son las nuevas costumbres que menciona el anuncio? ¿De qué forman parte?
4. ¿A qué actividad compara el desayuno el anuncio? ¿Por qué?
5. ¿Cómo desayuna la mayoría de los españoles? ¿Qué forma de verbo usa el anuncio en esta oración? ¿Por qué?
6. Según el anuncio, ¿es muy importante el desayuno? ¿Por qué?
7. ¿Qué ha editado Nestlé? ¿Cómo se llama? ¿Qué contiene?
8. Según el anuncio, ¿es fácil cambiar las costumbres?

B. Preguntas personales.

1. ¿Tiene Ud. la costumbre de tomar un buen desayuno? ¿En qué consiste, generalmente, su desayuno?
2. ¿Piensa Ud. que es importante tomar un buen desayuno?
3. ¿Tiene Ud. costumbres saludables? ¿Cuáles son?
4. ¿Es fácil para Ud. cambiar las costumbres?

Para conversar más

A. Su dieta. Hágale estas preguntas a un compañero (una compañera) de clase. Él o ella tiene que inventar respuestas cómicas, si es posible.

1. ¿Qué tomaste en el desayuno/el almuerzo/la cena ayer?
2. ¿Qué legumbres/carnes/frutas te gustan especialmente?
3. ¿En qué plato pones mucho/a azúcar/sal/aceite, generalmente?
4. ¿Cuándo necesitas mucho/a pimienta/helado/mantequilla, por lo general?

Suggestion B: Have pairs of students present their dialogues to class.

B. Teatro. Invente diálogos con varios compañeros.

1. You are a grocer. A little girl or boy comes into your store and asks for a few things, but does not have enough money to pay for it all. A customer who knows the family explains the child's situation, trying to be understanding.
2. You are eating in a restaurant. Your waiter or waitress is not very efficient. You ask for _____, but she or he does not seem to understand and offers various excuses. Expand the conversation as far as your vocabulary will permit.

Motivo cultural

Meals in Hispanic countries can differ significantly from meals in the United States, both in what they consist of and when they are eaten. Breakfast, whether eaten at home or out, is usually simple: coffee with milk and a bun or some crackers, with or without marmalade. Lunch (**el almuerzo** or **la comida**) is the most important meal of the day. It is usually served between 2:00 and 3:00 p.m. in Spain and around 1:00 p.m. in Spanish America. Supper (**la cena**) is generally lighter and is served much later than it is in the United States. In Spain, dinnertime can be as late as 10:00 p.m., although in Spanish America it is usually between 7:00 and 8:00 p.m., depending on the country and whether the locale is rural or urban.

Restaurant menus in Spanish America feature many tasty na-

tional dishes, including **cazuela,** a kind of stew; **empanadas,** meat pies; and **ceviche,** raw fish marinated in lemon juice. As you probably know, Mexican food can be very spicy: when ordering at a restaurant in Mexico, ask if the food contains **ají** or **chile** (*hot chile peppers*). Of course, one of the things you will not want to miss in Spain is the famous **paella valenciana,** a rice dish containing seafood and sometimes chicken or pork.

Cultural expansion: While single-plate meals are available (*platos combinados*), the usual pattern of dining in Hispanic countries calls for a *primer plato* (soup or vegetables), *segundo plato* (meat or fish with vegetables), salad (served with the meal, not before, as in the U.S.), dessert (frequently fruit), and coffee. Americans have the erroneous impression that Hispanic food is very spicy. This is only true of Mexican food. The cuisine of Spain, for instance, is one of the world's best-kept secrets. It is extremely varied, not spicy, puts a premium on freshness, and often includes fruit. Olive oil is preferred to butter for food preparation, an important reason for relatively low cholesterol level among Spaniards.

Vocabulario activo

Adjetivos

frito/a	fried
primero/a	first
rico/a	delicious
segundo/a	second
tercero/a	third

Sustantivos

LAS FRUTAS

la fresa	strawberry
el melocotón	peach
la naranja	orange
la pera	pear
la piña	pineapple
la sandía	watermelon
la uva	grape

LAS LEGUMBRES (HORTALIZAS, VERDURAS) (*VEGETABLES*)

la cebolla	onion
los frijoles	beans
el guisante	pea
la lechuga	lettuce
el maíz	corn
la papa, la patata	potato
el pepino	cucumber

el tomate	tomato
la zanahoria	carrot

LAS CARNES Y LOS MARISCOS (*MEATS AND SEAFOOD [SHELLFISH]*)

el atún	tuna
el bistec	steak
el camarón	shrimp
la carne de cerdo	pork
la carne de cordero	lamb
la carne (de res)	beef
la chuleta	chop
el pavo	turkey
el pescado	fish
el pollo	chicken
el salmón	salmon

LOS RECIPIENTES (*CONTAINERS*)

la bolsa	shopping bag
la botella	bottle
la caja	box
la lata	can
el paquete	package

OTROS SUSTANTIVOS

el aceite	oil
el almuerzo	dinner/lunch
el arroz	rice
el azúcar	sugar
el café con leche	coffee with milk
el café solo	black coffee
el carrito (de las compras)	shopping cart
la cena	dinner/supper
el cereal	cereal
los comestibles	food items, provisions
el desayuno	breakfast
la ensalada	salad
la harina	flour
el helado	ice cream
el huevo	egg

la mantequilla	butter
la mermelada	jam; marmalade
el panecillo	roll
la pimienta	pepper
el postre	dessert
la sal	salt
la sopa	soup
el supermercado	supermarket
la tostada	toast

Verbos

cenar	to have dinner
cocinar	to cook
cruzar	to cross
desayunar	to eat breakfast
subir	to go up

Otras palabras y expresiones

anoche	last night
bueno	well
como	as
con razón	no wonder
¡cuántos/as!	how many!
demasiado/a	too; too much
hacer las compras	to go shopping
más bien	rather
¡Por Dios!	For Heaven's sake!
por ejemplo	for example
por eso	for that reason
por favor	please
por fin	finally
por supuesto	of course
por teléfono	by (on the) telephone
¡Qué bueno!	How nice!
solamente	only
temprano	early

LECCIÓN 6

Mi casa

Hermosos balcones con flores en un edificio de apartamentos en Renaca, Chile.

METAS

Comunicación: In this lesson you will learn vocabulary and expressions related to your furniture and your house. You will talk about the different activities you do there, including getting along with your roommate and cleaning house. You'll give some orders—and even take a few!

Estructuras: 25. Irregular Preterites: **decir, traer, poner, saber, estar, tener** 26. Polite Commands; Negative Familiar Commands 27. Demonstrative Adjectives and Pronouns

GRÁFICOS

Las habitaciones

Las habitaciones*

A. la sala
B. el comedor
C. la cocina
D. el dormitorio
E. el cuarto de baño

Componentes y aparatos

1. la cocina (eléctrica/de gas)
2. el horno
3. el fregadero
4. el lavaplatos
5. el refrigerador
6. el ropero
7. el televisor
8. la bañera
9. el lavabo
10. el inodoro

Presentation: Model repeatedly the correct pronunciation of new words, since students will tend to pronounce some like their English counterparts: *refrigerador, televisión, teléfono, dormitorio.*

Actividades de la casa

apagar *to turn off*
cenar *to eat dinner/supper*
cocinar *to cook*
descansar *to rest*
limpiar *to clean*
llamar por teléfono *to call/phone*
mirar la televisión *to watch TV*
prender *to turn on*

Clarification: Point out that *televisor* refers to the set and *televisión* to the medium. When referring to watching a program, *televisión* is used.

Note: Students will learn *encender* along with other stem-changing verbs in *Lección 7.*

Actividades

A. ¿Cierto o falso? Corrija (*Correct*) las oraciones falsas.

1. Cocinamos en el lavabo.
2. Hay cocinas eléctricas y cocinas de gas.
3. Generalmente la leche está en el ropero.
4. Apagamos el refrigerador por la noche.
5. Freímos (*We fry*) huevos en el horno.
6. Lavamos los platos en el inodoro.

Emphasis: Point out information in footnote, explaining that *alcoba* corresponds to the English "alcove" and tends to be somewhat smaller than a *dormitorio* or *habitación.*

Expansion: Have students associate the words in A with those in B. Duplicate and distribute or write on the board. Then have students use verbs in complete sentences.

A	B
1. cocinar	a. televisor
2. llamar	b. teléfono
3. prender	c. cocina
4. limpiar	d. aspiradora
5. apagar	e. fregadero
	f. cena
	g. dormitorio
	h. el lavaplatos

*__Habitación__ and __cuarto__ can mean either *room* or *bedroom*. Other words for bedroom are __dormitorio, recámara__—used in Mexico—and __alcoba.__

Variation B: To lend more structure to Exercise B, write on board rooms of a house and several verbs: *el dormitorio / la cocina / el comedor / la sala — cocinar / comer / mirar la televisión / descansar.* Students in small groups list the different pieces of furniture, what room they are usually in, and what they are used for.

7. Prendemos el televisor para mirar la televisión.
8. Tomamos un baño en la bañera.
9. Cocinamos en el dormitorio.
10. Descansamos en el cuarto de baño.

B. Muebles (*Furniture*), componentes y aparatos. Nombre los muebles, componentes y aparatos de las diferentes habitaciones de su propia (*own*) casa y las actividades que Ud. asocia con ellos.

El sueño de María

 María's dream

◆ POLITE COMMANDS ◆

-ar:		
lavar	¡(no) lave(n)!	(*don't*) *wash!*
limpiar	¡(no) limpie(n)!	(*don't*) *clean!*
pasar	¡(no) pase(n)!	(*don't*) *pass!*
-er:		
barrer	¡(no) barra(n)!	(*don't*) *sweep!*
leer	¡(no) lea(n)!	(*don't*) *read!*
-ir:		
abrir	¡(no) abra(n)!	(*don't*) *open!*
decir	¡(no) diga(n)!	(*don't*) *say!*

Note: Explain that command construction *a* + infinitive (*¡A despertar!*) can be used with any infinitive: *¡A trabajar!* (Get to work! or Let's get to work!), *¡A estudiar!, ¡A leer!*, etc.

◆ IRREGULAR PRETERITES ◆

estar:	
estuve	*I was*
estuviste	*you were*
estuvo	*you were (he/she was)*
poner:	
puse	*I put*
pusiste	*you put*
puso	*you (he/she) put*

1. la alfombra
2. la aspiradora
3. el sillón
4. el sofá
5. el teléfono
6. la escoba
7. la mesa de centro

PEPA: *Lo siento,* señora. No vine ayer porque estuve enferma.
MARÍA: Está bien, Pepa, pero ahora, mientras yo leo, por favor, abra las ventanas, *pase la aspiradora* por la alfombra y limpie el *cristal* de la mesa de centro y los otros *muebles.*
PEPA: Muy bien, señora. *¿Algo más?*
MARÍA: Sí. *Ahí* está la escoba. Barra la cocina, por favor. Ah, y si *alguien llama por teléfono,* diga que *no estoy en casa.*
LA MADRE: María, *¡escucha!* ¿Qué haces? *¡A despertar!* ¿*Crees* que eres una gran *dama?* Pues bien, «señora», no lea más y, por favor, lave Ud. los platos *sucios* que puse en el fregadero esta mañana y (*gritando*) que *todavía* están allí.

I'm sorry

Note: Point out the idiom *pasar la aspiradora* (to vacuum) in the dialogue.

vacuum / glass

(pieces of) furniture

Anything else?

There / someone

calls on the phone / I'm not at home

listen! / Wake up! / Do you think

lady

dirty / shouting

still

MEMOPRÁCTICA

Try to use as many methods as possible to learn vocabulary. Say the words aloud, write them down, copy them onto flash cards for rapid recognition, have a friend say them to you, listen to them on tape and record them yourself. In addition, try to pantomime and visualize actions that involve them. By expanding your study techniques you'll find it easier to remember new vocabulary.

Memopráctica: Have students tell how they memorize words and how much time they are studying outside class. Encourage everyone to study sufficiently and efficiently.

Remind students that short, intensive study sessions at frequent intervals generally produce better results than long, infrequent sessions.

Actividades

Optional: In small groups, have a student leader (with answers) cue others to give affirmative informal commands.
MODELO: *poner →*
Pon la leche en
el refrigerador.
1. *abrir (Abre...)* **2.** *pasar (Pasa...)* **3.** *limpiar (Limpia...)* **4.** *lavar (Lava...)* **5.** *llamar (Llama...)* **6.** *barrer (Barre...)*

A. Su sueño. *Using appropriate verb forms, tell your "dream servant" (a classmate) to do something involving these words and phrases.*

> MODELO: cuarto de baño →
> Por favor, limpie el cuarto de baño primero.

1. las ventanas
2. la aspiradora
3. los platos sucios
4. «que no estoy en casa»
5. el cristal de la mesa de centro
6. la cocina

B. En casa (*At home*). Pregúntele a un compañero (una compañera) de clase.

1. ¿Cuántos/as teléfonos/televisores/habitaciones/aspiradoras hay en tu casa?
2. ¿Dónde tienes un sofá/una alfombra/un sillón?
3. ¿Qué trabajos domésticos haces en tu casa? (barrer/lavar/limpiar/pasar...)
4. ¿Te gusta cocinar? ¿Qué cocinas?
5. ¿Cuándo vas al mercado/supermercado? ¿Qué compras allí?
6. ¿Qué apagas por la noche?
7. ¿Dónde pones tu ropa/la comida/los platos?
8. ¿A qué hora cenas/desayunas?
9. ¿Llamas mucho por teléfono? ¿Tienes un teléfono en tu dormitorio?

Expansion C: Have students repeat the rooms, adding different items.

C. Los muebles y aparatos nuevos. Ud. y su amigo/a fueron de compras ayer y compraron varias cosas nuevas para su casa o apartamento. Diga qué cosas nuevas puso Ud. en las habitaciones indicadas. Luego diga también qué cosas puso su amigo/a en las habitaciones de su casa.

> MODELOS: sala →
> Puse una alfombra nueva en la sala.
> Mi amigo/a puso un sofá nuevo en la sala.

1. cocina
2. dormitorio
3. cuarto de baño
4. comedor
5. sala

Compañeros de cuarto

1. la cama
2. la mesa de noche
3. la cómoda
4. la lámpara
5. la máquina de escribir
6. el estante
7. el escritorio

◆ DEMONSTRATIVE ADJECTIVES ◆

	Masculine	*Feminine*
this	este	esta
these	estos	estas
that	ese	esa
those	esos	esas
that	aquel	aquella
those	aquellos	aquellas

◆ MORE IRREGULAR PRETERITES ◆

saber:

supe	*I knew; found out**
supiste	*you knew; found out*
supo	*you (he/she) knew; found out*

traer:

traje	*I brought*
trajiste	*you brought*
trajo	*you (he/she) brought*

decir:

dije	*I said*
dijiste	*you said*
dijo	*you (he/she) said*

Andrés *llega* a su cuarto y habla con Pepe.

ANDRÉS: Lo siento, pero necesito usar el escritorio esta noche. No fui a clase el lunes y no supe *hasta* hoy que tengo que leer este libro para mañana.

PEPE: Pero, Andrés, traje esta máquina de escribir de la universidad para *terminar* mi reporte. Es para aquel profesor *tan exigente* que dijo que no va a aceptar los reportes después de mañana. ¿Por qué no lees en tu cama? La lámpara de la mesa de noche tiene una *bombilla* potente y da muy buena *luz*.

ANDRÉS: De acuerdo, pero primero tienes que ayudarme a poner todos esos libros en el estante.

arrives

until

to finish / so demanding

lightbulb

light

Dialogue follow-up: Ask orally: **1.** *¿Quién está usando la máquina de escribir?* **2.** *¿Qué tiene que hacer Andrés?* **3.** *¿Qué necesita usar él?* **4.** *¿Qué tiene que terminar Pepe?* **5.** *¿Para quién es el reporte?* **6.** *¿Qué hay en la mesa de noche?*

Emphasis: Point out special meaning of *saber* in the preterite, as presented in footnote.

*Although the infinitive **saber** means *to know,* in the preterite it conveys the idea of finding (something) out.

Actividades

A.   Compañeros de cuarto. Complete las conversaciones con un compañero (una compañera) de clase.

1.   Andrés, ¿por qué necesitas usar el escritorio? (Tengo que...)
2.   Andrés, ¿por qué no leíste el libro antes? (Porque...)
3.   Pepe, ¿para qué trajiste la máquina de escribir? (Para...)
4.   Pepe, ¿qué dijo tu profesor? ¿Cómo es él? (...)
5.   Pepe, ¿por qué da buena luz la lámpara de la mesa de noche? (Porque...)

Variation B: Do as interview between two students.

B.   ¿Qué cree Ud. de su compañero/a de cuarto? Conteste las preguntas.

1.   ¿Supo Ud. algún detalle (*any details*) sobre su compañero/a de cuarto antes de (*before*) vivir con él/ella? ¿Cuáles?
2.   ¿Siempre pone él/ella su ropa en el ropero o la cómoda?
3.   ¿Usa las cosas de Ud. con frecuencia?
4.   ¿Siempre hace la cama? ¿Hizo la cama hoy?
5.   ¿Pone sus libros en el estante de Ud.?
6.   ¿Tiene mucha prisa, generalmente? ¿Por qué?
7.   ¿Trajo su propia (*own*) máquina de escribir o usa la máquina de Ud.?
8.   ¿Termina sus reportes a tiempo (*on time*)?
9.   ¿Qué tiene en su mesa de noche?
10.   ¿Cuándo llega a casa generalmente?

Note: Explain that *para afuera* indicates more openness to the outside world and that *para adentro* reveals a more private attitude. This latter approach, for security, modesty, or whatever reason, is the more traditional Hispanic attitude towards one's home.

VISTA CULTURAL

En los países hispánicos, como en los Estados Unidos, hay muchos tipos de casas, pero el concepto hispánico de «la casa» es un poco distinto del concepto norteamericano. Tradicionalmente, el español—o el mexicano o el argentino—no vive para fuera (*outside*), sino (*but rather*) para dentro (*inside*). En otras palabras, el interior es privado, no se ve de la calle. Muchas casas hispánicas tienen tapias (*walls*) a su alrededor (*surrounding them*) y rejas (*grilles*) en las ventanas. En el interior de la casa hay espacios abiertos como el bonito patio español de esta foto.

GRAMÁTICA ESENCIAL

25. Irregular Preterites: *decir, traer, poner, saber, estar, tener*

Pero, Andrés, traje esta máquina de escribir de la universidad para terminar mi reporte.

You have already learned the irregular preterite forms of **hacer, venir, dar, ir,** and **ser.** The following verbs are also irregular in the preterite: they bear no accent on the final syllable, and form the preterite on an irregular stem. They have been grouped according to the dominant letter in their preterite forms, to facilitate your memorization of them.

-j- { **decir:** dije, dijiste, dijo, dijimos, dijisteis, dijeron
traer: traje, trajiste, trajo, trajimos, trajisteis, trajeron

-u- { **poner:** puse, pusiste, puso, pusimos, pusisteis, pusieron
saber: supe, supiste, supo, supimos, supisteis, supieron
estar: estuve, estuviste, estuvo, estuvimos, estuvisteis, estuvieron
tener: tuve, tuviste, tuvo, tuvimos, tuvisteis, tuvieron

NOTE: There is no **i** in the endings of **dijeron** and **trajeron.**

Presentation: Explain that dominant letters (*j* and *u*) listed to left of verbs are offered as a memory aid. Note that designating *j* and *u* dominant letters is somewhat arbitrary; the intent is to facilitate students' memorization of these difficult forms. Also point out that *yo* and *Ud.* forms aren't accented on the last vowel, unlike regular preterites, and that all these irregular verbs take the same endings.

Initial oral drill: Students change to preterite: **1.** *digo* **2.** *tenemos* **3.** *están* **4.** *pongo* **5.** *traes* **6.** *decimos* **7.** *sé* **8.** *ponen* **9.** *está*

Actividades

A.   Viajes (*Trips*) y visitas. Complete según los modelos.

MODELO: Cuando (yo) <u>estuve</u> en Colombia, <u>hice muchas excursiones</u>.

1.   Cuando nosotros _____ en el Perú, _____.
2.   Cuando Uds. _____ en la Argentina, _____.
3.   Cuando ella _____ en el Brasil, _____.

Suggestion: Ask following questions with aid of prop: **1.** *¿Dónde puse el libro?* (Put a book on a desk.) **2.** *¿Qué puse allí?* **3.** *¿Es de Ud. el libro?* **4.** *¿No trajo Ud. el libro a clase?* **5.** *¿Qué dijo Ud.?*

Optional questions: 1. *¿Dónde estuvo anoche? ¿Con quién?* **2.** *¿Qué tuvo que hacer ayer? ¿A qué hora?* **3.** *¿Qué trajo a clase hoy?* **4.** *¿Cuántos hijos tuvieron sus padres?* **5.** *¿Qué hizo el año pasado en sus vacaciones?*

Reminder: Refer to Student Dyad Program in Instructor's Resource Kit for worksheets offering automatic drills for pair work.

MODELO: Ellos __vinieron__ por la tarde y __pusieron el coche en el garaje__ .

4. Nosotros _____ anoche y _____.
5. Vosotros _____ ayer y _____.
6. Tú _____ por la tarde y _____.

MODELO: Él dijo eso, y yo __tuve que contestar__ .

7. Ellas _____ eso, y tú _____.
8. Yo _____ eso, y Uds. _____.
9. Nosotras _____ eso, y vosotras _____.

MODELO: Ellas no __trajeron__ la aspiradora y yo __tuve que comprar una__ .

10. Él no _____ la lámpara y nosotros _____.
11. Tú no _____ la escoba y él _____.
12. Nosotros no _____ el teléfono y ellas _____.

MODELO: _____Supe_____ ayer que __estuviste__ enfermo.

13. Luisa _____ el domingo que vosotros _____ enfermos.
14. ¿(Tú) _____ el martes que yo _____ enfermo/a?
15. ¿(Vosotros) _____ ayer que nosotros _____ enfermos?

B. Una mañana de mala suerte (*luck*). Complete las oraciones lógicamente usando el pretérito.

1. 7:00 / yo / no venir...
2. 8:00 / tú / no decir...
3. 9:00 / él / no tener...
4. 10:00 / Uds. / no estar...
5. 11:00 / yo / no traer...
6. 12:00 / Uds. / no saber...

C. Un sueño. En grupos de tres, digan, por turno y en el pretérito, lo que le ocurrió a una persona en un sueño reciente. **Posibles expresiones:** estar en... , tener que... , saber... , etcétera

26. Polite Commands; Negative Familiar Commands

Está bien, Pepa, pero ahora, mientras yo leo, por favor, abra las ventanas, pase la aspiradora por la alfombra, y limpie...

A. Polite (formal) singular commands are formed by dropping the **-o** of the first-person singular of the present tense and adding the "opposite" vowel (**e**

for **-ar** verbs and **a** for **-er** and **-ir** verbs). Polite plural commands are formed by adding the opposite vowel plus **-n.** The pronouns **Ud.** and **Uds.** are frequently used with the commands.

Presentation: In groups of three, one student gives infinitive cue, another student polite singular command of verb, and third command in sentence. Example: *hablar; hable; Hable Ud. con el profesor.* Here are some verbs students can use: *escribir, comprar, no conversar, comer, no beber.*

Expansion: You may want to mention other verbs with spelling changes: *llegar, explicar.*

-ar (a → e): hablar → habl∅ → ¡hable Ud.! ¡hablen Uds.! *speak!*
-er (e → a): comer → com∅ → ¡coma Ud.! ¡coman Uds.! *eat!*
-ir (e → a): abrir → abr∅ → ¡abra Ud.! ¡abran Uds.! *open!*

The polite commands of most irregular verbs are also formed from the first-person singular of the present tense.

decir → dig∅ → ¡diga(n)! *say (tell)!*
hacer → hag∅ → ¡haga(n)! *do (make)!*
oír → oig∅ → ¡oiga(n)! *hear!*
poner → pong∅ → ¡ponga(n)! *put!*
salir → salg∅ → ¡salga(n)! *leave!*
tener → teng∅ → ¡tenga(n)! *have!*
traer → traig∅ → ¡traiga(n)! *bring!*
venir → veng∅ → ¡venga(n)! *come!*
ver → ve∅ → ¡vea(n)! *see!*

Three verbs do not follow the same rule; their command forms must be memorized.*

dar → ¡dé (den)! *give!*   ir → ¡vaya(n)! *go!*   ser → ¡sea(n)! *be!*

The spelling changes you learned with preterites in **Lección 5** also occur in some commands.

c → qu: buscar → ¡bus**que**(n)! *look for!*
g → gu: pagar → ¡pa**gue**(n)! *pay!*
z → c: cruzar → ¡cru**ce**(n)! *cross!*

To express a negative polite command, put **no** before the verb.

¡No hable Ud.!   ¡No vengan Uds.!

B. Negative familiar commands use the same form as **usted** plus a final **-s.** Compare these negative **Ud.** and **tú** commands.

	WITH **Ud.**	WITH **tú**
Regular Verbs	¡no trabaje Ud.! ¡no coma Ud.! ¡no escriba Ud.!	¡no trabajes tú! ¡no comas tú! ¡no escribas tú!
Irregular Verbs	¡no diga Ud.! ¡no salga Ud.! ¡no venga Ud.!	¡no digas tú! ¡no salgas tú! ¡no vengas tú!

*The command forms of **conocer** and **saber** are **conozca** and **sepa.** Their use will not be stressed in this book, as commands with these verbs are rare.

Actividades

A.　Una fiesta. *You're planning a twenty-fifth wedding anniversary party for your parents. What would you like to ask these guests to do or not do? Use polite commands to express your wishes.*

1. La señora García bebe mucho vino generalmente.
2. La señora Rivera siempre compra regalos muy caros.
3. Alonso Martínez, un buen amigo de su padre, cree que va a traer su trompeta.
4. El señor Ramírez dice malas palabras con frecuencia.
5. El jefe (*boss*) de su padre siempre grita.

B.　Para el profesor (la profesora). *Using the command form of the verbs, tell your instructor to do five things. Be frank.* **Possible verbs:** (no) enseñar, (no) hablar, (no) venir, (no) escribir, (no) decir, (no) ser tan exigente, (no) ir, (no) hacer

C.　Una excursión. *Imagine that you are a tour guide. Tell the tour participants what to do or not do using polite plural commands.*

1. no llegar tarde porque el autobús sale temprano
2. traer sólo dos maletas (*suitcases*)
3. ser responsables en el Museo del Prado y no tomar fotos allí
4. ver todos los cuadros (*paintings*) más importantes del museo
5. descansar un rato en el hotel en las horas libres
6. no hacer las maletas (*pack*) muy tarde
7. pagar la habitación del hotel un día antes de salir
8. poner el pasaporte en su bolsillo
9. tener todos los papeles en orden
10. apagar el televisor antes de salir de la habitación
11. no salir tarde del hotel
12. buscar a sus amigos en el aeropuerto

While you were explaining all of this to the group, Mrs. Jones was in the bus trying to find her camera. Now you will have to repeat all of the instructions above just for her.

D.　¡No hagas eso (*that*)! *A classmate states what she or he is going to do at your party: tell her or him not to.*

MODELO:　estudiar / Voy a estudiar toda la noche. →
　　　　　Por favor, no estudies toda la noche.

1. gritar
2. leer el periódico
3. traer vino y cerveza
4. venir tarde
5. ir a comprar cigarrillos (*cigarettes*)
6. mirar la televisión
7. beber mucho
8. abrir las ventanas
9. estar aburrido/a
10. salir de la fiesta a las 9:30

27. Demonstrative Adjectives and Pronouns

Lo siento, pero necesito usar el escritorio esta noche. No fui a clase el lunes y no supe hasta hoy que tengo que leer este libro para mañana.

A. There are three sets of demonstrative adjectives in Spanish.

	MASCULINE	FEMININE	
this *these*	este estos	esta estas	refers to persons or things near the speaker
that *those*	ese esos	esa esas	refers to persons or things at some distance from the speaker or near the person spoken to
that *those*	aquel aquellos	aquella aquellas	refers to persons or things even farther away from the speaker and the person spoken to

Suggestion A: Use real objects (*cuaderno, lápiz, dólar, bolígrafo, silla, reloj*) to illustrate use of demonstratives. For instance, take book and say *este libro*; point at student's book and say *ese libro*; place book in distant corner of room and say *aquel libro*.

Esta sala es muy bonita.	*This living room (near the speaker) is very pretty.*
Ese muchacho cocina muy bien.	*That boy (near the person spoken to) cooks very well.*
Voy a comprar aquella casa.	*I am going to buy that house (distant from both persons).*

Both the **ese** and **aquel** forms are also used to refer to things removed from the speaker in time. **Aquel** indicates a more distant time. Note that the verbs in the following examples are in the past tense.

Ese señor no dio su nombre.	*That man did not give his name.*
Aquellos momentos fueron muy felices.	*Those moments (long past) were very happy.*

B. Demonstrative pronouns take the place of nouns. They are spelled just like the adjective forms, except that they have a written accent. Compare the following.

DEMONSTRATIVE ADJECTIVE	DEMONSTRATIVE PRONOUN
Este refrigerador es caro.	Éste es caro.
This refrigerator is expensive.	*This one is expensive.*

The demonstrative pronoun must agree with the noun it replaces in both number and gender.

> ese teléfono → ése (*m. sing.*)
> aquellas lámparas → aquéllas (*f. pl.*)

C. The neuter demonstrative pronouns **esto, eso,** and **aquello** refer to an idea or a concept, not to a specific noun. They have no written accent.

> No me gusta esto (eso, aquello).   *I don't like this (that, that).*

Presentation C: Mention that *esto, eso,* and *aquello* are invariable in form.

Actividades

Optional: Give singular form as you point to object in classroom and have students change it to plural: *esta mesa, esa silla, aquel bolígrafo, esta pizarra, esa ventana, aquella puerta,* etc.

A. Identificaciones. *Identify the following items in the classroom, using the demonstrative adjectives* **este, ese,** *or* **aquel** *as appropriate, and describe each briefly.*

> MODELO: pizarra → Esa pizarra es negra.

1. sillas	4. ventana	7. libro
2. mesa	5. puerta	8. papeles
3. lápices	6. abrigo	

Optional oral questions:
1. ¿De quién es ese libro? (Point to book near student spoken to; *este* expected in answer.)
2. ¿Le gusta este reloj? (Hold up your own watch.) **3.** ¿Cómo se llama aquel edificio? (Point to distant building.) **4.** ¿De qué color son estos lápices? **5.** ¿Cómo se llama esto? (Point to any object close to you.) **6.** ¿Quién está en esa silla?

B. Cosas inútiles (*useless*). *You're cleaning out the house; tell the Goodwill agents what items they should take. Use these words to justify each decision:* **moderno/a, viejo/a, nuevo/a, (in)cómodo/a, sucio/a, demasiado, pequeño/a, grande, feo/a, antiguo/a, precioso/a.**

> MODELO: (ese) sillones →
> Lleven Uds. esos sillones porque son muy viejos.

este	1. sillón	2. lámparas	3. máquina de escribir
ese	4. alfombras	5. escritorio	6. estantes
aquel	7. cómoda	8. platos	9. cama

C. Regalos para la casa. *You've just received several duplicate gifts for your new house. Use demonstrative adjectives and pronouns to tell which gift is from whom.*

> MODELO: platos / Margarita, Tomás →
> Estos platos son de Margarita y aquéllos son de Tomás.

1. lavaplatos / Raúl, Margo

2. tres alfombras / Violeta, Ileana, el señor Garza
3. teléfonos / mi padre, Angelina
4. televisor / mi jefe, un amigo muy bueno

D. Desacuerdo. Exprese Ud. en español.

1. What is that?
2. I don't know.
3. This is not easy. I don't like this.
4. Don't say that. That's not true.

Para resumir y repasar

A. En persona: La casa de sus sueños. Ud. y su esposo/a compraron la casa de sus sueños. Hoy llaman a sus amigos para darles (*give them*) una descripción de la casa. Use estas preguntas para formar una descripción completa.

1. ¿Cuántas habitaciones tiene? ¿Qué muebles tienen en las habitaciones?
2. ¿Cómo es la cocina? ¿Qué aparatos contiene?
3. ¿Cuántos cuartos de baño hay? ¿Son grandes las bañeras?
4. ¿Cuánto pagaron por la casa?
5. ¿Por qué es ésta la casa de sus sueños?

B. Un desayuno especial. Cambie al pretérito los verbos en cursiva.

El viernes no *hago*[1] el desayuno en casa porque *salgo*[2] muy temprano para mis clases. Sólo *tomo*[3] café. Pero el sábado no *vengo*[4] a la universidad y por eso *voy*[5] a desayunar en una cafetería grande en mi barrio. ¡Mi desayuno del sábado *es*[6] enorme!

C. Para llegar a mi casa. Complete con **por** o **para**.

_____[1] llegar al Edificio Mérida, tienes que tomar el autobús que va _____[2] la Plaza de las Américas. Bajas (*You get off*) en la Calle Asunción y caminas _____[3] esa calle hasta llegar al parque. Allí hay solamente un edificio alto. Es el Edificio Mérida. Después de entrar _____[4] la puerta principal, caminas hacia (*towards*) la izquierda (*left*) _____[5] ver el ascensor (*elevator*). Subes hasta el piso (*floor*) once. Sales del ascensor y abres una gran puerta _____[6] entrar en mi sección. Es la primera puerta a la izquierda.

D. ¿Ser o estar?

A mí me gusta hacer las compras en la tienda de don Ramiro porque él _____[1] muy simpático. Yo sé que él _____[2] muy ocupado, pero siempre tiene tiempo para decir «Buenos días» a todos. Además, en la tienda de don Ramiro siempre hay frutas y legumbres buenas que _____[3] rebajadas; _____[4] muy buenas y muy baratas. Mi madre dice que sus precios _____[5] muy altos, pero ella no _____[6] contenta con los precios en ninguna (*any*) tienda.

COMUNICACIÓN

De la vida real

Note: Point out the numerous cognates and model their pronunciation: *instalación, sistemas modulares, confort permanente, prefabricado, ampliaciones futuras.*

¡Su Cabaña[a] Campestre[b]!

¿Qué espera para realizar ese sueño?

Ahora es cuando, con la facilidad y la rapidez de instalación de los sistemas modulares MULTYPANEL. En unas cuantas semanas viva y disfrute[c] esos encuentros[d] con la naturaleza en el confort permanente de su cabaña modular MULTYPANEL.

PREFABRICADO • AISLAMIENTO INTEGRADO[e] • RECUPERABLE[f] • AMPLIACIONES[g] FUTURAS

[a]*cabin*
[b]*country*
[c]*enjoy*
[d]*encounters*
[e]aislamiento... *built-in insulation*
[f]*moveable*
[g]*additions*

Actividades

A.   ¡Su cabaña campestre! Lea el anuncio y luego conteste las preguntas.

1.   ¿Cuántos cognados puede encontrar en este artículo? ¿Cuáles son?
2.   ¿Son fáciles o difíciles de construir estas cabañas campestres?
3.   ¿Qué ventajas (*advantages*) tienen estas cabañas?
4.   ¿Quiere Ud. comprar una casa como ésta? ¿Por qué (no)?

Usted diga el problema y
UN MAGO[a] EN CASA
se lo resuelve[b] fácil, rápida y económicamente

Ordene, hoy mismo,
UN MAGO EN CASA.

Cómo quitar el sarro.[c]

Cómo limpiar alfombras

Cómo instalar bocinas.

Cómo cortar el pelo de los niños.

Cómo reparar persianas.

Cómo quitar manchas.

[a]*magician*
[b]*se... solves it for you*
[c]*scale, sediment*

B. Un mago en casa. Primero lea el anuncio y defina las siguientes palabras en inglés.

1. quitar

(Since you know that **sarro** means *scale* or *sediment,* what do you think that this book would teach you to do with it?)

2. bocinas
3. cortar, pelo

(Are either of these words verbs? How do you know? What does a person usually do with a pair of scissors? What is the person in the picture doing with them?)

4. persianas
5. manchas

(Since you have guessed that **quitar** means *to remove,* can you guess from the picture what other item the book teaches you to remove?)

Ahora haga un resumen mental de las cosas que enseña este «mago». Luego, intente (*try*) venderle (*sell him/her*) el libro a un compañero (una compañera). Explíquele todas las cosas que puede aprender con este libro.

ᵃapartamentos
ᵇde... *servant's*
ᶜ*entry*
ᵈ*parking lots*
ᵉ*Doorkeeper*
ᶠ*intercom*
ᵍPlanta... *Electrical generator*
ʰ*We process*
ⁱ*loans*

C. Edificio Amazonas Park. Lea el anuncio y conteste las preguntas.

1. ¿Cuántos dormitorios tienen los apartamentos del Edificio Amazonas? ¿Cuántos baños?
2. ¿Qué precio tienen? (La unidad monetaria es el sucre.)
3. ¿Cómo son los muebles de cocina de estos apartamentos?
4. ¿Tiene parqueaderos el Edificio Amazonas? ¿Portero? ¿De qué tipo?
5. ¿Es necesario pagar el apartamento en efectivo (*in cash*)?

Ahora, déle a un compañero (una compañera) toda la información que Ud. tiene sobre los apartamentos del Edificio Amazonas.

Para conversar más

A. Mi propio (*own*) apartamento. Conteste las preguntas según su propio apartamento o use las preguntas para entrevistar (*to interview*) a un compañero (una compañera) de clase.

1. ¿Te gusta el apartamento? ¿Crees que es mucho o poco el alquiler (*rent*)?
2. ¿Qué muebles tiene el apartamento? ¿Qué otros muebles tienes que comprar? ¿Dónde venden muebles a precios muy buenos?
3. ¿Qué aparatos eléctricos debes comprar?

4. ¿A qué cuarto vas para descansar? ¿para dormir (*to sleep*)? ¿para escribir una carta?

5. ¿Qué usas para leer por la noche? ¿para lavar los platos? ¿para limpiar las alfombras sucias?

Variation B: Pairs of students could conduct their interviews on the telephone. It might even be possible to arrange for such calls between students from different classes.

B. Un nuevo apartamento. Imagine que Ud. es el propietario (la propietaria) de un edificio de apartamentos y un compañero (una compañera) quiere vivir en uno de sus apartamentos. Él/Ella necesita más información sobre el apartamento. Primero, haga una lista de la información que Ud. va a darle sobre...

1. el apartamento: ¿Cuántas habitaciones tiene? ¿Entra mucha luz? ¿Tiene alfombra? ¿Tiene ducha, o sólo bañera? ¿Es moderna o antigua la cocina? ¿Son de gas o son eléctricos los aparatos y la calefacción (*heat*)? ¿Están incluidos el gas y la electricidad en el precio del apartamento? ¿Cuánto cuesta?

2. el barrio: ¿Hay muchos edificios de apartamentos o hay más casas? ¿Hay transporte público? ¿Es tranquilo o hay mucho ruido (*noise*)? ¿mucho tráfico?

Ahora, converse con su compañero/a y déle toda la información.

MOTIVO CULTURAL

In the United States, many middle-class families, especially those with small children, prefer to live in houses in the suburbs, with the working members of the family commuting to work. In contrast, in Hispanic countries, most middle-class families live in houses or apartments in the city; only the very poor live on the outskirts of the city. The wealthy often have second homes—called **chalets**—farther out in the suburbs or in the country. This pattern is gradually changing, however, and many middle-class developments—called **colonias, urbanizaciones,** or **repartos,** depending on the country —are being built in the outlying areas of modern cities. Neverthe- less, the majority of people still prefer to live in cities, close to the bustle of the urban area and to where they work.

Vocabulario activo

Adjetivos

exigente	demanding
sucio/a	dirty

Sustantivos

HABITACIONES (*ROOMS*)

la cocina	kitchen
el comedor	dining room
el cuarto de baño	bathroom
el dormitorio	bedroom
la sala	living room

COMPONENTES Y APARATOS

la aspiradora	vacuum cleaner
la cocina (eléctrica/de gas)	(electric/gas) range
la escoba	broom
el fregadero	(kitchen) sink
el horno	oven
la lámpara	lamp
el lavaplatos	dishwasher
la máquina de escribir	typewriter
el refrigerador	refrigerator
el teléfono	telephone
el televisor	television set

Verbos

TRABAJANDO EN CASA

barrer	to sweep
lavar	to wash
limpiar	to clean
pasar la aspiradora	to vacuum

OTROS VERBOS

apagar	to turn off
creer	to think, believe
descansar	to rest
escuchar	to listen
gritar	to shout
llamar por teléfono	to call on the phone
llegar	to arrive
prender	to turn on
terminar	to end, finish

MUEBLES Y OTROS OBJETOS

la alfombra	rug
la bañera	bathtub
la bombilla	light bulb
la cama	bed
la cómoda	dresser, chest of drawers
el escritorio	desk, writing table
el estante	bookcase
el inodoro	toilet
el lavabo	washbasin
la mesa de centro	coffee table
la mesa de noche	nightstand
el ropero	clothes closet
el sillón	easy chair
el sofá	couch, sofa

OTROS SUSTANTIVOS

el cristal	glass
el reporte	report; paper (*for a class*)
el sueño	dream

Otras palabras y expresiones

¡a despertar!	wake up!
ahí	there
¿algo más?	anything else?
en casa	at home
hasta	until
Lo siento.	I'm sorry.
tan	so
todavía	still

Demostrativos

este, esta, estos, estas; ese, esa, esos, esas; aquel, aquella, aquellos, aquellas

éste, ésta, éstos, éstas; ése, ésa, ésos, ésas; aquél, aquélla, aquéllos, aquéllas

esto, eso, aquello

Lectura

Antes de leer

Reading in a foreign language often involves coping with words whose meaning you do not know. Learning how to deal with such words without using a dictionary will enable you to improve your reading comprehension in Spanish. One strategy is to try to figure out the word's meaning based on what you already know about the topic. Another is to use clues from the context, the part of the reading in which the word appears.

This reading may be partially familiar to you because it concerns the Christmas story of Mary, Joseph, and the baby Jesus. All the words in dark type are new, but you should be able to guess their meaning.

Probably the most difficult word you will have to figure out in this reading is the most important: **posadas.** Start by reading the opening paragraph. Which two of the following definitions of **posada** or **posadas** are found in this first paragraph?

1. a place to stay, an inn
2. a stable
3. the place Jesus was born
4. a Mexican tradition that dramatizes the events of the evening of Jesus's birth

If you guessed 1 and 4, you were correct. Were you also able to guess the meaning of **Navidad, Nochebuena,** and **Reyes Magos?** What are the English equivalents of these terms?

Now look at the second paragraph. Knowing the meaning of **cantar** probably will have allowed you to guess the meaning of **canción** and **cantantes,** but if you are still having trouble, the phrases in quotation marks give you another clue to the meaning of **canción.** Were you also able to define **peregrinos?** Why were Mary and Joseph traveling to Jerusalem? What are the people making a long journey to a specific place often called?

After reading the remainder of the selection, you may be able to state the other two interpretations of **posada(s)** given in the reading.

Las posadas

Las posadas son una tradición de la **Navidad** mexicana. *Recrean* el drama de la **Nochebuena,** cuando José y María no pudieron entrar en la **posada** del pueblo,[1] y tuvieron que pasar la noche en un *establo.* Fue allí donde nació el niño Jesús, y donde los **Reyes Magos** lo[2] **adoraron.**

5 Durante los días que preceden a la Navidad, los mexicanos **conmemoran** este drama de la siguiente forma: un grupo de personas canta[3] «Las posadas» enfrente de la casa de un amigo. En la *canción,* San José pregunta: «¿Quién les[4] da posada a estos **peregrinos,** que vienen cansados de andar[5] los caminos?» El *casero* de la posada contesta: «Por más que digáis 10 que venís **rendidos,** no damos posada a *desconocidos.*» Y el amigo, como el casero de la canción, les dice a los *cantantes* varias veces que no pueden entrar. Pero por fin comprende que los peregrinos son José y María, les abre la puerta y les da posada en su corazón.[6]

Los cantantes repiten esta misma **escena** varias veces cada noche en la 15 casa de diferentes amigos. Y cada vez, cuando terminan la canción, reciben una invitación para entrar.

En casas donde la familia espera[7] la visita de muchos cantantes, generalmente hay una mesa con una gran variedad de pasteles, tortas, dulces, helados, vinos y otros refrescos, tales como jugos de frutas tropicales y 20 «Flor de jamaica», que es una bebida típica de la Navidad.

If **crear** means *to create,* what would you guess **recrear** means?

The initial *-s* of some English words is equivalent to the **-es** of their Spanish counterparts. What might **establo** and **escena** mean?

Relate this noun to **cantar.**

Relate **casero** to **casa.**

The prefix **des-** is often translated as *un-* in English. You should also relate this noun to **conocer.**

Relate **cantantes** also to **cantar.**

Cultural expansion: In many countries, a typical Christmas treat is *turrón,* hard candy made of nougat that people buy for friends and relatives. In Mexico, *la torta de Reyes* is eaten on January 6th. A ring is baked into the cake and the person who finds the ring in his or her portion is thought to be the next one who will be married.

Después de leer

A. ¿Sí o no? Conteste sin mirar la lectura.

1. El niño Jesús nació en una posada.
2. Estas celebraciones ocurren después de la Navidad.
3. Los peregrinos vienen cansados de andar los caminos.
4. San José pregunta: «¿Quién les da posada a estos peregrinos?»
5. El casero siempre les da posada a desconocidos.
6. Por fin el casero permite entrar a los «peregrinos».
7. Los cantantes comen pasteles y toman refrescos en la casa de sus amigos.
8. Los cantantes repiten esta escena varias noches.

B. ¿Tiene Ud. buena voz? Cante el villancico. Noche de paz (*Night of Peace = Silent Night*).

Noche de paz, noche de amor,[a]
todo duerme[b] en derredor,[c]
sólo suenan[d] en la oscuridad
armonías de felicidad,
armonías de paz. (bis)[e]

Noche de paz, noche de amor,
todo duerme en derredor,
sobre el divino Niño Jesús
una estrella[f] esparce[g] su luz,
brilla[h] sobre el Rey. (bis)

---

[1]*town* [2]*him* [3]*sings* [4]*(to, for) them* [5]*caminar* [6]*heart* [7]*expects*
[a]*love* [b]*sleeps* [c]*en... (all) around* [d]*sound (resound)* [e]*repeat* [f]*star* [g]*sheds* [h]*it shines*

MOTIVO CULTURAL

The celebration of Christmas in Mexico traditionally begins several days prior to December 25. Many people still pay nightly visits to different friends singing Christmas carols, called **villancicos,** and recreating the scene described in the reading. For many, the celebration also extends beyond Christmas Day, since, according to Hispanic tradition, the **Reyes Magos** (*Three Wise Men*) deliver gifts to children on the Epiphany (January 6).

Repaso visual

Invente Ud. oraciones completas sobre los dibujos. Considere las siguientes preguntas: ¿Qué objetos hay en el dibujo? ¿Quiénes son las personas que están en los dibujos? ¿Dónde están? ¿Qué hacen? ¿Con quiénes conversan?

Examen de repaso 2

A. Complete.

¿ESTE, ESTA, ESTOS O ESTAS?

—¿Qué hacen Uds. _____¹ días?

—Nada, realmente. Sólo tenemos _____² trabajo por una semana. Vendemos _____³ legumbres y _____⁴ frutas.

¿ESE, ESA, ESOS O ESAS?

—_____⁵ cine es muy barato.

—Sí, pero _____⁶ barrio es malo.

—¿Por qué?

—Porque _____⁷ calles no tienen muchas luces.

¿ÉSE, ÉSA, ÉSOS O ÉSAS?

—Juan, quiero comprar un plato; quiero _____⁸ que está allí.

—Muy bien, Rafael. ¿Tus libros son _____⁹ que están allí?

—Sí, voy a comprar _____¹⁰ grandes, los otros, no.

B. Un misterio. Complete con la primera persona del presente del verbo.

Hoy (yo: traer¹) flores para mi madre, pero no está en casa. No (saber²) dónde está. (Yo: Poner³) las flores en su dormitorio. Entonces (oír⁴) que dos personas hablan en la sala y (salir⁵) del dormitorio. En la sala (ver⁶) a dos personas que no (conocer⁷). Son sus vecinos (*neighbors*). Me dicen que mi madre fue al hospital porque está muy enferma. (Yo: Ir⁸) a su dormitorio, (tomar⁹) las flores y (llamar¹⁰) un taxi para ir al hospital.

C. Otro misterio. Llene los espacios en blanco según la versión en inglés.

Anoche _____¹ _____² casa a las tres. _____³ a mi _____⁴ y _____⁵ la puerta. _____⁶ _____⁷ una persona extraña cerca de mi _____.⁸ No _____⁹ nada, pero di la vuelta y _____¹⁰ rápido. _____¹¹ en la _____¹² y _____¹³ a la policía. Desgraciadamente, el individuo _____¹⁴ antes de la llegada de la policía. ¿Qué _____¹⁵ yo entonces? _____¹⁶ _____¹⁷ mi amiga. ¿Qué _____¹⁸ ella? Que esa persona sólo _____¹⁹ a mi casa para robar algo.

Last night I arrived home at 3:00. I went up to my bedroom and opened the door. I saw a strange person near my bed. I didn't say anything, but turned and left quickly. I went into the living room and called the police. Unfortunately, the individual left before their arrival. What did I do then? I called my friend. What did she say? That the person only came to my house to steal something.

D. ¿Con o sin **a?**

Vamos _____¹ entrar aquí para ver _____² Juana. Sé que viene _____³ esta cafetería todas las tardes. Toma _____⁴ un café y visita _____⁵ un amigo que

142

trabaja aquí. También mira _____[6] los cuadros, porque la cafetería es, además, una galería de arte. El problema es que veo _____[7] su amigo, pero no _____[8] Juana.

E. Vocabulario. Complete o identifique.

1. un marisco delicioso: _____[1]
   dos legumbres verdes: _____,[2] _____[3]
   tres frutas amarillas: _____,[4] _____,[5] _____[6]
2. el _____[7] de las compras
   la _____[8] de sopa
   la _____[9] de cereal
   el _____[10] de harina
   la _____[11] de aceite
3. ¿Qué verbo asocia Ud. con estas expresiones?
   platos sucios: _____[12]
   aspiradora: _____[13]
   escoba: _____[14]
   horno: _____[15]

F. Dé mandatos formales.

MODELO: Uds. / llamar ahora. → Llamen Uds. ahora.

1. Ud. / venir temprano
2. Uds. / hablar con Alicia
3. Ud. / ser mi amigo
4. Uds. / no comer con ellos
5. Uds. / traer los platos
6. Ud. / no ir a esa fiesta

G. Dé los mandatos familiares correspondientes a los infinitivos.

La madre dice: «Niño, (salir[1]) de la sala; no (mirar[2]) la televisión ahora. (Ir[3]) a la cocina y (lavar[4]) los platos que están en el fregadero. Después (poner[5]) la mesa. ¡Ah! Y si alguien llama, no (decir[6]) que estoy en casa.»

H. ¿Para o por? Complete.

Doña Rosa sale _____[1] el supermercado _____[2] la puerta principal de su casa, y camina _____[3] la plaza _____[4] tomar el autobús. En el supermercado, doña Rosa compra azúcar _____[5] preparar un postre rico _____[6] la cena. Paga cien pesos _____[7] el azúcar. El postre es _____[8] su esposo. Doña Rosa llama _____[9] teléfono y explica a su esposo que la cena va a estar lista (*ready*) _____[10] las 7:00.

Mis diversiones

Los estudiantes se divierten en una fiesta en la Universidad de Puerto Rico.

METAS

Comunicación: In this lesson you will talk about music, television, movies, and other types of entertainment and pastimes. You'll also practice expressions you need for activities such as going to a store to get a videotape.

Estructuras: 28. Stem-Changing Verbs 29. Polite Command Forms of Stem-Changing Verbs 30. Present Participle of Stem-Changing Verbs 31. Stem Changes in the Preterite 32. Direct Object Pronouns 33. Position of Direct Object Pronouns

GRÁFICOS

El concierto de rock

1. el bajo
2. la batería
3. el/la cantante
4. el/la fanático/a
5. la guitarra principal

Verbs

aplaudir	*to applaud*
asistir (a)	*to attend*
gozar (de)	*to enjoy*
tocar	*to play (a musical instrument)*

Other Nouns

el billete/el boleto*	*ticket*
la canción	*song*
el conjunto/el grupo	*group*

Prepositions

al lado de	*beside*	detrás de	*behind*
delante de	*in front of*	encima de	*on top of*
debajo de	*underneath*	cerca de	*near*
lejos de	*far from*		

Expressions of Admiration

¡Estupendo! ¡Fabuloso!	
¡Fantástico! ¡Fenomenal!	
¡Qué bien (mal) toca (canta)!	*How well (badly) he/she plays (sings)!*
¡Qué horrible!	*How horrible!*
¡Qué bueno (malo)!	*How good (bad)!*

Actividades

A. Su conjunto favorito. Hágale estas preguntas a un compañero (una compañera) y luego conteste las preguntas de él (ella).

1. ¿Cómo se llama tu conjunto favorito? ¿Cuántos miembros tiene?
2. ¿Quién es el/la cantante principal? ¿Quién toca la guitarra? ¿el bajo? ¿la batería?

---

*El boleto is the word for *ticket* in most of Spanish America; **el billete** is preferred in Spain. **La entrada** is also heard in some countries.

3. ¿Qué tipo de música tocan?
4. ¿Cuáles son sus discos (*records*) más populares? ¿Cuál es tu canción favorita?
5. ¿Fuiste este verano a un concierto de este grupo? ¿Estuviste cerca o lejos del escenario (*stage*)? ¿Cuánto pagaste por el boleto? ¿Asistieron muchos fanáticos? ¿Gozaron y aplaudieron mucho?

B.   Las reacciones de un fanático. ¿Qué hace y dice Ud. cuando oye a...

1. los Rolling Stones?
2. Bruce Springsteen?
3. Paul Simon?
4. Madonna?

5. Janet Jackson?
6. David Bowie?
7. Prince?
8. los Talking Heads?

C.   ¿Dónde está Loli? Use preposiciones (**delante de, detrás de,** etcétera) para indicar dónde está Loli en relación con las otras personas y los objetos de los dibujos.

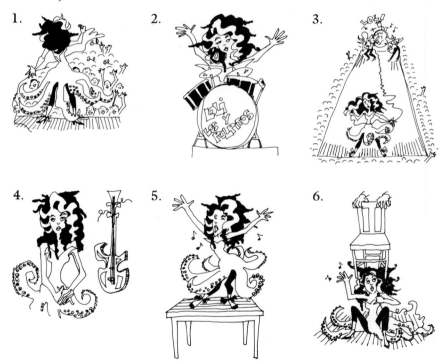

D.   Sus gustos musicales. Conteste.

1. ¿Le gusta asistir a los conciertos donde amplifican mucho la música? Explique.
2. ¿De qué goza más en un concierto de rock, de los cantantes o de los músicos? ¿Es importante el ambiente (*atmosphere*) para Ud.?

Optional: If you or any of your students sing and/or play an instrument, you may want to prepare a song or two for presentation in class.

3. ¿Asiste Ud. frecuentemente a los conciertos de rock? ¿Por qué (no)? ¿Son muy caros? ¿Canta Ud. las canciones de sus grupos favoritos?
4. ¿Toca Ud. un instrumento musical? ¿Cuál? ¿Escribe Ud. canciones?

Cada loco con su tema

To Each His Own

◆ STEM-CHANGING VERBS ◆	
puedo	*I can*
puede	*you (he/she) can*
quiero	*I want*
quiere	*you (he/she) want(s)*
prefiero	*I prefer*
prefiere	*you (he/she) prefer(s)*
juego	*I play*
juegan	*you (pl.) (they) play*
enciendo	*I turn on*
enciende	*you (he/she) turn(s) on*
duermo	*I sleep*
duerme	*you (he/she) sleep(s)*

Note: Model pronunciation of these stem-changing forms for students.

1. los audífonos
2. el disco
3. la casetera
4. el tocadiscos
5. el disco compacto

A. bailar
B. dormir una siesta
C. jugar a las cartas
D. mirar una telenovela (*soap opera*)
E. oír casetes*

Cultural expansion: The pronunciation of *casete* is not yet standardized in Spanish. This is also true of other words related to modern technology like *vídeo,* which many people write with no accent and pronounce with stress on the *e.*

Note: You may want to ask several students to read this narrative aloud.

En el *salón de recreo todo el mundo* puede hacer cosas diferentes. *Algunos* bailan con la música de los discos que Pablo pone en el tocadiscos. Teresa, que es un poco tímida, no quiere bailar; prefiere oír el casete que *grabó* del nuevo disco compacto de Loli y los pulpitos. Oye el casete en su casetera con los audífonos. Otros
5 estudiantes juegan a las *cartas,* y Víctor enciende el televisor para mirar una telenovela. ¿Y yo? Bailo *mal* y canto *peor.* Por eso, busco un *lugar* tranquilo *sin ruido* para descansar y *duermo una siesta.* ¡Cada loco con su tema!

recreation room / everybody / Some

recorded

cards
badly / worse / place / without
noise / I take a nap

---

*Some native speakers don't pronounce the second **e** in **casete,** but most do.

Actividades

A. En el salón de recreo. ¿Qué hacen las personas del dibujo?

1. Pablo
2. Teresa
3. Víctor
4. Ana y Alberto
5. Celia y Juan
6. el narrador

B. ¿Qué actividades prefiere Ud.? Ahora imagine que Ud. hace las actividades del ejercicio A. Escriba lo que (*what*) Ud. hace y luego ordene las actividades según sus preferencias personales.

> MODELO: Pablo pone discos en el tocadiscos. →
> Pongo discos en el tocadiscos.

C. Ahora, ¿qué hacen sus compañeros? Pregúntele a otro/a estudiante...

1. si le gusta bailar y qué bailes prefiere (el tango, el vals, el merengue, la música disco, la cumbia, la salsa, el rock, la lambada*)
2. si baila bien o mal y en qué lugar le gusta bailar
3. si prefiere oír música en la radio,† en su casetera con audífonos o en su tocadiscos
4. qué discos, casetes o discos compactos quiere comprar, y cuánto dinero puede gastar en ellos
5. si graba los discos, casetes o discos compactos de sus amigos
6. qué quiere mirar en la televisión hoy

D. Música en vivo (*live*). Lea este anuncio de Puerto Rico a la izquierda y conteste las preguntas.

1. ¿Cómo se llama este conjunto? ¿Cómo es su música?
2. ¿Cuánto cuesta contratar a este conjunto? ¿Es caro, según el anuncio?
3. ¿En qué lugares puede ser la fiesta?
4. ¿Qué significa «llama con tiempo para tu cita»?

[a]nunca... *never before seen*
[b]de... *according to your budget*
[c]*porch in a private home*
[d]*appointment*

Note C: The names of types of Hispanic music won't mean much to most students. Bring records or cassettes to class or prepare tape with several samples and have them listen to it in language lab. Tell students that some well-known American rock musicians, aware of importance of U.S. Spanish-speaking market, have recorded in Spanish —for instance, Linda Ronstadt, Gloria Estefan, and Los Lobos.

MOTIVO **CULTURAL**

Although English and American pop/rock music is very well known and admired in all Spanish-speaking countries, you would probably spend as much time dancing to a salsa or cumbia rhythm as to a pop/rock beat if you went to a party in a Latin American country.

***El tango** originated in Argentina, whereas **el merengue** and **la cumbia** are from the Dominican Republic and Colombia, respectively. **La salsa** is partly Cuban and partly Puerto Rican. **La lambada** is Brazilian.
†**El radio** is used in most of Hispanic America, **la radio** in Spain.

En la tienda de vídeos

1. el vídeo*

◆ STEM-CHANGING PRETERITES ◆	
durmió	*you (he/she) slept*
sintió	*you (he/she) felt*

◆ STEM-CHANGING POLITE COMMANDS ◆		
ie:	¡piense Ud.!	*think! (sing.)*
	¡piensen Uds.!	*think! (pl.)*
ue:	¡vuelva Ud.!	*return, come back! (sing.)*
	¡vuelvan Uds.!	*return, come back! (pl.)*

◆ DIRECT OBJECT PRONOUNS ◆			
lo	*him, it (m.)*	los	*them (m.)*
la	*her, it (f.)*	las	*them (f.)*

DEPENDIENTA: Buenos días, señor, ¿quiere comprar este vídeo?

PEPE: No, quiero *devolverlo* y *alquilar* otro para mi novia. Le gustan *tanto* las *películas,* que cuando no puede ir al cine, las ve en casa. — *return it / rent* — *so much / films*

DEPENDIENTA: Esta semana los alquilamos *a mitad de precio.* ¿*Qué le parece* «El *espía* que durmió aquí»? ¿O *tal vez* «El planeta X», de ciencia ficción? — *at half price / How do you like* — *spy / perhaps*

PEPE: *Mejor* llevo «Cuando Julieta sintió el *amor*». Mi novia prefiere las películas románticas y las musicales. — *Better (It's better that) / love*

DEPENDIENTA: Ud. *debe* alquilar dos. Son una *ganga.* Piénselo. — *ought / bargain*

PEPE: No, gracias, sólo quiero uno. ¿Cuánto *le debo*? — *do I owe you*

DEPENDIENTA: Tres mil cuatrocientas pesos (Pepe paga). Muy bien, señor. Muchas gracias y vuelva *pronto*. — *soon*

Presentation: In preparation for the extemporaneous dialogue called for in Exercise B that follows, have students dramatize dialogue several times in small groups. Then see how many *Pepes* can respond to questions of *dependientas* without referring to the dialogue.

Actividades

A. ¿Cierto o falso? Corrija las oraciones falsas.

1. Pepe quiere comprar un vídeo.
2. La novia de Pepe no ve películas en casa.
3. La tienda alquila los vídeos a mitad de precio esa semana.
4. La novia de Pepe prefiere las películas de ciencia ficción.
5. Pepe decide alquilar un vídeo.
6. Una película se llama «Cuando Julieta durmió aquí».

Cultural expansion: The use of videotapes has spread over the Hispanic world just as quickly as in the U.S. Every shopping mall in large cities has at least one store where movies can be rented, and many smaller towns also have video stores.

*****Vídeo** can also mean *VCR.*

Expansion B: *Un diálogo original.* With a classmate, dramatize the dialogue but change video titles to reflect your own interests. Change other parts of the dialogue also in order to add original touches of your own.

Optional: *Su vídeo favorito. ¿Cómo se llama? ¿Quiénes actúan en el vídeo? ¿Qué tipo de película es (romántica, de ciencia ficción, de horror, musical, un drama)? ¿Lo compró o solamente lo alquiló?*

Optional: *¿Qué le parece? Dé una opinión sincera.* **1.** Grateful Dead **2.** Barry Manilow **3.** *la ciencia ficción* **4.** *las comedias musicales* **5.** *las películas de acción (¿un título?)*

Optional: Have students bring to class favorite album, novel, magazine, etc. Working in small groups, each student should tell why he or she likes it.

B. La tienda de vídeos. *You enter a video store to rent or buy one or more videos. Use the suggestions below as a guide for your conversation with the clerk (a classmate). Go over this activity several times, changing roles with your classmate.*

1. —Buenas tardes, ¿qué desea Ud.?
   —Buenas tardes, quiero...
2. —¿Qué tipo de película quiere Ud.?
   —Quiero una película romántica (de ciencia ficción, de horror, musical, dramática).
3. —¿Qué le parecen las películas de espías, como las de Sean Connery? ¿O tal vez... ?
   —Sí (No), me gustan las de... Mejor llevo...
4. —¿Quiere comprar o alquilar el (los) vídeo(s)? Piénselo. Hoy lo(s)...
   —Lo(s) quiero...
5. —¿Sólo quiere un (dos, tres) vídeo(s)? Ud. debe llevar más. ¡Son una ganga!
   —Quiero uno (dos, tres, etcétera) porque lo(s)... ¿Cuánto le debo?
   —... Muchas gracias y vuelva pronto.

C. ¿Qué hizo Ud.? *Answer the following questions using the direct object pronouns in place of the nouns.*

1. **los vídeos:** ¿Los compró o los alquiló? ¿Por qué?
2. **la cantante:** ¿La aplaudió mucho o poco? ¿Por qué?
3. **su disco compacto:** ¿Lo trajo a la fiesta? ¿Por qué (no)?
4. **la telenovela:** ¿La vio hoy o anoche?
5. **las películas románticas:** ¿Las prefiere a las películas de aventuras?

VISTA CULTURAL

Optional: Play a Gloria Estefan Spanish recording for the class. Students probably won't be able to distinguish very many words at this point, but one of them may want to take the record home and write down any words learned in class that appear in the songs.

¡Triunfan los artistas hispanos en el mundo del espectáculo! Por ejemplo, Gloria Estefan, la cantante de la orquesta Miami Sound Machine, recibe aplausos ya en todo el mundo (*world*), de Londres a Tokio, del Parque Central de Nueva York a las capitales de Sudamérica. Ahora ella y otros artistas hispanos unen (*unite*) en su música la nostalgia de una patria distante con las tradiciones y la lengua de los Estados Unidos.

GRAMÁTICA ESENCIAL

28. Stem-Changing Verbs

Teresa no quiere bailar;
prefiere oír el casete que
grabó.

Some verbs in Spanish change the stressed stem vowel of the infinitive in four of the six conjugated forms of the present tense. You used two of these forms in the first part of this lesson. As you learn the complete conjugation, it may be helpful to visualize the overall pattern of change as a capital L.

Verbs of all three conjugations (**-ar, -er,** and **-ir**) show these stem changes.

e → ie **querer** (*to want*)		o → ue **poder** (*to be able to*)	
quiero	queremos	puedo	podemos
quieres	queréis	puedes	podéis
quiere	quieren	puede	pueden

Other verbs with these changes include the following:

e → ie		o → ue	
comenzar	*to begin*	almorzar	*to eat lunch*
encender	*to turn on*	costar	*to cost*
entender	*to understand*	devolver	*to return* (something)
pensar	*to think*	dormir	*to sleep*
perder	*to lose*	encontrar	*to find*
preferir	*to prefer*	morir	*to die*
sentir	*to feel; be sorry about*	volver	*to return*

NOTE: The verb **jugar** (*to play a game*) changes **u** to **ue: juego, juegas, juega, jugamos, jugáis, juegan. Llover** (*to rain*) and **nevar** (*to snow*) are used only in the third person singular.

Llueve mucho en Miami, pero nunca nieva.	*It rains a lot in Miami, but it never snows.*

Note: You can add to list *cerrar* (*ie*) and *recordar* (*ue*). Remind students that verbs formed by adding prefixes to another verb are conjugated like parent verb. *Volver,* for instance, is parent of *devolver* (to return, give back), *envolver* (to wrap; to involve), and *revolver* (to stir).

Optional: For extra practice with stem-changing verbs, use following transformations: **1.** singular → plural: *duermo, sirve, prefieres, muere, pido* **2.** plural → singular: *piensan, volvemos, dormís, repiten, pensamos* **3.** present → preterite: *comienzo, encuentro, pienso* **4.** preterite → present: *volví, comenzaron, entendimos.*

A few **-ir** verbs change the stressed stem vowel of the infinitive to a single vowel: **e → i.**

pedir (*to ask for, request*)

pido	pedimos
pides	pedís
pide	piden

Other verbs with this change include **repetir** (*to repeat*) and **servir** (*to serve*).

In future lessons, infinitives whose stressed stem vowel undergoes change will be presented in lists as follows: **pensar (ie), volver (ue), servir (i).**

MEMOPRÁCTICA

Sometimes an artificial pattern will help you remember a particular conjugation or construction. For example, an L-shaped pattern clearly illustrates where the vowel changes occur in stem-changing verbs. This group of verbs is also referred to as "shoe verbs" (**la conjugación del zapato**) because the shape also resembles a shoe or boot. Try to create learning aids like these whenever possible.

---

29. Polite Command Forms of Stem-Changing Verbs

Muchas gracias y vuelva pronto.

As you learned in **Lección** 6, the polite command forms are formed by dropping the **-o** of the first person singular of the present tense and adding the "opposite" vowel. Since the stressed vowels in stem-changing verbs change in the first-person singular (**e** to **ie, o** to **ue,** and **e** to **i**), this change also appears in the polite command forms.

e → ie	o → ue	e → i
¡Piense Ud.!	¡Vuelva Ud.!	¡Pida Ud.!
¡Piensen Uds.!	¡Vuelvan Uds.!	¡Pidan Uds.!

Two of the spelling changes you learned with the preterite tense in **Gramática 21** are also found in the stem-changing verbs whose infinitives end in **-zar** and **-gar.** These verbs, therefore, undergo two changes: (1) the change in the stem and (2) the spelling change in the verb ending in order to preserve the sound of the stem consonant.

comenzar	**z → c**	¡Comien**c**e Ud.!
jugar	**g → gu**	¡**J**ue**gu**e Ud.!

Suggestion: Explain that verbs ending in *-gar* and *-car* change *g* to *gu* and *c* to *qu* in polite commands, even if they are not radical changing: *llegar → ¡llegue!, tocar → ¡toque!.*

30. Present Participle of Stem-Changing Verbs

The following verbs change **e** to **i** or **o** to **u** in the stem of the present participle.

e → i				o → u			
pedir	→	p**i**diendo	*asking for*	dormir	→	d**u**rmiendo	*sleeping*
repetir	→	rep**i**tiendo	*repeating*	morir	→	m**u**riendo	*dying*
servir	→	s**i**rviendo	*serving*				

Emphasis: Point out that all verbs in this list are *-ir* verbs. *-ar* verbs and most *-er* verbs do not change their stem in the present participle: *comenzar → comenzando, pensar → pensando, volver → volviendo.* Mention that *-er* verbs whose roots end in vowels insert *y* in present participle: *creer → creyendo, leer → leyendo,* etc.

Actividades

A. Complete con el presente del verbo indicado.

UN ANUNCIO

¿Todavía lleva Ud. ese viejo abrigo cuando (llover[1]) o cuando (nevar[2])? ¿(Querer[3]) comprar un abrigo nuevo, pero no (encontrar[4]) abrigos buenos y baratos? ¿(Pensar[5]) que la ropa elegante siempre (costar[6]) mucho? ¿(Perder[7]) mucho tiempo buscando gangas? Pues, visite «California». Tenemos abrigos excelentes a mitad de precio.

PEPE Y SU NOVIA

Pepe (preferir[8]) oír música, pero su novia (querer[9]) mirar la televisión. Ella (encender[10]) el televisor porque la telenovela (comenzar[11]) a las ocho. Pepe no (entender[12]) por qué le gustan tanto las telenovelas. (Pensar[13]) que son estúpidas porque todos (morir[14]) de amor.

EN UN BAR

Entro en un bar y (pedir[15]) una cerveza. El camarero (*waiter*) dice que lo (sentir[16]), pero que no (poder[17]) servirme porque los bares no (servir[18]) alcohol a los menores. Yo (pensar[19]) que esto no es justo y (volver[20]) a casa muy triste.

B. Invente preguntas para hacerle a un compañero (una compañera) según el ejercicio A.

> MODELO: —¿Adónde puedes ir si quieres comprar un abrigo?
> —Si quiero comprar un abrigo, puedo ir a...

C. ¡No haga eso! *Although don Guillermo always wants to know what you are doing, he is usually rather disapproving. Tell him (a classmate) some of the things you do and listen while he tells you not to do them and recommends something else instead.*

> MODELO: (Alquilar) películas de horror. →
> —Alquilo películas de horror.
> —No alquile Ud. películas de horror; alquile películas cómicas.

1. (Pedir) dinero a los amigos.
2. (Jugar) a las cartas por la mañana.
3. (Pensar) constantemente en mis problemas.
4. (Almorzar) en la cafetería.
5. (Repetir) los mismos chistes muchas veces.
6. (Volver) a casa a las cinco de la tarde.
7. (Dormir) una siesta antes de comer.
8. (Servir) café antes de la cena.
9. (Encender) todas las lámparas de la casa.
10. (Comenzar) a cocinar a las seis.

D. Aprenda los diálogos de memoria. *Pay particular attention to the words in italics.*

1. —Teresa, *¿quieres* bailar?
—No, *prefiero* oír este casete. ¿No ves que Armando está *durmiendo*?

2. —*Pida* un bistec. ¿No le gusta la carne?
—Sí, me gusta, pero si como mucho, *duermo* mal.

3. —¿Qué *piensa* Ud. de las fiestas de doña Clarines?
    —Mire Ud., cuando *vuelvo* a casa... tomo una aspirina.

4. —¿Por qué *comienza* Ud. a trabajar tan temprano?
    —Porque *almuerzo* en casa a la una. Mi familia y yo siempre *almorzamos* juntos (*together*).

Now, covering the words and looking only at the drawings, recreate the dialogues.

E. Los niños tienen hambre. Cambie los verbos indicados al presente progresivo (**estar** + *present participle*). Después, conteste las preguntas usando también el presente progresivo.

El niño y su hermanita *duermen* una siesta en el sofá. Se despiertan (*They wake up*) y el niño dice que quiere comer. La hermanita *repite* que tiene hambre también. En ese momento, su madre *llama:* «¡A comer, niños, ya (*already*) *sirvo* la cena!»

1. ¿Qué hacen el niño y su hermanita?
2. ¿Qué repite la hermanita?
3. ¿Qué hace la madre?

Optional: ¿Qué está haciendo Ud. en este momento? Describa sus acciones y también las acciones de algunos compañeros con el presente progresivo. Use cinco verbos por lo menos. **Posibilidades:** mirar, encender, buscar, jugar, tocar, estudiar, repetir, alquilar, servir, etcétera.

31. Stem Changes in the Preterite

—¿Qué le parece «El espía que durmió aquí»?
—Mejor llevo «Cuando Julieta sintió el amor».

Many stem changes in the present tense do not occur in the preterite: **pienso** → **pensé; enciendes** → **encendiste; vuelven** → **volvieron.** Some -**ir** verbs, however, change the **e** to **i** or the **o** to **u** in the third-person singular and plural of the preterite.

servir (*to serve*)	dormir (*to sleep*)
serví	dormí
serviste	dormiste
sirvió	durmió
servimos	dormimos
servisteis	dormisteis
sirvieron	durmieron

The following verbs undergo similar changes.

morir (m*u*rió, m*u*rieron)　　repetir (rep*i*tió, rep*i*tieron)
pedir (p*i*dió, p*i*dieron)　　sentir (s*i*ntió, s*i*ntieron)
preferir (pref*i*rió, pref*i*rieron)

The preterite forms of **querer** and **poder** are similar to those of the irregular preterites you learned in **Lección** 6 (**Gramática esencial 25**). They attach the preterite ending to an irregular stem (**quis-** and **pud-**) and are not accented on the final syllable.

querer: quise, quisiste, quiso, quisimos, quisisteis, quisieron
poder:　pude, pudiste, pudo, pudimos, pudisteis, pudieron

Like **saber, querer** and **poder** have English equivalents in the preterite that are different from that of the infinitive.

querer:	Quiero leer el libro.	*I want to read the book.*
	Quise leer el libro.	*I tried to read the book.*
	No quise leer el libro.	*I refused to read the book.*
poder:	Puedo cantar.	*I can (am able to) sing.*
	Pude cantar.	*I could (and did) sing.*
	No pude cantar.	*I couldn't (and didn't) sing.*

Review: Remind students of the similar irregular preterites they learned in *Gramática esencial 25* by having them do rapid *hoy/ayer* oral transformation drill: **1.** *(hoy) digo* → *(ayer) dije* **2.** *(hoy) traes* → *(ayer) trajiste* **3.** *(hoy) pone* → *(ayer) puso* **4.** *sabemos* → *supimos* **5.** *estáis* → *estuvisteis* **6.** *tienen* → *tuvieron*

Emphasis: Note the special preterite meanings presented, and remind students of the preterite meaning of *saber*.

Actividades

A.　Cambie los verbos al pretérito.

UN CLIENTE DESCONTENTO

¿Sabe Ud. por qué no *vuelvo*[1] a ese café? Porque *pido*[2] chocolate y *repito*[3] tres veces: «¡Muy caliente (*hot*)!», pero el camarero lo *sirve*[4] frío.

LAS NOTICIAS

Víctor *enciende*[5] el televisor y *ve*[6] en las noticias un accidente de automóviles. ¡Víctor *siente*[7] mucho este accidente! *Piensa*[8] que *es*[9] horrible, porque en él *mueren*[10] muchas personas.

EL CONCIERTO DE LOLI Y LOS PULPITOS

Muchos fanáticos *duermen*[11] en la calle el martes para comprar los boletos temprano el miércoles. ¡Otros *vuelven*[12] a casa porque *prefieren*[13] dormir en la cama!

B. Variación. Invente preguntas para hacerle a otro compañero (otra compañera) según los segmentos del ejercicio A.

> MODELO: ¿Por qué no volviste a ese café?
> ¿Qué pediste?
> ¿Qué repetiste tres veces?, etcétera

Optional: Ask students what happened last night at home: **1.** ¿A qué hora volvió Ud. a casa ayer? **2.** ¿Sirvió Ud. una cena, pidió una pizza o no cenó anoche? **3.** ¿Repitió el vocabulario que aprendió ayer en la clase de español o prefirió hacer otra actividad? **4.** ¿Quiso estudiar los verbos para hoy? ¿Pudo estudiarlos? **5.** ¿Vio a un amigo suyo o a una amiga suya anoche? ¿Qué hicieron? **6.** ¿Cuántas horas durmió anoche?

C. «El taco verde». Con un compañero (una compañera), presente este diálogo en clase, cambiando los infinitivos al pretérito.

—¿Qué (tú: comer[1]) en El taco verde?

—(Yo: Pedir[2]) tacos, pero Emilio y Carmen (preferir[3]) las enchiladas. También (ellos: pedir[4]) chile con carne. Todo estaba (*was*) tan delicioso que (ellos: repetir[5]) (*to have seconds*) varias veces. ¡No sé cómo (ellos: poder[6]) comer tanto!

—¡Estupendo!

—No, no (ser[7]) estupendo. Cuando (nosotros: volver[8]) a casa, mis amigos (sentir[9]) terribles náuseas. (Ellos: Ir[10]) en ambulancia al hospital.

—¿Y (morir[11]) los dos?

—Claro que no, pero no (querer[12]) volver nunca a El taco verde.

32. Direct Object Pronouns

—¿Quiere comprar este vídeo?
—No, quiero devolverlo y alquilar otro para mi novia.

In the **Gráficos** section you have already used some of the direct object pronouns. A direct object answers the question *whom?* or *what?* For example: *He buys foreign products.* Question: *He buys what?* Answer: *foreign products* (the direct object). *María called Juan.* Question: *María called whom?* Answer: *Juan* (the direct object). Direct object pronouns take the place of nouns that function as direct objects, and may refer to people or things. Here are all the direct object pronouns.

	SINGULAR		PLURAL
me	*me*	nos	*us*
te	*you (fam.)*	os	*you (fam.)*
lo*	*you (pol.)/him/it*	los	*you (pol.)/them*
la	*you (pol.)/her/it*	las	*you (pol.)/them*

El profesor **me** llamó anoche. — *The professor called me last night.*

Ellos no **nos** consultan. — *They don't consult us.*

¿Quién **te** invitó? — *Who invited you (fam. sing.)?*

Ya no **os** necesita. — *He no longer needs you (fam. pl.).*

¿Dónde está tu disco? No **lo** veo. — *Where is your record? I don't see it.*

¿Los vídeos? ¿No **los** tienes tú? — *The videocassettes? Don't you have them?*

¿Sus guitarras? ¡No **las** veo! — *Their guitars? I don't see them!*

Presentation: Hold up or point to props or photos and ask questions to which students respond affirmatively or negatively: **1.** *lápiz: ¿Lo ve? (Lo veo.)* (**tiza, cuadernos, papeles, reloj, libros**) **2.** *camisa: ¿La vende? (No la vendo.)* (**zapatos, pantalones, suéter, chaqueta, calcetines**) **3.** *edificio: ¿Lo compran Uds.? (No lo compramos.)* (**coches, banco, guitarras, casa, elefante, etcétera**)

Optional: Students are often confused when they have to switch object pronouns in question-answer sequences. Ask these questions to practice pronoun switching: **1.** *¿Me escucha Ud.?* **2.** *¿Lo/La escucho a Ud.?* **3.** *¿Me llamó Ud. ayer?* **4.** *¿Lo/La llamé a Ud. anoche?* **5.** *¿Los conozco a todos Uds.?* **6.** *¿Me conocen Uds.?* **7.** *¿Me entienden Uds. cuando hablo español?* **8.** *¿Los entiendo a Uds. cuando hablan?* **9.** *¿Lo/La ayuda un amigo cuando Ud. lava su coche?* **10.** *¿Los invitó una persona a Ud. y a sus amigos a comer el sábado?*

Optional:
MODELO: —*¿Alquilas vídeos de horror a veces?*
—*No, nunca los alquilo.*
Posibilidades: *ver / la película... , gustarte / las escenas románticas... , devolver / el vídeo... , mirar / el programa... , encontrar / los libros...*

Actividades

A. Un mal amigo. *You and some of Fernando's other friends have had bad experiences with Fernando. Retell your stories by changing* **me** *in the story below to correspond to the friends mentioned.*

Fernando es un mal amigo. No *me* invitó a su fiesta. Por eso, cuando Diana y Orlando llegaron a la fiesta, *me* buscaron por todas partes (*everywhere*), pero no *me* vieron. Entonces, *me* llamaron por teléfono y *me* invitaron a ir con ellos al cine.

1. tú
2. María (Fernando es un mal amigo de María. No...)
3. nosotros
4. vosotras
5. Ramón y Silvia (Fernando es un mal amigo de Ramón y Silvia. No...)

B. Nuestro conjunto. Esta noche es la primera vez (*time*) que toca su nuevo conjunto. Pregúntele a su amigo/a si trajo todas las cosas que Uds. necesitan.

MODELO: ¿Trajiste el bajo? → Sí, lo traje. (No, no lo traje.)

1. la cantante
2. los audífonos
3. la batería
4. las guitarras
5. el disco compacto

---

*In Spain, **le** is frequently used in place of **lo** and **la** to express *him* and *you* (*pol.*). You will learn more about these pronouns in **Gramática 40**.

33. Position of Direct Object Pronouns

Son una ganga. Piénselo.

Direct object pronouns precede conjugated verbs and negative commands. They follow and are attached to affirmative commands.

Su guitarra es bonita. ¿Cuándo la toca Ud.?	*Your guitar is beautiful. When do you play it?*
Esos discos son muy caros; no los compre Ud.	*Those records are very expensive; don't buy them.*
No quiero esos audífonos, Paco. ¡Véndelos!	*I don't want those earphones, Paco. Sell them!*

When a conjugated verb is combined with an infinitive or present participle, the direct object pronoun may either precede the conjugated verb or be attached to the infinitive or present participle.

Felipe no quiere verme. ⎱ Felipe no me quiere ver. ⎰	*Felipe does not want to see me.*
Ella está llamándote. ⎱ Ella te está llamando. ⎰	*She is calling you.*

NOTE: In the case of present participles and affirmative commands, an accent mark must be added in order to preserve the stress pattern of the original verb form.

Actividades

A. ¡Escuche Ud.! Déle las siguientes instrucciones al nuevo empleado (*employee*) de su cine.

MODELO: Venda los billetes a las seis y media →
Véndalos a las seis y media.

1. Abra las puertas a las siete.
2. Sirva la Coca-Cola a las siete y cuarto.
3. Encienda el proyector a las siete y veinte y cinco.

4. Comience la película a las siete y media.
5. Repita estas instrucciones para la película de las nueve.

    MODELO: No venda cerveza aquí. → No la venda aquí.

6. No encienda el proyector hasta las siete y veinte y cinco.
7. No use la casetera durante (*during*) la película.
8. No lea el periódico durante la película.
9. No encienda las luces hasta las once.
10. No barra los salones hasta las once y cuarto.

B. ¡De acuerdo! Ahora imagine que Ud. es el empleado (la empleada) y que está repitiendo las instrucciones y los comentarios de su jefe (*boss*).

    MODELO: Voy a vender los billetes. → Voy a venderlos.
      or Los voy a vender.

1. No voy a vender los billetes hasta las siete.
2. Voy a comenzar la película a las siete y media.
3. No voy a limpiar el salón inmediatamente.
4. No voy a encender las luces ahora.
5. Voy a repetir las instrucciones.

Para resumir y repasar

A. En persona: Un concierto. Invite a un amigo (una amiga) a un concierto. Dígale quién toca y canta, dónde es el concierto, a qué hora comienza, cuándo termina, qué pueden hacer después, etcétera.

B. ¡Ayer limpié toda la casa! Dé un resumen de lo que Ud. hizo en casa ayer. Invente frases, con los verbos en el pretérito.

1. llevar / platos / a / cocina
2. poner / platos / en / lavaplatos
3. encender / lavaplatos
4. devolver / comida / a / refrigerador
5. barrer / cocina
6. lavar / ropa / sucia
7. limpiar / muebles
8. no tener tiempo / no poder pasar / aspiradora
9. descansar / en / sofá
10. encender / televisor

C. ¿Hacer o no hacer? Con un compañero (una compañera) invente cinco mandatos afirmativos y cinco mandatos negativos (para hacerle al profesor [a la profesora] o a otro/a estudiante). **Verbos posibles:** buscar, decir, llegar, pagar, escribir, venir, ser

COMUNICACIÓN

De la vida real

¿TE GUSTA LA MÚSICA?

¡wow!

¡NO TE PIERDAS LA VIDA, SECRETITOS Y CANCIONES DE LOS SUPER-ÍDOLOS DEL ROCK!

rei america inc.

THE CLASH

TINA TURNER

TALKING HEADS

BRYAN FERRY

PETER GABRIEL

PRINCE

[a]*Lyrics*
[b]*memento*
[c]*successful*
[d]*gossip*
[e]*superstars*
[f]*hechos... unpublished facts*
[g]*giro... money order*
[h]*gastos... handling and mailing expenses*

★ Letras[a] y canciones más populares de cada autor en dos idiomas (español e inglés)... ¡para que tú también cantes!

★ Fotografías en colores de los más inolvidables conciertos de rock... ¡oh, un recuerdo[b] fantástico!

★ Los orígenes de las canciones más exitosas[c] e historias[d] personales de las superestrellas[e] del rock... ¡hechos inéditos![f]

PIDE TU LIBRO-ARTISTA FAVORITO, ¡YA!

NO TE DUERMAS ...

SÍ quiero recibir los siguientes libros. Por favor, envíemelos a:

Nombre _____ Apellido _____ Apto. _____

No. de la Calle _____ Zona Postal _____

Ciudad _____ Estado _____

TÍTULO	PRECIO	TOTAL
☐ The Clash	US$ 7.95	
☐ Tina Turner	US$ 7.95	
☐ Peter Gabriel	US$ 7.95	
☐ Prince	US$ 7.95	
☐ Bryan Ferry	US$ 7.95	
☐ Talking Heads	US$ 7.95	

FORMA DE PAGO ☐ CHEQUE ☐ GIRO POSTAL[g]

SUB-TOTAL:
Pedidos de Florida, agregar 6% de impuesto:
GASTOS DE MANEJO Y ENVÍO[h] US$ 2.00
GRAN TOTAL:

R.E.I. AMERICA, INC.
6355 N.W. 36th Street. Virginia Gardens. Miami, Fl. 33166.

A. ¿Le gusta la música? Lea el anuncio y conteste las siguientes preguntas.

1. ¿Qué contienen los libros?
2. ¿En qué idioma están las canciones? ¿Para qué?
3. ¿De qué son las fotografías?
4. ¿Qué tipo de historias personales contienen los libros?

Después, complete el formulario de pedidos (*order form*) con la siguiente información: su nombre y dirección, los libros que Ud. quiere comprar, cuánto cuestan, el costo en total y la forma de pago que quiere usar. (*Did you guess what* **impuesto** *means?*)

Luego, pensando en las respuestas que Ud. dio a las otras preguntas, hable de los siguientes puntos con un compañero (una compañera).

• por qué Ud. decidió pedir estos libros
• la dirección adónde van a llegar
• cuánto costó cada uno y cuánto pagó en total
• cómo pagó

▼ **Soldadito español**, de Antonio Giménez Rico. 1988. 96 minutos. Con Maribel Verdú, Juan Luis Galiardo. Un chico pretende librarse de la mili. Para ello, intentará la objeción de conciencia, después se convertirá en Testigo de Jehová y, por último, intentará dejar embarazada a su novia. Comedia.

```
tve1
 2.15.—Música N.A.
 3.00.—Pero... ¿esto qué es?
 4.10.—El martes que viene.
 5.20.—Hablemos de sexo.
 6.05.—Tendido cero.
 6.55.—Entre líneas.
 7.25.—Rockopop.
 8.20.—Corrupción en Miami.
 9.05.—Los mapaches.
 9.30.—Compañeros.
10.00.—Santa Misa.
11.00.—Avance telediario.
11.05.—Concierto.
12.05.—Pueblo de Dios.
12.35.—Campo y mar.
13.05.—El salero.
14.00.—Nuestra Europa.
14.30.—Domingo revista.
```

```
15.00.—Telediario fin de semana.
15.30.—El tiempo.
15.35.—Calimero.
16.05.—La comedia: Golfus de Roma.
17.45.—Dibujos animados.
18.10.—Juego de niños.
18.40.—Alf.
19.05.—Waku waku.
19.35.—Doce del patíbulo.
20.30.—Telediario fin de semana.
21.00.—El tiempo.
21.08.—En portada.
21.55.—Domingo cine. Soldadito español.
23.40.—Avance Telediario.
23.45.—Opera.
```

ᵃpretende... *tries to free himself*
ᵇservicio militar*
ᶜ*will try*
ᵈ*Witness*
ᵉdejar... *to make pregnant*

Note: The 24-hour time notation system is used in some countries in television program listings: 15:30 = 3:30 P.M.; 20:00 = 8:00 P.M.

B. Domingo, 6. Lea la lista de programas y la descripción de la película *Soldadito español* y conteste las siguientes preguntas.

1. ¿Qué programa comienza a las 8:20 de la mañana? ¿Es un programa norteamericano? ¿Cómo se llama en inglés?
2. ¿Qué programa presentan a las 3:30 de la tarde?
3. ¿Qué película presentan hoy? ¿a qué hora? ¿Es una película de ciencia ficción? ¿De qué año es? ¿Quién es el director de la película? ¿Cómo se llaman los actores? ¿Qué hace el joven para no tener que ir a la «mili»?
4. ¿Qué programas religiosos presentan hoy?

Para conversar más

A. Su opinión sobre las diversiones. Pregúntele a un compañero (una compañera).

1. ¿Qué piensas del cine de hoy? ¿de los programas de televisión? ¿de los programas de radio?

---

*En España el servicio militar es obligatorio para los jóvenes.

2. ¿En qué países hacen buenas películas? ¿Te gustan las películas extranjeras (*foreign*)? ¿Cuáles? ¿Qué película buena viste recientemente? ¿La viste solo, o con un amigo o amiga? Si el periódico dice de una película «sólo para mayores», ¿qué entiendes?

3. ¿Qué diversiones baratas (caras) hay en tu ciudad? ¿Cuáles prefieres?

4. ¿Tocas un instrumento? ¿Lo tocas bien, mal o así así? ¿Te gusta cantar? ¿Qué tipo de canciones cantas? ¿Tocas o cantas en un grupo? ¿Cómo se llama el grupo? ¿Son Uds. famosos?

B. Organizando una fiesta. Un estudiante llama a «Los socios» (página 148) para contratarlos para una fiesta. Otro estudiante es un miembro del conjunto y da la información.

C. Los super-ídolos. Dígale a un compañero (una compañera) todo lo que Ud. sabe de su super-ídolo favorito/a. ¿Es soltero/a o casado/a? ¿Es una persona a quien le gusta el escándalo? ¿Qué tipo de artista es? ¿Sólo toca, o también canta y baila?

MOTIVO CULTURAL

Although most Hispanic countries produce movies, the film industry is especially important in Spain, Mexico, and Argentina. In recent years outstanding films have been produced in hispanic countries, including the Argentine film *La historia oficial*, Spaniard Pedro Almodóvar's *Mujeres al borde de un ataque de nervios,* which was nominated for an Academy Award for best foreign film in 1988, and the Puerto Rican film *Lo que le pasó a Santiago*, which was also nominated for an Academy Award in 1989. Many Hispanic actors and actresses, such as Ricardo Montalbán, Anthony Quinn, and Raúl Juliá, are well known in this country.

Vocabulario activo

Sustantivos

LA MÚSICA

los audífonos	earphones
el bajo	bass
la batería	drum set
la canción	song
el/la cantante	singer
el casete	cassette
la casetera	cassette player
el conjunto	(musical) group
el disco	record
el disco compacto	compact disc
el/la fanático/a	fan
la guitarra (principal)	(lead) guitar
el tocadiscos	record player

OTROS SUSTANTIVOS

el amor	love
el billete, el boleto	ticket
las cartas	(playing) cards
la ciencia ficción	science fiction
la cita	appointment
la ganga	bargain
el lugar	place
la película	film, movie
el ruido	noise
el salón de recreo	recreation room
la telenovela	soap opera
el vídeo	videotape; VCR

Verbos

almorzar (ue)	to eat lunch
alquilar	to rent
aplaudir	to applaud
asistir (a)	to attend
bailar	to dance
cantar	to sing
comenzar (ie)	to begin
costar (ue)	to cost
deber	to owe; must, ought to
devolver (ue)	to return (*something*)
dormir (ue, u)	to sleep
encender (ie)	to turn on
encontrar (ue)	to find
entender (ie)	to understand
gozar (de)	to enjoy

grabar	to record
jugar (ue)	to play (*a game*)
llover (ue)	to rain
morir (ue, u)	to die
nevar (ie)	to snow
pedir (i, i)	to ask for; to order
pensar (ie)	to think
perder (ie)	to lose
poder (ue)	to be able, can
preferir (ie, i)	to prefer
querer (ie)	to want; to love
repetir (i, i)	to repeat
sentir (ie, i)	to feel; to be sorry
servir (i, i)	to serve
tocar	to play (*a musical instrument*)
volver (ue)	to return, come back

Preposiciones

al lado de	next to
cerca de	near
debajo de	underneath
delante de	in front of
detrás de	behind
encima de	on top of
lejos de	far from

Expresiones de admiración

¡Estupendo!, ¡Fabuloso!, ¡Fantástico!, ¡Fenomenal!	
¡Qué bien (mal) toca (canta)!	How well (badly) he/she plays (sings)!
¡Qué bueno/malo/ horrible!	How good/bad/horrible!

Otras palabras y expresiones

algunos/as	some
a mitad de precio	at half price
dormir una (la) siesta	to take a nap
mal	badly, poorly
mejor	better
peor	worse; worst
pronto	soon, right away
¿Qué le parece... ?	How do you like . . . ?
sin	without
tal vez	perhaps
tanto	so much
todo el mundo	everybody

Otros tiempos, otros lugares

Muchas ciudades hispanoamericanas como Santo Domingo en la República Dominicana, Cartagena en Colombia y Lima en el Perú conservan todavía el sabor colonial en sus calles y edificios.

METAS

Comunicación: In this lesson you will learn the names of Hispanic countries, their capitals, and their location. You will talk about things you used to do in your childhood, and describe events in the past. You will also learn about the oldest colonial city founded in the western hemisphere, as well as two legends from the sixteenth century.

Estructuras: 34. Basic Meanings of the Imperfect Tense 35. Regular Forms of the Imperfect Tense 36. Irregular Imperfects: **ir, ser, ver** 37. Preterite and Imperfect Tenses Contrasted

GRÁFICOS

Países, capitales y habitantes del mundo hispánico

Countries, Capitals, and Inhabitants of the Hispanic World

Note: Students may require assistance in pronouncing correctly names of countries, capitals, and inhabitants. Model pronunciation while pointing out countries on large classroom map of Mexico and Central and South America.

Cultural expansion: Within Mexico, Guatemala, and Panama, the capital cities are referred to simply as *México, Guatemala,* and *Panamá,* respectively.

	PAÍS	CAPITAL	HABITANTE
1.	México	(Ciudad de) México	mexicano/a
2.	Cuba	La Habana	cubano/a
3.	la República Dominicana	Santo Domingo	dominicano/a
4.	Puerto Rico	San Juan	puertorriqueño/a
5.	Guatemala	(Ciudad de) Guatemala	guatemalteco/a
6.	Honduras	Tegucigalpa	hondureño/a
7.	El Salvador	San Salvador	salvadoreño/a
8.	Nicaragua	Managua	nicaragüense
9.	Costa Rica	San José	costarricense
10.	Panamá	(Ciudad de) Panamá	panameño/a
11.	Venezuela	Caracas	venezolano/a
12.	Colombia	Bogotá	colombiano/a
13.	el Ecuador	Quito	ecuatoriano/a
14.	el Perú	Lima	peruano/a
15.	Bolivia	La Paz	boliviano/a
16.	Chile	Santiago	chileno/a
17.	la Argentina	Buenos Aires	argentino/a
18.	el Paraguay	Asunción	paraguayo/a
19.	el Uruguay	Montevideo	uruguayo/a
20.	España	Madrid	español(a)

MEMOPRÁCTICA

It is much easier to learn the names of the countries and their capitals if you visualize their location. When you look at a map, try to relate countries to each other and make a point of observing shapes and special details. Note, for instance, that Cuba, Puerto Rico, and the Dominican Republic are islands in the Caribbean; Cuba is the largest one and is shaped like a crocodile, while Puerto Rico is the smallest of the three. In South America, Bolivia and Paraguay are the only countries with no access to the ocean. After studying this map, draw your own blank map and test yourself by filling in the countries and their capitals.

Review: Remind students that these country names are generally accompanied by definite article: *la Argentina, el Brasil, el Canadá, el Ecuador, los Estados Unidos, el Japón, el Paraguay, el Perú, la República Dominicana, el Uruguay.* Also mention that definite article is part of these names: *El Salvador, La Habana, La Paz.*

porque *era* el puerto principal en el Nuevo *Mundo. Servía de* puerto de entrada a los conquistadores y, *al mismo tiempo,* de puerto de salida al oro y a los otros productos que mandaban a Europa.

A pesar de su importancia *estratégica,* Santo Domingo *se guardaba* mal de los piratas que venían de diferentes islas del Caribe. En 1586 Sir Francis Drake *saqueó* la ciudad—*hasta* atacó la catedral—abandonándola sólo después de recibir 25.000 ducados, las *monedas* de oro que usaban los españoles.

Hoy día hay otra ciudad al lado de la ciudad colonial: la moderna de grandes hoteles y preciosos parques.

it was / World / It served as

at the same time

In spite of / strategic / guarded herself

sacked

even

coins

Nowadays

Suggestion: Drill pronunciation of words in dialogue: *aniversario, quinientos, descubrimiento, hemisferio, conquistadores, importancia estratégica, catedral.*

MOTIVO CULTURAL

Santo Domingo was founded in 1496 by Bartolomeo Colón, brother of Cristóbal Colón (Christopher Columbus), as the capital of the first Spanish colony in the New World. It was the seat of the New World's first bishopric (1504), the first Spanish viceroyship (1509), the first cathedral (1521), and the first university (1538). Santo Domingo became the point of departure for most of the expeditions of discovery and conquest of the other Caribbean islands and the American mainland. The reputed remains of Columbus are buried in Santo Domingo's cathedral.

Alcázar means *castle* or *fortress.* The alcázar shown on the previous page was built as a residence in 1510 by Diego Colón, Christopher Columbus's son, and was sacked by Sir Francis Drake in 1586.

Actividades

A. Santo Domingo. *First read the brief passage aloud several times. It is important to hear the words and feel the rhythm of the sentences. Then try to recreate the various sentences (there are only six!) without referring back to the text.*

1. En 1992 se celebró...
2. Santo Domingo es...
3. Tenía...
4. Servía de... y al mismo tiempo...
5. A pesar de su importancia estratégica...
6. En 1586...
7. Hoy día...

B. ¿Tiene Ud. buena memoria? Conteste.

1. ¿Qué descubrimiento importante ocurrió en 1492?
2. ¿Quién hizo este descubrimiento?
3. ¿Por qué tenía gran importancia para España Santo Domingo?
4. ¿Quiénes entraban al Nuevo Mundo por Santo Domingo?
5. ¿Y qué producto mandaban a Europa por este puerto?
6. ¿De dónde venían los piratas?
7. ¿Qué pidió por abandonar la ciudad Sir Francis Drake?
8. ¿Qué hay hoy día al lado de la ciudad colonial de Santo Domingo?

La composición de René

1. las montañas
2. la nieve
3. esquiar

◆ OTHER IMPERFECTS ◆	
era	*I (he/she/it) was (you were)*
éramos	*we were*
iba	*I (you/he/she/it) went*
íbamos	*we went*
veía	*I (you/he/she/it) saw*
veíamos	*we saw*
había	*there was, there were*
me gustaba(n)	*I used to like*

La profesora pidió una composición para mañana y René la escribe. Dice *así:*   thus *(as follows)*

Recuerdos de Bolivia   Memories

Cuando era niño, vivía con mis padres en La Paz. *Como* Bolivia no tiene costas, no   Since
iba a la playa en el verano. Sólo fui una *vez,* en un *viaje* que *hicimos* con nuestros   time / trip / we took (made)
vecinos a Lima en *Navidad.* Bolivia y el Perú están en el hemisferio *sur,* y allí es   neighbors / Christmas / southern
verano en diciembre. Naturalmente, había mucha gente en la playa entonces.
Todavía *recuerdo* esas *vacaciones* como las mejores de mi *juventud.*   I remember / vacation / youth

En La Paz *raras veces* había nieve en el invierno, pero veíamos mucha nieve   seldom
cuando íbamos *de excursión* a las montañas. En el *monte* Chacaltaya, a una hora de   on an excursion / mount
la capital, hay un gran centro de esquí, y *de niño,* me gustaba mucho esquiar.   as a child

Actividades

Optional: Additional oral practice: **1.** ¿Cuándo va Ud. a la playa? **2.** ¿Va más frecuentemente ahora, o iba más de niño? ¿Por qué? **3.** ¿Cuál es mejor, el esquí en la nieve o el esquí acuático? **4.** ¿En qué lugares de los Estados Unidos hace más calor en el verano? **5.** ¿Va Ud. a veces de excursión a las montañas? ¿Adónde va?

A. Recuerdos de Bolivia. ¿Recuerda Ud. el contenido de la composición de René? Complete sin *(without)* consultar el texto.

1. Cuando era niño, vivía...
2. No íbamos a la playa en el verano porque...
3. Fui una vez en un viaje con...
4. En Bolivia y en el Perú es verano en el mes de... porque...
5. Todavía recuerdo esas vacaciones como...
6. En invierno, en La Paz raras veces...
7. Veía mucha nieve cuando...
8. De niño, me gustaba...

B. Cuando Ud. era niño/a. Conteste.

1. ¿Había mucha nieve donde Ud. vivía?
2. ¿Adónde iba Ud. durante el verano? ¿a la playa? ¿de excursión?
3. ¿Veía mucho a sus parientes? ¿Por qué (no)?
4. ¿Qué le gustaba hacer? ¿Todavía le gusta?
5. ¿Cómo era Ud. de niño/a? ¿tímido/a? ¿simpático/a? ¿atlético/a? ¿estudioso/a? ¿solitario/a?

VISTA CULTURAL

«Es tan grande la ciudad como Sevilla y Córdoba. Son las calles de ella... muy anchas (*wide*) y muy derechas (*straight*)... Hay calles de caza (*hunted game*) donde venden todo linaje de aves (*birds*)... venados (*deer*) y perros pequeños... Hay calles de herbolarios, donde hay todas las raíces (*roots*) y yerbas medicinales que en esta tierra (*land*) se hallan (*are found*). Hay casas como de boticarios donde se venden las medicinas hechas... Hay casas como de barberos... Hay casas donde dan de comer y beber por precio... »

Éstas son algunas de las re-

acciones que el conquistador Hernán Cortés escribió en una de sus *Cartas de relación* después de visitar la capital azteca de Tenochtitlán en 1519. La ciudad tenía entonces aproximadamente 60.000 casas y 200.000 habitantes.

Note: Cortés's letters describe many aspects of Aztec society in great detail. While the Spanish text is too difficult for first-year students, you might want to read some of his letters and summarize them in English for the class. Have students read the portion of his letter here. Stress the historical importance of such a document. Model pronunciation of *Sevilla, Córdoba, linaje de aves, perros pequeños, calles de herbolarios, raíces y yerbas medicinales, Tenochtitlán.*

GRAMÁTICA ESENCIAL

34. Basic Meanings of the Imperfect Tense

Servía de puerto de entrada a los conquistadores y al mismo tiempo, de puerto de salida al oro y los otros productos que mandaban a Europa.

You learned the first of the two simple past tenses used in Spanish, the preterite, in **Lección** 5. The second, the imperfect, is used to express the actions and states described on the following page.

A. Continued actions without any indication of their beginning or end, often expressed in English by the past progressive (*was working, were singing,* and so on)

¿Qué hacían Uds. cuando llamé? —Yo miraba una telenovela y René escribía una composición.	*What were you doing when I called? —I was watching a soap opera and René was writing a composition.*

B. Customary actions in the past, often expressed in English by *used to* + verb, by *usually,* or *would* when it means *used to*

Ya no viajo, pero antes viajaba mucho.	*I no longer travel, but I used to travel a lot before.*
Elena caminaba cinco millas todos los sábados.	*Elena would (used to) walk five miles every Saturday.*

C. Descriptions of physical or emotional conditions as well as states of mind and feeling (*I thought, he wished, she loved, I feared,* and so on)

La casa era grande y estaba en una montaña.	*The house was large and it was on a mountain.*
Ella pensaba que tú y yo éramos hermanos.	*She thought (She imagined) that you and I were brothers.*
A René le gustaba mucho esquiar.	*René liked skiing a lot.*

Note, however, that the preterite is used when a reaction or a particular instant is expressed or implied.

Cuando nos vio juntos, ella pensó que tú y yo éramos hermanos.	*When she saw us together (at that moment), she thought that you and I were brothers.*
A René no le gustó lo que Ud. dijo.	*René didn't like what you said.*

D. Time of day and other divisions of time in the past

Eran sólo las seis, pero como era invierno ya era de noche.	*It was only six o'clock, but as it was winter it was already dark (night).*

Review: Before introducing imperfect, say these sentences in present and ask students to change to preterite: **1.** *Hago el café por la mañana.* **2.** *Mi hermano y yo comemos huevos en el desayuno.* **3.** *Salgo de casa a las 8:00.* **4.** *¿A qué hora sale Ud.?* **5.** *El profesor no viene a clase.* **6.** *Por eso, todos vamos a la cafetería.* **7.** *Carmela pide un vaso de agua, pero yo pido una Coca-Cola.*

Emphasis: Alert students to cues that indicate that imperfect must be used in Spanish: "was/were + -ing"; "usually," "would" (customary actions); physical descriptions; descriptions of states of mind and feelings; divisions of time in the past.

35. Regular Forms of the Imperfect Tense

Santo Domigo es la ciudad más antigua del hemisferio occidental. Tenía gran importancia para España en el siglo XVI porque era el puerto principal en el Nuevo Mundo.

In the **Gráficos** section of this lesson, you used several forms of the imperfect of various verbs. Here are all of the imperfect tense forms of regular verbs.

viajar	creer	salir
(*to travel*)	(*to believe*)	(*to leave*)
viajaba	creía	salía
viajabas	creías	salías
viajaba	creía	salía
viajábamos	creíamos	salíamos
viajabais	creíais	salíais
viajaban	creían	salían

The imperfect endings of **-er** and **-ir** verbs are the same. Stem-changing verbs do *not* change their stem vowels in the imperfect (**pensaba, volvía, servían**).

NOTE: The accent is used on the first-person plural endings of **-ar** verbs (**-ábamos**) and on the **-i-** in all **-er/-ir** endings.

Actividades

A. La vida de Santo Domingo. Repita esta narración varias veces, cambiando el sujeto (**nuestro vecino**) por uno de los sujetos indicados.

Todas las noches **nuestro vecino** *contaba* (*told*) cosas interesantes sobre Santo Domingo. *Hablaba* mucho del castillo que hay allí y, también, *describía* la gran catedral de la ciudad. *Mostraba* (*He showed*) fotografías o *ponía* películas de la sección colonial de la capital. Entonces *vivía* en Chicago, pero siempre *repetía* que *sentía* nostalgia por Santo Domingo.

1. tú
2. vosotros
3. yo
4. nosotras
5. ellos

B. Más narraciones. En estas narraciones se usa el tiempo pretérito. Cámbielas por narraciones similares en el imperfecto, usando las frases indicadas.

1. Ayer *almorcé* en la cafetería de la universidad. *Pedí* tacos y enchiladas. *Pasé* allí un rato hablando con mis amigos y también le *escribí* una carta a mi novia. Cuando *salí, vi* a Margarita y la *saludé* en español. (**Todos los días...**)
2. Cuando mi abuelo *volvió* a California de su viaje anual (**sus viajes anuales**) a Chile, *trajo* muchos regalos para todos nosotros. Le *preguntamos* muchas cosas sobre la ciudad de Santiago y él *contestó* todas nuestras preguntas. También *visitó* mi clase de español, *habló* con mi profesora chilena y le *dijo* que su país le *gustó* mucho. (**Cada vez que mi abuelo...**)

36. Irregular Imperfects: *ir, ser, ver*

En La Paz raras veces había nieve en el invierno, pero veíamos mucha nieve cuando íbamos de excursión a las montañas.

ir	ser	ver
iba	era	veía
ibas	eras	veías
iba	era	veía
íbamos	éramos	veíamos
ibais	erais	veíais
iban	eran	veían

NOTE: The irregular form **hay** has a regular imperfect: **había**. Just as **hay** means *there is* or *there are*, **había** means *there was* or *there were*.

Había muchos turistas en el museo.

There were many tourists at the museum.

Actividades

A. ¿Qué hacía Ud. cuando... ? Complete las oraciones con la forma apropiada del infinitivo.

—¿Qué hacía Ud. cuando era niño/a?
—Cuando era niño/a yo...

1. (esquiar) en el invierno
2. (ir) a las montañas con mis padres
3. (ver) la televisión los sábados por la mañana
4. no (poder) salir solo/a
5. (ver) a mis amigos todos los días

B. Transformaciones. Estas narraciones están en el presente. Cámbielas al pasado usando el tiempo imperfecto de los verbos.

Los Castillo *son*[1] muy ricos y *viajan*[2] mucho. Muchas veces *van*[3] a Suiza (*Switzerland*), porque les *gusta*[4] esquiar, y en la ciudad donde ellos y yo *vivimos*[5] casi nunca *hay*[6] nieve. Mis hermanos y yo no *vamos*[7] a Suiza porque *somos*[8] pobres, pero cuando *vemos*[9] que muchos de nuestros amigos no *pueden*[10] ir tampoco (*either*), no *decimos*[11] nada.

37. Preterite and Imperfect Tenses Contrasted

Como Bolivia no tiene costas, no iba a la playa en el verano. Sólo fui una vez, en un viaje que hicimos con nuestros vecinos a Lima en Navidad.

A. The preterite narrates past actions, while the imperfect depicts or characterizes qualities or states. In other words, the preterite narrates and the imperfect describes.

El general vino, vio y conquistó.	*The general came, saw, and conquered.*
Había mucha nieve y yo tenía frío.	*There was a lot of snow and I was cold.*

B. The preterite is used when the duration of the action is limited in some way, such as when its beginning or end is expressed or implied, or when the sentence indicates how long the action lasted or how many times it happened.

La semana pasada trabajé sólo dos días, pero trabajé diez horas diarias.	*Last week I worked only two days, but I worked ten hours each day.*
Mi familia vivía en Buenos Aires cuando yo era joven; vivimos allí tres años.	*My family lived in Buenos Aires when I was young; we lived there for three years.*

Note that when there is more than one past action in the same sentence, as in the last example, it is possible to express some of them in the imperfect and others in the preterite. This is also possible when an ongoing action (expressed in the imperfect) is interrupted by an action that is completed or limited in some way (expressed in the preterite).

Dormía una siesta cuando Pedro abrió la puerta y me despertó.	*I was taking a nap when Pedro opened the door and woke me up.*

Actividades

A. El diario de un profesor. ¿Pretérito o imperfecto? *Read the following passage in English and tell whether you would use the imperfect or the preterite for the verbs indicated. Explain your choices. Do not translate the passage.*

I arrived[1] late at my office this morning. Four students were[2] already waiting to see me. One was[3] Paul Johnson. I grumbled[4] to myself because he came[5] to

Presentation: Give some expressions generally associated with the preterite: *ayer, anoche, una vez, dos veces, de pronto, de repente* (suddenly). Warn students that these don't always signal preterite, depending on meaning of sentence: In *Anoche llovía cuando llegamos a casa,* imperfect of *llovía* is used to signify "it was raining," but action of *llover* is viewed as complete in *Anoche llovió mucho.*

see me before class nearly every day. There was[6] nothing wrong with his ability to learn. He just didn't study[7] enough. Anyway, I talked[8] to him one more time, and to my great surprise, he showed[9] me a very interesting paper he wrote[10] for another class just the week before.

B.   El secreto de Jorge. ¿Pretérito o imperfecto?

Mi hermana y yo (caminar[1]) por la calle hablando y mirando a la gente cuando (salir[2]) de su casa nuestro amigo Jorge. Lo (invitar[3]) a caminar con nosotros. (Él: Estar[4]) triste y mi hermana le (preguntar[5]) por qué. No (él: contestar[6]). En ese momento (él: ver[7]) a un policía que (entrar[8]) en el pequeño café La Cantina Alegre. Entonces nos (él: decir[9]) adiós y (tomar[10]) un autobús. ¡Qué misterio!

C.   Entrevista. Pregúntele a un compañero (una compañera) qué hacía y cómo era cuando era más joven.

> MODELO: **cuántas horas, estudiar** →
> ¿Cuántas horas estudiabas todos los días cuando eras más joven?

1. dónde, jugar
2. cuántos amigos, tener
3. qué discos, gustarte
4. qué programas, ver
5. qué deportes, preferir
6. qué lugares, visitar
7. saber, español
8. ganar, mucho dinero

Para resumir y repasar

A.   En persona: Viviendo en Santo Domingo. Imagine que Ud. vivía en esta hermosa ciudad dominicana. Invente varias oraciones para describir lo que Ud. hacía de niño/a.

SUGERENCIAS (*SUGGESTIONS*):

1. visitar / explorar / estudiar los antiguos edificios
2. ir / ver / las playas
3. mirar la playa / las calles / el puerto
4. entrar / a la catedral / al parque / al distrito colonial

B.   Una fiesta. Un amigo le pregunta a Ud. sobre la fiesta a la que asistió anoche. Conteste según el modelo.

> MODELO: ¿Quién te invitó?   (Alberto y Juana) →
> Alberto y Juana me invitaron.

1. ¿A qué hora llegaste a su casa?   (8:30)
2. ¿A qué hora empezaron a bailar?   (9:30)
3. ¿Qué conjunto vino a la fiesta?   (Loli y los pulpitos)
4. ¿Tocaste tu guitarra con ellos?   (sí)
5. ¿Qué bebisteis vosotros?   (Coca-Cola y vino)
6. ¿A qué hora volviste a casa?   (1:30)

COMUNICACIÓN

Texto: Dos *leyendas* y dos nombres

legends

Algunos españoles que exploraban la parte norte de Sudamérica en el siglo XVI, *oyeron a los nativos hablar* sobre una tribu donde había solamente mujeres. Estas mujeres tenían relaciones amorosas sólo ocasionalmente. Cuando *nacía* una niña, la madre la *criaba,* pero si nacía un niño, lo *enviaba* a la
5 tribu del padre. Recordando a las Amazonas de la mitología *griega,* los españoles llamaron «Amazonas» a esta región.

Cuando el conquistador español don Juan Ponce de León era gobernador de Puerto Rico, oyó la leyenda de la fuente de la juventud que, según los indios, estaba en la isla de Biminí. Ponce de León, que era un poco viejo, decidió *bañarse*
10 en esa fuente, y salió con tres *barcos* a buscarla. No la encontró; *en cambio,* llegó en abril de 1512 a una región de la America del Norte. Como era un día de *Pascua Florida,** el explorador le dio el nombre de «la Florida» a este lugar.

heard the natives speak

was born / raised / sent
Greek

Optional: Have students summarize in their own words the historical importance of Ponce de Leon's search for the fountain of youth.

to bathe

ships / instead

Easter

En San Juan, Puerto Rico: Una estatua en honor de Juan Ponce de Léon, conquistador español y gobernador de Puerto Rico.

A. Hablando del texto. Haga un resumen de las leyendas sin mirar el texto.

LAS AMAZONAS

1. explorar / Sudamérica
2. haber / tribu
3. nacer / niña
4. nacer / niño
5. recordar / Amazonas

LA FLORIDA

6. oír / leyenda
7. decidir / bañarse
8. salir / tres barcos
9. llegar / América del Norte
10. ser / Pascua Florida

B. Hablando más del texto. Ud. es un nativo sudamericano y un explorador español le pregunta sobre esa tribu de mujeres. Conteste sus preguntas. Use su imaginación.

ESPAÑOL:

¿Viven otras tribus en esta región?
¿Y no hay hombres en esa tribu?
¿Qué pasa cuando nace un niño?
¿Y si nace una niña?
¿Y son valientes esas mujeres?
¿Qué más sabe Ud. sobre ellas?

USTED:

_____
_____
_____
_____
_____
_____

*The word **Pascua** can mean both *Christmas* and *Easter* in Spanish. (A common way to say *Merry Christmas* is **Felices Pascuas.**) Whenever confusion is possible, *Easter* is referred to as **Pascua Florida** or **Pascua de Resurrección.**

De la vida real

Gracias a los
Alemanes,
Belgas,
Daneses,
Españoles,
Franceses,
Griegos,
Holandeses,
Ingleses,
Irlandeses,
Italianos,
Luxemburgueses,
Portugueses,
que nos confían
sus operaciones financieras.

Y gracias también a los Austriacos, Finlandeses, Noruegos, Suecos y Suizos.

CL CREDIT LYONNAIS ESPANA

Los países europeos ahora tienen una gran unión económica y política. Este anuncio es una sencilla y elocuente afirmación de la unidad de Europa. Lea el anuncio y asocie los habitantes europeos con sus respectivos países.

Italia	Luxemburgo	Inglaterra
Irlanda	Finlandia	Austria
Dinamarca	Alemania	Francia
Suecia	Holanda	Noruega
Grecia	Portugal	España
Bélgica	Suiza	

¿Por qué les da las gracias a los habitantes de estos países este grupo bancario?

¿Sabe Ud. los nombres de todas las capitales de estos países? Asocie los países con las siguientes capitales.

Dublín	Bruselas	Oslo
Ginebra	Copenhagen	Estocolmo
Berlín	París	Atenas
La Haya	Lisboa	Luxemburgo
Roma	Viena	Helsinki
Londres		

Para conversar más

A. Un explorador famoso. Ud. es Ponce de León de regreso de (*returning from*) su viaje. Conteste las preguntas de un periodista (*journalist*).

PERIODISTA: PONCE DE LEÓN:

Sr. Ponce de León, ¿cree Ud. que existe realmente la fuente de la juventud?   _____

¿Por qué tiene Ud. interés en encontrarla?   _____

¿Pudo Ud. bañarse en esa fuente?   _____

¿Llegó Ud. a algún (*any*) lugar?   _____

¡Ah! Ya veo. ¿Tiene nombre ese lugar?   _____

Y ¿por qué lo llamó Ud. así?   _____

B. Opiniones.

1. ¿Cree Ud. que existió la tribu de las Amazonas? ¿Por qué (no)? ¿Qué otra leyenda de la mitología griega conoce Ud.?
2. ¿Qué otra historia (*story*) conoce sobre el nombre de un lugar geográfico?
3. Ponce de León llegó a la Florida accidentalmente. ¿Qué otros descubrimientos importantes y accidentales conoce Ud.?

C. Viajes y excursiones.

1. Descríbale a un compañero (una compañera) un viaje que Ud. hizo el año pasado. Él (Ella) debe hacerle preguntas para saber más de ese viaje.
2. Para celebrar el aniversario de 1992, Ud. quiere repetir uno de los viajes de Colón. Examine el mapa del Motivo cultural, escoja una ruta y explíquele a un compañero (una compañera) lo que Ud. va a ver en ese viaje.

MOTIVO CULTURAL

Christopher Columbus made four trips to the New World. The first was, of course, in 1492; the last one took place in 1503. Shortly, thousands of Spanish conquistadores were traveling regularly to the New World on dozens of sailing vessels. Trade routes and outposts were quickly established, from the Dominican Republic to Mexico, from Colombia to Florida.

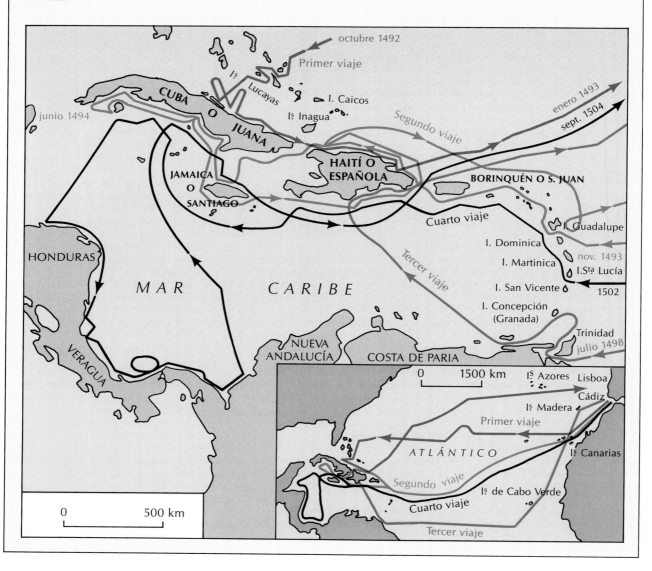

Vocabulario activo

Sustantivos

LOS PUNTOS CARDINALES

el este, el oriente	east
el norte	north
el oeste, el occidente	west
el sur	sur

LOS LUGARES

la capital	capital
el castillo	castle
la catedral	cathedral
la costa	coast
la entrada	entrance, entry
el hemisferio	hemisphere
la isla	island
el mar	sea
la montaña	mountain
el monte	mount, mountain
el mundo	world
el país	country
la playa	beach
el puerto	port
la salida	exit

LA GENTE

el conquistador/la conquistadora	conquistador
el/la habitante	inhabitant
el pirata	pirate

OTROS SUSTANTIVOS

el descubrimiento	discovery
el esquí	skiing
la juventud	youth
la moneda	coin
la Navidad	Christmas
la nieve	snow
el oro	gold
el pasado	past
el recuerdo	memory
el siglo	century
las vacaciones	vacation
el/la vecino/a	neighbor
la vez	time
el viaje	trip

Verbos

abandonar	to abandon
atacar	to attack
celebrar	to celebrate
esquiar	to ski
guardar(se)	to guard (itself)
mandar	to send
recordar (ue)	to remember
saquear	to sack (*a city*)
viajar	to travel

Otras palabras y expresiones

a pesar de	in spite of
al mismo tiempo	at the same time
así	in this manner, thus; as follows
como	since, as
de excursión	on an excursion
de niño/a	as a child
hacer un viaje	to take a trip
hasta	even
hoy día	nowadays
raras veces	seldom
sin	without

La persona

Estos amigos en Guadalajara, México, se sienten muy felices hoy.

METAS

Comunicación: In this lesson you will learn vocabulary and expressions related to the parts of the body and to different emotional and physical states. You will also practice talking about daily activities.

Estructuras: 38. Reflexive Constructions 39. Position of Reflexive Pronouns 40. Indirect Object Pronouns 41. Position of Indirect Object Pronouns 42. **Gustar** and Verbs Like **gustar**

GRÁFICOS

El cuerpo

Enrique · Leticia · Lázaro · Claudia · Don Tomás · Juan

The Body

1. la boca
2. el brazo
3. la cabeza
4. la cara
5. el dedo
6. el dedo del pie
7. la espalda
8. la cintura
9. la mano
10. la nariz
11. el ojo
12. la oreja
13. el pelo
14. el pie
15. la pierna

Descripciones

alto/a *tall* — bajo/a *short*
delgado/a *thin* — gordo/a *fat*
largo/a *long* — corto/a *short*
lacio/a *straight* — rizado/a *curly*

castaño/a *brown*
negro/a *black*
rubio/a *blond(e)*

Verbos

saludar *to greet*
dar la mano *to shake hands*

Actividades

A. Cubra (*Cover*) la lista y dé las palabras que corresponden a cada (*each*) número del dibujo.

B. Un examen «mitológico».

1. El cíclope tiene sólo un _____.
2. El monstruo «Big Foot» tiene dos grandes _____.
3. El elefante Dumbo tiene dos grandes _____.
4. La _____ de Pinocho se transforma cuando él no dice la verdad.
5. Según la mitología, Medusa tenía serpientes en el _____.

C. ¿Cómo son? Describa a las personas del dibujo. ¿Quién es alto/a, bajo/a, gordo/a, delgado/a? ¿Quién tiene el pelo largo, lacio, rizado, corto, rubio, castaño, negro? ¿Cuál es el problema especial de don Tomás?

Ahora, describa a cinco compañeros de clase, empezando por el pelo.

D. Accesorios especiales. ¿Qué parte del cuerpo asocia Ud. con los siguientes objetos?

1.   2.   3.   4.   5.    6.   7.   8.

¡Anímate, hombre!

Cheer up!

1. mojado/a (*wet*)
2. el lavabo
3. la toalla
4. el jabón
5. la ducha
6. el intercomunicador
7. el espejo

◆ REFLEXIVE VERBS ◆

Infinitive	Present
llevarse bien/mal *to get along well/badly*	me llevo bien/mal te llevas bien/mal se lleva bien/mal
secarse *to dry oneself*	me seco te secas se seca
peinarse *to comb (one's hair)*	me peino te peinas se peina
ponerse *to put on (clothing)*	me pongo te pones se pone

Antonio *acaba de llegar* al edificio donde vive su hermano Raúl. Le habla por el intercomunicador.

has just arrived

ANTONIO: ¿Qué me dices... ? *¿Te estás bañando* ahora? Raúl, la fiesta es a las nueve.

You are bathing

RAÚL: Ay, no tengo ganas de ir. No me gusta la comida que sirven los tíos y no me llevo bien con los primos. ¡Son tan *aburridos* todos!

boring

ANTONIO: No seas *necio,* Raúl, tú sabes muy bien que no podemos *faltar.* ¿Por qué no te secas, te peinas y te pones *algo* rápido? *¡Es hora de irnos***!

foolish / to be absent
something / It's time to go!

RAÚL: *Tranquilo,* hombre. ¿Por qué *te enojas* conmigo? *Ahora mismo me afeito.*

(Be) Calm / get mad / Right now
I shave (I'll shave)

ANTONIO: Está bien, no me enojo. ¡Es que ya son las nueve menos veinte!

---

*The use of **ir** in the reflexive gives the verb a slightly different meaning. **Ir** = *to go;* **irse** = *to go away* ("*to get out of here*").

Actividades

A. Dos hermanos. Describa la escena entre Antonio y Raúl.

1. ¿Quién está mojado? ¿Por qué?
2. ¿Quién habla por el intercomunicador? ¿Por qué?
3. ¿Quién tiene una toalla? ¿Por qué?
4. ¿Qué tiene que hacer Raúl rápidamente? (Tiene que secarse...)
5. ¿Adónde van los dos hermanos?
6. ¿Por qué no tiene ganas de ir Raúl?
7. ¿Quién se enoja? ¿Por qué? ¿Tiene razón?

B. ¿Tiene Ud. buena memoria? Sin mirar la actividad A, hable de Raúl y Antonio.

C. Preguntas personales. Un compañero (Una compañera) lee las preguntas y Ud. contesta.

1. ¿Qué usas cuando te bañas / te secas? (Cuando me baño, uso...)
2. ¿A qué hora te bañas / te afeitas / te peinas por la mañana?
3. ¿Cómo sabes cuando un amigo se enoja? ¿Qué haces?
4. ¿Qué haces si estás mojado/a / si vas a llegar tarde a una fiesta / si quieres bañarte y no hay jabón / si quieres peinarte y no hay espejo?
5. ¿Te enojas frecuentemente? ¿Por qué (no)?

¿Catorce horas entre las sábanas?

Fourteen Hours Between the Sheets?

1. la sábana
2. la almohada
3. el despertador

◆ STEM-CHANGING REFLEXIVE VERBS ◆

Present	Preterite
acostarse (ue) *to go to bed*	
me acuesto	me acosté
te acuestas	te acostaste
dormirse (ue, u) *to fall asleep*	
me duermo	me dormí
te duermes	te dormiste
despertarse (ie) *to wake up*	
me despierto	me desperté
te despiertas	te despertaste
sentirse (ie, i) *to feel*	
me siento	me sentí
te sientes	te sentiste

1. ¿Se acuesta a las diez de la mañana? **2.** ¿Se duerme durante la clase? **3.** ¿Se despierta a las dos de la tarde? **4.** ¿Se siente contento/a cuando hay examen?

SILVIA: Me desperté muy *tarde* esta mañana y *no me levanté* hasta las diez.

ALICIA: *¿No funcionó* tu despertador o es que te acostaste muy tarde?

SILVIA: No usé el despertador. Anoche me acosté a las ocho y... me dormí *en cuanto* puse la cabeza en la almohada... y sin *quitarme la ropa.*

ALICIA: ¡No lo creo! ¿Catorce horas entre las sábanas? *¿Qué te pasó?*

SILVIA: *Al sentarme* a la mesa para *merendar,* me sentí muy *débil...* y la cabeza *así de grande* (*indicándole* a Alicia con las manos muy *separadas*).

ALICIA: ¿Cómo te sientes ahora?

SILVIA: Todavía *bastante* débil.

late / I didn't get up

Didn't . . . work

as soon as / taking my clothes off

What happened to you?

Upon sitting down / to eat a snack / weak
this big / indicating to her / separated

quite

Actividades

A. Conclusión nueva. Con un compañero (una compañera), haga los papeles (*play the roles*) de Alicia y Silvia. Traten de (*Try to*) terminar el diálogo de una manera original.

ALICIA

1. ¿Te acostaste... ?
2. ¡No lo creo! ¿Catorce... ?
3. ¿Cómo... ?

SILVIA

Sí, y me dormí...
Al sentarme... débil...
...débil

B. Un repaso. Ahora imagine que Ud. es Silvia. ¿Qué hizo Ud. ayer y hoy por la mañana?

1. acostarse / anoche / 8:00
2. dormirse / pronto
3. quitarse / la ropa
4. despertarse / muy tarde / esta mañana
5. no levantarse / hasta / 10:00
6. sentirse / ___¿?___

C. Su rutina nocturna. Invente varias oraciones para describir su rutina cada noche. **Posibilidades:** quitarse la ropa, acostarse, almohada, sábanas, dormir, despertador, levantarse

VISTA CULTURAL

La típica casa hispánica está orientada hacia (*toward*) el interior, pero el hispano generalmente se orienta hacia el exterior. Es decir (*That is to say*), muchas personas hispánicas prefieren pasar mucho tiempo fuera de casa, caminando, tomando café, hablando con sus amigos, etcétera.

GRAMÁTICA ESENCIAL

38. Reflexive Constructions

¿Por qué no te secas, te peinas y te pones algo rápido?

A reflexive construction in Spanish consists of a verb and one of the following pronouns: **me, te, se, nos, os, se.**

<table>
<tr><td colspan="4" align="center">bañarse (to bathe)</td></tr>
<tr><td>(yo)</td><td>me baño</td><td>(nosotros)</td><td>nos bañamos</td></tr>
<tr><td>(tú)</td><td>te bañas</td><td>(vosotros)</td><td>os bañáis</td></tr>
<tr><td>(Ud.)</td><td rowspan="3">se baña</td><td>(Uds.)</td><td rowspan="3">se bañan</td></tr>
<tr><td>(él)</td><td>(ellos)</td></tr>
<tr><td>(ella)</td><td>(ellas)</td></tr>
</table>

In a reflexive construction the action of the verb refers back to the subject of the sentence or clause rather than to its object. Compare the following.

NONREFLEXIVE CONSTRUCTION

(verb—object)

Levanto la silla.
I'm lifting the chair.

¿Lavas el coche?
Are you washing the car?

REFLEXIVE CONSTRUCTION

(subject—verb)

Me levanto.
I get (myself) up.

¿Te lavas las* manos?
Are you washing your hands?

Some Spanish verbs, like **lavarse,** are expressed reflexively in English with the word *self* (*selves*): **Se lava.** (*He/She is washing himself/herself.*) Other verbs must

---

*The definite article (not a possessive adjective, as in English) is generally used with parts of the body and articles of clothing to indicate possession in Spanish.

      Me pongo **la** chaqueta.   *I'm putting on my jacket.*

simply be memorized as having reflexive meaning in Spanish, since they are not usually expressed reflexively in English.

acostarse (ue)	*to go to bed*	bañarse	*to bathe*
despertarse (ie)	*to wake up*	levantarse	*to get up*

Some verbs, used reflexively, indicate a change often expressed in English with *to get* or *become,* or *to fall* (*asleep, in love, down, etc.*).

Se cansaron.	*They got tired.*
Se enoja.	*He gets mad.*
Nos perdimos.	*We got lost.*

When a stem-changing verb is used reflexively, you must keep in mind which pronoun is used as well as the change in the root of the verb.

Reminder: You may want to remind students of the "shoe verb" memory aid for stem-changing reflexive verbs.

Me desp**ie**rto temprano.	*I wake up early.*
Se ac**ue**sta tarde.	*He goes to bed late.*
Se s**i**ntió mal.	*She felt bad (ill).*

You can identify verbs used reflexively in Spanish by the **-se** attached to the end of the infinitive. Other verbs used reflexively in this lesson include:

afeitarse	*to shave oneself*
alegrarse	*to be glad*
animarse	*to cheer up*
divertirse (ie, i)	*to have a good time*
dormirse (ue, u)	*to fall asleep*
llamarse	*to be named, called*
llevarse bien/mal	*to get along well/badly*
peinarse	*to comb (one's hair)*
ponerse	*to put on (clothing)*
prepararse	*to prepare oneself*
quitarse	*to take off (clothing)*
secarse	*to dry oneself*
sentarse (ie)	*to sit down*
sentirse (ie, i)	*to feel*
vestirse (i, i)	*to get dressed*

Note, however, that almost any Spanish transitive verb can be used with a reflexive meaning.

admirar (*to admire*) →	admirarse (*to admire oneself*)
mirar (*to look at*) →	mirarse (*to look at oneself*)
preguntar (*to ask*) →	preguntarse (*to ask oneself*)

Actividades

A. La rutina de Raúl. Raúl se levanta temprano para arreglarse (*to get ready*) muy rápido porque él y sus cuatro hermanos tienen un solo baño. Diga qué hace Raúl por la mañana.

MODELO: Raúl / despertarse / 5:30 →
Raúl se despierta a las cinco y media.

1. levantarse / 5:35
2. bañarse / 5:40
3. secarse / 5:50

4. afeitarse / 5:55
5. peinarse / 6:10
6. vestirse / 6:15

Follow-up A: Divide class into ''present'' half and ''preterite'' half. Give infinitive and point to one side or other for appropriate form: **1.** *bañarse, yo* **2.** *lavarse, nosotros* **3.** *afeitarse, tú* **4.** *vestirse, ellas* **5.** *peinarse, Ud.* **6.** *sentarse, yo* **7.** *dormirse, él* **8.** *acostarse, nosotras*

Optional oral questions: **1.** *¿Se despierta Ud. a las 7:00?* **2.** *¿Se levantan Uds. a las 7:30?* **3.** *¿Se bañan entonces?* **4.** *¿Se preparan Uds. para los exámenes luego?* **5.** *¿Se duermen en la biblioteca?*

Suggestion D: Ask students to prepare short speech based on this exercise also.

Su hermano Orlando se levanta quince minutos después que Raúl y sigue (*follows*) la misma rutina todos los días. Diga la rutina que siguió Orlando ayer.

MODELO: Orlando / despertarse / 5:45 →
Orlando se despertó a las seis menos cuarto.

B. La vida diaria. Complete, usando el presente de la forma reflexiva o no-reflexiva del verbo indicado.

1. Yo _____ a los niños. Yo _____ y abro los ojos. despertar(se)
2. Él _____ el paquete grande. Él _____ temprano. levantar(se)
3. Yo _____ los cuchillos. ¿Tú no _____ nunca? lavar(se)
4. Yo _____ a los dos niños en la misma silla. Ellas _____ en esas sillas. sentar(se)
5. Yo _____ gran satisfacción. Ella _____ enferma. sentir(se)
6. Ella _____ ocho horas anoche. ¿Ud. no _____ hasta la una? dormir(se)

Ahora, imagine que estas cosas pasaron ayer y cambie los verbos al pretérito.

C. Tu rutina. Hágale estas preguntas a un compañero (una compañera).

1. ¿A qué hora te despiertas generalmente? ¿Te levantas inmediatamente? ¿Te despiertas a la misma (*same*) hora todos los días?
2. ¿Te vistes rápidamente? ¿Qué te pones generalmente para venir a clase? ¿Te miras en el espejo antes de salir de casa?
3. ¿A qué hora(s) te sientas a comer durante el día?
4. ¿Te quitas los zapatos cuando llegas a casa?
5. ¿A qué hora te pones el pijama por la noche generalmente? ¿A qué hora te acuestas? ¿Te duermes inmediatamente?

Ahora, prepare un monólogo para la clase sobre la rutina diaria de su compañero/a.

D. Problemas de la vida. Diga Ud....

1. cómo se anima cuando está triste
2. si se perdió la primera vez que vino a esta clase
3. cómo se lleva con sus hermanos (sus padres, sus hijos)
4. si se alegra cuando recibe una carta de un amigo (una amiga) y por qué (no)
5. cómo se divierte los fines de semana (*weekends*)
6. por qué se enoja con los amigos generalmente
7. cómo se prepara para un examen
8. cómo se siente antes y después de un examen

39. Position of Reflexive Pronouns

—¿Qué te pasó?
—Al sentarme a la mesa
para merendar, me sentí
muy débil...

Reflexive pronouns, like direct object pronouns, precede conjugated verbs and
negative commands. However, they follow and are attached to affirmative
commands, and may follow and be attached to infinitives and present participles as well.

PRECEDING

Tú siempre **te** despiertas temprano.	*You always wake up early.*
¿Por qué no **se** sienten bien?	*Why don't they feel well?*
No **se** levante.	*Don't get up.*

FOLLOWING AND ATTACHED

Sién**tese** Ud. aquí, por favor.	*Sit here, please.*

PRECEDING OR FOLLOWING

Juanita no $\begin{cases} \textbf{se} \text{ quiere acostar.} \\ \text{quiere acostar}\textbf{se.} \end{cases}$ *Juanita doesn't want to go to bed.*

Los niños $\begin{cases} \textbf{se} \text{ están sentando} \\ \text{en este momento.} \\ \text{están sentándo}\textbf{se} \text{ en} \\ \text{este momento.} \end{cases}$ *The boys are sitting down at this instant.*

NOTE: As with direct object pronouns, remember to add an accent when a
reflexive pronoun is attached to an affirmative command or a present
participle.

Actividades

A. ¿Qué quiere hacer Ud.? Cambie según los modelos.

MODELOS: ¿Quiere Ud. prepararse? →
Pues, prepárese Ud.

¿No quiere Ud. prepararse? →
Pues, no se prepare Ud.

1. ¿Quiere Ud. levantarse?
2. ¿Quiere Ud. peinarse?
3. ¿Quiere Ud. lavarse?
4. ¿Quiere Ud. afeitarse?
5. ¿No quiere Ud. bañarse?
6. ¿No quiere Ud. sentarse?

Ahora, invente preguntas similares para hacerle a un compañero (una compañera).

B. En este momento. Cambie según el modelo.

MODELO: ¿Va a lavarse pronto? (en este momento) →
Estoy lavándome en este momento.
Me estoy lavando en este momento.

1. ¿Quiénes se levantan ahora? (nosotros)
2. ¿Te lavas las manos ahora? (no, la cara)
3. Te afeitas con agua fría, ¿verdad? (no, agua caliente)
4. ¿Se peina él? (sí, ahora mismo)
5. ¿Quién es esa persona que se sienta en mi silla? (el profesor)

C. Diálogos en miniatura. Con un compañero (una compañera) de clase, complete los diálogos siguientes. Luego invente otro diálogo con otro verbo reflexivo.

AFEITARSE

—Bueno, (yo) _____[1] ahora.
—¿No (tú) _____[2] anoche?
—No, _____[3] ayer por la mañana.
—¿Por qué tienes que _____[4] todos los días?

ACOSTARSE

—¿A qué hora _____[5] Uds. hoy?
—Muy temprano, porque anoche no _____[6] hasta la medianoche (*midnight*).
—Pues, _____[7] ahora, si quieren, porque nosotros nos vamos a _____[8] inmediatamente.

40. Indirect Object Pronouns

Y la cabeza así de grande (indicándole a Alicia con las manos muy separadas).

An indirect object (noun or pronoun) expresses *to whom* or *for whom* something is done. For example, in the sentence *He gave the boy a dollar* (*He gave a dollar to the boy*), *the boy* is an indirect object. Here are the Spanish indirect object pronouns.

SINGULAR		PLURAL	
me	(*to, for*) *me*	nos	(*to, for*) *us*
te	(*to, for*) *you* (*fam.*)	os	(*to, for*) *you* (*fam.*)
le	(*to, for*) *you* (*pol.*), *him, her, it*	les	(*to, for*) *you* (*pol.*), *them*

Le presté mi despertador.

I lent her (you [pol.]*, him) my alarm clock.*

Les abrió la puerta.

She opened the door for them.*

The indirect object pronoun is also used in Spanish to refer to the person from whom something is taken, removed, purchased, and so on.

No les va a quitar el jabón a ellos.

He's not going to take away the soap from them.

Le compré las almohadas a la señora García.

I bought the pillows from Mrs. García.

NOTE: In Spanish the indirect object pronoun is generally used even when the indirect object noun to which it refers is expressed.

Él les habla a los alumnos.

He speaks (to them) to the students.

41. Position of Indirect Object Pronouns

The same principles governing the position of direct object pronouns apply to indirect object pronouns. They precede conjugated verbs and negative commands and follow and are attached to affirmative commands. When used in conjunction with infinitives and present participles, indirect object pronouns may either be attached to the infinitive or present participle or precede the conjugated verb.

---

*In this example *for* is not expressed with **para;** the meaning of the English preposition *for* is expressed by the Spanish indirect object pronoun.

Le di a la joven diez dólares para ir al mercado.	*I gave the girl ten dollars to go to the market.*
No le dé la mano a él.	*Don't shake his hand.*
¿Va Ud. a decirle a ella dónde está Juan?	
¿Le va Ud. a decir a ella dónde está Juan?	*Will you tell her where Juan is?*
Está enseñándole italiano.	
Le está enseñando italiano.	*She is teaching him Italian.*
¡Háblame, Juan!	*Speak to me, Juan!*

Indirect object pronouns can be emphasized or clarified by adding the following prepositional phrases: **a mí***... , **a ti...** , **a Ud./él/ella...** , **a nosotros...** , **a vosotros...** , **a Uds./ellos/ellas...** .

Ellos me hablan a mí, no a ti.	*They are talking to me, not to you.*
Le di el jabón a él, no a Ud.	*I gave the soap to him, not to you.*

NOTE: The prepositional phrase may precede or follow the verb.

Le mandaron a él una carta.	
A él le mandaron una carta.	*They sent him a letter.*

Actividades

A. Preparando una cena típica. Lea la oración y ponga el pronombre en el lugar apropiado. Si hay más de una posibilidad, invente dos oraciones.

> MODELO: (te) Yo hablo luego. → Yo te hablo luego.

1. (os) Quiero preparar una cena típica.
2. (me) Compre Ud. las legumbres.
3. (nos) Pero, ¿no dijeron quiénes van a venir hoy?
4. (les) No pregunten Uds. dónde almuerzan.
5. (le) ¿Va a preguntar eso María?

B. Las invitaciones. Cambie según el modelo. Dé todas las posibles oraciones.

> MODELO: Miguel habla a la muchacha. → Miguel le habla.

1. Mandamos una nota a la profesora.
2. Estamos escribiendo una carta personal a los señores Salcedo.
3. ¿Vas a mandar una invitación a tus amigos de curso?
4. Hablé al doctor Vallejo en persona.
5. ¿Qué dijiste a esa señorita venezolana?

Optional: Ask students to conjugate the verbs and provide the appropriate indirect object pronouns for the following: **1.** (*nosotros*) / *mandar* / *reloj (a Pepe)* **2.** (*ellos*) / *devolver* / *los dos regalos (a nosotros)* **3.** ¿(*tú*) / *comprar* / *una camisa (a él)*? **4.** (*ella*) / *presentar* / *el libro de poesía (a las dos estudiantes)* **5.** ¿(*él*) / *dar* / *jabón (a vosotras)*?

Expansion B: **6.** *Voy a escribir a la amiga de Miguel.* **7.** *Pregunta a tu abuela si recibió tu invitación.* **8.** *¿Mandaste una invitación a la tía Susana?*

Emphasis: Stress footnote. Remind students of other such couplets: *tu, tú; el, él.*

---

*To distinguish **mí** (the object of a preposition) from **mi** (possessive adjective), an accent is added to the former.

C.   Complete Ud. según el modelo. *The words in parentheses tell you to whom the indirect object pronoun refers.*

MODELO: (hijas)   _Les_ hablé _a ellas_ .

1.   (señoritas) El jefe no _____ dijo eso _____.
2.   (vosotros) La muchacha _____ sirvió _____ el almuerzo.
3.   (María) ¿ _____ escribió _____?
4.   (sobrino) El abuelo _____ trajo _____ estos suéteres.
5.   (nosotros) ¿Qué _____ dieron _____ los clientes?
6.   (señora) Don Carlos _____ explicó el problema _____.
7.   (yo) El profesor _____ dio una nota muy buena _____.
8.   (tú) ¿ _____ mandó Alicia una invitación a la fiesta?

42. *Gustar* and Verbs Like *gustar*

Ay, no tengo ganas de ir.
No me gusta la comida que
sirven los tíos y no me llevo
bien con los primos.

You have already used **me gusta(n), te gusta(n),** and **le gusta(n)** to express *I like, you like,* and *he/she/it likes.* You will have no trouble using all of the forms of **gustar** correctly if you remember that although **gustar** expresses the idea of *liking,* it actually means that something *is pleasing (to me, him, you, us, . . .*). Since you must tell to whom something is pleasing, the indirect object pronouns are always used with **gustar.** In addition, just as the verb changes in English when more than one thing is pleasing to someone (two things *are* pleasing), **gusta** changes to **gustan** when you are talking about two or more objects. Here is the complete conjugation of **gustar** in the present tense, with all of the indirect object pronouns.

Presentation: Explain it's best to avoid using *gustar* with people: expressions like *Me gustas* aren't accepted socially except between lovers. Alternate: *Me caes bien* (*simpático/a*). Remind students that "it" as object of *gustar* is not expressed in Spanish.

One thing is pleasing (*to me, you, him, us, . . .*):

Me gusta ⎫
Te gusta ⎪
Le gusta ⎬ el verano.
Nos gusta ⎪
Os gusta ⎪
Les gusta ⎭

Several things are pleasing (*to me, you, him, us, . . .*):

Me gustan ⎫
Te gustan ⎪
Le gustan ⎬ los deportes
Nos gustan ⎪ de invierno.
Os gustan ⎪
Les gustan ⎭

Note the following relationships:

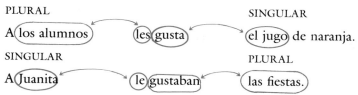

PLURAL   SINGULAR
A los alumnos   les gusta   el jugo de naranja.

SINGULAR   PLURAL
A Juanita   le gustaban   las fiestas.

NOTE: The indirect object pronoun must be used even when the indirect
object noun is present in the sentence. It is also common to use the
prepositional phrases given on page 193 to clarify which noun **le** and
les refer to, as well as for emphasis with the other pronouns.

A mí me gusta la nieve.   *I like the snow.*
A Elena le gusta viajar.   *Elena likes to travel.*

In the **gustar** construction, the prepositional phrases are most often placed
before the verb.

    Other verbs and phrases in similar constructions include **encantar** (*to love
something*), **hacer falta** (*to need*), **interesar** (*to interest*), and **parecer** (*to seem*).

Nos encanta viajar en auto.   *We love to travel by car.*
Le hace falta jabón.   *He needs soap.*
¿No te interesan los deportes?   *Aren't you interested in sports?**
Me parece increíble.   *It seems incredible to me.*

Actividades

A. ¿Que les gusta? Describa lo que les gusta a estas personas.

    MODELO: la ducha (a él) → Le gusta la ducha.

1. los abrazos de sus amigos (a ellos)
2. los besos de mi novio/novia (a mí)
3. el barrio de nuestra abuela (a nosotros)
4. el jugo de naranja (a ti)
5. las excursiones al campo (a ella)

B. Preguntas personales. Hágale estas preguntas a un compañero (una compañera) de clase.

1. ¿Qué te interesa más, poner tu dinero en el banco o hacer un viaje? ¿Te
interesa un viaje a Centro América? ¿Por qué (no)?
2. ¿Qué país realmente te encanta? ¿Por qué?
3. ¿Te encanta la ciudad en que vives? ¿Por qué (no)? ¿Te hace falta un coche
en esta ciudad? Explica por qué.
4. ¿Te parece fácil o difícil escribir una composición en español? ¿Por qué?

---

*Note the literal meaning of these sentences: *Traveling by car delights us; Soap is necessary to him;
Don't sports interest you?*

C.   Narraciones breves. Cambie las palabras indicadas, adaptando las narraciones a las personas indicadas.

1.   *Me* encantaban las fiestas, pero también *me* gustaba mucho leer, especialmente libros de historia, porque la historia *me* interesaba mucho. (**A mis amigos...**)

2.   *A Isabel le* hacía falta pollo para preparar el plato principal de la cena. *A toda la familia le* gustaba mucho el pollo, y *a Isabel le* parecía que con arroz con pollo en el menú la cena iba a ser un éxito (*success*). (**A nosotras...**)

3.   *A los estudiantes* no *les* interesaba la geografía, pero *les* gustaba conocer las costumbres (*customs*) hispánicas. *Les* hacía falta conocer estas costumbres para comprender mejor a los hispanos. (**A Gloria...**)

Suggestion C: Assign students to reconstruct brief situations they have actually experienced. If possible, they should use these verbs: *me encantaba(n), me gustaba(n), me interesaba(n), me hacía(n) falta, me parecía,* etc.

Para resumir y repasar

A.   En persona: Una fiesta de Navidad. Imagine que Ud. va con un amigo (una amiga) especial a una fiesta de Navidad. Ud. tiene que llevar un pequeño regalo para otra persona. Pero, nada resulta como Ud. esperaba. Primero, su reloj no funciona y Ud. casi no tiene tiempo para vestirse. Después, descubre que su regalo no sirve. Dígale a un compañero (una compañera) algo sobre su noche especial, su reloj, su regalo, etcétera.

B.   Una gran cena. Conteste según el modelo.

MODELO: ¿Encontraste la receta? (sí, ayer) →
          Sí, la encontré ayer.

1.   ¿Preparaste una gran cena la semana pasada? (no, anoche)
2.   ¿Invitaste a tus primas ayer? (no, el lunes)
3.   ¿No comió tu tío el pescado? (sí, después del postre)
4.   ¿No trajeron tus amigos vino el martes? (no, ayer)
5.   ¿Lavaron tus hermanos los platos? (sí, esta mañana)

C.   ¿Pretérito o imperfecto?

Mientras (*While*) _____ (yo: afeitarse[1]), mi hermano _____ (llamar[2]) por el intercomunicador. Me _____ (decir[3]) que ya _____ (ser[4]) las nueve menos veinte y que la fiesta _____ (comenzar[5]) pronto. _____ (Yo: Enojarse[6]) porque _____ (necesitar[7]) más tiempo para bañarme y vestirme. _____ (Él: Insistir[8]) en que no _____ (haber[9]) más tiempo. Entonces _____ (yo: decidir[10]) no ir a la fiesta.

D.   Errores. Éstas son las observaciones de un estudiante que no sabe mucho de los países hispánicos. Haga las correcciones necesarias.

1.   Guatemala está en el hemisferio sur y allí es invierno en junio.
2.   Bolivia tiene playas muy hermosas.
3.   Es posible esquiar en las montañas de Puerto Rico.
4.   La Paz es la capital del Paraguay.

COMUNICACIÓN

De la vida real

Note: In contrast to most pieces of realia used in *Motivos de conversación,* this one contains a lengthy narrative. You may want to use it as a reading, assigning short segments to different groups and having them work together to figure out each one.

^a*majority*
^b*contentas*
^c*gordas*
^d*hay... es necesario*
^e*sacarle... to get the most out of*
^f*tenemos*
^g*dejando... stopping from*
^h*taking advantage of*
ⁱ*te... will be necessary*
^j*cuantos... the more physical exercises that are done*
^k*se... one gets thin*
^l*lead to*
^m*effort*
ⁿ*unleashes*
^o*to burn*
^p*fats*
^q*swimming*
^r*Neither*
^s*forget*
^t*stairs*
^u*en... instead of*
^v*de... at once*
^w*dejar... stop being*
^x*los... others*
^y*Cease*
^z*complaining*
^{aa}*Por... lastly*

La mayoría[a] de las mujeres no se sienten felices[b] con el cuerpo que tienen; unas porque son demasiado gruesas,[c] otras porque son demasiado delgadas. No obstante, hay que[d] aprender a vivir con lo que tenemos y sacarle el mayor partido[e] posible a lo positivo que poseemos.[f]

LA IMAGEN

HAY que cambiar la actitud que tienes en relación a tu cuerpo, dejando de[g] proclamar tus defectos y aprovechando[h] tus cualidades. Si no optas por ese cambio no existen buenas intenciones que te valgan.[i] Pero habrá que hacer ejercicios físicos y ciertos ajustes de tipo psicológico.

Muchos creen que cuantos más ejercicios físicos se hagan[j] más rápido se adelgaza.[k] No es verdad. Primero, porque los excesos conducen[l] al aburrimiento, y consecuentemente, al abandono; segundo, porque el esfuerzo[m] muscular intenso desprende[n] ácido lacteo, que fatiga el músculo y le impide de seguir trabajando de forma coherente, al tiempo que bloquea la capacidad de quemar[o] grasas.[p] Lo mejor, según los expertos, es practicar algún tipo de ejercicio moderado, media hora al día, 3 a 5 veces por semana. Andar en bicicleta (movible o fija), la natación,[q] la gimnasia rítmica o «jazz», las caminatas o los ejercicios aeróbicos suaves son algunos ejemplos. Cada sesión debe terminar con 6 u 8 minutos de ejercicios de relajamiento. Tampoco[r] olvides[s] la gimnasia diaria que puedes hacer durante el día: como subir y bajar escaleras[t] en vez de[u] usar el ascensor; si la distancia que tienes que recorrer es pequeña hazla a pie en vez de ir en coche, etc. Igual de importante que el ejercicio es aprender a vivir con nuestro propio cuerpo. Decídete de una vez[v] a dejar de ser[w] la perfeccionista que encuentra siempre defectos cuando se compara con los demás.[x] Cesa[y] de una vez por todas de quejarte[z] de lo que te falta. Contémplate objetivamente y busca tus cualidades, empezando así a sacarles partido. No hay nadie perfecto y por eso lo importante es que estemos bien con nosotros mismos.

Por último,[aa] no olvides que más importante que tener un cuerpo bonito es lo que somos interiormente.

Conocemos mujeres bellísimas que despiertan la admiración por su belleza y... nada más. En cambio otras, menos «favorecidas» atraen a todos.

El secreto está en la personalidad que proyectan y en su vivacidad y simpatía.

A. La imagen. Conteste.

1. ¿Por qué no se sienten felices con el cuerpo que tienen la mayoría de las mujeres? ¿Qué hay que aprender a hacer? ¿A qué debemos sacarle el mayor partido posible?

2. ¿Qué hay que cambiar? ¿Qué debes dejar de proclamar? ¿Qué habrá que hacer entonces?

3. ¿Es verdad que se adelgaza más rápido haciendo muchos ejercicios? ¿A qué conducen los excesos? ¿Qué desprende el esfuerzo muscular intenso? ¿Qué le impide entonces?

4. ¿Qué tipo de ejercicios debes hacer, según los expertos? ¿Cuántas veces por semana? ¿Qué ejemplos de estos ejercicios da el artículo? ¿Cuáles son otras actividades que no debes olvidar?

5. ¿Qué debes decidir de una vez? ¿Cómo debes contemplarte? ¿Qué debes buscar? ¿Qué es más importante que tener un cuerpo bonito?

B. Menos calorías. Dígale a un compañero (una compañera) varias cosas sobre estas píldoras (*pills*). Por ejemplo: ¿Cómo se llaman? ¿Qué contienen? ¿Dónde puede comprarlas? ¿Qué le ayudan a perder? ¿Qué puede hacer para saber más sobre ellas? ¿Cuántas hay en el envase?

[a]*are in excess*
[b]*package*

Para conversar más

A. ¿Qué cree Ud.? Ahora, hable de sí mismo/a (*yourself*).

1. ¿Es Ud. perfeccionista? ¿Por qué es importante saber eso?
2. ¿Se siente Ud. feliz con su cuerpo? Explique.
3. ¿Qué hace Ud. para cambiar su imagen? (¿Sólo tiene buenas intenciones?)
4. ¿Qué ejercicios prácticos hace Ud. durante el día?
5. ¿Se puede contemplar a sí mismo/a objetivamente? ¿Qué buenas cualidades tiene Ud.?

B. Nuestro cuerpo. Comente con sus compañeros de clase.

1. Aunque (*Even though*) siempre hay una imagen de la persona perfecta, esta imagen no es siempre la misma. Piense por ejemplo en Marilyn Monroe, Twiggy y Christi Brinkley o en Robert Redford, Clint Eastwood y Michael Jackson. ¿Cuál de ellos corresponde a su imagen ideal?

2. Somos lo que comemos. ¿Qué come Ud.? ¿mucho azúcar? ¿muchas hortalizas y frutas? ¿mucha carne? ¿yogurt? ¿helado y pasteles? ¿Por qué es importante lo que comemos?

3. ¿Por qué es perder peso (*losing weight*) una obsesión en los Estados Unidos? Según Ud., ¿cuál es la mejor manera de perder peso?

C. Por la mañana.

1. Using as many of the reflexive verbs presented in this chapter as possible, make a list of infinitives that could be used to describe what you do during a typical morning.
2. After you have completed the list, conjugate the verbs and add other necessary details to describe a typical morning in your life.
3. Express what you did yesterday morning (preterite) and compare it to what you used to do in a typical morning as a child (imperfect).
4. Use your list of verbs to describe a typical morning in the lives of others: **sus padres, un amigo (una amiga), el profesor (la profesora).**
5. Use the verbs to ask a classmate questions about a typical morning in his or her life.

MOTIVO CULTURAL

Possibly two of the most prevalent stereotypes of Hispanics are those of the excitable, emotional person and the slow-paced, even lazy, one.

The fact that gestures are used more frequently in Spanish-speaking countries than they are in the United States probably leads many North Americans to believe that Hispanics are highly excited or angry when, in fact, they may simply be more expressive about what they are saying than is customary for English speakers. Gestures play an important role in communication in the Hispanic world, serving to add emphasis to what is being said or to subtly add positive or negative nuances to the verbal message they accompany. Be careful when you begin to use this physical "vocabulary," as it is easy to overuse gestures or to use them at

the wrong time. Note how Hispanics you know use gestures, and try to follow their lead.

Although the stereotypical "laid-back" Hispanic lifestyle may still be found in rural areas, the pace of life in large Hispanic urban centers rivals that of metropolitan areas in any of the industrialized countries. The majority of Hispanics value punctuality, and the tradition of the **siesta** is mostly a thing of the past.

Cultural expansion: You may want to demonstrate some common gestures used by Hispanics, such as: (1) *¡Un momento!* (index finger and thumb held half an inch apart) (2) *¡Ven/Venga!* (hand held palm down with fingers moving toward palm) (3) *¡Excelente!* or *¡Estupendo!* (fingers pulled together at tips, touched to pursed lips, and then opened as they are pulled away from the mouth) (4) *¡No!* (index finger moved in side-to-side motion) (5) *tacaño/a* (tapping the elbow with the palm of the other hand).

Vocabulario activo

Adjetivos

aburrido/a	boring
débil	weak
castaño/a	brown
corto/a	short (*in length*)
lacio/a	straight
largo/a	long
mojado/a	wet
necio/a	foolish
rizado/a	curly
rubio/a	blond(e)
tranquilo/a	calm

Sustantivos

EL CUERPO

la boca	mouth
el brazo	arm
la cabeza	head
la cara	face
la cintura	waist
el dedo	finger
el dedo del pie	toe
la espalda	back
la mano	hand
la nariz	nose
el ojo	eye
la oreja	ear
el pelo	hair
el pie	foot
la pierna	leg

OTROS SUSTANTIVOS

la almohada	pillow
el despertador	alarm clock
la ducha	shower
el espejo	mirror
el intercomunicador	intercom
el jabón	soap
la sábana	sheet
la toalla	towel

Verbos

VERBOS REFLEXIVOS

acostarse (ue)	to go to bed
afeitarse	to shave oneself
alegrarse	to be(come) happy
animarse	to cheer up
bañarse	to bathe oneself
cansarse	to get tired
despertarse (ie)	to wake up
divertirse (ie, i)	to have a good time
dormirse (ue, u)	to fall asleep
enojarse	to get angry
lavarse	to wash oneself
levantarse	to get up
llamarse	to be called, call oneself
llevarse bien/mal	to get along well/badly
peinarse	to comb (one's hair)
perderse (ie)	to get lost
ponerse	to put on (*clothing*)
prepararse	to prepare oneself
quitarse	to take off (*clothing*)
secarse	to dry oneself
sentarse (ie)	to sit down
sentirse (ie, i)	to feel
vestirse (i, i)	to get dressed

OTROS VERBOS

funcionar	to function, work
indicar	to indicate
merendar (ie)	to snack
saludar	to greet

Otras palabras y expresiones

acabar de + *inf.*	to have just (*done something*)
ahora mismo	right now
al + *inf.*	upon (*doing something*)
algo	something
así de grande	this big
bastante	quite, rather
dar la mano	to shake hands
en cuanto	as soon as
entre	between, among
es hora de + *inf.*	it's time (*to do something*)
¡No lo creo!	I don't believe it!
¿Qué te pasa/pasó?	What is happening/ happened to you?
tarde	late

Lectura

Antes de leer

Since it is not necessary to know every word to understand a reading in Spanish, you should learn to determine which words to look up in the dictionary. To decide whether to take the time to use a dictionary, it is often useful to identify the reading's function.

One way to determine the function of a text is to look at the verbs that are used. After examining the title of the following reading selection, as well as the photograph and some of the notes (to get an idea of what the selection is about), read through the first paragraph and make a list of the verbs.

Did you find all of the following verbs?

salió	**descubrió**	**hicieron pensar**
llevaron	**vivían**	**dieron**

What tense are these verbs in?

Now do a quick reading of the first paragraph and determine whether these verbs (and the phrases they are found in) are used mainly to

1. narrate the history of the islands
2. describe the islands
3. narrate the discovery and naming of the islands
4. describe the people who discovered the islands

Do you think it is important to understand completely the meaning of each of these verbs and the phrases in which they are found in order to have a clear notion of the content of the paragraph? In your own words, give a short synopsis of the paragraph.

Now scan the second paragraph and make a list of the verbs. Did you find the following verbs?

hay	**pesan**	**dieron**
parecen	**son**	**tienen**

What tense are most of the verbs in? Compare them to the verbs in the first paragraph. Read the second paragraph and decide whether these verbs (1) describe actions or (2) introduce descriptions.

What types of words give most of the information in this paragraph? Make a list of at least five of the phrases in which these words are found.

201

Note that it is not necessary for you to know the meaning of every one of these nouns and adjectives, once you realize that the function of this paragraph is to describe a series of birds and animals. Grasping this general notion may be sufficient for the time being.

Cultural expansion: Bring map of South America to class; have students locate Galápagos Islands and calculate distance between them and coast of South America. Just for fun, have one student investigate with travel agent how to get to islands, how much it would cost, what tourist facilities are there, etc.

Note: This text presents only a few animal names. If there is time, present others: *vaca, toro, caballo, mula, burro, oveja, cabra, gallina, pato, ardilla, camello, león, tigre, elefante, jirafa, cebra, mono, gorila, delfín, tiburón, ballena, etc.*

Una iguana gigantesca entre las rocas de las Islas Galápagos

Las Islas Galápagos

En 1535, *Fray* Tomás de Berlanga, un *fraile* dominico español, salió de Panamá navegando hacia el sur, pero las corrientes marinas llevaron su barco a una isla *desconocida* al oeste del Ecuador. Así descubrió accidentalmente un archipiélago de quince pequeñas islas. El paisaje[1] desolado sin vida humana, el *suelo* de origen volcánico y los animales raros que allí vivían hicieron pensar a los españoles que ésta era una tierra *embrujada,* y por eso el primer nombre que dieron a estas islas fue «Islas *Encantadas*».

En la fauna y la flora de las Islas Galápagos hay especies únicas en el mundo: iguanas negras y *rojizas,* enormes lagartos[2] con cresta, *ciempiés* tan grandes que parecen serpientes, y pájaros[3] extraños.[4] Hay también tortugas[5] gigantescas que pesan[6] más de 180 kilos, y esta clase de tortugas, llamadas «galápagos», son las que dieron a las islas el nombre que hoy tienen.

El explorador más famoso de la región fue Charles Darwin, quien *concibió* allí su teoría de la evolución. Él escribió en su diario: «Me llamaron mucho la atención las características de los fósiles de Sur América y las especies del archipiélago de Galápagos. Estos hechos[7], especialmente los últimos, son el origen de mis ideas... .»

Actualmente hay una estación de estudios biológicos de la UNESCO que lleva el nombre de Charles Darwin en la isla de Santa Cruz. Las islas pertenecen[8] al Ecuador, pero otros países también ayudan a mantener este centro dedicado a estudiar las extrañas formas de vida de la zona.

Fray = shortened form of **fraile** (*monk*).

You know **conocer.** Can you guess the meaning of this adjective?
You understand **origen volcánico.** What do you think **suelo** means here?
Bruja means *witch.* What English adjective describes something or someone under a witch's spell? This is a synonym of **embrujadas.**

This is a derivative of **rojo.** / What is the English name for an animal that has a hundred feet?

The English cognate of this verb has a different ending, but it is easy to guess if you read the end of the sentence.

At the present time (a false cognate)

---

[1]*landscape* [2]*lizards* [3]*birds* [4]*strange* [5]*turtles* [6]*weigh* [7]*facts* [8]*belong*

Después de leer

A. ¿Comprendió Ud.? Escoja (*Choose*) la respuesta correcta en cada caso.

1. Fray Tomás de Berlanga...

   a. era un naturalista
   b. descubrió Panamá
   c. era un explorador
   d. era un religioso español

2. Cuando Fray Tomás descubrió las islas Galápagos, allí no había...

   a. hombres y mujeres
   b. iguanas
   c. lagartos con cresta
   d. galápagos

3. Las islas se llamaron primero «Islas Encantadas» porque...

   a. a las personas que vivían allí les encantaban
   b. esta clase de tortugas abundaba allí
   c. el paisaje (*landscape*) era desolado y había allí animales extraños
   d. eran muchas islas

4. Las islas Galápagos fueron muy importantes en la vida de Darwin porque...

   a. él las descubrió
   b. concibió allí su teoría de la evolución
   c. perdió en ellas su diario
   d. murió allí

5. La UNESCO mantiene una estación en las islas Galápagos para...

   a. estudiar el diario de Charles Darwin
   b. defender al Ecuador
   c. estudiar los animales de este lugar
   d. colonizar el archipiélago

B. ¿Tiene Ud. buena memoria? Las descripciones de la columna derecha corresponden a los animales de la columna izquierda, pero en diferente orden. ¿Cuál es el orden correcto?

1. las iguanas
2. los ciempiés
3. las tortugas
4. los lagartos

   a. parecen serpientes
   b. pesan más de 180 kilos
   c. tienen cresta
   d. son de color negro y rojizo

C. Vocabulario. ¿Qué adjetivos uso para referirme a algo o a alguien que...

1. es de la orden religiosa de Santo Domingo?
2. no conozco?
3. está solitario?
4. fue víctima de una bruja?
5. no es común?
6. está relacionado con el mar?
7. es excepcionalmente grande?
8. tiene relación con la biología?

D. Complete sin consultar el texto.

Fray Tomás de Berlanga, un _____¹ dominico, salió de Panamá navegando hacia el _____², pero las corrientes marinas llevaron su _____³ a una isla al _____⁴ del

Ecuador. Actualmente, hay una _____⁵ de la UNESCO que lleva el _____⁶ de Charles Darwin en la isla de Santa _____.⁷ Las islas pertenecen a _____,⁸ pero otros países también ayudan a _____⁹ este centro dedicado a _____¹⁰ las extrañas _____¹¹ de vida de la zona.

E. Para escribir. Ud. es Fray Tomás de Berlanga o el famoso explorador Charles Darwin. Describa sus primeras impresiones de las islas Galápagos. Diga algo de su fauna, su nombre, el posible uso de las islas en el futuro, etcétera.

Repaso visual

Describa los dibujos. Considere las siguientes preguntas: ¿Qué objetos hay en los dibujos? ¿Quiénes son las personas que están en los dibujos? ¿Dónde están? ¿Qué hacen?

Examen de repaso 3

A. Excusas variadas. Complete estas excusas, poniendo un pronombre en el lugar apropiado.

1. La lección, no _____ pude _____ estudiar _____, porque _____ presté _____ mi libro a una amiga. (*it, fem. / her*)
2. Si el profesor pregunta por mí, _____ digan _____ que estoy enfermo. (*him*)
3. ¿Los vídeos? _____ voy _____ a _____ devolver _____ mañana; mi hermano _____ tiene _____ ahora. (*them / them*)
4. ¿ _____ esperabas _____ en la Plaza de Armas? Pues yo _____ estaba _____ esperando _____ en la Calle Luz. (*me / you, fam.*)

B. ¿Pretérito o imperfecto?

(Ser¹) las cinco cuando (yo: salir²) de casa. (Ver³) que (llover⁴) y (volver⁵) para buscar el paraguas (*umbrella*). Pero no (estar⁶) en el ropero. Lo (buscar⁷) por toda la casa, pero no lo (encontrar⁸) ¡Claro! Mi hermano lo (tener⁹). (Yo: Estar¹⁰) enojado porque (tener¹¹) prisa y mis amigos me (esperar¹²). Entonces, (llamar¹³) un taxi.

C. Los gustos de mi familia. Complete usando la forma apropiada de **gustar, encantar, hacer falta, interesar** o **parecer.**

1. A mi padre _____ _____ las novelas de espías.
2. A mis hermanos _____ _____ la playa.
3. A mi _____ _____ estudiar más para el examen mañana.
4. A mi madre _____ _____ las canciones románticas de Julio Iglesias.
5. A todos nosotros _____ _____ el helado de chocolate.

D. Un anuncio. Dé la forma apropiada de los infinitivos.

¿(Querer¹) Ud. bailar con su novia pero (preferir²) invitarla al cine porque (pensar³) que ir a un centro nocturno (*nightclub*) (costar⁴) mucho? Pues, (visitar⁵) Ud. Tropical! (Pedir⁶) nuestro descuento especial para estudiantes y (comenzar⁷) inmediatamente a divertirse con nuestra estupenda música.

E. Cambie las palabras indicadas por las nacionalidades de las personas.

1. mis amigos *de Caracas*
2. la profesora *de Quito*
3. el cantante *de Madrid*
4. un vecino *de Managua*
5. los estudiantes *de San Juan*
6. la señorita *de San José*

F. La rutina de mi familia. Complete con la forma apropiada del verbo y el pronombre reflexivo apropiado.

Yo (acostarse¹) muy tarde; por eso no me gusta (levantarse²) temprano. A veces no oigo el despertador y mi madre me dice: «¡(Despertarse³), José!» Mi padre siempre (bañarse⁴) primero y luego (afeitarse⁵). A veces mi hermanito no quiere (lavarse⁶) antes de ir al colegio y mi madre le dice: «¡Juanito, (lavarse⁷) la cara y las manos ahora mismo!» Todos nosotros (sentarse⁸) a desayunar a las siete y media.

G. Vocabulario. Complete.

1. Cosas que tengo en mi casa. En el baño tengo _____ para lavarme, un _____ para mirarme y una _____ para secarme. En mi cama tengo una _____ y _____.
2. Sé mucha historia y también mucha geografía. Por ejemplo, sé que en 1992 se celebran los 500 años del _____ de _____ por Cristóbal Colón. También sé que Bolivia está al _____ del Ecuador, que no tiene _____ y que por esta razón los bolivianos no pueden ir a la _____ en el verano.

H. Una clase loca. Cambie los verbos indicados al presente progresivo.

Todo el mundo (*Everyone*) *habla* durante la clase. La profesora *repite* lo que explicó antes, pero como nadie la puede oír, ella *pide* silencio. Yo *me muero* de sueño y mi amigo Luis *duerme*.

Coches y carreteras

¿Tiene Ud. prisa? —En la Avenida de la Reforma de la Ciudad de México, hay mucho tráfico a todas horas.

METAS

Comunicación: In this lesson you will learn vocabulary and expressions related to automobiles, street maps, and highway and traffic problems. You will learn to use Spanish to figure out a map, talk about an accident, explain your car's deficiencies, and give directions.

Estructuras: 43. The Perfect Tenses 44. Irregular Past Participles 45. Two Object Pronouns 46. **Se** with Direct Object Pronouns

GRÁFICOS

El coche

1. el asiento
2. el volante
3. los frenos
4. el acelerador
5. el/la chofer/el conductor (la conductora)
6. la llanta/la goma
7. la rueda
8. el faro
9. el motor
10. la llave
11. el parabrisas
12. el limpiaparabrisas
13. el baúl/el maletero
14. el policía/la mujer policía*
15. la gasolinera

No estacionar; No aparcar *No parking*
poner una multa *to give a ticket (a fine)*

Cultural expansion: Vocabulary related to the car varies a great deal depending on the country. Tires, for instance, are called *llantas* in most of Spain and South America and *gomas* in the Caribbean area. As for the word *chofer,* the tendency in Spanish America is to place the stress on the *e* while in Spain it is stressed on the *o* and has a written accent.

Actividades

A. Cubra la lista y dé la palabra que corresponde a cada número del dibujo.

B. ¿Tiene Ud. buena memoria? ¿Qué palabra asocia Ud. con las siguientes situaciones?

1. Una muchacha cruza (*crosses*) la calle; está leyendo una carta y no mira el tráfico. Un auto viene rápidamente.

   a. motor   b. asiento   c. frenos

2. Son las 11:00 de la noche. Vuelvo a casa en auto, pero no voy por las calles principales porque no veo bien el camino (*way*).

   a. ruedas   b. faros   c. llantas

3. El policía escribe algo en un papel y lo pone en el parabrisas.

   a. multa   b. asiento   c. volante

4. No sé qué hacían esos jóvenes con mi carro, pero ahora tengo que ir a la gasolinera.

   a. llantas   b. cuadros   c. acelerador

Emphasis: Point out footnote. You may want to stress other gender problems in current Spanish: el músico / la música, el químico / la química.

*Whereas **el policía** means *policeman,* **la policía** means *the police* in the more general sense of the police force.

5. Ese señor salió del bar y subió a su auto. Él es la causa del accidente.

   a. gasolinera   b. ruedas   c. chofer

6. El espacio es pequeño, pero creo que puedo estacionar mi coche.

   a. gasolinera   b. acelerador   c. volante

7. Ese carro iba muy rápido por la carretera porque el chofer tenía prisa.

   a. parabrisas   b. frenos   c. acelerador

8. Es ilegal estacionar en esta calle.

   a. policía   b. motor   c. llave

9. Está lloviendo y hay agua en el parabrisas.

   a. maletero   b. limpiaparabrisas   c. gomas

10. Siempre llevo una llanta extra en el coche.

    a. frenos   b. baúl   c. asiento

Buscando la carretera de Montevideo a Punta del Este*

⊗ el peatón y el chofer

*Vea Vista cultural, p. 211.

◆ **PRESENT PERFECT TENSE** ◆

-ar: examinar

| he examinado | *I have examined* |
| ha examinado | *you (he/she/it) have (has) examined* |

-er: comprender

| he comprendido | *I have understood* |
| ha comprendido | *you (he/she/it) have (has) understood* |

-ir: venir

| he venido | *I have come* |
| ha venido | *you (he/she/it) have (has) come* |

1. el Correo Central
   Main Post Office
2. la catedral   *cathedral*
3. la estación del ferrocarril   *train station*
4. la Jefatura de Policía
   Police Headquarters
5. el Palacio Municipal
   City Hall

   la avenida (Av.)
   la carretera/la autopista
   highway/superhighway
   la esquina   *corner*

Un conductor perdido *se dirige a* un *peatón*.

CHOFER: He examinado el mapa *con cuidado,* pero parece que no lo he comprendido bien. ¿Quiere *explicármelo,* por favor? Busco la carretera que va a Punta del Este.

PEATÓN: Voy a *explicárselo.* Ud. ha venido *mal. Siga* por la Avenida 18 de Julio. En la Plaza Independencia, *doble a la derecha* y *dé la vuelta a* la plaza. Entre en la calle Florida y *siga todo derecho* hasta la esquina con la Rambla Sur. Ahí *doble a la izquierda* y siga por la Rambla Sur, que *se convierte en* la carretera de Punta del Este. Tiene que *pasar por* dos pequeños parques que están a la derecha y el cementerio a la izquierda. No es difícil, pero lea los *letreros.*

CHOFER: ¿Es un viaje corto?

PEATÓN: No es corto, pero *tampoco* es muy largo. Y es muy *agradable.*

CHOFER: *Mil* gracias. Adiós.

PEATÓN: *De nada.* ¡Ay! ¡Un momento! ¡*Caramba!* La calle Florida *está en obras.*

addresses / pedestrian

carefully

explain it to me

explain it to you / the wrong way / Continue
turn right / go around
go straight ahead

turn left

becomes / to pass by

signs

neither / pleasant

Many (A thousand)

You are welcome. / Darn it!
is closed for repairs

Optional: Drill vocabulary by giving definitions and asking students to produce the corresponding words orally. **1.** *es adonde llevo las cartas (el Correo Central)* **2.** *es una iglesia importante (la catedral)* **3.** *es donde llegan los trenes (la estación del ferrocarril)* **4.** *es la intersección de dos calles (la esquina)* **5.** *es donde los conductores pueden ir muy rápido (la carretera o la autopista)*

Suggestion: Dramatize dialogue with pairs of students.

MOTIVO CULTURAL

In the city of Montevideo there are several Ramblas, which are very beautiful drives alongside the coastline. In Spain, the word **rambla** has a slightly different meaning: it refers to a wide avenue divided by a tree-lined promenade. The **Rambla** in the city of Barcelona, in northeastern Spain, is famous worldwide.

Actividades

A. El mapa de Montevideo. Conteste.

1. ¿Ha examinado con cuidado el mapa el conductor? ¿Por qué tiene que explicárselo el peatón?
2. ¿Qué tiene que hacer el chofer para llegar a la calle Florida desde (*from*) la Avenida 18 de Julio?
3. ¿Qué debe leer el conductor, según el peatón?
4. ¿Cómo es el viaje que va a hacer el chofer?
5. El peatón dijo que la calle Florida está en obras. ¿Qué otra calle puede tomar el conductor desde la Plaza Independencia?
6. ¿Cómo se llama la plaza más grande del mapa? ¿Qué otras plazas hay en la Avenida 18 de Julio?
7. ¿En qué se convierte la Rambla Gran Bretaña?
8. ¿En qué esquina está la Jefatura de Policía?
9. Ud. quería ir a la catedral. Subió por la calle Rondeau y ahora está en la estación del ferrocarril. ¿Ha venido mal? ¿Cómo debe ir?

Expansion B: In pairs, have students give each other directions from one street corner to another.

Suggestion B: Students should prepare carefully enough to be able to give directions quickly and easily.

B. ¿Quiere Ud. explicármelo, por favor? Déle instrucciones a un peatón (un compañero [una compañera]) para ir a los lugares indicados de Montevideo. Use el diálogo como modelo para explicárselo.

Variation B: Put map of your institution's neighborhood on board and ask students to tell how to get from one place to another.

1. la estación del ferrocarril → la Jefatura de Policía
2. el Palacio Municipal → el Correo Central
3. la Plaza Independencia → la Jefatura de Policía
4. la Plaza Libertad → el Cementerio Central

La dama y el tigre

Cultural expansion: It has long been customary in many Hispanic countries for women to be police officers. They act at every level, from directing traffic to investigating serious crimes.

The Lady and the Tiger

1. la acera
2. el semáforo
3. el camión
4. la camioneta
5. la señal de tráfico
6. las esposas

manejar/conducir *to drive*
parar *to stop*

◆ IRREGULAR PAST PARTICIPLES ◆

hacer: hecho	
he hecho	*I have done*
ha hecho	*you (he/she/it) have (has) done*
ver: visto	
he visto	*I have seen*
ha visto	*you (he/she/it) have (has) seen*
decir: dicho	
he dicho	*I have said*
ha dicho	*you (he/she/it) have (has) said*
poner: puesto	
he puesto	*I have put*
ha puesto	*you (he/she/it) have (has) put*

Note: *Esposa* means both "handcuff" and "wife," spawning many jokes in Hispanic countries. "To drive" is generally *conducir* in Spain but *manejar* in Spanish America.

LA MUJER POLICÍA: ¡Qué *choque*! Hombre, ¿qué ha hecho Ud.? ¿Por qué ha subido a la acera?

TOMÁS: ¡Pero si yo no he visto la acera!

LA MUJER POLICÍA: ¿Tampoco ha visto Ud. este camión con que ha *chocado*?

TOMÁS: Pues sí, pero cuando iba a parar, *en frente del* semáforo, un tigre y una señorita muy elegante cruzaban la calle... y...

LA MUJER POLICÍA: *La verdad es que* Ud. no puede manejar porque ha bebido demasiado. *¡Vaya sueño!* Déme su *carnet de conducir*. Ud. está *borracho* y la *ley* prohíbe manejar así.

TOMÁS: ¿Qué ha dicho? ¡Borracho! ¡Que no puedo manejar!

LA MUJER POLICÍA: No discuta más. *Está detenido*.

TOMÁS: *¡Dios mío!** Me ha puesto las esposas. ¿Es éste otro sueño?

collision

collided

in front of

The truth is that

What a dream! / driver's license

drunk / law

You are under arrest.

For Heaven's sake!

Suggestion: Based on the information in the dialogue, have students prepare a scene before the judge with Tomás and the policewoman giving their individual versions of the accident.

---

*¡Dios mío!, literally *My God!*, is a very common expression in Spanish and it is not considered irreverent.

Actividades

A. Vamos a hablar de Tomás.

1. ¿Adónde ha subido Tomás? ¿Por qué?
2. ¿Con qué ha chocado él? ¿Por qué? Según Tomás, ¿quiénes han cruzado la calle?
3. ¿Por qué ha dicho la mujer policía que Tomás no puede manejar?
4. ¿Cree Ud. que ha bebido mucho este conductor? ¿Por qué (no)?
5. ¿Qué le ha puesto la mujer policía a Tomás?

B. Y ahora, vamos a hablar de Ud.

1. ¿Ha bebido Ud. demasiado alguna vez (*ever*)? ¿Cuándo?
2. Ud. no ha manejado cuando ha bebido demasido, ¿verdad? ¿Qué ha hecho?
3. ¿Ha visto Ud. alguna vez un tigre en la calle? ¿un choque? ¿Cuándo? ¿Qué pasó?
4. ¿Cuántas multas le ha puesto a Ud. la policía? ¿Lo/La han detenido alguna vez?
5. ¿Ha dicho Ud. siempre la verdad? ¿Por qué (no)?

C. Pregúntele a un compañero (una compañera)...

1. si tiene carnet de conducir, si le gusta manejar, ¿por qué (no)?
2. si tiene un auto (o si no tiene, si quiere comprar uno), ¿qué tipo?
3. si es difícil aparcar en la universidad, ¿por qué (no)?
4. si ha tenido problemas con la ley, si le han puesto una multa alguna vez, ¿por qué?
5. si, cuando es peatón (peatona), cruza la calle cuando el semáforo está en rojo

Variation C: Students can answer questions in written form and/or present the information to the class.

VISTA CULTURAL

Esta foto es de Punta del Este, un balneario (*beach resort*) muy elegante que está en el Atlántico, al este de la ciudad de Montevideo, Uruguay.

Punta del Este es un lugar caro y exclusivo; le llaman la Riviera de Sudamérica. Sus playas son preciosas y extensas, y las familias ricas del Uruguay y otros países sudamericanos pasan allí los meses del verano: diciembre, enero, febrero y marzo. También es importante por las actividades que se celebran en esta ciudad. Todos los años hay un festival internacional de cine, ha sido varias veces el sitio de reunión de la Organización de Estados Americanos (OEA en español, OAS en inglés) y John F. Kennedy firmó (*signed*) allí en 1962 el pacto que se llamó «Alianza para el Progreso».

GRAMÁTICA ESENCIAL

43. The Perfect Tenses

He examinado el mapa con
cuidado, pero parece que
no lo he comprendido bien.

A. The present perfect tenses in Spanish are made up of a conjugated form
of the verb **haber** and a past participle (**participio pasado**). The present tense
of the auxiliary verb **haber** (*to have*) is conjugated as follows.

he	hemos
has	habéis
ha	han

Regular past participles are formed by dropping the infinitive ending and
adding **-ado** for **-ar** verbs and **-ido** for **-er** and **-ir** verbs.

-ar: examinar → examin**ado** *examined*
-er: entender → entend**ido** *understood*
-ir: salir → sal**ido** *gone out*

Here is the present perfect tense in all three conjugations.

-ar: dar		-er: ser		-ir:* recibir	
he dado	*I have given*	he sido	*I have been*	he recibido	*I have received*
has dado	*you have given*	has sido	*you have been*	has recibido	*you have received*
ha dado	*you have (he/she/ it has) given*	ha sido	*you have (he/she/ it has) been*	ha recibido	*you have (he/she/ it has) received*
hemos dado	*we have given*	hemos sido	*we have been*	hemos recibido	*we have received*
habéis dado	*you have given*	habéis sido	*you have been*	habéis recibido	*you have received*
han dado	*you/they have given*	han sido	*you/they have been*	han recibido	*you/they have received*

*-**Er** and **-ir** verbs whose stems end with a strong vowel (**a, e,** or **o**) require a written accent on
the **i** of the past participle ending: **leer → leído, traer → traído, oír → oído.**

To make a present perfect verb negative, place **no** before the form of **haber.**

Juan **no ha** hablado.   *Juan has not spoken.*

Place all object pronouns before the helping verb. If the sentence is negative, **no** precedes the object pronoun(s).

Él **(no) me lo** ha dado.   *He has (not) given it to me.*

To form a question in the present perfect, put the subject after the past participle.

¿Han venido las señoras?   *Have the ladies come?*
¿Ha lavado Juan el coche?   *Has Juan washed the car?*

The present perfect in Spanish does not always have an exact equivalent with the English present perfect. In addition to expressing *to have done something,* it can also express the simple past.

¡Pero si yo no he visto la acera!   *But I didn't see the sidewalk!*

B.   Once you have learned the present perfect, you can easily form the pluperfect (*I had given, you had given,* and so on). Just combine the imperfect of **haber (había, habías, había, habíamos, habíais, habían)** with the past participle of another verb.

había preparado	*I had prepared*	habíamos charlado	*we had chatted*
habías traído	*you had brought*	habíais bebido	*you had drunk*
no había comido	*you/he/she/it had not eaten*	no habían chocado	*you/they had not collided*

When two past actions are presented in the same sentence, the pluperfect indicates which action happened first. This tense is used frequently in Spanish.

Cuando el chofer vio el camión,   *When the driver saw the truck he*
ya **había chocado** con él.   *had already collided with it.*

Actividades

Variation A: Substitute pluperfect for present perfect. Any exercises in this section can also illustrate pluperfect. (Remind students to change demonstratives as necessary.)

A.   Vacaciones y pasatiempos (*pastimes*). Dé el participio pasado del infinitivo.

Todos hemos (viajar[1]) este año. Tomás ha (ir[2]) a Acapulco y Juliana y sus padres han (visitar[3]) Costa Rica. Yo no he (estar[4]) en otros países; mis viajes han (ser[5]) cortos, pero agradables.

Esta semana Marta y yo hemos (jugar[6]) al tenis cinco veces y ella ha (ganar[7]) cinco veces. Eso quiere decir que he (perder[8]) cinco veces. Juan y Pedro me han (invitar[9]) a jugar con ellos, pero he (tener[10]) que decirles que no me interesa jugar más.

B. Mis actividades hoy. Según el modelo, describa lo que Ud. ha hecho antes de venir a clase hoy. **Verbos posibles:** comer, caminar, estudiar, conversar, ir, llegar, entrar

> MODELO: salir, 8:15 → He salido de casa a las 8:15.

C. El viaje de mi familia. Mi familia va a hacer un viaje en auto y todos hemos cooperado preparando el coche. Cambie los verbos al presente perfecto para indicar lo que hemos hecho.

Pedro *limpia*[1] los faros y el parabrisas y *lava*[2] el resto del coche. Yo *ajusto*[3] los asientos, mi hermana Cecilia *revisa* (checks)[4] el aire de las llantas y mi padre *lleva*[5] el coche a la gasolinera y *llena*[6] el tanque de gasolina. Mi madre también *ayuda*,[7] pero de manera diferente. Ella *prepara*[8] sándwiches deliciosos para comer en el camino, *compra*[9] los refrescos y lo *pone*[10] todo en una cesta (*basket*). Ahora imagine que Ud. está describiendo los preparativos para un viaje que hicieron el año pasado. (Pedro había limpiado...)

44. Irregular Past Participles

¿Qué ha dicho? ¡Borracho!

A few past participles are irregular in Spanish; most of them are given below. You can now form the past participle for every verb studied in this text.

abrir:	**abierto**	*opened*		poner:	**puesto**	*put, placed*
decir:	**dicho**	*said, told*		romper:	**roto**	*broken*
escribir:	**escrito**	*written*		ver:	**visto**	*seen*
hacer:	**hecho**	*done; made*		volver:	**vuelto**	*returned*
morir:	**muerto**	*died*				

Actividad

Mi abuela en su coche. Cambie según el modelo.

> MODELO: ella / volver / a casa / temprano →
> Ella ha vuelto a casa temprano.

1. mi abuela / abrir / la puerta
2. ella / subir / al coche

3. ella / poner la llave / en el coche
4. ella / manejar mal
5. yo / verla / chocar / con un camión
6. el chofer del camión / no morir, afortunadamente
7. él / sólo / romperse / el brazo
8. dos policías / llegar / en ese momento
9. ellos / escribir / algo
10. mi abuela / volver / a su coche / muy triste

Now can you retell this story in your own words?

45. Two Object Pronouns

He examinado el mapa con cuidado, pero parece que no lo he comprendido bien. ¿Quiere explicármelo, por favor?

When an indirect and a direct object pronoun appear together, the indirect always precedes the direct. They are never separated by other words in the sentence.

Él **me lo** dio.	*He gave it to me.*
Ella no quiere explicár**telo.**	*She does not want to explain it to you.*
No **nos lo** lea.	*Don't read it to us.*

NOTE: Double object pronouns follow the same placement rules that apply to single object pronouns.

Actividades

A. ¿Quién lo hace? Complete poniendo los pronombres en el lugar apropriado.

1. (te lo) ¿El coche? Luis _____ presta _____ con mucho gusto.
2. (nos los) ¿Los frenos? El mecánico _____ va a _____ ajustar _____.
3. (te los) ¿Los letreros? Tú no sabes español. Yo _____ voy a _____ leer _____.
4. (me lo) ¿El carnet de conducir? El policía _____ ha _____ pedido _____.
5. (me lo) ¿El dinero para pagar la multa? Mis amigos no _____ quieren _____ prestar _____.

B. Una persona contradictoria. Ud. va con su compañero/a en el coche. Llegan a una gasolinera y cuando Ud. pide algo, su compañero/a lo/la contradice.

> MODELO: (El mapa) Explíquenoslo. →
> No nos lo explique.

1. (La gasolina) Pónganosla Ud.
2. (El parabrisas) Límpienoslo.
3. (Los letreros) Léanoslos.
4. (Las puertas) Ábranoslas.
5. (Las instrucciones) Dénoslas.
6. (El volante) Ajústenoslo.

C. Hagan Uds. lo mismo ahora, usando esta vez **me.**

> MODELO: (El mapa) Explíquemelo. →
> No me lo explique.

46. *Se* with Direct Object Pronouns

—Busco la carretera que va a Punta del Este.
—Voy a explicárselo. Ud. ha venido mal.

If both object pronouns are in the third person, whether singular or plural, the indirect object pronoun changes from **le (les)** to **se.** Study the following examples.

Le dimos **el volante al chofer.**

Se lo dimos.   *We gave it to him.*

Les dimos **la gasolina a las muchachas.**

Se la dimos.   *We gave it to them.*

Le dimos **los mapas a Juan.**

Se los dimos.   *We gave them to him.*

Les dimos **las instrucciones a las señoritas.**

Se las dimos.   *We gave them to them.*

This pattern also applies, of course, to any other combinations of third persons, singular or plural: *them to you (sing.), it to you (pl.), you to them (masc.), her to them (fem.),* and so on.

NOTE: If the meaning of **se** is unclear, clarify it with a prepositional phrase (**a Ud., a él, a ella,** etc.), as explained in **Gramática esencial** 41.

Se lo dimos a ellas.   *We gave it to them.*

Actividades

A. Un encuentro con un policía. Cambie según el modelo.

MODELO: El policía le indicó al chofer que debía parar inmediatamente. →
Se *lo* indicó.

1. El policía le dijo al chofer que la ley prohibía estacionar allí. Se _____ dijo.
2. Después el policía le pidió el carnet de manejar. Se _____ pidió.
3. El chofer le explicó sus razones al policía. Se _____ explicó.
4. El policía le devolvió el carnet y no le puso una multa. Se _____ devolvió y no se _____ puso.
5. El chofer le dio las gracias al policía. Se _____ dio.

B. Una compra imposible. Dé los pronombres apropiados en el orden correcto.

MODELO: El dependiente le enseñó (*showed*) las llantas a Alberto. →
  Se   las   enseñó.

1. Entonces el dependiente le enseñó a Alberto una lista de precios. _____ _____ enseñó.
2. Alberto le pidió un precio más bajo. _____ _____ pidió.
3. El dependiente le explicó a Alberto su situación. _____ _____ explicó. No podía bajarle el precio. No _____ _____ podía bajar.
4. Alberto le dijo su problema. _____ _____ dijo. No tenía suficiente dinero.
5. El dependiente no quiso escucharle sus razones. No quiso escuchar _____ _____.
6. Alberto no le compró las llantas. No _____ _____ compró. Le dio las gracias al dependiente y salió. _____ _____ dio y salió.

C. En una gasolinera. Cambie las palabras indicadas por pronombres, según el modelo.

MODELO: Voy a explicarle *mi problema al empleado.* →
Voy a explicárselo.

1. Primero, el dueño le pone *aceite a un coche.*
2. También les da *instrucciones a dos empleados.*
3. Después, el dueño le explica *el mapa a un automovilista perdido.*
4. Juan, un empleado, está llenándome *el tanque de gasolina.*
5. Pepe, otro empleado, está vendiéndole *dos faros a una señorita.*
6. Después Pepe va a cambiarles *las llantas a dos clientes.*

Para resumir y repasar

A. En persona: Un coche especial. Imagine que le han hecho un coche especial y Ud. ha podido hacer un viaje extraordinario. Describa el coche y su viaje. ¿Cuáles son los aspectos más interesantes de los dos?

B. Guillermito y su hermano. *Every time Guillermito's mother accuses him of doing or not doing something, he puts the blame on his older brother, José. With a classmate, do this dialogue, playing the part of Guillermito.*

MODELO: No te llevas bien con tus primos, Guillermito.
Yo me llevo bien con mis primos, José no se lleva bien con ellos.

1. No te lavaste las manos.
2. Te secaste con mi toalla.
3. Nunca te vistes bien.
4. Te quitaste los zapatos en la cocina.
5. Te enojaste con tu abuela.
6. No te peinaste.

C. Los hermanos Mendoza son antipáticos. Complete las quejas (*complaints*) que tengo sobre ellos con el pronombre del objeto directo o indirecto apropiado. ¿Por qué no soy amigo de los hermanos Mendoza? Porque...

1. (a su madre) No _____ llaman cuando van a llegar tarde a casa.
2. (a sus vecinos) No _____ saludan cuando los ven en la calle.
3. (a sus amigos) No _____ pagan el dinero que _____ deben.
4. (a ti) Tú eres mi mejor amigo, pero ellos no _____ quieren.
5. (a mí) Además, no _____ devolvieron el disco que yo (a ellos) _____ presté.

COMUNICACIÓN

De la vida real

[a]*driving*
[b]*to use something for the first time*

SAQUELE[a] A SU CARRO USADO EL MEJOR PRECIO DEL MERCADO.

El precio Sprint

Venga ahora mismo a su Concesionario[b] Chevrolet con su automóvil usado. Se lo recibimos al mejor precio del mercado como parte de pago[c] de un Chevrolet Sprint modelo 90, con garantía de 2 años ó 40.000 kilómetros.

Concesionarios Chevrolet.

La gente amable[d]

[a]*Get from*
[b]*authorized dealer*
[c]*payment*
[d]*nice*

A. ¡Muévete con Honda! Lea este anuncio de México y luego conteste las siguientes preguntas.

1. ¿De qué marca (*brand*) son las motos?
2. ¿Cree Ud. que es necesario tener carnet de conducir para manejar una moto en México? ¿Necesita Ud. un carnet aquí en los Estados Unidos?
3. ¿Para quiénes son los cursos de manejo?
4. ¿Cuánto cuestan los cursos?
5. ¿Por qué cree Ud. que los distribuidores Honda ofrecen cursos de manejo?

B. Concesionario Chevrolet. Primero lea el anuncio buscando la información para contestar las preguntas. Luego imagine que Ud. trabaja en este concesionario Chevrolet en Bogotá, Colombia, y conteste las siguientes preguntas de un compañero (una compañera) que entra a comprar un coche.

1. ¿Vende Ud. carros japoneses o carros norteamericanos?
2. Yo ya tengo un carro. ¿Qué voy a hacer con él si compro un carro nuevo?
3. ¿Cuánto me va a dar Ud. por mi carro?
4. ¿Qué modelo Sprint vende Ud. ahora?
5. ¿Qué garantía tiene este modelo?

C. Un caso sin esperanzas (*hopeless*). Complete la narración con la palabra apropiada.

Optional: Ask questions about this joke: **1.** *¿Qué lugar cruzaba la carretera?* **2.** *¿Qué no había en el desierto?* **3.** *¿Por qué paró el coche?* **4.** *¿Qué necesitaba el hombre?* **5.** *¿Dónde se puso él la mano?* **6.** *¿Cómo era el otro carro?* **7.** *¿Qué era el otro chofer?*

antiguo	desierto (*desert*)	paró
ayuda (*help*)	esqueleto	roto
carretera	frente (*forehead*)	solo
cruzaba		

Un chofer iba por una _____[1] que _____[2] el _____.[3] No había casas, árboles ni gente. De pronto (*Suddenly*), su coche _____.[4] Se había _____.[5] El hombre necesitaba _____.[6] Se puso la mano en la _____[7] y miró el horizonte. Pero el hombre no estaba _____.[8] Otro chofer, un _____,[9] en un carro muy _____[10] también miraba con la mano en la frente.

D. Lea varias veces la narración anterior y cuéntele a la clase el chiste sin mirar el libro.

Para conversar más

Suggestion A: Encourage student pairs to invent own scenarios in addition to five given.

A. Ud. es el policía (la mujer policía). Dígale a un compañero (una compañera) de clase, quien va a ser el/la chofer, qué debe hacer en estas situaciones. *Take turns playing the roles.*

> MODELO: Ha llovido mucho esta mañana; un señor viejo no puede parar su auto muy bien.
> (parar cuando llueve / usar los frenos) →
> Si quiere Ud. parar cuando llueve, use los frenos con cuidado varias veces, no sólo una vez.

1. Es invierno; el chofer no puede ver bien.
   (volver a casa / no manejar ahora)
2. Un señor ha bebido demasiado.
   (bajar del coche / hablar con el policía [la mujer policía])
3. Un joven no tiene su carnet de manejar.
   (acompañarme a la estación / llamar a sus padres)

4. Un niño juega en la calle.
   (venir un coche / no parar)
5. Hay un accidente de automóviles.
   (estar borracho/a / pagar una multa)

Suggestion B: You may want to have students take notes on their partner's answers and report them to the class or to another student.

Optional: Have students invent a scavenger hunt in which they provide directions (oral or written) for student "hunters."

B. Preguntas personales.

1. ¿Sabe Ud. manejar? ¿Cuándo aprendió a manejar? ¿Quién le enseñó a manejar?
2. ¿Cuál es la velocidad máxima permitida (kilómetros o millas por hora) en las carreteras nacionales? ¿Le han puesto a Ud. una multa alguna vez? ¿Por qué (no)?
3. ¿Cuánto cuesta la gasolina ahora (por litro o galón)?
4. ¿Qué usa Ud. para manejar de noche? ¿y cuándo llueve?

C. Reacciones. ¿Qué va a hacer Ud. en estas situaciones? *Answer in the present, trying to use the double pronoun construction whenever possible.*

1. Ud. ha visto un accidente de coches y al joven que lo causó. ¿A quién se lo dice? ¿Por qué se lo dice? ¿Qué pasa entonces? ¿Cómo lo ayuda?
2. Un viajero está perdido. ¿Ud. le da el mapa que tiene o se lo vende? ¿Por qué? ¿Qué más hace Ud.?
3. Ud. ha bebido demasiada cerveza. ¿Se lo dice a sus amigos? ¿Por qué (no)? ¿Qué hace entonces? ¿Debe manejar su coche?

MOTIVO CULTURAL

Small cars are very popular in Spain because of the extremely high price of gasoline there. Given that gasoline can cost from $.80 to $.90 per liter (more than $3 per gallon), most people must drive economical cars. Small cars are also popular because they can negotiate the narrow streets common in the oldest areas of Spanish cities.

The automobile has caused many of the same problems in Spain and other Hispanic countries as in the United States. Air pollution, for example, is a serious problem in some urban areas. Mexico City has considered a variety of radical measures to reduce air pollution, including banning particular groups of motorists on certain days of the week and installing oxygen booths on street corners for people with breathing difficulties.

Vocabulario activo

Adjetivos

agradable	pleasant
borracho/a	drunk

Sustantivos

COCHES Y CARRETERAS

el acelerador	gas pedal
el asiento	seat
el baúl	trunk
el camión	truck
la camioneta	station wagon
el carnet de manejar/ conducir	driver's license
el conductor/la conductora	driver
el/la chofer	driver
el choque	collision
el faro	headlight
los frenos	brakes
la gasolina	gasoline
la gasolinera	gas(oline) station
la goma	tire
el letrero	(road/street) sign
el limpiaparabrisas	windshield wiper
la llanta	tire
la llave	key
el maletero	trunk
el motor	motor
la multa	fine
el parabrisas	windshield
el peatón	pedestrian
la policía	police (force)
el policía/la mujer policía	policeman/policewoman
la rueda	wheel
el semáforo	traffic light
la señal de tráfico	traffic sign
el volante	steering wheel

CALLES Y LUGARES DE LA CIUDAD

la acera	sidewalk
la autopista	superhighway
la avenida	avenue
la carretera	highway
el correo central	main post office
la esquina	corner
la estación del ferrocarril	train station
la jefatura de policía	police headquarters
el palacio municipal	city hall
la rambla	scenic drive, boulevard

OTROS SUSTANTIVOS

la dama	lady
las esposas	handcuffs
la ley	law
el tigre	tigre

Verbos

aparcar	to park
conducir	to drive
convertirse (en)	to become
chocar	to collide, crash
dirigirse (a)	to address, direct oneself to
doblar	to turn
estacionar	to park
explicar	to explain
manejar	to drive
parar	to stop
pasar (por)	to pass (by)
seguir	to continue; to follow

PARTICIPIOS PASADOS

abierto	opened
dicho	said
escrito	written
hecho	done; made
muerto	dead
puesto	put, placed
roto	broken
visto	seen
vuelto	returned

Otras palabras y expresiones

a la derecha	to the right
a la izquierda	to the left
¡Caramba!	Darn it!
con cuidado	with care, carefully
dar la vuelta a	to go around
de nada	you are welcome
¡Dios mío!	For Heaven's sake!
en frente de	in front of
está detenido	you are under arrest
está en obras	is closed for repairs
poner(le) las esposas	to handcuff (someone)
poner(le) una multa	to give (someone) a ticket (a fine)
todo derecho	straight ahead
tampoco	neither
¡Vaya + *noun*!	What a _____!
la verdad es que	the truth is that

La presencia hispánica

Una familia hispánica en Austin, Texas, celebra el Día de Acción de Gracias (*Thanksgiving*). —¡A mí me encanta el pavo!

METAS

Comunicación: In this lesson you will learn about the major Hispanic groups in the United States and some of their cultural traditions. You'll witness a parade, visit a Cuban neighborhood in Miami, talk with classmates about Hispanic soap operas and discuss the Mexican legend of the Virgin of Guadalupe. You will also learn to express in Spanish a wish or request that someone do something, as well as your feelings about another person's actions.

Estructuras: 47. Subjunctive Mood: General Statement 48. Forms of the Present Subjunctive 49. Stem and Spelling Changes in the Present Subjunctive 50. Subjunctive with Verbs of Volition (Will) 51. Subjunctive with Verbs of Emotion

GRÁFICOS

El Desfile de la Hispanidad

Columbus Day Parade

1. la muchedumbre
2. la bandera
3. la carroza
4. la reina
5. el caballo (montar a caballo)
6. el traje regional, el traje de charro
7. los mariachis
8. el/la cónsul (de España)
9. el embajador/la embajadora (del Perú)
10. el alcalde/la alcaldesa (de la ciudad)
11. el gobernador/la gobernadora (del estado) (*state*)
12. el locutor/la locutora

MOTIVO CULTURAL

On Columbus Day, the twelfth of October, Hispanics commemorate their ties to Spain, as well as the history and characteristics common to all Hispanic groups. Cities in the United States with large Hispanic populations often celebrate Columbus Day with parades that include traditional music and dancing, as well as people dressed in their regional costumes.

Actividades

A.   Identificaciones. ¿Quién es? Un(a) estudiante lee una oración y otro/a estudiante adivina (*guesses*) la identidad de la persona.

1. Soy joven y bonita y voy en una carroza.
2. Somos el público que mira el desfile.
3. Soy la figura política más importante de la ciudad.
4. Y yo soy la figura política más importante del estado.
5. Nosotros representamos a nuestros países en los Estados Unidos.
6. Hablo por el micrófono describiendo el desfile.

¿De qué hablo? Un(a) estudiante lee una oración y otro/a estudiante adivina lo que describe.

7. el traje típico que llevan los hombres mexicanos
8. un vehículo especial para desfiles
9. el símbolo de un país
10. un animal que montamos
11. la ropa típica de una región
12. grupo de músicos

B. El Desfile de la Hispanidad. Complete.

En el Desfile de la Hispanidad se ven muchas _____[1] y en una de ellas va la _____[2]. Los espectadores forman una _____[3] en las aceras. Muchos llevan la _____[4] de su país o la de los Estados Unidos. Los _____[5] tocan una música muy alegre y muchas personas bailan. Un hombre pasa montado en un _____[6], vestido con un traje _____[7]. En una plataforma, el _____[8], la _____[9], la _____[10] y el _____[11] presiden el desfile. Una _____[12] describe el evento para el radio o la televisión.

Suggestion B: Test listening comprehension and review vocabulary by asking questions based on paragraph: **1.** ¿Dónde va la reina del desfile? **2.** ¿Qué llevan muchas de las personas que están en la acera? **3.** ¿Qué hacen los mariachis? **4.** ¿Dónde monta el charro? **5.** ¿Quiénes presiden el desfile? **6.** ¿Quién describe el evento?

En la Sagüesera*

In Southwest Miami

1. el cartel
2. la carnicería
3. la heladería

◆ PRESENT SUBJUNCTIVE ◆

desean que aprendas	*they want you to learn*
desean que aprendan	*they want them to learn*
desean que aprendamos	*they want us to learn*
quiero que entres	*I want you to enter*
quiero que entren	*I want them to enter*
quiero que entremos	*I want us to enter*

*****Sagüesera** is a corruption of the English *southwest,* and refers to the part of the city in which Cubans first concentrated.

ANITA: ¿Viste el cartel de esa carnicería? ¿Es que aquí los *comerciantes* tienen   *merchants*
que *anunciar* que hablan inglés?   *advertise*

PEPE: Sí, porque la *mayoría* de la gente que vive en este barrio es cubana.   *majority*
Muchos, que *ya no* eran jóvenes cuando llegaron a Miami, sólo saben   *no longer*
español. *Aunque, por supuesto,* todos desean que sus hijos y nietos   *Although / of course*
aprendan bien los dos *idiomas.* Yo, por ejemplo, soy bilingüe. Pero es *lo*   *languages*
mismo donde vives en California, ¿no?   *the same*

ANITA: Sí. Aunque después de varias generaciones, algunos mexicano-americanos ya no hablan español.

PEPE: Ay, Anita, *no conversemos más.* Quiero que entremos en la heladería.   *let's not talk any longer*
Tienen el mejor mantecado* de toda la Sagüesera.

Actividades

Expansion A, B: *Otras
tiendas: peluquería, pes-
cadería, relojería. ¿Cómo
se llama la persona que
arregla el pelo (vende
pescado, arregla relojes)?*

A. En la Sagüesera. Conteste.

1. ¿Cómo se llama la carnicería? ¿Qué dice el cartel?
2. ¿Por qué anuncian los comerciantes que hablan inglés?
3. ¿Cómo eran los cubanos cuando llegaron a Miami?
4. ¿Qué dice Pepe que desean todos los cubanos?
5. ¿Dónde hay también muchas personas bilingües?
6. ¿Qué les pasa a algunos mexicano-americanos después de varias generaciones?
7. ¿Dónde quiere Pepe que entren él y Ana?
8. ¿Qué van a tomar Pepe y Ana?

B. Dos versiones. Un(a) estudiante lee una oración y otro/a estudiante la
repite, pero cambia las palabras indicadas por palabras sinónimas.

1. En *la tienda donde venden carne* hay *un letrero* que anuncia que hablan inglés.
2. Muchos cubanos no eran muy jóvenes cuando llegaron a Miami, y por eso
ahora hablan solamente *una lengua.*
3. *Claro que* en California también hay muchas personas *que hablan dos idiomas.*
4. En *la tienda de helados* venden *helado hecho de huevos, leche y azúcar.*

ESTUDIO DE PALABRAS

The suffix **-ería** is often combined with the name of an item to form the
word for a shop in which that item is sold or repaired. Similarly, many
names of tradespersons are formed by adding the suffix **-ero/a** after
dropping the final vowel.

---

*A **mantecado** is a type of ice cream very popular in many Hispanic countries. It is made with
milk, egg yolks, and sugar.

OBJETO	TIENDA	VENDEDOR(A)
helado	heladería	heladero/a
pastel (*cake*)	pastelería	pastelero/a
fruta	frutería	frutero/a

A. ¿Qué venden en estas tiendas?

1. una camisería*
2. una carnicería*
3. una florería
4. una cafetería*
5. una papelería
6. una lechería
7. una panadería*
8. una mueblería

B. ¿Cómo se llama la persona que vende o arregla (*repairs*)...

1. relojes?
2. zapatos?
3. sombreros?
4. libros?
5. leche?
6. carne?
7. joyas (*jewelry*)?
8. pescado?

El santo de doña Guadalupe†

◆ OTHER PRESENT SUBJUNCTIVES ◆

me sorprende que (tú) sigas
I am surprised that you go on

quiere que (ella) conozca
he wants her to meet

le molesta que (él) llegue
it bothers her that he arrives

me alegro de que (tú) puedas
I am happy that you can

Adjetivos
dominante   *domineering*
honrado/a   *honest*
soberbio/a *haughty*

---

*Note that in some cases, the final vowel may be changed or dropped, and additional letters may be added.

†Each day in the Catholic calendar is dedicated to several saints. Hispanics celebrate their **día del santo** on the day dedicated to the saint whose name they bear. If you have a common name like **María, Carmen, Josefa, José,** or **Juan,** everybody will know that you should be congratulated on September 12, July 16, March 19, or June 24, respectively. **La Virgen de Guadalupe** is the patroness of Mexico, and the day dedicated to her is December 12.

JESÚS*: Mamá, me sorprende que sigas viendo esa telenovela tan tonta.

MADRE: El *argumento* es muy interesante, hijo. Teresa, la *protagonista*, es po- — *plot / main character*
bre, pero honrada, y un joven muy rico *está enamorado* de ella. — *is in love with*

JESÚS: Ya lo sé. Y cuando él la besa, ella se convierte en princesa.

MADRE: No *te burles*, Jesús, esta *historia* es muy realista. El joven quiere que su — *make fun / story*
madre, doña Guadalupe, conozca a Teresa. El *día del santo* de la — *saint's day*
señora, que es también el día de su *cumpleaños,* la lleva a la fiesta que — *birthday*
hay en su casa. Pero a doña Guadalupe, que es dominante y soberbia,
le molesta que su hijo llegue con una muchacha pobre y...

JESÚS: ¡Ay, mamá! Me alegro de que tú puedas *disfrutar* con eso, pero tengo — *enjoy yourself*
que irme. No quiero *perderme* el concierto de rock. — *miss*

Note: Explain that in some countries it is common to name a child after saint honored on day child was born. In this case, one celebrates both birthday and saint's day on same date.

Note: Mention some nicknames for names mentioned here: *Maruja, Maricusa, Marita, Mariíta* for *María; Carmita, Carmina, Carmencita* for *Carmen; Fefa, Fefita, Josefita, Josefina* for *Josefa; Pepe, Pepito, Pepín, Joseíto* for *José; Juancho, Juanito, Juanín* for *Juan; Chucho, Jesusito* for *Jesús.*

Optional A: Ask questions orally: **1.** *Según Jesús, ¿cómo es la telenovela?* **2.** *¿Cómo se llama la protagonista?* **3.** *¿Cómo es Teresa?* **4.** *¿Qué día celebra su santo y su cumpleaños doña Guadalupe?* **5.** *¿Cómo es doña Guadalupe?* **6.** *¿Adónde va Jesús?*

Suggestion B: Some students may want to investigate what saint corresponds to their birthday and report to class briefly about it.

Suggestion D: Have students write this episode in groups of three and perform in class. The class will award Oscars to the best actors and script writers.

Actividades

A. Una telenovela interesante. ¿Comprendió Ud. el diálogo? Diga si estas oraciones son ciertas o falsas. Corrija las oraciones falsas.

1. Jesús se alegra de que su madre siga viendo la telenovela.
2. Él cree que la telenovela es muy realista.
3. La protagonista de la telenovela se llama Guadalupe.
4. Un joven muy rico está enamorado de la protagonista.
5. El novio de la muchacha es soberbio y dominante.
6. Teresa se convierte en princesa.
7. El joven quiere que su novia conozca a su madre.
8. Hay una fiesta en casa de doña Guadalupe el 12 de diciembre.
9. Doña Guadalupe se alegra de que su hijo llegue con una muchacha honrada.

B. Preguntas personales. Hágale estas preguntas a un compañero (una compañera) y luego contéstelas cuando él (ella) se las pregunte a Ud.

1. ¿Sabes cuál es el día de tu santo? ¿Celebras tu santo? ¿Por qué (no)?
2. ¿Cuándo es tu cumpleaños? ¿Qué haces ese día?
3. ¿Te llaman muchos amigos el día de tu cumpleaños?
4. ¿Qué haces cuando un buen amigo olvida (*forgets*) tu compleaños?
5. En tu opinión, ¿por qué ve mucha gente telenovelas? ¿Ves tú una telenovela?

C. ¿Tiene Ud. buena memoria? Cuente el argumento de la telenovela sin mirar el texto.

D. ¿Qué hizo doña Guadalupe? Continúe el episodio de la telenovela, inventando lo que pasó el día de la fiesta entre la señora, su hijo y Teresa.

***Jesús** is a common Spanish name. Hispanics don't consider it disrespectful for a person to bear Jesus's name.

VISTA CULTURAL

Las telenovelas son el tipo de programa más popular en el mundo hispánico. Los hispanos que viven en los Estados Unidos pueden ver tres o más canales con programas exclusivamente en español, y una gran parte de la programación diaria de estos canales se compone de (*is composed of*) telenovelas. Las telenovelas hispanas son menos largas que las «soap operas» de los Estados Unidos. Después de varios meses, terminan con un final feliz.

La escena de este minidiálogo es muy típica de la vida hispánica en nuestro país. Si Ud. visita un hogar hispánico cualquier (*any*) noche, es muy probable que encuentre a la familia viendo una telenovela.

La mayoría de las telenovelas que se ven en los Estados Unidos se producen en México, pero algunas vienen de la Argentina y muchas de Venezuela. Este país ha exportado muchos programas en los últimos años.

Cultural expansion: In addition to local Hispanic channels in cities with large Hispanic populations, there are two national Hispanic networks in the U.S.A.: *Univisión* and *Telemundo.* A third network, *Galavisión,* originates in California and is seen on cable TV. Each channel shows five or more *telenovelas* daily. Unlike American soap operas, most *telenovelas* are shown after 7 P.M.

GRAMÁTICA ESENCIAL

47. Subjunctive Mood: General Statement

All verb forms that you have studied previously, with the exception of direct and indirect commands, belong to the *indicative* mood. In this and future lessons you will study some tenses of the *subjunctive* mood.

Unlike the indicative, which conveys direct statements or asserts factual certainties, the subjunctive is tinged with subjectivity. It expresses implied commands, the intellectual or emotional involvement of the speaker with an event, projections into an indefinite or uncertain future, anticipations or suppositions regardless of time, contrary-to-fact assumptions, and even statements of fact when they are considered the result of mere chance.

A typical sentence containing the subjunctive is a statement that includes a main clause (one that can stand alone) and a dependent clause whose full meaning is understood only in relation to the main clause. Study the following formula.

Subject 1 + main verb + **que** + subject 2 + dependent verb
(indicative)   (subjunctive)

MAIN CLAUSE   DEPENDENT CLAUSE
Yo deseo   que Ud. **hable.***
I want   *you to speak.*

This lesson and subsequent ones will examine the different uses of the subjunctive in the following categories: in noun clauses, in adjective clauses, and in adverb clauses. For the first category, the subjunctive in noun clauses, examine the following summary to get a general idea about what concepts in the main clause trigger the subjunctive in the dependent clause.

1. *Verbs of volition* (*will*): wanting, wishing, preferring, advising, requesting, commanding, permitting, and so on (**Lección 11**)
2. *Verbs of emotion:* feeling happiness, pleasure, or surprise; hoping; regretting; fearing; and so on (**Lección 11**)
3. *Verbs of doubt, disbelief, and denial* (**Lección 12**)
4. *Impersonal expressions* containing any of the above concepts (**Lección 12**)

Presentation: Stress subject change that occurs in most sentences requiring subjunctive. Write this sentence on board: *Yo deseo que Ud. hable.* Ask: *¿Quién desea? ¿Quién va a hablar?*

Optional: Give direct command to student and have him/her give similar, indirect command referring to a classmate: *Cierre la puerta.* → *Que (name of classmate) cierre la puerta.* **1.** *Cante una canción en español.* **2.** *Escriba una composición.* **3.** *Describa un traje de charro.* **4.** *Llame al gobernador.* **5.** *Monte a caballo ahora.* **6.** *No mire la telenovela.*

48. Forms of the Present Subjunctive

Quiero que entremos en la heladería.

HELADOS

---

*The dependent clause can also stand alone as an indirect command: **Que lo traiga Jorge** (*Let Jorge bring it*).

You have already used the third persons singular and plural of the present subjunctive in polite commands. To form the present subjunctive of all six persons of regular and irregular verbs in Spanish, drop the **-o** of the first person singular of the present indicative and add the subjunctive endings to the stem.

	COMMANDS	PRESENT SUBJUNCTIVE OF REGULAR VERBS	
habl**ø** ↓ habl-	**-ar:** (no) hable, (no) hablen →	hable hables hable	hablemos habléis hablen
com**ø** ↓ com-	**-er:** (no) coma, (no) coman →	coma comas coma	comamos comáis coman
viv**ø** ↓ viv-	**-ir:** (no) viva, (no) vivan →	viva vivas viva	vivamos viváis vivan

Note that for **-ar** verbs the predominant vowel in the present subjunctive is **e;** for **-er** and **-ir** verbs, it's **a.** As mentioned earlier, it may be helpful to think of these as the "opposite" vowels.

	COMMANDS	PRESENT SUBJUNCTIVE OF IRREGULAR VERBS	
dig**ø** ↓ dig-	(no) diga, (no) digan →	diga digas diga	digamos digáis digan

Like **decir,** the following irregular verbs preserve the irregularity of the first person singular of the present indicative throughout the six forms of the present subjunctive: **conocer (conozca, conozcas, conozca, conozcamos, conozcáis, conozcan), hacer (haga, hagas,** and so on), **oír, poner, salir, tener, traer, venir,** and **ver.**

Actividad

Los deseos de mi familia. Conteste las preguntas usando el presente de subjuntivo de los verbos indicados.

1. ¿Qué desea mi madre? Mi madre desea que yo... (salir con ella de compras, traer carne de la carnicería, hacer las camas, poner la mesa, tener mis tareas hechas antes de cenar)

Presentation: Write present indicative and present subjunctive of *hablar, comer,* and *vivir* on board. Students can remember forms more easily if they realize that vowels in subjunctive endings are opposite of indicative endings: *-ar: a → e; -er, -ir: e → a.* Next, ask questions that students answer affirmatively: **1.** *¿Desea Ud. que su amigo hable inglés (coma en la cafetería, viva en esta ciudad)?* **2.** *¿Quiere Ud. que nosotros hablemos en español (comamos en su casa, vivamos en su barrio)?* **3.** *¿Desea su mamá que Ud. no hable tanto por teléfono (coma bien, viva con ella)?* **4.** *¿Quiero que Uds. hablen bien el español (no coman en clase, vivan muchos años)?*

2. ¿Qué no quiere mi padre? Mi padre no quiere que mis hermanos... (oír tanta música, ver tantas telenovelas, venir tarde a casa, fumar [*to smoke*])

3. ¿Qué desea mi hermana? Mi hermana desea que tú... (invitarla a tomar un helado, llevarla a ver el desfile, venir a casa esta noche, comprarle un mantecado)

4. ¿Qué quieren mis abuelos? Mis abuelos quieren que todos nosotros... (hablar español en casa, conocer las tradiciones hispánicas, aprender a bailar bailes cubanos, llevar trajes regionales)

49. Stem and Spelling Changes in the Present Subjunctive

A doña Guadalupe le molesta que su hijo llegue con una muchacha pobre.

The consonantal changes found in the first person singular of the preterite and in the **Ud.** commands appear throughout the present subjunctive.

c → qu:	(buscar) busque, busques, busque, busquemos, busquéis, busquen
g → gu:	(llegar) llegue, llegues, llegue, etcétera
g → j:	(dirigir) dirija, dirijas, dirija, etcétera
z → c:	(comenzar) comience, comiences, comience, etcétera

The vowel changes of **-ar** and **-er** stem-changing verbs are found in all singular forms and in the third person plural of the present subjunctive.

e → ie:	(pensar) piense, pienses, piense, pensemos, penséis, piensen
o → ue:	(volver) vuelva, vuelvas, vuelva, volvamos, volváis, vuelvan

Stem-changing **-ir** verbs that have **i** or **u** in third-person preterite forms have the following changes in the first and second persons plural of the subjunctive in addition to the **ie** or **ue** change in the other persons:

e → ie / e → i:	(sentir) sienta, sientas, sienta, sintamos, sintáis, sientan
o → ue / o → u:	(dormir) duerma, duermas, duerma, durmamos, durmáis, duerman
e → i / e → i:	(pedir) pida, pidas, pida, pidamos, pidáis, pidan

Actividad

Escenas de la vida. Dé las formas del presente de subjuntivo correspondientes a los infinitivos.

No quiero que tú (repetir[1]) el nombre de ese «amigo». No (comenzar[2]) a hablarme de él. No quiero que (pensar[3]) que olvido sus ofensas. No quiero que tú (sentirse[4]) mal, pero prefiero que no lo (volver[5]) a ver.

El profesor recomienda que no nos (dormir[6]) en clase, que (comenzar[7]) a practicar los verbos y que (buscar[8]) en el diccionario las palabras nuevas. Él quiere también que Sofía (dirigir[9]) la práctica.

Dígale a Elvira que queremos que ella (almorzar[10]) con nosotros, que (ella: llegar[11]) temprano a la cafetería, (buscar[12]) la mesa que tenemos reservada, se (sentar[13]) y le (pedir[14]) al camarero (*waiter*) que le (servir[15]) un refresco.

50. Subjunctive with Verbs of Volition (Will)

—Te recomiendo
que lleves paraguas.

—No queremos
que Ud. fume.

—¿Mamá, prefieres
que no salga?

If the main clause of a sentence contains a verb of volition (will) expressing wanting, preferring, ordering, requesting, advising, and so on, and if there is a change in subject in the dependent clause, the verb in the dependent clause *must be in the subjunctive.* The dependent clause is introduced by **que.** Here are some frequently used verbs of volition; you have already seen many of them.

1. *Wanting:* **desear, querer**

    Yo quiero (deseo) **que** Ud. nos **escriba.**   *I want you to write to us.*

2. *Preferring:* **preferir**

    ¿Prefieres **que** te **hablemos** en español?   *Do you prefer that we speak to you in Spanish?*

Presentation: Stress presence of two subjects in example sentences even if they are not expressed. Also stress that while "that" is frequently omitted in English, *que* is always used in Spanish.

3. *Ordering or commanding:* **mandar** (*to order*), **(no) permitir, dejar** (*to permit*)

Nos manda (Nos permite, Nos deja) **que salgamos.**   *He orders (permits) us to leave.*

4. *Advising or requesting:* **aconsejar** (*to advise*), **pedir (i), recomendar (ie)**

Yo le voy a aconsejar a ella **que no fume** más.   *I'm going to advise her not to smoke any more.*

Note that the verbs in numbers 3 and 4 require the use in the main clause of an indirect object pronoun (**me, te, le, nos, os, les**) corresponding to the subject of the dependent clause.

Important: If there is no change of subject in the two clauses, Spanish requires the use of the infinitive. Compare the following.

Él quiere que yo lo compre.   *He wants me to buy it. (Who wants? **He.** Who buys? **I do.**)*

Él quiere comprarlo.   *He wants to buy it. (Who wants? **He.** Who buys? **He does.**)*

Actividades

Suggestion: Test listening comprehension by reading these sentences aloud. Ask students to write *I* (indicative) or *S* (subjunctive), depending on verbal mood they hear: **1.** *La joven que escribe la carta es mi hermana.* **2.** *¿Me permite Ud. que fume aquí?* **3.** *Mi mamá prefiere que yo no salga.* **4.** *Yo no salgo si llueve.* **5.** *Los alumnos que duermen en clase no aprenden.* **6.** *El doctor nos aconseja que no fumemos.* **7.** *¿Quién es aquí la persona que fuma?* **8.** *Te recomiendo que lleves paraguas.* **9.** *Quiero que la joven escriba una carta.* **10.** *Ellos dicen que piensan venir temprano.* **11.** *La profesora no quiere que durmamos en clase.* **12.** *¿Lleva Ud. paraguas al desfile?*

Suggestion A: For change of pace, have students vary subjects in sentences.

A. ¡Vamos al desfile! Un(a) estudiante lee una oración y menciona un sujeto; otro/a estudiante pone el nuevo sujeto en la oración y cambia el infinitivo por el subjuntivo.

MODELO: Armando quiere conocer a la reina. (Ud.) →
Armando quiere que Ud. conozca a la reina.

1. Ramón prefiere llevar traje de charro. (yo)
2. Queremos llegar temprano. (Uds.)
3. El gobernador desea saludar la bandera. (los policías)
4. Nosotros no queremos bailar en la calle. (vosotras)
5. Todos prefieren seguir tocando. (la banda)
6. Mi madre aconseja no volver muy tarde. (nosotras)
7. El alcalde pide hablar a la muchedumbre. (la reina)

B. Recomendaciones. Exprese una recomendación según el modelo. *Expand your sentences so that they contain a subjunctive and a touch of originality.*

MODELO: Ud. sabe que su amigo no va a clases. →
Le recomiendo (aconsejo, pido) que estudie mucho si desea recibir un título (*degree*) este año.

1. Ud. sabe que dos amigos duermen menos de cinco horas cada noche.
2. Un joven quiere comprar un auto nuevo.
3. Una señora desea consultar a un abogado.
4. Un señor quiere visitar muchos países extranjeros (*foreign*).
5. Unos amigos le preguntan si hay un buen restaurante en esta ciudad.

C. Doña Guadalupe y su hijo. Esta señora es dominante; siempre le dice a su hijo qué debe y qué no debe hacer. Exprese los mandatos afirmativos y negativos que le da a su hijo según el modelo.

MODELO: salir de aquí → Te pido que salgas de aquí.

1. pensar en las diferencias de clases sociales
2. buscar una novia de tu clase
3. salir con la hija de mi amiga
4. no venir a mi fiesta con Teresa
5. escuchar mis recomendaciones

51. Subjunctive with Verbs of Emotion

—Temo que llueva el día del desfile.

A Ana y a Pepe les molesta que este señor fume.

—Me alegro de que pongan (*they show*) el desfile por televisión.

These verbs express projections into the future, suppositions, or subjective attitudes (**Gramática esencial 48**). Regardless of the particular meaning conveyed, they regularly require the use of the subjunctive. The most common verbs of this type are **alegrarse de** (*to be glad*), **esperar** (*to hope*), **sentir** (**ie, i**) (*to be sorry, regret*), and **temer** (*to be afraid of*). **Gustar** also belongs in this group, as do two verbs using the **gustar** construction: **sorprender** (*to surprise*) and **molestar** (*to bother*).

Me alegro de que Ud. conozca al gobernador.
I am glad that you know the governor.

Espero que Ud. reciba buenas noticias en la carta.
I hope (that) you get good news in the letter.

Sentimos que ella esté enferma.
We regret that she is ill.

Temen que gastemos demasiado.
They are afraid (that) we may spend too much.

A Pérez le gusta (sorprende, molesta) que Ud. haga ese trabajo.
Pérez is pleased (surprised, bothered) that you are doing that work.

Actividades

A. En la Sagüesera. Un(a) estudiante lee una oración y otro/a estudiante inventa una segunda oración.

> MODELO: —Espero que su amiga quiera entrar en la heladería.
> —Y yo espero que le gusten los helados de frutas tropicales.

1. Siento que mis amigos no hablen mucho español.
2. Temo que el heladero no entienda a mis amigos.
3. Me sorprende que este cartel diga que se habla inglés.
4. Siento que aquí no sirvan hamburguesas.
5. Me alegro de que te guste el mantecado.
6. Espero que también tengan helado de piña.

B. Los sentimientos (*feelings*) de doña Guadalupe. Un compañero (una compañera) hace el papel de doña Guadalupe, quien expresa sus sentimientos. Ud. se los transmite a la clase. ¡Cuidado! Debe usar la construcción del verbo **gustar** en todos los casos.

> MODELO: *Me* molesta que *mi* hijo no tenga amigos de su clase social. →
> *A doña Guadalupe le* molesta que *su* hijo no tenga amigos de su clase social.

1. *Me* gusta que *mi* hijo visite lugares elegantes.
2. *Me* sorprende que *mi* hijo quiera a una muchacha pobre.
3. *Me* molesta que la familia de Teresa no tenga dinero.
4. No *me* gusta que *mi* hijo traiga a Teresa a *mi* casa.
5. No *me* sorprende que los invitados (*guests*) *nos* critiquen.
6. *Me* molesta que *mi* hijo no *me* obedezca (*obey*).

C. Confesiones de un(a) estudiante. Complete según sus sentimientos personales.

1. Siento que _____.
2. Me alegro de que _____.
3. Temo que _____.
4. Me gusta que _____.
5. Me molesta que _____.
6. Espero que _____.

Para resumir y repasar

A. En persona: Unas vacaciones difíciles. Ud. y un grupo de amigos están tratando de (*are trying*) decidir adónde quieren ir en las vacaciones que van a tomar juntos (*together*). Ud. quiere ir a Nueva York para ver el desfile de la Hispanidad, pero otro amigo quiere ir a Disney World. Él cree que el desfile es tonto y lo/la critica a Ud. por su decisión. Explíqueles a sus amigos por qué prefiere ir a Nueva York, qué espera ver en el desfile y también diga lo que Ud. piensa del comportamiento (*behavior*) del otro amigo. Éstos son algunos verbos que Ud. puede usar: **desear, querer, preferir, dejar, alegrarse de, esperar, sentir, gustar, molestar.** Por ejemplo: Mi amigo quiere que vayamos a Disney World, pero a mí me molesta que no se ponga de acuerdo con nosotros.

B. **¿Me lo, me las, se lo, se la, se los o se las?**

1. Ayer le pedí el auto a mi padre. ____ ____ pedí.
2. Le prometí manejar con prudencia. ____ ____ prometí.
3. Entonces, él me dio las llaves. ____ ____ dio.
4. Necesitaba gasolina, y un peatón me explicó dónde había una gasolinera. ____ ____ explicó.
5. En la gasolinera, un empleado le puso gasolina al coche. ____ ____ puso.
6. Como no tenía mucho dinero, le di al empleado mi tarjeta de crédito. ____ ____ di.

C. Ponga cada verbo en el pretérito perfecto (*present perfect*).

Hice[1] lo que Ud. me *mandó.*[2] *Compré*[3] un regalo para Augusto, *volví*[4] a casa, *puse*[5] el regalo en su dormitorio y lo *desperté.*[6]

Esta mañana *vi*[7] un terrible accidente donde *murieron*[8] dos personas. El policía *abrió*[9] la puerta del auto y *vio*[10] a las víctimas, pero no *dijo*[11] nada. *Volvió*[12] a cerrar la puerta y *escribió*[13] un reporte del accidente.

Suggestion: Show pictures of new and old basilicas of Guadalupe. Explain that new basilica was built because old church was sinking; in fact, this is second church to sink in same location. Because of conditions of subsoil in Mexico City, Palacio de Bellas Artes and column com-

COMUNICACIÓN

memorating independence in Paseo de la Reforma have had similar problems.

Texto: La Virgen de Guadalupe

Soy de Santa Fe, pero mi familia es mexicana. Cuando era niña, mi abuelita, que era de San Luis Potosí,* me contó la historia de la Virgen de Guadalupe, nuestra patrona.

En 1531 un indio *humilde,* llamado Juan Diego, se presenta un día en casa del *Obispo* y explica que vio a la Virgen y que Ella lo *envía* porque desea que *construyan* una iglesia en su honor. Pero *nadie* lo cree porque lo consideran un indio ignorante.

Juan Diego vuelve otro día a casa del Obispo. Dice que la Virgen siente mucho que no hagan lo que Ella quiere y que envía una *prueba* de que Juan Diego dice la verdad. Aunque es el 12 de diciembre, Juan Diego trae *docenas* de rosas *envueltas* en su tilma.† Hay también una imagen muy hermosa de la Virgen *pintada* en la tilma; esta vez todos creen al indio.

Miles de devotos visitan la Basílica de Nuestra Señora de Guadalupe, en la Ciudad de México.

humble

Bishop / sends
they build / nobody

proof

dozens / wrapped
painted

Note: Remind students to make use of cognates in passage when trying to understand its meaning. This *Texto* has numerous cognates. Suggest that students focus on first few letters of such words in order to guess meaning: *historia, humilde, construyan,* etc.

---

*San Luis Potosí is both the name of a state located in the north of Mexico and the name of its capital. It is an important commercial, industrial, and mining center, with oil deposits as well.
†A **tilma** is a large piece of cotton cloth that Mexican peasants wear like a cloak, fastened by a knot on one shoulder.

La *Basílica* de Guadalupe está en la Ciudad de México, en un lugar llamado «la Villa», y cientos de personas la visitan todos los días. El 12 de diciembre hay allí grandes muchedumbres.

church that has been given special honors and privileges

Algunos mexicanos no son muy religiosos, pero todos respetan a su patrona, y los mexicano-americanos también celebramos su fiesta con mucha alegría.

Cultural expansion: As last paragraph of reading suggests, Mexicans have special affinity for Virgin of Guadalupe, even though they may not be particularly religious. Her appearance to Juan Diego, a poor man of humble origins, has placed her on side of poor.

A.   Hablando del texto. ¿Cierto o falso? Corrija las oraciones falsas.

1.   La Virgen de Guadalupe es la patrona de México.
2.   Un indio humilde era el Obispo de México en 1531.
3.   Juan Diego vio a la Virgen en el mes de junio.
4.   Juan Diego llevaba rosas en su tilma como prueba.
5.   La Basílica de Guadalupe está en «la Villa».
6.   Los mexicano-americanos no celebran la fiesta de Guadalupe.

B.   Hablando más del texto. Reconstruya la leyenda de la Virgen de Guadalupe sin consultar el texto.

1.   1531 / Juan Diego
2.   Obispo / explicar
3.   Virgen / querer
4.   nadie / creer
5.   la Virgen / sentir
6.   rosas / tilma
7.   imagen / pintada

De la vida real

Con Fernando Carrillo y Catherine Fullop

Dos mundos diferentes vinculados[a]
por un amor desafiante[b]...

Así es PASIONARIA

De lunes a viernes   ● TELEMUNDO

CONSULTE LOS HORARIOS[c]
DE SU CANAL LOCAL   CONQUISTANDO

[a]*linked*
[b]*rebellious*
[c]*schedule*

A. «Pasionaria». Ésta es una telenovela venezolana que ha sido muy popular recientemente entre los hispanos de los Estados Unidos. Lea este anuncio y conteste las preguntas.

1. ¿Quiénes son el actor y la actriz protagonistas de «Pasionaria»?
2. ¿Qué sugiere (*suggests*) la expresión «dos mundos diferentes» con respecto a los protagonistas?
3. ¿Qué días no presentan esta telenovela?
4. Ud. quiere ver «Pasionaria», pero no sabe a qué hora la presentan en su canal local. ¿Qué debe hacer?

B. «Pasionaria». Con un compañero (una compañera) invente la historia de esta telenovela, contestando estas preguntas e inventado otros detalles (*details*). ¿Cómo son los protagonistas? ¿Cómo son sus «dos mundos diferentes»? ¿Por qué es desafiante su amor?

Para conversar más

A. Entrevista. Haga estas preguntas personales a un compañero (una compañera).

1. ¿Cuántos años lleva tu familia en los Estados Unidos?
2. ¿Qué antepasados tuyos (*ancestors of yours*) fueron inmigrantes? ¿De qué origen son/eran tus abuelos?
3. ¿Qué personas de tu familia hablan otro idioma?
4. ¿Cuántos hispanos hay, aproximadamente, en tu ciudad o pueblo?
5. Además del inglés, ¿qué otras lenguas se hablan en tu ciudad o pueblo?

B. Ud. es el locutor (la locutora) que narra el Desfile de la Hispanidad. ¿Qué le dice Ud. al público que ve el programa por televisión? ¿Cómo describe la escena del gráfico en la página 224?

C. Un(a) estudiante es el locutor (la locutora) y otro/a estudiante es el embajador (la embajadora) del Perú. Preparen un diálogo siguiendo las indicaciones. Usen también su imaginación.
Cosas que pregunta el locutor (la locutora):

1. su opinión del desfile
2. si es la primera vez que viene a este desfile
3. si le gusta la carroza
4. su opinión sobre Miss Hispanidad
5. si el Perú mandó un grupo musical o de baile al desfile
6. si...

MOTIVO CULTURAL

According to some experts, by the year 2000 there will be forty million Hispanics in the United States.

More than 50 percent of Hispanics currently residing in the United States are of Mexican origin. Mexican-Americans have varying levels of acculturation: many speak Spanish well and conserve Mexican traditions, whereas others have become totally Americanized. Although many Mexican-Americans—such as Katherine Dávalos Ortega, the Treasurer of the United States—have achieved a high degree of visibility in this country, as a group, Mexican-Americans have had many social and economic problems. The Chicano movement that began in the 1960s was organized in an effort to eradicate some of these problems. César Chávez, one of its leaders, has dedicated his life to this movement.

Puerto Ricans have been American citizens since 1917. Although some want total independence for Puerto Rico, the results of several elections indicate that the majority prefers the current status: commonwealth of the United States.

Because Puerto Rico is a very small island with a large number of inhabitants, many Puerto Ricans have come to the continent in search of better opportunities. The following Puerto Ricans have become quite famous in the enter-

tainment industry: José Ferrer, Erik Estrada, Chita Rivera, Rita Moreno, Raúl Juliá, José Feliciano.

Although Cubans in the United States are a relatively small group (approximately 500,000), they have had a great impact. Most of the political refugees of the 1960s were from the middle and upper classes, and today many occupy important positions in business and industry. Roberto Goizueta, for instance, is the first foreign president of Coca-Cola.

Although Mexicans, Puerto Ricans, and Cubans are the most frequently mentioned Hispanic populations in the United States, there are also large groups of immigrants from all the other Hispanic countries. The most recent wave of immigration has come from Central America. This group is already quite large, especially in California.

Cultural expansion: Many people in the U.S. no longer consider Spanish a foreign language, since more than 20 million native speakers of Spanish now live here. Continual influx of Mexicans and Central Americans along with growth rate of Hispanic-American population lead most experts to predict Hispanics will compose largest minority in country by turn of the century. For years Los Angeles has been considered second largest city in world in terms of Mexican inhabitants (even larger than Guadalajara and Monterrey). The diversity and vitality Hispanic traditions give to southwestern United States and major metropolitan centers are, of course, well known by people of those areas.

Vocabulario activo

Sustantivos

EL ESTADO (*STATE*)

el alcalde/la alcaldesa	mayor
la bandera	flag
el/la cónsul	consul
el embajador/la embajadora	ambassador
el gobernador/la gobernadora	governor

LAS CELEBRACIONES

el caballo	horse
la carroza	float
el cumpleaños	birthday
el charro	Mexican cowboy
el desfile	parade
el locutor/la locutora	TV or radio announcer
el mantecado	type of ice cream
los mariachis	mariachi band
la muchedumbre	crowd
la reina	queen
el (día del) santo	saint's day
el traje regional	regional costume

OTROS SUSTANTIVOS

el argumento	plot
la carnicería	meat market
el cartel	sign
el/la comerciante	merchant
la heladería	ice cream parlor
la historia	story
el idioma	language
la mayoría	majority
el/la protagonista	main character

Adjetivos

dominante	domineering
honrado/a	honest
realista	realistic
soberbio/a	haughty

Verbos

aconsejar	to advise
anunciar	to advertise
burlarse	to make fun of, mock
dejar	to allow, permit
disfrutar	to enjoy
esperar	to hope
fumar	to smoke
molestar	to bother
permitir	to permit
recomendar (ie)	to recommend
sorprender	to surprise
temer	to be afraid

Otras palabras y expresiones

aunque	although
estar enamorado/a de	to be in love with
lo mismo	the same
montar a caballo	to ride a horse
por supuesto	of course
ya no	no longer

¿Cómo te sientes?

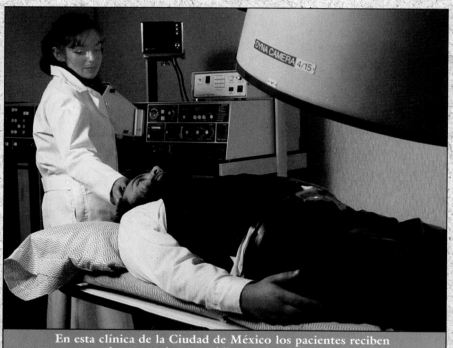

En esta clínica de la Ciudad de México los pacientes reciben los tratamientos médicos más modernos.

METAS

Comunicación: In this lesson you will learn vocabulary and expressions related to doctors, medicines, and illnesses. You will visit a doctor's office, describe symptoms, and suggest remedies. You will also learn to express doubt and uncertainty about actions or states and to express comparisons and superlative statements.

Estructuras: 52. Irregular Present Subjunctives: **dar, estar, ir, saber, ser** 53. Forms of the Present Perfect Subjunctive 54. Subjunctive with Verbs of Disbelief, Doubt, and Denial 55. Subjunctive with Impersonal Expressions 56. Comparatives and Superlatives

GRÁFICOS

En la sala de emergencias

In the Emergency Room

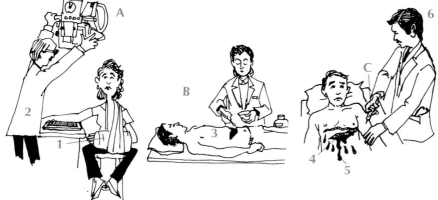

1. el brazo roto
2. el enfermero/la enfermera
3. el herido/la herida (*wounded person*)
4. la herida
5. la sangre
6. el médico/la médica (el doctor/la doctora)
7. la venda
8. las gotas (para los ojos)
9. las pastillas
10. la quemadura
11. la pomada, el ungüento

la presión arterial alta (baja) *high (low) blood pressure*

A. sacar(le) una radiografía
B. curar
C. poner(le) una inyección
D. tener dolor de estómago
E. dar(le) un ataque al corazón
F. dar(le) oxígeno
G. tomar(le) la presión
H. tener fiebre
I. poner(le) el termómetro

tener dificultad para respirar
to have difficulty in breathing

Actividades

A. Estudie el dibujo y el vocabulario y luego dé la palabra o expresión correspondiente a cada número y a cada letra sin consultar la lista.

B. Ud. es el médico (la médica) o el enfermero (la enfermera) en la sala de emergencias. Escoja en la columna de la derecha el tratamiento más apropiado para cada caso. A veces hay más de una posibilidad.

1. un brazo roto	a. dar una pastilla
2. un ojo irritado	b. poner pomada
3. una herida, mucha sangre	d. poner el termómetro
4. un ataque al corazón	c. sacar una radiografía
5. fiebre alta	f. poner una inyección
6. una quemadura	g. dar oxígeno
7. el dolor de estómago	h. poner una venda
8. la presión arterial alta (baja)	i. dar aspirinas
9. dificultad para respirar	j. tomar la presión
	k. curar
	l. poner gotas

ESTUDIO DE PALABRAS

Many Spanish scientific terms are similar to those in English. Pronounce the following words, being careful to avoid English sound patterns.

LAS ENFERMEDADES (*ILLNESSES*)	LOS REMEDIOS (*REMEDIES*) Y LOS TRATAMIENTOS (*TREATMENTS*) MÉDICOS	LA NUTRICIÓN
la alergia	el análisis	las calorías
la anemia	el antibiótico	los carbohidratos
la apendicitis	el antihistamínico	los minerales
la artritis	la aspirina	las proteínas
el cáncer	el diagnóstico	las vitaminas
la diabetes	el examen	
la epilepsia	la inyección	
la hepatitis	la operación	
la indigestión	la transfusión	
la parálisis		
la tuberculosis		
el tumor		
la úlcera		

Suggestion: Again, model pronunciation to avoid English pronunciation of cognates. Practice the names of these illnesses and remedies by giving definitions orally or writing them on the board and having students produce the appropriate word in each case. **1.** *una irritación del estómago, frecuentemente de origen nervioso (la úlcera)* **2.** *un tumor maligno (el cáncer)* **3.** *la inmovilidad de una parte del cuerpo (la parálisis)* **4.** *un exceso de azúcar en la sangre (la diabetes)* **5.** *la extrema sensibilidad a ciertas sustancias (la alergia)* **6.** *el tener pocos glóbulos rojos en la sangre (la anemia)* **7.** *el remedio universal para el dolor de cabeza (la aspirina)* **8.** *el procedimiento de darle sangre a una persona (la tranfusión)* **9.** *el remedio para las infecciones (el antibiótico)* **10.** *toman su nombre de las letras del alfabeto (las vitaminas)*

MOTIVO CULTURAL

Hispanic countries have fewer laws governing the sale of medicines or pharmaceuticals than the United States does, making it possible to purchase all types of medicine in pharmacies without a prescription. Hispanic countries have instituted a rotating system (called **estar de guardia** in Spain and **estar de turno** in Spanish America) to ensure that at least one pharmacy in each urban district is open all night for emergencies. The system is set up so that one pharmacy is open on Mondays, another on Tuesdays, and so on. Generally, newspapers publish the list of pharmacies so designated for a particular night. The duties of Hispanic pharmacists are also considerably broader than those of their North American counterparts. Pharmacists in Hispanic countries frequently advise customers on the best medicines to take, make diagnoses in less serious cases, and even give injections.

En la farmacia de don Tomás

◆ IRREGULAR VERBS ◆

Present Indicative	Present Subjunctive
ser:	
eres	...que seas
es	...que sea
son	...que sean
ir:	
vas	...que vayas
va	...que vaya
van	...que vayan
haber:	
hay	...que haya

1. la curita
2. las pastillas para la tos

Verbos
doler (ue)   *to hurt, ache*
cuidarse   *to take care of oneself*

DON TOMÁS:	¿Qué te pasa, Silvia?
SILVIA:	¡Ay, don Tomás, cómo me duele la cabeza! Ya tomé dos aspirinas y el dolor *no se me quita.*
DON TOMÁS:	¿Tienes también fiebre y *dolor de garganta?* Es posible que sea *gripe.*
SILVIA:	No creo que tenga fiebre, pero sí me duele la garganta y tengo *tos.*
DON TOMÁS:	Entonces es un simple *catarro.* Compra pastillas para la tos y este antihistamínico. Te aconsejo que te vayas ahora a casa, tomes el antihistamínico y te acuestes.
SILVIA:	Pero don Tomás, esta noche voy con mis amigas a un baile. Es probable que no haya otro baile como éste en mucho tiempo. ¿Me dice Ud. que no vaya?
DON TOMÁS:	No te digo que no vayas, pero sí te recomiendo que te cuides. La *salud* es *lo primero.*

Side glosses: won't go away / (a) sore throat / flu / (a) cough / cold / health / the first (most important) thing

La tensión le roba vitaminas al cuerpo. **Vita-Stress** las repone con su fórmula de Alta Potencia.

Actividades

A. Hágale estas preguntas a un compañero (una compañera).

1. ¿Qué le pasa a Silvia? ¿Qué tomó ella?
2. Según don Tomás, ¿qué es posible que sea la enfermedad de Silvia?
3. ¿Qué no cree Silvia?
4. ¿Qué otros síntomas tiene Silvia?
5. ¿Qué quiere don Tomás que Silvia compre?
6. ¿Qué le aconseja don Tomás a Silvia?
7. ¿Adónde va ella esta noche? ¿Por qué quiere ir?
8. ¿Qué le recomienda don Tomás? ¿Por qué?

B. Preguntas personales.

1. ¿Qué toma Ud. cuando le duele la cabeza?
2. ¿Qué toma si tiene dolor de garganta? ¿tos? ¿fiebre?
3. ¿Cuándo son más comunes los catarros? ¿y la gripe?
4. ¿Cuándo usa Ud. una curita? ¿y una venda?
5. Si hay un baile y Ud. tiene gripe, ¿va o se queda en casa? ¿y si tiene un simple catarro?
6. ¿Cree Ud. que la salud es lo primero? ¿Qué otras cosas son también importantes en la vida?

En la consulta* del dentista

At the Dentist's Office

la caries *cavity*
el/la dentista *dentist*
el empaste (empastar) *filling (to fill [a cavity])*
la muela *molar (tooth)*

Suggestion: Assign the roles of *Madre, Juanito,* and *Dentista* and have students act out this dialogue.

Follow-up: Ask orally: **1.** ¿Qué hace el niño? **2.** ¿Qué trata de hacer la madre? **3.** ¿Qué le va a dar el dentista a Juanito si es valiente? **4.** ¿Qué no quiere Juanito que haga el dentista? **5.** Según el dentista, ¿por qué no va a dolerle el empaste a Juanito? **6.** ¿Qué escribe el dentista? **7.** ¿Qué le pide el dentista a la enfermera? **8.** ¿Para quién es el calmante?

El niño grita, *llora* y *patalea*. La madre *trata de* calmarlo.   *cries / kicks / tries to*

MADRE: No llores, Juanito. Es necesario que estés *quieto* y abras la boca.   *still*

DENTISTA: Juanito, quiero que sepas que tienes caries en una muela y tengo
que empastarla. Si eres *valiente* te doy un premio después.   *courageous*

JUANITO: (Gritando otra vez.) ¡No quiero que me *saque* una muela! ¡No   *pull out*
quiero que me ponga una inyección! ¡No quiero que me dé un
premio!

DENTISTA: No voy a sacarte la muela, sólo voy a empastártela. Y no va a
dolerte nada; la inyección es de anestesia.

Juanito grita, llora y patalea por más de diez minutos. Finalmente, el dentista
escribe una *receta* y llama a la enfermera.   *prescription*

DENTISTA: Lucila, por favor, tráigame este *calmante* de la farmacia ahora mis-   *tranquilizer*
mo.

MADRE: Pero, doctor, ¿es necesario que le dé un calmante a Juanito?

DENTISTA: No, señora, el calmante es para mí.

*En algunos países se dice *consultorio*.

VISTA CULTURAL

En los países hispánicos existe una larga tradición en el uso de remedios caseros (hechos en casa). La mayor parte de estos remedios son cocimientos (*infusions*) de hierbas, como las de la foto. Son especialmente comunes en Hispanoamérica, primero porque mucha gente confía (*trust*) en ellos, pero también porque mucha gente no tiene acceso a tratamientos modernos por razones económicas. Claro que la curación con hierbas no es necesariamente una práctica supersticiosa de la gente pobre e ignorante. De hecho (*As a matter of fact*), muchas medicinas modernas, como la quinina, por ejemplo, se derivan de hierbas medicinales.

Actividades

A. En la consulta del dentista. Dé el subjuntivo de los infinitivos.

1. Niño, quiero que no (llorar) y que (estar) quieto.
2. No dejes que el doctor (sacarme) una muela o (ponerme) una inyección.
3. Juanito, quiero que (saber) que tienes caries en una muela.
4. Doctor, ¿cree Ud. que (ser) necesario que (darle) un calmante a Juanito?

B. Calmando a un niño. ¿Qué dice Ud. para calmar a un niño que...

1. grita antes de entrar en el consultorio?
2. llora cuando ve al dentista?
3. grita, llora y patalea cuando el dentista va a ponerle una inyección?

Suggestion C: This exercise can also be assigned as a written task, or as a short discussion topic for small groups to share experiences.

C. Su opinión personal. Conteste. *Answer quickly, changing verb forms and object pronouns as appropriate.*

1. ¿Le gusta que...
   a. el dentista le ponga una inyección?
   b. el dentista le empaste una muela?
   c. la enfermera le saque una radiografía?
2. ¿Prefiere que...
   a. lo/la examine un dentista o una dentista?
   b. no le den calmantes?
   c. un amigo lo acompañe si van a sacarle una muela?
3. ¿Es posible que...
   a. a veces no sean necesarias las radiografías?
   b. algunas pastas de dientes eviten (*prevent*) las caries?
   c. algunas personas tomen demasiados calmantes?

GRAMÁTICA ESENCIAL

52. Irregular Present Subjunctives: *dar, estar, ir, saber, ser*

—No llores, Juanito. Es necesario que estés quieto.
—Juanito, quiero que sepas
que tienes caries en una
muela y tengo que em-
pastarla.

You are already familiar with some of the following verb forms since, as
explained in **Gramática esencial 48,** polite direct commands are subjunctive
forms.

dar:	dé,* des, dé, demos, deis, den
estar:	esté, estés, esté, estemos, estéis, estén
ir:	vaya, vayas, vaya, vayamos, vayáis, vayan
saber:	sepa, sepas, sepa, sepamos, sepáis, sepan
ser:	sea, seas, sea, seamos, seáis, sean

NOTE: The present subjunctive form for **hay** (*there is, there are*) is **haya.**

Quiero que haya medicinas para   *I want (there to be) medicines for*
   todos.   *all.*

Actividades

A.   Buenos deseos. Su amigo está en el hospital. Exprese sus deseos con la
forma subjuntiva del verbo indicado.

Espero que...

1.   tu enfermedad (no ser) seria.
2.   los médicos (no darte) demasiadas medicinas.

---

*The accent is used on the first- and third-person singular forms of **dar** to distinguish them from
the preposition **de.**

3. tú (estar) en un buen hospital.
4. tus amigos (ir) a verte.
5. las enfermeras (ser) simpáticas.
6. los médicos (saber) curarte pronto.
7. no (haber) complicaciones durante la operación.

B. Pobre Juanito. Invente oraciones según el modelo.

MODELO: Sus padres / querer / él / ir al hospital →
Sus padres quieren que vaya al hospital.

1. La señora Barrios / preferir / la enfermera / no darle calmantes / a Juanito
2. El doctor / desear / todos nosotros / ir / a verlo
3. Ellos / alegrarse de / haber / una clínica cerca de su casa
4. Yo / esperar / Juanito / estar bien / pronto
5. Nosotros / temer / sus abuelos / no saber la verdad

53. Forms of the Present Perfect Subjunctive

The present subjunctive forms of the auxiliary verb **haber** are irregular.

PRESENT INDICATIVE		PRESENT SUBJUNCTIVE	
he	hemos	haya	hayamos
has	habéis	hayas	hayáis
ha	han	haya	hayan

The present subjunctive forms of **haber** are combined with the past participle to form the present perfect subjunctive. The present perfect subjunctive is used in the same types of situations (with verbs of will and emotion) that you have already learned with the present subjunctive.

Espero que la enfermera haya ve- *I hope the nurse has come.*
nido.
Nos alegramos de que lo hayan *We are happy they have seen him.*
visto.

Presentation: Remind students that in contrast with *hay* and *haya*, which are used only in singular to mean "there is/are," plural forms of *haber* are used when it is auxiliary verb.

Actividad

Un accidente en mi barrio. Ud. oyó por la radio que hubo un accidente de tránsito en su barrio, pero no sabe todos los detalles (*details*). Usando los verbos indicados, exprese lo que siente sobre el accidente.

MODELO: (Temer) La ambulancia / no llegar a tiempo →
Temo que la ambulancia no haya llegado a tiempo.

1. (Esperar) Uno de los vehículos / no ser el coche de mi padre
2. (Esperar) Los choferes / no morir
3. (Temer) Las víctimas / perder mucha sangre
4. (Esperar) Las heridas / no ser demasiado serias
5. (Temer) Uno de los conductores / estar borracho
6. (Sentir) El locutor / no dar más detalles

54. Subjunctive with Verbs of Disbelief, Doubt, and Denial

No creo que tenga fiebre,
pero sí me duele la garganta
y tengo tos.

A. Verbs like **creer** and **estar seguro/a de** (*to be sure about*) express certainty when used affirmatively. They then call for the indicative in the dependent clause.

Creo que es médico.	*I believe (that) he is a doctor.*
Estoy seguro de (Me parece) que nuestra clínica es mejor.	*I am sure (It seems to me) that our clinic is better.*

When used negatively, however, these verbs and expressions generally connote uncertainty and require the subjunctive in the dependent clause.

No creemos que tenga cáncer.	*We don't believe he has cancer.*
No está seguro de que Juana tenga suficientes pastillas para la tos.	*He isn't sure that Juana has enough cough drops.*

In questions with **creer** the indicative or subjunctive may be used, depending on the certainty or uncertainty of the questioner.

¿Cree Ud. que ella se siente bien hoy?	*Do you believe that she is feeling well today? (Maybe she does.)*
¿Crees que tengamos suficientes pastillas?	*Do you think we have enough pills? (The questioner doesn't think so.)*

B. **Dudar** (*to doubt*) and **negar (ie)** (*to deny*), in direct contrast to the preceding verbs, express uncertainty or denial when used affirmatively. They then require the subjunctive in the dependent clause.

Niego que estén en ese hospital.   *I deny (that) they are in that hospital.*

Dudamos que tengan los mismos síntomas.   *We doubt (that) they have the same symptoms.*

Actividades

A. ¿Están enfermos Juanito y Silvia? Cambie los verbos al subjuntivo.

¿Juanito? El doctor niega que...

1. (haber) que llevarlo al hospital.
2. él (tener) una infección en el brazo.
3. él (necesitar) antibióticos.
4. la herida (ser) muy profunda.
5. él (tener) fiebre.

¿Silvia? El doctor no cree que...

6. le (doler) la cabeza.
7. ella (ser) alérgica a la penicilina.
8. ella (necesitar) una transfusión de sangre.
9. ella (ir) al trabajo hoy.
10. ella (poder) tener un resfriado.

B. En el hospital. La abuela tiene que ir al hospital. Complete con la forma apropiada del verbo entre paréntesis.

—Carlos, siento mucho que mi abuela (*tener*[1]) que (*ir*[2]) al Hospital General, porque allí siempre (*haber*[3]) mucho ruido. Sé que a veces los pacientes (*gritar*[4]) en su habitación y temo que eso (*poder*[5]) molestar a mi abuela.

—¿Crees que eso (*ocurrir*[6]) en el Hospital General? No lo creo. (*Yo: Conocer*[7]) personalmente al director del hospital y estoy seguro de que él nunca (*permitir*[8]) eso. Además, me parece que allí las enfermeras (*ser*[9]) muy responsables. Lo siento, Bárbara, pero dudo que tú (*tener*[10]) razón esta vez.

C. Noticias de la clase. Invente oraciones originales para decirles a sus compañeros de clase que...

1. you believe that the instructor isn't coming to class tomorrow.
2. you are sure that he or she has been ill.
3. you doubt that he or she has been in the hospital.
4. you don't believe there's a test tomorrow, but you don't doubt there'll be one soon.
5. you are not sure you are prepared for a test.

55. Subjunctive with Impersonal Expressions

Es probable que no haya otro baile como éste en mucho tiempo.

Because impersonal expressions in Spanish often convey the speaker's subjectivity, most of them require the subjunctive in the dependent clause.

Es preciso (Es necesario) que vengas mañana.	*It is necessary that you come tomorrow.*
Es lástima (Es mejor) que no esté aquí.	*It's a pity (It's best) that he isn't (won't be) here.*
Es probable (Es posible) que ella no sepa eso.	*It's probable (It's possible) that she doesn't know that.*

Note: Most impersonal expressions are formed with *ser*. Some exceptions: *Está claro* (It is evident), *Vale más* (It is better), *¡Qué lástima!* (What a pity!), *¡Ojalá!* (I hope!).

When impersonal expressions express certainty, however, they require the indicative in the dependent clause.

Es verdad (Es cierto, Es obvio, Es seguro, Es evidente) que no tiene dinero.	*It's true (It's true, It's obvious, It's a sure thing, It's evident) that he has no money.*

If expressions of certainty are negative, they may call for the subjunctive since a measure of doubt is then cast on that certainty.

No es verdad que sea tan rico.	*It isn't true that he is so rich.*

When there is no expressed subject in the subordinate clause, impersonal expressions are followed by the infinitive. Compare the following.

Es importante que estudies.	*It is important that you study.*
Es importante estudiar.	*It is important to study.*

Actividades

Suggestion A: Have students form groups of two or three to complete this exercise, so that they can discuss their choice of mood in each item.

A. Una enfermedad grave. Complete la narración, decidiendo entre el indicativo y el subjuntivo de los verbos indicados.

Ayer don Guillermo entró en el hospital. Es posible que él no (saber) _____[1] qué tiene, pero es evidente que (estar) _____[2] muy enfermo. Su familia cree que su enfermedad (ser) _____[3] cáncer. Es preciso que el médico (decirle)

_____4 a don Guillermo la verdad, porque es probable que (tener) _____5 que operarlo pronto. Es lástima que yo no (poder) _____6 ir a verlo, porque es obvio que él (necesitar) _____7 ahora a sus amigos.

B. Haga un diálogo con un compañero (una compañera) entre un paciente y su dentista.

MODELO: ¿importante / yo / visitar al dentista / con frecuencia? →
—¿Es importante que yo visite al dentista con frecuencia?
—Sí, es importante que Ud. visite al dentista cada seis meses.

1. ¿seguro / el azúcar / producir / caries?
2. ¿mejor / la gente / no comer / dulces?
3. ¿probable / yo / tener / caries?
4. ¿preciso / Ud. / hacerme / dos empastes?
5. ¿cierto / Ud. / querer / sacarme una muela?
6. ¿necesario / Ud. / ponerme / una inyección de anestesia?
7. ¿importante / yo / pagarle / hoy?
8. ¿obvio / todos / deber / cuidarnos los dientes?

56. Comparatives and Superlatives

A. With adjectives and adverbs

To make a comparison of equality, use **tan** + *adjective (adverb)* + **como.**

Juan es **tan** bajo **como** Tomás.	*Juan is as short as Tomás (is).*
Ella canta **tan** bien **como** él.	*She sings as well as he (does).*

If the comparison is unequal, use **más (menos)** + *adjective (adverb)* + **que.**

Alberto es **más (menos)** saludable **que** su hermano.	*Alberto is healthier (less healthy) than his brother.*
Ella camina **más** rápidamente **que** yo.	*She walks faster than I do.*

Spanish adds the definite article to **más (menos)** and drops **que** to form the superlative (in comparing more than two items).

Carlos es **el** (estudiante) **más** guapo del grupo.	*Carlos is the best-looking (student) in the group.*
Su casa es **la más** antigua.	*Their house is the oldest.*

Note that after the superlative *in* is expressed by **de** in Spanish.

B. With nouns

To make an equal comparison, use **tanto (-a, -os, -as)** + *noun* + **como.**

El doctor Gil pone **tantas** inyecciones **como** su enfermera.	*Doctor Gil gives as many injections as his nurse (does).*

Note that **tanto** agrees in number and gender with the noun it modifies.

If two nouns are compared unequally, use **más (menos)** + *noun* + **que.**

> Ella tiene **más (menos)** proble-
> mas **que** yo.

> *She has more (fewer) problems
> than I (do).*

C. Irregular forms

The following chart presents several unequal irregular comparisons and their superlative forms.

		COMPARATIVE		SUPERLATIVE	
bueno/a	*good*	mejor	*better*	el/la mejor	*the best*
malo/a	*bad*	peor	*worse*	el/la peor	*the worst*
grande	*large*	más (menos) grande	*larger (smaller)*	el/la más (menos) grande	*the largest (the smallest)*
		mayor	*older*	el/la mayor	*the oldest*
pequeño/a	*small*	más (menos) pequeño/a	*smaller (larger)*	el/la más (menos) pequeño/a	*the smallest (the largest)*
		menor	*younger*	el/la menor	*the youngest*

> Es el **peor** hospital de la ciudad.
> Elisa es mi hermana **mayor** y
> Tomás mi hermano **menor.**

> *It is the worst hospital in the city.*
> *Elisa is my older sister and Tomás*
> *my younger brother.*

Más (menos) grande and **más (menos) pequeño** refer to difference in size; **mayor** and **menor** refer to age or special status.

Usually **mejor** and **peor** precede the nouns they modify, while **mayor** and **menor** follow them.

Actividades

A. La familia Aguilar. Diga con oraciones completas quién es (quiénes son)...

Don Guillermo
Padre
42 años

Doña Dora
Madre
39 años

Alberto
25 años

Pablito
13 años

Marisa
10 años

1. el/la más bajo/a de la familia
2. más grande que Marisa
3. tan alto/a como don Guillermo
4. menor que Alberto
5. el/la mayor de la familia
6. más fuerte (*strong*) que Pablito
7. el/la más pequeño/a de la familia
8. el/la más fuerte de la familia
9. tan bajo/a como la madre
10. el/la menor de la familia

Optional: Students use following components to form comparison:
1. una clínica, un hospital
2. este doctor, aquella doctora 3. el tabaco, el alcohol 4. la enfermedad del corazón, el cáncer 5. un resfriado, la gripe

Optional oral questions:
1. ¿Quién es más alto, (student's name) o (student's name)? 2. ¿Quién es mayor (menor), Ud. o yo? 3. ¿Quién tiene las manos (los pies) más pequeños/as, ella/él o yo? 4. ¿Cuántos/as hermanos/as tiene Ud.? ¿Quién es el/la más inteligente de todos/as? 5. ¿Quién es el mejor profesor (la mejor profesora) de esta clase? (El único [La única], naturalmente.)

Expansion A: After students have done this exercise, give orally your own story about your uncle to practice listening comprehension: Mi tío Rodolfo es un caso extremo. Visita a su médico todas las semanas y, con frecuencia, dos veces por semana. Si no tiene el pulso rápido, entonces lo tiene demasiado lento. Si tiene algún dolor en un músculo del brazo, en seguida piensa que sufre un ataque al corazón. En invierno le da miedo el aire frío; y en verano el aire caliente. Lo curioso es que tiene 98 años. ¡Nunca va a morir! Students answer questions orally or in writing: 1. ¿Cuántos años tiene mi tío? 2. ¿Qué le da miedo en verano? ¿Y en invierno? 3. ¿Qué piensa si tiene un dolor en algún músculo del brazo? 4. ¿Por qué le preocupa el pulso a veces?

B.   Dos amigas con gripe. Exprese en español.

1.   Mi amiga y yo tenemos gripe, pero yo estoy (*worse than her*) _____.
2.   Tengo (*the best doctor in the city*) _____ y he tomado (*as many medicines as*) _____ mi amiga, pero me siento muy mal.
3.   A ella le duele la cabeza, pero no le duele (*as much as*) _____ a mí.
4.   Es obvio que mi amiga va a curarse (*faster than*) _____ yo aunque voy a tomar (*more medicines than*) _____ ella.

C.   Gustos y preferencias. Pregúntele a un compañero (una compañera).

1.   ¿Prefieres que tu novio/a sea mayor o menor que tú? ¿Prefieres que sea más o menos alto/a que tú?
2.   ¿Qué crees que es mejor: estudiar por la noche o por la mañana? ¿Por qué?
3.   ¿Cuál es la mejor película que has visto este año? ¿y la peor? ¿Por qué?
4.   ¿Quién es tu mejor amigo/a? ¿Es mayor o menor que tú? ¿Quién es el menor de tus amigos?
5.   ¿Qué es peor, tener gripe o tener catarro? ¿Por qué?

Para resumir y repasar

A.   En persona: Su pobre tío. Ud. tiene un tío que es hipocondríaco. Siempre está en la consulta del médico o en la sala de emergencias. Cuéntele (*Tell*) a un compañero (una compañera) algunos de los problemas médicos que su tío cree que tiene. ¿Qué le dicen los médicos? ¿Qué le recomiendan? ¿Creen que los problemas de su tío son imaginarios o reales? ¿Qué le aconsejan?

B.   Haz lo que yo hago. Complete con la forma apropiada del presente de subjuntivo.

MODELO: Llego a las 6:00 y quiero que Ud.... →
          Llego a las 6:00 y quiero que Ud. llegue a las 6:00 también.

1.   Yo pienso estudiar mucho hoy y espero que tú...
2.   Sara siempre vuelve a casa temprano y prefiere que yo...
3.   Ellos duermen ocho horas y quieren que nosotros...
4.   Busco los libros que perdí y deseo que Uds....
5.   Ella no le pide dinero a nuestra madre y no quiere que nosotros le...
6.   Mi hermana aprende dos idiomas y me aconseja que yo _____ otro idioma también.
7.   El profesor llega a clase antes de las 8:00 y pide que los estudiantes _____ a esa hora también.
8.   Ya no fumo y me molesta que tú _____ aquí.
9.   Mis padres salen con mi hermano menor y ellos quieren que mi hermano mayor _____ con él también.
10. Tengo mucha hambre; me sorprende que los niños no...

COMUNICACIÓN

De la vida real

Pepto-Bismol
EN TABLETAS...
LLÉVELAS SIEMPRE CONSIGO,[a]
PORQUE UNO[b] NUNCA SABE.

FÁCILES DE LLEVAR...
FÁCILES DE TOMAR.

Donde quiera[c] que vaya, lleve Pepto-Bismol en tabletas.
Al igual que[d] Pepto líquido, las tabletas de Pepto-Bismol
alivian la acidez, la indigestión y hasta la diarrea.

Pepto-Bismol en tabletas.

LA MISMA MEDICINA, EL MISMO ALIVIO.

[a]*with oneself*
[b]*one (a person)*
[c]*Donde... Wherever*
[d]*Al... The same as*

A. Pepto-Bismol. Primero lea el anuncio.
Después, imagine que Ud. es el señor que está
comiendo y su compañero/a es el señor viejo.
Hágale a un compañero (una compañera)
estas preguntas.

1. ¿Es éste un remedio líquido?
2. ¿Por qué debo llevar las tabletas siempre
   conmigo (*with me*)?
3. ¿Cree Ud. que estoy comiendo mucho?
4. ¿Qué alivian estas tabletas?
5. ¿Qué diferencia hay entre el Pepto-Bismol
   en tabletas y el líquido?

B. La antivariólica. Conteste las preguntas.

1. El perro ataca a un hombre que está
   enfermo de viruela (*small pox*). ¿Qué
   síntoma tiene él de esta enfermedad?
2. ¿Tiene miedo este hombre de que el
   perro contraiga (*contract*) su enfermedad?
3. ¿De qué tiene miedo él? ¿de la rabia, o de
   la viruela?
4. ¿Cree el otro hombre que el perro va a

¿LO[a] HIZO VACUNAR?

SI... TIENE LA ANTIVARIOLICA

[a]*Lo... Did you have him vaccinated?*

C. El egiptólogo. Conteste las preguntas.

1. ¿Qué mira el egiptólogo?
2. Generalmente, ¿es fácil o difícil leer las recetas médicas?
3. ¿Es mala la letra (*handwriting*) de los médicos? ¿Es necesario un egiptólogo para descifrarlas?
4. ¿Cree Ud. que este chiste es cómico? ¿Por qué (no)?

Para conversar más

A. Preguntas comunes de un médico. Primero lea las preguntas para tener una idea general de sus respuestas. Luego, practique los papeles de médico/a y paciente con un compañero (una compañera).

1. Buenos días, joven, ¿cómo está hoy?
2. Y ¿dónde siente Ud. dolores?
3. ¿Desde (*Since*) cuándo tiene Ud. tos?
4. ¿Qué medicinas ha tomado Ud. ya?
5. ¿Tiene Ud. dolor de cabeza con frecuencia?
6. Bueno, lleve Ud. esta receta a su farmacia. ¿Cuál es su farmacia?

B. Soluciones médicas. ¿Qué dice Ud. en las siguientes (*following*) situaciones?

1. La mamá viene con un niño que tiene una herida. Ud. es médico/a y dice: «Señora, _____ ».
2. Un amigo está enfermo. Ud. sabe que no debe trabajar y por eso le dice: «_____».
3. Su padre tiene la presión arterial alta. La solución es fácil; Ud. le dice: «_____».
4. Su hermano come demasiado. Su recomendación: «_____».
5. Un amigo (Una amiga) necesita ejercicio todos los días. Le dice Ud.: «_____».

6. Una señora le dice que el beber vino y el fumar son muy malos hábitos. Ud. le contesta: «_____».
7. Alguien (*Someone*) le dice: «Ud. necesita hacer gimnasia». Ud. responde: «_____».
8. Todos hablan del mismo tema: la importancia de una buena alimentación (*nutrition*). Alguien le pregunta: «Y Ud., ¿qué piensa?» Ud. contesta: «_____».

C. Teatro. Con un compañero (una compañera) invente Ud. diálogos sobre las siguientes situaciones.

1. Ud. no se siente bien y le pide varios favores a su compañero/a de cuarto.
2. Ud. tiene un catarro, pero quiere ir a una fiesta. Su madre (padre) cree que no debe ir.
3. Ud. quiere calmar a un niño que grita y llora.

MOTIVO CULTURAL

In many Spanish-speaking countries, the word *hospital* refers to a government-subsidized public health facility where patients aren't charged any fees. Frequently, however, these hospitals lack modern equipment and provide less than ideal care. People who can afford the expense go to private hospitals called *clínicas*, which are well equipped and provide patients much better services. Many countries also have hospitals meant for emergencies only—called *casas de socorro* or *hospitales de urgencia*—that perform services similar to those provided by emergency rooms in the United States.

Family unity in the Hispanic culture is such that the family member will often stay with the patient in the hospital. Hispanics use the services of a nurse only for specialized treatments; routine care of a

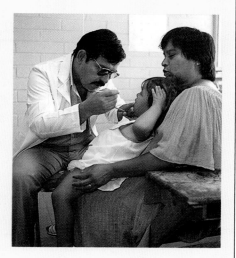

sick person is considered a labor of love and is therefore performed by members of the person's family.

Until recently, most doctors in Hispanic countries made house calls. Although many still do, this practice is becoming less common in large cities.

Vocabulario activo

Adjetivos

quieto/a	still
valiente	courageous

Comparativos y superlativos

el (la, los, las) más _____	the most _____
más (menos) _____ que	more (less) _____ than
tan _____ como	as _____ as
tanto (-a, -os, -as) _____ como	as much (many) _____ as

Sustantivos

LA SALA DE EMERGENCIAS (*THE EMERGENCY ROOM*)

el ataque al corazón	heart attack
el brazo roto	broken arm
el catarro	cold
la dificultad para respirar	difficulty in breathing
el dolor de estómago	stomachache
el dolor de garganta	sore throat
la enfermedad	illness
la fiebre	fever
la gripe	flu
la herida	wound
la presión arterial alta (baja)	high (low) blood pressure
la quemadura	burn
la sangre	blood
la tos	cough

LAS PERSONAS (*PERSONS*)

el/la doctor(a)	doctor
el/la enfermero/a	nurse
el/la herido/a	wounded person
el/la médico/a	medical doctor

LA FARMACIA

el calmante	tranquilizer
la curita	band-aid
las gotas (para la nariz, para los ojos)	(nose, eye) drops
la pastilla	tablet, pill
la pomada, el ungüento	ointment
la receta	prescription
la venda	bandage

LA CONSULTA DEL DENTISTA (*DENTIST'S OFFICE*)

la caries	cavity
el/la dentista	dentist
el empaste	filling
la muela	molar (tooth)

TRATAMIENTOS MÉDICOS Y DENTALES (*MEDICAL AND DENTAL PROCEDURES*)

curar	to cure
dar(le) oxígeno	to give (one) oxygen
empastar	to fill in (*cavity*)
poner(le) el termómetro	to take (one's) temperature
poner(le) una inyección	to give a shot
sacar(le) una muela	to extract a tooth
sacar(le) una radiografía	to take an X-ray
tomar(le) la presión	to take (one's) blood pressure

Verbos

cuidarse	to take care of oneself
doler (ue)	to hurt, ache
dudar	to doubt
llorar	to cry
negar (ie)	to deny
patalear	to kick, stamp

Expresiones impersonales

es cierto	it's true
es evidente	it's evident
es importante	it's important
es (una) lástima	it's a pity
es mejor	it's better
es necesario	it's necessary
es obvio	it's obvious
es posible	it's possible
es preciso	it's necessary
es probable	it's probable
es seguro	it's certain

Otras palabras y expresiones

dar(le) un ataque al corazón	to have a heart attack
el dolor no se me quita	the pain won't go away
estar seguro/a de	to be sure of
tener dificultad para respirar	to have difficulty in breathing
tratar de + *inf.*	to try to (*do something*)

Lectura

Antes de leer

Presentation: This reading is considerably longer than earlier *lecturas*. You could practice reading a couple of paragraphs aloud so that students get the feel of the intonation and the rhythm of a sustained context. You could even read a lengthy passage and have them follow along silently. Encourage them to concentrate carefully so as to understand as much as they possibly can.

Before proceeding with this reading, translate the title, looking up any words you don't know.

Now let's see how well you did. **Bellos** may refer to a group of men or to a mixed group of men and women. In this case, it refers to the former. Once you have discovered that **bisturí** means *scalpel,* you should be able to translate the title as "The Beautiful Men and the Scalpel." Now you know that the topic of this selection is surgery performed on men. Can you guess what kind of surgery, given that the men are referred to as *beautiful*?

Initially skimming a text alerts you to the general content. Rereading then becomes a process of expansion, of "fleshing out" your first impressions. Skim this selection by reading only the topic sentence of each paragraph. Check your general comprehension by indicating whether the following statements are true or false.

1. En el pasado, los clientes de los cirujanos plásticos eran principalmente hombres.
2. Las mujeres querían parecer jóvenes o corregir sus defectos físicos.
3. Hoy existen más tabúes y prejuicios que antes sobre la cirugía estética.
4. En el mundo de hoy es importante ser guapo.
5. Los hombres tienen miedo de que los acusen de frívolos.
6. La mayor parte de los pacientes de cirugía estética son hombres jóvenes.
7. Los primeros síntomas de que una persona es vieja son evidentes después de los 40 años.
8. Los políticos son los mejores clientes de los cirujanos plásticos.

Suggestion: This passage could be used as a listening exercise sometime after you have completed the exercise in its present format (i.e., for review).

Explain that English terms are often used in Spanish in connection with modern medical techniques originating in this country. The words "lifting" and "restyling" in the article are good examples of this practice.

Because of the traditional image of Hispanic men as *machos*, plastic surgery has been slow in gaining acceptance among Hispanic men although, as stated in the article, the number of men who have plastic surgery is increasing.

Correct Answers: Items 1, 3, 6, and 8 are false. Can you restate these statements so that they are correct according to the article?

Los bellos y el bisturí

Hasta no hace mucho,[1] la clientela de los cirujanos plásticos eran casi exclusivamente mujeres que querían recuperar la juventud o corregir sus rasgos[2] antiestéticos. Hoy, según el doctor Antonio de la

---

[1]Hasta... *Until recently*   [2]*features*

Fuente, uno de los más prestigiosos cirujanos plásticos de España, entre el
5 20 y el 25 *por ciento* de las operaciones de la nariz y alrededor del[3] 15 por
ciento de los «liftings» o estiramientos[4] de la piel,[5] se hacen a personas del
sexo masculino.

Muchos tabúes y *prejuicios* han caído a causa de[6] la necesidad de ser
guapos[7] y mantener el *aspecto juvenil* que imponen[8] los tiempos modernos.
10 «Sin embargo,[9] todavía no se ha perdido el *temor* del pasado. Cuando un
hombre me llama para recomendarme a algún amigo o pariente que quiere
operarse, en general, pide que no comentemos nada de su cirugía porque
nadie[10] lo sabe. Eso no ocurre con las mujeres, que generalmente lo
confiesan *con total naturalidad,* tal vez porque no esconden[11] su
15 coquetería[12]», *cuenta* el doctor de la Fuente.

«El varón[13] sigue pensando que se le puede acusar de frívolo, aunque[14]
los jóvenes comienzan a *superar* el trauma. Esperamos que el ''lifting'' de
varones aumente en los próximos[15] años hasta constituir el 25 por ciento
del total de operaciones de este tipo», *añade.*
20 La mayor parte de la clientela la constituyen hombres de 40 o más
años—cuando comienzan a advertirse[16] los primeros síntomas visibles de la
vejez—con un nivel[17] socio-económico y cultural *elevado* y un trabajo que
los obliga a tener una *relación* abierta con el público.

Los políticos son los que más se resisten a un «restyling» quirúrgico,
25 «posiblemente porque tengan miedo de que se note[18] el tratamiento y eso
les haga perder votos o credibilidad. En cambio,[19] hay importantes
banqueros y mucha gente del mundo del *espectáculo* que recurren[20] a estos
métodos sin temores», *señala* de la Fuente. «Y cada vez más».[21]

CAMBIO 16/España

Después de leer

A. Reemplace las palabras indicadas con los sinónimos de la lista.

a. a causa de
b. alrededor de
c. aumenta
d. cada vez más
e. esconden
f. estiramientos de la piel
g. nivel
h. notarse
i. próximos
j. rasgos
k. se operan
l. temor
ll. varones
m. la vejez

En el pasado, las mujeres querían cambiar algunas *características*[1] de su cara
o su cuerpo. Hoy, también muchos *hombres*[2] de *posición*[3] social importante
tienen operaciones[4] de la nariz y se hacen «*liftings*».[5]

Aunque los hombres se operan *más y más,*[6] todavía persiste el *miedo*[7]
masculino. Las mujeres, generalmente, hablan de sus operaciones, pero los
hombres *no dejan que nadie sepa de*[8] sus operaciones.

A los cuarenta años comienzan a *advertirse*[9] los síntomas de *los muchos
años.*[10] Muchos hombres se operan entonces, *por*[11] su trabajo, que les exige
(demands) mucho contacto con el público.

El número de varones que visita a los cirujanos plásticos *es más numeroso*[12]
cada día y probablemente en los años *siguientes*[13] el «lifting» entre ellos va a ser
más o menos[14] un 25 por ciento del total de las operaciones de este tipo.

---

[3]alrededor... *around (approximately)* [4]*stretching* [5]*skin* [6]a... *because of* [7]atractivos [8]*impose* [9]Sin... *However* [10]*nobody* [11]*hide*
[12]*affectation* [13]hombre [14]*although* [15]*next (coming)* [16]*to become noticeable* [17]*level* [18]se... *is noticed* [19]En... *On the other hand* [20]*resort*
[21]cada... *more and more*

Optional: **1.** ¿Quién es Antonio de la Fuente? **2.** ¿Por qué confiesan su cirugía con más naturalidad las mujeres? **3.** ¿Qué edad tiene la mayor parte de la clientela masculina de los cirujanos plásticos? **4.** ¿Qué nivel socio-económico y cultural tienen los clientes de los cirujanos plásticos? **5.** ¿Con quién tienen relación estos clientes en su trabajo?

B. Comprensión. Conteste según la lectura.

1. ¿Por qué razones iban las clientas a los cirujanos plásticos?
2. ¿Qué necesidad imponen los tiempos modernos a los hombres?
3. ¿Por qué no quieren los hombres que el doctor comente sobre su cirugía?
4. ¿A qué porcentaje del total espera el doctor de la Fuente que aumenten los estiramientos de la piel hechos en hombres?
5. ¿A qué edad comienzan a advertirse los primeros síntomas de la vejez?
6. ¿Por qué, probablemente, se resisten a operarse los políticos?
7. ¿Qué profesiones tienen muchos de los pacientes que se hacen este tipo de cirugía?

C. Opiniones. Hágale preguntas a un compañero (una compañera).

1. ¿Debe operarse una persona que tiene una nariz enorme? ¿Y si la tiene excesivamente pequeña?
2. ¿Debe estirarse la piel un hombre viejo? ¿Por qué (no)? ¿Debe comentarlo con los amigos una persona que se hace una operación de cirugía plástica? ¿Debe decírselo a todo el mundo o no debe decírselo a nadie?
3. ¿Es importante tener un aspecto juvenil? ¿Por qué (no)?
4. Si Ud. sabe que un político se ha hecho una operación de cirugía plástica, ¿vota por él? ¿Por qué (no)?
5. ¿Qué actores y actrices famosos se han hecho operaciones plásticas? ¿En qué parte del cuerpo se hicieron la operación? ¿Aprueba Ud. lo que hicieron? ¿Por qué (no)?

Repaso visual

Describa los dibujos. Considere las siguientes preguntas: ¿Qué objetos hay en los dibujos? ¿Quiénes son las personas que están en los dibujos? ¿Dónde están? ¿Qué hacen?

Examen de repaso 4

A. Un coche nuevo. Cambie los objetos directos e indirectos por pronombres.

> MODELO: Don José le dio *el dinero a Marta.* → Don José se lo dio.

1. Don José le ha comprado *un automóvil a su hija Marta.*
2. Marta le *dio las gracias a su padre.*
3. Ella *me* explicó *esto* en una carta.
4. Yo les di *la noticia a todos mis amigos.*
5. Mi hermano y yo le pedimos *un coche nuevo a mi padre.*
6. Mi padre *nos* dijo *a nosotros* que no tenía el dinero.

B. Adela, mi amiga la novelista. Exprese en español.

1. ¿Es verdad que tu amiga Adela _____ dos novelas? (*has written*)
2. Sí, pero (yo) no las _____. (*have seen*)
3. ¿Te _____ cuál de las novelas es mejor? (*has she told*)
4. No. Las compré, pero no las _____ todavía. (*have opened*)
5. ¿Por qué no? —Porque (yo) no _____ tiempo. (*have had*)

C. Diálogo entre dos amigos. Dé la forma apropiada del verbo indicado.

PEDRO: Prefiero que mis compañeros de apartamento no (saber[1]) que fui al médico, ni (*nor*) que estoy enfermo.

PABLO: ¿No quieres que yo les (decir[2]) la verdad?

PEDRO: No, por favor. Es mejor que no lo (saber[3]); por eso no quiero que el médico (llamar[4]) a casa.

PABLO: No creo que él (haber[5]) llamado todavía. Te aconsejo que (ir[6]) a hablar con él en su consultorio. Dudo que alguien te (ver[7]) entrar allí.

PEDRO: También te pido que no (hablar[8]) de esto con nadie.

PABLO: Lo siento, Pedro, pero ya se lo (haber[9]) dicho a mi hermana. Espero que no te (molestar[10]) mucho. Creo que ella (ser[11]) una persona discreta.

PEDRO: La verdad es que me sorprende que se lo (haber[12]) dicho. Ella siempre quiere (saber[13]) todo lo que hago. Es obvio que no (ser[14]) muy discreta. Ahora es seguro que (ir[15]) a tener que darle explicaciones.

D. Vocabulario. Complete.

Problemas del coche

1. Es difícil parar este coche porque no tiene buenos _____.
2. Necesito gasolina y no hay _____ en este barrio.
3. Hay mucha nieve en la calle y no tenemos _____ para la nieve.
4. En esta esquina no se puede _____ a la izquierda; espero que el policía no me ponga una _____.
5. No puedo manejar de noche; uno de los _____ está roto porque tuve un _____ con otro auto.

Celebraciones hispánicas

6. El Día de la Hispanidad, también llamado Día de la _____, hay un _____ muy grande en las calles de mi ciudad. La reina y otras chicas bonitas van en una _____ muy adornada. Un charro pasa montado a _____ y el _____ de la ciudad, el _____ del estado y los otros representantes aplauden con entusiasmo.

7. Nací (*I was born*) el 12 de diciembre y me llamo Guadalupe, así que celebro mi _____ y mi _____ el mismo día.

En el consultorio médico

8. —Doctor, ¿tengo la temperatura alta?
—Sí, Ud. tiene _____, y como además tiene _____ de cabeza, le aconsejo que tome dos aspirinas. Además, le voy a poner una _____ de antibióticos y le voy a dar unas _____ para la nariz y _____ para la tos.

E. Haz lo que yo hago. Complete con la forma apropiada del presente de subjuntivo.

MODELO: Llego temprano y quiero que Ud. ... →
Llego temprano y quiero que Ud. llegue temprano también.

1. Hoy almuerzo con Octavio y espero que Ud. ...
2. Pablo se dirige al cónsul y desea que yo...
3. Voy a un concierto el sábado y les pido a mis amigos que...
4. Siempre me siento cerca de la pizarra y te aconsejo que tú...
5. Pienso mucho en mi novio y espero que él...
6. El jefe (*boss*) perdió sus llaves, las busca y nos manda que...
7. Mi madre sólo duerme cinco horas y le molesta que nosotras...
8. Mi padre vuelve a casa temprano y no permite que yo...
9. Ya he comenzado a estudiar para el examen y les recomiendo que Uds. ...
10. Voy a pedirle a mi padre que no fume más y necesito que vosotros...

F. Comparaciones en mi familia. Complete.

1. Tu casa es grande, pero la casa de mi familia es _____.
2. Aunque tienes muchos hermanos, no tienes _____ hermanos _____ yo.
3. De mis hermanos, Pepe es el que tiene más años. Es el _____. Él pesa 60 kilos y yo 80; él es _____ gordo que yo.
4. Mi hermanita sólo tiene siete años. Ella es la _____.
5. Hay muchas madres buenas, pero creo que mi madre es la _____ madre _____ mundo.
6. No quiero a mis dos primos. Antonio es malo y Enrique es el _____ de los dos.

La madre Tierra

La vegetación exuberante de la selva tropical se ve en el parque nacional El Yunque en Puerto Rico.

METAS

Comunicación: In this lesson you will learn vocabulary and expressions related to nature: you will describe a landscape, comment on your favorite season, and discuss natural disasters. You will also be able to dream a little while discussing your plans for the future.

Estructuras: 57. Future Tense of Regular Verbs 58. Future Tense of Irregular Verbs 59. The Future of Probability 60. Affirmatives and Negatives 61. Uses of **pero, sino,** and **sino que**

GRÁFICOS

La tierra y el cielo

Earth and Sky

El paisaje (landscape)

1. el sol	4. el bosque	7. el río	10. la piedra	13. el mar/el océano
2. la nube	5. el valle	8. el árbol	11. la luna	14. la arena
3. la montaña	6. el lago	9. el camino	12. la estrella	15. la colina/la loma

Listening comprehension: Read following definitions and have students state or write down nouns defined: **1.** *regiones entre montañas donde el hombre cultiva la tierra (valles)* **2.** *soles muy distantes que vemos por la noche en el cielo (estrellas)* **3.** *vapor en masas de color blanco, negro o gris que vemos en el cielo (nubes)* **4.** *gran volumen de agua en una concavidad de la tierra (lago)* **5.** *montaña muy pequeña (loma o colina)* **6.** *origen de la luz que ilumina la tierra (sol)* **7.** *satélite de la tierra (luna)*

Actividades

A. Asociaciones. Con un compañero (una compañera) de clase, decida qué sustantivos se asocian con estas palabras.

1. el agua	4. la colina	7. la playa
2. el cielo	5. el mar	8. el camino
3. la noche	6. el día	9. los árboles

B. Un examen sobre la naturaleza (*nature*). Conteste.

1. ¿Qué puede Ud. ver en el cielo durante (*during*) la noche?
2. ¿De qué color son generalmente el sol, las nubes, el cielo y el mar?
3. ¿Qué valles de los Estados Unidos puede nombrar Ud.?
4. ¿Cuáles son los ríos más importantes de los Estados Unidos? ¿de Sudamérica?
5. ¿Qué mar separa España de África? ¿Qué mar está entre el norte de España y el oeste de Francia?
6. ¿Qué bosque famoso está en Alemania?

La primavera

1. la mariposa
2. las hojas
3. el pájaro
4. la rama

El verano

5. la ola
6. nadar
7. el bote de vela/el velero

El otoño

8. las hojas secas
9. el rastrillo
10. caer
11. el bulto
12. el cubo de la basura

El invierno

13. el muñeco de nieve
14. la pala
15. los copos de nieve

Warm-up: Say following words and ask students which season they associate with each: **1.** *la mariposa* **2.** *las hojas secas* **3.** *la pala* **4.** *el bote de vela* **5.** *el pájaro* **6.** *la playa* **7.** *el muñeco de nieve* **8.** *el rastrillo* **9.** *nadar* **10.** *las hojas verdes*

pasaré	*I will spend*
pasarás	*you will spend*
veré	*I will see*
verás	*you will see*
iré	*I will go*
irás	*you will go*

◆ IRREGULAR FUTURES ◆

saldré	*I will go out*
saldrás	*you will go out*
podré	*I will be able to*
podrás	*you will be able to*

Have students describe the scenes of the four seasons in their own words.

Antonio está *quitando* la nieve *frente a* su casa. — *removing / in front of*

ANTONIO: *¡Qué lata!* Cuando caían las hojas en el otoño, *pasaba* el día con el rastrillo en la mano, *recogiendo* hojas secas, haciendo bultos y llevándolos al cubo de la basura. Ahora que han llegado el invierno y los copos de nieve, *seguramente* pasaré todo el *tiempo* usando la pala. — *What a nuisance! / I used to spend gathering / surely (probably) / time*

TERE: A mí tampoco me gusta el invierno. La *única* persona de mi familia que disfruta del invierno es mi hermanito porque le encanta hacer muñecos de nieve. — *only*

ANTONIO: *Sueño con* la *llegada* de la primavera. *Brillará* el sol y saldré al *campo.* Veré mariposas y *oiré de nuevo* cantar a los pájaros en las ramas de los árboles. — *I dream about / arrival / will shine / country / I will hear again*

TERE: Pues yo no sueño con la primavera *sino* con el verano. Iré todos los días a la playa. Podré nadar, *navegar* en un bote de vela, o simplemente acostarme en la arena *blanda* a mirar las olas y *broncearme.* — *but (rather) / sail / soft / to get a tan*

ANTONIO: ¡Bonitos sueños! Pero, por el momento, te daré una pala y así me ayudas a quitar la nieve.

Actividades

A. ¿Cierto o falso? Corrija (*Correct*) las afirmaciones falsas.

1. En la primavera, Antonio recogió las hojas secas con una pala.
2. Tere es la única persona de su familia que disfruta del invierno.
3. El hermanito de Tere hace bultos con las hojas secas y las lleva al cubo de la basura.
4. Antonio no sueña con la llegada de la primavera sino con la llegada del invierno.
5. En la primavera brilla el sol y los árboles tienen hojas verdes en las ramas.
6. En la playa hay mariposas y pájaros en las ramas.
7. También podrá acostarse en la nieve blanda y broncearse.

B. Ud. tiene una amiga panameña que va a vivir en Boston por un año. Su amiga no ha visto antes la variedad de las cuatro estaciones. Explíquele en qué estaciones ella va a hacer las siguientes cosas.

MODELO: quitar / nieve →
En el invierno quitarás mucha nieve frente a tu casa.

1. pasar tiempo / recogiendo / rastrillo
2. ver / muñecos de nieve
3. salir al campo
4. oír cantar / pájaros
5. poder navegar / velero
6. ir a nadar / a la playa

C. Debate sobre las estaciones. Formen grupos de cuatro estudiantes. Cada estudiante va a defender una estación. Usen estas preguntas como guía.

¿Qué estación prefiere Ud.? Descríbala. ¿Por qué le gusta? ¿Qué estación no le gusta? ¿Por qué? ¿Es mejor vivir en un país tropical o en un país de clima frío? ¿Por qué?

Fenómenos y desastres de la naturaleza

1. el terremoto
2. el tornado
3. el huracán
4. la inundación
5. el relámpago
6. la lluvia
7. el volcán

Affirmatives
algo *something*
siempre *always*
también *too, also*

Negatives
nada *nothing*
nunca *never, not ever*
tampoco *neither, not either*

SR. GIL: (Leyendo el periódico.) El huracán Amelia llegará mañana al sureste de los Estados Unidos. *Se esperan* lluvias torrenciales y también inundaciones. *Are expected*

SRA. GIL: Paco, por favor, lee algo más *alegre*. No puedo oír nada sobre desastres o *guerras*. *Me pongo* muy nerviosa. *happy, cheerful* / *wars* / *I get*

SR. GIL: A mí no me gustan estas noticias tampoco. Nunca habíamos tenido tantos desastres *seguidos:* la erupción de un volcán en Centroamérica, un terremoto en la América del Sur, un tornado en Kansas y ahora un huracán. (*Se ve* un relámpago en el cielo y *se oye* un *trueno*.) *in a row* / *Is seen / is heard / thunder*

SRA. GIL: ¡Jesús! Aquí vamos a tener también *tormenta*. ¡Y yo con tanto miedo de los truenos! Voy a *rezarle* a Santa Bárbara. *a storm* / *pray*

Motivo cultural

Saint Barbara is the patron saint of artillerymen and also provides protection from storms. An ancient Spanish saying states: **"Acordarse de Santa Bárbara sólo cuando truena,"** which refers to those who remember their friends only in time of need. Because Saint Barbara is a legendary figure and there is no evidence that she ever existed, her name is no longer on the official list of saints in the Catholic Church. It is difficult, however, to eradicate tradition, and many Hispanics devoted to this saint still pray to her during storms.

Optional questions: 1. ¿Quién es la patrona de las tormentas? 2. ¿Qué dice un antiguo dicho? 3. ¿A quiénes se refiere este dicho? 4. ¿Por qué ya no está Santa Bárbara en la lista de santos de la iglesia católica? 5. ¿Por qué le rezan todavía muchos hispanos?

Actividades

A. Malas noticias. Conteste.

1. ¿Por qué se esperan inundaciones?
2. ¿Qué quiere la Sra. Gil que su esposo lea?
3. ¿Qué tipo de noticias no le gustan a la Sra. Gil? ¿Tiene la misma opinión el Sr. Gil?
4. ¿Qué desastres menciona el Sr. Gil?
5. ¿Por qué le sorprenden al Sr. Gil estos desastres?
6. ¿Por qué piensa la Sra. Gil que ellos van a tener también tormenta?
7. ¿Qué va a hacer ella? ¿Por qué?

B. Fenómenos naturales. ¿De qué hablo?

1. Es una montaña con fuego en el centro.
2. Son vientos muy fuertes (*strong*).
3. La tierra se mueve (*moves*).
4. Una luz cruza muy rápidamente el cielo.
5. El viento se mueve en forma de espiral.
6. El agua cae de las nubes.

Expansion B: Ask questions: 1. ¿En qué partes del mundo hay grandes volcanes? (en Centro y Sudamérica, Hawai, Japón, etc.) 2. ¿En qué estaciones del año tenemos huracanes? (en otoño, a finales del verano) 3. ¿Qué vemos en el cielo cuando hay una tormenta eléctrica? (relámpagos) 4. ¿Qué oímos, a veces, en una tormenta? (truenos)

ESTUDIO DE PALABRAS

In Spanish, diminutive endings are often added to words to express smallness, affection, or intensity of emotion. Many nicknames, for example, are formed that way. The most common diminutive endings are **-ito/a: árbol → arbolito; Tomás → Tomasito.**

Words ending in a vowel drop the vowel before adding the diminutive ending: **pájaro → pajarito; Luisa → Luisita.** Sometimes one or more additional letters are inserted before the diminutive ending: **pan → panecito; fuente → fuentecita.**

Reemplace cada diminutivo con la palabra original.

1. En el librito que leía Anita, había ilustraciones con maripositas entre las florecitas y fotografías de arbolitos con pajaritos en las ramas.
2. Me gustó mucho esa playita. El mar estaba azulito y había muchos botecitos. Un niñito, que jugaba en la arena con su palita, me dijo adiós.

VISTA CULTURAL

Los seis países de la América Central se extienden en un área total más pequeña que el estado de Texas, y en su paisaje son muy similares unos a los otros. En este paisaje predominan las cordilleras (*mountain ranges*), muchas de ellas volcánicas, que son continuación del sistema que comienza en Alaska. Entre las montañas hay fértiles valles con un suelo rico para la agricultura.

Guatemala, como se ve en esta foto del famoso lago Atitlán rodeado de (*surrounded by*) volcanes, es una región muy montañosa. Tiene el pico (*peak*) más alto de la América Central y 27 volcanes activos. Por esta razón, hay erupciones volcánicas y terremotos con frecuencia.

GRAMÁTICA ESENCIAL

57. Future Tense of Regular Verbs

Ahora que han llegado el invierno y los copos de nieve, seguramente pasaré todo el tiempo usando la pala.

Note: Use of the future is not very common in conversational Spanish; most natives show preference for the form *ir a* + infinitive. However, in written Spanish and more formal speech the future is used frequently.

Presentation: Mention that only future form that doesn't have written accent is *nosotros* form.

Most verbs in Spanish form the future by adding the endings shown below to the complete infinitive:

-é	-emos
-ás	-éis
-á	-án

	ENTRAR	VOLVER	ABRIR
	entraré	volveré	abriré
	entrarás	volverás	abrirás
	entrará	volverá	abrirá
	entraremos	volveremos	abriremos
	entraréis	volveréis	abriréis
	entrarán	volverán	abrirán

The future is the tense expressed with the auxiliaries *will* and *shall* in English.

Abriré la tienda mañana. *I shall open the store tomorrow.*
Volveremos pronto. *We will return soon.*

NOTE: In conversational Spanish the present tense is often used to refer to the immediate future, especially when an adverb of time (**mañana, esta tarde,** and so on) makes future meaning clear.

Te veo mañana. *I'll see you tomorrow.*

Warm-up: Say following statements and ask students to substitute future form for *ir a* + infinitive construction: **1.** *El sol va a brillar mucho en la primavera.* **2.** *Vamos a nadar en la playa.* **3.** *¿Vas a dormir la siesta en la arena?* **4.** *¿Van a ir Uds. con sus amigos?* **5.** *Voy a volver temprano a casa.* **6.** *Vais a oír cantar a los pájaros.* **7.** *Mis amigos van a alquilar un bote.* **8.** *¿Ud. va a caminar por la playa?*

Actividades

A. Escenas de la naturaleza. Ponga las siguientes narraciones en el futuro.

1. ¡Qué hermosa *es* la escena! El sol *brilla* mucho, las nubes *son* muy blancas y el pequeño río *corre* hacia (*towards*) el mar.
2. Yo *voy* a la playa, *nado* un poco y *alquilo* un bote de vela. Después *duermo* la siesta acostado en la arena.
3. *Llueve* esta noche. No *vemos* las estrellas y tampoco la luna. Los relámpagos *cruzan* el cielo y *oímos* los truenos.

Suggestion B: Have students report to class what they have learned about each other in interviews.

Optional: Change to future: **1.** ¿Con quién va Ud. al centro hoy? **2.** ¿Cuánto cuesta un vestido de seda? **3.** El dependiente no baja el precio. **4.** ¿Me compras un traje? **5.** ¿Vuelves a las 5:00?

4. El huracán Amelia *llega* mañana a la Florida. Mis amigos que viven en Miami *leen* la noticia en el periódico, *se sienten* nerviosos y *deciden* viajar al norte.

B. Planes para el futuro. Pregúntele a un compañero (una compañera)...

1. cuándo celebrará su cumpleaños
2. si organizará una fiesta
3. a quiénes verá el fin de semana
4. cuánto dinero necesitará este semestre
5. a dónde irá este verano
6. si preferirá pasar sus vacaciones en las montañas o en la playa

58. Future Tense of Irregular Verbs

Podré nadar, navegar en un bote de vela, o simplemente acostarme en la arena blanda a mirar las olas y broncearme.

It's easier to learn these forms if you group them as follows:

1. Verbs whose future stem is the infinitive minus the **e** of the ending:

   hab(e)r-, pod(e)r-, quer(e)r-, sab(e)r-

haber:	habré, habrás, habrá, habremos, habréis, habrán
poder:	podré, podrás, podrá, podremos, podréis, podrán
querer:	querré, querrás, querrá, querremos, querréis, querrán
saber:	sabré, sabrás, sabrá, sabremos, sabréis, sabrán

2. Verbs that substitute a **d** for the **e** or **i** of the infinitive ending:

   poner → pon(d)r-, salir → sal(d)r-, tener → ten(d)r-, venir → ven(d)r-

poner:	pondré, pondrás, pondrá, pondremos, pondréis, pondrán
salir:	saldré, saldrás, saldrá, saldremos, saldréis, saldrán
tener:	tendré, tendrás, tendrá, tendremos, tendréis, tendrán
venir:	vendré, vendrás, vendrá, vendremos, vendréis, vendrán

3. Verbs whose future stems are unique:

decir:	diré, dirás, dirá, diremos, diréis, dirán
hacer:	haré, harás, hará, haremos, haréis, harán

Note that the future of **haber** is combined with the past participle to form the future perfect.

Habré llegado para entonces.	*I will have arrived by then.*
¿Lo habrán comprado antes del lunes?	*Will they have bought it before Monday?*

Actividades

Warm-up: Write first person of irregular verbs on board to serve as guide and ask: **1.** *¿Podrá Ud. ir al cine esta noche con sus amigos?*   **2.** *¿Tendrán Uds. suficiente dinero?*   **3.** *¿Qué película querrán ver sus amigos?*   **4.** *¿Sabrá Ud. a qué hora comienza la película?*   **5.** *¿Se pondrá Ud. abrigo si va al cine?*   **6.** *¿A qué hora saldrán Uds. de casa?*   **7.** *¿Tendrá Ud. tiempo para comer antes de salir?*   **8.** *¿Habrá lugares para estacionar el coche cerca del cine?*   **9.** *Si sus amigos no quieren ir al cine, ¿qué hará Ud.?*

Optional: Have students work with partner, one of them playing fortune teller who predicts future of his/her partner.

A.   Lucía y Lolita van a ver a una adivinadora (*fortuneteller*) para saber su futuro. Lea lo que la adivinadora les dice y conteste.

A Lucía:

Pronto tendrá Ud. un nuevo novio. Saldrán siempre juntos y se querrán (*will love each other*) mucho. Este hombre le dirá palabras muy románticas y le comprará flores todos los días.

1.   ¿Qué tendrá pronto Lucía?
2.   ¿Quiénes saldrán siempre juntos y se querrán mucho?
3.   ¿Qué hará este hombre?

A Lolita:

Ud. y yo tendremos algunos accidentes en el futuro, pero las dos sabremos superarlos (*overcome them*). Ud. podrá conseguir un buen trabajo; pondrá mucho dinero en el banco y pronto será rica.

4.   ¿Qué les pasará a Lolita y a la adivinadora?
5.   ¿Qué podrá conseguir Lolita?
6.   ¿Qué hará ella con su dinero?
7.   ¿Qué será pronto Lolita?

B.   Si esto pasa, ¿qué hará Ud.?

> MODELO: Ud. invita a dos amigos a comer y llegan muy tarde. ¿Qué les dirá Ud.? →
> Yo les diré, «¿por qué llegaron tan tarde?»

1.   Ud. va por la calle y un señor muy elegante le pide que le dé dinero.
2.   Si mañana hace frío, ¿qué ropa se pondrá Ud.? Y si llueve, ¿qué llevará?
3.   Ud. no vino a clase el viernes, pero el profesor lo/la vio esa noche en una discoteca. ¿Qué le dirá Ud. el lunes?
4.   Un amigo que ganó la lotería le hará un regalo. ¿Qué regalo querrá Ud.?
5.   Mañana habrá un examen de la Lección 13. ¿Qué parte sabrá Ud. contestar mejor? ¿Qué partes de la lección no sabrá bien?

59. The Future of Probability

The future tense is also used in Spanish to express probability or conjecture. This usage has no exact equivalent in English and is often translated as: *I wonder, can, must,* and *probably.*

Note: Explain to students that this usage of the future tense is quite common and is probably the one they will hear most often in conversational Spanish.

¿De quién será este rastrillo?   *I wonder whose rake this is.*
No encuentro mi pala, ¿dónde estará?   *I can't find my shovel; where can it be?*

Actividad

Reacciones y conjeturas. Un(a) estudiante lee una frase y otro/a estudiante reacciona haciendo una conjetura según las indicaciones.

MODELO: Hubo un terremoto en Guatemala. (haber / heridos) →
Habrá muchos heridos en los hospitales.

1. En esa región llovió constantemente por 48 horas. (tener / inundaciones)
2. Vemos muchos relámpagos en el cielo. (oír / truenos)
3. Hay muchos pájaros y mariposas en el campo. (ser / primavera)
4. Tengo muchos árboles en mi jardín. (recoger en otoño / hojas secas)
5. Juan siempre va a la playa, pero nunca entra en el mar. (saber / nadar)
6. Mi madre le reza mucho a Santa Bárbara. (tener miedo / truenos)
7. Mis amigos tienen una casa cerca de un lago. (pasar / vacaciones)

60. Affirmatives and Negatives

Paco, por favor, lee algo más alegre. No puedo oír nada sobre desastres o guerras.

	AFFIRMATIVES		NEGATIVES	
Pronoun (*Used instead of a noun*)	algo alguien	*something* *someone*	nada nadie	*nothing* *nobody*
Adjective (*Used with a noun*)	algún (alguno/a/os/as)	*some; any*	ningún (ninguno/a)	*no, not any*
Adverb (*Used with a verb*)	siempre alguna vez también	*always* *ever* *also*	jamás nunca tampoco	*never, not ever* *neither, not either*

¿Ha venido alguien?   *Has anyone come?*
No, no ha venido nadie.   *No, no one (nobody) has come.*

The personal **a** is required when **alguien** or **nadie** is a direct object.

¿Viste a alguien aquí?   *Did you see someone here?*
No, no vi a nadie.   *No, I didn't see anybody.*

The adjectives **alguno** and **ninguno** are shortened to **algún** and **ningún** before a masculine singular noun. The plurals of **ningún (ninguno/a)** are rarely used.

¿Tienes algunas monedas?   *Do you have any coins (money)?*
No, no tengo ninguna   *No, I don't have any.*
(moneda).

All the negatives in the chart above can be placed either before or after the verb. If they are placed after, **no** must precede the verb. The resulting double or triple negative, while incorrect in English, is necessary in Spanish.

No lo veo nunca. (*or* Nunca lo   *I never see him.*
veo.)
No me dice nunca nada.   *He never tells me anything.*
A mí no me gustan nada las   *I don't like winter storms at all.*
tempestades de invierno.   *—I don't either.*
—Y a mí tampoco.

Actividades

A.   Excursiones y visitas. Cambie las oraciones según los modelos.

MODELO: Nunca he visto el mar. → No he visto nunca el mar.

1.   Nunca vamos a la playa.
2.   Tampoco hacemos excursiones a las montañas.
3.   Nadie conoce el camino del lago.
4.   Jamás subiré a un volcán.
5.   Nada es como me gusta.

MODELO: No llueve nunca en esta región. →
         Nunca llueve en esta región.

6.   ¿No vino a verme nadie?
7.   ¿No me llamó nadie?
8.   Ella no me ha visitado nunca.
9.   No pasará nada si ella no viene.
10.   No me ha llamado jamás.

B.   Rumores falsos. Ud. escribe para un periódico y tiene que negar ciertos rumores falsos. Dé la versión contraria en cada caso.

1.   Alguien dijo que venía un tornado.
2.   También tendremos inundaciones.
3.   En esta provincia hay terremotos algunas veces.
4.   Anoche tuvimos mucha lluvia y vimos algunos relámpagos en el cielo.
5.   Algunas personas creen los rumores falsos.
6.   Aquí siempre pasa algo.

61. Uses of *pero, sino,* and *sino que*

Pues yo no sueño con la primavera sino con el verano.

A statement containing the word *but* usually consists of two parts, which can be represented graphically in this way:

FIRST PART	BUT	SECOND PART
He is rich,	*but*	*he doesn't spend much money.*
Él es rico,	pero	no gasta mucho dinero.

If the first part is affirmative, *but* is always expressed with **pero.**

Gana $400,00, **pero** gasta
$500,00.

*He earns $400.00, but he spends
$500.00.*

If the first part is negative, the following applies.

1. *But* = **pero,** if it means *however:*

    No es un huracán, **pero** hace
    mucho viento.

    *It isn't a hurricane, but (however)
    it is very windy.*

2. *But* = **sino** if the second part is an incomplete thought—for example, just a noun or an infinitive.

    No veía estrellas **sino** nubes.

    *He didn't see stars but (only)
    clouds. (second part is just a
    noun:* **nubes***)*

    No nos prometió bailar **sino**
    cantar.

    *She didn't promise us to dance but
    to sing. (second part is just an
    infinitive:* **cantar***)*

3. *But* = **sino que** if it means *on the contrary* or *instead* and introduces a conjugated verb:

    No llegaron al volcán, **sino que**
    volvieron al pueblo.

    *They didn't arrive at the volcano,
    but (on the contrary) they re-
    turned to the village.*

Presentation: Explain that "but" is translated as *pero* if it means "however, on the other hand, yet," but as *sino* if it means "but rather."

Related constructions: You may want to mention *no sólo (solamente)... sino (que) también (además)...* : *Aquí no sólo hace frío, sino que también nieva mucho.* Also, when "but" follows an affirmative statement and means "except," its more common Spanish equivalents are *menos* and *excepto: Leí todo el libro menos (excepto) la última parte. Todos mis compañeros estaban en la fiesta menos (excepto) tú.*

Actividades

A. Las estaciones. Complete con **pero, sino** o **sino que.**

La primavera

1. No llueve ahora, _____ lloverá pronto, porque en abril llueve mucho.

2. El pájaro que veo en la rama no come, _____ está cantando.
3. No hay pájaros entre las flores, _____ mariposas.

El verano

4. Veo a mucha gente en la arena, _____ pocas personas están nadando.
5. Mi amiga no dijo que tenía miedo de las olas, _____ no sabía nadar.
6. No montaremos en bote de vela, _____ practicaremos el esquí acuático.

El otoño

7. Las hojas secas no son verdes, _____ tienen tonos de amarillo, rojo y café.
8. No me gusta recoger las hojas, _____ acostarme en ellas.
9. Todavía no hace mucho frío, _____ ya los árboles no tienen hojas.

El invierno

10. No uso un rastrillo para limpiar la nieve, _____ una pala.
11. El muñeco de nieve no lleva zapatos, _____ sí lleva sombrero.
12. Hoy no hace mucho frío, _____ todavía hay mucha nieve en la calle.

B. Complete lógicamente.

1. No he visto nunca un tornado, pero...
2. Algunos países no quieren paz (*peace*) sino...
3. No dice que alquilará un bote, sino que...
4. El ciclón no llegará a esta región, pero...
5. No tengo miedo de los truenos, sino...

Para resumir y repasar

A. En persona: El futuro de la madre Tierra. Muchos científicos dicen que la temperatura de la Tierra está subiendo a causa del efecto invernadero (*greenhouse effect*). Algunos dicen que el clima y las estaciones cambiarán drásticamente. Descríbale a un compañero (una compañera) de clase cómo se imagina Ud. el clima y las estaciones en el año 2100.

B. Juanito está enfermo otra vez. Dé el presente de subjuntivo correspondiente a cada infinitivo.

Es lástima que Juanito (estar[1]) enfermo hoy. Dudo que su enfermedad (ser[2]) seria, pero quiero que (estar[3]) en la cama toda la mañana y que (ir[4]) al médico por la tarde. Es muy posible que el médico (saber[5]) inmediatamente cuál es el problema y que le (dar[6]) una medicina sin esperar el resultado de los análisis.

C. Observaciones médicas. ¿Subjuntivo o indicativo? Complete con la forma apropiada del infinitivo.

1. Es evidente que la Dra. Pendás (ser) una médica excelente y es una lástima que yo no (poder) ir a consultarla.
2. Dudo que tu abuelita (tener) cáncer y espero que (curarse) muy pronto.
3. Estoy seguro de que ésa (ser) la medicina que me recetó la médica.

4. Es necesario que todos (tomar) vitaminas para tener buena salud.
5. El profesor no cree que a Silvia le (doler) la cabeza; él está seguro de que ella lo (decir) como excusa para no examinarse.

COMUNICACIÓN

¡Mas reciclaje[a] ahora en Queens!

De la vida real

[a]*recycling*
[b]*Board (Committee)*
[c]*cardboard*
[d]*glass (objects)*
[e]*ser... recibir una multa*
[f]*flat*
[g]*inches*
[h]*tying them up*
[i]*de su casa*
[j]*container*
[k]*enclosed*
[l]*even though*
[m]*reimbursement*
[n]*glass*
[o]*tin*
[p]*smooth*

Junta[b]Comunitaria #7

Efectivo inmediatamente, el Departamento de Sanidad recogerá y reciclará sus **revistas, catálogos** y **cartones[c]corrugados** junto con sus periódicos, metales y cristales[d].

Recuerde, el reciclaje es ley en Nueva York. Usted tiene que separar los materiales mencionados del resto de su basura, o puede ser multado[e].

Cómo reciclar

- **Periódicos, revistas, catálogos, cartones corrugados aplastados:**[f] Usted (o su super) pueden hacer bultos de hasta 18 pulgadas[g]de altura, amarrándolos[h]con cordón resistente.

- **Cristal, metal, papel de aluminio:** Continúe limpiándolos y ponga sus cristales, metales y papeles de aluminio caseros[i]en el recipiente[j]azul de reciclaje de su edificio.

- Si no conoce su Día de Reciclaje, chequee el mapa adjunto[k].

- Ponga su bulto de papeles **al lado** (no dentro) de su recipiente de reciclaje, al borde de la acera, **la noche anterior** a su día de Reciclaje, todas las semanas, aunque[l]llueva.

Si usted vive en un edificio de apartamentos, pregunte a su superintendente dónde colocar sus materiales de reciclaje.

Depósito de 5¢: Continúe devolviendo botellas y latas vacías al almacén para reembolso,[m]o déselas a los niños o a los sin hogar de su barrio. Estas son también alternativas excelentes para el reciclaje.

NYC Departamento de Sanidad

Ayude a reducir la basura de Nueva York. Recicle por favor.

Qué reciclar

Sí Periódicos
Revistas
Catálogos
Cartones corrugados
(cajas aplastadas)

Latas (atún, sopa, alimentos de animales domésticos)
Botellas de vidrio[n](jugo, vino, etc.)
Frascos de vidrio (alimentos para niños, mermelada, etc.)
Papel de aluminio y de hojalata[o] (recipientes de torta o de comida para llevar)

No Guías telefónicas
Libros de tapa dura o blanda
Cartón gris liso[p](de cereal o cajas de zapatos, cajas de camisas)

Envases de aerosol o atomizadores ("sprays")
Latas de pintura o recipientes de productos químicos
Plásticos
Cerámicas
Bombillas eléctricas
Espejos

Impreso en papel reciclado, naturalmente.

A. ¡Más reciclaje ahora en Queens! Lea el aviso (*notice*) y conteste las preguntas.

1. ¿Qué va a hacer, efectivo inmediatamente, el Departamento de Sanidad de Nueva York?
2. ¿Qué puede pasarle a Ud. si no separa los materiales para reciclar del resto de la basura?
3. ¿Cómo debe preparar los periódicos, revistas y cartones para el reciclaje?
4. ¿Dónde debe poner el bulto de papeles para reciclarlo? ¿Cuándo? ¿Y si llueve?
5. Si una persona vive en un edificio de apartamentos, ¿qué debe preguntarle al superintendente?
6. ¿Cuáles son otras alternativas para el reciclaje?

B. Ud. es empleado/a del Departamento de Sanidad. Prepare un diálogo con un compañero (una compañera) que llama por teléfono y pregunta qué debe hacer con los siguientes objetos.

1. los periódicos y revistas
2. los objetos de cristal y metal
3. las botellas de plástico de Coca-Cola
4. las latas de atún y sopa
5. los espejos

C. Clasificación. En este aviso de la página anterior, aparece una lista que tiene el título «Qué reciclar». Léale a un compañero (una compañera) algunos de los objetos de esta lista. Él (Ella) tendrá que decirle si los objetos que Ud. menciona se pueden reciclar o no.

D. Nadie tiene derecho a destruir el ambiente de tus hijos. Lea este anuncio de Venezuela y conteste las preguntas.

1. ¿Qué cosas quema y tala la gente?
2. ¿Qué tipo de contaminación menciona el anuncio?
3. ¿Qué tipo de caza critica el anuncio? ¿y qué tipo de ruido?
4. ¿Qué debemos cuidar todos?
5. ¿Cree Ud. que tiene razón el autor del anuncio? ¿Por qué (no)?

Note: Ad is from Venezuela. Take opportunity to explain that in Hispanic countries, as in U.S., concern for protection of environment is growing. In Caracas, for instance, overpopulation has created serious problems: excessive noise, pollution, and continual traffic jams. Existence of *Ministerio del Ambiente y de los Recursos Naturales* and of ads like this exemplify attempts by Venezuelan government to solve environmental problems.

Nadie tiene derecho[a] a destruir el ambiente[b] de tus hijos

El hombre todos los días recibe un paraíso. Pero hay quienes, cada día, se empeñan en[c] destruirlo. La quema[d] y la tala[e] de bosques y sabanas; la contaminación del aire, de los ríos y las playas; la caza[f] indiscriminada y la producción de ruidos molestos[g] deterioran el ambiente de nuestros hijos. Al recuperar[h] el ambiente se recupera el hombre.

Cuida que no sea destruído el ambiente de tus hijos.

[a]*right*
[b]*environment*
[c]*se... are bent on*
[d]*burning*
[e]*cutting*
[f]*hunting*
[g]*annoying*
[h]*Al... Upon recuperating*

Note: This ad provides excellent reading and pronunciation practice as well as an up-to-date word of caution about how we treat our environment.

Para conversar más

Suggestion B: Students can prepare short speeches about their own plans or those of an imaginary person at home and present them in class. Classmates can then ask questions based on speeches.

Cultural expansion: This *Motivo* refers to traditional *dicho* (saying). Proverbs, axioms, and refrains have been popular with Spanish authors for centuries; authors from Middle Ages to present have collected and disseminated them. While today such pithy sayings are not considered basis of philosophy, as they were in Middle Ages, they are still looked upon as interesting dimension of a people and its cultural expression.

A. ¿De qué hablamos? *In groups of three, invent cues for your classmates to guess what natural phenomenon or place you are talking about. Some possibilities are given below; continue with your own ideas.*

MODELO: Es un río. Es muy grande. Está en una selva tropical. Este río cruza una gran parte del territorio del Brasil. ¿Cómo se llama?
→ El río Amazonas.

1. isla / cerca de la Florida / su capital es La Habana / _____
2. hay mucho viento / el viento va en dirección circular / _____
3. la tierra se mueve / es muy peligroso estar en una ciudad en estos momentos / _____

B. Predicciones. Describa sus planes, usando verbos en el futuro.

MODELO: la familia →
Tendré un esposo (una esposa) inteligente y tres niños hermosos y listos... como yo.

1. su vida personal
2. sus estudios
3. el futuro de este planeta

MOTIVO CULTURAL

According to an old Spanish saying, during one's life a person should have a child, write a book, and plant a tree. Most people cannot do these three things, but this saying indicates the Hispanic concern for creativity in all its forms: biological, intellectual, and natural.

An important aspect of Spanish literature is poetry inspired by nature. The following fragment from **"El viaje definitivo,"** by the Spanish poet Juan Ramón Jiménez (1881–1958), relates his meditations about death with the humble things of everyday life. He tells us sadly that life and nature will go on even after his death:

EL VIAJE DEFINITIVO

Y yo me iré; y estaré solo, sin
  hogar, sin árbol
verde, sin pozo blanco,
sin cielo azul y plácido...
Y se quedarán los pájaros cantando.

THE FINAL JOURNEY

*And I will depart and will be
  all alone,
with no home, no green tree, no
  whitewashed well,
no blue, placid sky . . .
And the birds will remain,
  singing.*

Juan Ramón Jiménez
(1881–1958)

Vocabulario activo

Adjetivos

alegre	happy, cheerful
blando/a	soft
seco/a	dry
seguido/a	in a row
único/a	only

Sustantivos

LA TIERRA Y EL CIELO (*EARTH AND SKY*)

la arena	sand
el bosque	forest
el camino	road
el campo	countryside
la colina	hill
el copo de nieve	snowflake
la estrella	star
la hoja	leaf
el lago	lake
la loma	hill
la luna	moon
la mariposa	butterfly
el muñeco de nieve	snowman
la nube	cloud
el océano	ocean
la ola	wave
el paisaje	landscape
el pájaro	bird
la piedra	stone
la rama	branch
el río	river
el sol	sun
el valle	valley

FENÓMENOS Y DESASTRES DE LA NATURALEZA
(*PHENOMENA AND DISASTERS OF NATURE*)

el huracán	hurricane
la inundación	flood
la lluvia	rain
el relámpago	lightning
el terremoto	earthquake
la tormenta	storm
el tornado	tornado
el trueno	thunder
el volcán	volcano

OTROS SUSTANTIVOS

el bote de vela	sailboat
el bulto	bundle
el cubo de la basura	garbage pail
la guerra	war
la llegada	arrival
la pala	shovel
el rastrillo	rake
el tiempo	time
el velero	sailboat

AFIRMATIVOS

algo	something
alguien	someone
algún (alguno/a/os/as)	some; any
alguna vez	ever
siempre	always
también	also

NEGATIVOS

jamás	ever, never
nada	nothing
nadie	nobody
ningún (ninguno/a)	no, not any
nunca	never
tampoco	neither

Otras palabras y expresiones

de nuevo	again
frente a	in front of
ponerse + *adj.*	to become, get + *adj.*
¡Qué lata!	What a nuisance!
seguramente	surely; probably

Verbos

brillar	to shine
broncearse	to get a tan
caer	to fall
nadar	to swim
navegar	to sail
pasar	to spend
quitar	to remove
recoger	to gather, pick up
rezar	to pray
soñar (ue) (con)	to dream (about)

De viaje por España

Este pastor y sus ovejas tienen al fondo la catedral y el Alcázar de Segovia.

METAS

Comunicación: In this lesson you will learn vocabulary and expressions related to travel: packing a bag, staying in a hotel, participating in sports, and visiting different points of interest. You will talk about playing a game of tennis, going to the beach, and eating in a restaurant.

Estructuras: 62. Conditional of Regular Verbs 63. Uses of the Conditional 64. Conditional of Irregular Verbs 65. Ordinal Numbers 66. Stressed Possessive Adjectives and Possessive Pronouns

GRÁFICOS

Haciendo la maleta

Los cosméticos

11. la crema (para la cara)
12. la loción (para las manos)
13. la laca   *hair spray*
14. el estuche de maquillaje   *make-up kit*
15. la barra para los labios / el lápiz labial / el creyón de labios
16. el perfume
17. el agua de colonia
18. el colorete   *rouge*
19. la sombra para los ojos   *eyeshadow*

Las joyas

20. el anillo (de brillantes)   *(diamond) ring*
21. los pendientes / los aretes (de plata)   *(silver) earrings*
22. el collar (de perlas)
23. la pulsera (de oro)   *(gold) bracelet*

Para el viaje

1. la maleta
2. el maletín

Para la higiene personal

3. el peine
4. el cepillo para el pelo
5. el cepillo de dientes
6. la pasta de dientes ∘

7. la máquina de afeitar
8. la loción de afeitar   *after-shave lotion*
9. el champú   *shampoo*
10. el desodorante

Actividades

A. Cubra la lista de palabras y luego identifique los objetos.

B. Personas interesantes. Comente sobre cada uno de estos individuos. ¿Qué cosas necesitan usar? ¿Qué deben hacer? ¿Qué no pueden hacer o usar?

Raúl   Daniel   Ana   Paco   Victoria

Expansion D: Ask these questions: **1.** *¿Cuál es su perfume favorito?* **2.** *¿Les gusta a todos los miembros de su familia la misma pasta de dientes?* **3.** *¿Prefiere Ud. peinarse con un peine o con un cepillo?* **4.** *(para una chica) ¿Cuáles son algunos de los colores de moda en que viene la sombra de ojos?* **5.** *(para un hombre) ¿Prefiere Ud. afeitarse con máquina eléctrica o con navaja (straight razor)? ¿Por qué?*

C. Asociaciones. ¿Con qué partes del cuerpo asocia Ud. las siguientes cosas?

1. la crema
2. el peine
3. el anillo
4. la pulsera
5. el desodorante
6. «Giorgio»
7. la barra
8. la pasta
9. la laca
10. la máquina de afeitar
11. los aretes

D. Sus preferencias. Invente un monólogo para explicar qué cosméticos y accesorios Ud. o alguien que Ud. conoce prefieren. ¿Son muy caros?

En la *recepción* de un hotel de Barcelona

Front Desk

1. el botones
2. el ascensor/el elevador
3. la(s) escalera(s)
4. el jugador
5. la jugadora
6. la raqueta
7. la pelota

Note: *Botones* is term for "bellhop" because of buttons on uniform.

◆ REGULAR CONDITIONALS ◆

-ar:	
me gustaría	*I would like*
nos gustaría	*we would like*

-er:	
sería	*I/you/he/she/it would be*
serías	*you would be*

-ir:	
preferiría	*I/you/he/she/it would prefer*
preferirías	*you would prefer*

Presentation: Model pronunciation of conditional, since it can be quite a mouthful for students.

Una conversación en Barcelona en 1992, el año de los Juegos Olímpicos.

EMPLEADO: Señoritas, aquí tienen la llave. El botones les llevará las maletas en unos minutos. Tienen la habitación número ciento once, en el primer *piso*.* Los ascensores están a su derecha y las escaleras a su izquierda.   *floor*

ALICIA: ¡Primer piso! ¿Tendremos una buena *vista*? Reservamos el mes *pasado*...   *view   last*

EMPLEADO: Es un *milagro* que tengan habitación. Todo el mundo ha venido a Barcelona a ver los Juegos Olímpicos.   *miracle*

---

*En los países hispánicos el primer piso equivale al segundo de los Estados Unidos.

ILEANA: Hablando de los Juegos... Nos gustaría ver alguna *competencia.*   *competition*
¿Sería posible *conseguir* billetes?   *obtain*

EMPLEADO: ¡Eso *sí que* sería un milagro señorita! Todos están *agotados.*   *indeed / sold out*

ALICIA: Bueno, Ileana, mañana *intentaremos* conseguir algunos *de todas*   *we'll try*
maneras.   *anyway*

ILEANA: Sí, y *mientras tanto, aunque* preferiría ver jugadores profesionales,   *in the meantime / although*
también nosotras podemos competir. Esta tarde alquilaremos ra-
quetas y pelotas y jugaremos un buen *partido* de tenis en la *cancha*   *match / court*
del hotel.

ALICIA: Buena idea. Y *la que* pierda el partido, pagará la cena.   *the one who*

Actividades

Optional: Ask these
questions: **1.** ¿Quién llevará las maletas a la habitación? **2.** ¿Dónde están
los ascensores? ¿Y las escaleras? **3.** ¿En qué piso
está la habitación 111?
4. ¿Por qué es un milagro
que Ileana y Alicia tengan
habitación? **5.** ¿Por qué
no pueden conseguir bi-
lletes para ver alguna
competencia olímpica las
chicas? **6.** ¿Qué alqui-
larán Ileana y Alicia? **7.**
¿Dónde jugarán ellas un
partido? **8.** ¿Qué hará la
chica que pierde el partido?

Suggestion B: Exercise
can also be done in pairs
with students addressing
each other with *tú.*

A. Diálogo en la recepción del hotel. Imagine que Ud. y dos compañeros/as
son el empleado (E), Alicia (A) e Ileana (I). Completen el diálogo. Pueden
cambiar o inventar detalles.

(E)   Aquí tienen... El botones les llevará... a su habitación. Tienen la habitación número ciento once en el...

(A)   ¡Primer piso! Pero no tendremos... Reservamos...

(E)   Es un milagro... Todo el mundo ha venido a Barcelona...

(I)   Nos gustaría ver... ¿Sería posible conseguir... ?

(E)   ¡Eso sí que sería... ! Los billetes están...

(A)   Mañana... , de todas maneras.

(I)   Yo preferiría ver... pero mientras tanto, nosotros/as podemos competir.
Esta tarde alquilaremos... y jugaremos... en la... del hotel.

(A)   Y la que pierda el partido...

B. Ud. y los deportes (*sports*). Conteste estas preguntas según sus preferencias deportivas.

Si a Ud. le gusta jugar al tenis...

1.   ¿Cuándo comenzó a jugar al tenis? ¿Cuántas veces juega por semana?
2.   ¿Qué tipo de raqueta tiene? ¿Dónde la compró? ¿Preferiría tener otro tipo
de raqueta?
3.   ¿Con quién(es) juega? Usualmente, ¿pierde o gana Ud.? ¿Es Ud. un
jugador bueno (una jugadora buena)?

Si Ud. no juega al tenis...

1.   ¿No ha intentado nunca jugar al tenis? ¿Por qué no juega Ud. ahora?
2.   ¿Le gustaría aprender a jugar al tenis? ¿Por qué (no)?
3.   ¿Qué otros deportes practica Ud.?

Fin de semana en Mallorca*

Weekend

◆   IRREGULAR CONDITIONALS   ◆

querer:	
querrías	*you would want*
querrían	*they would want*
decir:	
dirías	*you would say*
dirían	*they would say*
hacer:	
haría	*I would do*
haríamos	*we would do*
poder:	
podría	*I could*
podríamos	*we could*
tener:	
tendría	*I would have*
tendríamos	*we would have*

Stressed Possessive Adjectives and Pronouns

el/la mío/a   *mine*
el/la tuyo/a   *yours*

1. el bañador / el traje de baño
2. el bañador de dos piezas
3. la bolsa de playa
4. la loción bronceadora
5. las gafas de sol
6. la sombrilla
7. el salvavidas
8. la piscina

ALICIA: ¡Qué sol hace! Deberíamos alquilar una sombrilla.

ILEANA: *¡De ninguna manera!* Compré un bañador de dos piezas para broncearme bien. ¿Querrías regresar *pálida* de tus vacaciones? ¿Qué dirían nuestros amigos? No creerían que estuvimos en Mallorca.

By no means!

pale

ALICIA: Tienes razón. Préstame tu loción bronceadora. Dejé la mía esta mañana en la piscina.

ILEANA: *Cógela tú misma.* Está en la bolsa de playa.

Get it yourself

ALICIA: No decidimos lo que haríamos esta noche.

ILEANA: Podríamos comer en La Lonja. *Se especializa* en mariscos.

It specializes

ALICIA: ¡Magnífica idea! La parrillada† de mariscos es mi plato preferido. ¿Cuál es el tuyo?

ILEANA: El mío es el bistec con papas fritas, pero en La Lonja tendría que pedir algún plato de pescado. Tal vez una paella‡, que me gusta mucho.

---

*Mallorca es una isla que está en el mar Mediterráneo, cerca de Barcelona.
†Plato de carne o mariscos cocinados a la parrilla (*grilled*).
‡Plato típico español que consiste en arroz, mariscos y azafrán (*saffron*).

Cultural expansion: Students may be interested in the names of some of the many *mariscos* popular in the Hispanic world: *gambas* or *camarones* (shrimp) (*Lección 5*), *mejillones* (mussels), *langosta* (lobster), *langostino* (prawn), *pulpo* (octopus), *calamares* (squid), *percebes* (goose barnacles), *almejas* (clams).

Suggestion: Give definitions orally and students give the word corresponding to each definition. **1.** *el traje que uso cuando voy a la playa* **2.** *donde llevo la toalla y otros artículos que uso en la playa* **3.** *la loción que me pongo para broncearme con el sol* **4.** *lo que llevo para protegerme los ojos del sol* **5.** *el parasol que uso en la playa* **6.** *objeto que uso para flotar en el agua* **7.** *donde nado cuando no nado en el mar* **8.** *lo contrario de bronceado*

Suggestion: Point out the Balearic Islands on a map and explain to students that they are a popular vacation spot not only for Spaniards but also for many other Europeans.

Actividades

A. Un fin de semana en Mallorca. Un estudiante que no comprendió bien el diálogo escribió estas oraciones falsas. Corríjalas, explicando por qué son falsas.

1. Alicia quiere alquilar un salvavidas.
2. A Ileana le gusta estar pálida.
3. Ileana no llevaría de ninguna manera un bañador de dos piezas.
4. A Ileana no le importa la opinión de sus amigos.
5. La loción broncaadora de Alicia está en la playa.
6. Ileana coge la loción broncaadora de la bolsa de playa.
7. La Lonja se especializa en platos de carne.
8. El plato preferido de Alicia es el bistec con papas fritas.

B. Sus actividades. Invente oraciones explicando qué haría Ud. en un fin de semana en Mallorca.

1. en la playa: alquilar, llevar, broncearse, nadar
2. en La Lonja: comer, pedir, beber, conversar

C. Artículos de playa. ¿Para qué sirven estas cosas? Invente oraciones completas.

1. una bolsa de playa
2. la loción broncaadora
3. un traje de baño
4. las gafas de sol
5. un salvavidas
6. una sombrilla

VISTA CULTURAL

Ésta es una foto de las Ramblas de Barcelona. Aquí hay cafés al aire libre, tiendas y también muchos puestos (*stands*) en donde se venden flores, pájaros, revistas y toda clase de mercancía. Las Ramblas es uno de los sitios más populares para el paseo, una vieja costumbre que se conserva en toda España. Por la tarde, cuando la gente sale de su trabajo, no se va a casa inmediatamente, sino que se queda (*stays*) unas horas en la calle caminando, haciendo algunas compras, hablando con los amigos o tomando algo en un café.

GRAMÁTICA ESENCIAL

62. Conditional of Regular Verbs

Nos gustaría ver alguna competencia. ¿Sería posible conseguir billetes?

All regular verbs in Spanish form the conditional by adding the following endings to the complete infinitive. When pronouncing these forms, be careful to stress the accented *í*.

-ía	-íamos
-ías	-íais
-ía	-ían

	DEJAR	BEBER	PREFERIR
	dejaría	bebería	preferiría
	dejarías	beberías	preferirías
	dejaría	bebería	preferiría
	dejaríamos	beberíamos	preferiríamos
	dejaríais	beberíais	preferiríais
	dejarían	beberían	preferirían

Suggestion: Again, model pronunciation of these verbs.

Expansion: Write following sentences on board: *¿Qué dijo Ud.? —Dije que llamaría al botones (hablaría con el empleado, compraría un traje de baño, comería un bistec, escribiría una carta, viviría un año en Chile).* Then ask *¿Qué dije yo?, ¿Qué dijo él/ella?,* and so on.

MEMOPRÁCTICA

Have you noticed any similarities the conditional shares with any of the other tenses you've learned? You probably related the conditional to the future right away, but did you also notice that the conditional endings are exactly the same as the imperfect endings of regular **-er** and **-ir** verbs? Remember, however, that the endings are attached to the complete infinitive in the conditional tense.

	IMPERFECT	CONDITIONAL
comer	**comía**	**comería**
escribir	**escribía**	**escribiría**

63. Uses of the Conditional

The conditional expresses English *would + verb.**

Yo no entraría en el mar sin salvavidas porque no sé nadar.	*I wouldn't go in the ocean without a life preserver because I can't swim.*
No sé qué perfume comprar. ¿Cuál comprarías tú?	*I don't know which perfume to buy. Which one would you buy?*

A past tense calls for the conditional, as the present calls for the future.

Dice que irá, pero no lo creo.	*He says he will go but I don't believe him.*
Dijo que iría, pero no fue.	*He said he would go but he didn't.*

Emphasis: Stress use of conditional to report what person said she/he would do. Ask question of student A, to be answered with future tense; then have student B report on A's reply: *¿Adónde irá Ud. el sábado?* → *Iré al cine.* → *(A's name) dijo que iría al cine.*

Actividades

Optional: 1. *¿Qué preferiría comer esta noche?* **2.** *¿Con quién iría Ud. al cine?* **3.** *¿A cuál de sus amigos llamaría por teléfono?* **4.** *¿Qué le gustaría hacer mañana?*

A. Los planes de mis amigas. Conteste estas preguntas para expresar lo que sus amigas dijeron que no harían.

MODELO: ¿Comerá Alicia con nosotras esta tarde?
No, dijo que no comería con nosotras.

1. ¿Comprará Alicia otra raqueta?
2. ¿Jugarán al golf Ileana y Alicia?
3. ¿Nadará Ileana en la piscina mañana?
4. ¿Irán ellas a la playa por la tarde?
5. ¿Necesitará Ileana gafas de sol?

B. Con quinientos dólares en la mano... Pregúntele a un compañero (una compañera) cómo gastaría su dinero.

C. No estoy de acuerdo. Ud. y sus amigos tienen diferentes ideas y opiniones en todo. Indique su opinión usando el condicional e inventando detalles originales.

MODELO: Queremos ir a Barcelona este año.
Yo no iría a Barcelona. Preferiría ir al sur de España.

1. Reservaremos una habitación en el Hotel Colón.
2. Vamos a nadar en la piscina.
3. Jugaremos un partido de tenis.
4. Pensamos alquilar un coche.
5. Subiremos en el ascensor.

---

*Remember that when *would* means *used to,* the imperfect tense, not the conditional, is used.

En esa época pescábamos en el lago todos los domingos.	*At that time we would fish (used to fish) at the lake every Sunday.*

64. Conditional of Irregular Verbs

¿Querrías regresar pálida de
tus vacaciones? ¿Qué dirían
nuestros amigos?

1. Verbs whose conditional stem is the infinitive minus the **e** of the ending:

    hab(e)r, pod(e)r, quer(e)r, sab(e)r

    haber: habría, habrías, habría, habríamos, habríais, habrían
    poder: podría, podrías, podría, podríamos, podríais, podrían
    querer: querría, querrías, querría, querríamos, querríais, querrían
    saber: sabría, sabrías, sabría, sabríamos, sabríais, sabrían

2. Verbs that substitute a **d** for the **e** or **i** of the infinitive ending:

    poner → **pon(d)r, salir** → **sal(d)r, tener** → **ten(d)r, venir** → **ven(d)r**

    poner: pondría, pondrías, pondría, pondríamos, pondríais, pondrían
    salir: saldría, saldrías, saldría, saldríamos, saldríais, saldrían
    tener: tendría, tendrías, tendría, tendríamos, tendríais, tendrían
    venir: vendría, vendrías, vendría, vendríamos, vendríais, vendrían

3. Verbs whose conditional stems are unique:

    decir: diría, dirías, diría, diríamos, diríais, dirían
    hacer: haría, harías, haría, haríamos, haríais, harían

Note that the conditional of **haber** is combined with the past participle to
form the conditional perfect.

Nos habría gustado ver el partido.	*We would have liked to see the match.*

Nosotros no habríamos hecho
  ese viaje.
	*We wouldn't have taken (made)
	  that trip.*

Presentation: Review irregular past participles (*Lección 10; Gramática esencial 44*) before explaining formation of conditional perfect.

Actividades

Suggestion A: After students complete this dialogue with the correct conditionals, assign the roles of Luis, Jaime, the pedestrian, and the clerk and have students act out the dialogue in class.

A.   Luis y Jaime no tienen habitación. Complete con el condicional del verbo
indicado.

1. Nuestra prima dijo que nos (reservar) una habitación en un hotel de
    Barcelona. ¿Por qué no lo (haber) hecho?

2. (A un peatón) —Señor, ¿(saber) Ud. decirnos dónde hay un buen hotel? —Sigan todo derecho por esta calle.

3. (Al empleado del hotel) —No reservamos habitación aquí, pero ¿(tener) Ud. una habitación para nosotros?

4. —¿(Querer) Uds. una habitación con una cama matrimonial? No tengo habitaciones vacías de dos camas.

5. —¿No (poner) Ud. una cama adicional en la habitación?

6. —Lo (hacer) con gusto, señor, pero en esa habitación no (poder) poner dos camas. No hay espacio.

7. —De saber (*If we knew*) que (tener) este problema, no (haber) venido.

8. (Luis a Jaime) —Bueno, en el parque hay buenos bancos. (Nosotros: Poder) dormir allí.

B.   Situaciones. Lea y conteste.

1. hacer un viaje: Maribel y Sandra, los Pirineos, montañas y pueblos
   a. ¿A quiénes les gustaría hacer un viaje?
   b. ¿Adónde querrían ir?
   c. ¿Qué podrían ver allí?
   d. ¿A Ud. le gustaría ir con ellas? ¿Por qué (no)?

2. comprar perfumes y cosméticos: Carmen y yo, una boutique
   a. ¿Qué querríamos comprar?
   b. ¿Adónde tendríamos que ir para comprar eso?
   c. ¿Qué diferentes perfumes podríamos comprar?
   d. ¿Qué haría Ud. en esa boutique?

3. ir a la playa: tú, los compañeros, arena, «¡Qué fantástico!»
   a. ¿Adónde irías?
   b. ¿Quiénes vendrían a visitarte?
   c. ¿Dónde jugaríais todos?
   d. ¿Qué dirían todos?

C.   Situaciones difíciles.

¿Qué le diría Ud. ...

1. a un señor en la calle que le pregunta algo en español?
2. a un amigo (una amiga) que no quiere trabajar?
3. al profesor que lo/la vio en una fiesta después de que Ud. le dijo que estaba enfermo/a?

¿Qué haría Ud. ...

4. si comienza a llover cuando Ud. está en la calle sin paraguas (*umbrella*)?
5. si un buen amigo (una buena amiga) lo/la invita a cenar y a Ud. no le gusta lo que se sirve?
6. si un amigo (una amiga) le pide una cantidad considerable de dinero?

65. Ordinal Numbers

Tienen la habitación número ciento once, en el primer piso.

Ordinal numbers generally precede the nouns they modify and must agree with them in gender and number. Ordinal numbers are not common in Spanish beyond ten.

primero	*first*	quinto	*fifth*	octavo	*eighth*
segundo	*second*	sexto	*sixth*	noveno	*ninth*
tercero	*third*	séptimo	*seventh*	décimo	*tenth*
cuarto	*fourth*				

Vivo en la Quinta Avenida. ¿Y Ud.?   *I live on Fifth Avenue. And you?*

Even these numerals are replaced at times by cardinals in everyday language.

Quiero examinar el volumen cinco.   *I want to examine the fifth volume (volume five).*

Remember that **primero** is used with dates to express the first of the month, but that cardinal numbers are used for all other dates.

El primero (tres) de noviembre es mi cumpleaños.   *The first (third) of November is my birthday.*

NOTE: Remember that **primero** and **tercero** are shortened to **primer** and **tercer** before a masculine singular noun: **primer autobús, tercer día.**

Presentation: Explain that in everyday language only cardinal numbers are used after *décimo*. So Alfonso the Thirteenth is *Alfonso XIII* (*Trece*). Take opportunity to mention that definite article is not used in Spanish with names of kings, queens, and popes.

Follow-up: Ask these questions: **1.** ¿Quién fue la primera persona que vio Ud. esta mañana? **2.** ¿En qué piso estamos ahora? **3.** ¿Qué día es su cumpleaños? **4.** ¿Cómo se llama el presente Papa? **5.** ¿Cómo se llama el rey de España? **6.** ¿Cómo se llama una calle elegante de Nueva York? **7.** ¿Qué día se celebra la independencia de los Estados Unidos? **8.** ¿Qué sinfonía de Beethoven es muy famosa? **9.** ¿Qué grados hay en la escuela primaria? **10.** ¿Qué grados hay en la escuela secundaria?

Actividades

A. Hablando del tenis. Exprese en español.

1. Vamos a jugar en _____ cancha. (*the third*)
2. Tendremos _____ partido. (*the second*)
3. _____ jugadora ganó la competencia el año pasado. (*the fourth*)
4. Fue su _____ competencia. (*first*)
5. Este año la competencia es _____ de octubre. (*the seventh*)

B. Conteste según el modelo. *Always use the next number in your answer.*

MODELO: ¿Vio Ud. el primer programa? →
No, no vi el primero. Vi el segundo.

1. ¿Va Ud. de vacaciones la tercera semana de enero?
2. ¿Va a volver la primera semana de febrero?
3. ¿Fue éste el segundo baile de la fiesta?
4. ¿Fue ése el octavo regalo que recibió ella?
5. ¿Jugó Ud. en el noveno partido?
6. ¿Puso Ud. sus libros en el séptimo estante?
7. ¿Es el viernes el quinto día de la semana?
8. Según la Biblia, ¿descansó Dios el sexto día después de crear el mundo?

66. Stressed Possessive Adjectives and Possessive Pronouns

—La parrillada de mariscos
es mi plato preferido.
¿Cuál es el tuyo?
—El mío es el bistec con
papas fritas.

Both possessive adjectives and pronouns agree in number and gender with the noun they modify or refer to.

POSSESSIVE ADJECTIVES

yo	→ mío/a/os/as *mine, of mine*	nosotros	→ nuestro/a/os/as *ours, of ours*
tú	→ tuyo/a/os/as *yours, of yours*	vosotros	→ vuestro/a/os/as *yours, of yours*
él	→ suyo/a/os/as* *his, of his*	ellos, ellas	→ suyo/a/os/as* *theirs, of theirs*
ella	→ suyo/a/os/as* *hers, of hers*	Uds.	→ suyo/a/os/as* *yours, of yours*
Ud.	→ suyo/a/os/as* *yours, of yours*		

*You may clarify **suyo/a/os/as** by using the alternates **de él, de ella, de Ud., de ellos, de ellas, de Uds.**

Stressed possessive adjectives follow the noun or the verb **ser.**

Fui a la playa con una **amiga mía.**	*I went to the beach with a girl friend of mine.*
Las pelotas de tenis **son suyas** pero la raqueta **es mía.**	*The tennis balls are theirs but the racket is mine.*

Possessive pronouns have the same form as stressed possessive adjectives but they are preceded by the definite article.

¿Las bolsas de playa? Aquí está **la mía,** pero no sé donde está **la tuya.**	*The beach bags? Here is mine but I don't know where yours is.*
Mis zapatos están en el dormitorio; **los vuestros** están en la sala.	*My shoes are in the bedroom; yours are in the living room.*

Actividades

A. Nuestros objetos de uso personal. Dé un color para cada objeto de la lista. Dos compañeros/as darán colores diferentes. Contesten según el modelo.

> MODELO: el maletín → mi maletín es de color café →
> el maletín mío es gris → el mío es verde

1. el cepillo de dientes
2. los peines
3. las maletas
4. la sombrilla
5. la bolsa de playa
6. los zapatos
7. el traje de baño
8. el coche
9. la raqueta

B. Vamos a jugar al tenis. Conteste según el modelo, inventando los detalles necesarios.

> MODELO: Nuestra cancha preferida es la cancha del parque Martí. ¿y la vuestra? →
> La nuestra es la cancha de la universidad.

1. Veo que tu raqueta es cara. ¿y la suya (la de ella)?
2. Mis amigos juegan muy bien al tenis. ¿y los vuestros?
3. Sus cosas están en el asiento del coche. ¿y las nuestras?
4. Tus pelotas están aquí. ¿y las mías?
5. La ropa que llevo cuando juego al tenis es blanca. ¿y la suya (la de Ud.)?
6. El tenis es mi deporte favorito. ¿y el tuyo?

Para resumir y repasar

A. En persona: ¿Qué haría Ud.? Dígale a un compañero (una compañera) lo que haría Ud. en las siguientes situaciones.

1. Ud. llega al hotel donde hizo reservaciones y el empleado le dice que no hay ninguna reservación en su nombre.

Suggestion B: Point to object and tell students it is yours. Ask student A to contradict you; student B will agree with A and tell rest of class. For example: *Este libro es mío.* → A: *No, no es suyo, es mío.* → B: *Es verdad, es el libro de él (ella).*

Suggestion A: Some of the *En persona* exercises also lend themselves to be presented in the form of dialogues. Assign the roles and have students act them out.

2. Ud. gana un viaje a Hawaii. La única condición es que Ud. tiene que hacer el viaje esta noche.
3. Ud. llegó a Madrid hoy para sus vacaciones, pero su maleta no va a llegar hasta la próxima (*next*) semana porque la aerolínea la mandó a Malasia. ¿Qué cosas compraría mientras tanto?
4. Ud. llega a Barcelona el mismo día que empiezan los Juegos Olímpicos y no encuentra billete para ninguna competencia.

B. Una excursión al campo. Complete con la forma correcta del verbo.

1. Mis amigos niegan que (nosotros: estar) perdidos.
2. ¿Estás segura de que (haber) un lago cerca de aquí?
3. No creo que (nosotros: haber) traído suficiente comida.
4. Hay nubes en el cielo. Es evidente que (venir) una tormenta.
5. Es preciso que (nosotros: llegar) a la carretera pronto.

C. Exprese en español.

JOSÉ: Alberto es ＿＿1 alto ＿＿2 tú. (*as . . . as*)
CARLOS: No, yo soy un poco ＿＿3 él. (*taller than*)
JOSÉ: ¿Sí? Yo pensaba que él era ＿＿4 la clase. (*the tallest in*)
CARLOS: No pensemos ＿＿5 (*so much*) en Alberto. Tenemos que hacer ＿＿6 trabajo ＿＿7 él. (*as much as*)

COMUNICACIÓN   **Andalucía**

5 días / days   (A-226)

SALIDAS:[a] **MARTES**

De la vida real

[a]*departures*
[b]*mosque*
[c]*overnight lodging*
[d]*Moorish palace*
[e]*settled*
[f]*beautifully*

SIGNIFICADO DE LOS SÍMBOLOS:
Autocar aire acondicionado / Air Conditioned Bus
Autocar de butacas reclinables / Bus with reclining seats
Radio-Cassette / Radio-Cassette

ITINERARIO:

Día 1.° MADRID - CORDOBA - SEVILLA
Salida de nuestra TERMINAL, Plaza de Oriente, 8, a las 8.00 horas, hacia Ocaña, Puerto Lápice, Manzanares y el Paso de Despeñaperros, entrando en Andalucía, Bailén y Córdoba. **Almuerzo y visita** de su famosa Mezquita[b] siguiendo hasta Sevilla. **Cena y alojamiento**[c]

Día 2.° SEVILLA
Desayuno, almuerzo y alojamiento. Visita de sus más importantes monumentos: la Catedral, el Alcázar, el Parque de María Luisa, etc. Tarde libre.

Día 3.° SEVILLA - RONDA - GRANADA
Desayuno y salida hacia Ronda, ciudad pintorescamente asentada[e] sobre montañas. **Visita y almuerzo.** Por la tarde, continuación a Granada. **Cena y alojamiento.**

Día 4.° GRANADA
Desayuno, almuerzo y alojamiento. Visita de la ciudad, bellamente[f] situada al pie de Sierra Nevada. Tarde libre.

Día 5.° GRANADA - UBEDA - MADRID
Desayuno y salida hacia Ubeda. **Visita y almuerzo.** Continuación a Aranjuez, para llegar a Madrid, por la tarde, de nuevo a nuestra TERMINAL.

FIN DEL VIAJE

Cultural expansion: As a result of the Moorish occupation of the south of Spain from the eighth century to 1492, the architecture and monuments in this area show an Arabic influence. The Mosque of Córdoba (*la mezquita*), built from the eighth to the tenth centuries, is an architectural wonder because none of its 850 columns obstruct the view of the center of the mosque, where ceremonies were performed. A must for any visitor of Granada is a tour of the Alhambra, a palace of the Moorish kings.

A. Andalucía. Primero lea el anuncio. Luego, imagine que Ud. trabaja en la compañía que organiza esta excursión. Conteste las preguntas de un(a) cliente (un compañero [una compañera]) que quiere más información sobre la excursión.

1. ¿Sale todos los días esta excursión?
2. ¿Cuántos días dura (*lasts*) la excursión?
3. ¿Cuánto tiempo estaremos en Córdoba? ¿Qué haremos allí?
4. ¿Qué día llegamos a Sevilla? ¿Visitaremos todos los monumentos? ¿Cuáles visitaremos?
5. ¿Pasará la excursión por alguna ciudad en las montañas?
6. ¿Tendremos algún tiempo libre durante la excursión?
7. ¿Qué comodidades ofrece el autocar en que viajaremos?

Mi verano en Ibiza*

N.° 975/30-7-90

Lea el chiste y conteste.
Según el hombre:

1. ¿Qué pasa con el agua de esta playa?
2. ¿Por qué no puede él broncearse?
3. ¿Qué problemas hay con las discotecas? ¿los restaurantes? ¿el tráfico?
4. ¿Qué llevan los turistas alemanes?
5. ¿Cuál es la única suerte (*luck*) del hombre?

Según Ud.:

6. ¿Cuál es la actitud de la mujer en el primer cuadro? ¿Por qué?
7. ¿Cuál es la reacción de la mujer cuando llega el otro hombre?
8. ¿Por qué se va ella? ¿Hizo bien o mal?
9. ¿Qué cree Ud. que hará el hombre ahora?
10. ¿Se ha bañado Ud. en playas contaminadas? ¿Por qué (no)?
11. ¿Se ha quejado (*complained*) Ud. alguna vez de algo en sus vacaciones? ¿De qué?

Cultural expansion: Spain's current population is approximately 40 million. Tourism is a vital industry in Spain; usually, there are as many foreign visitors in a year as there are residents. Until recent years, prices there were lower than those of northern Europe. This is changing with the integration of Spain into the European Common Market, but the country is still a favorite vacation spot for many foreign tourists, as well as home to many foreign retirees. German, English, and American colonies are scattered along the southeastern and southern coasts of Spain.

ᵃllenas... *full of*
ᵇ*hole*
ᶜ*very crowded*
ᵈ*lousy*
ᵉMenos... *Fortunately*

*Ibiza, como Mallorca, forma parte del archipiélago balear que está en el mar Mediterráneo, cerca de la costa oriental de España.

Para conversar más

A. La excursión a Andalucía. ¿Qué haría Ud. si decidiera ir en la excursión del anuncio?

1. ¿Buscaría un compañero (una compañera) de viaje? ¿Quién sería?
2. ¿Se quedaría en un hotel con piscina?
3. ¿Qué ropa llevaría? ¿Qué tipo de maleta llevaría? ¿Qué cosméticos o accesorios pondría en la maleta?
4. ¿Qué otras cosas llevaría? ¿una cámara? ¿un libro para hacer apuntes (*notes*) sobre el viaje? ¿fotos de su familia o amigos? ¿Por qué?

B. Sus diversiones preferidas. Hágale estas preguntas a un compañero (una compañera).

1. ¿Cómo preferirías divertirte en un viaje a España? Habla de varias actividades que te gustaría hacer.
2. ¿Te gustaría viajar en autobús por España? ¿en tren? ¿alquilar un coche? ¿Por qué (no)?
3. ¿Qué evento te parece más interesante: los Juegos Olímpicos o la Exposición Mundial de Sevilla? ¿Por qué?
4. En España, ¿preferirías pasar el tiempo en la playa o visitar las ciudades?
5. ¿Qué te gusta hacer en la playa?
6. ¿Sabes navegar en un bote de vela? ¿Cuándo y dónde aprendiste a hacerlo?
7. ¿Nadas bien? ¿Te gusta nadar en el mar o prefieres nadar en las piscinas?

MOTIVO CULTURAL

The year 1992 brought millions of tourists to Spain not only to see the Olympic Games in Barcelona, but also to attend the celebration of the 500-year anniversary of the discovery of the New World at the World's Fair in Sevilla.

The construction completed in preparation for these events began in 1988 and included the construction of superhighways in Sevilla, the modernization of the railway system, the restoration of the Santa María de las Cuevas Monastery (where Christopher Columbus lived for several years), and the construction of replicas of Columbus's three ships: the Niña, the Pinta, and the Santa María.

The site chosen for Expo. '92, the biggest world's fair to date, was an island in the center of the Guadalquivir river, which runs through Sevilla. The fair's theme was historic, presenting the five hundred years of technological and scientific advances since the discovery of the New World. The many attractions offered to the thousands of daily visitors ranged from taking a ride on the monorail, to dining in one of over 90 restaurants open to the public.

Suggestion: Bring in current articles and/or photographs of these events in Spain. Encourage student discussion of the events, the consequences they have had for Spain, and whether they have served to increase awareness of Spain as well as Hispanic culture and history in the non-Hispanic world.

Vocabulario activo

Adjetivos

agotado/a	sold out
mismo/a	myself, yourself, himself, herself, etc.
pálido/a	pale
pasado/a	past; last
preferido/a	favorite

Sustantivos

HACIENDO LA MALETA

el cepillo de dientes	toothbrush
el cepillo para el pelo	hairbrush
el champú	shampoo
el desodorante	deodorant
la maleta	suitcase
el maletín	carry-on bag (small suitcase)
la máquina de afeitar	(electric) shaver
la pasta de dientes	toothpaste
el peine	comb

EN LA PLAYA

el bañador (de dos piezas)	(two-piece) swimming suit
la bolsa de playa	beach bag
las gafas de sol	sunglasses
la loción bronceadora	suntan lotion
el salvavidas	life preserver
la sombrilla	sun shade; beach umbrella
el traje de baño (de dos piezas)	(two-piece) swimming suit

LOS DEPORTES (*SPORTS*)

la cancha	court
el/la jugador(a)	player
el partido	match, game
la pelota	ball
la piscina	swimming pool
la raqueta	racket
el tenis	tennis

LOS COSMÉTICOS Y LAS JOYAS (*JEWELRY*)

el agua de colonia	cologne
el anillo (de brillantes)	(diamond) ring
los aretes (de plata)	(silver) earrings
la barra para los labios	lipstick
el colorete	rouge

el collar (de perlas)	(pearl) necklace
la crema (para la cara)	(face) cream
el creyón de labios	lipstick
el estuche de maquillaje	make-up kit
la laca	hair spray
el lápiz labial	lipstick
la loción (para las manos)	(hand) lotion
la loción de afeitar	after-shave lotion
los pendientes (de plata)	(silver) earrings
el perfume	perfume
la pulsera (de oro)	(gold) bracelet
la sombra para los ojos	eyeshadow

OTROS SUSTANTIVOS

el ascensor	elevator
el botones	bellboy
la competencia	competition
el elevador	elevator
la(s) escalera(s)	stairs; staircase
el fin de semana	weekend
el milagro	miracle
el piso	floor
la recepción	front desk (*of a hotel*)
la vista	view

Verbos

coger	to get; to take hold of
conseguir	to obtain
especializarse (en)	to specialize (in)
intentar	to try

Otras palabras y expresiones

aunque	although
de ninguna manera	by no means
de todas maneras	anyway
mientras tanto	in the meantime
sí que	indeed

ORDINAL NUMBERS

primer(o), segundo, tercer(o), cuarto, quinto, sexto, séptimo, octavo, noveno, décimo

STRESSED POSSESSIVE ADJECTIVES

mío, mía, míos, mías; tuyo, tuya, tuyos, tuyas; suyo, suya, suyos, suyas; nuestro, nuestra, nuestros, nuestras; vuestro, vuestra, vuestros, vuestras; suyo, suya, suyos, suyas

De viaje por Hispanoamérica

Las ruinas de Machu-Picchu, la ciudad legendaria de los incas.

METAS

Comunicación: In this lesson you will learn vocabulary and expressions related to transportation and travel. You will make requests concerning your travel needs, converse about your plans, and express your reactions to your travel experiences.

Estructuras: 67. Regular Endings of the Imperfect Subjunctive 68. Imperfect Subjunctive of Irregular and Stem-Changing Verbs 69. Sequence of Tenses with the Subjunctive 70. The Construction **hace... que**

GRÁFICOS

Los transportes

Puntos de partida y llegada
(*Departure and Arrival*)
el aeropuerto *airport*
la estación del ferrocarril
railroad station
la estación / la terminal de
autobuses *bus station,*
terminal
la parada de autobuses / de
taxis *bus stop; taxi stand*
el puerto *port*

Verbos
aterrizar *to land*
despegar *to take off* (an
airplane)
facturar el equipaje *to check*
baggage

Expansion: Ask these personal
questions: **1.** *¿Prefiere Ud. viajar
en avión, tren o autobús?* **2.**
*¿Cuántos viajes (vuelos) hace al
año?* **3.** *¿Prefiere un asiento de
ventanilla o de pasillo? ¿Por qué?*
4. *¿Tiene Ud. miedo cuando el
avión despega? ¿Y cuando
aterriza?* **5.** *¿Vive Ud. cerca de
una estación de autobuses? ¿de un
aeropuerto? ¿de una estación del
ferrocarril?* **6.** *¿Cómo va generalmente al aeropuerto (a la
estación)?* **7.** *¿Siempre lleva mucho o poco equipaje? ¿Por qué?*
8. *¿Qué viajes ha hecho este año
(mes)?*

1. el avión
2. los pasajeros
3. el asiento de ventanilla
4. el asiento de pasillo

5. la aeromoza,* la azafata
6. el/la auxiliar de vuelo†
7. el horario electrónico
8. el equipaje

9. el barco
10. el tren
11. el taxi
12. el autobús / el ómnibus‡

Actividades

A. Asociaciones. ¿Qué vehículos asocia Ud. con...

1. el aire?
2. las carreteras?

3. una estación?
4. la gasolina?

5. la aeromoza?
6. el mar?

---

*Aeromoza** is used in Spanish America.
†**El auxiliar de vuelo** is quite a common term now, since there are numerous male flight
attendants.
‡**El ómnibus** is the preferred word in many Hispanic countries.

B. Definiciones. Invente oraciones para definir en español estos objetos, lugares y personas.

1. la estación de autobuses
2. un pasajero
3. un horario electrónico
4. un asiento de pasillo
5. el puerto
6. un asiento de ventanilla
7. una auxiliar de vuelo
8. el equipaje

C. ¿Dónde están las personas que dicen las siguientes frases?

1. ¿Desea café o té, señor?
2. Señorita, ¿quiere Ud. facturar el equipaje?
3. Por favor, ¿cuál de estos trenes va a Michoacán?
4. Señores pasajeros, aterrizaremos en cinco minutos.
5. ¿A qué hora despega el avión para Valparaíso?
6. ¡Viene una tormenta! ¡Mira qué olas tan grandes!
7. ¡Atención, señores pasajeros! El ómnibus para Rosario saldrá en diez minutos.

El *contratiempo* de Elena

Mishap

◆ VERBOS REGULARES ◆	
Pretérito de indicativo	*Imperfecto de subjuntivo*
	-ar: confirmar
confirmaron	que (yo) confirmara
	que (Ud./él/ella) confirmara
	que (ellos/ellas) confirmaran
	-er: perder
perdieron	que (yo) perdiera
	que (Ud./él/ella) perdiera
	que (ellos/ellas) perdieran
	-ir: decidir
decidieron	que (yo) decidiera
	que (Ud./él/ella) decidiera
	que (ellos/ellas) decidieran

1. el/la agente
2. el boleto / billete de ida (de ida y vuelta)
3. el viajero / la viajera

Adjetivos

contrariado/a *upset*
lleno/a *full*
preocupado/a *worried*
vacío/a *empty*

Cuando compré el boleto de ida y vuelta para mi viaje a Sudamérica, *escogí* para el *I chose*
regreso un asiento de ventanilla en la sección *delantera* del avión. Me *advirtieron* *return / front / warned*
que era necesario que confirmara la reservación de vuelta veinticuatro horas antes
del *vuelo. Olvidé* hacerlo y mis amigos no me lo recordaron. Por eso iba muy *flight / I forgot*
5 preocupada *camino del* aeropuerto. ¡Sería terrible que perdiera mi asiento! *on my way to*
   Así *ocurrió.* Cuando llegué, la agente de la *línea aérea* me dijo: «Lo siento, *happened / airline*
pero le dimos su asiento a otro pasajero *hace diez minutos*». Me informó además *ten minutes ago*
que el avión iba lleno y me pidió que decidiera entre ir en el único asiento vacío,
que estaba en la sección de *fumadores,* o esperar hasta el día siguiente. Estaba muy *smokers*
10 contrariada, pero *no tuve más remedio que* esperar, porque soy alérgica al *humo.* *I had no choice but / smoke*

Suggestion: Model parts of reading, especially italicized subjunctive phrases, for students to repeat. Drill imperfect subjunctive forms by stating third-person plural forms of preterite and having students give imperfect subjunctives: **1.** *hablaron* **2.** *escogieron* **3.** *olvidaron* **4.** *esperaron* **5.** *decidieron* **6.** *compraron* **7.** *perdieron*

Suggestion A: Have students use questions in A to prepare oral summary of reading rather than answer each question as discrete item. Encourage them to talk about questions without constantly referring back to them by keeping in mind these cues for each question: **1.** *boleto* **2.** *asiento* **3.** *necesario* **4.** *nerviosa* **5.** *terrible* **6.** *agente* **7.** *vacío* **8.** *contrariada* **9.** *esperar*

Suggestion C: Divide students in pairs and ask them to prepare skits before class. Have students present as many skits as time allows; rest of class can pose questions after each presentation.

Actividades

A. El contratiempo de Elena. Conteste.

1. ¿Qué clase de boleto compró Elena?
2. ¿Qué asiento escogió ella para el regreso? ¿En qué sección del avión estaba?
3. ¿Qué le advirtieron que era necesario hacer?
4. ¿Por qué iba preocupada Elena camino del aeropuerto?
5. ¿Qué le parecía a ella que sería terrible?
6. ¿Qué le dijo la agente de la línea aérea cuando ella llegó al aeropuerto? ¿Qué le informó además?
7. ¿Qué le pidió a Elena la agente? ¿Dónde estaba el único asiento vacío?
8. ¿Cómo se sintió Elena?
9. ¿Por qué no tuvo más remedio que esperar?
10. ¿Puede explicar Ud. en sus propias palabras el contratiempo de Elena?

B. Complete sin consultar el texto. Haga después una oración con cada expresión.

1. la estación de...   3. la sección de...   5. el auxiliar de...
2. el boleto de...   4. el asiento de...   6. la agente de...

C. Un viajero (una viajera) y un(a) agente. Complete este diálogo y represéntelo en clase con un compañero (una compañera).

VIAJERO/A: Señor (Señorita), salgo en el vuelo _____ a las _____. Tengo el asiento _____.

   AGENTE: Tenía, señor (señorita). Lo siento mucho, pero _____ hace cinco minutos.

VIAJERO/A: ¡Dios mío! Olvidé _____ y mis amigos _____.

   AGENTE: Sólo hay un asiento vacío en este vuelo en la sección de _____.

VIAJERO/A: Pero, mire Ud., el problema es que yo _____.

   AGENTE: Entonces, no tiene más remedio que _____.

VIAJERO/A: _____

La tarjeta de Elena

Querida[a] mamá:

Hace sólo dos horas[b] que aterrizamos en Lima, pero quería que supieras que llegué bien, por eso decidí escribirte en seguida.[c] Lima es una ciudad maravillosa y me gustaría que estuvieras aquí conmigo.[d]

Carmen nos pidió a Marta y a mí que fuéramos con ella a Arequipa, pero yo prefiero ir a Machu-Picchu. La excursión sale pasado mañana.[e]

Ahora voy corriendo al correo para comprar sellos, porque creo que cierran[f] a las seis.

Besos[g] de

Elena

Sra. Luisa Pérez de García
Marbella del Caribe,
Apto. 43
Isla Verde
Puerto Rico 00919

VERBOS IRREGULARES	
Pretérito de indicativo	*Imperfecto de subjuntivo*
-ar: estar	
estuvieron	estuvieras
	estuviéramos
-er: saber	
supieron	supieras
	supiéramos
-ir: ir	
fueron	fueras
	fuéramos

[a]*Dear*
[b]*Hace... Only two hours ago*
[c]*en... at once*
[d]*with me*
[e]*pasado... day after tomorrow*
[f]*they close*
[g]*kisses*

1. la tarjeta / la postal
2. el sello / la estampilla
3. la dirección

MOTIVO CULTURAL

The ancient Incan city of Machu-Picchu, now in ruins, is located near the city of Cuzco, Peru. The trip from Cuzco to Machu-Picchu takes four hours by train. These mysterious ruins are hidden high among the mountain peaks; the civilized world did not know of their existence until Hiram Bingham, a North American explorer, discovered them in 1911.

Located in the mountainous southern region of the country, Arequipa is Peru's second city in importance. It is often called the *white city* because of the ash from nearby Misti volcano that falls on its houses, making them appear white.

Optional: If possible, bring pictures of Machu-Picchu and Arequipa to class. Review *Motivo cultural* with these questions: **1.** ¿Qué es Machu-Picchu? **2.** ¿Dónde está? **3.** ¿En qué condiciones está hoy? **4.** ¿Cuánto tarda el viaje en tren de Cuzco a Machu-Picchu? **5.** ¿Cuándo supo el mundo civilizado que existían estas ruinas? **6.** ¿Está Arequipa en el sur o en el norte del Perú? **7.** ¿Es Arequipa una ciudad grande? ¿Cómo lo sabe Ud.? **8.** ¿Qué es el Misti? **9.** ¿Por qué se llama Arequipa «la ciudad blanca»?

Actividades

A. La tarjeta de Elena. Conteste.

1. ¿Cuánto tiempo hace que Elena llegó a Lima?
2. ¿Por qué decidió escribirle a su madre tan pronto?
3. Según Elena, ¿cómo es Lima?

4. ¿Qué le gustaría a Elena?
5. ¿Adónde quería Carmen que ella y Marta fueran?
6. ¿Adónde prefiere ir Elena?
7. ¿Por qué va Elena corriendo al correo?

B. Cambie las palabras indicadas por palabras sinónimas.

1. El avión de Elena *llegó a* Lima hace sólo dos horas.
2. Elena le escribió *inmediatamente* a su madre.
3. En la *postal* le decía que Lima es una ciudad *estupenda*.
4. La excursión a Machu Picchu sale *el día después de* mañana.
5. Elena quería ir *muy rápidamente* al correo para comprar *estampillas*.

Vista Cultural

Algunas fiestas en Hispanoamérica tienen su origen en el folklore indígena, otras, en la tradición católica; pero la mayoría de ellas son una combinación de estas dos influencias. La celebración del Día de los Muertos (el dos de noviembre) que vemos en esta foto, por ejemplo, une costumbres católicas e indígenas.

Gramática Esencial

67. Regular Endings of the Imperfect Subjunctive

Me advirtieron que era necesario que confirmara la reservación.

The imperfect subjunctive is generally used in the same way as the present subjunctive, but for past events. To form the imperfect subjunctive, delete the third-person plural ending of the preterite tense and add the imperfect subjunctive endings.

Suggestion: Model pronunciation of imperfect subjunctive forms. You might point out -se forms in footnote and conjugate three verbs in chart with that ending: e.g., *trabajase, comiésemos, recibiesen.*

trabajar (TRABAJ~~ARON~~)	**comer** (COM~~IERON~~)	**recibir** (RECIB~~IERON~~)
trabaj**ara** trabaj**aras** trabaj**ara**	com**iera** com**ieras** com**iera**	recib**iera** recib**ieras** recib**iera**
trabaj**áramos** trabaj**arais** trabaj**aran**	com**iéramos** com**ierais** com**ieran**	recib**iéramos** recib**ierais** recib**ieran**

Note that the endings for **-er** and **-ir** verbs are the same in the imperfect subjunctive.*

68. Imperfect Subjunctive of Irregular and Stem-Changing Verbs

...quería que supieras que llegué bien... y me gustaría que estuvieras aquí conmigo.

Since the third-person plural of the preterite is used as the stem for the imperfect subjunctive, its irregularities are found throughout the imperfect subjunctive conjugation. Irregular verbs with similar imperfect subjunctive endings are grouped together in the following chart.

---

*The imperfect subjunctive has a second set of endings that is used less frequently: **-ar** verbs: **-ase, -ases, -ase, -ásemos, -aseis, -asen; -er** and **-ir** verbs: **-iese, -ieses, -iese, -iésemos, -ieseis, -iesen.**

KEY STEM LETTER	THIRD-PERSON PLURAL PRETERITE	IMPERFECT SUBJUNCTIVE
f	**ir:** fueron **ser:** fueron	fuera, fueras, fuera, etc. fuera, fueras, fuera, etc.
j	**decir:** dijeron **traer:** trajeron	dijera, dijeras, dijera, etc. trajera, trajeras, trajera, etc.
s	**poner:** pusieron **querer:** quisieron	pusiera, pusieras, pusiera, etc. quisiera, quisieras, quisiera, etc.
u	**poder:** pudieron **saber:** supieron	pudiera, pudieras, pudiera, etc. supiera, supieras, supiera, etc.
v	**tener:** tuvieron **estar:** estuvieron	tuviera, tuvieras, tuviera, etc. estuviera, estuvieras, estuviera, etc.
i	**venir:** vinieron **hacer:** hicieron **dar:** dieron	viniera, vinieras, viniera, etc. hiciera, hicieras, hiciera, etc. diera, dieras, diera, etc.

Dar and **estar** take the **-er, -ir** endings even though they are **-ar** verbs.
Decir, traer, ir, and **ser** drop the **i** of the imperfect subjunctive
ending: **trajera, trajeras; fuera, fueras,** and so on.

The **-ir** stem-changing verbs that change **o** to **u** and **e** to **i** in the third-person
plural preterite feature the same change throughout the imperfect subjunctive
(**Gramática esencial** 31).

THIRD-PERSON PLURAL PRETERITE	IMPERFECT SUBJUNCTIVE
dormir: durmieron	durmiera, durmieras, durmiera, durmiéramos, durmierais, durmieran
pedir: pidieron	pidiera, pidieras, pidiera, pidiéramos, pidierais, pidieran

Other verbs in this group are **divertirse (ie, i), morir, preferir, repetir,
sentir,** and **servir.**

Presentation: Write infinitives on board. Ask one student to give third-person plural preterite form and another to give imperfect subjunctive form: **1.** *divertirse* **2.** *morir* **3.** *preferir* **4.** *repetir* **5.** *dormir* **6.** *pedir* **7.** *sentir* **8.** *servir*

Review: Read these sentences and have students indicate whether imperfect subjunctive or preterite form is used: **1.** *Era lástima que no llegaran antes.* **2.** *Yo no sé qué dijeron ellos.* **3.** *Les pedí que no me sirvieran carne.* **4.** *¿A qué hora llegaron los niños?* **5.** *Eran las 10:00 cuando nos sirvieron la cena.* **6.** *No era posible que dijeran eso.* **7.** *Esperaba que no se sintieran mal.* **8.** *Era imposible que se sintieran tan mal.*

Actividades

A. Pepito y Juanito van a México. Pepito ha olvidado muchas cosas sobre el
viaje y le hace varias preguntas a Juanito. Complete sus respuestas cambiando
los infinitivos al imperfecto de subjuntivo.

P: Cuando anunciamos que haríamos un viaje a México, ¿qué nos desearon
nuestros amigos?

Note: Usage of imperfect subjunctives is not treated until *Gramática esencial 69.* This *Actividades* section stresses only forms; for that reason, students do not have to decide here between subjunctive or indicative usage. *All* these answers require imperfect subjunctive.

Suggestion B: Change subject pronouns of some sentences to give students practice in quickly changing corresponding verb forms.

J: Nos desearon que (poder[1]) visitar muchos lugares, que (divertirnos[2]) mucho, que (traerles[3]) muchos regalos y que (tener[4]) tiempo para verlo todo.

P: Juanito, ¿qué le pediste al agente cuando compraste los boletos?

J: Le pedí al agente que (darme[5]) buenos asientos, que (decirme[6]) la hora del vuelo, que (mandar[7]) los boletos a mi casa y que (hacernos) también una reservación para la vuelta.

P: Juanito, olvidé lo que me recordaste que hiciera antes de salir para el aeropuerto.

J: ¡Pero qué mala memoria tienes, Pepito! Te recordé que (confirmar[8]) la reservación, que (traer[9]) tu cámara, que (llamar[10]) un taxi temprano y que no (estar[11]) nervioso.

B. Complete con el imperfecto de subjuntivo correspondiente a cada infinitivo.

En tren

Eran las 2:00 y yo no había almorzado. Le pedí al conductor del tren que me (servir[1]) algo de comer si no quería que me (morir[2]) de hambre allí mismo. Él me explicó que era lástima que yo no (traer[3]) nada para comer y que (sentir[4]) tanta hambre, porque en ese tren no había ni comedor ni cocina. Me aconsejó que me (dormir[5]).

Problemas de dinero

A mi padre no le gustó que mi prima y yo le (pedir[1]) dinero al banco para hacer nuestro viaje. Nos aconsejó que no (repetir[2]) este error, pero nos deseó que nos (divertir[3]) mucho y hasta nos dio dinero para gastarlo como nosotros (preferir[4]). ¡Qué buen padre tengo!

Una invitación a cenar

Mi madre llamó a mi padre a la oficina; quería que él le (decir[1]) a su jefe que (venir[2]) a cenar a casa. Después me pidió que (ir[3]) al supermercado y (traer[4]) tomates y manzanas. Prefería que los tomates no (estar[5]) verdes y que las manzanas (ser[6]) grandes. Ella esperaba que yo le (dar[7]) la comida a mi hermanito, que (poner[8]) la mesa, y también que (hacer[9]) y (servir[10]) el café al final de la comida. Me dijo que era lástima que yo no (saber[11]) cocinar. (Yo: Querer[12]) aprender, ¡pero no es fácil!

69. Sequence of Tenses with the Subjunctive

¡Sería terrible que perdiera mi asiento! ...y me pidió que decidiera entre ir en el único asiento vacío...

There is always a relationship between the tense of the main verb and the tense of the verb in the dependent clause. This relationship is called the *sequence of tenses,* and certain sequences are fairly standard.

A. The present subjunctive is most commonly used in the dependent clause after the following:

1. present indicative

> Yo **deseo** que Ud. **vaya** en avión.   *I want you to go by plane.*

2. future indicative

> Yo le **pediré** que **compre** un boleto de ida y vuelta.   *I will ask him to buy a round-trip ticket.*

3. command

> **Dígale** que **confirme** su reservación.   *Tell him to reconfirm his reservation.*

B. The imperfect subjunctive is most commonly used after the following:

1. imperfect indicative

> **Queríamos** que Ud. nos **reservara** una habitación.   *We wanted you to reserve a room for us.*

2. preterite

> Mi madre me **pidió** que le **escribiera** a menudo.   *My mother asked me to write to her often.*

3. conditional

> Yo **preferiría** que Ud. **viniese** en tren.   *I would prefer that you come by train.*

It is also possible to use the imperfect subjunctive when the main verb is in the present tense. Note that this same tense sequence is also used in English, as in the sentence below.

> Me **molesta** que mi amigo no **llegara** a tiempo.   *It bothers me that my friend didn't arrive on time.*

All the rules that call for the use of the present subjunctive (after verbs of wanting, commanding, prohibiting and permitting, emotion, disbelief, doubt, and denial, as well as after most impersonal expressions) also apply to the imperfect and other subjunctive tenses.

Review: Review forms of future tense of sample verb to help students distinguish between future and imperfect subjunctive. Point out that for second person singular and third person singular and plural, only difference between future and imperfect subjunctive forms is an accent mark.

Listening comprehension: To practice distinguishing use of present and imperfect subjunctive, write these on board: (1) *regrese(n)* (2) *regresara(n)*. Students write 1 or 2, as appropriate, as you read following: **1.** *Ella le pidió que no...* **2.** *Yo esperaría que Uds....* **3.** *Ellos querían que Uds....* **4.** *Yo le recomendaré a Marta que...* **5.** *Sería muy posible que él...* **6.** *Les dije varias veces a ellas que...* **7.** *Ud. desea que su amigo...* **8.** *Prohíbales a los muchachos que...*

Actividades

A. Un crucero (*cruise*) por el Caribe. Complete.

1. Tenemos sólo una hora y es posible que no lleguemos al puerto a tiempo. → Teníamos sólo una hora y era posible...
2. Le diremos al taxista que vaya muy rápido. → Le dijimos al taxista...
3. Mi familia va a sentir mucho que perdamos el barco. → Mi familia sentiría...
4. Nos sorprende que no haya muchos viajeros en el puerto. → Nos sorprendió...
5. Dudamos que todos estén ya en el barco. → Dudábamos...
6. Voy allí con mi equipaje porque quiero que me la facturen. → Fui allí con mi equipaje porque quería...
7. El empleado me pide que le dé mis papeles. → El empleado me pidió...
8. El boleto dice: «4 de junio»; ¡es imposible que el barco salga el día 3! → El boleto decía «4 de junio»; ¡era imposible... !

B. Reacciones y sentimientos de un viajero. Use la expresión indicada y el tiempo correcto del subjuntivo.

> MODELO: el taxi / costar tanto (Me molestaba...) →
> Me molestaba que el taxi costara tanto.

1. el agente / darme un buen asiento (Me alegro de que...)
2. el avión / estar tan lleno (Me sorprendió...)
3. algunos pasajeros / fumar tanto (No me gustaba...)
4. las azafatas / hablar español (No podía creer...)
5. mi equipaje / perderse (Tengo miedo de...)
6. él / ponerse el cinturón (Dígale...)
7. el vuelo / llegar temprano (Dudo...)
8. mi familia / no esperarme en el aeropuerto (Sentiría...)

C. Cambie al pasado las siguientes narraciones.

En un autobús

Intento[1] subir al autobús con mi perro Marcelo, pero el chofer no me *deja*[2] que *suba.*[3] Me *explica*[4] que no se *permite*[5] que los pasajeros *lleven*[6] animales en los autobuses. Marcelo *es*[7] mi mejor amigo, y no *puedo*[8] creer que alguien lo *clasifique*[9] como un animal. Por eso, *cuento*[10] (*count*) mi dinero. *Es*[11] posible que *tenga*[12] suficiente para tomar un taxi. *Espero*[13] que al chofer del taxi le *gusten*[14] los perros.

La fiesta en el barco

El capitán *desea*[1] que los viajeros se *diviertan*[2] mucho en su fiesta. Todos *sentimos*[3] que ésta *sea*[4] la última noche del viaje. Nos *piden*[5] a todos que nos *vistamos*[6] elegantemente, porque *es*[7] una noche de gala. *Siento*[8] mucho que mi amiga *esté*[9] enferma y no *pueda*[10] ir, pero el doctor le *recomienda*[11] que se *quede*[12] en cama porque *está*[13] muy mareada (*seasick*).

70. The Construction *hace... que*

Hace sólo dos horas que
aterrizamos en Lima.

A. **Hace** + *period of time* + **que** + *present or present progressive tense* expresses
how long something has been going on.

<table>
<tr><td>Hace tres años que vivo en México.</td><td>*I have been living in Mexico for three years.*</td></tr>
<tr><td>Hace media hora que estamos esperando el autobús.</td><td>*We have been waiting for the bus for half an hour.*</td></tr>
</table>

B. **Hace** + *period of time* + **que** + *preterite tense* tells how long ago something happened.

<table>
<tr><td>Hace varias semanas que mis padres reservaron esa habitación.</td><td>*My parents reserved that room several weeks ago.*</td></tr>
</table>

C. To ask both how long something has been going on and how long ago
something happened, use the construction **¿Cuánto/a/os/as** + *period of time* +
hace que... ?

<table>
<tr><td>¿Cuánto tiempo (Cuántos minutos) hace que Uds. están esperando el autobús?</td><td>*How long (How many minutes) have you been waiting for the bus?*</td></tr>
<tr><td>¿Cuánto tiempo (Cuántas semanas) hace que tus padres reservaron esa habitación?</td><td>*How long (How many weeks) ago did your parents reserve that room?*</td></tr>
</table>

Note: Warn students about the possible confusion between *¿Cuánto tiempo hace que... ?* (How long has it been . . .?) and *¿Qué tiempo hace?* (What's the weather like?) Give examples of *tiempo* referring to the concept of hourly time, to time of day, and to weather. Also remind them of the meaning of *vez* to avoid confusion with this term.

Actividades

A. Viejos deseos. Complete, expresando deseos personales.

MODELO: muchos años / desear →
Hace muchos años que deseo hacer un viaje a la Argentina.

1. más de tres meses / querer
2. varias semanas / desear
3. unos días / tener ganas de
4. algunos años / soñar con
5. mucho tiempo / planear
6. más de una hora / desear

B.   Ud. está de visita en la Ciudad de México y llama a su amigo Agustín por teléfono. Dígale cuánto tiempo hace que pasaron los eventos indicados.

> MODELO: El avión aterrizó a las diez. (Son las once.) →
> Hace una hora que el avión aterrizó.

1.   Ud. llegó a México el 16 de junio. (Hoy es 23 de junio.)
2.   Ud. terminó sus exámenes el 23 de mayo. (Hoy es 23 de junio.)
3.   Ud. encontró el número de Agustín en la guía de teléfonos a las doce menos diez. (Ahora son las doce.)
4.   Hoy Ud. se despertó a las nueve. (Son las doce.)
5.   Su amigo Orlando lo/la llamó a las 11:35. (Son las 12:05.)
6.   Orlando compró boletos para un viaje a Taxco el viernes. (Hoy es domingo.)

C.   Entrevista al revés (*in reverse*). Hágale las preguntas a un compañero (una compañera).

1.   —¿... ?
—Hace cinco años que vivo en la misma dirección.
2.   —¿... ?
—Hace ocho meses que estudio español.
3.   —¿... ?
—Hace cuatro horas que desayuné.
4.   —¿... ?
—Hace sólo tres semanas que estoy trabajando.
5.   —¿... ?
—Hace seis meses que compré mi coche.
6.   —¿... ?
—Hace dos años que sé manejar.

Para resumir y repasar

A.   En persona: Un viaje terrible. Imagine que Ud. hizo un viaje al Perú con un amigo (una amiga) el año pasado. Esta persona ya no es su amigo/a porque no se llevaron bien en el viaje. Él (Ella) hizo muchas cosas que le molestaron a Ud. y nunca quería hacer lo que Ud. quería hacer. Dígale a un compañero (una compañera) qué pasó en este viaje. ¿Cuánto tiempo hace que viajaron? ¿Qué cosas quería hacer él (ella) que no le interesaron a Ud.? ¿Qué quería hacer Ud.? ¿Qué hizo su amigo/a que le molestó a Ud.? ¿Por qué le molestó? ¿Qué habría preferido Ud. que su amigo/a hiciera?

B.   Planes de viaje Cambie al condicional.

Mi tío quiere ir a Patagonia, en el sur de Argentina, en el mes de marzo. *Dice que* será[1] agradable viajar en marzo, porque no *hará*[2] calor. *Saldrá*[3] de Buenos Aires, *irá*[4] en su coche por carreteras entre montañas y pampas y *disfrutará*[5] de paisajes muy hermosos. Creo que varios miembros de mi familia *querrán*[6] ir con mi tío, pero sé que él *preferirá*[7] viajar solo.

C. ¿De quién es? Conteste cada pregunta dos veces, la primera vez afirmativamente y la segunda de manera negativa diciendo de quién es (quiénes son) el (los) objeto(s).

MODELO: ¿Es tuya esa postal? →
Sí, es mía. → No, no es mía, es suya.

1. ¿Son vuestros esos sellos de correo?
2. ¿Es de ellos este boleto?
3. ¿Es mío el asiento A6?
4. ¿Son nuestros esos equipajes?
5. ¿Son tuyas estas postales?
6. ¿Es de Uds. ese taxi?

COMUNICACIÓN

De la vida real

A. Hotel Crillón. Lea rápidamente este menú. ¿Reconoce Ud. las palabras **ananá, faturas, manteca, panceta** y **pomelo**? Éstas son palabras usadas en la Argentina para comestibles que Ud. conoce por otros nombres. Haga una lista de los sinónimos de estas palabras que conoce. Imagine que Ud. se hospeda en el Hotel Crillón y está en el comedor del hotel para desayunar. Usando este menú, prepare un diálogo con el camarero (la camarera) [un compañero (una compañera)].

HOTEL Crillón
BUENOS AIRES

DESAYUNO CONTINENTAL
Continental Breakfast

— Café americano / American coffee
— Té / Tea
— Café express / Express coffee
— Chocolate
— Jugo pomelo / Graperfruit Juice
— Café con leche / Coffee with milk
— Jugo naranja / Orange juice
— Jugo tomate / Tomato juice
— Jugo Ananá / Pineapple juice

Incluye: faturas, tostadas, manteca y mermelada
Rolls - toast - butter and marmalade included.

DESAYUNO Crillón

— Café americano / American coffee
— Jugo naranja / Orange juice
— Fritos / Fried
— Café express / Express coffee
— Jugo pomelo / Grapefruit juice
— Revueltos / Scrambled
— Café con leche / Coffee with milk
— Jugo tomate / Tomato juice
— Omelette
— Té / Tea
— Jugo ananá / Pineapple juice
— Con: / With:
— Chocolate
— Yoghurt
— Panceta / Bacon
— Cereales / Corn flakes
— Huevos / Eggs
— Jamón / Ham
— Ensalada de frutas / Fruit salad
— Pasados por agua / Boiled
— Salchicha / Sausage

Incluye: faturas, tostadas, manteca y mermelada
Rolls, toast, butter and marmalade included.

Note: Point out that words that vary from country to country usually describe the most common items of everyday life. Ask students if they can remember any of the following synonymous terms they have learned: *el estudiante / el alumno; el almacén / los almacenes; el coche / el carro / el automóvil; el boleto / el billete; el bolso / la bolsa / la cartera; los vaqueros / los jeans; la papa / la patata; la habitación / el cuarto; el dormitorio / la recámara; el chofer / el conductor; la azafata / la aeromoza / el auxiliar de vuelo.*

Suggestion: Have small groups of students practice ordering a meal in a restaurant. One is the waiter or waitress and the others order from the menu given. At the end they should ask for the *cuenta* and the server will add everything up.

Porque tenemos muchas horas de vuelo le ofrecemos...
¡ Vacaciones en la playa !

Venezuela lo tiene todo. 2.800 kilómetros de costa en el mar del Caribe.
Las playas más extensas, la selva[a] virgen donde se esconden profundos secretos de agua y vida. Ríos como mares. Naturaleza en toda su belleza.[b]
Y una infraestructura moderna para disfrutar plenamente de tus vacaciones.
Paraíso[c] de las compras, Venezuela es el país de la gente amable[d] que habla como nosotros.
Anímate.[e] Sé de los primeros en descubrir el secreto mejor guardado del Caribe. Este verano ven. Ven a Venezuela.

Venezuela
EL SECRETO DEL CARIBE
CORPORACION DE TURISMO DE VENEZUELA

[a]*jungle*
[b]*beauty*
[c]*Paradise*
[d]*friendly*

Para disfrutar el sol, la arena y la brisa del mar en las playas de nuestro país, Mexicana le ha reservado los mejores vuelos. Goce[a] al máximo cada momento rodeado de[b] paisajes espectaculares y una divertidísima vida nocturna.[c]
Descubra con Mexicana que "en el mar, la vida es más sabrosa".[d]
Utilice nuestros excelentes planes de crédito: CVM (Crédito para Viajes a la Medida)[e] y la práctica Tarjeta de Crédito Millonaria.

RESERVACIONES:
660-44-44

Compre con su agente de viajes, no le cuesta más.

[a]Disfrute
[b]rodeado... *surrounded by*
[c]de la noche
[d]*pleasant*
[e]a... *customized*

mexicana

Con muchas horas de vuelo
mexicana
primera línea aérea de Latinoamérica

Cultural expansion: Ads meant for the Hispanic public often contain references that may be meaningless to people from other cultures. The ad from Mexico, for instance, quotes a song popular throughout the Hispanic world: "*En el mar la vida es más sabrosa...*" You might also call attention to use of *Ud.* in Mexican ad (addressed to Spanish Americans) and use of *tú* in ad from Venezuela (addressed to Spaniards). While in Spanish America the *Ud.* form is still preferred in advertisements, in Spain *tú* is most common form of address for T.V. commercials and magazine/newspaper ads.

B. ¡Vacaciones en la playa! O en Venezuela. Imagine que Ud. es agente de viajes y su compañero/a es su cliente. Él (Ella) no puede decidir entre ir de vacaciones a México o a Venezuela. Explíquele las ventajas (*advantages*) de cada lugar, usando la lista siguiente, inventando más detalles.

MÉXICO

1. las playas
2. el servicio aéreo de Mexicana
3. los paisajes
4. la vida nocturna
5. los planes de crédito de Mexicana

VENEZUELA

6. las costas
7. las playas
8. la selva
9. los ríos
10. las compras
11. la gente

Suggestion: Both ads are suitable for pronunciation practice; have students imitate a radio or television announcer.

Para conversar más

A. Un viaje a Hispanoamérica. Escoja un país y describa un viaje (real o imaginario) que Ud. hizo allí. Las siguientes palabras pueden ayudarlo:

vacaciones	vuelo	edificios
agencia de viajes	horario electrónico	monumentos
hacer las maletas	avión	museos
taxi	hotel	espectáculos (*shows*)
aeropuerto	ciudad	parques
línea aérea	calles	restaurantes

B. Preguntas personales. Pregúntele a un compañero (una compañera).

1. ¿Qué medio de transporte prefieres? ¿Por qué?
2. ¿Qué vuelos largos has hecho? ¿Qué viajes interesantes?
3. ¿Crees que es buena idea que no se permita fumar en los vuelos cortos? ¿Por qué (no)?
4. ¿Tienes miedo de volar? ¿Por qué (no)?
5. ¿Prefieres un asiento de ventanilla o un asiento de pasillo? ¿Por qué?
6. ¿Has hecho un viaje largo en tren? ¿en autobús? ¿en barco?
7. ¿Has tenido contratiempos en algún viaje? ¿Qué contratiempos?
8. ¿Qué transporte usas para viajes locales en tu ciudad o pueblo?
9. Para estos viajes locales, ¿qué transporte es más rápido? ¿más cómodo? ¿más económico?

MOTIVO CULTURAL

The countries of South America offer the traveler incredible variety. There is something for everyone. Those interested in Indian cultures will be happy in Machu Picchu or in Bolivia visiting Lake Titicaca, the picturesque markets, or the pre-Incan ruins of Tiahuanaco. Anyone interested in less common areas can travel on the Amazon River or to the Galápagos Islands (part of Ecuador), where species of prehistoric animals still exist. On the other hand, people who prefer city life will enjoy visiting Buenos Aires—the Paris of America—, Santiago de Chile, Caracas, or any of the other great capitals.

Vocabulario activo

Adjetivos

contrariado/a	upset
delantero/a	front
lleno/a	full
preocupado/a	worried
próximo/a	next
querido/a	dear
vacío/a	empty

Sustantivos

LOS TRANSPORTES

la aeromoza	stewardess
el aeropuerto	airport
el/la agente	agent
el asiento de pasillo/de ventanilla	aisle/window seat
el autobús	bus
el/la auxiliar de vuelo	flight attendant
el avión	plane
la azafata	stewardess
el barco	ship
el boleto, el billete de ida/de ida y vuelta	one-way/round-trip ticket
el equipaje	baggage
la estación de autobuses	bus station
el horario (electrónico)	(electronic) schedule
la línea aérea	airline
el ómnibus	bus
la parada de autobuses/de taxis	bus stop/taxi stand
el/la pasajero/a	passenger
el tren	train
el/la viajero/a	traveler
el vuelo	flight

OTROS SUSTANTIVOS

el contratiempo	mishap, disappointment
la dirección	address
la estampilla	stamp
el/la fumador(a)	smoker
el humo	smoke
la postal	postcard
el regreso	return
el sello	stamp
la tarjeta	postcard

Verbos

advertir (ie, i)	to warn, inform
anunciar	to announce
aterrizar	to land
confirmar	to confirm
decidir	to decide
despegar	to take off
escoger	to choose
ocurrir	to happen
olvidar	to forget
recordar (ue)	to remind

Otras palabras y expresiones

camino de + lugar	on one's way to + place
conmigo	with me
en seguida	at once
facturar el equipaje	to check baggage
no tener más remedio (que)	to have no choice (but)
pasado mañana	day after tomorrow
por eso	that's why

Lectura

Antes de leer

When attempting to guess the meaning of a new word, you are often told to examine its context. The following are some practical hints to help you discover the meaning of new words within their contexts.

1. Look for capitalized letters within sentences. Capitalization indicates these words are proper nouns and tells you there is no need to look these words up in the dictionary. Scan the reading, examining the marginal notes and the definitions at the bottom of the page, and make a list of all the proper nouns you find.
2. Watch for compound words containing words you know. Knowing part of a compound word will often help you guess its meaning. For example, turn to the first paragraph of the reading, where you will find the word **recorrido.** Since you know that **corrido** is the past participle of **correr,** can you guess the meaning of **recorrido** from the context of the sentence? Now scan the reading and use this hint to guess the meaning of **cafetaleras, embarque** (both in the second paragraph), and **inolvidable** (in the last paragraph).
3. Compare related forms of a new word to clarify its meaning. For instance, in the fifth paragraph of the reading, you see the word **arrastrado.** Once you know that the verb **arrastrar** means *to drag,* can you guess the meaning of **fui arrastrado**?
4. Examine clauses joined by **de.** Since **de** indicates possession, origin, or composition, the words of these phrases are probably closely related. The following phrases are found in the first two paragraphs of this reading: **habitación del hotel, regiones montañosas de selva, punto de embarque.** What others can you find?
5. Look for clauses separated by commas (also by parentheses, dashes, colons, and semicolons). They may clarify the preceding word or another clause in a series. Note, for example, the information the following clauses give about the words that precede them:

    Pejibaye, **nuestro punto de embarque** (from the second paragraph)...
    Fernando, **nuestro guía** (from the fourth paragraph)...

Viaje por el río Reventazón

Lo primero[1] que me preguntaron, después de *instalarme* en una cómoda[2] habitación del hotel Irazú de San José, fue si ya había recorrido el río Reventazón. Al contestar que no, el gerente[3] me inscribió[4] en una excursión que salía a la mañana siguiente.

5 El viaje comenzó a las 7:30, con un trayecto en autobús por regiones montañosas de selva,[5] plantaciones cafetaleras y puentes[6] improvisados, hasta llegar a Pejibaye, nuestro punto de embarque.

Después de inflar nosotros mismos las *balsas* de goma,[7] recibimos unas *breves* recomendaciones de cómo remar,[8] el uso de los salvavidas y qué hacer
10 en caso de caer al agua. Entonces entramos en el río.

La rápida corriente nos *atrapó* de inmediato, llevándonos a través de[9] grandes rocas y vertiginosos remolinos.[10] A medida que[11] avanzábamos, las condiciones de la corriente variaban de manera abrupta, siendo nuestra única orientación el rugir[12] de las aguas que nos esperaban tras cada recodo.[13]
15 Fernando, nuestro guía,[14] gritaba: «¡Remen, remen! ¡Hacia adelante! ¡Atrás, atrás... a la derecha!»

Al sentir que la presión del agua era *menor*, todos dejamos de remar, levantando los brazos en triunfo... demasiado prematuro. El torbellino[15] que *se agitaba* a nuestras espaldas succionó la balsa, *sumergiéndonos* en un mar de
20 espuma.[16] Por fin no pude más[17] y, obedeciendo a Fernando, que me hacía señas,[18] me solté[19] y fui arrastrado por la corriente.

Recordé las instrucciones que me habían dado al iniciarse el *paseo:* «No intente nadar, flote sobre la espalda, con las rodillas *dobladas* sobre el pecho y evite[20] que el agua lo voltee».[21] Había que respirar[22] cuando la espuma no me
25 cubriera y sobre todo, no debía perder la calma.

Gracias a Dios, *no me entró el pánico* y pude llegar hasta un recodo donde el agua perdía gran parte de su fuerza[23] y allí me quedé en la orilla,[24] exhausto, a esperar a que me recogieran, lo cual ocurrió media hora más tarde.

Eran las 19:30 horas cuando el autobús me dejó en mi hotel, como si[25]
30 nada hubiera pasado... como si horas antes no hubiera vivido una inolvidable aventura en las aguas de espuma blanca de uno de los ríos «*salvajes*» de Costa Rica.

HOMBRE DE MUNDO, México

Notas al margen

What is a good word to express "installing myself"?

What might they be inflating other than life preservers to travel on a river?
An adjective related to brevity.

Think of *trap*.

You know that **menor** can mean *younger*. What do you think it means in this context?
The English verb has a "t" in the last syllable. / *Sub...* in English.

You know that a **paseo** is a *stroll*. What other meaning does it have here?
You know **doblar** means to turn. What other meaning might it have when referring to a position with your knees on your chest?
Pánico is a noun. What is the English equivalent of this phrase?

The English cognate is spelled without an "l" and replacing the "j" with a "g."

Suggestion: To review this reading assign 1 or 2 students to each of the 8 paragraphs. Allow a couple of minutes for each group to review his/her paragraph. Then go around the class quickly, having each one make a comment without looking at his/her paragraph.

Después de leer

A. Cuestionario. Pregúntele a un compañero (una compañera).

1. ¿Dónde está el río Reventazón?
2. ¿Cómo es este río?

---

[1]Lo... *The first thing* [2]*comfortable* [3]*manager* [4]*me... signed me up* [5]*jungle* [6]*bridges* [7]*rubber* [8]*to row* [9]*a... through* [10]*whirlpools* [11]A... *As* [12]*roar* [13]*turn* [14]*guide* [15]remolino [16]*foam* [17]*no... I gave up* [18]*gestures* [19]*me... I let myself go* [20]*avoid* [21]*turn over* [22]*to breathe* [23]*strength* [24]*shore* [25]*como... as if*

3. ¿Qué transportes usó este viajero en la excursión?
4. ¿Qué le pasó a la balsa donde iba el narrador?
5. ¿Qué hizo él entonces?

B. Identificaciones. Diga qué palabra corresponde a cada definición.

a. atrapar
b. corriente
c. espuma
d. gerente
e. inflar
f. puente
g. remar
h. remolino
i. selva

1. El director de un hotel.
2. Construcción que sirve para pasar un río.
3. Un sinónimo de *jungla*.
4. Movimiento giratorio (*revolving*) de una masa de agua.
5. Sinónimo de *capturar*.
6. Masa de agua que avanza.
7. Lo que hacemos para avanzar una balsa.
8. Lo que flota sobre un líquido cuando se agita mucho.
9. Llenar (*fill*) con aire un objeto flexible.

C. Imagine que Ud. es Fernando, el guía de la excursión, y que el resto de la clase son los viajeros. Déles instrucciones de cómo prepararse, qué hacer en caso de accidente, etcétera.

D. Ud. es el viajero (la viajera). Cuente el viaje como una experiencia personal. ¿Fue peligroso (*dangerous*)? ¿Qué le pasó? ¿Le gustó? ¿Volvería?

Repaso visual

Describa los dibujos. Considere las siguientes preguntas: ¿Qué objetos hay en los dibujos? ¿Quiénes son las personas que están en los dibujos? ¿Dónde están? ¿Qué hacen?

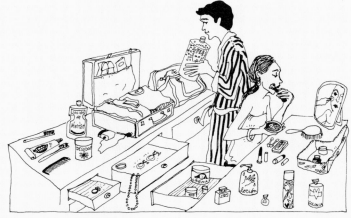

Examen de repaso 5

A. La señora Gil. Complete con **pero, sino** o **sino que.**

1. La Sra. Gil no había oído la noticia en el radio, _____ la había leído en el periódico.
2. El periódico no decía que en la Florida había un tornado, _____ esperaban un huracán.
3. El huracán no llegará a la región donde viven los Gil, _____ esperan inundaciones allí.
4. A la Sra. Gil no le gusta leer noticias de guerras y desastres, _____ de cosas alegres.
5. Ella no le reza a San Francisco cuando hay truenos, _____ a Santa Bárbara.

B. Mis planes para el sábado. Complete con la forma apropiada del futuro.

Cuando me levante, (poner[1]) la televisión para oír las noticias. ¿Qué (decir[2]) el locutor? Creo que (hacer[3]) buen tiempo y probablemente (querer[4]) ir a la playa con mis primos que (venir[5]) de Santiago. Pero si hay una tormenta inesperada, no (nosotros: poder[6]) nadar y (tener[7]) que quedarnos (*stay*) en casa.

C. Un terremoto reciente. Conteste, usando más de un negativo en su respuesta.

1. ¿Hay *alguna* noticia nueva sobre el terremoto?
2. ¿Tuvieron Uds. *alguna vez* un terremoto así?
3. ¿Oyó Ud. *algo* en la televisión sobre las víctimas?
4. ¿Le dijo *alguien* cuántas víctimas hay?
5. ¿Viven *algunos* de sus amigos en la zona del terremoto?
6. No me gustan las noticias de desastres. ¿Le gustan a Ud.?

D. Coincidencias. Conteste, usando un posesivo enfático como en el modelo.

MODELO: Mi maleta es pequeña. ¿y *la tuya*? →
La mía es pequeña también.

1. Tu maleta está en el ropero. ¿y *la mía*?
2. Mis perfumes son caros. ¿y *los tuyos*?
3. Mi máquina de afeitar es muy buena. ¿y *la de él*?
4. Nuestros anillos son de oro. ¿y *los vuestros*?
5. Nuestra habitación está en el quinto piso. ¿y *la de ellos*?

E. El apartamento de mi familia. Cambie las palabras indicadas por el número ordinal que sigue.

1. Vivimos en la *Quinta* Avenida desde el *31 de enero*.
2. Nuestro edificio es el *primero* de la calle.
3. Nuestro apartamento está en el *octavo* piso.
4. Este es el *sexto* apartamento donde vivimos.

F. Mi viaje a Buenos Aires. Cambie al pasado.

Mis tíos me *piden*[1] que *vaya*[2] a Buenos Aires a visitarlos este verano. Mis amigos *desean*[3] que me *divierta*[4] mucho, que *tenga*[5] tiempo para visitar muchos lugares interesantes y que les *traiga*[6] muchos regalos. Mi madre me *recuerda*[7] que *haga*[8] la maleta con tiempo, que no *ponga*[9] mi pasaporte en la maleta y que *salga*[10] temprano para el aeropuerto.

G. Vocabulario. Descripciones y narraciones. Complete.

1. ¡Qué hermoso día! El cielo está muy azul y no hay ni una _____. Los _____ cantan en los árboles y las _____ vuelan entre las flores.
2. La playa está llena de personas que toman el sol acostadas en la _____. Como quiero protegerme del sol, en la bolsa de playa llevo _____ para los ojos y loción _____. También llevo un _____ para peinarme.
3. Mi amiga Elena viaja por el Perú. No me escribió una carta, pero me mandó una _____ muy bonita. Como no sabe dónde vivo ahora, me la mandó a la _____ de mi madre. Compró en el correo un _____ muy bonito para poner en la postal, porque sabe que los colecciono.

Las relaciones humanas

Playa, sol y alegría en Málaga, España

METAS

Comunicación: In this lesson you will learn vocabulary and expressions related to friends, sweethearts, and weddings. You will gossip about friends and family members, go to a wedding, and talk about your interpersonal relationships.

Estructuras: 71. Reciprocal Constructions 72. Passive Constructions 73. Impersonal **se** 74. Relative Pronouns **que** and **lo que**

GRÁFICOS

Una boda elegante

An Elegant Wedding

1. el novio
2. la novia
3. el anillo de compromiso*
4. los anillos de boda

5. el suegro *father-in-law*
6. la suegra *mother-in-law*
7. el padrino *best man*

8. la madrina *maid of honor*
9. el champán
10. los canapés *hors d'oeuvres*

Sentimientos y expresiones

A. abrazar / el abrazo *to embrace / embrace*
B. besar / el beso *to kiss / kiss*
C. brindar / el brindis *to toast / toast*
D. enamorarse (de) *to fall in love (with)*
E. felicitar / la felicitación *to congratulate / congratulation*
F. tener celos / los celos *to be jealous / jealousy*

Otros verbos y sustantivos

amar / el amor *to love / love*
casarse (con) *to get married (to)*
divorciarse (de) / el divorcio *to get divorced / divorce*
odiar / el odio *to hate / hate*
prometer / la promesa *to promise / promise*

Cultural expansion: The words *padrino* and *madrina* do not correspond exactly to "best man" and "maid of honor." In most Hispanic countries, the *padrino* is the father of the bride and the *madrina* is the groom's mother. If either or both are deceased or unavailable, older relatives (often an uncle or an aunt) substitute for them.

Warm-up A: Ask for antonyms, for rapid oral practice: **1.** *casarse (divorciarse)* **2.** *suegro (suegra)* **3.** *padrino (madrina)*

Actividades

A. Amigos, novios y esposos. Estudie la lista de palabras y luego complete.

1. Mi amiga Ileana siempre besa a sus amigos cuando los saluda, pero yo prefiero _____ a los míos.
2. La gente siempre come _____ y toma _____ en las bodas.
3. La persona con quien Ud. se casa es su _____.
4. En la boda, el novio pone el _____ en el dedo de la _____.
5. Siempre _____ con una copa de champán en una boda.

*In Spain it is customary to give the fiancée an engagement bracelet instead of an engagement ring; in Spanish America, a ring is given.

6. La madre de su esposo (esposa) es su _____.

7. Lo contrario de amar es _____.

B. Una historia de amor. Complete la historia con la forma apropiada de las palabras de la lista.

anillo de compromiso	odio	brindis
casarse	boda	celos
felicitar	enamorarse	amor
divorcio	besar	padrino
prometer	amar	promesa

En mayo del año pasado conocí a Julia y me _____[1] de ella casi inmediatamente. Una noche quise darle un beso, pero ella me preguntó: «¿Por qué me quieres _____[2]? ¿Es que me _____[3]?» Me sorprendió tanto su pregunta y estaba tan nervioso que no pude declararle el _____[4] que sentía. En octubre nos hicimos (*we became*) novios. Yo ya quería _____[5] con ella y ella conmigo. No tenía mucho dinero, pero le di un precioso _____[6]. ¡Le encantó su pequeño brillante! Celebramos nuestra _____[7] en junio de este año. Fue una ceremonia un poco diferente, pues yo le _____[8] algunas cosas, por ejemplo, que nunca tendría _____[9] de ella aunque la viera con otro hombre. Ella también me hizo algunas _____[10]. Después de la ceremonia, mi mejor amigo, el _____[11] de la boda, nos _____[12] con un abrazo y ofreció un _____[13] con la copa de champán en la mano. Nos deseó mucha felicidad y que nunca llegaran el _____[14] y el _____[15] a nuestro hogar.

MEMOPRÁCTICA

Being able to paraphrase or define terms quickly and succinctly can "save" you when you don't know or can't think of a particular word. Exercise C calls for practice of this type.

Expansion D: **1.** ¿Cuándo abraza Ud. a sus amigos?   **2.** ¿En qué ocasiones los felicita?   **3.** ¿Cuándo tiene Ud. celos de su novio/a (su amigo/a)?   **4.** ¿Con qué licor prefiere brindar Ud.?   **5.** ¿Hay muchas personas divorciadas en su familia?   **6.** ¿Es fácil o difícil divorciarse en el estado donde Ud. vive?   **7.** En su opinión, ¿es posible enamorarse a primera vista (instantáneamente) de una persona? ¿Se ha enamorado Ud. así alguna vez?   **8.** ¿Cuánto cuesta, más o menos, un buen anillo de compromiso?   **9.** Si ha sido Ud. padrino o madrina de alguna boda, ¿de quién era la boda?   **10.** ¿Le gustaría casarse con una boda elegante, o prefiere una simple ceremonia civil? ¿Por qué?

Expansion C: **9.** el abrazo   **10.** el divorcio   **11.** los canapés   **12.** una promesa

C. Definiciones.

MODELO: el padrino →
Es el amigo del novio; trae el anillo a la ceremonia.

1. el suegro
2. la boda
3. el anillo de boda
4. la madrina
5. el odio
6. la felicitación
7. divorciarse
8. el anillo de compromiso

D. Conteste.

1. ¿Tiene Ud. novio/a?
2. ¿Le ha dado a alguien o ha recibido de alguien un anillo de compromiso?
3. ¿Piensa Ud. (*Do you intend*) casarse? ¿Por qué (no)?
4. ¿Es fácil casarse ahora? ¿Por qué (no)?
5. ¿Cuánto cuesta, más o menos, una boda elegante hoy?

Abrazos y besos... fáciles y difíciles

◆ RECIPROCAL ACTIONS ◆	
se saludan	*they greet each other*
se odian	*they hate each other*
se quieren	*they love each other*
se abrazan	*they embrace each other*
se besan	*they kiss each other*
nos peleamos	*we fight with each other*
nos pegamos	*we hit each other*

ÁNGEL: Papá, ¿por qué no se saludaron ayer en la boda el tío Alfonso y el tío Enrique?

PADRE: Bueno, hijo, están *peleados*. Tuvieron un *disgusto* serio hace años. Es un *cuento* muy largo...

estranged / quarrel

story

ÁNGEL: ¿Es que se odian?

PADRE: ¡*En absoluto!* Pero *supongo* que ellos piensan que no se quieren mucho.

Not at all! / I suppose

ÁNGEL: ¿Y qué piensas tú?

PADRE: ¿Yo? Pues... que *en el fondo* se quieren, como dos hermanos.

deep down

ÁNGEL: Entonces, ¿por qué no se abrazan y se besan como Miguelito y yo después que nos peleamos y nos pegamos?

PADRE: Ah, mi Angelito... *Lo malo* con los *mayores* es que no todo *se arregla* tan fácilmente entre ellos. Pero... ¡ven aquí y dame un abrazo! Y tú, Miguelito, dame un beso.

The bad thing / adults / is fixed

Actividades

A. Ud. es el padre. Conteste las preguntas de Ángel sin consultar el texto.

1. Papá, ¿por qué no se saludaron ayer el tío Alfonso y el tío Enrique?
2. ¿Se odian mis tíos?
3. ¿Y qué piensas tú?
4. ¿Por qué mis tíos no se abrazan y se besan como Miguelito y yo después que nos peleamos y nos pegamos?

B. Un cuento. Describa un disgusto (antiguo o reciente) que Ud. haya tenido con su hermano o hermana. Use estas preguntas como guía.

1. ¿Cuál fue la causa del disgusto?
2. ¿Quién tuvo la culpa (*was at fault*)?
3. ¿Se pegaron Uds. o sólo se insultaron?
4. ¿Cómo terminó el disgusto? ¿Se abrazaron y se besaron Uds.?

C. Preguntas personales. Conteste.

1. ¿Cree Ud. que es importante que los hermanos, jóvenes o viejos, se abracen y se besen? ¿Por qué (no)?

2. ¿Se pelean Ud. y sus hermanos (amigos, padres) frecuentemente?
3. En su opinión, ¿es posible que dos personas que se quieren en el fondo, se peleen constantemente? ¿Puede dar ejemplos?
4. En su opinión, ¿qué es lo malo de los disgustos y las peleas (*fights*)? ¿Por qué?
5. ¿Por qué cree Ud. que es más fácil que se arregle todo entre los niños que entre los mayores?

La amistad

Friendship

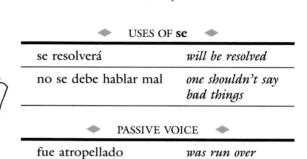

◆ USES OF **se** ◆

se resolverá	*will be resolved*
no se debe hablar mal	*one shouldn't say bad things*

◆ PASSIVE VOICE ◆

fue atropellado	*was run over*

JUAN: ¿Carlos? ¡No lo puedo *soportar*! *No me hace caso últimamente.*
LOLA: Anoche *traté de* aconsejarlo y se puso de mal humor.
PACO: Antes era una persona *amable,* pero ahora todo le molesta. Parece que odia a su *propia* familia.
MARIBEL: *Discúlpenme,* pero creo que Uds. están *equivocados.* Lo que pasa es que Carlos está muy preocupado estos días. Sus padres se divorciaron hace un mes y un tío suyo fue atropellado por un coche la semana pasada. Por eso, tengan paciencia con él. Todo se resolverá.
MARÍA: Estoy de acuerdo con Maribel. Además, no se debe hablar mal de los amigos.

put up with / He doesn't pay attention to me lately.
I tried to
friendly, polite

own

Excuse me / wrong

Suggestion: Point out practical expressions used in dialogue: *no (poder) soportar, hacerle caso (a alguien), tratar de, ponerse de mal humor, molestarle (a uno), discularse, estar equivocado, tener paciencia, estar de acuerdo, (no) se debe.*

Actividades

Expansion A, B: Ask these personal questions:
1. ¿Soporta a todos sus amigos (hermanos, profesores)? **2.** ¿Qué hace cuando un amigo no le hace caso? **3.** ¿Siempre está Ud. de acuerdo con sus padres? Explique.
4. ¿Tiene celos de algún amigo (alguna amiga)? ¿De quién? ¿Por qué?
5. ¿Generalmente tiene Ud. mucha paciencia? Explique. **6.** ¿Realmente odia Ud. a alguna persona? ¿A quién? ¿Por qué?

A. Los problemas de Carlos. Conteste.

1. ¿A quién no soporta Juan? ¿Por qué?
2. ¿Qué trató de hacer anoche Lola? ¿Con qué resultado?
3. ¿Cómo era Carlos antes? ¿Qué le molesta últimamente, según Paco? ¿A quiénes parece odiar?
4. ¿Por qué se disculpa Maribel? ¿Qué les explica a sus amigos?
5. ¿Qué hicieron los padres de Carlos hace un mes?
6. ¿Qué le pasó a su tío?
7. ¿Es optimista la actitud de Maribel con relación a la situación de Carlos? ¿Qué dice ella?
8. ¿Qué piensa María?

B. Ud. y sus amigos. Con un compañero (una compañera) invente un diálogo similar a «La amistad», tomando como base estos verbos.

1. soportar, hacer caso
2. tratar de aconsejar, ponerse de mal humor

3. molestar, parecer
4. creer, estar
5. tener paciencia, no hablar mal

VISTA CULTURAL

La entrega (*handing over*) de las arras forma parte de las bodas religiosas en muchos países hispánicos. La palabra **arras** es de origen germánico y se refiere a la prenda (*pledge*) que una persona da cuando hace un contrato con otra. En la boda, el novio le da a la novia las arras, que son trece monedas de plata (o de oro si el novio puede) como símbolo del compromiso (*commitment*) que contrae con ella.

GRAMÁTICA ESENCIAL

71. Reciprocal Constructions

Papá, ¿por qué no se saludaron ayer en la boda el tío Alfonso y el tío Enrique?

Reciprocal actions are expressed in English with *each other* or *one another*. In Spanish, reciprocal actions are expressed with the reflexive pronouns **se, nos,** and **os.**

Los buenos amigos siempre se ayudan.	*Good friends always help one another.*
Hace diez años que Luis y yo nos conocemos.	*Luis and I have known each other for ten years.*
¿Os queréis mucho?	*Do you love each other a lot?*

Suggestion: Remind students of the reflexive *se* construction they learned in *Lección 9.* Ask them to explain the difference in meaning between the two constructions, giving examples.

Warm-up: Ask students to give the equivalent reciprocal construction for each of these sentences: **1.** *Yo saludo a Alfonso y Alfonso me saluda a mí. Alfonso y yo...* (nos saludamos) **2.** *Yo ayudo a mi hermana y mi hermana me ayuda a mí. Mi hermana y yo...* (nos ayudamos) **3.** *Alfonso no le habla a Enrique y Enrique no le habla a Alfonso. Alfonso y Enrique...* (no se hablan) **4.** *Juan no soporta a Carlos y Carlos no soporta a Juan. Juan y Carlos...* (no se soportan) **5.** *Miguel le pega a Ángel y Ángel le pega a Miguel. Miguel y Ángel...* (se pegan) **6.** *Tú conoces a Maribel y Maribel te conoce. Tú y Maribel...* (os conocéis)

Actividades

A. Las relaciones humanas. Forme oraciones lógicas, combinando las personas con las acciones.

PERSONAS

1. los novios
2. los padres y los hijos
3. los amigos que viven en diferentes ciudades
4. los enemigos
5. la novia y su suegra
6. los compañeros de clase
7. los primos
8. la persona que da una fiesta y sus invitados

ACCIONES

a. detestarse
b. llamarse por teléfono
c. odiarse
d. ayudarse
e. darse la mano
f. mirarse mucho a los ojos
g. no hablarse
h. saludarse con afecto
i. respetarse y quererse
j. besarse
k. escribirse

B. Tu mejor amigo/a y tú. Conteste, según su experiencia personal, las preguntas que le hará un compañero (una compañera).

1. ¿Cuánto tiempo hace que tu mejor amigo/a y tú se conocen?
2. ¿Se ven Uds. con frecuencia?
3. ¿Cuántas veces a la semana se llaman por teléfono?
4. ¿Se pelean Uds. a veces? ¿frecuentemente? ¿nunca?
5. Cuando se ven en la calle, ¿se dan la mano? ¿se abrazan? ¿se besan?

72. Passive Constructions

...y un tío suyo fue atropellado por un coche la semana pasada. Por eso, tengan paciencia con él. Todo se resolverá.

The term *active voice* is used when the subject of a sentence is the doer of the action; the term *passive voice* is used when the subject receives the action of the verb. Compare these sentences:

ACTIVE VOICE

John wrote the letters.
subject verb

PASSIVE VOICE

The letters were written (by John).
subject verb

A. Spanish has a true passive construction that employs a form of the verb **ser** with a past participle. In this construction the past participle functions as an adjective; that is, it agrees with the subject in gender and number. This construction is used when the doer of the action (the agent) is expressed or strongly implied.

Los novios fueron presentados por el padre de ella. (*Note:* **novios → presentados**)
Su libro fue publicado (por la Editorial Castalia). (*Note:* **libro → publicado**)

The bride and groom were presented (introduced) by her father.
Her book was published (by the Castalia Publishing Co.).

The true passive voice is seldom heard in spoken Spanish. It is used occasionally in written Spanish, but much less frequently than in English. It is presented here for recognition only; you will not be asked to use it.

B. If the agent is not stated and the recipient of the action is one or more things, or a non-individualized group of people, the passive voice is usually expressed in Spanish with a reflexive construction. The verb will be in the third-person singular or plural, depending on whether the recipient of the action is singular or plural. The recipient usually follows the verb.

VERBO SINGULAR

Se prepara una recepción magnífica.
A magnificent reception is being prepared.
Se abrirá la puerta a las doce.
The door will be opened at twelve.

VERBO PLURAL

Se contrataron camareros adicionales.
Additional waiters were hired.
Se servirán canapés con el champán.
Hors d'oeuvres will be served with the champagne.

This construction is very common in Spanish and is seen in signs, newspaper classified advertisements, public notices, and so on.

Se habla español.
Se necesitan obreros.
Se alquilan trajes de novia.

Spanish (is) spoken.
Workers wanted (are needed).
Wedding gowns (are) rented.

Se alquila habitación a persona mayor. © 5762045.
Se necesitan camareros/as. Arturo Soria, 247.
Se necesita mujer para office. Jornada continua. Urbanización Rivas. © 6663525.
Se necesita dependiente para bar familiar. Urgente. © 2671833.
Se necesita dependienta pastelería con experiencia. © 7856797.

C.   A third-person plural verb in the active voice is another common alternative for the passive voice when the agent is not stated. This construction is equivalent to the impersonal use of *they* in English.

La boda será aplazada y los regalos serán devueltos.	*The wedding will be postponed and the gifts will be returned.*
Aplazarán la boda y devolverán los regalos.	*They will postpone the wedding and return the gifts.*

Actividades

A.   Preparativos para una boda. Primero, complete el ejercicio usando **se** con un verbo de tercera persona. Luego, un compañero (una compañera) cambiará la oración usando la tercera persona del plural.

En presente

> MODELO: (consultar) los libros de etiqueta → Se consultan los libros de etiqueta. → Consultan los libros de etiqueta.

1.   (recibir) los regalos de los invitados
2.   (discutir) después el plan de la boda
3.   (escoger) el vestido de la novia

En pretérito

> MODELO: (alquilar) un Cadillac blanco →
> Se alquiló un Cadillac blanco → Alquilaron un Cadillac blanco.

4.   (repetir) varias veces la marcha nupcial
5.   (pagar) los billetes para el viaje al Japón
6.   (comprar) champán para el banquete

En futuro

> MODELO: (planear) una luna de miel (*honeymoon*) maravillosa →
> Se planeará una luna de miel maravillosa. → Planearán una luna de miel maravillosa.

7.   (necesitar) más muebles para la casa
8.   (traer) los canapés por la tarde
9.   (celebrar) la boda en la iglesia

B.   Anuncios y letreros. Invente oraciones según el modelo y luego expréselas en inglés.

> MODELO: traducir / documentos → Se traducen documentos de todo tipo. (*Documents of all kinds [are] translated.*)

1.   procesar / divorcios
2.   comprar / muebles viejos
3.   alquilar / apartamento
4.   necesitar / chofer
5.   dar clases / guitarra
6.   vender / carro

73. Impersonal *se*

Además, no se debe hablar mal de los amigos.

Se followed by a third-person singular verb may have a general or impersonal meaning usually expressed in English by *one, you, they,* or *people* (*in general*).

Se trabaja mucho aquí.	*People (One) work(s) hard here.*
En algunas bodas se baila mucho.	*At some weddings they dance a lot.*
Se come bien en este restaurante.	*You eat well in this restaurant.*

Note that in most cases this construction is used with intransitive verbs; that is, verbs that don't take a direct object.

If the verb is reflexive, **uno** (*one*) is used.

A veces uno se equivoca sin darse cuenta.	*Sometimes one makes a mistake without realizing it.*
Uno se divierte mucho en una boda.	*One enjoys oneself a lot at a wedding.*

Actividad

¿Qué se hace? Use el **se** impersonal para decir lo que hace la gente.

> MODELO: Cuando estamos en España salimos mucho. →
> En España se sale mucho.

1. Comemos siempre muy bien en El Jorocho.
2. Duermen mucho los domingos.
3. Hablas con los amigos frecuentemente.
4. Camino por el campo en la primavera.
5. En el verano, vamos a la playa los fines de semana.
6. Todo el mundo grita mucho en un partido de fútbol.

74. Relative Pronouns *que* and *lo que*

Lo que pasa es que Carlos está muy preocupado estos días.

The relative pronoun **que** (*that, which, who*) refers back to a noun (person, place, or thing) already mentioned, but without breaking the speaker's line of thought; thus, the clause with **que** is not separated by commas.

Los regalos que han comprado son estupendos.	*The gifts (that) they have bought are wonderful.*
El señor que vino es mi padrino.	*The gentleman who came is my best man.*

Note that **que** must always be used in Spanish even though *that* can be omitted in English.

Lo que (*what, that which*) refers to a statement, an idea, or an action that is understood but not specified.

Lo que dice no me interesa.	*What he says doesn't interest me.*
No me gusta lo que ella hace.	*I don't like what (that which) she is doing.*

Actividades

A. Identificaciones. Ud. va a una fiesta en su barrio con un nuevo compañero (una nueva compañera) de clase. Forme oraciones escogiendo elementos de cada columna para identificar a las personas que están en la fiesta.

MODELO: El señor joven que bebe vino es mi tío Alberto.

1.	La mujer	habla francés	mi sobrinito
2.	El muchacho	baila con Juan	mi profesor de español
3.	El señor viejo	está vestida de blanco	Dolores Castillo
4.	El niño	baila tan bien	la suegra de mi primo
5.	La señora vieja	está al lado de la ventana	mi vecino Tomás
6.	El señor joven	habla con mi hermano	mi abuela
7.	La señorita	nos mira	mi tío Alberto
8.	La chica	bebe vino	mi amigo Ernesto
9.	El joven	lleva un plato con canapés	mi prima Olga

Suggestion: Point out that the relative *que* follows a noun while *lo que* appears by itself: *Las palabras que dijo* / *Lo que dijo; Las cosas que compramos ayer* / *Lo que compramos ayer*. *Lo que* never refers to people. You may want to explain that *el que, la que, los que,* and *las que* are used for people: *el hombre que vino a comer → el que vino a comer; la camarera que sirvió el champán → la que sirvió el champán; los invitados que vinieron a la fiesta → los que vinieron a la fiesta; las jóvenes que me presentaron ayer → las que me presentaron ayer.* Note that *el/la/los/las que* refer to nouns that have already been mentioned or are generally understood.

B. Regalos de boda. **¿Que** o **lo que?** Complete el diálogo.

—¿Dijiste _____[1] todo esto es _____[2] compraste ayer?

—Estás equivocada. Dije _____[3] los paquetes _____[4] están en la mesa son los regalos de boda.

—¿Te gustó todo _____[5] te dieron?

—Sí. Por ejemplo, este mantel, _____[6] es importado de Francia. Eso es _____[7] me dijo la persona _____[8] me lo regaló.

—¿Y qué es _____[9] te regalaron tus padres?

—Me regalaron _____[10] más necesitaba: ¡dinero!

Para resumir y repasar

A. En persona: ¡Qué desastre de boda! Usando los siguientes detalles e inventando otros, imagine lo que pasó en esta boda. Luego, descríbasela a un compañero (una compañera).

1. El padrino está enamorado de la novia y no quiere ir a la ceremonia.
2. Los padres del novio piensan que los padres de la novia escogieron un champán muy barato.
3. El novio olvida las promesas que debe hacerle a la novia durante la ceremonia.
4. La madrina ve que el novio besa a otra mujer antes de la ceremonia.
5. La novia y un amigo del novio se abrazan apasionadamente.
6. Los tíos de la novia se pelearon ayer.

B. Fuimos a una boda. **¿Imperfecto o pretérito?** Complete con la forma correcta del infinitivo.

Mi vecina Julita (casarse[1]) el sábado en la catedral y (invitarnos[2]) a mi novio y a mí. Aunque estamos en abril, (hacer[3]) mucho frío y el cielo (estar[4]) gris (*gray*). Julita (llevar[5]) un traje precioso de seda y (ser[6]) evidente que (estar[7]) muy contenta. Cuando (terminar[8]) la ceremonia, Julita nos (saludar[9]) a todos. A mí (abrazarme[10]) y (besarme[11]). La fiesta de la boda (ser[12]) estupenda, pero mi novio y yo (beber[13]) demasiado champán.

C. Diagnósticos del médico. Decida si se debe usar el subjuntivo o no.

1. Es verdad que (Ud.: tener) una úlcera, pero es probable que (curarse) con una dieta especial.
2. No creo que su enfermedad (ser) seria y dudo que (necesitar) ir al hospital.
3. Es lástima que Ud. no (haber) venido a verme antes, pero estoy seguro de que no (ser) demasiado tarde.
4. Creo que al paciente (dolerle) mucho la herida y es evidente que (haber) perdido mucha sangre; es mejor que (yo: ponerle) una inyección ahora.
5. Sra. Gutiérrez, es posible que la fiebre le (bajar) con aspirinas; si no le baja, es necesario que (Ud.: tomar) antibióticos.
6. Don Agustín, es importante que (Ud.: seguir) mis indicaciones y (cuidarse).

COMUNICACIÓN

De la vida real

¡Aprenda el arte de enamorar por carta!

CÓMO ESCRIBIR CARTAS DE AMOR es la guía[a] más completa que se haya publicado sobre la correspondencia amorosa. En este original libro, el lector[b] encontrará las orientaciones indispensables sobre el arte de escribir y comunicarse con el ser amado.[c]

Cómo Escribir Cartas de AMOR

¡El arte de enamorar por cartas!
¡El libro más completo sobre cartas de amor!
¡Aprenda a expresar todo su amor en cartas!

Además,
CARTAS DE AMOR DE
FIGURAS HISTÓRICAS
MODELOS ILUSTRATIVOS
A LA VENTA[d] EN SU LIBRERÍA O PUESTO[e] DE
REVISTAS FAVORITO

[a]*guide*
[b]*reader*
[c]ser... *loved one*
[d]A... *For sale*
[e]*stand*

LAS LISTAS DE MODA

Montar[a] la lista de bodas en El Corte Inglés está de moda.[b] Y es que no todos pueden ofrecer, al mismo tiempo, la mayor variedad de artículos y los mejores servicios:
• 10%* de descuento en todas sus compras en El Corte Inglés, seis meses antes y tres después de la boda.
• Regalo del 10% del importe[c] total de su lista.

• Precios especiales para "La luna de miel"[d] en nuestra agencia de viajes.
• Seguimiento[e] por ordenador[f] del estado de su lista.
• Posibilidad de recibir regalos desde cualquier centro de El Corte Inglés en España.

El Corte Inglés
toda una lista de ventajas.[g]

[a]*Set up*
[b]está... *is fashionable*
[c]*value*
[d]luna... *honeymoon*
[e]*Following*
[f]*computer*
[g]*advantages*

A. ¡Aprenda el arte de enamorar por carta! Lea el anuncio y conteste.

1. ¿Qué aprenderá el lector con este libro?
2. ¿Cómo se describe el libro en el anuncio?
3. ¿Qué encontrará el lector en el libro?
4. Este libro también incluye cartas de amor de figuras históricas. ¿Qué figuras históricas aparecerán en este libro?
5. ¿Dónde se vende *Cómo escribir cartas de amor*?
6. ¿Compraría Ud. un libro así? ¿Por qué (no)?

B. Las listas de boda (*bride's registry*). Estudie el anuncio y conteste.

1. ¿Cómo se llama este almacén? ¿Dónde está?
2. ¿Qué está de moda?
3. ¿Cuánto ofrece de descuento El Corte Inglés?
4. ¿Qué ofrece El Corte Inglés para la luna de miel?
5. ¿Cuáles son las ventajas de montar la lista de boda en El Corte Inglés?

C. ¡Solitarios! Estudie este anuncio y conteste las preguntas.

¡SOLITARIOS!
¿DESEA CONTRAER MATRIMONIO?
El Club de Relacionamiento Humano, A. C., le pondrá en comunicación con personas de su mismo nivel[a] y sus mismos intereses. Solicite[b] folleto[c] gratis al 592-38-67, o escríbanos:
Pisicóloga ANA VICTORIA SEGURA T.,
"CLUB DE RELACIONAMIENTO HUMANO", A. C.
VALLARTA 1, Desp. 109-"B", México 4, D. F.
"La vida, si no se comparte,[d] no se disfruta"

[a]*level*
[b]*Request*
[c]*pamphlet*
[d]*se. . . is shared*

1. ¿A quién se dirige este anuncio?
2. ¿Cuál es el propósito (*purpose*) del club?
3. ¿A quién deben escribir los interesados?
4. ¿Está Ud. de acuerdo con esta oración:
   «La vida, si no se comparte, no se disfruta»?

Para conversar más

A. Ideas personales. ¿Cuáles de las siguientes opiniones acepta (o no acepta) Ud.? Explique su opinión. *Use the statements as springboards from which to express personal opinions.*

1. Un divorcio es mejor que un mal matrimonio.
2. Las causas principales del divorcio son (a) los problemas financieros y (b) una mala división del trabajo en casa.
3. Hay otras causas del divorcio igualmente importantes. Por ejemplo: la incompatibilidad y el no tener intereses comunes.

Expansion B: 9. ¿Se casará Ud. algún día? 10. ¿Se casará por la iglesia o por lo civil? 11. ¿Adónde irá a pasar su luna de miel?

B. Cuestionario psicológico.

1. ¿Se pone Ud. de mal humor fácilmente? ¿Cuándo?
2. Cuando Ud. le promete a un amigo (una amiga) que va a hacer algo, ¿siempre trata de hacerlo? Explique.
3. ¿Le es fácil o difícil disculparse con los amigos si Ud. está equivocado/a en algo? ¿Por qué?
4. ¿Cree que realmente odia a alguien? ¿A quién? ¿Por qué?
5. ¿Hace Ud. mucho caso de sus amigos? ¿Cómo les demuestra (*show*) su amistad?
6. Generalmente, ¿tiene Ud. paciencia con otras personas? ¿Con quién(es) no tiene Ud. paciencia?
7. ¿Cómo saluda Ud. a sus amigos generalmente? ¿Los abraza? ¿Los besa?
8. ¿Ha tenido celos alguna vez? ¿Por qué (no)?

Optional: Ask students to imagine they are attending a wedding and observing the people present. They use phrases from A and the appropriate subjunctive form of verbs in B to talk about what they see. (Put these on the board or duplicate for students' use.)
A: 1. *Quiero que los novios...* **2.** *Espero que Uds....* **3.** *Me alegro de que el padre...* **4.** *Siento que la mamá...* **5.** *Temo que el novio...* **6.** *Quiero que tú...* **7.** *Prefiero que el abuelo...* **8.** *Deseo que los invitados...*
B: *tener dinero, divertirse, bailar, no hablar mal del novio, asistir a, (no) beber demasiado, estar cómodo/a, (no) preocuparse, abrazar, venir, ponerse de buen humor, casarse*

MOTIVO CULTURAL

As you have seen so far in *Motivos de conversación,* the word **novio/a** has a few different meanings in Spanish: *sweetheart, betrothed, bridegroom/bride, newlywed.* It is not used as loosely as *boyfriend/girlfriend* is in the United States.

Courtships and engagements in Hispanic countries usually last longer than in the United States, most often progressing from going out with a group of friends to a bona fide courtship that may last a number of years before an engagement takes place. The engagement, in turn, may go on for a number of years before the couple decides to marry. Young people usually live at home until they are married, saving their money for their future married life, even if the ceremony does not take place until they are in their thirties.

Vocabulario activo

Adjetivos

amable	pleasant, polite
equivocado/a	mistaken
peleado/a	estranged
propio/a	own

Sustantivos

LA BODA (*WEDDING*)

el anillo de boda	wedding ring
el anillo de compromiso	engagement ring
el brindis	toast
el canapé	hors d'oeuvre
el champán	champagne
la felicitación	congratulations
la madrina	bridesmaid, maid of honor
el/la novio/a	sweetheart, bridegroom/ bride, fiancé/fiancée
el padrino	best man
el/la suegro/a	father-in-law/mother-in-law

OTROS SUSTANTIVOS

el abrazo	embrace, hug
la amistad	friendship
los celos	jealousy
el cuento	story
el disgusto	quarrel
el divorcio	divorce
los mayores	adults, grown-ups
el odio	hatred

Verbos

abrazar	to embrace
amar	to love
arreglar	to arrange; to fix
besar	to kiss
brindar	to toast
casarse (con)	to get married (to)
disculparse	to excuse oneself, apologize
divorciarse (de)	to get divorced (from)
enamorarse (de)	to fall in love (with)
felicitar	to congratulate
odiar	to hate
pegar	to hit
pelear	to fight
prometer	to promise
querer	to love
resolver (ue)	to solve, resolve
soportar	to tolerate, put up with
suponer	to suppose

Otras palabras y expresiones

en absoluto	not at all
en el fondo	deep down
hacer caso a/de	to pay attention to, be considerate of
lo malo	the bad thing
lo que	what, that which
ponerse de mal/buen humor	to get in a bad/good mood
tener celos	to be jealous
tratar de + *inf.*	to try (*to do something*)
últimamente	lately

El dinero y los negocios

La Bolsa de Buenos Aires, Argentina. —¿Qué transacciones me recomienda Ud.?

METAS

Comunicación: In this lesson you will learn vocabulary and expressions useful in business and banking. You will talk about cashing and depositing checks, opening a checking and a savings account, visiting an office, and even witnessing a bank robbery. You will also learn some interesting facts about the monetary units of Hispanic countries.

Estructuras: 75. Subjunctive in Adjective Clauses 76. Subjunctive in Clauses Modifying Indefinite Persons or Things 77. Subjunctive in Clauses Modifying Negative Antecedents 78. *If*-Clauses

G RÁFICOS

Inversiones y ahorros

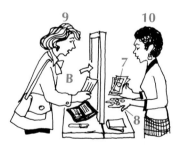

Investments and Savings

1. la tarjeta de crédito
2. la (tarjeta de) identificación/el carnet de identidad
3. la libreta de cheques, la chequera
4. la alcancía
5. el interés (el ocho por ciento)
6. las cuentas a largo plazo (*long-term accounts*)
7. los billetes
8. las monedas
9. el/la cliente/a
10. el/la empleado/a del banco (bancario/a)

A. ahorrar   *to save*
B. cambiar/hacer efectivo un cheque   *to cash a check*
C. abrir una cuenta corriente/de cheques   *to open a checking account;* abrir una cuenta de ahorros   *to open a savings account*
D. firmar   *to sign*

Cultural expansion:
Many Hispanic countries issue government *tarjetas* or *carnets de identidad* to all their citizens. Unlike in the United States, where a driver's license is the most common document used for identification, in Spanish-speaking countries, the *carnet* is used for general as well as political identification.

Actividades

A. Asociaciones. Elimine la palabra o frase que no tenga relación directa con la palabra o frase indicada.

1. cambiar un cheque

   a. firmar   b. la libreta de cheques   c. la inversión

2. abrir una cuenta de ahorros

   a. interés a largo plazo   b. la alcancía   c. la chequera

3. ir de compras

   a. la tarjeta de crédito   b. la empleada bancaria   c. los billetes

4. ahorrar

   a. la cuenta corriente   b. la cuenta a largo plazo   c. las monedas

B. Definiciones. ¿De qué o de quién hablo?

1. Pongo allí monedas.
2. Es una cuenta de la que no puedo sacar dinero inmediatamente.
3. Sirve para confirmar nuestra identidad.
4. Es el dinero que el banco me paga si tengo una cuenta de ahorros.
5. Es la persona que hace negocios con un banco.
6. Es dinero de metal.

C. Conteste.

1. ¿Qué tarjeta(s) de identificación tiene Ud? ¿En qué circunstancias la(s) usa?
2. ¿Qué interés gana hoy una cuenta de ahorros común? ¿y una a largo plazo?
3. En su opinión, ¿cuál es la mejor inversión: comprar un auto o comprar una casa? ¿Por qué?
4. ¿Tiene Ud. una alcancía? ¿Cómo ahorra?
5. ¿Tiene Ud. tarjeta de crédito? ¿Cuál? ¿Cuánto tiene que pagar de intereses si no paga el total al final del mes?

En la oficina

◆   SUBJUNCTIVE IN ADJECTIVE CLAUSES   ◆

papel que tenga mi membrete
paper that has my letterhead

no hay nada que resulte...
there is nothing that is . . .

busque un sobre que sea bastante grande
look for an envelope that is big enough

1. el/la secretario/a
2. el intercomunicador
3. la máquina de escribir
4. el membrete
5. la libreta de taquigrafía
6. el sobre
7. la computadora/el ordenador
8. el archivo
9. la carpeta
10. la copiadora
11. la impresora

JEFA: (Por el intercomunicador) Por favor, traiga la libreta de taquigrafía; voy a dictarle una circular. Quiero que la *imprima* en papel
que tenga mi membrete personal, y que haga después diez copias.

SECRETARIA: Lo siento, señorita; la impresora no funciona.

JEFA: No hay nada que resulte tan *inútil* como una computadora cuando no imprime la impresora. Bueno, la puede *pasar a máquina.*
Otra cosa: en el archivo hay dos carpetas de López y *Cía.* Necesito la carpeta que tiene el nombre en rojo. Busque un sobre que
sea bastante grande y *meta* en él la carpeta con los documentos
que le di ayer.

SECRETARIA: Muy bien, señorita.

boss
print

useless
type up
(Compañía) *Co.*

put

Suggestion: Dialogue
contains several cog-
nates difficult to pro-
nounce. Practice *intercomunicador, computadora,
transcriba, documentos.*

Actividades

Note: Exercises A and B
can be done in small
groups.

Note: Business-oriented
students may be interest-
ed in learning it is easy
for someone who knows
shorthand in English to
take dictation in Spanish,
since in major shorthand
systems both languages
use same characters.

Optional: General questions. **1.** *¿Cuál es la diferencia entre una carta y
una circular?* **2.** *¿Cuál es
la ventaja* (advantage) *de
escribir algo en taquigrafía?* **3.** *¿Qué necesita
tener Ud. para usar la copiadora que hay en la bi-
blioteca?* **4.** *¿Por qué es
útil saber escribir a má-
quina y usar una compu-
tadora? ¿Sabe Ud. hacer
estas dos cosas?*

Expansion B: Without referring back to the items
in the text, have students
describe the functions of
or offer definitions for the
following: **1.** *la carpeta*
2. *el sobre* **3.** *la copiadora* **4.** *el membrete*
5. *la impresora*

Additional review items:
1. *la cuenta a largo plazo*
2. *el banco* **3.** *la libreta
de cheques* **4.** *la alcancía* **5.** *los billetes*

A. ¿Cierto o falso? Corrija las afirmaciones falsas.

1. La jefa habla con su secretaria por teléfono.
2. La jefa quiere dictar una circular a su secretaria.
3. La jefa quiere que la circular no tenga membrete.
4. La computadora no funciona.
5. La secretaria va a pasar la carta a máquina.
6. La jefa cree que la impresora es inútil.
7. La jefa necesita las dos carpetas de López y Cía.
8. Es necesario un sobre que sea grande para meter en él la carpeta.

B. ¿Qué se usa en una oficina para...

1. escribir cartas?
2. imprimir cartas?
3. organizar las carpetas?
4. escribir lo que dicta el jefe/la jefa?
5. hablar con alguien que está en otra habitación?
6. hacer copias de una carta?

C. El secretario (La secretaria). Ud. es el jefe (la jefa) y un compañero (una
compañera) de clase es el secretario (la secretaria). Ud. tiene una reunión muy
importante y le pide a su secretario/a que haga las cosas indicadas. Pero él
(ella) siempre tiene una excusa por no hacerlas (no puede encontrar la carpeta,
no funciona la copiadora, etcétera).

MODELO: traer la libreta de taquigrafía →
—Por favor, traiga la libreta de taquigrafía que tiene la carta que
dicté esta mañana.
—Lo siento, pero no sé donde está la libreta.

1. buscar la carpeta de la compañía...
2. traerle una taza de café a su oficina
3. escribirles a... una carta pidiendo...
4. hacer copias para...
5. imprimir la carta en un papel que tenga membrete
6. pasar la carta a máquina

En la ventanilla del banco

1. las hojas de depósito
2. el asaltante
3. la ventanilla
4. el/la cajero/a
5. el bolsillo
6. el revólver
7. la nota
8. la cola
9. el/la cómplice

◆ IMPERFECT SUBJUNCTIVE IN *IF*-CLAUSES ◆

Si tuviera dinero para hacer un cheque, no robaría bancos.
If I had money to write a check, I wouldn't rob banks.

Si Ud. activara la alarma, yo tendría que usar el revólver...
If you were to activate the alarm, I would have to use the revolver . . .

CAJERA: Señor, para depositar un cheque necesita una hoja de depósito, y para cambiarlo, una identificación que tenga su firma.

ASALTANTE: Señora, esto no es un cheque, sino una nota. Si tuviera dinero para hacer un cheque, no robaría bancos.

CAJERA: (Leyendo *en voz baja*) «Si Ud. coopera no *pasará* nada; pero si Ud. activara la alarma, yo tendría que usar el revólver que llevo en el bolsillo. Tengo además un cómplice *al final* de la cola. Quiero billetes que *no estén marcados*». (Hablando al asaltante) ¿Quiere que le dé una bolsa para los billetes, o los lleva en la mano?   *in a low voice / will happen*   *at the end*   *unmarked*

ASALTANTE: Déme el dinero y *no se preocupe*. Tengo una bolsa.   *don't worry*

Actividades

Suggestion A, C: Both exercises are appropriate for small-group work.

Variation B: Exercise can be done as dialogue. One student is police officer and asks questions of witness: *¿Dónde estaba Ud.? ¿Tenía el hombre un revólver? ¿Era alto, bajo, gordo, delgado? ¿Tenía bigote? ¿De qué color era la bolsa que llevaba? ¿Cómo era su cómplice?*, etc.

A. ¿Quién soy? Un(a) estudiante lee las descripciones y otro/a estudiante hace una conjetura de quién es esa persona.

1. Llevo un revólver en el bolsillo.
2. Tengo mucho miedo, pero voy a activar la alarma.
3. Estoy al final de la cola y también tengo un revólver.
4. Le doy dinero de su cuenta de ahorros a una clienta.
5. Escribo una nota y obligo a la cajera a darme el dinero.

B. ¿Es Ud. un buen (una buena) testigo/a (*witness*)? Mire por unos segundos el dibujo del banco de la página 342. Cierre el libro. Imagine que un compañero (una compañera) es miembro de la policía y descríbale la escena.

C. Diálogo en el banco. Usando los elementos que se dan, invente un diálogo con un compañero (una compañera).

CAJERA: depositar o cambiar un cheque / hoja de depósito / identificación

ASALTANTE: cheque / nota / tener dinero para hacer un cheque / no robar bancos / cooperar / no pasar nada / activar la alarma / usar revólver / llevar bolsillo / cómplice / final de la cola / querer billetes / no estar marcados

CAJERA: ¿querer bolsa / billetes / llevar en la mano?

ASALTANTE: dar dinero / no preocuparse / tener bolsa

En su opinión, ¿qué pasaría si la cajera no le diera el dinero al asaltante? Invente un final para el diálogo.

ESTUDIO DE PALABRAS

No Spanish words end in **t, k,** or **m.** For this reason, many English words that end in these consonants have Spanish cognates that end in a vowel.

A. *The Spanish cognates of the following words appear in the* **Gráficos** *section. Do you remember them?*

1. credit
2. client
3. document
4. deposit
5. percent
6. bank
7. check
8. alarm

B. *The Spanish cognates of these words also appear in* **Gráficos.** *Give them without consulting that section.*

1. to rob
2. to activate
3. to cooperate
4. to deposit
5. to dictate
6. to result
7. investment
8. accomplice
9. interest
10. note
11. copy
12. identification
13. revolver
14. intercom

VISTA CULTURAL

En los últimos años se ha visto una verdadera explosión de máquinas y métodos que facilitan nuestro acceso a la información: el correo electrónico, las máquinas FAX, los teléfonos portátiles, etcétera. España y otros países hispanos han incorporado estos avances a su vivir diario con gran rapidez. Ahora es posible mandar una carta de Chicago a Caracas o a Barcelona en unos pocos segundos.

Los avances tecnológicos permiten, por ejemplo, al hombre común obtener dinero rápidamente, gracias al cajero automático del banco, y al investigador científico seguir la destrucción de la selva amazónica, gracias a las fotografías de los satélites.

GRAMÁTICA ESENCIAL

75. Subjunctive in Adjective Clauses

The first subjunctive group you studied involved noun clauses. Adjective clauses constitute the second large group of statements that can call for the use of the subjunctive. When a noun in the main clause is described by the entire dependent clause, this clause is referred to as an *adjective clause.* As the following chart illustrates, the entire statement introduced by **que** modifies the noun **sobre** in the main clause.

MAIN CLAUSE CONTAINING A NOUN	QUALIFYING STATEMENT FUNCTIONING AS AN ADJECTIVE
Necesito **un sobre** *I need an envelope*	**que** sea grande. *that is large.*

The use of the subjunctive in adjective clauses can be divided into two categories: (1) subjunctive in clauses modifying indefinite persons or things (**Gramática esencial** 76) and (2) subjunctive in clauses modifying negative antecedents (**Gramática esencial** 77).

76. Subjunctive in Clauses Modifying Indefinite Persons or Things

Quiero que la transcriba en papel que tenga mi membrete personal.*

---

*In this sentence the boss is not referring to a particular piece of paper but to any paper that has her personal letterhead.

Suggestion: You may want to briefly review noun clauses (*Gramática 47, 50, 51, 54, 55*) by giving some examples students learned earlier. Volition: *Quiero que vengas. Prefieren que no vayamos. Mi padre no deja que yo salga. Te aconsejo que no fumes.* Emotion: *Me alegro de que estés aquí. Esperan que vayamos. Le molesta que ella hable tanto. Sentimos que esté enferma.* Disbelief, doubt, and denial: *No creo que él lo sepa. Dudan que me conozcan. Negamos que estén en la casa. Están seguros de que no estamos en casa.* Impersonal expressions: *Es preciso que la esperes. Es probable que ella no lo sepa todavía. Es importante que trabajemos mucho. Es seguro que no tiene dinero.* Have students identify the noun clause in each sentence. Also ask them to explain in their own words why they are called noun clauses and why those presented in *Gramática* 75 are called adjective clauses.

The subjunctive is used in the adjective clause if the latter describes an *indefinite person, object,* or *event.*

Necesito un dependiente que me **ayude** en mi trabajo.	*I need a clerk (any clerk) who will help me in my work.*

NOTE: If the words *some* or *any* can be inserted before the main-clause noun in English, it is probably indefinite.

If the person, object, or event is definite, however, the indicative—not the subjunctive—is used in the adjective clause.

Conozco a una cajera que **sabe** español.	*I know a cashier who knows Spanish.*

Note that the personal **a** used above is required since **una cajera** is a definite person. Remember, too, that the personal **a** is also required when **alguien** or **nadie** is a direct object.

¿Conoce Ud. a alguien que **pueda** aconsejarme?	*Do you know anyone who can advise me?*
No conozco a nadie que **quiera** hacer una inversión ahora.	*I don't know anyone who wants to make an investment now.*

Listening practice: Read these sentences aloud and have students write each subjunctive verb they hear: **1.** *Busco un banco que me cambie este cheque.* **2.** *Tenemos un cajero que trabaja mucho.* **3.** *Quieres hablar con alguien que sepa mucho español.* **4.** *¿Conoces a un actor que sea famoso?* **5.** *Busco una amiga que me preste dinero.* **6.** *Necesitan una secretaria que escriba bien a máquina.* **7.** *Tengo una copiadora que funciona muy bien.* Reading the sentences a second time, ask students to explain the choice of mood in each sentence.

Actividades

A. Asuntos (*Issues*) financieros. Complete con la forma apropiada del infinitivo.

Busco una inversión que (ser[1]) buena. Tengo una cuenta de ahorros que (pagar[2]) sólo el 6 por ciento de interés, pero necesito una cuenta que (pagar[3]) un mínimo de un 8 por ciento. Debo hablar con una persona que (entender[4]) mucho de negocios y que (querer[5]) aconsejarme en esto.

Necesito una calculadora que (funcionar[6]) bien, pero no quiero una calculadora que (costar[7]) más de $30. ¿Hay alguna tienda que (estar[8]) cerca donde (vender[9]) calculadoras buenas y baratas?

Héctor vive en un apartamento que (ser[10]) muy caro, porque no hay apartamentos que (ser[11]) baratos en este barrio. Busca un compañero que (pagar[12]) la mitad del alquiler. ¿Hay algún estudiante en la universidad que (necesitar[13]) apartamento?

B. Cambie los párrafos anteriores al pasado. *Use the imperfect indicative for the main verb and decide between the imperfect indicative and the imperfect subjunctive form of the verb in parentheses.*

MODELO: Buscaba una inversión que fuera buena... .

77. Subjunctive in Clauses Modifying Negative Antecedents

No hay nada que resulte tan inútil como una computadora cuando no imprime la impresora.

Emphasis: Explain that answers to questions like *¿Hay alguien que... ?*, *¿Conoces a alguien que... ?*, and *¿Tienes... que... ?* take indicative if they are affirmative and subjunctive if they begin with *no*. Remind students that several negatives in same sentence is common and correct in Spanish: *No encuentro nunca a nadie que me preste dinero.*

Note: Alert students to fact that if sentence begins with *nadie, ningún, nunca,* etc., instead of *no*, and does not contain adjective clause, indicative is used: *Nadie me presta dinero nunca; Ningún cajero habla español en ese banco; Nunca he usado una computadora.*

When an adjective clause modifies a noun in a negative main clause, its verb must be in the subjunctive.

En ese banco no tienen cajeros que **hablen** español.	*At that bank they don't have tellers who speak Spanish.*
No había nadie allí que **pudiera** ayudarle.	*There was no one there who could help him.*

Actividades

Follow-up A: Do as written exercise and then repeat orally, changing main verb: **1.** *Para mi trabajo compré una computadora que no...* **2.** *Hay una persona mayor que...* **3.** *Conozco a una persona que...* **4.** *Cuando trabajo, uso vestidos (trajes) que no...* **5.** *Aquí hay alguien que...* **6.** *Hay varias soluciones que...* **7.** *Aquí tenemos muchos empleados que...* **8.** *Encontré inversiones que...*

Optional B: Ask students to complete these partial sentences logically, using subjunctive or indicative. Present them orally, on board, or on photocopies: **1.** *Voy a llamar a varias personas que...* **2.** *¿Ha venido alguien que... ?* **3.** *Hablé con el empleado que...* **4.** *Sé que hay algunos candidatos que...* **5.** *Recomiéndeme una persona que...* **6.** *Necesito un libro que...* **7.** *Es un trabajo que...* **8.** *¿Hay estudiantes que... ?*

A. En la oficina. Complete las oraciones de la izquierda usando las frases de la derecha. ¡Cuidado con el tiempo del verbo!

1. Para mi trabajo quiero una computadora que no _____.
2. Cuando trabajo, prefiero usar ropa que no _____.
3. Aquí no tenemos empleados que _____.
4. ¿Sabe Ud. encontrar inversiones que _____?
5. ¿Hay alguien aquí que _____?
6. No hay soluciones que _____.

a. no ser inteligente
b. costar mucho
c. ser fáciles
d. dar mucho dinero
e. ser muy elegante
f. saber la respuesta

B. Preguntas y respuestas. En grupos de tres, un(a) estudiante hace las preguntas, otro/a estudiante las contesta afirmativamente y otro/a las contesta negativamente.

MODELO: ¿Conoces una secretaria que sepa usar una computadora? →
Sí, conozco a una secretaria que sabe usar una computadora.
No, no conozco a ninguna secretaria que sepa usar una computadora.

1. ¿Hay por aquí un banco que tenga un cajero automático?
2. ¿Hay un banco cerca donde yo pueda cambiar un cheque?
3. ¿Hay algún autobús que vaya a ese barrio?
4. ¿Conoce Ud. a alguien que trabaje allí?
5. ¿Hay otra persona que pueda ayudarme?

78. *If*-Clauses

Si tuviera dinero para hacer un cheque, no robaría bancos.

Although many sentences containing *"if-clauses" do not* require the subjunctive, the following types of conditional statements always call for the use of the imperfect subjunctive in the *if*-clause.

1. Contrary-to-fact conditions
When a speaker speculates about conditions known to be contrary to the facts, he or she uses a subjunctive verb form in the *if*-clause. The main or "result" clause expresses the consequences of that hypothesis and requires a verb in the conditional.

Si la niña tuviera una alcancía, ahorraría algún dinero.	*If the girl had a piggy bank (she does not), she would save some money.*
Él abriría una cuenta de ahorros si fuese inteligente.	*He would open a savings account if he were intelligent (I know he isn't).*

2. Improbable future actions and conditions
If the speaker speculates about a future action that is not likely to take place, he or she can convey uncertainty by using a subjunctive verb form in the *if*-clause.

Si Ana viniera mañana, podría firmar los documentos.	*If Ana should come tomorrow (and I doubt that she will), she could sign the documents.*
Iría a trabajar el sábado si mi jefe me lo pidiera.	*I would go to work on Saturday if my boss were to ask me (and it is not likely he will).*

Note that the *if*-clause may either precede or follow the main clause. In both instances, the conditional is used in the main clause and the imperfect subjunctive is used in the *if*-clause.

Ya puede comprar con su tarjeta Cajamadrid.

····· servicio

Actividades

A. Buscando excusas. Un(a) estudiante le pide a otro/a que haga algo. El otro (La otra) contesta con una excusa, según las indicaciones.

> MODELO: Por favor, cómprame algo en la tienda. (No tengo tiempo.) →
> Te compraría algo si tuviera tiempo.

1. Ven con nosotros al cine esta tarde. (No puedo.)
2. Por favor, llévanos al cine en tu coche. (Mi coche no funciona.)
3. Entonces, camina con nosotros por el parque. (No hace buen tiempo.)
4. ¿Quieres comer después en el restaurante Las Milpas? (La comida allí no es buena.)
5. ¿Quieres prestarme diez dólares? (No tengo dinero.)

B. Ud. es consejero financiero (consejera financiera). Aconseje a las siguientes personas, usando el imperfecto de subjuntivo de los infinitivos indicados.

Su amigo Juanito tiene muchas deudas (*debts*) y sus amigos no quieren prestarle dinero.

—Juanito, si tú no (gastar¹) tanto, no tendrías tantas deudas. Si (abrir²) una cuenta de ahorros en un banco y (poner³) allí una parte de tu sueldo (*salary*) todas las semanas, no necesitarías pedir dinero a tus amigos. Y si no les (pedir⁴) dinero constantemente a tus amigos, tendrías más amigos.

La Srta. Aguilar necesita comprar un auto, pero es nueva en el pueblo y el banco no quiere prestarle dinero.

—Srta. Aguilar, si Ud. (ser⁵) una residente antigua de este pueblo, tendría crédito establecido en todas partes. Y si Ud. (conocer⁶) a personas que (poder⁷) garantizarla y esas personas (firmar⁸) su solicitud (*application*), el banco le prestaría el dinero para comprar el auto. Otra solución sería que su jefe (querer⁹) anticiparle dinero de su sueldo.

C. Mi sueño imposible. Invente discursos breves sobre lo que Ud. haría si fuera posible.

> MODELO: ir, dar → ¡Estoy tan cansada de estudiar! Iría ahora mismo a España o a México si mis padres me dieran el dinero para comprar un boleto de ida y vuelta. ¡También iría si sólo pudiera comprar un boleto de ida!

1. comer, tener
2. visitar, conocer
3. casarme, amar
4. hacer, decir
5. vivir, saber

D. Complete estas narraciones con el imperfecto de subjuntivo de los infinitivos.

Sueños Si yo (ganar¹) la lotería, pondría una parte del dinero en una cuenta de ahorros a largo plazo y compraría una casa que (tener²) jardín y piscina y que (estar[3]) en un buen barrio. También ayudaría a mis amigos si ellos lo (necesitar[4]) y les prestaría dinero si me lo (pedir[5]).

No soy un héroe Si un bandido (robar[6]) el banco y yo (estar[7]) allí, no sería un héroe. Si él me (amenazar[8]) (*threaten*) con un revólver y me (mandar[9]) acostarme en el suelo, lo haría sin protestar. También le daría mi dinero si él me lo (exigir[10]) (*demand*). Lo miraría bien si (poder[11]), para describirlo después a la policía. Le diría a la policía todo lo que (recordar[12]) del robo. Y si lo (capturar[13]), iría a identificarlo.

Para resumir y repasar

A. En persona: El nuevo secretario (la nueva secretaria). Otro socio (Otra socia) (*partner*) de su compañía y Ud. han decidido emplear un secretario (una secretaria). Hablen de la persona que buscan, usando la siguiente lista de habilidades (*skills*) y otras que Uds. inventen.

> MODELO: ahorrar dinero →
> *Socio/a 1:* Quiero una persona que nos ayude a ahorrar más dinero.
> *Socio/a 2:* De acuerdo. No quiero ninguna persona que no sepa ahorrar el dinero de la compañía.

1. hablar con los clientes
2. llevar las cuentas corrientes de la compañía
3. saber usar las computadoras
4. escribir rápido a máquina
5. saber taquigrafía
6. organizar nuestros archivos

B. En el restaurante El Gamberro. Exprese en español.

1. One eats well in El Gamberro.
2. Yes, but you pay (one pays) a lot too.
3. That's why you never see many people there.
4. And that's why you get such good service.
5. You're right, you (one) can have a great time in El Gamberro.

C. Reacciones a un banquete. Exprese en español, usando la forma apropiada de los siguientes verbos con *se*:

apagar   decorar   contratar   cubrir   poner

_____[1] las mesas de muchos platos y canapés. _____[2] algunas luces del salón para crear (*to create*) un ambiente íntimo. _____[3] las flores en floreros muy elegantes. _____[4] veinte camareros para servir la cena. _____[5] el salón con papeles de muchos colores.

Optional D: Review subjunctive in *if*-clauses by having students complete following, to be distributed or read aloud: **1.** *Iría a consultar con un abogado si...* **2.** *Yo le escribiría al presidente si...* **3.** *Organizaría una fiesta para todos mis amigos si...* **4.** *Yo me casaría si...* **5.** *Compraría muchas cosas si...* **6.** *Yo iría con Ud. si...*

Optional: Write the following cues on the board or duplicate them for distribution. Have students do them orally or in writing, as a review. *Modelo: recibir (pretérito) / las invitaciones → Se recibieron las invitaciones.* **1.** *escoger (pretérito) / el día para la boda* **2.** *pagar (pretérito) / el alquiler de la iglesia* **3.** *preparar (pretérito) / la lista de invitados* **4.** *mandar (pretérito) / las invitaciones* **5.** *planear (pretérito) / la ceremonia* **6.** *abrir (futuro) / las puertas para la recepción a las tres* **7.** *servir (futuro) / muchos canapés* **8.** *comprar (futuro) / 50 botellas de champán* **9.** *recibir (futuro) / más de 300 regalos* **10.** *terminar (futuro) / la recepción a las cinco*

COMUNICACIÓN

De la vida real

Suggestion: Have several students read the announcement aloud as fast and as dramatically as they can, as if it were a radio commercial.

Suggestion: Point out although this convention is not followed in ***Motivos,*** accent marks are generally omitted on capitalized letters in Spanish, as in this ad. Ask students to identify any words in the ad that would have accent marks if the text weren't printed in capital letters.

ATARI® Portfolio
UN VERDADERO ORDENADOR COMPATIBLE PC DE BOLSILLO, QUE SE PUEDE CONECTAR A UNA IMPRESORA O INTERCAMBIAR[a] INFORMACION CON OTROS ORDENADORES, PARA PODER TRABAJAR EN CUALQUIER[b] MOMENTO Y EN CUALQUIER LUGAR, EL AVION, LA OFICINA, EL COCHE, LA UNIVERSIDAD... TODA LA POTENCIA[c] DE UN ORDENADOR AHORA EN SUS MANOS.
49.900 PTS +I.V.A. P.V.P.

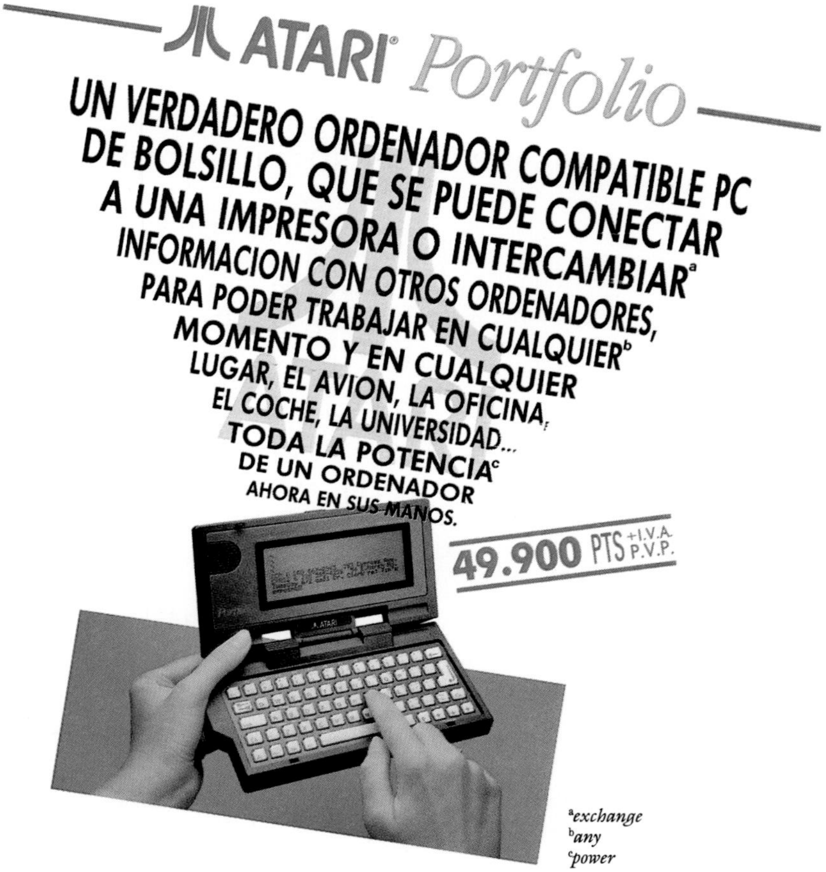

[a]*exchange*
[b]*any*
[c]*power*

A. Atari Portfolio. Primero, lea el anuncio fijándose en las ventajas de este ordenador. Luego, imagine que Ud. es un cliente (una clienta) que quiere comprar un ordenador. Entra en una tienda y le explica al vendedor (a la vendedora) qué cualidades debe tener el ordenador que Ud. busca. El vendedor (La vendedora) le explicará por qué debe comprar un Atari Portfolio.

MODELO: ordenador compatible / llevar a casa →
CLIENTE/A: Necesito un ordenador compatible que yo pueda llevar a casa para trabajar.

VENDEDOR(A): El Atari Portfolio es perfecto para Ud. porque es un ordenador compatible de bolsillo. Es tan pequeño que Ud. lo puede llevar a casa o a cualquier otra parte sin dificultad.

1. mi secretario / conectar / las impresoras de la oficina / imprimir
2. intercambiar información / el ordenador de mi jefe
3. llevar y poder usar en el avión
4. tener suficiente potencia
5. no costar más de 60.000 pesetas

M E M O P R Á C T I C A

Memorization can be made easier by using your *visual memory* to the fullest extent. Often you can remember a word because of its association with a drawing or picture or even because of its location on a page. Your familiarity with checks should tell you at once what the various blank lines are for on the check in the following exercise.

Note: Emphasize the *Memopráctica*. You may want to add a few comments about the importance of fixing new words and expressions firmly in one's mind by repeating them over and over.

B. Banco de la Nación. Examine este cheque y conteste las preguntas.

```
BANCO DE LA NACIÓN

Antonio Oyarzún                                    281
Calle Luz, Nº 2973             1 _____
Santiago, Chile

Páguese a la orden de  2 _____  $ 3 _____

_____

Anotación _____           4
           07893  100227  1458  217  028
```

1. fecha
2. nombre del acreedor (la persona que recibe el cheque)
3. importe del cheque (la cantidad [*amount*])
4. firma del deudor (la persona que paga con el cheque)

1. ¿Cómo se llama el banco?
2. ¿Sabemos quién es el dueño de la libreta de cheques? Explique.
3. Hablando de cheques, ¿qué otra palabra hay para decir «cantidad»?
4. ¿Cómo se llama la persona para quien se hace el cheque?
5. ¿Qué nombre podemos dar a la persona que firma el cheque?
6. ¿Qué nos dicen los números que aparecen en la última línea del cheque?
7. Cerca de la fecha hay un número. ¿Qué nos dice ese número?

---

*Note that impersonal orders such as **Páguese** call for a polite command followed by **se: ¡Dígase!** (*Tell!*); **Escríbase!** (*Write!*); **¡Póngase!** (*Put!*); and so on.

^a*monthly payments*

C. Como caída del cielo. Conteste a base del anuncio.

1. ¿Cómo interpreta Ud. la expresión «Como caída del cielo»?
2. Si una persona tiene esta tarjeta, ¿cómo puede pagar sus compras?
3. Además de comprar a crédito, ¿qué hará una persona con esta tarjeta?
4. ¿Dónde puedo obtener esta tarjeta?
5. ¿De qué otra manera puedo obtenerla?

Para conversar más

A. ¿Busca Ud. la perfección? Descríbale a un compañero (una compañera) la idea que tiene Ud. de las siguientes personas y cosas.

> MODELO: el empleo perfecto →
> Busco un empleo que me pague muchísimo dinero (que me dé seis semanas de vacaciones cada año, que me permita vivir donde yo quiera, etcétera).

1. el profesor perfecto (la profesora perfecta)
2. el jefe perfecto (la jefa perfecta)
3. la computadora perfecta
4. el banco perfecto
5. la universidad perfecta

B. Gente rara. Pregúntele a un compañero (una compañera) si conoce a alguien que...

> MODELO: tener mucho dinero pero no querer gastarlo →
> ¿Conoces a alguien que tenga mucho dinero pero no quiera gastarlo?

1. haber robado un banco
2. no trabajar nunca
3. ahorrar el dinero en una alcancía
4. usar más de diez tarjetas de crédito
5. llevar una pistola

C. Cuestionario bancario. Haga estas preguntas a un compañero (una compañera) de clase.

1. ¿Tienes una cuenta corriente o una cuenta de ahorros en el banco? ¿Prefieres usar una tarjeta de crédito en vez de (*instead of*) pagar con un cheque? ¿Por qué (no)?
2. En tu banco, ¿piden algo para confirmar tu identidad cuando presentas un cheque personal?
3. ¿Es bueno el servicio de tu banco? ¿Cómo se llama tu banco?
4. ¿Te gustaría trabajar en un banco? ¿Por qué (no)?

MOTIVO CULTURAL

Bolivia, Colombia, Cuba, Chile, Mexico, the Dominican Republic, and Uruguay all use the **peso** as their monetary unit, although its value in relationship to the dollar differs from country to country. Here is a list of the monetary units of the other Hispanic countries.

la Argentina	el austral	Nicaragua	el córdoba
Costa Rica	el colón	Panamá	el balboa
el Ecuador	el sucre	el Paraguay	el guaraní
El Salvador	el colón	el Perú	el inti
España	la peseta	Puerto Rico	el dólar
Guatemala	el quetzal	Venezuela	el bolívar
Honduras	el lempira		

In many cases, the name of a country's money has a traditional or historical origin. Five of these currencies carry the name of a historical figure: **Colón** (Columbus); **Sucre** and **Bolívar,** two South American patriots; **Lempira,** an Indian chief who fought against the conquistadors; and **Balboa** (Vasco de Núñez de Balboa), the Spanish conquistador who discovered the southern coast of Panama.

The origin of some of the other names is also quite interesting: the **quetzal** is a beautiful Central American bird that the Mayas worshipped; the **guaraní** is a Paraguayan Indian tribe and also the name of the second official language of this country; and **inti** is the name of the Incan sun god.

Cultural expansion: Encourage students to check financial section of newspaper to get idea of current exchange rates. Ask them to report how many currencies of Spanish-speaking countries are regularly listed. Students can also obtain up-to-date information about foreign currencies from local banks.

Suggestion: If you have coins or bills from Hispanic countries, bring them to class. Explain that *el austral* replaced *el peso* as monetary unit of Argentina a few years ago, and even more recently *el inti* was created in Peru to replace *el sol.* These changes were made because inflation and devaluation of national currency had made it necessary to use figures with many zeros for everyday transactions.

Vocabulario activo

Adjetivos

inútil	useless
marcado/a	marked

Sustantivos

AHORROS E INVERSIONES (*SAVINGS AND INVESTMENTS*)

la alcancía	piggy bank
el billete	bill
el/la cajero/a	teller
el carnet de identidad	ID card
la circular	letter
el/la cliente/a	client
la cuenta a largo plazo	long-term account
la cuenta corriente/de cheques	checking account
la chequera	checkbook
el/la empleado/a de banco (bancario/a)	banker; bank employee
la hoja de depósito	deposit slip
el interés	interest
la libreta de cheques	checkbook
la (tarjeta de) identificación	ID card
la ventanilla	window

EN LA OFICINA

el archivo	filing cabinet
la carpeta	folder
la compañía	company
la computadora	computer
la copia	copy
la copiadora	copying machine
la impresora	printer
el/la jefe/a	boss
la libreta de taquigrafía	shorthand pad
el membrete	letterhead
la nota	note
el ordenador	computer
el/la secretario/a	secretary
el sobre	envelope

OTROS SUSTANTIVOS

el asaltante	robber
el bolsillo	pocket
la cola	line (of people)
el/la cómplice	accomplice
el revólver	revolver

Verbos

ahorrar	to save
cooperar	to cooperate
depositar	to deposit
firmar	to sign
imprimir	to print
pasar	to happen
robar	to rob

Otras palabras y expresiones

abrir una cuenta de ahorros/corriente	to open a savings/checking account
al final	at the end
cambiar/hacer efectivo un cheque	to cash a check
en voz baja	in a low voice
no se preocupe	don't worry
pasar a máquina	to type

El mundo del trabajo

Mujeres policías en Lima, Perú. —¿En qué podemos servirle?

METAS

Comunicación: In this lesson you will learn vocabulary and expressions related to the world of work. You will consider various job opportunities, talk about different professions, and discuss your own career plans.

Estructuras: 79. Subjunctive in Adverbial Clauses 80. Subjunctive in Adverbial Clauses of Purpose and Proviso 81. Subjunctive in Adverbial Clauses of Time 82. Subjunctive After **aunque**

GRÁFICOS

Carreras

Suggestion: Model pronunciation of difficult terms like *farmacéutico, odontología, psiquiatría, sociólogo.*

Professions, Careers

UNIVERSIDAD DEL ESTADO

Carrera (Título)	Años	Carrera (Título)	Años
Arquitectura	4	Medicina	
(el Arquitecto/la Arquitecta)		(el Médico/la Médica,	
Comercio/Administración de empresas		el Doctor/la Doctora)	6
[*businesses*]		(el Enfermero/la Enfermera)	3
(el Contador/la Contadora) [*Accountant*]	4	(el Veterinario/la Veterinaria)	6
Derecho [*Law*]		Odontología	
(el Abogado/la Abogada)	4	(el/la Dentista)	4
Farmacia		Pedagogía	
(el Farmacéutico/la Farmacéutica)	4	(el Maestro/la Maestra)	4
Ingeniería: Civil, de Minas, Eléctrica, Mecánica		Psiquiatría	
(el Ingeniero/la Ingeniera)	5	(el/la Psiquiatra)	5
		Química	
		(el Químico/la Química)	4
		Socio-Economía	
		(el Sociólogo/la Socióloga)	4
		(el/la Economista)	4
		(el Trabajador/la Trabajadora Social)	4

Matrícula (*Registration*)

Días de matrícula: agosto 1–5; Pago de derechos: agosto 1–5

Actividades

Expansion A: Additional sentences you could present orally: **1.** *Todo médico necesita un experto en la preparación de medicinas, o sea* (that is), *un (una) _____.* **2.** *Tuve un choque ayer. No quiero pagar para arreglar mi carro porque no fue mi culpa* (fault). *Voy a consultar a un (una) _____.* **3.** *Mi amiga está estudiando _____ porque quiere trabajar con su padre en una mina.* **4.** *Me*

A. Las profesiones. Dé el nombre del profesional o de la carrera de que se habla en cada oración.

1. Mi amigo quiere descubrir una nueva fórmula para un pesticida que no haga daño a los trabajadores agrícolas. Está estudiando _____.
2. Una maestra de la secundaria me recomendó que estudiara _____ porque me interesa mucho el estudio de los problemas sociales.
3. La persona que lleva todas las cuentas (*accounts*) de una compañía es el/la _____.
4. Cuando termine los estudios de _____, voy a trabajar en una instalación hidroeléctrica.

gustaría construir una casa moderna y cómoda para mi familia. Tengo que hablar con un (una) _____.
5. Aprecio mucho a las _____. Ellas ayudan a los médicos y cuidan a los pacientes del hospital.
6. Me duele una muela. Tengo que ver al (a la) _____. *7. Tendré que consultar a un (una) _____ para descubrir la causa de mi depresión.*

Optional: If you live in large city or in area with large Hispanic population, for extra practice you and students may be able to find ads and announcements similar to one given here.

5. Mi prima estuvo en Inglaterra para hacer un estudio que compara la economía de ese país con la del nuestro. Ella es _____.
6. Los abogados estudian _____.
7. Creo que me gustaría enseñar inglés. Este año empiezo los estudios de _____.
8. Cuando mi perrito está enfermo, lo llevo al _____.
9. Mi vecina tiene varios niños, no tiene empleo y no recibe ninguna ayuda. Debe hablar con un _____.
10. Cuando empezaron a construir el metro, llamaron a un _____.

B. Definiciones. Invente oraciones para dar una definición de las carreras o de lo que hacen los profesionales. *Try not to refer back to Exercise A.*

1. la administración de empresas
2. la ingeniería (civil, mecánica)
3. el sociólogo / la socióloga
4. el químico / la química
5. la odontología
6. el maestro / la maestra
7. la arquitectura
8. la psiquiatría

C. Mis planes. Diga Ud. cuál de las siguientes profesiones le gustaría practicar. Explique por qué, escogiendo entre las razones dadas e inventando otras.

1. abogado / abogada
2. contador / contadora
3. farmacéutico / farmacéutica
4. ingeniero / ingeniera
5. médico / médica
6. enfermero / enfermera

ayudar a los pobres / viejos / niños / enfermos
trabajar en un hospital / una gran empresa / una farmacia
ganar mucho dinero
hacer nuevos descubrimientos
inventar nuevas máquinas

Los *obreros* y el *dueño*

Variation C: As review or follow-up, have students write a brief paragraph on the profession of their choice.

Workers / Owner

1. la tubería
2. el fontanero (la fontanera), el plomero (la plomera)
3. el aislamiento
4. el carpintero (la carpintera)
5. el/la electricista
6. la escalera

◆ SUBJUNCTIVE IN ADVERBIAL CLAUSES ◆

antes de que se instale *before it's installed*	
hasta que me diga *until he tells me*	
a menos que se decida *unless he decides*	
para que sea *so that it will (may) be*	
después de que terminen *after they finish*	
con tal de que no se caiga *provided he doesn't fall*	

EL CARPINTERO: ¿Saben? El dueño quiere que yo termine las paredes antes de
que se instale el aislamiento. No sabe nada de *carpintería*.   *carpentry*

EL FONTANERO: Yo no puedo poner la tubería del *sótano* hasta que él me diga   *basement*
dónde quiere instalar la *lavadora* y la *secadora*. Tendré un   *washer / dryer*
verdadero problema a menos que se decida antes del lunes.   *real*

EL ELECTRICISTA: Mi caso es peor. Me ha pedido que no haga algunas conexiones, para que el precio del trabajo sea más bajo. Dice que
él las hará después de que el *albañil* y el *pintor* terminen su   *bricklayer / painter*
trabajo.

EL CARPINTERO: Sé que tiene problemas financieros...

EL ELECTRICISTA: Me gustaría *echarle una mano*, pero ¿por qué *no pinta* él la   *lend him a hand / doesn't he paint*
casa *en vez de* hacer las conexiones eléctricas? Pintar es más   *instead of*
fácil y menos *peligroso*... bueno, con tal de que no *se caiga* de   *dangerous / doesn't fall down*
la escalera y *se mate*.   *kill himself*

Actividades

A.   Asociaciones. ¿Qué palabras de la derecha asocia Ud. con los individuos
de la izquierda? *This exercise also reviews vocabulary from previous lessons.*

1. carpintero/a	a. las conexiones	g. una puerta más
2. fontanero/a	b. el aislamiento	h. el agua caliente
3. electricista	c. la cocina eléctrica	i. la lavadora
4. pintor(a)	d. la tubería	j. las luces
5. albañil	e. el cemento	k. el color
	f. las paredes	l. la escalera

B.   Ud. es el dueño (la dueña) de la casa que se está construyendo. Déles
instrucciones a los obreros.

> MODELO: (yo) querer / Uds. esperar / hasta que / yo pintar paredes →
> Quiero que Uds. esperen hasta que yo pinte las paredes.

1. (yo) querer / Uds. terminar paredes / antes de que / instalarse aislamento
2. (yo) aceptar / Uds. traer / joven para trabajar en mi casa / con tal de que /
el saber carpintería
3. (yo) esperar / Uds. no poner tubería / hasta que / yo decidir / dónde
poner lavadora y secadora
4. (yo) necesitar / Uds. pintar sótano / después de que / pintar baño y cocina
5. (yo) no querer / Uds. hacer las conexiones / para que / precio del trabajo /
no ser verdadero problema para mí
6. (yo) esperar / Uds. no dejar de trabajar / a menos de que / alguien caerse
y matarse
7. (yo) necesitar / Uds. echarme una mano / para que / la construcción / no
resultarme cara

C.   ¿Es Ud. una persona que echa una mano en su casa? ¿Cuáles de los
siguientes trabajos ha hecho Ud.? ¿Por qué (no)?

1. ¿Qué ha pintado Ud. en su casa? ¿la sala? ¿una puerta? ¿el garaje?
2. ¿Sabe Ud. hacer conexiones eléctricas? ¿Puede instalar un teléfono nuevo? ¿Sabe montar una computadora?
3. ¿Le molesta subirse a una escalera? ¿Se ha caído de una escalera alguna vez? Describa las circunstancias.
4. ¿Qué aparatos ha instalado? ¿la lavadora y la secadora? ¿otras cosas como tubería? ¿aislamiento? ¿estantes?
5. ¿Quisiera Ud. ser carpintero/a, albañil, pintor(a), fontanero/a o electricista? ¿Por qué (no)?

Las *reparaciones*

Repairs

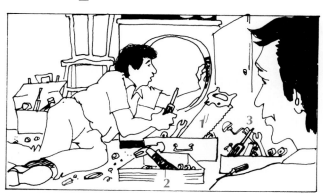

◆ EXPRESIONES VERBALES ◆	
cobrarme	*to charge me*
valer la pena	*to be worth the trouble*
hacer falta	*to be needed*
tener en cuenta	*to take into account*
montar una empresa	*to start a business*

1. el serrucho
2. el martillo
3. las herramientas

EL CLIENTE:	¿Cuánto me cobraría por *reparar* esta secadora?	*to repair*
EL TÉCNICO:	Quinientos cuarenta mil pesos.	
EL CLIENTE:	¿Tanto? Casi no vale la pena.	
EL TÉCNICO:	Las reparaciones no son baratas. Hacen falta herramientas especiales hasta para *ajustar* una *pieza* de poca importancia.	*adjust, fix / part*
EL CLIENTE:	¡Claro! ¡Ya sé que Ud. no va a usar un serrucho o un martillo!	
EL TÉCNICO:	Además, hay que tener en cuenta mis años de experiencia y el costo de montar una empresa *actualmente*.	*currently (at the present time)*
EL CLIENTE:	*¿Conque* Ud. ya no es *técnico* sino *empresario*? Ahora veo por qué el costo de estas reparaciones *ha aumentado* tanto.	*And so / technician / businessman has increased*

Actividades

A. Los trabajos de la casa. Conteste.

1. Generalmente, ¿dónde se instala la mayor parte de la tubería en una casa?
2. ¿Cuánto ganan actualmente por hora, más o menos, los carpinteros (los fontaneros, los electricistas)? ¿Por qué reciben un salario bastante alto algunos técnicos?

3. ¿Qué herramientas usan los carpinteros?
4. ¿Qué podría cortar Ud. con un serrucho?
5. ¿Qué debe tener en cuenta la persona que quiere hacer trabajos especializados en su propia casa?
6. ¿Puede explicar la diferencia entre un técnico de servicio y un empresario? ¿Quién gana más? ¿Por qué?
7. ¿Le gustaría a Ud. montar su propia empresa o preferiría trabajar para otra persona? Explique.

B. Una reparación en su casa. Con un compañero (una compañera) de clase, invente un diálogo basado en esta situación: Ud. quiere que un técnico (una técnica) le repare su lavadora (secadora, lavaplatos, refrigerador). Posibles preguntas: ¿Qué experiencia tiene él/ella? ¿Cuánto le va a cobrar? ¿Cuánto tiempo le va a tomar esta reparación? ¿Sólo va a ajustar las piezas, o hace falta comprar alguna pieza nueva? ¿Vale la pena reparar el/la (aparato), o sería mejor comprar un nuevo (una nueva)... ? ¿Qué se debe tener en cuenta para que no haya que hacer la misma reparación en el futuro?

VISTA CULTURAL

Elige bien tu profesión.
Elige bien tu futuro.

Elegir[a] bien o mal tu profesión influye[b] mucho en las posibilidades de encontrar un trabajo interesante. Y, ten por seguro, hoy en día no hay ninguna profesión que no te convenga[c] tan sólo por el hecho de ser mujer.[d] Lo que cuenta[e] son tus gustos y capacidades y que tu formación se corresponda con el trabajo existente.

Para que puedas decidir tu futuro libremente,[f] el Consejo Rector del Instituto de la Mujer ha puesto en marcha[g] el Plan para la Igualdad entre Mujeres y Hombres.
AHORA YA PUEDES ELEGIR

MINISTERIO DE CULTURA
Instituto de la Mujer

PLAN PARA LA IGUALDAD DE OPORTUNIDADES

[a]Escoger
[b]influences
[c]no... doesn't suit you
[d]por... due to the fact that you are a woman
[e]Lo... Lo importante
[f]freely
[g]ha... has put into motion

GRAMÁTICA ESENCIAL

79. Subjunctive in Adverbial Clauses

You've already studied the subjunctive in noun clauses and adjective clauses. In both cases the dependent clause containing the subjunctive is introduced by **que.** The third and final use of the subjunctive is in adverbial clauses. In this instance the dependent clause, introduced by an adverbial conjunction rather than by **que,** modifies the verb of the main clause.

MAIN CLAUSE CONTAINING A VERB	QUALIFYING STATEMENT FUNCTIONING AS AN ADVERB
Yo trabajo *I am working*	para que coma mi familia. *so that my family can eat.*

Here the clause introduced by the adverbial conjunction **para que** indicates the reason for working.

The use of the subjunctive in adverbial clauses can be divided into three categories: subjunctive in adverbial clauses of purpose and proviso, subjunctive in adverbial clauses of time, and subjunctive after **aunque.** The next three sections of the **Gramática esencial** will explain these categories.

80. Subjunctive in Adverbial Clauses of Purpose and Proviso

Me ha pedido que no haga algunas conexiones para que el precio del trabajo sea más bajo.

The adverbial conjunctions **para que** (*in order that, so that*), **a menos que** (*unless*), **con tal (de) que** (*provided that*), and **en caso de que** (*in case*) always require the use of the subjunctive in the dependent clause, because they stipulate a condition that does not yet exist.

Note: Common source of confusion for students is similarity between prepositions and conjunctions. Compound prepositions and conjunctions must be learned as single units, not separate words. Students must also be made aware of respective functions. Give them simple rule: Preposition introduces infinitive (among other words), while conjunction introduces conjugated verb.

Le dio ese libro **para que** entendiera mejor la psiquiatría.	*He gave him that book so that he would understand psychiatry better.*
No le daré crédito **a menos que** trabaje.	*I will not grant (give) him credit unless he works.*
Iré a ver al contador **con tal de que** Ud. vaya también.	*I will go to see the accountant on the condition that you go also.*
No lo reciba **en caso de que** venga a hacerle una entrevista.	*Do not receive him in case he comes to interview you.*

Actividades

Expansion A, B: After reviewing A and B, write these verbs and phrases on board: *arreglar una pared, instalar la tubería, trabajar, repararla, pintar mi cuarto.* Then ask following questions, which students answer using words on board: **1.** *¿Para qué lleva Ud. la máquina de afeitar al mecánico?* **2.** *¿Para qué llamará Ud. al fontanero?* **3.** *¿Para qué necesitamos un albañil?* **4.** *¿Para qué va a llamar al pintor?* **5.** *¿Para qué le pagan a Ud.?*

Optional: Read these sentences; students indicate whether they contain preposition or adverbial conjunction: **1.** *Conversaremos en español a menos que ellos no lo hablen.* **2.** *Lo invitaré a ir con tal de que lo vea.* **3.** *No me importa trabajar mucho con tal de ganar buen sueldo.* **4.** *Mi amiga irá a España en caso de tener dinero.* **5.** *Pediré vino en el restaurante con tal de que tú lo pidas también.*

A. Una recomendación. Complete con la forma correcta del verbo entre paréntesis.

En caso de que Ud. (necesitar[1]) un carpintero, llame a Carlos Suárez. Es muy bueno, pero cobra mucho. Por eso, no lo llame a menos que Ud. (tener[2]) bastante dinero. Carlos trabaja con cuidado para que su trabajo siempre (ser[3]) bueno; en mi casa el año pasado él no pudo hacer cierta reparación y salió en seguida para (comprar[4]) la herramienta apropiada. Vale la pena pagar mucho con tal de que el trabajo (quedar)[5] bien.

B. Para obtener un buen trabajo. Imagine que su compañero/a busca trabajo. Déle consejos según el modelo.

> MODELO: el día de la entrevista salir de tu casa temprano / para que / llegar a tiempo →
> El día de la entrevista sal de tu casa temprano para que llegues a tiempo.

1. llevar un traje / para que / la jefa tener una buena impresión
2. llegar a su oficina un poco temprano / a menos que / tú realmente no querer el empleo
3. hacerle tú preguntas sobre la compañía / para que / ver que tú tener mucho interés
4. no hablar mucho de ti mismo/a / a menos que / la jefa hacerte primero preguntas sobre ti
5. no pedir más dinero / con tal de que / el sueldo ser suficiente
6. después de la entrevista escribirle una carta / para que / ella saber que tú ser muy cortés

81. Subjunctive in Adverbial Clauses of Time

El dueño quiere que yo termine las paredes antes de que se instale el aislamiento.

A subjunctive is required whenever an expression of time introduces a statement about something that hasn't happened yet. If future time is not implied, a verb in the indicative is used. This is always the case when the main verb is in the present tense, indicates habitual action, or is in a past tense. Compare the uses in the chart below.

TIME EXPRESSION	WITH PRESENT OR PAST (INDICATIVE)	WITH FUTURE (SUBJUNCTIVE)
cuando	Siempre se lo doy cuando lo **pide.** *I always give it to him when he asks for it.*	Se lo daré cuando lo **pida.** *I'll give it to him when he asks for it.*
después (de) que	Fui después (de) que **llegaste.** *I went after you arrived.*	Iré después (de) que **llegues.** *I shall go after you arrive.*
hasta que	Siempre trabajaba hasta que ella **salía.** *He always worked until she left.*	Trabajará hasta que ella **salga.** *He will work until she leaves.*
tan pronto como	Comenzamos a pintar tan pronto como **vinieron.** *We began to paint as soon as they came.*	Comenzaremos a pintar tan pronto como **vengan.** *We will begin to paint as soon as they come.*

NOTE: Because of its meaning, the conjunction **antes (de) que** (*before*) is always used with the subjunctive.

Él no podrá volver antes de que terminen su trabajo el albañil y el pintor.

He won't be able to return before the bricklayer and the painter finish their work.

Actividades

Optional: For further practice after completing A, B, and C, write these infinitives on board: *ponerse, recibir, salir, sentarse, llamar, consultar, dar, escoger, tener, ver.* Then have students use them to complete following sentences: **1.** *Sentiremos menos frío después de que...* **2.** *Mandé un regalo a la novia tan pronto como...* **3.** *Preséntele la cuenta antes de que...* **4.** *Podíamos hablarle después de que...* **5.** *No saldré de aquí hasta que las muchachas...* **6.** *Estaba más contento después de que nosotros...* **7.** *Llámeme tan pronto como...* **8.** *Ud. lo instalará cuando...*

A. De ayer a mañana. Complete con la forma correcta del verbo entre paréntesis.

1. Esperaron hasta que el ingeniero (hacer) la instalación.
   Esperarán hasta que el ingeniero (hacer) la instalación.
2. Habló después de que la socióloga (terminar) la discusión.
   Hablará después de que la socióloga (terminar) la discusión.
3. No quería dar una opinión antes de que la arquitecta (anunciar) sus planes.
   No va a dar una opinión antes de que la arquitecta (anunciar) sus planes.
4. Comenzó sus estudios cuando (poder) ahorrar suficiente dinero.
   Comenzará sus estudios cuando (poder) ahorrar suficiente dinero.
5. Vino después de que yo (llamarlo).
   Vendrá después de que yo (llamarlo).

B. ¿Qué hará Ud. hoy tan pronto como... ? Invente un monólogo en serie, según el modelo.

   MODELO: Tan pronto como me levante hoy, me bañaré. Tan pronto como me bañe hoy,...

1. despertarse
2. ducharse
3. afeitarse
4. vestirse
5. desayunarse
6. salir de casa
7. tomar el autobús
8. ir a mis clases
9. ver a mis amigos
10. ___¿?___

C. Cambie rápidamente las acciones del ejercicio B al pasado.

   MODELO: Tan pronto como me levanté ayer, me bañé. Tan pronto como me bañé ayer,...

82. Subjunctive After *aunque*

If a speaker sees an event as a mere possibility when making a statement introduced by **aunque** (*although, even if*), he or she must use the subjunctive.

Presentation: Use of subjunctive after *aunque* depends strictly on speaker's attitude, although subjunctive is used more frequently when main verb is in future tense and indicative more often when main verb is in past.

Juan no será nunca un gran músico, aunque practique todos los días.	*Juan will never be a great musician even if he may practice every day.*
Aunque ella tenga dinero en efectivo, pagará con un cheque.	*Although she may have the cash, she will pay with a check.*

If the event is seen as a fact and not as a possibility, the speaker uses the indicative.

Juan no será nunca un gran músico, aunque practica todos los días.	*Juan will never be a great musician even though he practices every day.*
Aunque ella tendrá dinero en efectivo, pagará con un cheque.	*Although she will have the cash, she will pay with a check.*

In the last two sentences, *he practices every day* and *she will have the cash* are seen as actual facts.

Actividad

¿Subjuntivo o no? Complete con la forma apropiada del verbo entre paréntesis.

1. María es millonaria.
   Aunque ella (ser) rica, vive en una casa muy pequeña.
2. Su hermano Juan es muy simpático, pero no muy inteligente.
   Aunque Juan no (ser) un genio, siempre saca buenas notas porque estudia mucho.
3. Su otro hermano, Tomás, es un técnico muy bueno, pero siempre cobra precios razonables.
   Tomás hará un buen trabajo aunque no (cobrar) mucho.
4. Su padre vuelve hoy pero ella no sabe a qué hora llega el tren.
   Aunque él (llegar) tarde, lo esperamos para cenar.
5. María no necesita la ayuda de su padre, pero tal vez sus hermanos la necesiten.
   Su padre insiste en ayudarles, aunque no (necesitar) nada.

Para resumir y repasar

A. En persona: El buen profesional (La buena profesional). Hable con un compañero (una compañera) de las cualidades y habilidades necesarias para que una persona sea un buen profesional (una buena profesional) en las siguientes carreras.

Posibilidades: gustarle las matemáticas, ser bilingüe, conocer bien el cuerpo humano, ser un experto (una experta) en leyes, gustarle ayudar a la gente, tener paciencia, ser una persona analítica, seguir los últimos avances médicos, poder hablar en público, ser una persona comprensiva (*understanding*)

> MODELOS: contador(a) →
> Para que sea un buen contador (una buena contadora), una persona debe tener mucha experiencia con muchos tipos de cuentas.
> Con tal de que a una persona le guste trabajar con los números, será un buen contador (una buena contadora).

1. maestro/a	3. ingeniero/a	5. psiquiatra
2. abogado/a	4. médico/a	6. dentista

B. El asaltante y la cajera: acciones y reacciones. Complete las siguientes oraciones según el modelo.

MODELO: A la cajera: Si Ud. gritar, ...
          Si Ud. gritara, usaría este revólver.

1. Si Ud. cooperar conmigo, ...
2. Si Ud. no llamar a la policía, ...
3. Si Ud. darme billetes, ...

MODELO: Al asaltante: Si Ud. ahorrar dinero, ...
          Si Ud. ahorrara dinero, no tendría que robar bancos.

4. Si Ud. no tener un cómplice, ...
5. Si Ud. ser más... , ...
6. Si Ud. matar... , ...

COMUNICACIÓN

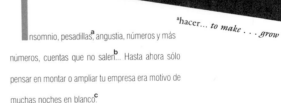

Cómo montar o hacer crecer[a] tu empresa sin perder el sueño.

[a]hacer... *to make . . . grow*

De la vida real

IGUALDAD DE LA MUJER EN EL PLAN DE EMPLEO

En el Plan de Empleo destacan[a] los programas de formación dirigidos a nuevas empresarias, que incluyen la posibilidad de conseguir apoyo[b] a las empresas promovidas[c] por mujeres durante su primer año de actividad.

[a]*nightmares*
[b]no... *don't come out right*
[c]en... *blank (sleepless)*
[d]*City Halls*
[e]*Labor Unions*
[f]puesto... *come to an agreement*
[g]*to create*
[h]*enterprising*

Insomnio, pesadillas,[a] angustia, números y más números, cuentas que no salen[b]... Hasta ahora sólo pensar en montar o ampliar tu empresa era motivo de muchas noches en blanco.[c]

Hoy, la Comunidad, Ayuntamientos,[d] Sindicatos[e] y Empresarios nos hemos puesto de acuerdo[f] para echarte una mano. Porque queremos crear[g] empleo. Y sabemos que eres tú quien puede hacerlo posible. Para eso está el Plan de Empleo en la Comunidad de Madrid. Dirigido a jóvenes. A pequeños y medianos empresarios. A gente tan emprendedora[h] como tú.

A. Plan de empleo. Conteste las preguntas.

1. Según el anuncio, ¿cómo es, para la mayoría de las personas, la experiencia de montar una empresa?
2. ¿Quiénes se han puesto de acuerdo para comenzar este plan?
3. ¿Por qué lo han comenzado?
4. ¿A quiénes está dirigido el plan?
5. ¿Es este plan sólo para los hombres?
6. ¿Qué incluyen los programas para las empresarias?

Importante Empresa

Solicita para trabajar en Caracas

Arquitecto
o Ingeniero Civil

Requisitos:
— Para realizar[a] asistenca técnica a la industria de la construcción
— Bilingüe (español-inglés)
— Con vehículo propio
— Dispuesto a[b] viajar

La Empresa Ofrece:
— Remuneración acorde con la experiencia
— Posibilidades amplias de desarrollo[c]
— Cursos de adiestramiento[d]
— Pólizas de vida[e] y de hospitalización, cirugía y maternidad
— Excelente ambiente de trabajo

Interesados favor enviar currículum vitae[f] al apartado 197, Puerto Cabello.

[a]*to fulfill, carry out*
[b]Dispuesto... *Prepared to*
[c]*development*
[d]*training*
[e]Pólizas... *Life insurance*
[f]currículum... *résumé*

B. Arquitecto o Ingeniero Civil. Primero lea el anuncio. Luego, imagine que Ud. es el empresario (la empresaria) que escribió este anuncio y descríbale a un compañero (una compañera) el empleado (la empleada) ideal para este puesto (*position*).

> MODELO: Busco un arquitecto (una arquitecta) que sea experto en asistencia técnica en proyectos de construcción.

Ahora, imagine que Ud. está buscando trabajo. Usando la lista de lo que la empresa del anuncio ofrece como modelo, describa la empresa ideal.

> MODELO: Busco una empresa que me ofrezca remuneración acorde con mi experiencia.

Para conversar más

A. Ud. y su carrera. Pregúntele a un compañero (una compañera).

1. ¿En qué te especializas? ¿Por qué?
2. ¿Qué otras carreras te interesan especialmente? ¿Por qué?

3. ¿Cuánto dinero esperas ganar?
4. ¿Qué papel han tenido tus padres en estas decisiones? ¿Qué te han aconsejado ellos?
5. ¿Decides a favor de una profesión por el dinero que se puede ganar o por otras razones? Explica.

B. Teatro. En colaboración con un compañero (una compañera), presente Ud. a la clase las siguientes conversaciones.

1. Una madre (Un padre) discute con su hijo/a sus planes para el futuro.
2. Dos amigos/as discuten sus estudios y la matrícula que tienen que pagar.
3. El dueño (La dueña) de un edificio habla de algunos problemas con un fontanero (una fontanera).

C. ¿Es Ud. una persona emprendedora? ¿Qué piensa Ud. de las siguientes ideas y acciones? ¿Le interesan o le dan miedo? ¿Cree que son positivas o negativas? ¿Por qué? Discuta sus reacciones con un compañero (una compañera).

1. ponerse de acuerdo con otros
2. echarles una mano a otros
3. manipular números y cuentas
4. perder el sueño
5. montar una empresa nueva
6. tener siempre una actitud positiva
7. promover la igualdad entre todos
8. inventar programas de formación
9. buscar el apoyo del Ayuntamiento
10. ampliar las posibilidades de las mujeres

MOTIVO CULTURAL

The business and professional worlds in the United States are experiencing radical changes in many areas, including new companies, new methods, new technologies, and new solutions. Nevertheless, many old problems still exist: unemployment, moonlighting that still doesn't provide people enough to live on, inflation, foreign debt, and so on. All these problems exist in Hispanic countries as well, and the solutions to them are not easily found.

Along with modern technological changes, come social changes. Perhaps the most important one today is the entrance of a large number of women into the professional and technical fields. For example, in some Hispanic countries today there are many professional women working as professors, lawyers, doctors, and so forth.

Vocabulario activo

Adjetivos

peligroso/a	dangerous
verdadero/a	real

Conjunciones adverbiales

a menos que	unless
antes (de) que	before
con tal (de) que	provided that
después (de) que	after
en caso (de) que	in case
hasta que	until
para que	in order that, so that
tan pronto como	as soon as

Sustantivos

CARRERAS, TRABAJADORES Y PROFESIONALES

el/la abogado/a	lawyer
la administración de empresas	business administration
el/la albañil	bricklayer
el/la arquitecto/a	architect
el/la carpintero/a	carpenter
el/la contador(a)	accountant
el derecho	law
el/la economista	economist
el/la electricista	electrician
el/la empresario/a	businessman/woman
el/la farmacéutico/a	pharmacist
el/la fontanero/a	plumber
la ingeniería	engineering
el/la ingeniero/a	engineer
el/la obrero/a	worker
la pedagogía	teaching
el/la pintor(a)	painter
el/la plomero/a	plumber
el/la psiquiatra	psychiatrist
la química	chemistry
el/la químico/a	chemist
el/la sociólogo/a	sociologist
el/la técnico/a	technician, serviceperson
el/la trabajador(a) social	social worker
el/la veterinario/a	veterinarian

HERRAMIENTAS Y MATERIALES (*TOOLS AND MATERIALS*)

el aislamiento	insulation
el martillo	hammer
el serrucho	saw
la tubería	plumbing, pipes

OTROS SUSTANTIVOS

la carpintería	carpentry
el/la dueño/a	owner
la empresa	company, business
la escalera	ladder; stairs
la lavadora	washing machine
la matrícula	registration
la reparación	repair
la secadora	(clothes) dryer
el sótano	basement
el título	degree; title

Verbos

caerse	to fall (down)
cobrar	to charge
matar(se)	to kill (oneself)
pintar	to paint

Otras palabras y expresiones

actualmente	currently
conque	and so
echar una mano	to lend a hand
en vez de	instead of
hacer falta	to be needed
montar una empresa	to start a business
tener en cuenta	to take into account
valer la pena	to be worth the trouble

Lectura

Antes de leer

You can more easily remember what you read if you understand the reading selection's underlying structure. To get a quick feeling for the reading's structure and topic, first read just the initial sentence of each paragraph. Together these sentences provide a fairly complete summary of the article. The following initial sentences are from the reading in this section, but in English and out of order. Number them 1–9 to indicate their correct order.

_____ Later they had to familiarize themselves with reveille at four in the morning, . . .

_____ The entrance into and the first days of the course in the Academy were not easy for these women.

_____ Likewise, the statistics about desertion from the academy indicate that women endure . . . better than men.

_____ The majority of the group admit that at the beginning of the course they felt somewhat afraid of handling weapons.

_____ Thirty-two women are graduating as detectives in Bogotá in "urban detective" course number 72.

_____ In the second place, once matriculated, the "blue berets" had to become accustomed to the disciplinary regimen . . .

_____ According to them, female detectives have an advantage over men in some tasks.

_____ Later the women had to get used to dressing daily in bluejeans, . . .

_____ On Colonel Murillo's desk there are résumés of more than fifty female aspirants . . .

The correct order is as follows: 4-2-8-6-1-3-7-5-9.

Now skim the entire selection and, referring back to the preceding exercise, ascertain how the reading is organized by dividing the paragraphs into the following thematic groups: (1) introduction, (2) the women's entry into and becoming accustomed to the military system, (3) the women's success in the academy, and (4) conclusion. Be sure to note the verb tenses used in each group.

Note: The recruitment, training, and deployment of female police officers is now quite common throughout the Hispanic world. Many countries have employed women as traffic officers for years. More recently, the opportunities available to Hispanic women in the various branches of criminology and police enforcement have been expanding rapidly.

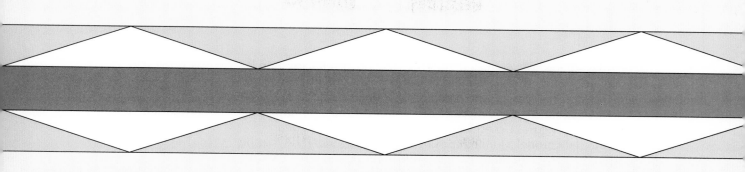

Las boinas azules

Treinta y dos mujeres se gradúan como detectives en Bogotá en el curso número 72 de «detectives urbanos». Son las primeras «boinas[1] azules», y no sólo están capacitadas[2] para *manejar* armas sino también para realizar[3] *labores* de inteligencia y contrainteligencia, desactivación de explosivos e
5 incluso para actuar como escoltas.[4]

El ingreso[5] y los primeros días del curso en la Academia no fueron fáciles para estas mujeres. En primer lugar, tenían que renunciar a casarse y casi abandonar los novios mientras durara el curso. Porque uno de los principales *requisitos* de admisión es que sean solteras entre los 20 y 26 años y que sean
10 bachilleres.[6]

En segundo lugar, una vez[7] *matriculadas,* las «boinas azules» tuvieron que acostumbrarse al régimen disciplinario de la academia, a la vida de *internado,* a las nuevas formas de vestir y a hablar un nuevo lenguaje[8]: el militar.

Luego tuvieron que familiarizarse con el toque de diana[9] a las cuatro de la
15 mañana, el baño con agua *helada* y la salida al comedor para desayunar a las cinco de la mañana. En seguida el arreglo[10] de los salones y la preparación del material didáctico hacia las seis de la mañana, para estar listas para las clases a las siete y media de la mañana.

Posteriormente las mujeres tuvieron que *habituarse* a vestir diariamente
20 con *bluyines,* buzos[11] grises y las ajustadas[12] botas.

La mayoría del grupo admite que al comenzar el curso sintieron algo de *temor* al manejar armas. «Al principio *temblábamos.* Creíamos que la subme- tralladora[13] se iba a *disparar* sola. Después nos fuimos familiarizando con las armas y actualmente las disparamos con mucha seguridad y precisión»,
25 asegura Mildred Mendoza.

Según ellas, las mujeres detectives aventajan[14] a los hombres en algunas labores. «Somos más *detallistas,* discretas e inflexibles. Tenemos a favor la intuición femenina y ésta, aunque no lo crean, ayuda mucho a detectar con más facilidad los riesgos[15].»

You have learned the meaning of this word in relation to automobiles. How would you translate it in relation to weapons? / The English cognate of **labores** is usually used in its singular form.

What would be another meaning for ''requisites''?

Relate to **matricular.**

Relate to ''a person completing an internship.''

If **helar** = *to freeze,* what does this adjective mean?

Think literally: ''habituate oneself.''

bluyines: pronounce clearly and guess. You have learned a different spelling of this English word. Remember the verb **temer.** / The English is close: ''trembl . . .'' What would a gun do all by itself?

If **detalle** = *detail,* what would this English adjective be?

---

[1]*berets* [2]*qualified, equipped* [3]*to carry out, perform* [4]*bodyguards* [5]*entrance* [6]*high school graduates*
[7]*una... once* [8]*lengua* [9]*toque... reveille* [10]*tidying up* [11]*sweatshirts* [12]*tight* [13]*submachine guns*
[14]*have an advantage over* [15]*risks*

30   Asímismo[16], las *estadísticas* de deserción en la academia señalan[17] que las   Examine without initial "e."
mujeres «aguantan»[18] más el régimen disciplinario y las pruebas[19] que los
hombres. Según el coronel José Jacinto Murillo, «la mujer se adapta más a las
exigencias[20] de la academia y tiende[21] a ser más *estable*. Quizá también esto   Again, delete the initial "e."
sea consecuencia de la rigurosa preselección que se hace del personal.»
35   En el escritorio del coronel Murillo reposan[22] las hojas de vida[23] de más de
50 mujeres aspirantes a ser detectives. Pero sólo habrá cupo[24] para treinta
nuevas «boinas azules».

CROMOS, Colombia

Después de leer

A. Preguntas y comentarios.

1. ¿Por qué cree Ud. que estas mujeres detectives se llaman «boinas azules»?
2. ¿Qué distintas labores realizan ellas?
3. En su opinión, ¿por qué tienen que ser solteras, jóvenes y bachilleres?
4. Describa Ud. los varios aspectos de la vida militar.
5. ¿Cree Ud. que las mujeres son más detallistas que los hombres? Dé ejemplos.
6. ¿Cree Ud. en la intuición femenina? Explique.
7. ¿A Ud. le gustaría ser una «boina azul»? ¿Por qué (no)?

B. De memoria. Aquí tiene los temas mencionados en la sección **Antes de leer.** ¿Puede Ud. hacer un comentario sobre cada uno, sin referirse a la lectura?

1. introducción
2. ingresar y acostumbrarse al régimen militar de la Academia
3. éxito (*success*) de las mujeres en la Academia
4. conclusión

Note C: The chart in 2 presents a portion of a circle. In a certain sense, as suggested in 1, the reading starts at the end and ends at the beginning (at the outset the first class of female recruits is graduating and at the conclusion the new class of recruits is beginning).

C. ¡Ud. es el/la detective!

1. Examine el primero y el último párrafos de la lectura. En cierto sentido podemos decir que la lectura comienza al final y termina al comienzo. ¿Por qué?
2. La estructura de la lectura podría representarse gráficamente así:

1 2 3 4 5 6 7 8 9 (párrafos)

```
futuro
presente
pasado
```

---

[16]*Likewise* [17]*indicate* [18]*endure* [19]*tests* [20]*demands* [21]*tends* [22]*lie* [23]*hojas... résumés* [24]*openings (room)*

¿Puede Ud. explicar esta representación? ¿Puede decir cuál es la forma general de la lectura? (Sugerencia: Imagine que la línea se proyecta al infinito. ¿Dónde terminará? No olvide la pregunta 1 de este ejercicio.)

3. La representación gráfica en 2 es lineal. ¿Puede Ud. inventar otra más clara, como un reloj quizá? ¿Cómo lo haría?

Repaso visual

Describa los siguientes dibujos.

Examen de repaso 6

A. Mi viaje. Dé la forma apropiada del verbo entre paréntesis.

Quería ir a la agencia de viajes para (hablar[1]) con el agente. Él me había dicho que (ir[2]) a su oficina a las tres. Mi jefe me dio permiso para que (yo: poder[3]) salir temprano. Me dijo que si (trabajar[4]) diez horas mañana, podría trabajar sólo seis hoy. Nunca esperé que él me (poner[5]) estas condiciones. Pero por fin le dije que así lo (hacer[6]). Llegué a la agencia de viajes con un increíble dolor de cabeza y tuve que pedirle al agente que me (dar[7]) dos aspirinas. Cuando le dije que mi esposa y yo queríamos (visitar[8]) Colombia, me dijo que era necesario que (pagar[9]) el billete de ida y vuelta al contado (*in cash*). ¡Otro dolor de cabeza! Pero ahora mi esposa se alegra mucho de que yo lo (haber[10]) pagado.

B. ¿Viene Alberto a la fiesta? Reacciones de varios individuos. Dé la forma apropiada de **venir**.

JUANA: Espero que Claudio _____.[1] Es un buen chico.

TOMÁS: Si él _____,[2] yo no le hablaré. ¡Es tan aburrido!

RAÚL: No sé si él piensa _____.[3] Pero si no _____,[4] no me interesaría la fiesta para nada.

CLARA: Pues, aunque él _____,[5] yo no me quedo aquí.

C. Las reacciones de Alberto. Dé la forma correcta del verbo entre paréntesis.

A JUANA: Iré a la fiesta para que tú y yo _____[1] (hablar).

A TOMÁS: Aunque _____[2] (tú: llegar) tarde, esperaré hasta que _____[3] (venir).

A RAÚL: Tampoco iría yo a menos que _____[4] (ir) tú.

A CLARA: Es lástima que no _____[5] (cantar) porque quisiera _____[6] (oír)te.

A LUISA: No hay otra amiga que _____[7] (ser) tan buena como tú.

A CARLOS: Necesitas amigos que te _____[8] (decir) la verdad.

A LULÚ: Me alegraba de _____[9] (poder) ayudarte.

D. ¿Quién(es)? Diga con el vocabulario apropiado quién...

1. hace las conexiones eléctricas en una casa nueva
2. pone toda la tubería en esa misma casa
3. hace los planes originales para el edificio nuevo
4. es la madre de la novia, desde el punto de vista del novio
5. le cambia los cheques en el banco
6. está en la cola para ayudar al asaltante del banco
7. repara las secadoras
8. arregla el divorcio entre Ud. y su esposo/a
9. pinta su casa
10. se ocupa de sus asuntos financieros

E. El día de la boda. Complete usando **se + el verbo** como equivalente de la voz pasiva.

1. (Recibir) muchos regalos de los invitados.
2. (Celebrar) la ceremonia en una iglesia muy grande.
3. (Decorar) la iglesia con muchas flores.
4. (Tocar) una hermosa marcha nupcial.
5. (Beber) mucho champán y otras bebidas.
6. (Servir) también canapés y comida internacional.

Appendix One: Verbs

A. Regular Verbs: Simple Forms

INFINITIVE PRESENT PARTICIPLE PAST PARTICIPLE	INDICATIVE						SUBJUNCTIVE		IMPERATIVE
	PRESENT	IMPERFECT	PRETERITE	FUTURE	CONDITIONAL		PRESENT	IMPERFECT[1]	
to speak *speaking* *spoken*	*I speak, do speak, am speaking, etc.*	*I was speaking, used to speak, spoke, etc.*	*I spoke, did speak, etc.*	*I shall (will) speak, etc.*	*I should (would) speak, etc.*		*(that) I (may) speak, etc.*	*(that) I (might) speak, etc.*	*speak* *don't speak* *let's speak*
hablar hablando hablado	hablo hablas habla hablamos habláis	hablaba hablabas hablaba hablábamos hablabais	hablé hablaste habló hablamos hablasteis	hablaré hablarás hablará hablaremos hablaréis	hablaría hablarías hablaría hablaríamos hablaríais		hable hables hable hablemos habléis	hablara hablaras hablara habláramos hablarais	habla tú no hables hable Ud. hablemos hablad no habléis
	hablan	hablaban	hablaron	hablarán	hablarían		hablen	hablaran	hablen Uds.
comer comiendo comido	como comes come comemos coméis	comía comías comía comíamos comíais	comí comiste comió comimos comisteis	comeré comerás comerá comeremos comeréis	comería comerías comería comeríamos comeríais		coma comas coma comamos comáis	comiera comieras comiera comiéramos comierais	come tú, no comas coma Ud. comamos comed no comáis
	comen	comían	comieron	comerán	comerían		coman	comieran	coman Uds.
vivir viviendo vivido	vivo vives vive vivimos vivís	vivía vivías vivía vivíamos vivíais	viví viviste vivió vivimos vivisteis	viviré vivirás vivirá viviremos viviréis	viviría vivirías viviría viviríamos viviríais		viva vivas viva vivamos viváis	viviera vivieras viviera viviéramos vivierais	vive tú, no vivas viva Ud. vivamos vivid no viváis
	viven	vivían	vivieron	vivirán	vivirían		vivan	vivieran	vivan Uds.

B. Regular Verbs: Perfect Forms

INDICATIVE						SUBJUNCTIVE	
PRESENT PERFECT	PLUPERFECT	PRETERITE PERFECT[2]	FUTURE PERFECT[2]	CONDITIONAL PERFECT[2]		PRESENT PERFECT[3]	PLUPERFECT[3]
I have spoken, etc.	*I had spoken, etc.*	*I had spoken, etc.*	*I shall (will) have spoken, etc.*	*I should (would) have spoken, etc.*		*(that) I (may) have spoken, etc.*	*(that) I (might) have spoken, etc.*
he has ha hemos habéis han	había habías había habíamos habíais habían	hube hubiste hubo hubimos hubisteis hubieron	habré habrás habrá habremos habréis habrán	habría habrías habría habríamos habríais habrían	hablado comido vivido	haya hayas haya hayamos hayáis hayan	hubiera hubieras hubiera hubiéramos hubierais hubieran

(each grouped with: hablado comido vivido)

[1]The imperfect subjunctive has another set of endings not used in *Motivos de conversación*: hablase, hablases; aprendiese, aprendieses; viviese, vivieses; hablásemos; aprendiésemos; vivieseis, viviesen
[2]These forms are not covered in *Motivos de conversación*.
[3]The pluperfect subjunctive also features the alternate set of endings: hubiese hablado, hubieses vivido, etc.

C. Irregular Verbs

This section gives only irregular forms, not entire verb conjugations. If a form is not listed, you can assume that it is regular.

andar *to walk; to go*

Preterite anduve, anduviste, anduvo, anduvimos, anduvisteis, anduvieron
Imperfect subjunctive anduviera, anduvieras, anduviera, anduviéramos, anduvierais, anduvieran

caer *to fall*

Present participle cayendo
Past participle caído
Present indicative caigo, caes, cae, caemos, caéis, caen
Preterite caí, caíste, cayó, caímos, caísteis, cayeron
Present subjunctive caiga, caigas, caiga, caigamos, caigáis, caigan
Imperfect subjunctive cayera, cayeras, cayera, cayéramos, cayerais, cayeran

dar *to give*

Present indicative doy, das, da, damos, dais, dan
Preterite di, diste, dio, dimos, disteis, dieron
Present subjunctive dé, des, dé, demos, deis, den
Imperfect subjunctive diera, dieras, diera, diéramos, dierais, dieran

decir *to say; to tell*

Present participle diciendo
Past participle dicho
Present indicative digo, dices, dice, decimos, decís, dicen
Preterite dije, dijiste, dijo, dijimos, dijisteis, dijeron
Present subjunctive diga, digas, diga, digamos, digáis, digan
Imperfect subjunctive dijera, dijeras, dijera, dijéramos, dijerais, dijeran
Future diré, dirás, dirá, diremos, diréis, dirán
Conditional diría, dirías, diría, diríamos, diríais, dirían
Imperative di

estar *to be*

Present indicative estoy, estás, está, estamos, estáis, están
Preterite estuve, estuviste, estuvo, estuvimos, estuvisteis, estuvieron
Present subjunctive esté, estés, esté, estemos, estéis, estén
Imperfect subjunctive estuviera, estuvieras, estuviera, estuviéramos, estuvierais, estuvieran

haber *to have*

Present indicative he, has, ha, hemos, habéis, han
Preterite hube, hubiste, hubo, hubimos, hubisteis, hubieron
Present subjunctive haya, hayas, haya, hayamos, hayáis, hayan
Imperfect subjunctive hubiera, hubieras, hubiera, hubiéramos, hubierais, hubieran
Future habré, habrás, habrá, habremos, habréis, habrán
Conditional habría, habrías, habría, habríamos, habríais, habrían

hacer *to do; to make*

Past participle hecho
Present indicative hago, haces, hace, hacemos, hacéis, hacen
Preterite hice, hiciste, hizo, hicimos, hicisteis, hicieron
Present subjunctive haga, hagas, haga, hagamos, hagáis, hagan
Imperfect subjunctive hiciera, hicieras, hiciera, hiciéramos, hicierais, hicieran
Future haré, harás, hará, haremos, haréis, harán
Conditional haría, harías, haría, haríamos, haríais, harían
Imperative haz

ir *to go*

Present participle yendo
Present indicative voy, vas, va, vamos, vais, van
Imperfect indicative iba, ibas, iba, íbamos, ibais, iban
Preterite fui, fuiste, fue, fuimos, fuisteis, fueron
Present subjunctive vaya, vayas, vaya, vayamos, vayáis, vayan
Imperfect subjunctive fuera, fueras, fuera, fuéramos, fuerais, fueran
Imperative ve

oír *to hear*

Present participle oyendo
Past participle oído
Present indicative oigo, oyes, oye, oímos, oís, oyen
Preterite oí, oíste, oyó, oímos, oísteis, oyeron
Present subjunctive oiga, oigas, oiga, oigamos, oigáis, oigan
Imperfect subjunctive oyera, oyeras, oyera, oyéramos, oyerais, oyeran
Imperative oye

poder *to be able, can*

Present participle pudiendo
Preterite pude, pudiste, pudo, pudimos, pudisteis, pudieron
Imperfect subjunctive pudiera, pudieras, pudiera, pudiéramos, pudierais, pudieran
Future podré, podrás, podrá, podremos, podréis, podrán
Conditional podría, podrías, podría, podríamos, podríais, podrían

poner *to put, place*

Past participle puesto
Present indicative pongo, pones, pone, ponemos, ponéis, ponen
Preterite puse, pusiste, puso, pusimos, pusisteis, pusieron
Present subjunctive ponga, pongas, ponga, pongamos, pongáis, pongan
Imperfect subjunctive pusiera, pusieras, pusiera, pusiéramos, pusierais, pusieran
Future pondré, pondrás, pondrá, pondremos, pondréis, pondrán
Conditional pondría, pondrías, pondría, pondríamos, pondríais, pondrían
Imperative pon

Like **poner: componer** *(to compose)*, **oponer** *(to oppose)*, **proponer** *(to propose)*

377

querer *to wish, want*
Preterite quise, quisiste, quiso, quisimos, quisisteis, quisieron
Imperfect subjunctive quisiera, quisieras, quisiera, quisiéramos, quisierais, quisieran
Future querré, querrás, querrá, querremos, querréis, querrán
Conditional querría, querrías, querría, querríamos, querríais, querrían

saber *to know*
Present indicative sé, sabes, sabe, sabemos, sabéis, saben
Preterite supe, supiste, supo, supimos, supisteis, supieron
Present subjunctive sepa, sepas, sepa, sepamos, sepáis, sepan
Imperfect subjunctive supiera, supieras, supiera, supiéramos, supierais, supieran
Future sabré, sabrás, sabrá, sabremos, sabréis, sabrán
Conditional sabría, sabrías, sabría, sabríamos, sabríais, sabrían

salir *to go out, leave*
Present indicative salgo, sales, sale, salimos, salís, salen
Present subjunctive salga, salgas, salga, salgamos, salgáis, salgan
Future saldré, saldrás, saldrá, saldremos, saldréis, saldrán
Conditional saldría, saldrías, saldría, saldríamos, saldríais, saldrían
Imperative sal

ser *to be*
Present indicative soy, eres, es, somos, sois, son
Imperfect indicative era, eras, era, éramos, erais, eran
Preterite fui, fuiste, fue, fuimos, fuisteis, fueron
Present subjunctive sea, seas, sea, seamos, seáis, sean
Imperfect subjunctive fuera, fueras, fuera, fuéramos, fuerais, fueran
Imperative sé

tener *to have*
Present indicative tengo, tienes, tiene, tenemos, tenéis, tienen
Preterite tuve, tuviste, tuvo, tuvimos, tuvisteis, tuvieron
Present subjunctive tenga, tengas, tenga, tengamos, tengáis, tengan
Imperfect subjunctive tuviera, tuvieras, tuviera, tuviéramos, tuvierais, tuvieran
Future tendré, tendrás, tendrá, tendremos, tendréis, tendrán
Conditional tendría, tendrías, tendría, tendríamos, tendríais, tendrían
Imperative ten

Like tener: detener (*to detain*), mantener (*to maintain*)

traer *to bring*
Present participle trayendo
Past participle traído
Present indicative traigo, traes, trae, traemos, traéis, traen
Preterite traje, trajiste, trajo, trajimos, trajisteis, trajeron
Present subjunctive traiga, traigas, traiga, traigamos, traigáis, traigan
Imperfect subjunctive trajera, trajeras, trajera, trajéramos, trajerais, trajeran

valer *to be worth*
Present indicative valgo, vales, vale, valemos, valéis, valen
Present subjunctive valga, valgas, valga, valgamos, valgáis, valgan
Future valdré, valdrás, valdrá, valdremos, valdréis, valdrán
Conditional valdría, valdrías, valdría, valdríamos, valdríais, valdrían

venir *to come*
Present participle viniendo
Present indicative vengo, vienes, viene, venimos, venís, vienen
Preterite vine, viniste, vino, vinimos, vinisteis, vinieron
Present subjunctive venga, vengas, venga, vengamos, vengáis, vengan
Imperfect subjunctive viniera, vinieras, viniera, viniéramos, vinierais, vinieran
Future vendré, vendrás, vendrá, vendremos, vendréis, vendrán
Conditional vendría, vendrías, vendría, vendríamos, vendríais, vendrían
Imperative ven

ver *to see*
Past participle visto
Present indicative veo, ves, ve, vemos, veis, ven
Imperfect indicative veía, veías, veía, veíamos, veíais, veían
Preterite vi, viste, vio, vimos, visteis, vieron
Present subjunctive vea, veas, vea, veamos, veáis, vean

D. Stem-Changing Verbs

1. e → ie and o → ue

comenzar *to begin*
Present indicative comienzo, comienzas, comienza, comenzamos, comenzáis, comienzan
Present subjunctive comience, comiences, comience, comencemos, comencéis, comiencen

volver *to return*
Present indicative vuelvo, vuelves, vuelve, volvemos, volvéis, vuelven
Present subjunctive vuelva, vuelvas, vuelva, volvamos, volváis, vuelvan
Imperative vuelve

Verbs with similar changes are as follows: **acostarse (ue)** (*to go to bed*), **cerrar (ie)** (*to close*), **costar (ue)** (*to cost*), **doler (ue)** (*to hurt*), **empezar (ie)** (*to begin*), **encontrar (ue)** (*to meet*), **entender (ie)** (*to understand*), **jugar (ue)** (*to play*), **llover (ue)** (*to rain*), **negar (ie)** (*to deny*), **nevar (ie)** (*to snow*), **pensar (ie)** (*to think*), **perder (ie)** (*to lose*), **querer (ie)** (*to wish, want*), **sentarse (ie)** (*to sit down*)

2. e → ie, i and o → ue, u

preferir *to prefer*
Present participle prefiriendo
Present indicative prefiero, prefieres, prefiere, preferimos, preferís, prefieren
Preterite preferí, preferiste, prefirió, preferimos, preferisteis, prefirieron

Present subjunctive prefiera, prefieras, prefiera, prefiramos, prefiráis, prefieran
Imperfect subjunctive prefiriera, prefirieras, prefiriera, prefiriéramos, prefirierais, prefirieran

dormir *to sleep*
Present participle durmiendo
Present indicative duermo, duermes, duerme, dormimos, dormís, duermen
Preterite dormí, dormiste, durmió, dormimos, dormisteis, durmieron
Present subjunctive duerma, duermas, duerma, durmamos, durmáis, duerman
Imperfect subjunctive durmiera, durmieras, durmiera, durmiéramos, durmierais, durmieran

Verbs with similar changes are as follows: **divertirse (ie, i)** (*to enjoy oneself*), **morir (ue, u)** (*to die*), **sentir (ie, i)** (*to feel*)

3. e → i, i

pedir *to ask for*
Present participle pidiendo
Present indicative pido, pides, pide, pedimos, pedís, piden
Preterite pedí, pediste, pidió, pedimos, pedisteis, pidieron
Present subjunctive pida, pidas, pida, pidamos, pidáis, pidan
Imperfect subjunctive pidiera, pidieras, pidiera, pidiéramos, pidierais, pidieran

Other -ir verbs of this type are as follows: **repetir (i, i)** (*to repeat*), **seguir (i, i)** (*to follow*), **servir (i, i)** (*to serve*)

E. Verbs with Spelling (Orthographic) Changes

1. c → qu

buscar *to look for*
Preterite busqué, buscaste, buscó, buscamos, buscasteis, buscaron
Present subjunctive busque, busques, busque, busquemos, busquéis, busquen

Like **buscar: explicar** (*to explain*), **sacar** (*to take out*), **significar** (*to mean*), **tocar** (*to play music*)

2. c → zc

conocer *to know, be acquainted*
Present indicative conozco, conoces, conoce, conocemos, conocéis, conocen
Present subjunctive conozca, conozcas, conozca, conozcamos, conozcáis, conozcan

Like **conocer: aparecer** (*to appear*), **ofrecer** (*to offer*)

3. z → c

comenzar (ie) *to begin*
Preterite comencé, comenzaste, comenzó, comenzamos, comenzasteis, comenzaron
Present subjunctive comience, comiences, comience, comencemos, comencéis, comiencen

Like **comenzar: cruzar** (*to cross*), **empezar (ie)** (*to begin*), **organizar** (*to organize*)

4. g → gu

llegar *to arrive*
Preterite llegué, llegaste, llegó, llegamos, llegasteis, llegaron
Present subjunctive llegue, llegues, llegue, lleguemos, lleguéis, lleguen

Like **llegar: jugar (ue)** (*to play*), **negar (ie)** (*to deny*), **pagar** (*to pay*)

5. g → j

corregir (i, i) *to correct*
Present indicative corrijo, corriges, corrige, corregimos, corregís, corrigen
Present subjunctive corrija, corrijas, corrija, corrijamos, corrijáis, corrijan

Like **corregir: dirigir** (*to direct*), **escoger** (*to choose*), **proteger** (*to protect*)

6. gu → g

seguir (i, i) *to follow*
Present indicative sigo, sigues, sigue, seguimos, seguís, siguen
Present subjunctive siga, sigas, siga, sigamos, sigáis, sigan

7. i → y

creer *to believe*
Preterite creí, creíste, creyó, creímos, creísteis, creyeron
Imperfect subjunctive creyera, creyeras, creyera, creyéramos, creyerais, creyeran

Like **creer: leer** (*to read*)

construir *to build, construct*
Present indicative construyo, construyes, construye, construimos, construís, construyen
Preterite construí, construiste, construyó, construimos, construisteis, construyeron
Present subjunctive construya, construyas, construya, construyamos, construyáis, construyan
Imperfect subjunctive construyera, construyeras, construyera, construyéramos, construyerais, construyeran

Like **construir: contribuir** (*to contribute*), **incluir** (*to include*)

Appendix Two: Punctuation, Capitalization, and Syllabication

A. Punctuation

Generally speaking, Spanish uses punctuation marks very much as English does. Note, however, the following exceptions:

1. Spanish uses inverted initial interrogation and exclamation marks.

   ¿Cómo se llama Ud.?
   ¡Qué clase!

2. Spanish uses dashes rather than quotation marks to set off the discourse of speakers.

   —Se lo daré ahora mismo—dijo el vendedor.

3. The comma is used more frequently in Spanish to separate adjectival and adverbial phrases of more than three or four words.

   Más hermosa que nunca, se presentó en la recepción, acompañada por su hermana.

   On the other hand, no comma is used in Spanish when a conjunction precedes the last item of a series.

   En ese cajón tengo lápices, bolígrafos, papel y sobres.

4. Spanish reserves quotation marks for words or phrases that are not being used in their normal sense, or to indicate that a passage is being quoted textually. In such instances most other punctuation marks usually go outside the quotation marks.

   Luego afirmó: «Reformarse es vivir».

B. Capitalization

The main differences between Spanish and English capitalization are the following:

1. Spanish does not capitalize adjectives of nationality, days of the week, or names of months. (In some Spanish American countries, however, the names of months are capitalized.)

   Era un señor uruguayo.
   Vendrá el lunes, 24 de noviembre.

2. In Spanish only the first letter of a title is capitalized.

   Elogio de la inteligencia y la imaginación

C. Dividing Words into Syllables

1. A single consonant forms a new syllable with the vowel(s) following it. Remember that **ch, ll,** and **rr** are single consonants in Spanish and cannot be separated.

   ca-ma   mu-cho   gui-ta-rra   ca-ba-llo

2. Most consonants followed by **l** or **r** form an indivisible group that counts as one consonant.

   la-bra-dor   a-pli-ca-ción   Pe-dro   ha-blo

3. Other groups of two consonants are divided in the middle.

   Car-men   Al-fre-do   es-tu-dia   Mar-ga-ri-ta

4. If more than two consonants occur between vowels, the last consonant or consonantal group forms a new syllable with the vowel(s) following it.

   cons-truc-ción   pers-pec-ti-va

5. Any combination of two or more vowels containing an **i** or **u** is considered one unit, except when there is a written accent on **i** or **u.**

   Ma-rio   con-ti-nuo   Ma-rí-a   con-ti-nú-o

Appendix Three: Answers to
Para resumir y repasar

LECCIÓN 1

B. 1. Cambie / Complete / Conteste / Repita / Responda **2.** Repita / Pronuncie / Diga **3.** Prepare / Invente / Haga **4.** Conteste / Repita / Haga **5.** Conteste **6.** Dé / Invente / Prepare / Haga **7.** Conteste / Responda **8.** Pronuncie / Diga **9.** Diga / Dé **10.** Invente **11.** Diga
C. 1. Buenos días. Bien, gracias. ¿Y Ud.? **2.** se llama... te llamas... eres... de (Los Ángeles)... de (Los Ángeles)
D. 1. 13 **2.** 21 **3.** 18 **4.** 26 **5.** 11
E. 1. Son las seis en punto. **2.** Son las once y diez y ocho (dieciocho). **3.** Son las nueve y cuarto.

LECCIÓN 2

B. 1. ¿Estudias español todos los días? **2.** ¿Trabajas en la biblioteca? **3.** ¿Deseas hablar dos lenguas? **4.** Preparas bien las lecciones? **5.** ¿Conversas con los compañeros de clase?
C. 1. Compro muchos libros (muchos lápices, muchos cuadernos, mucha tiza). **2.** Visitamos varias ciudades (varios países, varios barrios, varias plazas). **3.** Uso las palabras nuevas (los dibujos nuevos, el mapa nuevo, los lápices nuevos). **4.** Converso con las profesoras famosas (el inglés famoso, la francesa famosa, los españoles famosos).

LECCIÓN 3

B. 1. Toma jugo de naranja. **2.** Bebe una cerveza. **3.** Come un sándwich. **4.** Toma leche. **5.** Bebe vino. *Possible answers:* **1.** El hombre compra billetes de lotería. **2.** Es alto, simpático e inteligente. **3.** Es simpática, generosa y bonita. **4.** Discuten las noticias del día. **5.** Es alto, feo y rico.

LECCIÓN 4

B. 1. es, es **2.** es, está **3.** es, está **4.** Es **5.** es **6.** somos **7.** es **8.** ser **9.** estamos **10.** están

LECCIÓN 5

B. *Possible answers:* **1.** Hace mucho frío en enero en Alaska. **2.** Hace mucho calor en mayo en Acapulco.
3. Hace mucho viento en octubre en Chicago. **4.** Hace mucho sol en Los Ángeles en agosto. **5.** Hace fresco en San Antonio en diciembre. **6.** ...tengo frío. **7.** ...tengo hambre.
8. ...tengo cincuenta años. **9.** ...tengo que estudiar. **10.** ...tengo mucha sed.
C. 1. Sal de casa a las cinco de la tarde. **2.** Ve a la tienda de don Ramiro. **3.** Compra azúcar y plátanos. **4.** Dile a don Ramiro que necesitas plátanos y no bananas. **5.** Trae todas las compras a casa rápidamente.
6. Abre una lata de leche condensada. **7.** Lee las instrucciones de la receta. **8.** Haz mi postre favorito.

LECCIÓN 6

B. 1. hice **2.** salí **3.** tomé **4.** vine **5.** fui **6.** fue
C. 1. Para **2.** por **3.** por **4.** por **5.** para **6.** para
D. 1. es **2.** es **3.** están **4.** son **5.** son **6.** está

LECCIÓN 7

B. 1. Llevé los platos a la cocina.
2. Puse los platos en el lavaplatos.
3. Encendí el lavaplatos. **4.** Devolví la comida al refrigerador. **5.** Barrí la cocina. **6.** Lavé la ropa sucia.
7. Limpié los muebles. **8.** No tuve tiempo y no pude pasar la aspiradora. **9.** Descansé en el sofá.
10. Encendí el televisor.

LECCIÓN 8

B. 1. Llegué a su casa a las ocho y media. **2.** Empezamos a bailar a las nueve y media. **3.** Loli y los pulpitos vino a la fiesta. **4.** Sí, toqué mi guitarra con ellos. **5.** Nosotros bebimos Coca-Cola y vino. **6.** Volví a casa a la una y media.

LECCIÓN 9

B. 1. No, la preparé anoche. **2.** No, las invité el lunes. **3.** Sí, mi tío lo comió después del postre. **4.** Mis amigos lo trajeron ayer. **5.** Sí, mis hermanos los lavaron esta mañana.
C. 1. me afeitaba **2.** llamó **3.** dijo **4.** eran **5.** comenzaba **6.** me enojé **7.** necesitaba **8.** Insistió **9.** había **10.** decidí
D. 1. Bolivia y el Perú están en el hemisferio sur y allí es invierno en junio. **2.** Bolivia no tiene playas. **3.** Es posible esquiar en las montañas de Bolivia. **4.** La Paz es la capital de Bolivia.

LECCIÓN 10

B. 1. Yo me lavé las manos, José no se las lavó. **2.** No me sequé con tu toalla, José se secó. **3.** Yo me visto bien, José no se viste bien. **4.** No me quité los zapatos en la cocina, José se los quitó. **5.** No me enojé con mi abuela, José se enojó con ella.
C. 1. la **2.** los **3.** les, les **4.** te **5.** me, les

LECCIÓN 11

B. 1. Se lo **2.** Se lo **3.** Me las **4.** Me lo **5.** Se la **6.** Se la
C. 1. He hecho **2.** ha mandado **3.** He comprado **4.** he vuelto **5.** he puesto **6.** he despertado **7.** he visto **8.** han muerto **9.** ha abierto **10.** ha visto **11.** ha dicho **12.** ha vuelto **13.** ha escrito

LECCIÓN 12

B. 1. ...pienses estudiar hoy mucho también. **2.** ...vuelva a casa temprano también. **3.** ...durmamos ocho horas también. **4.** ...los busquen también. **5.** ...le pidamos dinero tampoco. **6.** aprenda **7.** lleguen **8.** fumes **9.** salga **10.** tengan hambre también.

LECCIÓN 13

B. 1. esté **2.** sea **3.** esté **4.** vaya **5.** sepa **6.** dé
C. 1. es, pueda **2.** tenga, se cure **3.** es **4.** tomemos **5.** duela, dice

LECCIÓN 14

B. 1. estemos **2.** hay **3.** hayamos **4.** viene **5.** lleguemos
C. 1. tan **2.** como **3.** más alto que

4. el más alto de **5.** tanto **6.** tanto **7.** como

LECCIÓN 15

B. 1. sería **2.** haría **3.** Saldría **4.** iría **5.** disfrutaría **6.** querrían **7.** preferiría
C. *Possible answers:* **1.** Sí, son nuestros. → No, no son nuestros, son suyos. **2.** Sí, es de ellos. → No, no es de ellos, es mía. **3.** Sí, es tuyo. → No, no es tuyo, es mío. **4.** Sí, son vuestros. → No, no son vuestros, son suyos. **5.** Sí, son mías. → No, no son mías, son tuyas.

LECCIÓN 16

B. 1. se casó **2.** nos invitó **3.** hacía **4.** estaba **5.** llevaba **6.** era **7.** estaba **8.** terminó **9.** saludó **10.** me abrazó **11.** me besó **12.** fue **13.** bebimos
C. 1. tiene, se cure **2.** sea, necesite **3.** haya, es **4.** le duele, ha, le

ponga **5.** baje, tome **6.** siga, se cuide

LECCIÓN 17

B. 1. Se come bien en El Gamberro. **2.** Sí, pero se paga mucho también. **3.** Es por eso que nunca se ve a mucha gente allí. **4.** Y es por eso se recibe buen servicio allí. **5.** Tienes razón, uno se divierte mucho en el Gamberro.
C. 1. se cubrieron **2.** se apagaron **3.** se pusieron **4.** se contrataron **5.** se decoró

LECCIÓN 18

B. *Possible answers:* **1.** ..., no pasaría nada. **2.** ..., no tendría que usar mi revólver. **3.** ..., los pondría en esta bolsa y me iría. **4.** ..., no me daría tanto miedo. **5.** ..., no haría esto (robaría bancos). **6.** ..., pasaría el resto de su vida en una prisión.

Appendix Four: Answers to *Exámenes de repaso*

EXAMEN DE REPASO 1

A. 1. el **2.** el **3.** la **4.** el
5. la **6.** el **7.** el **8.** el **9.** el
10. el **11.** el **12.** la
B. 1. Las sillas son nuevas. El mapa es
nuevo. Los dibujos son nuevos. La
cámara es nueva. **2.** La amiga es argentina. El señor es argentino. Las señoras son argentinas. Los profesores
son argentinos.
C. *Possible answers:* **1.** a. Yo deseo hablar español muy bien. b. Nosotros
necesitamos estudiar mucho hoy.
2. a. Juan y María leen la lección **3.**
b. Tú escribes una carta. **3.** a. Uds.
van a casa a las dos de la tarde. b. Ella
viene a la biblioteca con nosotras.
4. a. Él dice «Buenos días» todas las
mañanas. b. Vosotros hacéis la tarea
todos los días... **1.** b. *We need to
study a lot today.* **2.** b. *You are writing a letter.* **3.** b. *She comes to the
library with us.* **4.** b. *You (all) do the
homework everyday.*
D. 1. Son las tres menos diez. **2.**
Son las siete y cuarto. **3.** Son las
diez en punto.
E. 1. amarillo **2.** verde **3.** rojo,
blanco y azul
F. 1. cuatro mil seiscientos cincuenta
y ocho coches **2.** un millón de
mujeres **3.** mis zapatos **4.** nuestras
faldas
G. 1. es **2.** Es **3.** es **4.** son
5. están **6.** está **7.** es **8.** están
9. ser
H. *Possible answers:* **1.** Sí, (No, no)
tengo clases todos los días. **2.** Leo
las noticias en el periódico. **3.** En la
clase leo el diálogo, hago los ejercicios, pronuncio las palabras nuevas y
converso con el profesor (la profesora). **4.** Me gusta hablar con los
amigos. **5.** Sí, (No, no) voy al cine
mucho. Usualmente voy con...
I. 1. buenos precios **2.** Dónde
3. difíciles **4.** baratos pero buenos
5. enseñan varias clases **6.** son
7. joven y lista **8.** cincuenta y tres

EXAMEN DE REPASO 2

A. 1. estos **2.** este **3.** estas
4. estas **5.** Ese **6.** ese **7.** esas
8. ése **9.** ésos **10.** ésos
B. 1. traigo **2.** sé **3.** Pongo
4. oigo **5.** salgo **6.** veo
7. conozco **8.** Voy **9.** tomo
10. llamo
C. 1. llegué **2.** a **3.** Subí
4. dormitorio (habitación, alcoba)
5. abrí **6.** Vi **7.** a **8.** cama
9. dije **10.** salí **11.** Entré **12.** sala
deestar **13.** llamé **14.** salió
15. hice **16.** Llamé **17.** a **18.** pensó
19. vino
D. 1. a **2.** a **3.** a **4.** — **5.** a
6. — **7.** a **8.** a
E. 1. 1. el camarón, **2.** los guisantes,
3. la lechuga, **4.** la banana, **5.** la piña,
6. el melocotón **2. 7.** carrito, **8.** lata,
9. caja, **10.** el paquete, **11.** botella
3. 12. lavar, **13.** pasar, **14.** barrer,
15. cocinar
F. 1. Venga Ud. temprano. **2.** Hablen Uds. con Alicia. **3.** Sea Ud. mi
amigo. **4.** No coman Uds. con
ellos. **5.** Traigan Uds. los platos.
6. No vaya Ud. a esa fiesta.
G. 1. sal **2.** mires **3.** Ve
4. lava **5.** pon **6.** digas
H. 1. para **2.** por **3.** por
4. para **5.** para **6.** para **7.** por
8. para **9.** por **10.** para

EXAMEN DE REPASO 3

A. 1. no la pude estudiar (no pude
estudiarla), porque le presté...
2. mí,... díganle que... **3.** Los voy a
devolver (Voy a devolverlos) mañana,
mi hermano los tiene ahora. **4.** ¿Me
esperabas en... yo te estaba esperando
en... (yo estaba esperándote en...)
B. 1. Eran **2.** salí **3.** Vi
4. llovía **5.** volví **6.** estaba
7. busqué **8.** encontré **9.** tenía
10. Estaba **11.** tenía **12.** esperaban
13. llamé
C. 1. le interesan **2.** les gusta

(encanta) **3.** me hace falta **4.** le
parecen **5.** nos encanta (gusta)
D. 1. Quiere **2.** prefiere **3.** piensa
4. cuesta **5.** visite **6.** Pida
7. comience
E. 1. mis amigos venezolanos **2.** la
profesora ecuatoriana **3.** el cantante
español **4.** un vecino nicaragüense
5. los estudiantes puertorriqueños
6. la señorita costarricense
F. 1. me acuesto **2.** levantarme
3. Despiértate **4.** se baña **5.** se
afeita **6.** lavarse **7.** lávate **8.** nos
sentamos
G. 1. jabón, espejo, toalla, almohada,
manta **2.** aniversario, descubrimiento, América, sur, costa, playa
H. está hablando, está repitiendo, está
pidiendo, estoy muriéndome (me
estoy muriendo), está durmiendo

EXAMEN DE REPASO 4

A. 1. Don José se lo ha
comprado. **2.** Marta se las dio.
3. Ella me lo explicó en una carta.
4. Yo se la di. **5.** Mi hermano y yo se
lo pedimos. **6.** Mi padre nos lo dijo.
B. 1. ha escrito **2.** he visto **3.** ha
dicho **4.** he abierto **5.** he tenido
C. 1. sepan **2.** diga **3.** sepan
4. llame **5.** haya **6.** vayas **7.** vea
8. hables **9.** he **10.** moleste
11. es **12.** hayas **13.** saber **14.** es
15. voy (vas)
D. 1. frenos **2.** gasolineras
3. llantas **4.** doblar, multa **5.** faros,
choque **6.** Raza, desfile, carroza,
caballo, alcalde, gobernador
7. santo, cumpleaños **8.** fiebre, dolor,
inyección, gotas, pastillas
E. *Possible answers:* **1.** ...almuerce también con él. **2.** ...me dirija a él también. **3.** ...vayan también.
4. ...te sientes cerca también.
5. ...piense mucho en mí también.
6. ...nosotros las busquemos también.
7. ...durmamos mucho. **8.** ...llegue a
casa tarde. **9.** ...comiencen a estudiar
también **10.** ...no fuméis tampoco.

F. 1. más grande **2.** tantos, como **3.** mayor, menos **4.** menor **5.** mejor, del **6.** peor

EXAMEN DE REPASO 5

A. 1. sino que **2.** sino que **3.** pero **4.** sino **5.** sino
B. 1. pondré **2.** dirá **3.** hará **4.** querré **5.** vendrán **6.** podremos **7.** tendremos
C. 1. No, no hay ninguna noticia nueva sobre el terremoto. **2.** No, no tuvimos nunca (nunca tuvimos) un terremoto así. **3.** No, no oí nada sobre las víctimas. **4.** No, no me dijo nadie (nadie me dijo) cuántas víctimas hay. **5.** No, ninguno de mis amigos vive en la zona del terremoto. **6.** No, a mí no me gustan tampoco.
D. 1. La tuya está en el ropero también. **2.** Los míos son caros también. **3.** La de él (La suya) es muy buena también. **4.** Los nuestros son de oro también. **5.** La de ellos (La suya) está en el quinto piso también.
E. 1. Sexta, primero de febrero **2.** segundo **3.** noveno **4.** séptimo
F. 1. pidieron **2.** fuera **3.** desearon **4.** divirtiera **5.** tuviera **6.** trajera **7.** recordó **8.** hiciera **9.** pusiera **10.** saliera
G. 1. nube, pájaros, mariposas **2.** arena, gafas, bronceadora, peine **3.** postal, dirección, sello

EXAMEN DE REPASO 6

A. 1. hablar **2.** fuera **3.** pudiera **4.** trabajara **5.** pusiera **6.** haría **7.** diera **8.** visitar **9.** pagáramos **10.** haya
B. 1. venga **2.** viene **3.** venir **4.** viniera **5.** venga
C. 1. hablemos **2.** llegues **3.** vengas **4.** fueras **5.** cantes **6.** oírte **7.** sea **8.** digan **9.** poder
D. 1. el/la electricista **2.** el plomero (el fontanero) (la plomera, la fontanera) **3.** el arquitecto (la arquitecta) **4.** la suegra **5.** el cajero (la cajera) **6.** el/la cómplice **7.** el técnico (la técnica) **8.** el abogado (la abogada) **9.** el pintor (la pintora) **10.** el contador (la contadora)
E. 1. Se recibieron muchos regalos. **2.** Se celebró la ceremonia en una iglesia muy grande. **3.** Se decoró la iglesia con muchas flores. **4.** Se tocó una hermosa marcha nupcial. **5.** Se bebieron mucho champán y otras bebidas. **6.** Se sirvieron también canapés y comida internacional.

Vocabularies

The Spanish-English Vocabulary contains all the words that appear in the text, with some exceptions in the following categories: identical cognates, verb conjugations, regular past participles, absolute superlatives ending in -ísimo/a, adverbs ending in -mente, diminutives, and the proper names of individuals. The number in parentheses after some definitions refers to the lesson in which a word appears in an active (end-of-chapter) vocabulary list; vocabulary not included in an active vocabulary list is not numbered. *P* indicates words appearing in the preliminary lesson. The English-Spanish Vocabulary includes all words and expressions in the active vocabulary lists, as well as all vocabulary needed to do the English-to-Spanish translation exercises in the text.

The gender of nouns is indicated except for masculine nouns ending in **-o** and feminine nouns ending in **-a**. Stem and spelling changes are shown for verbs: **dormir (ue, u)**; **llegar (gu)**. Verbs having both are followed by two sets of parentheses: **comenzar (ie) (c)**. The conjugations of verbs marked *irreg.* are found in Appendix 1.

Words that begin with **ch, ll,** and **ñ** are found under separate headings, following the letters **c, l,** and **n,** respectively. Within words, **ch, ll,** and **ñ** follow **c, l,** and **n.** For example, **leche** would follow **lectura, ella** would follow **elude,** and **año** would follow **anuncio.**

The following abbreviations are used:

adj.	adjective	*Mex.*	Mexico
adv.	adverb	*n.*	noun
arch.	archaic	*obj. of prep.*	object of a preposition
Arg.	Argentina	*pl.*	plural
Col.	Colombia	*p.p.*	past participle
conj.	conjunction	*poss.*	possessive
d.o.	direct object	*prep.*	preposition
f.	feminine	*pron.*	pronoun
fam.	familiar	*refl. pron.*	reflexive pronoun
form.	formal	*s.*	singular
i.o.	indirect object	*Sp.*	Spain
inf.	infinitive	*Sp. Am.*	Spanish American
interj.	interjection	*sub. pron.*	subject pronoun
irreg.	irregular	*subj.*	subjunctive
L.A.	Latin America	*U.S.*	United States
m.	masculine		

Spanish-English Vocabulary

A

a to (P); **a veces** sometimes (1)
abajo below
abandonar to abandon (8)
abandono abandonment
abarrotado/a jam-packed
abierto/a *p.p.* open, opened (10)
abogado/a lawyer (18)
abrazar to embrace, hug (16)
abrazo embrace, hug (16)
abrigo coat (3)
abril April
abrir to open (2)
abrupto/a abrupt
absoluto: en absoluto not at all (16)
abuelo/a grandfather/grandmother
  (4); *m. pl.* grandparents
aburrido/a boring (9)
aburrimiento boredom
acabar de + *inf.* to have just (done
  something) (9)
academia academy
acceso access
aceite *m.* oil (5)
acelerador *m.* gas pedal (10)
aceptar to accept (3)
acera sidewalk
acidez *f.* heartburn
ácido acid
acomodar to accommodate
acompañar to accompany
acondicionado: aire (*m.*)
  acondicionado air conditioner;
  air-conditioning
aconsejar to advise (11)
acontecimiento event
acordarse (ue) to remember
acostarse (ue) to go to bed (9)
acostumbrarse to get used to
acreedor(a) payee (*on a check*)
actitud *f.* attitude
activar to activate (17)
actor/actriz actor/actress
actualmente currently (18)
actuar: actuar como to act; to work
  as
acuático/a water (*adj.*)
acuerdo: de acuerdo a/con
  according to; **ponerse** (*irreg.*) **de
  acuerdo** to agree
acusar to accuse

adaptarse to adjust to
adecuado/a appropriate, adequate
adelantar to get ahead
adelante forward; **de _____ en
  adelante** from _____ up (*prices*)
adelgazar (c) to lose weight
además besides; furthermore (4)
adiestramiento training
adiós good-bye (P)
adivinador(a) fortune-teller
adivinar to guess
adjunto/a enclosed
administración de empresas
  business administration (18)
admirar(se) to admire (oneself)
admisión *f.* admission
admitir to admit to
adonde where; **¿adónde?** (to) where?
adorar to worship
adornado/a ornamented, adorned
adorno ornament
adquirir (ie) to buy; to get
advertir (ie, i) to warn, inform (15);
  to notice
aéreo/a *adj.* air; **línea aérea** airline
aerolínea airline
aeromoza stewardess (15)
aeropuerto airport (15)
afectuosamente affectionately
afeitarse to shave (oneself)(9)
afirmación *f.* affirmation, statement
afortunado/a fortunate
agencia agency; **agencia de viajes**
  travel agency
agente *m., f.* agent (15)
agitar to agitate
agosto August
agotado/a sold out (14)
agradable *adj. m., f.* pleasant (10)
agregar (gu) to add
agrícola *m., f.* agricultural
agua *f.* (*but:* **el agua**) water (2); **agua
  de colonia** cologne (14)
aguantar to endure
ahí there (6)
ahora now (1); **ahora mismo** right
  now (9)
ahorrar to save (17)
ahorros savings
aire *m.* air; **al aire libre** outdoor(s)

aislamiento insulation (18)
ajustado/a snug, tight (*attire*)
ajustar to adjust (*mechanical*)
ajuste *m.* adjustment
al + *inf.* upon (doing something) (9)
ala *f.* (*but:* **el ala**) wing
albañil *m., f.* bricklayer (18)
albóndiga meatball
alcalde/alcaldesa mayor (11)
alcancía piggy bank (17)
alcázar *m.* palace, castle, fortress
alcoba bedroom
alegrarse to be(come) happy (9)
alegre happy, cheerful (13)
alegría joy, happiness
alemán *m.* German language;
  alemán/alemana German
  man/woman (1)
alergia allergy
alfombra rug, carpet (6)
alfombrado/a carpeted
algo something (9); **¿algo más?**
  anything else? (6)
alguien someone (13)
algún, alguno/a/os/as some (7); any
  (13)
alianza alliance
alimentación *f.* nourishment
alimento food
aliviar to relieve
alivio relief
almacén (*also* **almacenes**) *m.*
  department store (2); **almacén de
  ropa** clothing store
almohada pillow (9)
almorzar (ue) (c) to eat lunch (7)
almuerzo lunch (5)
alojamiento lodging
alquilar to rent (7)
alrededor around, about
alternativa option
alto/a tall (3)
altura height
aluminio aluminum
alumno/a student (1)
allí there
amable *m., f.* pleasant, polite (16)
amar to love (16)
amarillo/a yellow (3)
amarrar to tie

ambos/as both
ambiente *m.* environment, atmosphere (*indoors*)
ambulancia ambulance
amenazar (c) to threaten
amigo/a friend (P)
amistad *f.* friendship (16)
amor *m.* love (7)
amoroso/a love (*adj.*); loving, amorous
ampliar to expand
amplificar (qu) to amplify
amplio/a ample
análisis *m. s.* analysis, test
ananá *m.* pineapple (*Arg.*); **jugo de ananá** pineapple juice (*Arg.*)
ancho/a wide
andar *irreg.* to walk; **andar en bicicleta** to ride a bike
angustia anguish
anillo ring; **anillo de boda/de compromiso** wedding/engagement ring (16); **anillo de brillantes** diamond ring (14)
animados: dibujos animados cartoons
animarse to cheer up (9)
anoche last night
antepasado/a ancestor
anterior *m., f.* previous
antes (de) que before (18)
anticipar to advance (*money*)
antiguo/a old (2)
antipático/a nasty, unpleasant
antivariólica smallpox vaccination
anunciar to advertise (11); to announce (15)
anuncio advertisement
añadir to add
año year (4); **el año pasado** last year; **tener** (*irreg.*) _____ **años** to be _____ years old (4)
apagar (gu) to turn off (6)
aparato appliance, fixture
aparcar (qu) to park (10)
aparecer (zc) to appear
apariencia appearance
apartado: apartado postal post office box
apartamento apartment (2)
apasionadamente passionately
apellido last name, surname
aplastado/a flattened, crushed
aplaudir to applaud (7)
aplauso applause

aplazar (c) to postpone
apoyar to support
apoyo *n.* support
apreciar to appreciate
aprender to learn (4); **aprender de memoria** to memorize
aprobar (ue) to approve of
apropiado/a appropriate
aprovechar to take advantage of
aproximación *f.* consolation prize (*lottery*)
apto. (*abbreviation of* **apartamento**) apartment
apuntes *m. pl.* notes
aquel, aquella/os/as *adj.* that, those (6)
aquél, aquélla/os/as *pron.* that (one), those; the former (6)
aquello that, that thing (6)
aquí here (1)
aragonés/aragonesa from Aragón, Spain
árbol *m.* tree (2)
arena sand (13)
arete *m.* (**de plata**) (silver) earring (14)
argumento plot (11)
armario closet, wardrobe (6)
arrastrar to drag
arreglar to arrange; to fix (16); **arreglarse** to work out, be all right (16)
arreglo *n.* tidying up
arroz *m.* rice (5); **arroz con pollo** rice with chicken
arquitecto/a architect (18)
arterial: presión arterial alta/baja high/low blood pressure (12)
artista *m., f.* actor/actress; artist
asaltante *m., f.* robber (17)
ascensor *m.* elevator (14)
asegurar to assure
asentado/a situated
así in this manner, thus; as follows (8)
asiento seat (10); **asiento de pasillo/de ventanilla** aisle/window seat (15); **asiento delantero** front seat (15);
asistir (a) to attend (7)
asociar to associate
aspecto look, appearance; aspect

aspiradora vacuum cleaner (6); **pasar la aspiradora** to vacuum (6)
aspirante *m., f.* applicant, candidate
asunto matter
atacar (qu) to attack (8)
ataque *m.* attack; **ataque al corazón** heart attack (12); **ataque de nervios** nervous attack
atender (ie) to take care of, help (*in a store*)
aterrizar (c) to land (15)
atomizador *m.* atomizer
atrapar to trap
atrás: hacia atrás backward
atrasado/a delayed
atropellar to run over (*with a car*)
atún *m.* tuna (5)
audífonos earphones (7)
aumentar to increase
aun: aun cuando even though
aunque although (11) (14)
autobús *m.* bus (2); **estación** (*f.*) **de autobuses** bus station (15)
autocar *m.* *type of bus (Sp.)*
autoconfianza self-confidence
automóvil *m.* automobile, car (2)
autopista expressway (10)
auxiliar (*m., f.*) **de vuelo** flight attendant (15)
avance *m.* preview (*movie/TV*); *pl.* advance
avanzar (c) to advance
ave *f.* (*but:* **el ave**) bird
avenida (*abbreviation:* **avda.**) avenue (10)
aventajar to surpass
avión *m.* airplane (15)
aviso ad; notice; warning
ayer yesterday (P)
ayudar to help (4)
ayuntamiento municipal government
azafata stewardess (15)
azafrán *m.* saffron (*spice*)
azúcar *m.* sugar (5)
azul blue (3)

B

bachiller *m., f.* high school graduate
bachillerato high school studies
bailar to dance (7)
bailarín/bailarina dancer
baile *m.* dance
bajar to go down; to reduce (*a price*); **bajarse** to get off (*a vehicle*)

bajo *n.* bass (*musical instrument*) (7)
bajo/a short (*person*) (3); low
balcón *m.* balcony, window
balneario resort
balsa raft
banana banana (4)
bancario/a bank (*adj.*)
banco bank; bench (2)
bandera flag (11)
banquero/a banker
bañador *m.* (de dos piezas) (two-piece) swimming suit (14)
bañarse to bathe oneself (9)
bañera bathtub (6)
baño: baño de servicio bathroom for servants; **cuarto de baño** bathroom (6); **traje** (*m.*) **de baño** swimming suit (14)
bar *m.* bar, barroom (2)
barato/a inexpensive, cheap (2)
barbaridad *f.* a great deal, very large amount
barco ship (15)
barra para los labios lipstick (14)
barrer to sweep (6)
barrio neighborhood (2)
base: a base de based on
basílica type of church
bastante quite, rather (9); enough
basura garbage
batería drum set (7)
baúl *m.* trunk (10)
beber to drink (2)
bebida drink
belleza beauty
bello/a beautiful
beneficencia welfare; **Junta de Beneficencia** Welfare Board
besar to kiss (16)
beso kiss (16)
Biblia Bible
biblioteca library (1)
bien well; **muy bien, gracias** very well, thank you
bienvenido/a welcome
billete *m.* ticket (7); lottery ticket (2); **billete de ida/de ida y vuelta** one-way/round-trip ticket (15)
bistec *m.* steak (5)
bisturí *m.* surgeon's knife
blanco/a white (3); **espacio en blanco** blank (space); **noche** (*f.*) **en blanco** sleepless night
blando/a soft (13)

bloquear to block
blusa blouse (3)
bluyines *m. pl.* jeans
boca mouth (9)
bocina (loud)speaker
boda wedding (16); **boda religiosa** church wedding
boina beret
boleto ticket (7)
bolígrafo ballpoint pen (1)
bolívar *m. monetary unit of Venezuela*
bolsa bag (3); shopping bag (5); **bolsa de playa** beach bag (14)
bolsillo pocket (17)
bolso bag, purse (3)
bombero/a firefighter
bombilla light bulb (6)
bombón *m.* chocolate
bonificación *f.* bonus
bonito/a pretty, beautiful (2)
borde *m.* edge; **al borde de** on the verge of
bordo: a bordo on board
borracho/a drunk (10)
borrador *m.* eraser (1)
bosque *m.* forest
bota boot (3)
bote (*m.*) **de vela** sailboat (13)
botella bottle (5)
boticario/a pharmacist
botón *m.* button
botones *m. s.* bellboy (14)
brazo arm (9); **brazo roto** broken arm (12)
breve *m., f.* brief
brevedad: a la mayor brevedad posible as soon as possible
brillante *n. m.* diamond
brillar to shine (13)
brindar to toast (16); to offer
brindis *m.* toast (16)
brisa breeze
broncearse to get a tan (13); **loción** (*f.*) **bronceadora** tanning lotion
buen, bueno/a good (2)
bulto bundle
burlarse (de) to make fun (of), mock (11)
buscar (qu) to look for (3)
butaca seat (*at theater, movies*)
buzo sweatshirt, T-shirt (*Col.*)

C

caballero gentleman; knight

caballo horse; **montar a caballo** to ride a horse
cabaña hut, cabin
cabeza head (9)
cada each, every (4)
caducar (qu) to expire
caer(se) *irreg.* to fall (down) (13)
café *m.* coffee; café, restaurant (2); **café con leche** coffee with milk (5); **café solo** black coffee
cafetalero/a *adj.* coffee
cafetería coffee shop (2)
caja box (5)
cajero/a teller (17); cashier
calcetín *m.* sock (3)
calculadora calculator (1)
calefacción *f.* heating
calidad *f.* quality
caliente *m., f.* hot
calmante *m.* tranquilizer (12)
calor *m.* heat, warmth; **hacer** (*irreg.*) **calor** to be hot (out); **tener** (*irreg.*) **calor** to be (feel) warm
calle *f.* street (2)
cama bed (6); **cama matrimonial** double bed
cámara camera (2)
camarero/a waiter/waitress
camarón *m.* shrimp (5)
cambiar to change; **cambiar un cheque** to cash a check (17)
cambio: en cambio instead
caminar to walk (4)
caminata walk, hike
camino road (13); **camino de** + *place* on one's way to + *place* (15)
camión *m.* truck (10); bus (*Mex.*)
camioneta station wagon (10)
camisa shirt (3)
camiseta T-shirt (3)
campeonato championship
campestre *m., f.* country (*adj.*)
campo countryside (13)
canal *m.* TV channel
canapé *m.* hors d'oeuvre (16)
canción *f.* song (7)
cancha tennis court
cansado/a tired (3)
cansarse to get tired (9)
cantante *m., f.* singer (7)
cantar to sing (7)
cantidad *f.* amount, quantity
capa layer
capacidad *f.* capability
capacitado/a qualified

capital *f.* capital (8)
capitán/capitana captain
cara face (9)
¡caramba! darn it! (10)
caries *f.* cavity (12)
cariños affectionately (*closing to a letter*)
carne *f.* meat; **carne de cerdo/de cordero/de res** pork (5)/lamb (5)/beef (5)
carnet: carnet (*m.*) **de identidad** ID card (17); **carnet** (*m.*) **de manejar** driver's license (10)
carnicería meat market (11)
caro/a expensive (2)
carpeta folder (17)
carpintería carpentry (18)
carpintero/a carpenter (18)
carrera career
carretera highway (10)
carrito (de las compras) *m.* (shopping) cart (5)
carro car (2)
carroza float (*in a parade*) (11)
carta letter (2); playing card (7)
cartel *m.* sign (11)
cartera purse, handbag (3)
cartón *m.* cardboard
casa house, home (2); **casa de socorro** emergency hospital; **en casa** at home (6)
casado/a married (4)
casarse (con) to get married (to) (16)
casero/a *n.* gentleman/lady of the house; *adj.* home; **remedio casero** homemade remedy
casete *m.* cassette (7)
casetera cassette player (7)
casi almost (4)
caso: en caso (de) que in case that (18); **hacer** (*irreg.*) **caso a/de** to pay attention to (16)
castaño/a brown (9)
castillo castle (8)
catarro cold (*illness*) (12)
catedral *f.* cathedral (8)
catorce fourteen
causa: a causa de because of
caza hunting
cebolla onion (5)
celebrar to celebrate (8)
celos *m. pl.* jealousy (16); **tener** (*irreg.*) **celos de** to be jealous of (16)
cena dinner, supper (5)

cenar to eat dinner, dine (5)
centro downtown (2); **mesa de centro** coffee table (6)
Centroamérica Central America
cepillo brush; **cepillo de dientes** toothbrush (14); **cepillo de pelo** hairbrush (14)
cerca (de) near (7)
cereal *m.* cereal (5)
cerrar (ie) to close, shut
cerveza beer (2)
cesta basket
ceviche *m. dish made of marinated raw fish*
cielo sky (13); heaven
ciempiés *m. s.* centipede
ciencia ficción *f.* science fiction (7)
ciento one hundred (2); **por ciento** percent, percentage (17)
cierto/a certain; **es cierto** it's true (12)
cifra figure (*numerical*)
cinco five (P)
cincuenta fifty (2)
cine *m.* movie theater (2)
cintura waist (9)
cinturón *m.* belt
circular *f.* circular letter (17)
cirugía surgery
cirujano/a surgeon
cita appointment (7)
ciudad *f.* city (1)
ciudadano/a citizen
claro/a clear
clase *f.* class; **clase media** middle class; **compañero/a de clase** classmate (1); **sala de clase** classroom (1)
claxon *m.* horn (*car*)
cliente/a client, customer (17)
clima *m.* climate, weather
clínica clinic, hospital
club (*m.*) **de relacionamiento humano** Lonely Hearts Club
cobrar to charge (18); to collect
cocimiento medicinal tea
cocina kitchen (6); **cocina (eléctrica/de gas)** (electric/gas) range, stove (6)
cocinar to cook (5)
cocinero/a cook
coctel *m.* cocktail
coche *m.* car (2)
coger (j) to grab; to take hold of (14)

cognado cognate
cola line (*of people*) (17); **hacer** (*irreg.*) **cola** to stand in line
coleccionar to collect
colegio school; high school (*in some countries*)
colina hill (13)
colocar (qu) to place
colón *m. monetary unit of Costa Rica*
Colón: Cristóbal Colón Christopher Columbus
colonia colony; residential neighborhood; **agua** (*f. but:* **el agua**) **de colonia** cologne (14)
color (*m.*) **café** brown (3)
colorete *m.* rouge, blush (14)
colorido color
collar *m.* **(de perlas)** (pearl) necklace (14)
comedia comedy
comedor *m.* dining room (6)
comentar to comment
comentario commentary
comenzar (ie) (c) to begin (7)
comer to eat (2)
comercial: anuncio comercial ad, (TV) commercial
comerciante *m., f.* merchant (11)
comercio commerce, business (18)
comestibles *m. pl.* food items, provisions (5)
cómico/a comic(al)
comida food (4); (midday) meal; dinner (5)
como since; as (8); like; **como si** as if
¿cómo? how?; what? (P); **¿cómo es/son _____?** what is/are _____ like? (3)
cómoda dresser, chest of drawers (6)
comodidad *f.* comfort
cómodo/a comfortable (3)
compañero/a friend; associate; **compañero/a de clase** classmate (1); **compañero/a de cuarto** roommate
compañía (*abbreviation:* **Cía.**) company (17)
comparar to compare
compartir to share
competencia competition (14)
complejo: complejo residencial residential development
complejo/a complex, complicated
completo/a complete
complicación *f.* complication

cómplice *m., f.* accomplice (17)
componente *m.* component
componerse (*like* **poner**) **de** to consist of
comportamiento behavior
compra purchase; **ir** (*irreg.*) **de compras** to go shopping (3)
comprar to buy (2)
comprender to understand (4)
comprensivo/a understanding
compromiso commitment; **anillo de compromiso** engagement ring (16)
compuesto: estar (*irreg.*) **compuesto por** to consist of
computadora computer (17)
computarizado/a computerized
común *m., f.* common, ordinary
comunicación *f.* communication, connection
comunicar (**qu**) to convey; **comunicarse** to get in touch, call
comunidad *f.* community, group; **Comunidad Europea** European Community
comunismo communism
comunitaria: Junta Comunitaria Community Board
con with (1); **con cuidado** with care, carefully (10); **con gusto** gladly; **con razón** no wonder (5); **con respecto a** with regard to; **con tal (de) que** provided that (18)
concebir (**i, i**) to conceive
concertar (**ie**) to arrange
concesionario/a concessionary
concierto concert
condensada: leche (*f.*) **condensada** condensed milk
condición *f.* condition
conducir (*like* **producir**) to drive (10); to lead to
conductor(a) driver (10); conductor
conectar to connect
conexión *f.* connection; **conexión eléctrica** electrical connection
conferencia conference, convention
confesión *f.* confession
confiar to trust
confidencialidad *f.* confidentiality
confirmar to confirm, reconfirm (15)
confortable *m., f.* comfortable
congreso congress, convention
conjetura conjecture, guess

conjugar (**gu**) to conjugate
conjunto (*musical*) group (7)
conmemorar to commemorate
conmigo with me (15)
conocer (**zc**) to know (be acquainted with) (4)
conocimiento knowledge, notion
conque and so (18)
conquistador *m.* conquistador, explorer (8)
conquistar to conquer
consecuentemente consequently
conseguir (**i, i**) (**g**) to get, obtain (14)
consejero/a adviser
consejo advice; **consejo rector** executive board
conservar to preserve, keep
considerar to consider
consigo with you/him/her/them
consistir en to consist of
constituir (**y**) to constitute
construir (**y**) to construct, build
cónsul *m., f.* consul (11)
consulta doctor's office (12); consultation
consultorio doctor's office (12)
consumo consumption
contador(a) accountant (18)
contaminación *f.* pollution, contamination
contar (**ue**) to relate, tell; to count
contemplar to contemplate, examine
contener (*like* **tener**) to contain
contenido *s.* contents
contento/a happy (3), satisfied
contestar to answer, respond (1)
contigo with you
continente *m.* continent
continua: jornada continua full-time work
continuo/a continuous
contrabajista *m., f.* bass player
contradecir (*like* **decir**) to contradict
contraer (*like* **traer**) to contract, get (*a disease*); **contraer matrimonio** to marry, get married
contrainteligencia counterintelligence
contrariado/a upset (15)
contrario/a contrary, opposite
contrario: al contrario on the contrary

contratar to contract, hire
contratiempo mishap, disappointment (15)
contrato contract
contribuir (**y**) to contribute
convenir (*like* **venir**) to be convenient; to suit
conversación *f.* conversation
conversar to converse, talk (1)
convertirse (**ie, i**) (**en**) to become, turn into (10)
cooperar to cooperate (17)
copa wine glass (4)
copia copy (17)
copiadora copying machine (17)
copo de nieve snowflake (13)
coquetería coquetry, vanity
corazón *m.* heart; **ataque** (*m.*) **al corazón** heart attack (12)
corbata necktie (3)
cordero lamb
cordillera mountain range
córdoba *m. monetary unit of Nicaragua*
cordón *m.* cord, rope
coro choir
coronel(a) colonel
corregir (**i, i**) (**j**) to correct
correo post office (15), mail; **correo central** main post office (10)
correr to run
correspondencia correspondence
correspondiente *adj. m., f.* corresponding
corriente *f.* current (*water*); **corriente** *adj. m., f.* current; **cuenta corriente** checking account (17)
corrugado/a corrugated
cortar to cut
corte *m.* cut
cortés *m., f.* courteous
corto/a short (9)
cosa thing (1)
cosméticos cosmetics (14)
costa coast (8)
costar (**ue**) to cost (7)
costarricense *m., f.* Costa Rican
costo cost
costumbre *f.* custom
creación *f.* creation
crear to create
crecer (**zc**) to grow

crecimiento growth
credibilidad *f.* credibility
crédito credit; **tarjeta de crédito** credit card (3)
creer (y) to think, believe (6)
creo: ¡no lo creo! I don't believe it! (9)
cresta crest
creyón (*m.*) **de labios** lipstick (14)
criar to raise
cristal *m.* (*pane of*) glass (6)
criticar (qu) to criticize
crucero cruise
cruz *f.* (*pl.* **cruces**) cross
cruzar (c) to cross (10)
cuaderno notebook (1)
cuadro picture, painting
cual: el/la cual, los/las cuales which, who, whom
¿cuál(es)? what (is)?; which one(s)?
cualidad *f.* quality
cualquier(a) (just) any, whichever (one); **en cualquier momento** anytime
cuando when; **aun cuando** even though
¿cuándo? when? (1)
¿cuánto? how much?; **¿cuánto cuesta?** how much is it?; how much does it cost? (3)
cuánto/a/os/as how much/how many (3)
cuanto: en cuanto as soon as (9)
cuarenta forty (2)
cuarto *n.* room; quarter (*hour*); *adj.* fourth (14); **cuarto de baño** bathroom (6)
cuatro four (P)
cuatrocientos/as four hundred (2)
cubierto/a *p.p.* covered
cubiertos *m. pl.* silverware (4)
cubo de basura garbage pail (13)
cubrir(se) to cover (oneself)
cuchara spoon (4)
cucharita teaspoon (4)
cuchillo knife (4)
cuello collar (*in a garment*)
cuenta (a largo plazo) (long-term) account (17); **abrir una cuenta de ahorros/corriente** to open a savings/checking account (17); **cuenta corriente/de cheques** checking account (17); **darse**

(*irreg.*) **cuente (de)** to realize; **lo que cuente** what counts; **tener** (*irreg.*) **en cuenta** to take into account (18)
cuento story (16); short story
cuerpo body (9)
cuesta: ¿cuánto cuesta? how much is it?; how much does it cost?
cuestionario questionnaire
cuidado: con cuidado with care, carefully (10); **¡cuidado!** watch out!; **tener** (*irreg.*) **cuidado** to be careful
cuidar(se) to take care (of) (oneself) (12)
culpa: ¿quién tiene/tuvo la culpa? whose fault is/was it?
cultura culture; education
cumbia *dance from Colombia*
cumpleaños *m. s.* birthday (11)
cupo capacity, room (*space*)
curar to cure (12); **curarse** to cure oneself; to heal, get well
curita band-aid (12)
cursiva *s.* italics
curso course, class; school year
cuyo/a/os/as whose

CH

champán *m.* champagne (16)
champú *m.* shampoo (14)
chaqueta jacket (3)
charlar to chat
charro cowboy (*Mex.*) (11)
cheque (*m.*): **cambiar un cheque** to cash a check (17); **hacer** (*irreg.*) **efectivo un cheque** to cash a check (17); **cheque de viajero** traveler's check
chequear (*also* **checar [qu]**) to check
chequera checkbook (17)
chicano/a *American of Mexican descent*
chico/a boy/girl (3)
chisme *m.* piece of gossip
chiste *m.* joke
chocar (qu) to collide, crash (10)
chofer *m., f.* driver (10)
choque *m.* collision
chuleta chop (*meat*) (5)

D

dama lady (10)

danés/danesa Danish
daño: hacer (*irreg.*) **daño** to damage
dar *irreg.* to give (3); **dar las gracias** to say thanks; **dar la mano** to shake hands; **dar un paseo** to take a walk; **dar posada** to provide lodging; **dar(le) miedo** to scare; **dar(le) oxígeno** to give (one) oxygen (12); **darse cuenta (de)** to realize
dato fact; piece of information
de of; from (P); in; about; than (*before numeral*); **de donde** from where (P); **de excursión** on an excursion (8); **de inmediato** immediately; **de nada** you are welcome; **de vacaciones** on vacation
debajo de underneath (7)
deber to owe; must, ought to (7)
débil weak (9)
década decade
decidir to decide (15); **decidirse (a)** to make up one's mind (about)
décimo/a tenth (14)
decir *irreg.* to say, tell (2)
declarar to declare, state
decorar to decorate
dedicar (qu) to dedicate, devote
dedo finger (9); **dedo del pie** toe (9)
definir to define
dejar to allow, permit (11); to leave behind; **dejar de** + *inf.* to stop (*doing something*)
delante de in front of (7)
delantero/a front (15); **asiento delantero** front seat (15)
delgado/a thin (3)
delicioso/a delicious
demás: los/las demás the others, the rest
demasiado *adv.* too much, excessively (10)
demasiado/a *adj.* too, too many
demostrar (ue) to show, prove
dentista *m., f.* dentist (12)
dentro (de) inside, within
departamento apartment; **departamento de sanidad** sanitation department
dependiente/a salesclerk (3)
deporte *m.* sport
deportivo/a sport (*adj.*)
depositar to deposit (17)

depósito deposit; **hoja de depósito** deposit slip (17)
derecha right; **a la derecha** on/to the right (10)
derecho/a straight; **derecho** law (*career*) (18); **todo derecho** straight ahead (10); **facultad** (*f.*) **de derecho** law school
derechos de matrícula registration fees
derredor: en derredor round about, around
desacuerdo disagreement
desafiante *m., f.* defiant
desarrollo development; improvement
desastre *m.* disaster (13)
desayunar(se) to eat breakfast (5)
desayuno breakfast (5)
descansar to rest (6)
descanso *n.* rest
descifrar to decipher
desconocido/a *n.* stranger; *adj.* unknown
descontento/a discontent, dissatisfied
describir to describe
descubrimiento discovery (8)
descubrir to discover
descuento discount
desde since; from; **desde luego** of course
deseable *m., f.* desirable
desear to desire, want (2)
deseo desire, wish
desfile *m.* parade (11); **Desfile de la Hispanidad** Columbus Day Parade (11)
desgraciadamente unfortunately
desierto desert
desodorante *m.* deodorant (14)
desolado/a desolate
despegar (gu) to take off (15)
despertador: (reloj [*m.*]) despertador *m.* alarm clock (9)
despertarse (ie) to wake up (9); **¡a despertar!** wake up! (6)
desprender to get rid of, release
después *adv.* afterward, later (4); **después de** *prep.* after; **después de + inf.** after (*doing something*); **después (de) que** *conj.* after (18)
destacar(se) (qu) to stand out
destino destination
destruir (y) to destroy

detalle *m.* detail
detallista *m., f.* meticulous, detail-oriented
detener (*like* **tener**) to detain, stop
detenido: estar (*irreg.*) **detenido** to be under arrest (10)
deteriorar to deteriorate
determinado/a certain
detestar(se) to detest (each other)
detrás (de) behind (7)
deuda debt
deudor(a) payer (*on a check*)
devolver (ue) to return (something) (7)
día *m.* day (P); **al día siguiente** on the following day; **día del santo** saint's day (11); **hoy día** nowadays (9); **por el día** during the day; **todos los días** every day; **un día** someday
diagnóstico diagnosis
diálogo dialogue
diamante *m.* diamond
diana: toque (*m.*) **de diana** reveille
diario diary
diario/a daily
dibujo drawing (1)
diccionario dictionary (1)
diciembre *m.* December (P)
dictar to dictate
dicho/a *p.p.* said (10)
diecinueve (diez y nueve) nineteen (P)
dieciocho (diez y ocho) eighteen (P)
dieciséis (diez y seis) sixteen (P)
diecisiete (diez y siete) seventeen (P)
diente *m.* tooth (12); **cepillo de dientes** toothbrush; (14) **pasta de dientes** toothpaste (14)
diez ten (P)
diferencia difference
diferente *m., f.* different
difícil *m., f.* difficult (1)
dificultad (*f.*) **para respirar** difficulty in breathing (12)
Dinamarca Denmark
dinero money (3)
Dios *m.* God; **¡Dios mío!** my goodness! (10); **¡por Dios!** for heaven's sake!
diptongo diphthong
dirección *f.* address (15)
dirigir (j) to direct; **dirigirse (a)** to address (oneself) (to) (10); to go to

disciplinario/a disciplinary
disco record; **disco compacto** compact disc (7)
discoteca discotheque
discreto/a discreet
disculparse to excuse oneself, apologize (17)
discurso speech
discutir to argue; to discuss (2)
diseño design
disfraz (*pl.* **disfraces**) costume
disfrutar (de) to enjoy (11)
disgustado/a upset
disgusto quarrel (16)
disparar to shoot
dispuesto/a (a) ready/willing (to)
distancia distance
distinto/a different
distribuidor(a) distributor, dealer
distrito district
disturbio disturbance
diversidad *f.* diversity
diversión *f.* diversion, amusement
divertirse (ie, i) to have a good time (9)
divorciarse (de) to get divorced (from) (16)
divorcio divorce (16)
doblar to turn (10); to bend
doble *m.* double
doce twelve (P)
docena dozen
doctor(a) doctor (12)
dólar *m.* dollar
doler (ue) to ache, hurt, give pain (12)
dolor *m.* pain, ache; **dolor de cabeza** headache (12); **dolor de estómago** stomachache (12); **dolor de garganta** sore throat (12); **el dolor no se me quita** the pain won't go away (12)
doméstico/a domestic
dominante *m., f.* domineering (11)
domingo Sunday (P)
dominicano/a Dominican
dominico/a Dominican (*religious order*)
don title of respect before male first names
dónde where (P); **de donde** from where (P); **en donde** where, in which; **¿dónde?** where? (P); **¿de dónde?** from where? (P)

doña *title of respect before female first names*
dormir (ue, u) to sleep (7); **dormir una/la siesta** to take a nap; **dormirse** to fall asleep (9)
dormitorio bedroom (6)
dos: los/las dos two (P); both
doscientos/as two hundred (2)
dramático/a dramatic
ducado ducat (*old Spanish coin*)
ducha shower (6)
duda doubt; **sin duda** undoubtedly, without a doubt
dudar to doubt (12)
dueño/a owner (18)
dulce *n. m.* candy; *adj. m., f.* sweet
durante during
durar to last
duro/a hard (4)

E

economía economy
economista *m., f.* economist (18)
echar: echar de menos to miss, long for; **echar una mano** to lend a hand (18)
edad *f.* age
edificio de apartamentos apartment building (2); **edificio de oficinas** office building (2)
efectivamente effectively
efectivo: en efectivo *adj.* cash; **hacer efectivo (un cheque)** *m.* to cash (a check) (17)
efecto invernadero greenhouse effect
egiptólogo/a Egyptologist
ejemplo example; **por ejemplo** for example
él *sub. pron. m.* he, it; *obj. of prep.* him, it, himself
elaborar to produce, make
electricista *m., f.* electrician (18)
eléctrico/a electric; **aparato eléctrico** appliance (6); **cocina (eléctrica/de gas)** (electric/gas) stove (6)
electrónico: horario electrónico electronic schedule (15)
elegante *m., f.* elegant
elegir (i, i) (j) to elect, choose
elevado/a high
elevador *m.* elevator (14)
eliminar to eliminate

ella *sub. pron., f.* she, it; *obj. of prep.* her, it, herself
ellos/as *sub. pron.* they; *obj. of prep.* them, themselves
embajador(a) ambassador (11)
embarazada pregnant
embargo: sin embargo nevertheless, however
embarque: tarjeta de embarque boarding pass
embrujado/a bewitched
emergencia: sala de emergencia emergency room
empanada *turnover filled with meat*
empastar to fill in (*a tooth*) (12)
empaste *m.* filling (*for a tooth*) (12)
empeñarse (en) to insist (on)
empezar (ie) (c) to begin, start
empleado/a employee, clerk; **empleado/a de banco/bancario** banker, bank employee (17)
emplear to employ, hire
empleo job, position
emprendedor(a) enterprising
empresa company, business (18); **montar una empresa** to start a business (18)
empresario/a businessman/woman (18)
en in, on (1); **en casa** at home (6); **en cuanto** as soon as; **en efectivo** *adj.* cash; **en seguida** at once (15); **en vez de** instead of (18)
enamorado/a in love (3); **estar (*irreg.*) enamorado/a (de)** to be in love (with) (11)
enamorarse (de) to fall in love (with) (16)
encender (ie) to turn on (7)
encima de on top of, over (7)
encontrar (ue) to find (7)
encuentro *n.* encounter
encuesta poll, survey
enemigo/a enemy
enero January (P)
enfermedad *f.* illness (12)
enfermero/a nurse (12)
enfermo/a ill (3)
enfrente (de) in front (of)
enojado/a angered (9)
enojarse to get angry (9)
enorme *m., f.* enormous
ensalada salad (5)
enseñar to teach (1); to show

entender (ie) to understand (7)
entonces then (3)
entrada entrance, entry (8)
entrar (en) to enter (1)
entre between, among (9)
entregar (gu) to deliver, hand in
entretenimiento entertainment
entrevista interview
entrevistar to interview
envase *m.* container
enviar to send
envuelto/a *p.p.* wrapped
época epoch, time
equipaje *m.* baggage (15)
equipamiento *n.* equipping
equivaler (*like* **valer**) to be equivalent, equal to
equivocado/a mistaken (16)
equivocarse (qu) to make a mistake, be wrong
erradicar (qu) to eradicate
errar to err
escalera ladder (18); **escalera(s)** stair(s) (14)
escándalo scandal
escena scene
escenario stage (*of a theater*)
escoba broom (6)
escoger (j) to choose (15)
escolta escort; bodyguard
esconder to hide
escribir to write (2)
escrito/a *p.p.* written (10)
escritorio desk, writing table (6)
escuchar to listen to (6)
escuela school (4)
ese/a/os/as *adj.* that, those (6)
ése/a/os/as *pron.* that (one), that fellow/character; those (6)
esfuerzo effort
esmeralda emerald
esmero care, neatness
eso that, that thing (6)
espacio space; **espacio en blanco** blank (space)
espalda back (*of person*) (9); **a nuestras espaldas** behind us
español *m.* Spanish (*language*) (1)
esparcir (z) to spread
especial *m., f.* special
especialidad *f.* specialty
especializarse (c) (en) to specialize (in)
especie *f.* species

especificación *f.* specification
espectáculo show, pageantry
espectador(a) spectator, person in the audience
espejo mirror (9)
esperar to hope (11); to wait (for); to expect
espía *m., f.* spy
esposas *pl.* handcuffs; **poner(le)** (*irreg.*) **las esposas** to handcuff (10)
esposo/a husband/wife (4); *m. pl.* married couple
espuma foam
esqueleto skeleton
esquí *m.* skiing (8)
esquiar to ski (8)
esquina corner (10)
estable *m., f. adj.* stable
establecido/a *p.p.* established
establo stable
estación *f.* season (P); **estación de autobuses** bus station (15); **estación del ferrocarril** railroad station (10)
estacionar to park (10)
estadio stadium
estadística statistic
estado state
estampilla (postage) stamp (15)
estante *m.* bookcase (6)
estar *irreg.* to be (3); **estar de moda** to be in style; **estar de turno** to be open all night (*pharmacy*); **estar enamorado/a (de)** to be in love (with) (11); **estar seguro/a (de)** to be sure (of) (12); **estar verde** to be unripe
estatua statue
este *m.* east (8)
este/a/os/as *adj.* this/these (6)
éste/a/os/as *pron.* this (one), these; the latter (6)
estereotipo stereotype
estética *s.* aesthetics
estilo style
estiramiento stretching, lifting
estirar to stretch
esto this, this thing (6)
estómago: dolor (*m.*) **de estómago** stomachache (12)
estratégico/a strategic
estrecho/a narrow
estrella star (13)
estrenar to use something for the first time; to premiere (*a play, movie, etc.*)

estreno premiere (*of a play, movie, etc.*)
estricto/a strict
estructura structure
estuche (*m.*) **de maquillaje** makeup kit (14)
estudiante *m., f.* (male/female) student (P)
estudiar to study (1)
estudioso/a studious
estupendo/a stupendous, wonderful
estúpido/a stupid
etapa stage (*of a project, etc.*)
etiqueta etiquette
evidente: es evidente it's evident (12)
evitar to prevent
examen *m.* examination
excelente *m., f.* excellent
excesivamente excessively
exceso excess
excursión: de excursión on an excursion (8)
exhausto/a exhausted
exigencia demand
exigente *m., f.* demanding (6)
exigir (j) to demand, insist on
exiliado/a person in exile
existir to exist
éxito success
exitoso/a successful; popular; famous
experto/a expert
explicación *f.* explanation
explicar (qu) to explain (10)
explorador(a) explorer
explorar to explore
explosivo explosive
exportar to export
exposición exposition, exhibit
expresar(se) to express (oneself)
expresión f. expression
extenderse (ie) to extend
extenso/a extensive
extranjero/a foreigner
extraño/a *n.* stranger; *adj.* strange
extremo/a extreme

F

fabuloso/a fabulous
fácil *m., f.* easy (10)
facilidad: con facilidad easily
facilitar to facilitate
facturar el equipaje to check the baggage (15)
facultad *f.* university school; college

falda skirt (3)
falso/a false
falta: hacer(le) (*irreg.*) **falta (a uno)** to be lacking; to be needed (18)
faltar to be absent; **faltarle a uno** not to have; to need, be in need of; to be missing
fallar to fail
familiar *adj. m., f.* family
familiarizarse (c) to familiarize (oneself)
famoso/a famous
fanático/a fan (7)
fantasía fantasy
farmacéutico/a pharmacist (18)
farmacia pharmacy, drugstore
faro headlight (10)
fatigar (gu) to tire
fatura sweet roll (*Arg.*)
favor: a favor (de) in favor of; **haga (Ud.) el favor (de)** please; **por favor** please (5)
favorito/a favorite
febrero February (P)
fecha date (P)
felicidad *f.* happiness
felicitación *f.* congratulations (16)
felicitar to congratulate (16)
feliz *m., f.* (*pl.* **felices**) happy, joyful
femenino/a feminine
fenomenal *m., f.* phenomenal
fenómeno phenomenon (13)
feo/a ugly (2)
ferrocarril: estación (*f.*) **del ferrocarril** railroad station (10)
fértil *m., f.* fertile, rich
ficción *f.:* **ciencia ficción** science fiction
fiebre *f.* fever (12)
fiesta party (3)
figura (*human*) figure
fijarse to pay attention
fijo/a fixed, steady
fila row (*of seats*)
filete *m.* steak, fillet (*of beef or fish*)
filosofía philosophy
fin *m.* end, conclusion; **fin de semana** weekend (14); **por fin** finally (5)
final *m.:* **al final** at the end (17)
financiamiento financing
financiero/a financial; **asuntos financieros** financial matters
finca land, farm
firma signature
firmar to sign one's name (17)

físico/a physical
flan *m.* custard
flor *f.* flower (2); **Flor de Jamaica** *drink made from petals of the Jamaica plant (Mex.)*
florería flower shop
florero vase
flotar to float
folleto pamphlet, brochure
fondo: en el fondo deep down (16)
fontanero/a plumber (*Sp.*) (18)
forma form
formación *f.* training, education
formar to form, shape
formulario de pedido order blank
foto *f.* photo; **tomar fotos** to take photos (2)
fotografía photograph; **tomar fotografías** to take photographs (2)
fraile *m.* monk, friar
francés *m.* French (*language*) (1); **francés/francesa** Frenchman/Frenchwoman (1)
frasco flask, bottle
frase *f.* phrase
fraternidad *f.* fraternity
fray *title used before a monk's name*
frecuencia: con frecuencia frequently
frecuente *m., f.* frequent
fregadero kitchen sink (6)
freír (i, i) to fry (5)
freno(s) brake(s) (10)
frente *n. f.* forehead
frente a in front of (13); **en frente de** in front of (10)
fresa strawberry (5)
fresco: hacer (*irreg.*) fresco to be cool (*weather*) (4)
frijoles *m.* beans (5)
frío/a cold; **hacer (*irreg.*) frío** to be cold (out) (4); **tener (*irreg.*) frío** to be (feel) cold (4)
frito/a fried (5); **papas/patatas fritas** French fries
frívolo frivolous
fruta fruit (5)
frutería fruit stand (4)
frutero/a fruit vendor
fuego fire
fuente *f.* fountain (2)
fuerte *m., f.* strong
fuerza strength
fumador(a) smoker (15)
fumar to smoke (11)
función *f.* role; function

funcionamiento operation
funcionar to run, work, function (9)
furioso/a furious
fútbol *m.* soccer; **fútbol americano** football
futuro/a future

G

gafas (*f. pl.*) **de sol** sunglasses (14)
gala: de gala *adj.* elegant
galería de arte art gallery
galón *m.* gallon
galletitas cookies
ganar to earn (3); to win; **ganarse la vida** to earn a living
ganas: tener (*irreg.*) ganas de +*inf.* to feel like (doing something) (4)
ganga bargain (7)
garaje *m.* garage (10)
garantía guarantee, warranty
garantizar (c) to guarantee
garganta: dolor (*m.*) **de garganta** sore throat (12)
gasolina gasoline (10)
gasolinera service station (10)
gastar to spend (3)
gatito kitten (4)
gato cat (4)
general *n.* general (*rank*); **por lo general** generally
gente *f. s.* people (2)
geografía geography
gerente *m., f.* manager (18)
germánico/a Germanic
gigante/a *n.* giant
gigantesco/a gigantic
gimnasia: hacer (*irreg.*) gimnasia to do calisthenics
giratorio/a revolving
giro postal money order
glóbulo corpuscle (*blood*)
gobernador(a) governor (11)
goma tire (10)
gordo/a fat (3)
gotas para la nariz/los ojos nose/eye drops (12)
gozar (c) (de) to enjoy (7)
grabar to record (7)
gracias thank you (P); **dar (*irreg.*) las gracias** to say thanks; **muy bien, gracias** very well, thanks (P)
gracioso/a funny
grado degree (18)
graduarse (en) to graduate (from)
gran (*shortened form of* **grande,** *used before nouns*) great

grande large (2), big; **así de grande** this big (9)
grasa *n.* fat
gratis free, at no cost
grave *m., f.* serious
Grecia Greece
griego/a Greek
gripe *f.* flu (12)
gris *m., f.* gray
gritar to shout, scream (6)
grueso/a fat
grupo group
guapo/a handsome
guaraní *m. monetary unit of Paraguay*
guardado/a *p.p.* kept
guardar(se) to guard (oneself) (8)
guardia: estar (*irreg.*) de guardia to be open all night (*pharmacy*)
guatemalteco/a Guatemalan
guerra war (13)
guía *m., f.* guide (*person*); *f.* manual (*book*); **guía de teléfonos** telephone book
guisante *m.* pea (5)
guitarra (principal) (lead) guitar (7)
gustar(le) (a uno) to be pleasing (to one); to like (P)
gusto taste; **con gusto** gladly; **mucho gusto** (I am) pleased to meet you

H

haber *irreg.* to have (*auxiliary verb*); to be (*inf. form of* **hay**)
había there was/were
habilidad *f.* skill, ability
habitación *f.* room (6)
habitante *m., f.* inhabitant (8)
hábito habit
habituarse to get used to
hablar to speak (1)
hacer *irreg.* to do; to make (2); **hace diez minutos/una hora que llegué** I arrived ten minutes/one hour ago (15); **hace cinco años que vivo aquí** I have been living here for five years (15); **hacer buen/mal tiempo** to be good/bad weather (4); **hacer calor/fresco/ frío/sol/viento** to be hot/cool/ cold/sunny/windy (*weather*) (4); **hacer caso a/de** to pay attention to (16); **hacer cola** to stand in line; **hacer daño** to damage; **hacer**

efectivo (un cheque) to cash (a check) (17); **hacer gimnasia** to do calisthenics; **hacer preguntas** to ask questions; **hacer señas** to signal; **hacer un viaje** to take a trip (8); **hacer(le) falta (a uno)** to be lacking, needed (18); **hazme un favor** do me a favor (4)

hacia toward; about; **hacia abajo/ arriba** downward/upward; **hacia adelante/atrás** forward/backward; **hacia la derecha/la izquierda** toward/to the right/the left

haga (*subj. of* **hacer**): **haga (Ud.) el favor (de)** please

hallar to find

hambre *f.* (*but:* **el hambre**) hunger; **tener** (*irreg.*) **hambre** to be hungry (4)

hamburguesa hamburger

harina flour (5); **harina de maíz** corn flour

hasta until (6); even (8); **hasta luego/mañana** until later, soon/tomorrow (P); **hasta que** *conj.* until (18)

hay there is/are (P)

hecho/a *p.p.* done; made (10)

heladería ice cream parlor (11)

heladero/a ice cream vendor

helado ice cream (5)

hemisferio hemisphere (8)

herbolario/a vendor of herbs

heredar to inherit

herida wound (12)

herido/a wounded person (12)

hermano/a brother/sister (4)

hermoso/a beautiful, lovely; handsome

herramienta tool (18)

hielo ice

hierba grass; herb

hijo/a son/daughter (4)

hipocondríaco/a hypochondriac

hispanidad: Desfile (*m.*) **de la Hispanidad** Columbus Day Parade (11)

historia story (11); history

hogar *m.* home

hoja leaf (13); **hoja de depósito** deposit slip (17)

hojalata tin, tinplate

hola hello (P)

holandés/holandesa Dutch

hombre *m.* man (2)

hondureño/a Honduran

honrado/a honest (11)

hora hour; time; **¿a qué hora?** at what time?; **es hora de** + *inf.* it's time (*to do something*) (9); **¿qué hora es?** what time is it?

horario (electrónico) (electronic) schedule (15)

horizonte *m.* horizon

horno oven (6)

hortalizas *f. pl.* vegetables, greens (5)

hospedarse to stay (*at a hotel*)

hotel *m.* hotel (2)

hoy today (P); **hoy día** nowadays (8); **hoy mismo** today without fail

huevo egg (5); **huevos rancheros** *scrambled eggs with chili peppers and tomatoes* (*Mex.*); **huevos revueltos** scrambled eggs

humilde *m., f.* humble

humo smoke (15)

humor: ponerse (*irreg.*) **de buen/mal humor** to get in a good/bad mood (16)

huracán *m.* hurricane (13)

I

ida: de ida y vuelta round-trip (*adj.*) (15)

idealista *m., f.* idealistic

identidad *f.* identity

identificación: tarjeta de identificación ID card (17)

identificar (qu) to identify

idioma *m.* language (11)

ídolo idol

iglesia church (2)

ignorante *m., f.* ignorant; unaware

igual *m., f.* equal; **igual de** + *adj.* as _____ as; **igual que** the same as, just like

igualdad *f.* equality

igualmente equally

imagen *f.* image

imaginar(se) to imagine

imaginario/a imaginary

imitar to imitate

impaciente *m., f.* impatient

impacto impact

impedir (*like* **pedir**) to prevent (from)

imperfecto imperfect (*grammar*)

imponer (*like* **poner**) to impose

importancia importance

importante: es importante it's important (12)

importe *m.* total amount

impreso/a *p.p.* printed

impresora printer (*machine*) (17)

imprimir to print (17)

improvisado/a *p.p.* improvised

impuesto tax

incluir (y) to include

incluso *adv.* even

incómodo/a uncomfortable (3)

incompatibilidad *f.* incompatibility

incorporar to incorporate

increíble *m., f.* incredible

independencia independence

indicaciones *f. pl.* indications, directions

indicar (qu) to indicate (9)

indicativo indicative (*grammar*)

indígena *m., f.* indigenous, native

indio/a Indian

indiscriminado/a indiscriminate

individuo *n.* individual

industria industry

inédito/a unpublished

inesperado/a unexpected

infanta *Spanish princess*

infección *f.* infection

infinitivo infinitive (*grammar*)

infinito infinite

inflación *f.* inflation

inflar to inflate

influir (y) to influence

informar to inform

infraestructura facilities for tenants; infrastructure

ing. (*abbreviation of* **ingeniero/a**) engineer (18)

ingeniería engineering (18); **ingeniería mecánica** mechanical engineering; **ingeniería de minas** mining engineering

ingeniero/a engineer (18)

Inglaterra England

inglés *m.* English (*language*) (1); **inglés/inglesa** Englishman/ Englishwoman (1)

ingresar to enter (*as employee, student, etc.*)

ingreso entry, admission

iniciar(se) to begin

ininterrumpido/a uninterrupted

inmediatamente immediately

inmediato: de inmediato immediately

inmigrante *m., f.* immigrant
inmovilidad *f.* immobility
inodoro toilet (6)
inolvidable *m., f.* unforgettable
inscribir(se) to enroll, register, sign up
insistir (en) to insist (on)
insomnio insomnia
instalación *f.* installation
instalar to install; **instalarse (en)** to settle (down/in)
insultarse to exchange insults
integrar(se) to integrate (into)
inteligencia intelligence
intenso/a intense
intentar + *inf.* to try (to do something) (14)
intercambiar to interchange, exchange
intercomunicador *m.* intercom (9)
interés *m.* interest (17)
interesados: los/las interesados/as those interested
interesante *m., f.* interesting
interesar to interest; **interesarse (en)** to be interested (in)
interiormente inside
internado: vida de internado life as an internee
inti *m. monetary unit of Peru*
íntimo/a intimate
intuición *f.* intuition
inundación *f.* flood (13)
inútil *m., f.* useless (17)
invernadero: efecto invernadero greenhouse effect
inversión *f.* investment (17)
investigador(a) researcher
invierno winter (P)
invitado/a *n.* guest; *adj.* invited
invitar to invite
inyección *f.* injection (12); **poner(le)** (*irreg.*) **una inyección** to give a shot (injection) (12)
ir *irreg.* to go (3); **ir de compras** to go shopping (3)
Irlanda Ireland
irlandés/irlandesa Irishman/Irishwoman
irritado/a irritated (12)
isla island (8)
Italia Italy
italiano/a Italian
itinerario itinerary, route
izquierdo/a *adj.* left; **a la**

izquierda to/on the left; **de la izquierda** on the left

J

jabón *m.* soap (9)
Jamaica: flor (*f.*) **de Jamaica** *drink made from petals of the Jamaica plant* (*Mex.*)
jamás ever; never (13)
jamón *m.* ham (2)
Japón *m.* Japan
japonés/japonesa Japanese
jardín *m.* garden, yard
jarra pitcher (4)
jeans *m. pl.* jeans (3)
jefatura de policía police headquarters (10)
jefe/a boss (17)
jersey sweater (*Sp.*)
jornada working day; **jornada continua** full-time work
joven *n. m., f.* young man/woman (1); *adj. m., f.* young (3)
joya piece of jewelry (15); *pl.* jewelry (15)
juego game, match; flexibility
jueves *m. s.* Thursday (P)
jugador(a) player (14)
jugar (ue) (gu) to play (*a game, sport, etc.*) (7)
jugo juice; **jugo de ananá/pomelo/tomate** pineapple (*Arg.*)/grapefruit (*Arg.*)/tomato juice; **jugo de naranja** orange juice (2)
julio July (P)
junio June (P)
Junta: Junta de Beneficencia Welfare Board; **Junta Comunitaria** Community Board
junto/a/os/as together
justo/a just, fair
juvenil *m., f.* youthful
juventud *f.* youth (8)

K

kilo (*abbreviation of* **kilogramo**) kilogram
kilómetro kilometer

L

la *d.o. pron. f. s.* you (*form. s.*)/her/it
labio lip; **creyón** (*m.*) **de labios** lipstick; **lápiz** (*m.*) **labial/para los labios** lipstick (14)

labor *f.* work
laboral *adj. m., f. pertaining to labor or work*
laboratorio laboratory
laca hairspray (14)
lacio/a straight (9)
lácteo lactic
lado: al lado de next to (7)
lagarto lizard
lago lake (13)
lámpara lamp (6)
lana wool; **de lana** (made of) wool (3)
langosta lobster
lápiz *m.* (*pl.* **lápices**) pencil (1); **lápiz labial/para los labios** lipstick (14)
largo/a long (9); **a largo plazo** long term (17)
las *d.o. pron. f.* you (*pl.*); them
lástima: es (una) lástima it's a pity (12)
lata can (5); **qué lata** what a nuisance (13)
latino/a *adj.* Latin
Latinoamérica Latin America
lavabo washbasin (6)
lavadora washing machine (18)
lavaplatos *m. s.* dishwasher (6)
lavar to wash (6); **lavarse** to wash oneself (9)
lección *f.* lesson (1)
lector(a) reader
lectura reading
leche *f.* milk (2); **café** (*m.*) **con leche** coffee with milk (5)
lechuga lettuce (5)
leer (y) to read (2)
legumbre *f.* vegetable (5)
lejano/a distant, far away
lejos de far from (7)
lempira *m. monetary unit of Honduras*
lengua language (1)
lenguaje *m.* language
les *i. o. pron. pl.* to/for you; to/for them
letra letter (*of alphabet*); handwriting; lyrics (*of a song*)
letrero (road/street) sign (10)
levantarse to get up (9)
ley *f.* law (10)
leyenda legend
libertad *f.* liberty, freedom
librarse (de) to escape (from)
libre *m., f.* free; **al aire libre** outside, outdoor(s)

libremente freely
librería bookstore
libreta de cheques checkbook (17); **libreta de taquigrafía** shorthand pad (17)
libro book (1)
Lic. (*abbreviation of* **Licenciado/a**) *title before a lawyer's name*
liceo high school (*in some countries*)
líder *m., f.* leader
límite *m.* limit
limón *m.* lemon; **torta de limón** lemon pie
limpiaparabrisas *m. s.* windshield wiper (10)
limpiar to clean (6)
linaje *m. arch.* kind
línea line; **línea aérea** airline (15)
liquidación *f.* liquidation, sale
líquido/a liquid
liso/a smooth (*surface*); **cartón** (*m.*) **liso** noncorrugated cardboard
lista list
listo/a: estar (*irreg.*) **listo/a** to be ready (3); **ser** (*irreg.*) **listo/a** to be smart (3)
literario/a literary
litro liter
lo *d. o. pron.* you (*form. s.*)/it (*m. and neuter*); **lo cual** which; **lo** + *adj.* the (*adj.*) thing; **lo que** what, that which (16); **lo siento** I am sorry (about it) (6)
local *n. m.* place, premises; *adj. m., f.* local
localidad *f.* place, town
loción: loción bronceadora tanning lotion (14); **loción** (*f.*) **de afeitar** after-shave lotion (14); **loción para las manos** hand lotion (14)
loco/a crazy, silly
locutor(a) TV/radio announcer (11)
loma hill (13)
Londres London
los *d.o. pron. m.* you (*pl.*); them
lotería lottery; **billete** (*m.*) de lotería lottery ticket (2)
Ltda. (*abbreviation of* **Limitada**) incorporated (*referring to a business*)
luchar to fight, struggle
luego then; later (P); **desde luego** of course; **hasta luego** until later (P)
lugar *m.* place (7)
lujo luxury; **de lujo** deluxe
luna moon (13); **luna de miel** honeymoon

lunes *m. s.* Monday (P)
luneta seat (*at theater*)
luz *f.* (*pl.* **luces**) light (6)

LL

llamada call
llamar to call; ¿**cómo se llama Ud.?**/¿**cómo te llamas?** what is your name?; **llamar por teléfono** to call on the telephone (4); **llamarse** to call oneself, be named (P) (9)
llanta tire (10)
llave *f.* key (10)
llegada arrival (13)
llegar (**gu**) to arrive (6)
llenar (**de/con**) to fill (with)
lleno/a (**de**) full (of) (15)
llevar to wear (3); to take; to carry (4); **llevarse bien/mal** to get along well/badly (9)
llorar to cry (12)
llover (**ue**) to rain (7)
lluvia rain (13)

M

madre *f.* mother (4)
madrina bridesmaid, maid of honor (16)
maestro/a teacher
magnífico/a magnificent, great
mago/a magician; **los Reyes Magos** Three Wise Men, Magi
maíz *m.* corn (5)
mal *adv.* badly, poorly (7); *adj. shortened form of* **malo** *used before m. s. nouns*
maldito/a damned, cursed
maleta suitcase (14); **hacer** (*irreg.*) **la maleta** to pack
maletero trunk (*car*) (10)
maletín *m.* carry-on bag (14)
maligno/a malignant
malo/a bad (2); **lo malo** the bad thing (16)
mancha stain
manchado/a stained (3)
mandar to send (8); to order (*command*)
mandato command
manejar to drive (10); to handle; **carnet** (*m.*) **de manejar** driver's license
manejo *n.* driving; handling

manera manner, way; **de ninguna manera** by no means (14); **de todas maneras** at any rate
manipular to handle
mano *f.* hand (9); **dar** (*irreg.*) **la mano** to shake hands (9); **echar una mano** to lend a hand (18)
manteca butter (*Arg.*)
mantecado *type of ice cream* (11)
mantel *m.* tablecloth (4)
mantener (*like* **tener**) to maintain, keep; to support
mantenimiento upkeep
mantequilla butter (5)
manzana apple (4)
mañana tomorrow (P); **a la mañana siguiente** on the following morning; **pasado mañana** day after tomorrow (15)
mapa *m.* map (1)
mapache *m.* raccoon
maquillaje *m.* makeup; **estuche** (*m.*) **de maquillaje** make-up kit (14)
máquina machine; **máquina de afeitar** electric shaver (14); **máquina de escribir** typewriter (6); **pasar a máquina** to type (17)
mar *m.* sea (8)
maravilloso/a marvelous, wonderful
marca brand name
marcado/a marked (17)
marcha march; **marcha nupcial** wedding march (16); **poner** (*irreg.*) **en marcha** to set in motion
mareado/a seasick
margen *m.* margin
mariachis *m. pl.* mariachi band (11)
marino/a marine, nautical
mariposa butterfly (13)
marisco shellfish; *pl.* seafood (5)
mármol *m.* marble (2)
marquesina porch (*Puerto Rico*)
martes *m. s.* Tuesday (P)
martillo hammer (18)
marzo March (P)
más more (3); most; plus; **el/la/los/las más** _____ the most _____ (12); **más (menos)** _____ **que** more (less) _____ than (12); **más o menos** more or less
matanza slaughter
matar(se) to kill (oneself) (18)
matemáticas *f. pl.* mathematics
materia (school) subject
maternidad *f.* maternity

materno/a *adj. related to mother's side of family*

matrícula registration (18)

matrimonial: cama matrimonial double bed

matrimonio matrimony; **contraer** (*like* **traer**) **matrimonio** to get married

máximo/a maximum; **al máximo** to the maximum

mayo May (P)

mayor major; greater; older (4); **a la mayor brevedad posible** as soon as possible; **la mayor parte** most; **los mayores** adults, grown-ups (16); **premio mayor** first prize

mayoría majority (11)

mecánico/a mechanic; **ingeniería mecánica** mechanical engineering

mediano/a medium-sized

medianoche *f.* midnight

medicina medicine

médico/a medical doctor (12)

medida: a la medida customized; **a medida que** as

medio/a half; **clase** (*f.*) **media** middle class; **diez y media** ten-thirty; **medio de transporte** means of transportation

mejor better (7); best; **es mejor** it's better (12); **lo mejor** the best (thing)

melocotón *m.* peach (5)

membrete *m.* letterhead (17)

memoria memory; **aprender de memoria** to memorize

mencionar to mention

menor minor; younger; youngest (4); less, lesser, least; smaller, smallest

menos minus (P); less, fewer; **a menos que** unless (18); **más o menos** more or less; **menos mal** fortunately; **menos que** less than (12); **por lo menos** at least

mensualidad *f.* monthly payment

menudo: a menudo often

mercado market; **mercado común** common market

mercancía merchandise

merendar (ie) to snack

merengue *m. type of music from Dominican Republic*

merienda snack

mermelada jam, marmalade (5)

mes *m.* month (P)

mesa table (1); **mesa de centro**

coffee table (6); **mesa de noche** nightstand (6)

meta goal, objective

meter to put in; to place (17)

método method

metro subway (2)

mezcla mixture

mezquita mosque

mi(s) *poss.* my (2)

mí *obj. of prep. pron.* me, myself

miedo fear; **dar(le)** (*irreg.*) **miedo** to scare; **tener** (*irreg.*) **miedo** to be afraid (4)

miel: luna de miel honeymoon

miembro *m., f.* member

mientras while (4); **mientras tanto** in the meantime (14)

miércoles *m. s.* Wednesday (P)

mil *m.* (a) thousand (2)

milagro miracle (14)

mili *f.* military service (*Sp.*)

militar *adj. m., f.* military

milla mile

millón *m.* million (2)

millonario/a millionaire

mina mine; **ingeniería de minas** mining engineering

mínimo/a minimum, minimal

ministerio ministry

minuto minute

mío/a/os/as *poss. pron.* (of) mine (14)

mirar to watch, look at (2); **mirar la televisión** to watch television (6); **mirarse** to look at oneself, each other; **sin mirar** without looking

misa Mass

mismo/a/os/as same; very; myself, yourself, etc. (14); **ahora mismo** right now (9); **al mismo tiempo** at the same time (8); **allí mismo** right there; **hoy mismo** today; **lo mismo** the same thing (11)

misterio mystery

mitad *f.* half; **a mitad de precio** (at) half price (7)

mitología mythology

mochila backpack (1)

moda fashion, trend; **estar** (*irreg.*) **de moda** to be in style

moderado/a moderate

modismo idiom, idiomatic expression

mojado/a wet (9)

molestar to bother (11)

molestia inconvenience, nuisance

molesto/a annoying

momento moment; **en cualquier momento** anytime; **en este momento** at the present time; **por el momento** for the time being

moneda coin (8)

monetaria: unidad (*f.*) **monetaria** monetary unit

mono/a cute (4)

monólogo monologue

monstruo monster

montaña mountain (8)

montar to mount, ride; **montar a caballo** to ride a horse (11); **montar una empresa** to start a business (18)

monte *m.* mount, mountain (8)

morir (ue, u) to die (7); **morirse de sueño** to be extremely sleepy

mostrar (ue) to show

moto *f.* (*abbreviation of* **motocicleta**) motorcycle

motor *m.* motor, engine (10)

mover (ue) to move

movimiento movement

muchacho/a boy/girl (2)

muchedumbre *f.* crowd (11)

mucho/a lot, much (P); *pl.* many; **mucho gusto** (I am) pleased to meet you

mueble *m.* piece of furniture; *pl.* furniture (6)

mueblería furniture store

muela molar, tooth (12)

muelle (*m.*) **pesquero** fishing pier

muerte *f.* death

muerto/a *p.p.* dead (10)

mujer *f.* woman (2)

multa fine; **poner(le)** (*irreg.*) **una multa** to give (one) a ticket (a fine) (10)

mundo world (8)

muñeco de nieve snowman (13)

músculo muscle

museo museum

música music

músico/a musician

mutualista *adj. m., f.* mutual

muy very (P); **muy bien, gracias** very well, thank you (P)

N

nacer (zc) to be born

nacimiento birth

nacionalidad *f.* nationality

nada nothing, not anything (4, 13); **de nada** you are welcome (10); **nada de nuevo** nothing new (P)

nadar to swim (13)

nadie no one, nobody, not anyone (13)

naranja orange (5); **jugo de naranja** orange juice (2)

nariz *f.* nose (9); **gotas para la nariz** nose drops (12)

narrador(a) narrator

natación *f.* swimming

nativo/a native

naturaleza nature

naturalista *m., f.* naturalist

navegar (gu) to sail, navigate (13)

Navidad *f.* Christmas (8)

necesario/a necessary; **es necesario** it's necessary (12)

necesidad *f.* necessity, need

necesitar to need (2)

necio/a foolish (9)

negar (ie) (gu) to deny (12)

negocio business

negro/a black (3)

nervios *m. pl.* nerves; **ataque** (*m.*) **de nervios** nervous attack

nervioso/a nervous

nevar (ie) to snow (7)

ni neither, nor; **ni... ni** neither . . . nor; not even

nicaragüense *m., f.* Nicaraguan

nieto/a grandson/granddaughter (4)

nieve *f.* snow (8); **copo de nieve** snowflake (13); **muñeco de nieve** snowman (13)

ningún, ninguno/a no, not any (13); **de ninguna manera** by no means (14)

niño/a boy/girl (2); child (4); *m. pl.* children; **de niño/a** as a child (9)

nivel *m.* level

nocturno/a nocturnal; **centro nocturno** night club (*Mex.*)

noche *f.* night; evening; **buenas noches** good night/evening (P); **de/en/por la noche** in the evening, at night (1); **de noche** at night; **esta noche** tonight; **mesa de noche** nightstand (4); **Nochebuena** Christmas Eve; **toda la noche** all night; **todas las noches** every night

nombrar to name

nombre *m.* name (1)

norma norm

norte *m.* north (8); **América del norte** North America

Norteamérica North America

norteamericano/a North American

noruego/a Norwegian

nos *d. o. pron.* us; *i. o. pron.* to/for us; *refl. pron.* ourselves

nosotros/as *sub. pron.* we; *obj. of prep.* us

nota note (17); academic grade

notable *m., f.* remarkable, notable

notarse to be noticeable

noticias news (2)

novecientos/as nine hundred (2)

novela novel

novelista *m., f.* novelist

noveno/a ninth (14)

noventa ninety (2)

novia girlfriend, sweetheart (4); bride; fiancée (16)

noviembre *m.* November (P)

novio boyfriend, sweetheart (4); fiancé; groom (14); *pl.* boyfriends, sweethearts; fiancés; bride and groom

nube *f.* cloud (13)

nuestro/a/os/as *poss.* our (2); (of) ours (14); **a nuestras espaldas** behind us

Nueva York New York

nueve nine (P)

nuevo/a new (1); **de nuevo** again (13); **nada de nuevo** nothing new (P)

nulo/a not valid

número number (2)

numeroso/a numerous

nunca never, not ever (13)

nupcial: marcha nupcial wedding march (16)

nutritivo/a nourishing, nutritious

O

o or (3); **o... o** either . . . or

obedecer (zc) to obey

obispo bishop

objeto object

obligar (gu) to force, oblige

obligatorio/a obligatory

obras: está en obras is under repair (10)

obrero/a worker (18)

obstante: no obstante nevertheless, however

obtener (*like* **tener**) to obtain, get

obvio: es obvio it's obvious (12)

occidente *m.* west

océano ocean (13)

ocio leisure

octavo/a eight (14)

octubre *m.* October (P)

ocupado/a busy (3)

ocuparse de to take care of

ocurrir to happen, occur (15)

ochenta eighty (2)

ocho eight (2)

ochocientos/as eight hundred (2)

odiar to hate (16)

odio hatred (16)

odontología dentistry, dental surgery

oeste *m.* west (8)

ofensa offense

oferta offer

oficina office (17); **edificio de oficinas** office building (2)

ofrecer (zc) to offer

oír *irreg.* to hear (4)

ojo eye (9); **gotas para los ojos** eye drops; **sombra para los ojos** eyeshadow (14)

ola wave (13)

¡olé! *interj.* bravo!, Great!

olimpiada Olympiad

Olímpicos: Juegos (*m. pl.*) **Olímpicos** Olympic Games

olvidar to forget (15)

ómnibus *m. s.* bus (15)

once eleven (P)

operación *f.* operation

operarse to have an operation

oponer (*like* **poner**) to oppose

oportunidad *f.* opportunity, chance

optar (por) to choose, opt for

optimista *adj. m., f.* optimistic

opuesto *n.* opposite

oración *f.* sentence (3)

orden *m.* order; arrangement; *f.* religious order; **páguese a la orden de** pay to the order of (*on a check*)

ordenador *m.* computer (*Sp.*) (17)

ordenar to put in order; to order

oreja ear (9)

orgánica: química orgánica organic chemistry

organizar (c) to organize

orientado/a oriented

orientarse to point; to be geared to

oriente *m.* orient, east (8)

origen *m.* origin
originarse to originate
orilla bank (*of river*)
oro gold (8)
orquesta orchestra
os *d. o. pron.* you (*fam. pl.*); *i. o. pron.* to/for you (*fam. pl.*); *refl. pron.* yourselves (*fam. pl.*)
oscuridad *f.* darkness
otoño autumn, fall
otro/a *n.* another one; *adj.* other, another (2)
oxígeno: dar(le) (*irreg.*) **oxígeno** to give (one) oxygen (12)
ozono ozone

P

padre *m.* father (4); *pl.* parents (4)
padrino best man (16)
pagar (gu) to pay (3)
país *m.* country (8)
paisaje *m.* landscape (13)
pájaro bird (13)
pala shovel (13)
palabra word (1)
palacio municipal city hall (10)
pálido/a pale (14)
pan *m.* bread (4)
panecillo roll (5)
pantalones *m. pl.* pants (3); **pantalones cortos** *m. pl.* shorts (3); **pantalones vaqueros** jeans (3)
papa potato (5); **papas fritas** French fries
papel *m.* paper (1)
paquete *m.* package (5)
par *m.* pair
para: para que for, in the direction of (4); in order that (18)
parabrisas *m. s.* windshield (10)
parada stop; **parada de autobuses** bus stop; **parada de taxis** taxi stand (15)
parar to stop (10)
parecer (zc) to look like, seem; **qué le parece...** how do you like . . . (7)
pared *f.* wall (1)
parentesco family relationship
pariente *m., f.* relative
parque *m.* park (2)
parqueadero parking lot (*Col.*)
párrafo paragraph
parrilla: a la parrilla grilled
parrillada mixed grill

parte *f.* part; **formar parte (de)** to be part (of); **la mayor parte** most; **por todas partes** everywhere
participio participle (*grammar*); **participio pasado** past participle (*grammar*)
particularmente especially
partida departure
partido match, game (14)
partir to leave
pasado *n.* past (8)
pasado/a *adj.* past; last (14); **participio pasado** past participle (*grammar*); **pasado mañana** day after tomorrow (15); **la semana pasada** last week
pasajero/a passenger (15)
pasaporte *m.* passport
pasar to happen (17); **pasar a máquina** to type (17); **pasar la aspiradora** to vacuum (6); **pasar (por)** to pass (by) (10); **pasar el rato** to pass the time (of day); **¿qué te pasa/pasó?** what is happening/ happened to you? (9)
pasatiempo pastime
Pascua Florida Easter
pasear (por) to walk (along/in), stroll
paseo walk, stroll; **dar** (*irreg.*) **un paseo** to take a walk; **ir** (*irreg.*) **de paseo** to go for a walk
pasillo aisle, hall; **asiento de pasillo** aisle seat (15)
pasivo/a passive; **participio pasivo** past participle (*grammar*)
pasta de dientes toothpaste (14)
pastel *m.* pie; cake
pastelería pastry shop, bakery
pastelero/a pastry chef, baker
pastilla tablet, pill (12)
pata leg (*of animal*)
patalear to kick, stamp (12)
patata potato (5); **patatas fritas** French fries
patíbulo *s.* gallows
patio yard, central court, patio
patria homeland
patrocinador(a) sponsor
patrocinar to sponsor
patrona patroness; patron saint
pavo turkey (5)
paz *f.* peace; **Noche** (*f.*) **de Paz** "Silent Night" (*song*)
peatón, peatona pedestrian (10)

pecho chest
pedagogía teaching (18)
pedir (i, i) to ask for; to order (7)
pegar (gu) to hit (16)
peinarse to comb (one's hair) (9)
peine *m.* comb (14)
pelea fight
peleado/a estranged (16)
pelear to fight (16)
película film, movie (7)
peligroso/a dangerous (18)
pelo hair (9); **cepillo de pelo** hairbrush (14)
pelota ball (14)
pena: valer (*irreg.*) **la pena** to be worth the trouble (18)
pendientes *m. pl.* **(de plata)** (silver) earrings (*Sp.*) (14)
pensar (ie) to think (7); **pensar en** to think about
peor worse; worst (7)
pepino cucumber (5)
pequeño/a small, little (2)
pera pear (5)
perder (ie) to lose (7); **perder peso** to lose weight; **perderse** to get lost (9)
peregrino/a pilgrim, wayfarer
perfume *m.* perfume (14)
periódico newspaper (2)
periodista *m., f.* journalist
perla pearl (14)
permanecer (zc) to remain
permiso permission
permitir to permit, allow, let (11)
permitido/a allowed
pero but (1)
perrito puppy (4)
perro dog (4)
persiana venetian blind
pertenecer (zc) to belong
peruano/a Peruvian
pesadilla nightmare
pesar to weigh; **a pesar de** in spite of (8)
pescado (*caught*) fish (5)
pescador(a) fisherman/woman
peseta *monetary unit of Spain*
peso *monetary unit of Bolivia, Colombia, Cuba, Chile, the Dominican Republic, Mexico, Uruguay;* **perder (ie) peso** to lose weight
pesquero: muelle (*m.*) **pesquero** fishing pier

pico peak
pie *m.* foot (9); **a pie** on foot; **dedo del pie** toe
piedra stone (13)
piel *f.* skin; **de piel** (made of) leather (3)
pierna leg (9)
pieza piece; part
píldora pill
piloto *m., f.* pilot
pimienta pepper (5)
pintar to paint (18)
pintor(a) painter (18)
pintorescamente in a picturesque way
pintura paint
piña pineapple (5)
pirata *m., f.* pirate (8)
piscina swimming pool (14)
piso floor (14); apartment (*Sp.*)
pistola pistol
pizarra blackboard (1)
plácido/a placid
planear to plan
planta plant
plantar to plant (13)
plástico/a: cirugía plástica cosmetic surgery; **cirujano/a plástico/a** plastic surgeon
plata silver
plataforma platform
plátano banana (4)
plato plate (4); dish
playa beach (8); **bolsa de playa** beach bag (14)
plaza public square
plazo: a largo plazo long term
plenamente fully, completely
plomero/a plumber (18)
pluma feather
pluscuamperfecto pluperfect (*grammar*)
pobre poor (3)
poco/a (a) little (3); **unos pocos** a few
poder *irreg.* to be able, can (7)
poesía poetry
policía *m., f.* policeman/ policewoman; *f.* police (force) (10)
política *s.* politics (2)
político/a politician
póliza (insurance) policy
pollo chicken (5); **arroz** (*m.*) **con pollo** rice with chicken
pomada ointment (12)

pomelo grapefruit (*Arg., Sp.*); **jugo de pomelo** grapefruit juice
poner *irreg.* to put (4); **poner en marcha** to start, get going; **poner la mesa** to set the table (4); **poner la televisión** to turn the television on; **poner(le) una inyección** to give a shot (injection) (12); **poner(le) una multa** to give (one) a ticket (fine); **poner(le) el termómetro** to take (one's) temperature (12); **ponerse** to put on (*clothing*) (9); **ponerse** + *adj.* to become, get + *adj.* (13); **ponerse de mal humor** to get in a bad mood (16)
por for; through, in (4); on; because of; along, by; for the sake of, on behalf of; per; **por aquí** this way; **por avión** (by) airmail; **por ciento** percent (17); **por el día** during the day; **por Dios** for heaven's sake (5); **por ejemplo** for example (5); **por eso** for this reason, therefore (5); **por esta razón** for this reason; **por favor** please (5); **por fin** finally (5); **por lo general** generally; **por lo menos** at least; **por el momento** for the time being; **por qué** why (2); **por supuesto** of course (5, 11); **por teléfono** by/on (the) telephone; **por televisión** on television; **por último** finally; **tener** (*irreg.*) **por seguro** to be sure (*about something*)
porcentaje *m.* percentage
porque because (3)
portada front cover (*book*)
portafolio portfolio; folder
portátil *m., f.* portable
portero(a) doorman/woman (doorkeeper)
portugués/portuguesa Portuguese
posada inn, lodging; **dar** (*irreg.*) **posada** to provide lodging; *pl. traditional Mexican Christmas festivities*
poseer (**y**) to possess
posibilidad *f.* possibility
posibilitar to make possible
posible: es posible it's possible (12)
posición *f.* position
posponer (*like* **poner**) to postpone

postal *f.* postcard (15)
posteriormente later
postre *m.* dessert (5)
potencia potency, power
potente *m., f.* potent
pozo (water) well
pqte. *m.* (*abbreviation of* **paquete**) package
practicar (**qu**) to practice (1)
práctico/a practical
preceder to precede
precio price (3); **a mitad de precio** half price (7)
precioso/a pretty, lovely
preciso: es preciso it's necessary (12)
predicción *f.* prediction
predominar to predominate
prefabricado/a prefabricated
preferido/a favorite (14)
preferir (**ie, i**) to prefer (7)
pregunta question (1)
preguntar to ask (*a question*) (1); **preguntarse** to ask oneself; to wonder
prejuicio prejudice
premiado/a prize-winning
premio prize (4); **premio mayor** first prize
prenda garment, article of clothing; pledge
prender to turn on (6)
preocupado/a worried, concerned (15)
preocupe: no se preocupe don't worry (17)
preparar to prepare (1); **prepararse** to prepare oneself (9)
preparativos *m. pl.* preparation
presentar to present; to introduce
presente *adj. m., f.* present
presidir to preside
presión: presión (*f.*) **arterial alta/baja** high/low blood pressure (12); **tomar(le) la presión** to take (one's) blood pressure (12)
prestación *f.* loan, advance
préstamo loan (18)
prestar to lend (3)
prestigioso/a prestigious
presupuesto budget
pretender to try to
pretérito preterite, past (*tense*)
primaria: escuela primaria primary school

primavera spring(time) (P, 13)
primer *shortened form of* **primero,** *used before m. s. nouns*
primero/a first (5); **lo primero** the first thing
primo/a cousin (4)
princesa princess
principal *m., f.* main; **guitarra principal** lead guitar (7)
príncipe *m.* prince
principio: al principio in/at the beginning
prisa haste; **tener** (*irreg.*) **prisa** to be in a hurry (4)
prisionero/a prisoner
privado/a private
probable: es probable it's probable (12)
probar (ue) to prove
problema *m.* problem
procedimiento procedure
procesamiento processing
procesar to process
proclamar to proclaim, expose
producir (*irreg.*) to produce
profesión *f.* profession
profesor(a) professor (1)
profundo/a deep, profound
programa *m.* program
progresivo: presente (*m.*) **progresivo** present progressive (*grammar*)
prohibir to prohibit, forbid
promesa promise (16)
prometer to promise (16)
promover (ue) to promote
pronombre *m.* pronoun (*grammar*)
pronto soon, right away (7); **tan pronto como** as soon as (18)
pronunciar to pronounce (1)
propio/a own (16)
propósito purpose
protagonista *m., f.* main character, protagonist (11)
proteger (j) to protect
protestar to protest
proveedor(a) provider
próximo/a next (15)
proyectar to project
prudencia prudence, care
prueba proof; test
psicológico/a psychological
psicólogo/a psychologist
psiquiatra *m., f.* psychiatrist (18)

pto. (*abbreviation of* **puerto**) port (8)
pts. (*abbreviation of* **pesetas**) *monetary unit of Spain* (*pl.*)
publicar (qu) to publish
pueblo town, village
puente *m.* bridge
puerta door (1)
puerto port (8)
puertorriqueño/a Puerto Rican
pues... well . . . (P)
puesto *n.* stand (*newspaper, fruit, etc.*)
puesto/a *p.p.* put, placed (10)
pulgada inch
pulpito small octopus
pulsera (de oro) (gold) bracelet (14)
punto point; **en punto** sharp (*on time*) (P); **punto de vista** viewpoint
puro/a pure

Q

que which (3); who, that (1); than (12); **a menos que** unless (18); **antes (de) que** before (18); **con tal (de) que** provided that (18); **después (de) que** after (18); **en caso (de) que** in case (18); **hasta que** (*conj.*) until (18); **lo que** what, that, which (16); **más/menos que** more/less than; **para que** so that, in order that (18); **tener** (*irreg.*) **que** + *inf.* to have to (do something) (4)
¿qué? what?, which? (P); **¿a qué hora?** at what time?; **¿con qué?** with what?, with which?; **¿de qué?** of what?; **¿qué hay?** what's up? (P); **¿qué le parece?** what do you think?; **¿qué más?** what else?; **¿qué pasa/pasó?** what is happening/happened? (9); **¿qué tal?** how are you?; **¡qué... !** *interj.* how . . . !, what (a) . . . !; **¡qué bien!** (how) great!; **¡qué bueno!** how nice! (5); **¡qué lata!** what a nuisance (bother)! (13)
quedar(se) to remain, stay; to be; **quedarle grande (pequeño, bien) (a uno)** to be too large (too small, right) (for one) (3)
queja complaint
quemadura burn (12)
quemar to burn

querer *irreg.* to want (6, 7); to love (7, 16); **quererse** to love each other (16)
querido/a dear, beloved
queso cheese (2)
quetzal *monetary unit of Guatemala*
Quetzalcóatl *plumed serpent god of the Aztecs*
quien(es) who, whom
¿quién(es)? who?, whom? (P); **¿a quién(es)?** whom?, to whom?; **¿con quién(es)?** with whom?; **¿de quién(es)?** whose?
quieto/a still; quiet, calm (12)
química chemistry (18); **química orgánica** organic chemistry
químico/a *n.* chemist (18); *adj.* chemical
quince fifteen (P)
quinientos/as five hundred (2)
quinina quinine
quinto/a fifth (14)
quirúrgico/a surgical
quisiera I (you/he/she) would (really) like (*softened form*)
quitar to remove (13); **quitarse** to take off (*clothing*) (9); **el dolor no se me quita** the pain won't go away (12)
quizá(s) perhaps, maybe

R

rabia *s.* rabies
radiografía: sacar(le) (qu) una radiografía to take X rays (12)
raíz *f.* (*pl.* **raíces**) root
rama branch (*tree*) (13)
rambla scenic drive, boulevard (10)
ramo branch (*field, specialization*)
ranchero: huevos rancheros *scrambled eggs with chili peppers and tomatoes* (*Mex.*)
rapidez *f.* rapidity, speed
rápido *adv.* quickly
rápido/a *adj.* rapid, quick
raqueta racket (*sports*) (14)
raro/a odd, rare; **raras veces** seldom
rasgo feature (*face*)
rastrillo garden rake (13)
rato a while, short period of time (4); **pasar el rato** to pass the time (of day)

raza race (*breed*); **Día** (*m.*) **de la Raza** Columbus Day
razón *f.* reason; **con razón** no wonder (5); **(no) tener** (*irreg.*) **razón** to be right (wrong) (4); **por esta razón** for this reason
razonable *m., f.* reasonable
reacción *f.* reaction
real *m., f.* real; royal
realizar (c) to perform, carry out
realmente really
realzar (c) to enhance
rebajado/a reduced (*in price*) (3)
recámara bedroom (*Mex.*)
recepción *f.* reception; front desk (14)
receta recipe; prescription (12)
recetar to prescribe
recibir to receive
reciclaje *m. n.* recycling
reciclar to recycle
reciente *m., f.* recent
recientemente recently
recipiente *m.* container (5)
reclinable *m., f.* reclining
recodo turn (*road, river*)
recoger (j) to gather, collect (13)
recomendar (ie) to recommend (11)
reconocer (zc) to recognize
reconstruir (y) to reconstruct
recordar (ue) to remember (8); **recordar(le)** to remind (one) (15)
recorrer to travel, tour
rector: consejo rector executive board
recuerdo memory, remembrance (8)
recuperar to recuperate
recurrir to resort to
rechazar (c) to reject; to refuse
red *f.* net; network
redacción *f.* editing; wording
reducir (*like* **producir**) to reduce
reembolso refund
reemplazar (c) to replace, substitute
referirse (ie, i) to refer
reflexivo/a reflexive (*grammar*)
refresco cold drink
refrigerador *m.* refrigerator (6)
refugiado/a refugee (11)
regalar to give (*a gift*)
regalo gift, present
régimen *m.* set of rules
regional: traje (*m.*) **regional** regional costume/dress (11)
regla rule

regresar to return
regreso *n.* return (15)
regular to regulate
reina queen (11)
reja *s.* iron bars, grating
relación *f.* relation(ship)
relacionado/a related
relacionamiento: club (*m.*) **de relacionamiento humano** Lonely Hearts Club
relámpago lightning flash (13)
religioso/a religious; **boda religiosa** church wedding; **orden** (*f.*) **religiosa** religious order
reloj *m.* watch; clock (1)
remedio remedy; **no tener** (*irreg.*) **más remedio (que)** to have no choice (but) (15); **remedio casero** homemade remedy
remoto/a remote
rendido/a exhausted, worn out, very tired
renunciar to renounce, give up
reparación *f.* repair (18)
reparar to repair (18)
reparto residential neighborhood
repasar to review
repaso review
repetir (i, i) to repeat (7)
reponer (*like* **poner**) to replace, reinstate
reporte *m.* report; paper (*for a class*) (6)
reposar to rest, lie, be in a place
requerir (ie, i) to require
res: carne (*f.*) **de res** beef (5)
reserva reservation
resfriado *n.* cold (*illness*) (12)
residencial: complejo residencial residential development
residente *m., f.* resident
resistente *m., f.* strong
resistirse (a) to resist; to be reluctant (*to do something*)
resolver (ue) to resolve
respecto: con respecto a with regard to
respetar to respect
respeto respect
respirar to breathe; **dificultad** (*f.*) **para respirar** difficulty in breathing (12)
responder to respond, answer
responsable *m., f.* responsible
respuesta answer, reply

restaurante *m.* restaurant (2)
resto: el resto the rest, the remainder
resultado *n.* result
resultante *adj. m., f.* resulting
resultar to turn out to be, result
resumen *m.* summary
resumir to summarize
resurrección *f.* resurrection, revival
retener (*like* **tener**) to retain
reumatismo rheumatism
revés: al revés backward, reversed
revisar to check
revista magazine; **puesto de revistas** newspaper stand
revólver *m.* revolver (17)
revuelto: huevos revueltos scrambled eggs
rey *m.* king; *pl.* king and queen; **los Reyes Magos** Three Wise Men, Magi
rezar (c) to pray (13)
rico/a rich (3); delicious (5)
ridículo/a ridiculous
riesgo risk
riguroso/a rigurous
río river
riqueza richness, wealth
rito rite
rizado/a curly (9)
robar to rob, steal (17)
robo theft
roca rock, stone
rodeado/a (de) surrounded (by)
rodilla knee
rojizo/a reddish
rojo/a red (3)
ropa clothes, clothing (3); **almacén** (*m.*) **de ropa** clothing store
ropero (clothes) closet (6)
rosa rose
rosado/a pink (3)
rotativo/a rotating
roto/a broken; **brazo roto** broken arm (12)
rubio/a blond(e) (9)
rueda wheel (10)
rugir *n. m.* roaring
ruido noise (7)
ruinas *f. pl.* ruins
ruta route
rutina routine

S

sábado Saturday (P)
sabana savannah

sábana (bed)sheet
saber *irreg.* to know; (4); **saber +**
inf. to know how to (do
something) (4)
sabor *m.* flavor, taste
sabroso/a pleasant, enjoyable;
delicious
sacar (qu) to get, obtain; to take out;
sacar buenas notas to get good
grades (4); **sacar(le) una muela** to
extract a tooth (12); **sacar(le)**
partido to take advantage;
sacar(le) una radiografía to take X
rays (12)
sacrificio sacrifice
sagüesero/a *pertaining to the southwest*
area of Miami
sal *f.* salt (5)
sala living room (6); **sala de clase**
classroom (1); **sala de emergencia**
emergency room (12)
salario salary
salchicha sausage
salida exit, departure
salir *irreg.* to leave, go out (4)
salmón *m.* salmon (5)
salón (*m.*) **de recreo** recreation room
salsa *type of music*
salud *f.* health (12)
saludable *m., f.* healthy
saludar to greet, salute (9);
saludarse to greet each other (16)
saludo greeting (P)
salvadoreño/a Salvadoran
salvaje *m., f.* wild, unexplored
salvavidas *m. s.* life preserver
san *shortened form of* **santo,** *used*
before most m. saints' names
sandalia sandal (3)
sandía watermelon (5)
sándwich *m.* sandwich (2)
sangre *f.* blood (12)
sangría wine and fruit punch
sanidad: departamento de sanidad
sanitation department
santo/a saint; **día** (*m.*) **del santo**
saint's day (11)
saquear to sack (*a city*) (8)
sarro sediment
satélite *m.* satellite
satisfacción *f.* satisfaction
se (*impersonal*) one; *i. o. pron.* to you
(*form.*)/him/her/it/them; *refl. pron.*
(to) yourself/yourselves
(*form.*)/himself/herself/itself/

oneself/themselves; (to) each
other/one another
secadora dryer
secar(se) (qu) to dry (oneself) (9)
seco/a dry (13)
secretario/a secretary (17)
secreto secret
secundario/a secondary
sed *f.* thirst; **tener** (*irreg.*) **sed** to be
thirsty (4)
seda silk (3); **de seda** made of silk
seguido/a in a row; continued (13);
en seguida at once
seguir (i, i) (g) to follow; to continue
(10)
según according to
segundo/a *adj.* second
seguridad *f.* security; **cinturón** (*m.*)
de seguridad safety belt
seguro/a sure; **es seguro** it's certain
(12); **estar** (*irreg.*) **seguro/a (de)** to
be sure (of) (12); **tener** (*irreg.*) **por**
seguro to be sure (*about something*)
seis six (P)
seiscientos/as six hundred (2)
seleccionado/a selected
selva jungle (15)
sello stamp (15)
semáforo traffic light (10)
semana week (P); **fin** (*m.*) **de**
semana weekend (14); **la semana**
pasada last week; **todas las**
semanas every week
semestre *m.* semester
senador(a) senator
sencillo/a simple
sensibilidad *f.* sensibility
sensualidad *f.* sensuality
sentarse (ie) to sit down (9)
sentimiento feeling; sentiment
sentir(se) (ie, i) to feel (9); to regret,
be/feel sorry (7); **lo siento** I am
sorry (about it) (6)
seña: hacer (*irreg.*) **señas** to signal
señal: señal (*m.*) **de tráfico** traffic
sign (1)
señalar to indicate
señor *m.* gentleman, man; sir (P);
Mr.; *pl.* Mr. and Mrs., ladies and
gentlemen
señora lady, woman; madam; Mrs.
(P); wife
señorita young lady, young woman;
Miss (P)
sepa *present subjunctive of* **saber**

separar to separate
septiembre *m.* September (P)
séptimo/a seventh (14)
sequía drought
ser *irreg.* to be (3); **ser de** to be from
(P); to belong to; to be made of
serie *f. s.* series
serio/a serious
serpiente *f.* snake
serrucho saw (18)
servicio service; **baño de servicio**
bathroom for servants; **técnico/a**
de servicio serviceman/
servicewoman
servilleta napkin
servir (i, i) to serve (7)
sesenta sixty (2)
setecientos/as seven hundred (2)
setenta seventy (2)
sexo sex
sexto/a sixth (14)
sierra mountain range
siesta nap; **dormir (ue, u) una/la**
siesta to take a nap (7)
siete seven (P)
siglo century (8)
significado meaning
significar (qu) to mean, signify
siguiente *m., f.* following; **al día** (*m.*)
siguiente on the following day; **a**
la mañana siguiente on the
following morning
silencio silence
silla chair (1)
sillón *m.* easy chair (6)
símbolo symbol
simpático/a nice, pleasant (3)
sin without (8); **sin duda**
undoubtedly, without a doubt; **sin**
embargo however, nevertheless
sindicato union (*workers*)
sino but, rather; except; **sino que**
but, on the contrary (13)
sinónimo synonym
síntoma *m.* symptom; sign
sistema *m.* system
situación *f.* situation
situado/a located
soberbio/a haughty (11)
sobrar(le) (a uno) to have in excess
sobre *n. m.* envelope (17); *prep.* on,
upon; over, above, concerning,
about; **sobre todo** above all
sobrino/a nephew/niece (4)
sociedad *f.* society

socio (business) partner
sociología sociology
sociólogo/a sociologist (18)
socorro: casa de socorro emergency hospital
sofá *m.* sofa, couch (6)
sol *m.* sun (13); **gafas de sol** sunglasses (14); **hacer** (*irreg.*) **sol** to be sunny (4)
solamente only (5)
soldadito (*diminutive of* **soldado**) dear soldier
solicitar to seek, ask for, request (18)
solicitud *f.* application
solitario/a solitary, lonely
sólo only (1)
solo/a alone; single
soltarse (ue) to get loose; let oneself go
soltero/a *n.* unmarried person; *adj.* unmarried, single (4)
sombra para los ojos eyeshadow (15)
sombrero hat (3)
sombrilla beach umbrella, parasol
soñar (ue) to dream; **soñar con** to dream about (13)
sopa soup (5)
soportar to tolerate, put up with (16)
sorprender to surprise (11)
sorpresa surprise (4)
sostener (*like* **tener**) to maintain, support
sótano basement (18)
su(s) *poss.* your (*form. s., pl.*)/his/her/its, their (2)
suave *m., f.* mild
subametralladora submachine gun
subir to go up (5); to get on
subjuntivo subjunctive (*grammar*)
succionar to suck up
sucesivamente: y así sucesivamente and so on
sucio/a dirty (6)
sucre *m. monetary unit of Ecuador*
Sudamérica South America
sudamericano/a South American
Suecia Sweden
sueco/a Swedish
suegro/a father-in-law/mother-in-law
sueldo salary
suelo floor; soil
sueño dream (6); **morirse (ue, u) de sueño** to be extremely sleepy; **tener** (*irreg.*) **sueño** to be sleepy (4)

suerte *f.* luck
suéter *m.* sweater (3)
suficiente *m., f.* sufficient
sugerencia suggestion
sugerir (ie, i) to suggest
Suiza Switzerland
suizo/a Swiss
sujeto subject
sumergir (j) to submerge, sink
super *n. m., f.* (*abbreviation of* **superintendente**) superintendent (*U.S.*), building manager
superar to overcome
superestrella *m., f.* superstar
superlativo superlative (*grammar*)
supermercado supermarket (5)
supersticioso/a superstitious
suponer (*like* **poner**) suppose (16)
supuesto: por supuesto of course (5)
sur *m.* south (8)
sureste *m.* southeast (8)
surtido selection, assortment
sustancia substance
sustantivo noun
suyo/a/os/as *poss.* your (*form. s., pl.*)/his/her/its, theirs (15)

T

tabaco tobacco
tableta tablet
tabú *m.* taboo
tal such (a); **con tal (de) que** provided that (18); **¿qué tal?** what's up?; **tal vez** perhaps (7); **tales como** such as
tala *n.* tree felling
talar to cut down (*a tree*)
talla (*garment*) size
tampoco neither, not either (10, 13)
tan so (6); as (12); **tan... como** as . . . as (12); **tan pronto como** as soon as (18)
tanque *m.* gas tank
tanto/a as much, so much; *pl.* as many, so many (7); **tanto/a/os/as... como** as much (many) . . . as (12)
tapa appetizer (*Sp.*)
tapia outside wall
taquigrafía shorthand (17)
tarde *f.* afternoon; **buenas tardes** good afternoon (P); **de/en/por la tarde** in the afternoon, evening (1, 6); *adv.* late (9); **tarde o temprano** sooner or later

tarea homework
tarjeta card, calling card; postcard (15); **tarjeta de crédito** credit card (3); **tarjeta de identificación** ID card (17); **tarjeta postal** postcard
taxi *m.* taxi, cab (15)
taxista *m., f.* taxi driver
taza cup (4)
té *m.* tea
teatro theater
técnico/a technician (18); **técnico/a de servicio** serviceman/ servicewoman
tecnología technology
telediario newscast
telefónico/a *pertaining to the telephone*
teléfono telephone; **guía de teléfonos** telephone book; **llamar por teléfono** to call on the telephone (4); **por teléfono** by/on the telephone (6)
telenovela soap opera (7)
televisión: mirar la televisión to watch television (6); **por televisión** on television
televisor *m.* television set (6)
tema *m.* theme, topic
temblar (ie) to tremble, shake
temer to fear, be afraid (11)
temor (*m.*) fear
temperatura temperature (12)
tempestad *f.* storm
temporada season
temprano early (5)
tender (ie) to tend to
tenedor *m.* fork (4)
tener *irreg.* to have (2); **no tener más remedio (que)** to have no choice (but) (15); **(no) tener razón** to be right (wrong) (4); **¿qué tienes?** what's wrong? (4); **tener _____ años** to be _____ years old (4); **tener calor/frío** to be/feel hot/cold (4); **tener celos** to be jealous (16); **tener cuidado** to be careful (4); **tener en cuenta** to take into account (18); **tener ganas de** + *inf.* to feel like (doing something) (4); **tener hambre/sed** to be hungry/thirsty (4); **tener miedo** to be afraid (4); **tener paciencia** to be patient (16); **tener por seguro** to be sure (*about something*); **tener prisa** to be in a hurry (4); **tener que** + *inf.* to have to (do something) (4); **tener**

sueño to be sleepy (4); **tener suerte** to be lucky
tenis *m.* tennis; sneaker (3); **cancha de tenis** tennis court
teoría theory
tercer *shortened form of* **tercero,** *used before m. s. nouns* (14)
tercero/a third (14)
terminal: terminal (*m.*) **de autobuses** bus terminal (15)
terminar to end, finish (6)
termómetro: poner(le) (*irreg.*) **el termómetro** to take one's temperature (12)
terremoto earthquake (13)
territorio territory
tesorero/a treasurer
testigo *m., f.* witness
ti *obj. of prep. pron.* you, yourself (*fam. s.*)
tiempo time; weather; **a tiempo** on time; **al mismo tiempo** at the same time (8); **¿cuánto tiempo hace que** + *present?* how long + *present perfect?* (15); **hacer** (*irreg.*) **buen/mal tiempo** to be good/bad weather (4); **¿qué tiempo hace hoy?** what's the weather like today?; **tiempo completo/parcial** full-/ part-time (18)
tienda store (2); **tienda de animales** pet shop (4)
tierra land; earth, world (13); territory
tigre *m.* tiger (10)
tilma *large cotton cloak fastened by a knot on the shoulder* (*Mex.*)
tímido/a timid (7)
tinto: vino tinto red wine
tío/a uncle/aunt (4)
típico/a typical
tipo type
título degree; diploma (18); title
tiza chalk (1)
toalla towel (9)
tocadiscos *m. s.* record player (7)
tocar (qu) to play (*musical instrument*) (7)
todavía still, yet (6); **todavía no** not yet
todo/a all (1); every; everything; **de todos modos** in any case; **en todas partes** everywhere; **toda clase (de)** all kinds (of); **todo derecho** straight ahead (10); **todo el día/toda la mañana/tarde/noche**

all day/morning/afternoon/evening long; **todo el mundo** everybody (7); **todos** everyone; **todos los días** every day (2)
tomar: tomar fotos to take photos (2); **tomar(le) la presión** to take (one's) blood pressure (12)
tomate *m.* tomato (5); **jugo de tomate** tomato juice
tono tone
tonto/a dumb (3)
toque: toque (*m.*) **de diana** reveille
torbellino whirlpool
tormenta storm (13)
tornado tornado (13)
torta round cake, tart; **torta de limón** lemon pie
tortilla omelette; cornmeal pancake (*Sp. Am.*); **tortilla española** potato omelette
tortuga tortoise, turtle
tos *f.* cough (12)
tostada toast (5)
trabajador(a) social social worker (18)
trabajar to work (1)
trabajo *n.* work (4); job
tradición *f.* tradition
traducir (*like* **producir**) to translate
traer *irreg.* to bring (4)
tráfico traffic; **señal** (*m.*) **de tráfico** traffic sign (10)
tragedia tragedy
traje *m.* suit (4): **traje de baño** swimming suit (14); **traje regional** regional custom/dress (11)
tramitar to carry through, transact
tranquilo/a calm (9)
transcribir to transcribe
transferir (ie, i) to transfer
transformarse to transform
tránsito transit
transmitir to transmit
transporte *m.* transportation, means of transportation (16)
tras behind (*adv.*)
tratamiento treatment (12)
tratar de + *inf.* to try to (do something) (12, 16); **tratarse de** to be a matter of; to be
través: a través de through
trayecto trip, trek
trece thirteen (P)
treinta thirty (P, 2)
tren *m.* train (15); **en tren** by train

trescientos/as three hundred (2)
tribu *f.* tribe
trigo wheat
triste *m., f.* sad (3)
triunfar to triumph
triunfo triumph
trompeta trumpet
tronar (ue) to thunder
trono throne
trueno thunder (13)
tu(s) *poss.* you (*fam. s.*)
tú *sub. pron.* you (*fam. s.*)
tubería tubing, piping (18)
turista *m., f.* tourist
turno turn; **estar** (*irreg.*) **de turno** to be open all night (*pharmacy*)
tuyo/a/os/as *poss.* your, (of) yours (*fam. s.*) (14)

U

Ud(s). (*abbreviation of* **usted/ustedes**)
úlcera ulcer (12)
últimamente lately (16)
último/a last, latest; **por último** finally
un, uno/a a, an; one; **un día** someday
ungüento ointment (12)
único/a only (13)
unidad (*f.*) **monetaria** monetary unit
unir to join
universidad *f.* university
universitario/a *adj.* university
urbanización *f.* real estate development; residential neighborhood
urbano/a urban
urgencia urgency, emergency
urgente *m., f.* urgent
usar to use (1); to wear (3)
usado/a used
usted *sub. pron.* you (*form. s.*); *obj. of prep. pron.* you (*form. s.*)
ustedes *sub. pron.* you (*form. pl.*); *obj. of prep. pron.* you (*form. pl.*)
utilidades *f. pl.* profits
utilizar (c) to utilize, use
uva grape (5)

V

vacaciones *f. pl.* vacation (8); **de vacaciones** on vacation
vacío/a empty (15); available
vacunar to vaccinate

valenciano/a *from Valencia, Spain*
valer *irreg.* to be worth; **valer la pena** to be worthwhile (18)
válido/a valid
valiente *m., f.* courageous, brave
valor *m.* value
vals *m.* waltz
valle *m.* valley (13)
vaqueros *m. pl.* jeans (3)
variado/a varied
variar to change, be variable
variedad *f.* variety
varios/as several, various (1)
varón *m.* male
vaso (drinking) glass (4)
vecino/a neighbor (8)
vegetal *m.* vegetable
vegetariano/a vegetarian
vehículo vehicle
veinte twenty (2)
veinticinco twenty five (P)
veinticuatro twenty four (P)
veintidós twenty two (P)
veintinueve twenty nine (P)
veintiocho twenty eight (P)
veintiséis twenty six (P)
veintisiete twenty seven (P)
veintitrés twenty three (P)
veintiuno twenty one (P)
vejez *f.* old age
vela: bote (*m.*) **de vela** sailboat (13)
velero sailboat (13)
velocidad *f.* speed
venado deer
venda bandage, dressing (12)
vendedor(a) seller, vendor, salesperson
vender to sell (2)
venezolano/a Venezuelan
venir *irreg.* to come (2)
venta sale; **a la venta** for sale
ventaja advantage
ventana window

ventanilla window (*in a bank*) (17); **asiento de ventanilla** window seat (15)
ver *irreg.* to see (4); **a ver** let's see
verano summer(time) (P)
verbo verb (*grammar*)
verdad *f.* truth (1); **es verdad** it's true (2); **¿verdad?** really? (1)
verdadero/a true, real (18)
verde *m., f.* green (3); **estar** (*irreg.*) **verde** to be unripe
verduras *f. pl.* vegetables, greens
vestido dress (3); **vestido de novia** wedding gown
vestido/a (de) dressed (in)
vestir (i, i) to dress; **vestirse** to get dressed (9)
veterinario/a veterinarian (18)
vez *f.* (*pl.* **veces**) time (8); **a veces** sometimes; **alguna vez** ever (*in a question*) (13); **de una vez** once and for all; **en vez de** instead of (18); **otra vez** again; **tal vez** perhaps
viajar to travel (8)
viaje *m.* trip
viajero/a traveler (15); **cheque** (*m.*) **de viajero** traveler's check (17)
víctima *m., f.* victim
vida: vida de internado life as an internee
vídeo videotape (7)
vidrio glass
viejo/a *n.* old man/woman (2); *adj.* old (3)
viento wind; **hace viento** it's windy (4)
viernes *m. s.* Friday (P)
villancico Christmas carol
vinculado/a joined
vino wine; **vino tinto** red wine
Virgen *f.* Virgin Mary; **selva virgen** unexplored jungle
viruela smallpox

visita visit; **estar** (*irreg.*) **de visita** to be visiting
visitar to visit
vista view; **punto de vista** viewpoint
vitalidad *f.* vitality
vitamina vitamin
vivir to live (2)
volante *m.* steering wheel (10)
volar (ue) to fly
volcán *m.* volcano (13)
vólibol *m.* volleyball
voltear to turn over
volumen *m.* volume
volver (ue) to return (7); **volver a +** *inf.* to (do something) again
vosotros/as *sub. pron.* you (*fam. pl. Sp.*); *obj. of prep. pron.* you, yourselves (*fam. pl. Sp.*)
votar to vote
voto *n.* vote
voz (*pl.* **voces**) voice; **en voz baja** in a low voice (17)
vuelo flight (15); **auxiliar** (*m., f.*) **de vuelo** flight attendant (15)
vuelta return; **dar** (*irreg.*) **la vuelta** to go around (10); **de ida y vuelta** round-trip (15)
vuelto/a *p.p.* returned (10)
vuestro/a/os/as *poss.* your (*fam. pl. Sp.*) (2); (of) yours (*fam. pl. Sp.*) (15)

Y

y and (P)
ya already (8); **ya no** no longer (11);
yerba (*also* **hierba**) herb
yo *sub. pron.* I

Z

zanahoria carrot (5)
zapatero/a shoemaker
zapato shoe (3)
zona zone, region, area
zoología zoology

English-Spanish Vocabulary

A

abandon **abandonar** (8)
able: to be able **poder** *irreg.* (7)
about **de, sobre**
above **sobre, arriba, (por) encima (de)** (7)
accept **aceptar** (3)
accomplice **cómplice** *m., f.* (17)
according to **según** (3)
account **cuenta** (17); checking account **cuenta corriente/de cheques** (7); long-term account **cuenta a largo plazo** (17); savings account **cuenta de ahorros** (17); to take into account **tener** (*irreg.*) **en cuenta** (18)
accountant **contador(a)** (18)
ache *v.* **doler (ue)** (12)
acquainted: to be acquainted with **conocer (zc)** (4)
activate **activar** (17)
address **dirección** *f.* (15); to address **dirigirse (j) (a)** (12)
adjust **ajustar** (10)
administration: business administration **administración** (*f.*) **de empresas** (18)
adults **mayores** *m. pl.* (16)
advertise **anunciar** (11)
advise **aconsejar** (11)
afraid: to be afraid **temer** (11), **tener** (*irreg.*) **miedo** (4)
after (afterward) **después (de) (que)** (4) (18); one after another **seguidos/as** (13)
afternoon **tarde** *f.*; good afternoon **buenas tardes** (P); in the afternoon **por/de/en la tarde** (P)
again **de nuevo** (13); **otra vez**
agency: travel agency **agencia de viajes**
agent **agente** *m., f.* (15)
ago: a month ago **hace un mes** (15)
ahead: straight ahead **todo derecho** (10)
airline **línea aérea** (15)
airplane **avión** *m.* (15)
airport **aeropuerto** (15)
aisle: aisle/window seat **asiento de pasillo/ventanilla** (15)

alarm **alarma** (17); alarm clock **reloj** (*m.*) **despertador** (9)
all **todo/a/os/as** (1); all day/morning/night long **todo el día/la mañana/la noche;** not at all **en absoluto** (16)
allergy **alergia** (12)
allow **permitir** (11), **dejar** (11)
almost **casi** (4)
alone **solo/a**
along **por** (5)
along: to get along well/badly **llevarse bien/mal** (9)
already **ya** (8)
also **también** (1)
although **aunque** (11)
always **siempre** (4)
ambassador **embajador(a)** (11)
among **entre** (9)
and **y** (P)
angry **enojado/a** (9); to get angry **enojarse** (9)
announce **anunciar** (11) (15)
announcer (*TV or radio*) **locutor(a)** (11)
another **otro/a** (2)
answer *v.* **contestar** (1); (*form. command*) **¡conteste Ud.!**
any (*some*) **alguno/a/os/as** (13), **algunos/as** (17); not any **ningún, ninguno/a** (13)
anyone **alguien** (13), **alguno** (13)
anything: anything else **algo más** (6); not anything **nada** (4, 13)
apartment **apartamento, piso** (*Sp.*) (2); apartment building **edificio de apartamentos** (2)
apologize **disculparse** (16)
appetizers **canapés** *m. pl.* (16)
applaud **aplaudir** (7)
apple **manzana** (4)
appliance: electrical appliance **aparato eléctrico** (6)
appointment **cita** (7)
April **abril** *m.* (P)
archeology **arqueología** (18)
architect **arquitecto/a** (18)
are: there are **hay;** there aren't **no hay** (P)

argue **discutir** (2)
arm **brazo** (9)
around: to go around **dar** (*irreg.*) **la vuelta (a)** (10)
arrange **arreglar** (16)
arrest: you are under arrest **está detenido/a** (10)
arrival **llegada** (13)
arrive **llegar (gu)** (6)
as **como;** as . . . as **tan... como** (12); as many . . . as **tantos/as... como;** as much . . . as **tanto/a... como** (12); as soon as **en cuanto, tan pronto como** (18)
ask **preguntar** (1); to ask for **pedir (i, i)** (7); to ask questions **hacer** (*irreg.*) **preguntas** (7); asking (for) **pidiendo**
asleep: to fall asleep **dormirse (ue, u)** (9)
at **a, en** (1)
attack *v.* **atacar (qu)** (8)
attack *n.*: heart attack **ataque** (*m.*) **al corazón** (12); to have a heart attack **dar(le)** (*irreg.*) **un ataque al corazón** (12)
attend **asistir (a)** (7)
attention: to pay attention to **hacer** (*irreg.*) **caso a/de** (16)
August **agosto** (P)
aunt **tía** (4)
authority **autoridad** *f.* (11)
authorize **autorizar (c)**
automobile **auto(móvil)** *m.* (2), **carro** (2), **coche** *m.* (2)
autumn **otoño** (P) (13)
avenue **avenida** (10)

B

bachelor **soltero** (4)
back *n.* **espalda** (9)
backpack **mochila** (1)
backward **hacia atrás**
bad **mal, malo/a** (2); the bad thing **lo malo** (16)
badly **mal** (16)
bag: carry-on bag **maletín** *m.* (14)
baggage **equipaje** *m.* (15)
ball **pelota** (14)

ballpoint pen **bolígrafo** (P)
banana **banana** (4), **plátano** (4)
band **banda** (11)
band-aid **curita** (12)
bandage **venda** (12)
bank **banco** (17); bank employee **empleado/a de banco** (17); piggy bank **alcancía** (17)
banker **banquero/a** *m. f.;* **empleado/a de banco/bancario** (17)
bar **bar** *m.* (2)
bargain **ganga** (7)
basement **sótano** (18)
bass (*musical instrument*) **bajo** (7)
bathe (oneself) **bañar(se)** (9)
bathroom **(cuarto de) baño** (6)
bathtub **bañera** (6)
be **estar** *irreg.* (3); **ser** *irreg.* (3); to be _____ years old **tener** (*irreg.*) _____ **años** (4); to be able **poder** (*irreg.*); to be afraid **temer, tener** (*irreg.*) **miedo** (4); to be called **llamarse** (P); to be careful/hot/cold/hungry/in a hurry/sleepy/thirsty **tener** (*irreg.*) **cuidado/calor/frío/hambre/prisa/sueño/sed** (4); to be glad of **alegrarse de** (11); to be pleasing **gustar** (7); to be right/wrong **tener/no tener** (*irreg.*) **razón** (4); to be sorry **sentir (ie, i)** (7); to be sure (of) **estar seguro/a de** (12); to be worth **valer** (*irreg.*) (18)
beach **playa** (8); beach bag **bolsa de playa** (14)
bean **frijol** *m.* (5)
beautiful **bonito/a** (2); **hermoso/a**
because **porque** (3)
become **ponerse** (*irreg.*) + *adj.* (13); **convertirse (ie, i) en** (10)
bed **cama** (6); to go to bed **acostarse (ue)** (9)
bedroom **alcoba, cuarto, dormitorio** (6), **recámara** (*Mex.*) (6)
beef **carne** *f.* **(de vaca/de res)** (5)
beefsteak **bistec** *m.* (5)
beer **cerveza** (2)
before **antes (de) (que)** (18)
begin **comenzar (ie) (c)** (7)
behind *adv.* **detrás de** (7)
believe **creer (y);** I don't believe it **no lo creo** (9)
bellboy **botones** *m. s.* (14)
bench **banco** (2)

besides **además** (4)
best **el/la mejor** (12); best man **padrino** (16); the best thing **lo mejor** (12); it's best **es mejor** (12)
better **mejor** (12); better than **mejor que** (12); it's better **es mejor** (12)
between **entre** (9)
big **grande** *m., f.* (2); this big **así de grande** (9)
bilingual **bilingüe** (11)
bill (*to be paid*) **cuenta;** (*of money*) **billete** *m.* (17)
bird **pájaro** (13)
birthday **cumpleaños** *m. s.* (11)
black **negro/a** (3)
blackboard (chalkboard) **pizarra** (1)
blond(e) **rubio/a** (9)
blood **sangre** *f.* (12); blood pressure **presión** (*f.*) **arterial**
blouse **blusa** (3)
blue **azul** *m., f.* (3)
boat **barco;** sailboat **bote** (*m.*) **de vela** (13)
body **cuerpo** (9)
book **libro** (1)
bookcase (bookshelf) **estante** *m.* (6)
boot **bota** (3)
boring: to be boring **ser** (*irreg.*) **aburrido/a** (9)
boss **jefe/a** (17)
bother *v.* **molestar** (11)
bottle **botella** (5)
box **caja** (5)
boy **muchacho** (2), **niño** (2)
boyfriend **novio** (4)
bracelet **pulsera** (14)
brakes **frenos** *m. pl.* (10)
branch (*tree*) **rama** (13); (*field*) **ramo** (18)
bread **pan** *m.* (4)
breakfast **desayuno** (5); to eat breakfast **desayunar(se)** (5)
breathing: difficulty in breathing **dificultad** (*f.*) **para respirar** (12)
bricklayer **albañil** *m., f.* (18)
bride **novia** (16)
bridegroom **novio** (16)
bridesmaid **madrina** (16)
bring **traer** *irreg.* (4)
broken **roto/a** *p.p.* (10)
broom **escoba** (6)
brother **hermano** (4)
brown **color** (*m.*) **café** (3); **castaño** (8)
build **construir (y)**

building **edificio;** apartment/office building **edificio de apartamentos/oficinas** (2)
bundle **bulto** (13)
burn *n.* **quemadura** (12)
bus **autobús** *m.* (2), **ómnibus** *m.* (15)
business **comercio** (18), **empresa** (18), **negocio**
business administration **administración** (*f.*) **de empresas** (18)
businessman/woman **empresario/a** (18)
busy **ocupado/a** (3)
but **pero** (1); **sino; sino que** (13)
butter **mantequilla** (5)
butterfly **mariposa** (13)
buy *v.* **comprar** (2)
by **por** (5)

C

café **café** *m.* (2)
calculator **calculadora** (1)
call *v.* **llamar;** to call on the phone **llamar por teléfono** (4)
calm **quieto/a** (12), **tranquilo/a** (9)
camera **cámara** (2)
can *n.* **lata** (5); *v.* (to be able) **poder** (*irreg.*) (7)
cancer **cáncer** *m.* (12)
capital (*city*) **capital** *f.* (8)
car **auto(móvil)** *m.* (2), **carro** (2), **coche** *m.* (2)
card: credit card **tarjeta de crédito** (3); identification (ID) card **tarjeta de identificación** (17); playing cards **cartas** *f. pl.* (3)
care: to take care (of) **cuidar (de);** to take care of oneself **cuidarse** (12); with care, carefully **con cuidado, cuidadosamente**
careful: to be careful **tener** (*irreg.*) **cuidado** (4)
carpenter **carpintero/a** (18)
carpentry **carpintería** (18)
carpet **alfombra** (6)
carrot **zanahoria** (5)
carry **llevar** (4)
case: in case **en caso de que** (18)
cash *v.* **hacer** (*irreg.*) **efectivo/cambiar un cheque** (17)
cash: to pay in cash **pagar (gu) al contado**
cashier **cajero/a**

cassette **casete** *m.* (7); cassette player **casetera** (7)

castle **castillo** (8)

cat **gato/a** (4)

cathedral **catedral** *f.* (8)

cavity **caries** *f. s.* (12)

celebrate **celebrar** (8)

cent: percent **por ciento** (17)

century **siglo** (8)

cereal **cereal** *m.* (5)

certain: it's certain **es cierto** (12), **es seguro** (12)

chair **silla** (1); easy chair **sillón** *m.* (6)

chalk **tiza** (1)

chalkboard **pizarra** (1)

champagne **champán** *m.* (16)

charge *v.* **cobrar** (18)

chat *v.* **charlar, conversar** (1)

cheap **barato/a** (2)

check **cheque** *m.;* checkbook **libreta de cheques** (17), **chequera** (17); checking account **cuenta corriente/de cheques** (17)

check: to check the baggage **facturar el equipaje** (15)

cheer up **animar(se)** (9)

cheerful **alegre** *m., f.* (13)

cheese **queso** (2)

chemist **químico/a** (18)

chemistry **química** (18)

chest: chest of drawers **cómoda** (6)

chicken **pollo** (5)

child **niño/a;** as a child **de niño/a** (4)

choice: to have no choice (but) **no tener** (*irreg.*) **más remedio (que)** (17)

choir **coro** (7)

choose **escoger (j)** (15)

chop **chuleta;** lamb/pork chop **chuleta de cordero/de cerdo** (5)

Christmas **Navidad** *f.* (8); Christmas Eve **Nochebuena**

church **iglesia** (2)

circular **circular** *f.* (17)

city **ciudad** *f.* (1); city hall **palacio municipal** (10)

class **clase** *f.* (1)

classmate **compañero/a de clase** (1)

classroom **sala de clase** (1)

clean *v.* **limpiar** (6)

cleaner: vacuum cleaner **aspiradora** (6)

clerk **dependiente/a** (3)

clever **listo/a**

client **cliente/a** (17)

climate **clima** *m.*

clock **reloj** *m.* (1)

closet (*clothes*) **ropero** (6)

clothes (clothing) **ropa** (3)

cloud **nube** *f.* (13)

coast *n.* **costa** (8)

coat *n.* **abrigo** (3)

coffee **café** *m.* (2); black coffee **café solo** (5); coffee with milk **café con leche** (5)

coffee shop **cafetería** (2), **café** *m.* (2)

coin **moneda** (8)

cold (*illness*) **catarro** (12); to be cold (out) **hacer** (*irreg.*) **frío** (4); to be (feel) cold **tener** (*irreg.*) **frío** (4)

collect (*pick up, gather*) **recoger (j)** (13)

collide (with) **chocar (qu) (con)** (10)

collision **choque** *m.* (10)

cologne **agua** *f.* (*but:* **el agua**) **de colonia** (14)

comb *n.* **peine** *m.* (14); *v.* (*one's hair*) **peinarse** (9)

come **venir** *irreg.* (2); (*fam. command*) **ven** (4); come back **volver (ue)** (7)

comfortable **cómodo/a** (3)

commerce **comercio** (18)

commercial *n.* (*TV or radio*) **anuncio comercial**

compact disc **disco compacto** (7)

company **compañía** (17), **empresa** (17)

competition **competencia** (14)

computer **computadora** (17), **ordenador** *m.* (*Sp.*) (17)

concert **concierto** (7)

confirm **confirmar** (15)

congratulate **felicitar** (16)

congratulation **felicitación** *f.* (16)

conquistador **conquistador** *m.* (8)

consul **cónsul** *m., f.* (11)

consult **consultar**

continue **seguir (i, i) (g)** (10)

cook *v.* **cocinar** (5)

cool: to be cool (out) **hacer** (*irreg.*) **fresco** (4)

cooperate **cooperar** (17)

copy *n.* **copia** (17)

copy(ing) machine **copiadora** (17)

corn **maíz** *m.* (5)

corner **esquina** (10)

cosmetics **cosméticos** *m. pl.* (14)

cost *v.* **costar (ue)** (7); how much does it cost? **¿cuánto cuesta?** (3)

costume: regional costume **traje** (*m.*) **regional** (11)

couch **sofá** *m.* (6)

cough *n.* **tos** *f.* (12); cough drop **pastilla para la tos** (12)

count *v.* **contar (ue)**

country **país** *m.* (8); countryside **campo** (13), **paisaje** *m.* (13)

course *n.* **curso;** of course **desde luego, por supuesto** (11); **¡claro!;** of course not! **¡claro que no!**

court (*tennis*) **cancha** (14)

cousin **primo/a** (4)

cowboy **charro** (*Mex.*) (11)

crash *v.* **chocar (qu)** (10)

cream: (face) cream **crema (para la cara)** (14)

credit *n.* **crédito;** credit card **tarjeta de crédito** (3)

cross *v.* **cruzar (c)** (10)

crowd *n.* **muchedumbre** *f.* (11)

cry *v.* **llorar** (12)

cucumber **pepino** (5)

culture **cultura**

cup **taza** (4)

cure *v.* **curar;** to get cured **curarse** (12)

curly **rizado/a** (9)

currently **actualmente** (18)

cute **mono/a** (4)

D

dance *n.* **baile** *m.; v.* **bailar** (7)

dangerous **peligroso/a** (18)

darn it! **¡caramba¡** (10)

date *n.* (*appointment*) **cita;** (*calendar*) **fecha** (P)

daughter **hija** (4)

day **día** *m.* (P); day after tomorrow **pasado mañana** (15); the following day **al día siguiente;** saint's day **día del santo** (11)

daytime: in the daytime **de día**

dead **muerto/a** *p.p.* (10)

dear **querido/a** (15)

December **diciembre** *m.* (P)

decide **decidir** (15)

deep **profundo/a**

degree **grado; título** (18)

delicious **delicioso/a, rico/a** (5)

delight *v.* **encantar**

demanding *adj.* **exigente** *m., f.* (6)

dentist **dentista** *m., f.* (12)
deny **negar (ie) (gu)** (12)
deodorant **desodorante** *m.* (14)
department store **almacén** *m.,*
  almacenes *m. pl.* (2)
deposit *v.* **depositar** (17)
deposit *n.*: deposit slip **hoja de**
  depósito (17)
desire *v.* **desear** (2)
desk **escritorio** (6); front desk (*of a*
  hotel) **recepción** *f.* (14)
dessert **postre** *m.* (5)
diamond **diamante** *m.;* **brillante** *m.*
  (16)
dictate *v.* **dictar** (17)
dictionary **diccionario** (1)
die *v.* **morir (ue, u)** (7)
difficult **difícil** (1)
difficulty **dificultad** *f.* (12)
dining room **comedor** *m.* (6)
dinner **comida** (5), **cena** (5); to eat
  dinner **cenar** (5), **comer** (5)
direct (oneself) (to) **dirigir(se) (j) (a)**
  (10)
dirty **sucio/a** (6)
disagree: I disagree **no estoy de**
  acuerdo
disappointment **contratiempo** (15)
disaster **desastre** *m.* (13)
discover **descubrir**
discovery **descubrimiento** (8)
discuss **discutir** (2)
dish *n.* **plato** (4) (5)
dishwasher **lavaplatos** *m. s.* (6)
district **barrio** (2)
divorce *n.* **divorcio** (16); to get a
  divorce **divorciarse** (16)
do **hacer** *irreg.* (2)
doctor *n.* **doctor(a)** (12), **médico/a**
  (12); doctor's office **consulta** (12),
  consultorio (12)
dog **perro/a**
domineering **dominante** *m., f.* (11)
done **hecho/a** *p.p.* (10)
door **puerta** (1)
dot: on the dot **en punto** (P)
doubt *v.* **dudar** (12); *n.* **duda;**
  without a doubt **sin duda**
down **abajo;** deep down **en el fondo**
  (16); to go down **bajar**
downtown **centro** (2)
dramatic **dramático/a**
drawers: chest of drawers **cómoda** (6)

drawing **dibujo** (1)
dream *v.:* to dream (about) **soñar**
  (ue) (con) (13); *n.* **sueño** (6)
dress *v.* **vestir(se) (i, i)** (9); *n.*
  vestido (3); regional dress **traje**
  (*m.*) regional (11)
dresser (*furniture*) **cómoda** (6)
drink *v.* **beber** (2), **tomar** (2); *n.*
  bebida; soft drink **refresco**
drive *v.* **manejar** (10), **conducir** (*like*
  producir) (10)
drive *n.:* scenic drive **rambla** (10)
driver **chofer** *m., f.;* **conductor(a)**
  (10); driver's license **carnet** (*m.*) **de**
  manejar/conducir (10)
drop: cough drop **pastilla para la tos**
  (12); eye/nose drops **gotas** (*f. pl.*)
  para los ojos/la nariz (12)
drugstore **farmacia** (12)
drum set **batería** (7)
drunk **borracho/a** (10)
dry *v.* (oneself) **secar(se) (qu)** (9);
  adj. (*dried up*) **seco/a** (13)
dryer (*clothes*) **secadora** (18)
dumb **tonto/a** (3)
during **durante**

E

each **cada** (4)
ear **oreja** (9)
early **temprano** (5)
earn **ganar** (3); to earn a living
  ganarse la vida
earphone **audífono** (7)
earring **arete** (14) *m.;* **pendiente** *m.*
  (*Sp.*) (14)
earth **tierra** (13)
earthquake **terremoto** (13)
east **este** *m.* (8), **oriente** *m.* (8)
easy **fácil** *m., f.* (1); easy chair **sillón**
  m. (6)
eat **comer** (2); (*fam. command*)
  ¡come! (4); to eat dinner/supper
  cenar (5); to eat lunch **almorzar**
  (ue) (c) (7)
economist **economista** *m., f.* (18)
egg **huevo** (5)
eight **ocho** (P)
eight hundred **ochocientos/as** (2)
eighteen **diez y ocho** (P), **dieciocho**
  (P)
eighth **octavo/a** (14)
eighty **ochenta** (2)

either . . . or **o... o;** not either
  tampoco (13)
electrician **electricista** *m., f.* (18)
electronic: electronic schedule
  horario electrónico (15)
elevator **ascensor** *m.* (14), **elevador**
  m. (14)
eleven **once** (P)
else: anything else? **¿algo más?** (6)
embrace *v.* **abrazar (c)** (16); *n.*
  abrazo (16)
emergency **emergencia** (12)
employee **empleado/a**
empty **vacío/a** (15)
encounter *v.* **encontrar (ue)** (7)
end *v.* **terminar** (6); *n.* **final** *m.* (17);
  at the end **al final** (17)
engagement: engagement ring **anillo**
  de compromiso (16)
engineer **ingeniero/a** (18)
engineering **ingeniería** (18)
English **inglés/inglesa** (1); English
  language **inglés** *m.* (1)
enjoy **disfrutar (de)** (11), **divertirse**
  (ie, i) (11), **gozar (c) (de)** (7)
enough **bastante** (9)
enter **entrar (en)**
entrance **entrada** (8)
envelope *n.* **sobre** *m.* (17)
eraser **borrador** *m.* (1)
estranged **peleado/a** (16)
even *adv.* **hasta** (8)
evening: good evening **buenas**
  noches (P); in the evening
  por/de/en la noche (1)
ever (*in a question*) **alguna vez** (13);
  jamás (13)
every **cada** (4); every day **todos los**
  días
everybody **todo el mundo** (7)
everyone **todos** (7), **todo el mundo**
  (7)
evident: it's evident **es evidente** (12)
example **ejemplo;** for example **por**
  ejemplo (4)
excursion: on an excursion **de**
  excursión (8)
excuse (oneself) **disculpar(se)** (16)
exit *n.* **salida** (8)
expect **esperar**
expensive **caro/a** (2)
explain **explicar (qu)** (10)
expressway **autopista** (10)

extract: to extract a tooth **sacar(le)**
(**qu**) **una muela** (12)
eye **ojo** (9); eye drops **gotas** (*f. pl.*)
para los ojos; eye shadow **sombra
para los ojos** (14)

F

face *n.* **cara** (9)
fall *v.* **caer** *irreg.* (13; *n.* **otoño** (P,
13); to fall asleep **dormirse** (**ue, u**)
(9); to fall down **caerse** (18); to
fall in love (with) **enamorarse** (**de**)
(16)
fan (*audience*) **fanático/a** (7)
far (from) **lejos** (**de**) (7)
fat **gordo/a** (3)
father **padre** *m.* (4), **papá** *m.* (4)
father-in-law **suegro** (16)
favor *n.* **favor** *m.;* do me the favor
of (*fam. command*) **hazme el favor
de** (4)
favorite **preferido/a** (14)
fear *v.* **temer** (11)
feather **pluma**
feel **sentir(se)** (**ie, i**) (7)(9); to feel
like (*doing something*) **tener** (*irreg.*)
ganas de + *inf.* (4)
fever **fiebre** *f.* (12)
fewer: fewer than **menos que** (12)
fiancé/fiancée **novio/a** (16)
field (*of study*) **ramo;** (*countryside*)
campo (13)
fifteen **quince** (P)
fifth **quinto/a** (14)
fifty **cincuenta** (2)
fight *v.* **pelear** (16)
file (*filing cabinet*) **archivo** (17)
fill *v.* **llenar;** fill in **empastar** (12)
fillet **filete** *m.* (5)
filling *n.* **empaste** *m.* (12)
film **película** (7)
finally **por fin** (5)
financial **financiero/a** (17)
find *v.* **encontrar** (**ue**) (7), **hallar**
fine *n.* **multa** (10); *adv.* **bien;** fine,
thanks **muy bien, gracias** (P)
finger *n.* **dedo** (9)
finish *v.* **terminar** (6)
first **primer, primero/a** (5)
fish *n.* **pescado** (5)
fishing pier **muelle** (*m.*) **pesquero**
five **cinco** (P)
five hundred **quinientos/as** (2)

fix *v.* **arreglar** (16)
flag *n.* **bandera** (11)
flight **vuelo** (15); flight attendant
auxiliar (*m., f.*) **de vuelo** (15),
azafata (15), **aeromoza** (15)
float *n.* **carroza** (11)
flood *n.* **inundación** *f.* (13)
floor (*of building*) **piso** (14)
flour **harina** (5)
flower *n.* **flor** *f.* (2)
flu **gripe** *f.* (12)
folder **carpeta** (17)
follow **seguir** (**i, i**) (**g**) (10)
following **siguiente** (3); the
following day **al día siguiente**
food **comida** (4); food items
comestibles *m. pl.* (5)
foolish **necio/a** (9)
foot **pie** *m.* (9)
for (*in the direction of, in order to*)
para (5); (*through, in*) **por** (5); for
his sake **por él** (5); in exchange
for **por** (5)
foreign **extranjero/a**
forest **bosque** *m.* (13)
forget **olvidar** (15)
fork **tenedor** *m.* (4)
forty **cuarenta** (2)
fountain **fuente** *f.* (2)
four **cuatro** (P)
four hundred **cuatrocientos/as** (2)
fourteen **catorce** (P)
fourth **cuarto/a** (14)
French **francés/francesa** (1); French
language **francés** *m.* (1)
frequently **con frecuencia**
Friday **viernes** *m. s.* (P)
fried **frito/a** (5) (10)
friend **amigo/a** (P)
friendly **amable** *m., f.* (16)
friendship **amistad** *f.* (16)
from **de** (P); from where? **¿de dónde?**
(P); I am from **soy de** (P)
front: in front of **frente a** (13); **en
frente de** (10); front desk (*of a
hotel*) **recepción** *f.* (14); front seat
asiento delantero (15)
fruit **fruta** (5); fruit stand, fruit
store **frutería** (4)
full **lleno/a** (15)
fun: to make fun (of) **burlarse** (**de**)
(11)
function *v.* **funcionar** (9)

furious **furioso/a**
furniture **muebles** *m. pl.;* piece of
furniture **mueble** *m.* (6)
furthermore **además** (4)

G

game (*match*) **partido** (14)
garage **garaje** *m.* (10)
garbage **basura;** garbage pail **cubo de
la basura** (13)
gas(oline) **gasolina** (10); gas pedal
acelerador *m.* (10); gas station
gasolinera (10)
gather **recoger** (**j**) (13)
generous **generoso/a**
gentleman **señor** *m.* (P); old
gentleman **señor** (*m.*) **viejo** (2)
German **alemán/alemana** (1);
German language **alemán** *m.* (1)
get: to get divorced **divorciarse** (**de**)
(16); to get good grades **sacar** (**qu**)
buenas notas (4); to get married
casarse (**con**) (16); to get a suntan
broncearse (14); to get up
levantarse (9)
gift **regalo** (2)
girl **muchacha** (2), **niña** (4)
girlfriend **novia** (4)
give **dar** *irreg.* (3); to give a shot
(*injection*) **poner** (*irreg.*) **una
inyección** (12)
glad **contento/a** (3); to be glad
of/about **alegrarse de** (9)
glass (*wine*) **copa** (4); (*drinking*) **vaso**
(4); (*material*) **cristal** *m.* (6); glass
of wine **copa de vino**
go **(ir)se** *irreg.* (3); (don't) go (*form.
command*) **(no) vaya Ud.** (6); to go
to bed **acostarse** (**ue**) (9); to go
down **bajar;** to go out **salir** (*irreg.*)
(4); to go shopping **ir** (*irreg.*) **de
compras** (3); to go toward
dirigirse (**j**) **a;** to go up **subir** (5)
going: I am (not) going **(no) voy** (3)
gold *n.* **oro** (8)
good **buen, bueno/a** (2); good
afternoon **buenas tardes** (P); good
evening/night **buenas noches** (P);
good morning **buenos días** (P)
good-bye **adiós**
governor **gobernador(a)** (11)
grab **coger** (**j**) (14)

grade *n.* **nota;** to get good grades **sacar (qu) buenas notas** (4)
granddaughter **nieta** (4)
grandfather **abuelo** (4)
grandmother **abuela** (4)
grandparents **abuelos** *m. pl.*
grandson **nieto** (4)
grape **uva** (5)
grass **hierba**
great **gran, grande**
green *adj.* **verde** *m., f.* (3)
greet **saludar** (9)
greeting **saludo** (P)
ground *n.* **suelo**
group (*musical*) **conjunto** (7)
guard; to guard (oneself) **guardar(se)** (8)
guitar: (lead) guitar **guitarra (principal)** (7)

H

hair **pelo** (9)
hairbrush **cepillo para el pelo/cabello** (14)
hairspray **laca** (14)
half **mitad** *f.;* half price **a mitad** (*f.*) **de precio** (7)
ham **jamón** *m.* (2)
hammer *n.* **martillo** (18)
hand *n.* **mano** *f.* (9); to lend a hand **echar una mano** (18)
handbag (*small suitcase*) **maletín** *m.* (14)
handcuff *v.* **poner(le)** (*irreg.*) **las esposas** (10); handcuffs *n.* **esposas** *f. pl.* (10)
happen **pasar** (17); **ocurrir** (15); what's happening? **¿qué pasa?** (9)
happy **alegre** *m., f.* (13), **contento/a** (3), **feliz;** to become happy **alegrarse** (9)
hard **duro/a** (4)
hat **sombrero** (3)
hate *v.* **odiar** (16)
hatred **odio** (16)
haughty **soberbio/a** (11)
have **tener** *irreg.* (2); to have to **tener que** (4), **deber** (4); to have a good time **divertirse (ie, i)** (7)
he *sub. pron.* **él**
head **cabeza** (9)
headache **dolor** (*m.*) **de cabeza** (12); to have a headache **doler(le) (ue) (a uno) la cabeza** (12)

headlight **faro** (10)
health **salud** *f.* (12)
hear **oír** *irreg.* (4)
heart **corazón** *m.* (12); heart attack **ataque** (*m.*) **al corazón** (12)
heaven: for heaven's sake! **¡Dios mío!** (10)
hello **hola** (P)
help *v.* **ayudar** (4)
hemisphere **hemisferio** (8)
her *poss. adj.* **su(s)** (2); hers **suyo/a/os/as** (14); *obj. of prep. pron.* **ella**
here **aquí** (1)
highway **carretera** (10); superhighway **autopista** (10)
hill **colina, loma** (13)
hire *v.* (*rent*) **alquilar** (7)
his *poss. adj.* **su(s)** (2)
Hispanic **hispánico/a, hispano/a**
home *adv.* **a casa;** at home **en casa** (6)
honest **honrado/a** (11)
hope *v.* **esperar** (11)
hors d'oeuvres **canapés** *m. pl.* (16)
horse **caballo** (11); to ride a horse **montar a caballo** (11)
hot **caliente** *m., f.;* to be hot (out) **hacer** (*irreg.*) **calor** (4); to be (feel) hot **tener** (*irreg.*) **calor** (4)
hotel **hotel** *m.* (2)
hour **hora** (P)
house **casa** (2); apartment house **edificio de apartamentos** (2)
how? **¿cómo?** (P); how are you? **¿cómo está Ud.?** (*form.*), **¿cómo estás?** (*fam.*) (P); how many? **¿cuántos/as?** (3); how much does it cost? **¿cuánto cuesta?** (3)
however **pero** (1), **sin embargo**
hug *v.* **abrazar (c)** (16); *n.* **abrazo** (16)
hundred: one hundred **cien, ciento** (2)
hungry: to be (very) hungry **tener** (*irreg.*) **(mucha) hambre** (4)
hurricane **huracán** *m.* (13)
hurry *n.* **prisa;** to be in a hurry **tener** (*irreg.*) **prisa** (4)
hurt *v.* **doler (ue)** (12)
husband **esposo** (4)

I

I **yo** (P)

ice **hielo**
ice cream **helado** (5), **mantecado** (11)
identification (ID) card **tarjeta de identificación** (17)
if **si** (P)
ill **enfermo/a** (3)
illness **enfermedad** *f.* (12)
importance **importancia**
important: it's important **es importante** (12)
in **en** (1), **por** (5); in order that **para que** (18); in order to **para** (5)
indeed **sí que** (14)
indicate **indicar (qu)** (9)
inexpensive **barato/a** (2)
inhabitant **habitante** *m., f.* (8)
injury **herida** (12)
instead of **en vez de** (18)
insulation **aislamiento** (18)
intercom **intercomunicador** *m.* (9)
interest *v.* **interesar;** *n.* **interés** *m.* (17)
interesting **interesante** *m., f.*
into **en**
investment **inversión** *f.* (17)
invite **invitar**
irritated **irritado/a** (12)
is **es;** there is **hay** (P); is there? **¿hay?** (P)
island **isla** (8)
it *d. o. pron.* **la, lo**
its *poss. adj.* **su(s)** (2)

J

jacket **chaqueta** (3)
jam **mermelada** (5)
January **enero** (P)
jealous: to be jealous **tener** (*irreg.*) **celos** (16)
jealousy **celos** *m. pl.* (16)
jeans **pantalones** (*m. pl.*) **vaqueros** (3), **jeans** *m.* (3)
jewelry **joyas** *f. pl.*
job **trabajo** (4)
juice **jugo** (2)
July **julio** (P)
June **junio** (P)
just: to have just (done something) **acabar de + *inf.*** (9)

K

key **llave** *f.* (10)
kick *v.* (*stamp*) **patalear** (12)

kill *v.* **matar;** to kill oneself **matarse** (18)

kiss *v.* **besar** (16); *n.* **beso** (16)

kit: makeup kit **estuche** (*m.*) **de maquillaje** (14)

kitchen **cocina** (6)

kitten **gatito/a** (4)

knife **cuchillo** (4)

know (*someone*) **conocer (zc)** (4); (*a fact*) **saber** *irreg.* (4)

L

ladder **escalera** (18)

lady **señora** (P); young lady **señorita** (P)

lake **lago** (13)

lamb **carne** (*f.*) **de cordero** (5)

lamp **lámpara** (6)

land *v.* **aterrizar (c)** (15)

landscape **paisaje** *m.* (13)

language **lengua** (P), **idioma** *m.* (11)

large **grande** *m., f.* (2)

last (*in a series*) **último/a;** (*with expressions of time*) **pasado/a** (14); last night **anoche**

late **tarde** (9)

lately **últimamente** (16)

later **después** (4), **luego** (P), **más tarde** (4); see you later **hasta luego** (P)

law (*course of study*) **derecho** (18); **ley** (*f.*) (10)

lawyer **abogado/a** (18)

leaf *n.* **hoja** (13)

learn **aprender** (4)

leather: (made of) leather **(de) piel** (3)

leave *v.* **dejar** (11), **partir, salir** *irreg.* (4); (*fam. command*) **¡sal!** (4)

left: to the left **a la izquierda** (10)

leg **pierna** (9)

lend **prestar** (3)

less: less than **menos que/de** (12)

lesson **lección** *f.* (1)

let **dejar** (11); (*to rent*) **alquilar** (14)

letter **carta** (2); (*circular*) **circular** *f.* (17)

letterhead **membrete** *m.* (17)

lettuce **lechuga** (5)

library **biblioteca** (1)

life **vida** (4)

lifesaver **salvavidas** *m. s.* (14)

light **luz** *f.* (*pl.* **luces**) (6); lightbulb **bombilla** (6); traffic light **semáforo** (10)

lightning bolt **relámpago** (13)

like *v.* **gustar;** to feel like (doing something) **tener** (*irreg.*) **ganas de** + *inf.* (4); how do you like? (*form.*); **¿qué le parece?** (7); I like **me gusta(n);** you (*form.*)/he/she like(s) **le gusta(n)** (P)

likeable **simpático/a** (3)

line *n.* (*of people*) **cola** (17); to stand in line **hacer** (*irreg.*) **cola**

lipstick **barra para los labios** (14), **creyón** (*m.*) **de labios** (14), **lápiz** (*m.*) **labial/para los labios** (14)

listen (to) **escuchar** (6), **oír** *irreg.* (6); (*form. command*) **¡escuche Ud.!**

little **pequeño/a** (2), **poco/a;** a little **un poco** (3)

live *v.* **vivir** (2)

living: to earn a living **ganarse la vida;** living room **sala** (6)

long **largo/a** (9); all day/morning/night long **todo el día/toda la mañana/toda la noche;** long term **a largo plazo** (17)

longer: no longer **ya no** (11)

look (at) **mirar** (2); to look for **buscar (qu)** (3)

lose **perder (ie)** (7); to get lost **perderse** (9)

lot: a lot of **mucho/a/os/as** (P)

lotion: aftershave lotion **loción** (*f.*) **de afeitar** (14); hand lotion **loción** (*f.*) **para las manos** (14); suntan lotion **loción bronceadora** (14)

lottery: lottery ticket **billete** (*m.*) **de lotería** (2)

love *v.* **querer** (*irreg.*) (7); **amar** (16); *n.* **amor** *m.* (7); to be in love (with) **estar** (*irreg.*) **enamorado/a (de)** (11); to fall in love (with) **enamorarse (de)** (16)

lunch *n.* **almuerzo** (5); to eat lunch **almorzar (ue) (c)** (7)

M

madam **señora** (P)

made **hecho/a** *p.p.* (10)

maid: maid of honor **madrina** (16)

main character **protagonista** *m., f.* (11)

majority **mayoría** (11)

make **hacer** *irreg.* (2)

makeup kit **estuche** (*m.*) **de maquillaje** (14)

man **hombre** *m.* (2); best man **padrino** (16); old man **viejo** (2); young man **joven** *m.* (2)

manager **gerente** *m., f.* (18)

manner **manera;** in this manner **así** (8)

many **muchos/as**

map *n.* **mapa** *m.* (1)

March **marzo** (P)

marked **marcado/a** (17)

market *n.* **mercado;** meat market **carnicería** (11)

marmalade **mermelada** (5)

married **casado/a** (4); to get married (to) **casarse (con)** (16)

match *n.* (*game*) **partido** (14)

May **mayo** (P)

mayor **alcalde/alcaldesa** (11)

meal **comida** (5)

means: by no means **de ninguna manera** (14)

meantime: in the meantime **mientras tanto** (14)

meat **carne** *f.* (5); meat market **carnicería** (11)

medicine **medicina** (12)

memory **recuerdo** (8)

merchant **comerciante** *m., f.* (11)

milk **leche** *f.* (2)

million: one million **un millón** (2)

mine: of mine *poss. adj.* **mío/a/os/as** (14)

minus **menos** (P)

miracle **milagro** (14)

mirror *n.* **espejo** (9)

mishap **contratiempo** (15)

Miss **señorita** (P)

mistaken **equivocado/a** (16); to make a mistake **equivocarse (qu)** (16)

molar **muela** (12)

Monday **lunes** *m. s.* (P)

money **dinero** (3)

month **mes** *m.* (P); a month ago **hace un mes** (15)

mood: to get in a good/bad mood **ponerse** (*irreg.*) **de buen/mal humor** (16)

moon **luna** (13)

more **más** (3); more than **más que** (12)

morning **mañana** (P); all morning **toda la mañana;** good morning **buenos días** (P); in the morning **por/de/en la mañana** (P)

most: the most + *adj.* **el/la/los/las más + *adj.*** (12)

mother **madre** *f.* (4), **mamá** (4)

mother-in-law **suegra** (16)

motor **motor** *m.* (10)

mount *n.* **monte** *m.* (8)

mountain **montaña** (8)

mouth *n.* **boca** (9)

move *v.* **mover (ue)**

movie **película** (7); movie house (movies) **cine** *m.* (2)

much **mucho/a** (P); so much **tanto/a** (7); too much *adv.* **demasiado** (10)

music **música** (7)

must **deber** (7)

my *poss. adj.* **mi(s)** (2)

myself *poss. pron.* **yo mismo/a** (14)

N

name *n.* **nombre** (1); my name is **me llamo** (P); what's his/her name? **¿cómo se llama él/ella?** (P); what's your name? **¿cómo se llama Ud.?** (*form.*) (P), **¿cómo te llamas (tú)?** (*fam.*) (P)

nap *n.* **siesta;** to take a nap **dormir (ue, u) la/una siesta** (7)

napkin **servilleta** (4)

near *adv.* **cerca de** (7)

necessary: it's necessary **es necesario** (12), **es preciso** (12); to be necessary (for one) **hacer(le) (*irreg.*) falta (a uno)** (18)

necklace **collar** *m.* (14)

necktie **corbata** (3)

need *v.* **necesitar** (2)

neighbor **vecino/a** (8)

neighborhood **barrio** (2)

neither **tampoco** (10); neither . . . nor **ni... ni** (13)

nephew **sobrino** (4)

never **nunca** (13), **jamás** (13)

nevertheless **sin embargo**

new **nuevo/a** (1); nothing new **nada de nuevo** (P)

news **noticias** *f. pl.* (2)

newspaper **periódico** (2)

next **siguiente** *m., f.* (3); **próximo/a** (15)

nice **simpático/a** (3); how nice! **¡qué bueno!**

niece **sobrina** (4)

night **noche** *f.* (P); all night **toda la noche;** at night **de noche, por la noche** (P); good night **buenas noches** (P); last night **anoche**

nightstand **mesa de noche** (6)

nine **nueve** (P)

nine hundred **novecientos/as** (2)

nineteen **diez y nueve** (P), **diecinueve** (P)

ninety **noventa** (2)

ninth **noveno/a** (14)

no **no** (P); no longer **ya no** (11)

no one **ninguno/a** (13), **nadie** (13)

nobody **ninguno/a** (13), **nadie** (13)

none **ningún, ninguno/a** (13)

north **norte** *m.* (8)

nose **nariz** *f.* (9); nose drops **gotas** (*f. pl.*) **para la nariz** (12)

not: not any **ningún, ninguno/a** (13); not very **poco** (3)

note *n.* **nota** (17)

notebook **cuaderno** (1)

nothing **nada** (4); nothing new **nada de nuevo** (P)

November **noviembre** *m.* (P)

now **ahora** (1); right now **ahora mismo** (9)

nowadays **hoy día** (8)

nuisance: what a nuisance! **¡qué lata!** (13)

nurse *n.* **enfermero/a** (12)

O

obtain **conseguir (i, i) (g)** (14)

obvious: it's obvious **es obvio** (12), **es evidente** (12)

occur **ocurrir** (15)

ocean **océano** (13)

October **octubre** *m.* (P)

of **de** (P)

office **oficina** (17); doctor's office **consulta** (12), **consultorio** (12); office building **edificio de oficinas**

oil *n.* **aceite** *m.* (5)

ointment **pomada** (12), **ungüento** (12)

old **viejo/a** (2); (*things only*) **antiguo/a** (2); old man/woman **viejo/a** (2)

older **mayor** (4)

omelette **tortilla** (5)

on **en** (1); on (top of) **sobre** (7), **encima de** (7)

once: at once **en seguida** (15)

one **uno** (P)

one hundred **cien, ciento** (2)

onion **cebolla** (5)

only **sólo** (1), **solamente** (5), **único/a** (13)

open *v.* **abrir** (2); to open a savings account **abrir una cuenta de ahorros** (17)

open, opened **abierto/a** *p.p.* (10)

opera: soap opera **telenovela** (7)

or **o** (3)

orange **naranja** (5); orange juice **jugo de naranja** (2)

order *v.* **mandar** (*command*); (*to ask for*) **pedir (i, i)** (7)

order *n.*: in order that **para que** (18); in order to **para** (5)

other **otro/a** (2)

ought (to) **deber** (7); you ought to **debiera** (*form. s.*), **debieras** (*fam. s.*)

our *poss. adj.* **nuestro/a** (4)

oven **horno** (6)

over (*on top of*) **(por) encima de** (7)

overcoat **abrigo** (3)

owe **deber** (7)

own *adj.* **propio/a** (16)

owner **dueño/a** (18)

oxygen: to give (someone) oxygen **dar(le) (*irreg.*) oxígeno** (12)

P

package **paquete** *m.* (5)

pad: shorthand pad **libreta de taquigrafía** (17)

pain *n.* **dolor** *m.* (12); the pain won't go away **el dolor no se me quita** (12)

paint *v.* **pintar** (18)

painter **pintor(a)** (18)

pale *adj.* **pálido/a** (14)

pants **pantalones** *m. pl.* (3)

papa **papá** *m.* (2)

paper *n.* **papel** *m.* (1); (*class report*) **reporte** *m.* (6)

parade **desfile** *m.* (11)

paralysis **parálisis** *f.* (12)

parents **padres** *m. pl.* (4)

park *n.* **parque** *m.* (2)

park *v.* **aparcar (qu)** (10), **estacionar** (10)

parlor: ice cream parlor **heladería** (11)

party *n.* **fiesta** (3)

pass (by) **pasar (por)** (10)

passenger **pasajero/a** (15)

past **pasado/a** *p.p.* (10); *n.* **pasado** (8)

patient *n.* **paciente** *m., f.* (12); to be patient **tener** (*irreg.*) **paciencia** (4)

pay *v.* **pagar (gu)** (3); to pay attention to **hacer** (*irreg.*) **caso a/de** (16); to pay in cash **pagar (gu) al contado**

pea **guisante** *m.* (5)

peach **melocotón** *m.* (5), **durazno** (5)

pear **pera** (5)

pearl **perla** (14); **collar** (*m.*) **de perlas** pearl necklace (14)

pedal: gas pedal **acelerador** *m.* (10)

pedestrian **peatón** *m.* (10)

pen (*ballpoint*) **bolígrafo** (1)

pencil **lápiz** *m.* (*pl.* **lápices**) (1)

people **gente** *f. s.* (2)

pepper **pimienta** (5)

per **por;** percent **por ciento** (17)

perfume **perfume** *m.* (14)

perhaps **tal vez** (7)

permit *v.* **permitir** (11)

pet shop **tienda de animales** (4)

pharmacist **farmacéutico/a** (18)

pharmacy **farmacia** (12)

photograph *n.* **fotografía** (2)

pick up **recoger (j)** (13)

piggy bank **alcancía** (17)

pill **píldora** (12)

pillow **almohada** (9)

pineapple **piña** (5)

pink **rosado/a** (3)

pipe **tubería** (18)

pirate **pirata** *m., f.* (8)

pitcher **jarra** (4)

pity **lástima;** it's a pity **es (una) lástima** (12)

place *n.* **lugar** *m.* (7)

plant *v.* **plantar** (13)

plate **plato** (4)

play *v.* (*a game*) **jugar (ue) (gu) a** (7); (*a musical instrument*) **tocar (qu)** (7); (*a role*) **hacer** (*irreg.*) **un papel**

player **jugador(a)** (14); record player **tocadiscos** *m. s.* (7)

pleasant (*people*) **simpático/a** (3), **agradable** *m., f.* (10), **amable** *m., f.* (16)

please **por favor** (5) (*fam. command*)

pleased: pleased to meet you **encantado/a, mucho gusto** (P)

pleasing: to be pleasing (to someone) **gustar(le) (a alguien)** (P)

plot *n.* (*of story*) **argumento** (11)

plumber **fontanero/a** (*Sp.*), **plomero/a** (18)

plumbing **tubería** (18)

plus (*with numbers*) **más** (P)

pneumonia **pulmonía** (12)

pocket **bolsillo** (17)

police (force) **policía** (10); policeman **policía** *m.* (10); policewoman **mujer policía** (10)

police headquarters **estación** (*f.*) **de policía** (10)

polite **amable** *m., f.* (16)

politics **política** *s.* (2)

pool: swimming pool **piscina** (14)

poor **pobre** *m., f.* (3)

poorly **mal** (7)

pork **carne** (*f.*) **de cerdo** (5)

port (*sea*) **puerto** (8)

possible: it's possible **es posible** (12)

post office **correo** (15); main post office **correo central** (10)

postage stamp **sello** (15), **estampilla** (15)

postcard **tarjeta postal; tarjeta** (15)

potato **papa** (5), **patata** (5)

practice *v.* **practicar (qu)** (1)

pray **rezar (c)** (13)

prefer **preferir (ie, i)** (7)

prepare (oneself) **preparar(se)** (1)(9)

prescription **receta** (12)

present *n.* (*gift*) **regalo** (2)

president **presidente/a** (2)

pressure: high/low blood pressure **presión** (*f.*) **arterial alta/baja** (12); to take (one's) blood pressure **tomar(le) la presión** (*f.*) (12)

pretty **bonito/a** (2)

price **precio** (3); half price **a mitad de precio** (7)

print *v.* **imprimir** (17)

printer **impresora** (17)

prize **premio** (4)

probable: it's probable **es probable** (12)

probably **probablemente, seguramente** (13)

professor **profesor(a)** (P)

program *n.* **programa** *m.*

promise *n.* **promesa** (16)

pronounce **pronunciar** (1)

provided: provided that **con tal (de) que** (18)

psychiatrist **psiquiatra** *m., f.* (18)

pulse *n.* **pulso** (12)

puppy **perrito/a** (4)

purse **bolso** (3), **bolsa** (3), **cartera** (3)

put **poner** *irreg.*, **puesto/a** *p.p.* (10); (*fam. comm.*) **¡pon!** (4); to put on (*clothes*) **ponerse** *irreg.* (9); to put up with **soportar** (16)

Q

quarrel *n.* **disgusto** (16)

quarter: it's a quarter after one **es la una y cuarto** (P)

queen **reina** (11)

question *n.* **pregunta** (1)

quiet (calm) **tranquilo/a** (9)

quite **bastante** (9)

R

racket (*sports*) **raqueta** (14)

railroad station **estación** (*f.*) **del ferrocarril** (15)

rain *v.* **llover (ue)** (7); *n.* **lluvia** (13); it's raining **está lloviendo**

rake *n.* **rastrillo** (13)

range *n.* (*kitchen*) **cocina eléctrica/de gas** (6)

rather **bastante** (9)

read **leer (y)** (2)

ready **listo/a** (3)

real **verdadero/a** (18)

realistic **realista** *m., f.* (11)

really **realmente;** really? **¿verdad?** (1)

reason: for that reason **por eso** (5)

receive **recibir**

reception **recepción** *f.* (16)

recommend **recomendar (ie)** (11)

record *v.* **grabar** (7); *n.* (*phonograph*) **disco** (7); record player **tocadiscos** *m. s.* (7)

red **rojo/a** (3)

reduced **rebajado/a** *p.p.* (3)

refreshment **refresco**

refrigerator **refrigerador** *m.* (6)

refugee **refugiado/a** (11)

registration **matrícula** (18)

regret *v.* **sentir (ie, i)** (7)

relative *n.* **pariente** *m., f.* (4)
remedy *n.* **remedio** (12)
remember **recordar (ue)** (8)
remind **recordar (ue)** (15)
remove **quitar** (13)
rent *v.* **alquilar** (7)
repair *v.* **reparar** (18); *n.* **reparación** *f.* (18)
repairs: is closed for repairs **está en obras** (10)
repeat **repetir (i, i)** (7); (*form. command*) **¡repita Ud.!**
report *n.* **reporte** *m.* (6)
request *v.* **pedir (i, i)** (7)
resolve *n.* **resolver (ue)** (16)
rest *v.* **descansar** (6)
restaurant **café** *m.* (2), **restaurante** *m.* (2)
return *v.* (*to a place*) **volver (ue)** (7); (*objects*) **devolver (ue)** (7); *n.* **regreso** (15)
returned **vuelto/a** *p.p.* (10); **devuelto/a** *p.p.*
review *v.* **repasar**
revolver *n.* **revólver** *m.* (17)
rice **arroz** *m.* (5)
rich **rico/a** (3)
ride a horse **montar a caballo** (11)
right: (not) to be right **(no) tener** (*irreg.*) **razón** (4); to/on the right **a la derecha** (10); right? **¿verdad?** (1); right now **ahora mismo** (9)
ring *n.* **anillo;** diamond ring **anillo de brillantes** (14)
river **río** (13)
road **camino** (13); road sign **letrero** (10)
rob **robar** (17)
robber **asaltante** *m., f.* (17)
roll (*bread*) **panecillo** (5)
room *n.* **habitación** *f.* (6), **cuarto, recámara** (*Mex.*); dining room **comedor** *m.* (6): living room **sala** (6); recreation room **salón** (*m.*) **de recreo** (7)
rouge (*blush*) **colorete** *m.* (14)
round-trip ticket **billete** (*m.*)/**boleto de ida y vuelta** (15)
row: in a row **seguido/a** (13)
rug **alfombra** (6)
run *v.* **correr**

S

sack (*a city*) **saquear** (8)
sad **triste** *m., f.* (3)

said **dicho/a** *p.p.* (10)
sail *v.* **navegar (gu)** (13)
sailboat **bote** (*m.*) **de vela** (13), **velero** (13)
saint's day **día** (*m.*) **del santo** (11)
salad **ensalada** (5)
salary **sueldo**
sale **liquidación** (*f.*), **venta**
salesclerk **dependiente/a** (3)
salmon **salmón** *m.* (5)
salt **sal** *f.* (5)
same **mismo/a;** the same **lo mismo** (11)
sand **arena** (13)
sandal **sandalia** (3)
sandwich **sándwich** *m.* (2)
satisfied **contento/a** (3)
Saturday **sábado** (P)
save (*money*) **ahorrar**
savings **ahorros** *m. pl.* (17)
saw **serrucho** (18)
say **decir** *irreg.* (2); (*fam. command*) **¡di!** (4); you don't say! **¡no me diga!**
schedule **horario;** electronic schedule **horario electrónico** (15)
school **escuela** (4)
science fiction **ciencia ficción** (7)
sea **mar** *m.* (8)
seafood **marisco(s)** (5)
season **estación** *f.* (P)
seat *n.* **asiento** (10); aisle/window seat **asiento de pasillo/de ventanilla** (15)
second **segundo/a** (5); second of December **el dos de diciembre** (14)
secretary **secretario/a** (17)
see **ver** *irreg.* (4); let's see **a ver**
seek **solicitar** (18)
seem **parecer (zc)**
seen **visto/a** *p.p.* (10)
seldom **raras veces** (8)
sell **vender** (2)
send **mandar** (8)
sentence **oración** *f.* (3)
September **septiembre** *m.* (P)
serve *v.* **servir (i, i)** (7)
serviceman/servicewoman **técnico/a** (18)
set: television set **televisor** *m.* (7)
seven **siete** (P)
seven hundred **setecientos/as** (2)
seventeen **diez y siete** (P), **diecisiete** (P)

seventh **séptimo/a** (14)
seventy **setenta** (2)
several **varios/as**
shake: to shake hands **dar(se)** (*irreg.*) **la mano** (9)
shampoo **champú** *m.* (14)
sharp (*on time*) **en punto** (P)
shave (oneself) **afeitar(se)** (9)
shaver (*electric*) **máquina de afeitar** (14)
she *sub. pron.* **ella** (P)
sheet (*bed*) **sábana** (9)
shellfish **marisco(s)** (5)
shine *v.* **brillar** (13)
ship **barco** (15)
shirt **camisa** (3); T-shirt **camiseta** (3)
shoe **zapato** (3)
shop *n.* **tienda** (2); pet shop **tienda de animales** (4)
shopping: to go shopping **ir** (*irreg.*) **de compras** (3); shopping bag **bolsa** (5); shopping cart **carrito (de las compras)** (5)
short (*stature*) **bajo/a** (3); (*length*) **corto/a** (9); short term **a corto plazo** (17); short time **rato** (4)
shorter **más bajo/a; más corto/a** (12)
shorthand pad **libreta de taquigrafía** (17)
shorts **pantalones** (*m. pl.*) **cortos** (3)
shot: to give a shot **poner(le)** (*irreg.*) **una inyección** (12)
shout *v.* **gritar** (6)
shovel *n.* **pala** (13)
shower *n.* **ducha** (9)
shrimp **camarón** *m.* (5)
shut *v.* **cerrar (ie)** (7)
shy **tímido/a** (4)
sick **enfermo/a** (12)
sidewalk **acera** (10)
sign *v.* **firmar** (17); *n.* **cartel** *m.* (11); (*road/street*) **letrero** (10)
signature **firma** (17)
silk **seda** (3); made of silk **de seda** (3)
silver **plata** (14)
silverware **cubiertos** *m. pl.* (4)
since (*because*) **como** (8)
sing **cantar** (7)
singer **cantante** *m., f.* (7)
single (*unmarried*) **soltero/a** (4)
sink (*kitchen*) **fregadero** (6)
sir **señor** *m.* (P)
sister **hermana** (4)

sit down **sentarse (ie)** (9)
six **seis** (P)
six hundred **seiscientos/as** (2)
sixteen **diez y seis** (P), **dieciséis** (P)
sixth **sexto/a** (14)
sixty **sesenta** (2)
size (*clothes*) **talla** (3); (*shoes*) **número**
ski *v.* **esquiar** (8)
skiing *n.* **esquí** *m.* (8)
skin *n.* **piel** *f.*
skirt *n.* **falda** (3)
sky **cielo** (13)
sleep *v.* **dormir (ue, u)** (7)
sleepy: to be sleepy **tener** (*irreg.*)
  sueño (4)
small **chico/a, pequeño/a** (2)
smart **listo/a** (3)
smoke *v.* **fumar** (11); *n.* **humo** (15)
smoker **fumador(a)** (15)
snack *v.* **merendar (ie)** (9)
sneaker **tenis** *m.* (3)
snow *n.* **nieve** *f.* (8)
snowflake **copo de nieve**
snowman **muñeco de nieve** (13)
so **así** (P), **tan** (6); and so **conque**
  (18); so much **tanto/a**
soap **jabón** *m.* (9); soap opera
  telenovela (7)
sociologist **sociólogo/a** (18)
sock *n.* **calcetín** *m.* (3)
sofa **sofá** *m.* (6)
soft **blando/a** (13); soft drink
  refresco
sold out **agotado/a** *p.p.* (14)
solicit **solicitar** (18)
solve **resolver (ue)** (16)
some **algún, alguno/a/os/as** (13),
  algunos/as (7)
someone **alguien** (13), **alguno** (13)
something **algo** (9)
sometimes **a veces** (1)
son **hijo** (4)
song **canción** *f.* (7)
soon **pronto** (7); as soon as **tan
  pronto como** (18), **en cuanto** (9)
sore: sore throat **dolor** (*m.*) **de
  garganta** (12)
sorry: I am sorry **lo siento** (6); to
  be/feel sorry **sentir (ie, i)** (7)
soup **sopa** (5)
south *n.* **sur** *m.* (8)
Spain **España** (P)
Spanish **español(a)** (1); Spanish
  language **español** *m.* (1)
speak **hablar** (1); **dirigirse (j) a** (10)

specialize **especializarse (c)** (14)
spend (*money*) **gastar** (3); (*time*)
  pasar (13)
spite: in spite of **a pesar de** (8)
spoon *n.* **cuchara** (4)
spring(time) **primavera** (P) (13)
stained **manchado/a** (3)
stamp (*postage*) **sello** (15), **estampilla**
  (15)
stand: taxi stand **parada de taxis** (15)
star *n.* **estrella** (13)
start: start a business **montar una
  empresa** (18)
state *n.* **estado** (11)
station: bus station **estación** (*f.*) **de
  autobuses** (15); railroad station
  estación (*f.*) **del ferrocarril** (15);
  station wagon **camioneta** (10)
steak **bistec** *m.* (5)
steering wheel **volante** *m.* (10)
stewardess **azafata** (15), **aeromoza**
  (15)
still *adv.* **todavía** (6); *adj.* **quieto/a**
  (12)
stomach **estómago**; stomachache
  dolor (*m.*) **de estómago** (12)
stone **piedra** (13)
stop *v.* **parar** (10); to stop (doing
  something) **dejar de** + *inf.*
stop: bus stop **parada de autobuses**
  (15)
store *n.* **tienda** (2)
storm *n.* **tormenta** (13)
story **historia** (11), **cuento** (16)
stove **cocina (eléctrica/de gas)** (6)
straight (*hair*) **lacio/a** (9); straight
  ahead **todo derecho** (10)
strawberry **fresa** (5)
street **calle** *f.* (2); street sign **letrero**
  (10)
strong **fuerte**
student **alumno/a** (1), **estudiante**
  m., f. (P)
study *v.* **estudiar** (1)
subway **metro** (2)
sugar **azúcar** *m.* (5)
suit *n.* (*clothes*) **traje** *m.* (3)

T

table **mesa** (1); coffee table **mesa de
  centro** (6)
tablecloth **mantel** *m.* (4)
tablespoon **cuchara** (4)
tablet **pastilla** (12)

take **tomar; llevar** (4); to take a nap
  dormir (ue, u) la/una siesta (7);
  to take off (*clothing*) **quitarse** (9);
  to take off (*plane*) **despegar (gu)**
  (15); to take pictures **tomar fotos**
  (2); to take a trip **hacer** (*irreg.*) **un
  viaje** (8)
talk *v.* **conversar** (1), **charlar** (1)
tall **alto/a** (1)
taller **más alto/a** (12)
tan: to get a tan **broncearse** (13)
tape: tape recorder **grabadora**; tape
  player **casetera** (7)
taxi **taxi** *m.* (2)
teach *v.* **enseñar** (1)
teacher **maestro/a**
teaching (*career*) **pedagogía** (18)
teaspoon **cucharita** (4)
technician **técnico/a** (18)
telephone *n.* **teléfono**; to call on the
  telephone **llamar por teléfono** (4)
television **televisión** *f.*; television set
  televisor *m.* (6)
tell **decir** *irreg.* (2); (*narrate*) **contar
  (ue)**
teller **cajero/a** (17)
temperature **temperatura**; to take
  (one's) temperature **poner(le)**
  (*irreg.*) **el termómetro** (12)
ten **diez** (P)
tennis **tenis** *m.* (14)
tenth **décimo/a** (14)
term: short/long term **a corto/largo
  plazo** (17)
than **que** (12)
that *adj.* **ese/a** (6), **aquel/aquella** (6);
  pron. **ése/a** (6), **aquél/aquélla** (6),
  neuter **eso** (6), **aquello** (6); *conj.*
  que (1); that which **lo que** (16)
their *poss. adj.* **su(s)** (2)
theirs *poss. adj.* **suyo/a/os/as** (15)
them *d. o. pron.* **los, las**; *i. o. pron.*
  les; with them **con ellos/ellas**
then **entonces** (3), **luego** (3)
there **ahí** (6); there is/are **hay** (P)
these **estos/as** (6)
they **ellos/as** (P)
thin **delgado/a** (3)
thing **cosa** (1)
think **pensar (ie)** (7); **creer (y)** (6);
  to think about **pensar en**
third **tercer, terceno/a** (5)
thirsty: to be thirsty **tener** (*irreg.*) **sed**
  (4)
thirteen **trece** (P)

thirty **treinta** (2)

this *adj.* **este/a** (6); this (one) *pron.* **éste/a** (6), **esto** (6)

those *adj.* **esos/as** (6), **aquellos/as** (6); *pron.* **ésos/as** (6), **aquéllos/as** (6)

thousand: one thousand **mil** *m.* (2)

three **tres** (P)

three hundred **trescientos/as** (2)

throat: sore throat **dolor** (*m.*) **de garganta** (12)

through *prep.* **por** (5)

thunder **trueno** (13)

Thursday **jueves** *m. s.* (P)

thus **así** (8)

ticket **boleto** (7), **billete** *m.* (7); round-trip ticket **boleto/billete de ida y vuelta** (15); to give (one) a ticket **poner(le)** (*irreg.*) **una multa** (10)

tiger **tigre** *m.* (10)

time *n.* **hora, tiempo** (8), **vez** (*pl.* **veces**) (8); at times **a veces**; at the same time **al mismo tiempo** (8); at what time **¿a qué hora?** (P); full-/part-time **tiempo completo/parcial** (18); to have a good time **divertirse (ie, i)** (9); it's time to **es hora de** (9); what time is it? **¿qué hora es?** (P)

tire *n.* **llanta** (10), **goma** (10)

tired **cansado/a** (3); to get tired **cansarse** (9)

title **título** (8)

to **a** (P)

toast *n.* (*bread*) **tostada** (5); (*drinking*) **brindis** *m.* (16); *v.* (*to drink*) **brindar** (16)

today **hoy** (P)

toe **dedo del pie** (9)

toilet **inodoro** (6)

tolerate **soportar** (16)

tomato **tomate** *m.* (5)

tomorrow **mañana** (P); until (*I see you*) tomorrow **hasta mañana** (P)

too (*excessively*) **demasiado** (10); (*also*) **también** (1)

tool **herramienta** (18)

toothbrush **cepillo de dientes** (14)

toothpaste **pasta de dientes** (14)

tornado **tornado** (13)

toward **hacia**

towel *n.* **toalla** (9)

traffic **tráfico;** traffic light **semáforo** (10); traffic sign **señal** (*f.*) **de tráfico** (10)

train **tren** *m.* (15)

tranquilizer **calmante** *m.* (12)

transportation: modes of transportation **transportes** *m. pl.* (15)

travel **viajar** (8)

travel agency **agencia de viajes**

traveler **viajero/a** (15); traveler's check **cheque** (*m.*) **de viajero**

tree **árbol** *m.* (2)

trip **viaje** *m.* (8); to take a trip **hacer** (*irreg.*) **un viaje** (8)

trouble: to be worth the trouble **valer** (*irreg.*) **la pena** (18)

truck *n.* **camión** *m.* (10)

true: it's true **es cierto** (12), **es verdad** (12)

trunk **baúl** *m.* (10), **maletero** (10)

truth **verdad** *f.;* the truth is that **la verdad es que** (12)

try (to do something) **tratar de +** *inf.* (12) (16); **intentar** (14)

T-shirt **camiseta** (3)

Tuesday **martes** *m. s.* (P)

tuna **atún** *m.* (5)

turkey **pavo** (5)

turn *v.* **doblar** (10); to turn around **dar** (*irreg.*) **la vuelta** (10); to turn off **apagar (gu)** (6); to turn on **encender (ie)** (6)

twelve **doce** (P)

twenty **veinte** (P)

two **dos** (P)

two hundred **doscientos/as** (2)

type *v.* **pasar a máquina** (17)

typewriter **máquina de escribir** (6)

U

ugly **feo/a** (2)

ulcer **úlcera** (12)

umbrella **paraguas** *m. s.;* beach umbrella **sombrilla** (14)

uncle **tío** (4)

uncomfortable **incómodo/a** (3)

under(neath) **debajo de** (7)

understand **comprender** (4), **entender (ie)** (4), (7)

university **universidad** *f.* (1)

unless **a menos que** (18)

unmarried **soltero/a** (4)

until **hasta** (6), **hasta (que)** (18); until later/tomorrow **hasta luego/hasta mañana** (P)

up: to get up **levantarse** (9); to go up **subir** (5)

upon (doing something) **al +** *inf.* (9)

upset **disgustado/a, contrariado/a** (15)

us *d. o. pron.* **nos**

use *v.* **usar** (1)

useless **inútil** *m., f.* (17)

V

vacation **vacaciones** *f. pl.* (8)

vacuum cleaner **aspiradora** (6); to vacuum **pasar la aspiradora** (6)

valley **valle** *m.* (13)

vegetable **legumbre** *f.* (5)

very **muy** (P); not very **poco;** very well, thanks **muy bien, gracias** (P)

veterinarian **veterinario/a** (18)

videotape *n.* **vídeo** (7)

voice: in a low voice **en voz baja** (17)

volcano **volcán** *m.* (13)

W

waist **cintura** (9)

wait (for) **esperar;** (*form. command*) **¡espere Ud.!**

wake up (*command*) **¡a despertar!** (6); *v.* **despertarse (ie)** (9)

walk *v.* **caminar** (4)

wall **pared** *f.* (1)

want *v.* **desear** (2), **querer** (*irreg.*) (2, 7); I want **quiero** (3)

war *n.* **guerra** (13)

warn **advertir (ie, i)** (15)

wash *v.* **lavar** (6); to wash (oneself) **lavarse** (9)

washbasin **lavabo** (6)

washing machine **lavadora** (18)

watch *n.* **reloj** *m.*

watch *v.* **mirar** (2)

water **agua** *f.* (*but:* **el agua**) (2)

watermelon **sandía** (5)

wave *n.* (*water*) **ola** (13)

way: on one's way to **camino de** (15)

we *sub. pron.* **nosotros/as**

weak **débil** *m., f.* (9)

wear *v.* **llevar** (3), **usar** (3)

weather *n.* **tiempo** (13); to be bad/good weather **hacer** (*irreg.*) **mal/buen tiempo** (4); what's the weather like today? **¿qué tiempo hace hoy?**

wedding **boda** (16); wedding ring **anillo de boda** (16)

Wednesday **miércoles** *m. s.* (P)

week **semana** (P); last week **la semana pasada;** next week **la semana próxima**

weekend **fin** (*m.*) **de semana** (14)

welcome: you are welcome **de nada** (10)

well **bien, pues** (P); very well, thanks **muy bien, gracias** (P)

west **oeste** *m.* (8), **occidente** *m.* (8)

wet **mojado/a** (9)

what? **¿cómo?** (P); **¿qué?** (P); **¿cuál?;** what is he/she like? **¿cómo es?** (3); what's up?, what's new? **¿qué hay?** (P); what's wrong? **¿qué te pasa?;** what do you think? **¿qué te parece?**

what **lo que** (16)

what a + *n.* (*interj.*) **vaya** + *n.* (10)

wheel *n.* **rueda** (10); steering wheel **volante** *m.* (10)

when? **¿cuándo?** (1)

where? **¿dónde?** (P); where from? **¿de dónde?** (P); where to? **¿adónde?, ¿a dónde?**

which **que** (3); that which **lo que** (16)

which? **¿cuál(es)?, ¿qué?** (P)

while **mientras** (4); little while **rato** (4)

white **blanco/a** (3)

who **que** (1), **quien** (1)

who? **¿quién(es)?** (P)

whom: to whom? **¿a quién(es)?** (P); with whom? **¿con quién(es)?**

why: that's why **por eso** (15)

why? **¿por qué?** (2)

wife **esposa** (4)

win *v.* **ganar**

windshield **parabrisas** *m. s.* (10)

windshield wiper **limpiaparabrisas** *m. s.* (10)

window **ventana** (1); in a bank **ventanilla** (17); window seat **asiento de ventanilla**

windy: to be windy **hacer** (*irreg.*) **viento** (4)

wine **vino** (2)

wineglass **copa** (4)

winter(time) **invierno** (P, 13)

with **con** (1); with me **conmigo** (15); with you (*fam.*) **contigo** (15)

without **sin** (8)

woman **mujer** *f.* (2), **señora** (P); young woman **joven** *f.* (2); old woman **vieja** (2)

wool: (made of) wool **de lana** (3)

word **palabra** (1)

work *v.* **trabajar** (1); (*machine, car*) **funcionar** (9); *n.* **trabajo** (4)

worker **trabajador(a), obrero/a** (18); social worker **trabajador(a) social** (18)

world **mundo** (8)

worried **preocupado/a** (15)

worry: don't worry **no se preocupe** (17)

worse **peor** (7)

worst **peor** (7)

worth: (not) to be worth the trouble **(no) valer** (*irreg.*) **la pena** (18)

wound *n.* **herida** (12)

wounded person **herido/a** (12)

write **escribir** (2); (*form. command*) **¡escriba Ud.!**

writing table **escritorio** (6)

written **escrito/a** *p.p.* (10)

wrong: to be wrong **no tener** (*irreg.*) **razón** (4); what's wrong? **¿qué te pasa?, ¿qué tienes?** (4)

X

X rays: to take X rays **sacar(le) (qu) una radiografía** (12)

Y

year **año;** to be _____ years old **tener** (*irreg.*) _____ **años** (4)

yellow **amarillo/a** (3)

yes **sí** (P)

yesterday **ayer** (P)

yet: not yet **todavía no**

you *sub. pron.* **tú;** *sub. pron., obj. of prep.* **usted(es), vosotros/as**

young **joven** *m., f.* (3); young man/woman **joven** *m., f.*

younger **menor** (4)

your *pos. adj.* **tu(s), su(s), vuestro/a/os/as**

yours *poss. adj.* **tuyo/a/os/a, suyo/a/os/as; vuestro/a/os/as** (14)

youth **juventud** *f.* (8)

Index

The credit page constitutes a continuation of the copyright page.

About the Authors

Robert L. Nicholas is Professor of Spanish at the University of Wisconsin, Madison. His Ph.D. is from the University of Oregon; he has been at Wisconsin since 1965. His scholarly interests focus on the modern period of Spanish literature, especially the twentieth-century theater and novel. He has published numerous articles in addition to his books *The Tragic Stages of Antonio Buero Vallejo; Unamuno, narrador;* and *El sainete serio (crónica de tres generaciones)*. He has been the recipient of several research grants from the Graduate School of the University of Wisconsin, and for years directed teaching assistants in the beginning Spanish course at the University of Wisconsin. More recently he has served as departmental chairman. He has authored or coauthored several high school and college Spanish textbooks, including *¡En camino!* and *¡Adelante!*

María Canteli Dominicis, Professor of Spanish and coordinator of the Spanish division at St. John's University, New York, was born in Cuba and has been teaching college-level Spanish in the United States since 1961. She holds a degree of Doctora en Filosofía y Letras from the University of Havana and a Ph.D. from New York University. Professor Dominicis is the author of *Don Juan en el teatro español del siglo XX* and *Escenas cotidianas,* a textbook for intermediate-level conversation courses. She is also coauthor of a number of college textbooks, including *Casos y cosas* (an intermediate conversation text), *¡En camino!,* and *¡Adelante!*

Eduardo Neale-Silva (1905–1989) received his Ph.D. from the University of Wisconsin, Madison and taught there for fifty-one years before his retirement. The recipient of a John Simon Guggenheim Fellowship, the James Homer Herriott Professorship of Spanish, and several research grants from the Graduate School of the University of Wisconsin, he wrote many articles of literary criticism, including a biography of José Eustasio Rivera, *Horizonte humano,* and an exhaustive analysis of César Vallejo's *Trilce.* In 1987 he received the first prize in the essay category in the **Letras de Oro** contest sponsored by the University of Miami and the American Express Company. The award-winning book, published subsequently, is entitled *César Vallejo, cuentista.* For many years Professor Neale-Silva directed the University of Wisconsin's teaching methods course for graduate teaching assistants in Spanish. He was involved with many high-school and college textbook projects, including *¡En camino!* and *¡Adelante!*

MAR CARIBE

OCÉANO ATLÁNTICO

Barranquilla
Cartagena
Lago de Maracaibo
Caracas
VENEZUELA
Río Orinoco

GUYANA
SURINAM
GUAYANA FRANCESA

Manizales
Río Magdalena
Bogotá
COLOMBIA
Cali
Otavalo

ECUADOR

ECUADOR
Quito

Iquitos

Río Amazonas

Cajamarca

PERÚ

BRASIL

Machu Picchu
Písac
Lima
Cuzco
Ayacucho
Lago Titicaca

BOLIVIA
La Paz
Brasilia
Sucre
Potosí

PARAGUAY
Río Paraná

Río de Janeiro

Salta
Asunción
Iguazú

OCÉANO PACÍFICO

Río Uruguay

URUGUAY
Santiago
Montevideo
Buenos Aires
Punta del Este
Río de la Plata
CHILE

OCÉANO ATLÁNTICO

ARGENTINA

Temuco

América del Sur

| 0 | 200 | 400 | 600 | 800 Millas |

| 0 | 200 | 400 | 600 | 800 Kilómetros |

Estrecho de Magallanes

TIERRA DEL FUEGO